Fodor's 2001

Switzerland

by Nancy Coons

The complete guide, thoroughly up-to-date

Packed with details that will make your trip

The must-see sights, off and on the beaten path

What to see, what to skip

Mix-and-match vacation itineraries

City strolls, countryside adventures

Smart lodging and dining options

Essential local do's and taboos

Transportation tips, distances and directions

Key contacts, savvy travel tips

When to go, what to pack

Clear, accurate, easy-to-use maps

Books to read, videos to watch, background essay

Fodor's Switzerland 2001

EDITOR: Jennifer J. Paull

Editorial Contributors: Diane Conrad, Katrin Gygax, Jennifer McDermott, Kara Misenheimer, Helayne Schiff, Lito Tejada-Flores, Susan Rose, Susan Tuttle-Laube, Kay Winzenried
Editorial Production: Tom Holton
Maps: David Lindroth, *cartographer*; Bob Blake, *map editor*
Design: Fabrizio La Rocca, *creative director;* Guido Caroti, *art director;* Jolie Novak, *photo editor;* Melanie Marin, *photo researcher*
Cover Design: Pentagram
Production/Manufacturing: Robert B. Shields
Cover Photograph: Peter Guttman

Copyright

Special Sales

Fodor's Travel Publications are available at special discounts for bulk purchases for sales promotions or premiums. Special editions, including personalized covers, excerpts of existing guides, and corporate imprints, can be created in large quantities for special needs. For more information, contact your local bookseller or write to Special Markets, Fodor's Travel Publications, 280 Park Ave., New York, NY 10017. Inquiries from Canada should be directed to your local Canadian bookseller or sent to Random House of Canada, Ltd., Marketing Department, 2775 Matheson Boulevard East, Mississauga, Ontario L4W 4P7. Inquiries from the United Kingdom should be sent to Fodor's Travel Publications, 20 Vauxhall Bridge Road, London SW1V 2SA, England.

PRINTED IN THE UNITED STATES OF AMERICA

10 9 8 7 6 5 4 3 2 1

Important Tip

Although all prices, opening times, and other details in this book are based on information supplied to us at press time, changes occur all the time in the travel world, and Fodor's cannot accept responsibility for facts that become outdated or for inadvertent errors or omissions. So **always confirm information when it matters,** especially if you're making a detour to visit a specific place.

CONTENTS

Maps and Charts

ON THE ROAD WITH FODOR'S

EVERY TRIP is a significant trip. Acutely aware of that fact, we've pulled out all stops in preparing *Fodor's Switzerland 2001.* To guide you in putting together your Swiss experience, we've created multiday itineraries and neighborhood walks. And to direct you to the places that are truly worth your time and money, we've rallied the team of endearingly picky know-it-alls we're pleased to call our writers. Having seen all corners of the regions they cover for us, they're real experts. If you knew them, you'd poll them for tips yourself.

About Our Writers

Nancy Coons has been tracing ancestral trails in Switzerland since moving to Europe in 1987, when she also began covering Luxembourg, Belgium, and much of northeastern France for Fodor's. Based in her 300-year-old farmhouse in Lorraine, she has written on European culture and food for the *Wall Street Journal, European Travel & Life, Opera News,* and *National Geographic Traveler.*

Diane Conrad began traveling many years ago, when jumbo jets were a dream and flying was a pleasure. Now living in St. Moritz, she teaches English as a second language at the College of Tourism Management Graubünden. For this edition she revised the Graubünden chapter.

Katrin Gygax was born in Zürich. She moved to California when she was four, Vancouver when she was six, and didn't stop traveling for the next 28 years. Now based in Zürich with her own translating business, she also writes movie reviews for a Swiss fashion magazine, is working on a mystery-novel series, and sings whenever possible. For this edition she updated the Zürich, Eastern Switzerland, and Luzern and Central Switzerland chapters.

Geneva updater **Jennifer McDermott** arrived in the city at age 11 and can't quite imagine living anywhere else. Her career as a freelance writer and editor began in 1997 with the editorship of *The Illustrated Greek Wine Guide* (Olive Press,

1999), and she is a member of the Geneva Writers Group. She also writes poetry, monitors Geneva's cultural scene for a local radio station, and teaches theater to young people.

The first flight **Kara Misenheimer** took *anywhere* was to Switzerland. After more than a decade of constant contact with the country, she has mastered three of its national languages, some of its national sports, and none of its national efficiencies. She has performed with the Basel Opera and produced multimedia projects for Swiss and European organizations. Her current work in film, publishing, and international media spans cities on several continents—from Helvetia to Hollywood. For this edition she updated the Basel chapter.

Susan Rose, a writer, translator, and editor, is a native of California. She speaks French, German, and several animal languages including Sheep—many of which came in handy during the update of the Valais and Fribourg, Neuchâtel, and the Jura chapters. She holds advanced degrees in linguistics and documentary film, as well as a certificate in motherhood and intercultural family life. She lives next to a cow pasture near Fribourg.

Susan Tuttle-Laube has been showing Switzerland to family and friends since moving there in 1981. As an "outsider living on the inside," she enjoys discovering the details that make the difference between a good trip and a great one; in this edition, the Bern, Berner Oberland, and Ticino chapters benefited from her perspective. Her book *Inside Outlandish* (Bergli Books, Basel, Switzerland 1997) recounts her mostly humorous experiences as a foreigner living abroad.

Vaud updater **Kay Winzenried** made her first visit to Switzerland in 1980 and has returned every year since. Now a dual citizen by marriage, she has lived in both the French- and German-speaking regions. She's used the centrally located country as a base for travels throughout Europe and a solo trip around the world, and as a training site for high-altitude trekking. Hiking with friends, exploring vineyards, and dining—be it rustic or haute cuisine—are her pleasures.

We'd also like to thank the staff of the Swiss regional tourist offices, as well as Erika Lieben and Evelyne Mock of the Switzerland Tourism office in New York, for their help with questions big and small.

Don't Forget to Write

Keeping a travel guide fresh and up-to-date is a big job. So we love your feedback—positive and negative—and follow up on all suggestions. Contact the Switzerland editor at editors@fodors.com or c/o Fodor's, 280 Park Avenue, New York, New York 10017. And have a wonderful trip!

Karen Cure

Karen Cure
Editorial Director

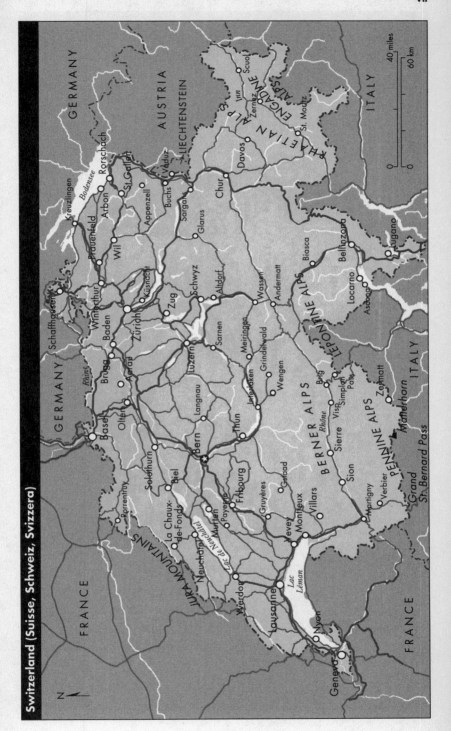

Switzerland (Suisse, Schweiz, Svizzera)

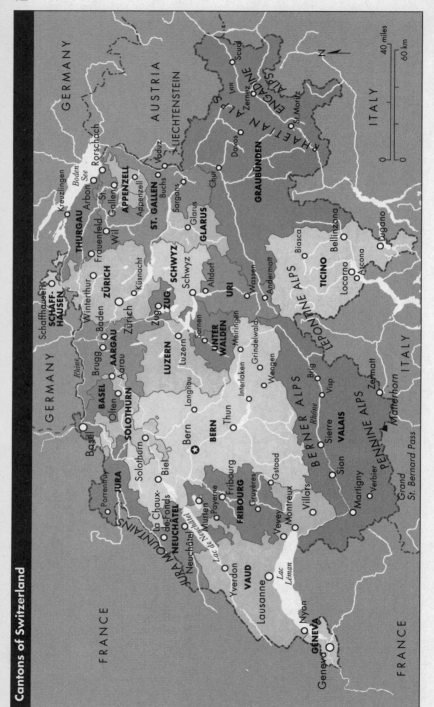

Cantons of Switzerland

SMART TRAVEL TIPS A TO Z

Basic Information on Traveling in Switzerland, Savvy Tips to Make Your Trip a Breeze, and Companies and Organizations to Contact

AIR TRAVEL

BOOKING

When you book **look for nonstop flights** and **remember that "direct" flights stop at least once.** Try to avoid connecting flights, which require a change of plane.

CARRIERS

When flying internationally, you must usually choose among a domestic carrier, the national flag carrier of the country you are visiting, and a foreign carrier from a third country. You may, for example, choose to fly Swissair to Switzerland. National flag carriers have the greatest number of nonstops. Domestic carriers may have better connections to your hometown and serve a greater number of gateway cities. Third-party carriers may have a price advantage.

Switzerland also has a couple of smaller airline. **KLM-Alps/Air Engiadina** uses small planes to make short-hop flights within Switzerland and to other European cities. **Crossair,** based in Basel's EuroAirport, has direct routes between several Swiss cities, as well as international flights.

➤ MAJOR AIRLINES: **Air Canada** (☎ 800/776–3000) to Geneva and Zürich. **American Airlines** (☎ 800/433–7300) to Zürich. **Delta** (☎ 800/221–1212) to Zürich. **Swissair** (☎ 800/221–4750) to Geneva, Zürich, and Basel.

➤ FROM THE U.K.: **Aer Lingus** (☎ 020/8899–4747) from Manchester. **British Airways** (☎ 0345/222–111). **Crossair** (☎ 020/7439–4144). **Easy-Jet** (☎ 0870/600–0000). **Swissair** (☎ 020/7434–7300).

➤ SMALLER AIRLINES: **KLM-Alps/Air Engiadina** (☎ 0848/848328 for reservations). **Crossair** (☎ 0848/852000 for reservations).

CHECK-IN & BOARDING

Assuming that not everyone with a ticket will show up, airlines routinely overbook planes. When everyone does, airlines ask for volunteers to give up their seats. In return, these volunteers usually get a certificate for a free flight and are rebooked on the next flight out. If there are not enough volunteers, the airline must choose who will be denied boarding. The first to get bumped are passengers who checked in late and those flying on discounted tickets, so **get to the gate and check in as early as possible,** especially during peak periods.

Always **bring a government-issued photo I.D. to the airport.** You will be asked to show it before you are allowed to check in.

For 20 SF per bag round-trip, air travelers on Swissair and partner airlines holding tickets or passes on Swiss Federal Railways can forward their luggage to their final destination, allowing them to make stops on the way unencumbered; the baggage is retrieved from the train station of the final destination. Baggage check-in and issuance of boarding passes are also possible at 102 train stations in Switzerland. A "Fly-Rail Baggage" brochure is available free of charge, in English, from the **Swiss Federal Railways** (☎ 0900/300300; 1.19 SF/min).

CUTTING COSTS

The least expensive airfares to Switzerland must usually be purchased in advance and are nonrefundable. It's smart to **call a number of airlines, and when you are quoted a good price, book it on the spot**—the same fare may not be available the next day. Always **check different routings** and look into using different airports. Travel agents, especially low-fare specialists (☞ Discounts & Deals, *below*), are helpful.

Consolidators are another good source. They buy tickets for scheduled international flights at reduced rates from the airlines, then sell them at prices that beat the best fare available directly from the airlines, usually without restrictions. Sometimes you can even get your money back if you need to return the ticket. Carefully read the fine print detailing penalties for changes and cancellations, and **confirm your consolidator reservation with the airline.**

When you **fly as a courier,** you trade your checked-luggage space for a ticket deeply subsidized by a courier service. There are restrictions on when you can book and how long you can stay.

➤ CONSOLIDATORS: **Cheap Tickets** (☎ 800/377–1000). **Discount Airline Ticket Service** (☎ 800/576–1600). **Unitravel** (☎ 800/325–2222). **Up & Away Travel** (☎ 212/889–2345). **World Travel Network** (☎ 800/409–6753).

➤ COURIERS: **Air Courier Association** (✉ 15000 W. 6th Ave., Suite 203, Golden, CO 80401, ☎ 800/282–1202, www.aircourier.org).

International Association of Air Travel Couriers (✉ 220 S. Dixie Hwy. No. 3, Box 1349, Lake Worth, FL 33460, ☎ 561/582–8320, FAX 561/582–1581, www.courier.org).

Now Voyager Travel (✉ 74 Varick St., Suite 307, New York, NY 10013, ☎ 212/431–1616, FAX 212/219–1753 or 212/334–5243,www.nowvoyager-travel.com).

DOMESTIC FLIGHTS

The entire country of Switzerland is smaller in area than the state of West Virginia, so flying from one region to another is a luxury that, considering how efficient the trains are, few travelers require—unless there's a convenient connection from your intercontinental arrival point (Geneva, Zürich) to a lesser airport (Basel, Bern, Lugano, St. Moritz). Crossair (☞ Smaller Airlines, *above*) is Switzerland's domestic airline, servicing local airports and various Continental cities as well: Brussels,

Düsseldorf, Florence, Nice, Paris, London, and Venice.

ENJOYING THE FLIGHT

For more legroom, **request an emergency-aisle seat.** Don't sit in the row in front of the emergency aisle or in front of a bulkhead, where seats may not recline. If you have dietary concerns, **ask for special meals when booking.** These can be vegetarian, low-cholesterol, or kosher, for example. On long flights try to maintain a normal routine in order to help fight jet lag. At night, **get some sleep.** By day, **eat light meals, drink water** (not alcohol), and **move around the cabin** to stretch your legs.

Many carriers have prohibited smoking on all their international flights; others allow smoking only on certain routes or certain departures, so **contact your carrier regarding its smoking policy.** Swissair, which does not allow smoking, stocks Nicorette gum.

FLYING TIMES

Flying time is just under two hours from London, seven hours from New York, 10 hours from Chicago, and 14 hours from Los Angeles.

HOW TO COMPLAIN

If your baggage goes astray or your flight goes awry, complain right away. Most carriers require that you **file a claim immediately.**

➤ AIRLINE COMPLAINTS: U.S. Department of Transportation **Aviation Consumer Protection Division** (✉ C-75, Room 4107, Washington, DC 20590, ☎ 202/366–2220, airconsumer@ost.dot.gov, www.dot.gov/airconsumer). **Federal Aviation Administration Consumer Hotline** (☎ 800/322–7873).

AIRPORTS

The major gateways are Zürich's Kloten Airport (ZRH) and Geneva's Cointrin Airport (GVA).

➤ MAJOR AIRPORTS: Geneva: **Cointrin International Airport** (☎ 022/7177111). Zürich: **Kloten Airport** (☎ 01/8121212; 1571060 at.86 SF/min.).

➤ OTHER AIRPORTS: Lugano: **Aeroporto Lugano-Agno** (☎ 091/

6101212). Bern: **Belpmoos** (☎ 031/9602121). Basel/Mulhouse: **EuroAirport** (✉ Just across the border in France, ☎ 061/3253111). Sion: (✉ Rte. de Aeroport, ☎ 027/3222480). Upper Engadine: (✉ Samedan, ☎ 081/8525433).

BIKE TRAVEL

BIKE MAPS

Local tourist offices are the best places to get cycling maps for specific areas; you can also contact **Cartes Cyclistes** (✉ VCS/ATE, Velokarten, Postfach, CH-3360 Herzogenbuchsee, ☎ 062/9565656, FAX 062/9565699, www.vcs-ate.ch).

BIKE RENTALS

Ever the transit expert, Switzerland links bicycles and trains; you can rent bikes at 230 train stations. Bikes can be returned to any station, but if you drop off a bike at a different station from where you picked it up, there's a 6 SF service charge per bike, with arrangement at time of pickup, or a 12 SF per bike charge without prior notification. Rates for standard bikes are 16 SF per half day, 20 SF per day, and 80 SF per week. Mountain bikes are 21 SF per half day, 26 SF per day, or 104 SF per week. Groups get reductions according to the number of bikes. Individuals must make a reservation by 6 PM the day before they plan to use the bike, groups a week in advance. A daily train pass for a bike costs 15 SF (10 SF with a half-price pass).

BIKES IN FLIGHT

Most airlines accommodate bikes as luggage, provided they are dismantled and boxed. For bike boxes, often free at bike shops, you'll pay about $5 from airlines (at least $100 for bike bags). International travelers can sometimes substitute a bike for a piece of checked luggage at no charge; otherwise, the cost is about $100. Domestic and Canadian airlines charge $25–$50.

BOAT & FERRY TRAVEL

All of Switzerland's larger lakes are crisscrossed by elegant steamers, some of them restored paddle steamers. Their café-restaurants serve drinks, snacks, and hot food at standard mealtimes; toilet facilities are provided. Service continues year-round but is greatly reduced in winter. Unlimited travel is free to holders of the Swiss Pass. If you are not traveling by train, **consider the Swiss Boat Pass,** which for 35 SF allows half-fare travel on all boats January 1–December 31. The Swiss Card, Swiss Pass, or the Flexipass (☞ Train Travel, *below*) may also be used for boat travel.

BUS TRAVEL

Switzerland's famous yellow postbuses, with their stentorian tritone horns, link main cities with villages off the beaten track and even crawl over the highest mountain passes. Both postbuses and city buses follow posted schedules to the minute: You can set your watch by them. You can pick up a free schedule for a particular route in most postbuses; full schedules are included in train schedule books. You can also check the Swiss Post Web site (☞ Web Sites, *below*). Watch for the yellow sign with the picture of a bus. Postbuses cater to hikers: walking itineraries are available at some postbus stops.

There's also a special scenic postbus route, the *Palm Express*. This route (summer only) runs from St. Moritz to Lugano via the Maloja Pass and Italy. Reservations can be made at any train station or tourist office.

DISCOUNT PASSES

The Swiss Pass (☞ Train Travel, *below*) gives unlimited travel on the postbuses.

BUSINESS HOURS

BANKS & OFFICES

Businesses still close for lunch in Switzerland, generally from 12:30 to 2, but this is changing, especially in larger cities. All remain closed on Sunday, and a few stay closed through Monday morning. Banks are open weekdays from 8:30 to 4:30.

GAS STATIONS

Gas station kiosks are usually open daily from 6:30 AM until 9 PM. Automatic pumps, which accept major credit cards and Swiss bank notes, are in service 24 hours a day.

MUSEUMS & SIGHTS

Museums generally close on Monday. There is, however, an increasing trend toward staying open late one night a week, usually on Thursday or Friday evening.

SHOPS

Shops are generally open every day but Sunday, though a few stay closed through Monday morning. Smaller stores close for an hour or two for lunch. Stores in train stations often stay open until 9 PM; in the Geneva and Zürich airports, shops are open on Sunday.

CAMERAS & PHOTOGRAPHY

It may seem impossible to *not* take a good picture when facing a gorgeous Alpine view, but keeping a few tips in mind can make your shots even better. Particularly when snapping mountain scenery, **include something of known size in the picture** to give a sense of scale. Also, **consider the light**; at sunrise or sunset you can capture spectacular colors, while the effects of storm clouds can be very dramatic. And if you find yourself itching to photograph those black-and-white cows? Remember to show them in context in order to make it an evocative travel picture.

➤ PHOTO HELP: **Kodak Information Center** (☎ 800/242–2424). *Kodak Guide to Shooting Great Travel Pictures,* available in bookstores or from Fodor's Travel Publications (☎ 800/533–6478; $16.50 plus $5.50 shipping).

EQUIPMENT PRECAUTIONS

Always **keep your film and tape out of the sun.** Carry an extra supply of batteries, and **be prepared to turn on your camera or camcorder** to prove to security personnel that the device is real. Always **ask for hand inspection of film,** which becomes clouded after repeated exposure to airport X-ray machines, and **keep videotapes away from metal detectors.**

CAR RENTAL

If booked from overseas, rates in Zürich and Geneva begin at $45 a day and $178 a week for an economy car with air-conditioning, a manual transmission, and unlimited mileage. This does not include the 7.6% tax on car rentals. Try to arrange for a rental before you go; rentals booked in Switzerland are considerably more expensive.

➤ MAJOR AGENCIES: **Alamo** (☎ 800/522–9696; 020/8759–6200 in the U.K.). **Avis** (☎ 800/331–1084; 800/331–1084 in Canada; 02/9353–9000 in Australia; 09/525–1982 in New Zealand). **Budget** (☎ 800/527–0700;0870/607–5000 in the U.K., through affiliate Europcar). **Dollar** (☎ 800/800–6000; 0124/622–0111 in the U.K., through affiliate Sixt Kenning; 02/9223–1444 in Australia). **Hertz** (☎ 800/654–3001; 800/263–0600 in Canada; 020/8897–2072 in the U.K.; 02/9669–2444 in Australia; 09/256–8690 in New Zealand) **National Car Rental** (☎ 800/227–7368; 020/8680–4800 in the U.K., where it is known as National Europe).

CUTTING COSTS

To get the best deal, **book through a travel agent who will shop around.** Do **look into wholesalers,** companies that do not own fleets but rent in bulk from those that do and often offer better rates than traditional car-rental operations. Payment must be made before you leave home.

➤ WHOLESALERS: **Auto Europe** (☎ 207/842–2000 or 800/223–5555, FAX 800–235–6321, www.autoeurope.com). **Europe by Car** (☎ 212/581–3040 or 800/223–1516, FAX 212/246–1458, www.europebycar.com). **DER Travel Services** (✉ 9501 W. Devon Ave., Rosemont, IL 60018, ☎ 800/782–2424, FAX 800/282–7474 for information; 800/860–9944 for brochures; www.dertravel.com). **Kemwel Holiday Autos** (☎ 800/678–0678, FAX 914/825–3160, www.kemwel.com).

INSURANCE

When driving a rented car, you are generally responsible for any damage to or loss of the vehicle. Before you rent, see what coverage your personal auto-insurance policy and credit cards already provide.

Before you buy collision coverage, check your existing policies—you may already be covered. However, collision policies that car-rental companies sell for European rentals usually do not include stolen-vehicle coverage.

REQUIREMENTS & RESTRICTIONS

In Switzerland your own driver's license is acceptable. However, an International Driver's Permit is a good idea; it's available from the American or Canadian automobile association, and, in the United Kingdom, from the Automobile Association or Royal Automobile Club. These international permits are universally recognized, and having one in your wallet may save you a problem with the local authorities.

SURCHARGES

Before you pick up a car in one city and leave it in another, **ask about drop-off charges or one-way service fees,** which can be substantial. Note, too, that some rental agencies charge extra if you return the car before the time specified in your contract. To avoid a hefty refueling fee, **fill the tank just before you turn in the car,** but be aware that gas stations near the rental outlet may overcharge.

CAR TRAVEL

EMERGENCY SERVICES

All road breakdowns should be called in to the central Switzerland-wide emergency number, 140. If you are on the autoroute, pull over to the shoulder and look for arrows pointing you to the nearest orange radio-telephone, called Bornes SOS; use these phones instead of a mobile phone because with them police can locate you instantly and send help. There are SOS phones every kilometer (½ mi), on alternate sides of the autoroute.

FROM THE U.K. BY FERRY

In addition to the relatively swift (and expensive) Channel Tunnel (Chunnel), on which cars piggyback on trains to cross the channel from Dover to Boulogne, there are many drive-on/drive-off car ferry services across the Channel, but only a few are suitable as a means of getting to Switzerland. The situation is complicated by the different pricing systems operated by ferry companies and the many off-peak fares, and by the tolls

charged by France on some of its motorways; these add up, particularly if you drive long distances. To avoid the tolls, **take a northerly route through Belgium or the Netherlands and Germany,** where motorways are free. The crossings for this route are Felixstowe or Dover to Zeebrugge; Sheerness to Vlissingen; and Ramsgate to Dunkirk. All these Continental ports have good road connections, and Switzerland can be reached in a day of hard driving.

GASOLINE

Unleaded (*sans plomb* or *bleifrei*) gas costs around 1.29 SF per liter, and super costs around 1.32 SF per liter. Leaded fuel is no longer available. Prices are slightly higher in mountain areas. **Have some 10 SF and 20 SF notes available,** as many gas stations (especially in the mountains) offer vending-machine gas even when they're closed. Simply slide in a bill and fill your tank. Many of these machines also now accept major credit cards with precoded PIN numbers (☞ Money, *below*). You can get a receipt if you ask the machine for it.

PARKING

Parking areas are clearly marked. Blue or red zones are slowly being replaced by white zones only. Each city sets its own time allotments for parking; the limits are signposted. A *disque* (provided in rental cars or available free from banks or police stations) must be placed clearly in the front window noting the time of arrival. Metered parking is often paid for at communal machines; these vary from city to city. Some machines simply accept coins and dispense tickets. At others you'll need to punch in your parking space number, then add coins. The ticket for parking may or may not have to be placed in your car window; this information is noted on the machine or ticket. Parking in public lots normally costs 2 SF for the first hour, increasing by 1 SF every half hour thereafter.

ROAD CONDITIONS

Swiss roads are well surfaced but wind around considerably—especially in the mountains—so **don't plan on achieving high average speeds.** When estimating likely travel times, look carefully at the map: There may be only 32 km (20 mi) between one point and another—but there may be an Alpine pass in the way. There is a well-developed highway network, though some notable gaps still exist in the south along an east–west line, roughly between Lugano and Sion. A combination of steep or winding routes and hazardous weather means some roads will be closed in winter. Signs are posted at the beginning of the climb.

To find out about road conditions, traffic jams, itineraries, and so forth, you can turn to two places: The **Swiss Automobile Club** (☎ 031/3283111, FAX 031/3110310) has operators standing by on weekdays from 8 to 5 to provide information in all languages from their information center at ☎ 031/3121515. Dues-paying members of the **Touring Club of Switzerland** (☎ 022/4172424, FAX 022/4172020) may contact the organization for similar information. Note that neither of these numbers gets you breakdown service (☞ *below*). For frequent and precise information in Swiss languages, you can dial 163, or tune in to local radio stations.

RULES OF THE ROAD

Driving is on the right. Priority is given to the driver on the right except when merging into traffic circles, when priority is given to the drivers coming from the left. In built-up areas the speed limit is 50 kph (30 mph); on main highways, it's 80 kph (50 mph); on expressways, the limit is 120 kph (75 mph). Pass on the left only. It is not legal to make a right-hand turn on a red light. The blood-alcohol limit is .08.

Children under age seven are not permitted to sit in the front seat. **Use headlights** in heavy rain or poor visibility and in road tunnels—they are compulsory. Always **carry your valid license and car-registration papers;** there are occasional roadblocks to check them. **Wear seat belts** in the front- and backseats—they are required.

To use the main highways, you must display a sticker, or *vignette,* in the lower left-hand corner of the windshield. You can buy it at the border (cash only; neighboring foreign currencies can be changed). It costs 40 SF and can also be purchased from any post office and from most gas stations; it's valid to the end of the year. Cars rented within Switzerland already have these stickers; if you rent a car elsewhere in Europe, **ask if the company will provide the vignette for you.**

Traffic going up a mountain has priority except for postbuses coming down. A sign with a yellow post horn on a blue background means that postbuses have priority.

In winter **use snow chains,** compulsory in some areas and advisable in all. Snow-chain service stations have signs marked SERVICE DE CHAÎNES À NEIGE or SCHNEEKETTENDIENST; snow chains are available for rent.

If you have an accident, even a minor one, you must call the police.

CHILDREN IN SWITZERLAND

In Swiss hotels and restaurants, children are generally warmly welcomed. (If your kids volunteer the magic words "hello," "goodbye," "please," and "thank you" in the local language, the door will open even wider.) Children's meals are often available on menus; otherwise, you can usually request one and prices will be adjusted.

If you are renting a car, don't forget to **arrange for a car seat** when you reserve.

Supervised playrooms are available in some of the better Swiss hotels, and many winter resorts also provide lists of reliable baby-sitters. For recommended local sitters, **check with your hotel desk.**

CHILDREN'S CAMPS & HOLIDAY COURSES

Every summer some 120 private schools in Switzerland offer leisurely language study and recreation courses for primary and secondary school-age children from around the world. Summer camps similar to those in the United States are also available. Ask Switzerland Tourism (☞ Visitor Information, *below*) for a copy of

"Holiday and Language Courses," a list of camps and summer programs in Switzerland.

FLYING

If your children are two or older, **ask about children's airfares.** As a general rule, infants under two not occupying a seat fly at greatly reduced fares or even for free. When booking, **confirm carry-on allowances** if you're traveling with infants. In general, for babies charged 10% of the adult fare you are allowed one carry-on bag and a collapsible stroller; if the flight is full, the stroller may have to be checked, or you may be limited to fewer pieces of carry-on luggage.

Experts agree that it's a good idea to use safety seats aloft for children weighing less than 40 pounds. Airlines set their own policies: U.S. carriers usually require that the child be ticketed, even if young enough to ride free, since the seats must be strapped into regular seats. Do **check your airline's policy about using safety seats during takeoff and landing.** And since safety seats are not allowed everywhere in the plane, get your seat assignments early.

When reserving, **request children's meals or a freestanding bassinet** if you need them. But note that bulkhead seats, where you must sit to use the bassinet, may lack an overhead bin or storage space on the floor.

LODGING

Most hotels in Switzerland allow children under a certain age to stay in their parents' room at no extra charge, but others charge for them as extra adults; be sure to **find out the cutoff age for children's discounts.** The Swiss Hotel Association has listings of family hotels throughout the country.

➤ ORGANIZATIONS: Swiss Hotel Association (✉ Monbijoustr. 130, Postfach, CH-3001 Bern, ☎ 031/3704111, FAX 031/3704444, www.swisshotels.ch).

SIGHTS & ATTRACTIONS

Places that are especially appealing to children are indicated by a rubber duckie icon ℧ in the margin.

The Adult Plus version of the **Swiss Museum Passport** (☞ Discounts & Deals, *below*) allows free entrance to five children age 16 and under at participating museums.

TRANSPORTATION

Families traveling together in Switzerland should **buy an STS Family Card,** a special pass (20 SF if purchased in Switzerland with the purchase of a Swiss Pass or Europass) that allows children under 16 to travel free on trains, postbuses (☞ Bus Travel, *above*), and boats when accompanied by ticket-holding parents or guardians. The pass is valid for one year. Adults must hold a valid Swiss Pass, Swiss Card, Swiss Transfer Ticket, or Eurail tariff ticket to obtain the STS Family Card, available at any Swiss train station, for their children (☞ Train Travel, *below*).

CONSUMER PROTECTION

Whenever shopping or buying travel services in Switzerland, **pay with a major credit card** so you can cancel payment or get reimbursed if there's a problem. If you're doing business with a particular company for the first time, **contact your local Better Business Bureau and the attorney general's offices** in your own state and in the company's home state, as well. Have any complaints been filed? Finally, if you're buying a package or tour, always **consider travel insurance** that includes default coverage (☞ Insurance, *below*).

➤ BBBs: **Council of Better Business Bureaus** (✉ 4200 Wilson Blvd., Suite 800, Arlington, VA 22203, ☎ 703/276–0100, FAX 703/525–8277 www.bbb.org).

CUSTOMS & DUTIES

When shopping, **keep receipts** for all purchases. Upon reentering the country, **be ready to show customs officials what you've bought.** If you feel a duty is incorrect or object to the way your clearance was handled, note the inspector's badge number and ask to see a supervisor. If the problem isn't resolved, write to the appropriate authorities, beginning with the port director at your point of entry.

IN AUSTRALIA

Australian residents who are 18 or older may bring home $A400 worth of souvenirs and gifts (including jewelry), 250 cigarettes or 250 grams of tobacco, and 1,125 milliliters of alcohol (including wine, beer, and spirits). Residents under 18 may bring back $A200 worth of goods. Prohibited items include meat products. Seeds, plants, and fruits need to be declared upon arrival.

➤ INFORMATION: **Australian Customs Service** (Regional Director, ✉ Box 8, Sydney, NSW 2001, ☎ 02/9213–2000, FAX 02/9213–4000).

IN CANADA

Canadian residents who have been out of Canada for at least seven days may bring home C$500 worth of goods duty-free. If you've been away less than seven days but more than 48 hours, the duty-free allowance drops to C$200; if your trip lasts 24–48 hours, the allowance is C$50. You may not pool allowances with family members. Goods claimed under the C$500 exemption may follow you by mail; those claimed under the lesser exemptions must accompany you. Alcohol and tobacco products may be included in the seven-day and 48-hour exemptions but not in the 24-hour exemption. If you meet the age requirements of the province or territory through which you reenter Canada, you may bring in, duty-free, 1.14 liters (40 imperial ounces) of wine or liquor *or* 24 12-ounce cans or bottles of beer or ale. If you are 16 or older, you may bring in, duty-free, 200 cigarettes and 50 cigars. Check ahead of time with Revenue Canada or the Department of Agriculture for policies regarding meat products, seeds, plants, and fruits.

You may send an unlimited number of gifts worth up to C$60 each duty-free to Canada. Label the package UNSOLICITED GIFT—VALUE UNDER $60. Alcohol and tobacco are excluded.

➤ INFORMATION: **Revenue Canada** (✉ 2265 St. Laurent Blvd. S, Ottawa, Ontario K1G 4K3, ☎ 613/993–0534; 800/461–9999 in Canada, FAX 613/957–8911, www.ccra-adrc.gc.ca).

IN NEW ZEALAND

Homeward-bound residents 17 or older may bring back $700 worth of souvenirs and gifts. Your duty-free allowance also includes 4.5 liters of wine or beer; one 1,125-milliliter bottle of spirits; and either 200 cigarettes, 250 grams of tobacco, 50 cigars, or a combination of the three up to 250 grams. Prohibited items include meat products, seeds, plants, and fruits.

➤ INFORMATION: **New Zealand Customs** (Custom House, ✉ 50 Anzac Ave., Box 29, Auckland, New Zealand, ☎ 09/359–6655, FAX 09/359–6732).

IN SWITZERLAND

Entering Switzerland, an overseas visitor 17 years or older may bring in 400 cigarettes or 100 cigars or 500 grams of tobacco; 2 liters of alcohol up to 15 proof; and a liter of alcohol over 15 proof. When entering from a European country, tobacco is restricted to 200 cigarettes or 50 cigars or 250 grams of tobacco. Medicine, such as insulin, is allowed for personal use only.

IN THE U.K.

If you are a U.K. resident and your journey was wholly within the European Union (EU), you won't have to pass through customs when you return to the United Kingdom. If you plan to bring back large quantities of alcohol or tobacco, check EU limits beforehand.

➤ INFORMATION: **HM Customs and Excise** (✉ Dorset House, Stamford St., Bromley, Kent BR1 1XX, ☎ 020/7202–4227).

IN THE U.S.

U.S. residents who have been out of the country for at least 48 hours (and who have not used the $400 allowance or any part of it in the past 30 days) may bring home $400 worth of foreign goods duty-free. U.S. residents 21 and older may bring back 1 liter of alcohol duty-free. In addition, regardless of your age, you are allowed 200 cigarettes and 100 non-Cuban cigars. Antiques, which the U.S. Customs Service defines as objects more than 100 years old, enter duty-free, as do original works of art done entirely by hand, including paintings, drawings, and sculptures.

You may also send packages home duty-free: up to $200 worth of goods for personal use, with a limit of one parcel per addressee per day (except alcohol or tobacco products or perfume worth more than $5); label the package PERSONAL USE and attach a list of its contents and their retail value. Do not label the package UNSOLICITED GIFT, or your duty-free exemption will drop to $100. Mailed items do not affect your duty-free allowance on your return.

➤ INFORMATION: **U.S. Customs Service** (✉ 1300 Pennsylvania Ave. NW, Washington, DC 20229, www. customs.gov; ☎ 202/354–1000 for inquiries; complaints c/o ✉ Office of Regulations and Rulings; registration of equipment c/o ✉ Resource Management, ☎ 202/927–0540).

DINING

The restaurants we list are the cream of the crop in each price category. Properties indicated by an ✕☯ are lodging establishments whose restaurant warrants a special trip (and will accommodate non–hotel guests). In regional chapters price charts appear in the dining subsection of the Pleasures and Pastimes section, which follows each chapter introduction. In chapters devoted to a single city, price charts appear in the introductions to the dining section. Unless otherwise noted, the restaurants listed in this guide are open daily for lunch and dinner.

RESERVATIONS & DRESS

Reservations are always a good idea: we mention them only when they're essential or not accepted. Book as far ahead as you can, and reconfirm as soon as you arrive. We note dress only when men are required to wear a jacket or a jacket and tie.

DISABILITIES & ACCESSIBILITY

In Switzerland most forms of public transportation offer special provisions, and accessible hotels are available in many areas of the country.

➤ LOCAL RESOURCES: **Mobility International Schweiz** (✉ Froburgstr. 4,

CH-4600 Olten, ☎ 062/2068835, FAX 062/2068839, www.mis-infothek.ch) for information on special tours and travel.

➤ COMPLAINTS: **Disability Rights Section** (✉ U.S. Department of Justice, Civil Rights Division, Box 66738, Washington, DC 20035-6738, ☎ 202/514–0301 or 800/514–0301; TTY 202/514–0301 or 800/514–0301, FAX 202/307–1198) for general complaints. **Aviation Consumer Protection Division** (☞ Air Travel, *above*) for airline-related problems. **Civil Rights Office** (✉ U.S. Department of Transportation, Departmental Office of Civil Rights, S-30, 400 7th St. SW, Room 10215, Washington, DC 20590, ☎ 202/366–4648, FAX 202/366–9371) for problems with surface transportation.

DRIVING

Foreign visitors with either the Disabled Badge of their country or the International Wheelchair Badge mounted inside the windshield of their car are entitled to use parking spaces reserved for people with disabilities throughout the country. Motorists who cannot walk unaided can obtain a special permit for parking privileges, as well as the international badge mentioned above, from the local police authority.

RESERVATIONS

When discussing accessibility with an operator or reservations agent, **ask hard questions.** Are there any stairs, inside *or* out? Are there grab bars next to the toilet *and* in the shower/tub? How wide is the doorway to the room? To the bathroom? For the most extensive facilities meeting the latest legal specifications, **opt for newer accommodations.**

TRAIN TRAVEL

Throughout the Swiss Federal Railways, wheelchairs are often available; inform the particular station ahead of time that you will need one. In addition, ramps or lifts and wheelchair-accessible toilets have been installed in more than 100 stations. All Inter-City and long-distance express trains and more than two-thirds of the country's regional shuttle trains now have wheelchair compartments. A brochure describing services for disabled travelers is available (in French, German and Italian) from the Swiss Federal Railways (☞ Train Travel, *below*).

TRAVEL AGENCIES

In the United States the Americans with Disabilities Act requires that travel firms serve the needs of all travelers. Some agencies specialize in working with people with disabilities.

➤ TRAVELERS WITH MOBILITY PROBLEMS: **Access Adventures** (✉ 206 Chestnut Ridge Rd., Rochester, NY 14624, ☎ 716/889–9096, dltravel@prodigy.net), run by a former physical-rehabilitation counselor. **Care-Vacations** (✉ 5–5110 50th Ave., Leduc, Alberta T9E 6V4, ☎ 780/986–6404 or 877/478–7827, ℻ 780/986–8332, www.carevacations.com), for group tours and cruise vacations. **Flying Wheels Travel** (✉ 143 W. Bridge St., Box 382, Owatonna, MN 55060, ☎ 507/451–5005 or 800/535–6790, ℻ 507/451–1685, www.flyingwheels.com).

➤ TRAVELERS WITH DEVELOPMENTAL DISABILITIES: **Sprout** (✉ 893 Amsterdam Ave., New York, NY 10025, ☎ 212/222–9575 or 888/222–9575, ℻ 212/222–9768, sprout@interport.net, www.gosprout.org).

DISCOUNTS & DEALS

Besides the various discount transportation passes (☞ Boat & Ferry Travel, *above and* Train Travel, *below*), there is a discount pass for Swiss museums. For a flat fee (30 SF for one month), the **Swiss Museum Passport** grants free entrance to more than 250 museums throughout the country. You can buy the passports at the participating museums, many local tourist offices, and the main office.

Be a smart shopper and **compare all your options** before making decisions. A plane ticket bought with a promotional coupon from travel clubs, coupon books, and direct-mail offers may not be cheaper than the least expensive fare from a discount ticket agency. And always keep in mind that

what you get is just as important as what you save.

➤ DISCOUNT MUSEUM PASS: **Swiss Museum Passport Office** (✉ Hornbachstr. 50, CH-8034 Zürich, ☎ 01/3898456, ℻ 01/3898400, www.museums.ch/pass).

DISCOUNT RESERVATIONS

To save money, **look into discount reservations services** with toll-free numbers, which use their buying power to get a better price on hotels, airline tickets, even car rentals. When booking a room, always **call the hotel's local toll-free number** (if one is available) rather than the central reservations number—you'll often get a better price. Always ask about special packages or corporate rates.

When shopping for the best deal on hotels and car rentals, **look for guaranteed exchange rates,** which protect you against a falling dollar. With your rate locked in, you won't pay more, even if the price goes up in the local currency.

➤ AIRLINE TICKETS: ☎ 800/FLY-4–LESS. ☎ 800/FLY-ASAP.

➤ HOTEL ROOMS: **International Marketing & Travel Concepts** (☎ 800/790–4682, imtc@mindspring.com). **Steigenberger Reservation Service** (☎ 800/223–5652, www.srs-worldhotels.com). **Travel Interlink** (☎ 800/888–5898, www.travelinterlink.com).

PACKAGE DEALS

Don't confuse packages and guided tours. When you buy a package, you travel on your own, just as though you had planned the trip yourself. Fly/drive packages, which combine airfare and car rental, are often a good deal. If you **buy a rail/drive pass,** you may save on train tickets and car rentals. All Eurail- and Europass holders get a discount on Eurostar fares through the Channel Tunnel.

ELECTRICITY

To use your U.S.-purchased electric-powered equipment, **bring a converter and adapter.** The electrical current in Switzerland is 220 volts, 50 cycles alternating current (AC); wall outlets take Continental-type hexagonal-shape plugs, which have two or three round prongs.

If your appliances are dual-voltage, you'll need only an adapter. Don't use 110-volt outlets, marked FOR SHAVERS ONLY, for high-wattage appliances such as blow-dryers. Most laptops operate equally well on 110 and 220 volts and so require only an adapter.

EMBASSIES

➤ AUSTRALIA: Consulate, ✉ chemin de Fins 2; ✉ Case Postale 172, CH-1211 Geneva, ☎ 022/7999100.

➤ CANADA: ✉ Kirchenfeldstr. 88, CH-3005 Bern, ☎ 031/3573200.

➤ UNITED KINGDOM: ✉ Thunstr. 50, CH-3015 Bern, ☎ 031/3597700.

➤ UNITED STATES: ✉ Jubiläumstr. 93, CH-3001 Bern, ☎ 031/3577011.

EMERGENCIES

Anglo-Phone (☎ 1575014), an English-language hot line, gives information on what to do in an emergency, in addition to many other topics. Lines are open 9–7 on weekdays and 9–1 on Saturday. Calls cost 2.13 SF per minute.

➤ CONTACTS: Police (☎ 117). Ambulance (☎ 144).

ENGLISH-LANGUAGE MEDIA

BOOKS

It's quite easy to find English-language books, especially in major cities. Most bookstores have a selection of fiction and nonfiction; kiosks at train stations and airports stock some as well.

NEWSPAPERS & MAGAZINES

You can find the *International Herald Tribune* at newsstands and kiosks throughout Switzerland. *USA Today* and some British newspapers are also often available.

TELEVISION

BBC World, BBC Prime, CNN, and CNBC are generally available on cable channels in hotels.

ETIQUETTE & BEHAVIOR

In Switzerland it's polite to **say hello and goodbye** to everyone you speak to, from policemen to cashiers. The standard gesture for greeting and goodbye is a simple handshake. When doing business, only use your counterpart's first name if he or she uses your given name first.

GAY & LESBIAN TRAVEL

For resources Switzerland, a good starting poin Dialogai (✉ 11–13 rue de la Na ttion, CH-1211 Geneva, ☎ 0. 9064040, FAX 022/9064044), wl h has a library, tea-room, bar, ana an English-speaking staff. You can pick up a copy of its guide, which lists gay-friendly contacts for Switzerland's French-speaking region and neighboring France (it's in French only).

➤ GAY- & LESBIAN-FRIENDLY TRAVEL AGENCIES: Different Roads Travel (✉ 8383 Wilshire Blvd., Suite 902, Beverly Hills, CA 90211, ☎ 323/651–5557 or 800/429–8747, FAX 323/651–3678, leigh@west.tzell.com). Kennedy Travel (✉ 314 Jericho Turnpike, Floral Park, NY 11001, ☎ 516/352–4888 or 800/237–7433, FAX 516/354–8849, main@kennedytravel.com, www.kennedytravel.com). Now Voyager (✉ 4406 18th St., San Francisco, CA 94114, ☎ 415/626–1169 or 800/255–6951, FAX 415/626–8626, www.nowvoyager.com). Skylink Travel and Tour (✉ 1006 Mendocino Ave., Santa Rosa, CA 95401, ☎ 707/546–9888 or 800/225–5759, FAX 707/546–9891, skylinktvl@aol.com, www.skylinktravel.com), serving lesbian travelers.

HEALTH

Switzerland's reputation for impeccable standards of cleanliness is well earned. But even at the foot of an icy-pure 2,000-m (6,560-ft) glacier, you'll find the locals drinking bottled mineral water; you'll have to wrangle with the waiter if you want tap water with your meal. This is as much a result of the tradition of expecting beverages in a café to be paid for as it is a response to health questions. If you're traveling with a child under two years old, you may be advised by locals not to carry him or her on excursions above 2,000 m (6,560 ft); check with your pediatrician before leaving home. Adults should limit strenuous excursions on the first day at extra-high-altitude resorts, those at 1,600 m (5,248 ft) and above. Adults with heart problems may want to avoid all excursions above 2,000 m (6,560 ft).

OVER-THE-COUNTER REMEDIES

Basic over-the-counter medicines are available from pharmacies. You can ask for them by using a major brand name.

HOLIDAYS

Jan. 1, Apr. 13 (Good Friday), Apr. 15–16 (Easter Sunday and Monday), May 1 (Labor Day), May 24 (Ascension), June 3–4 (Whitsunday/Pentecost), Aug. 1 (Swiss National Holiday), and Dec. 24–26.

INSURANCE

The most useful travel insurance plan is a comprehensive policy that includes coverage for trip cancellation and interruption, default, trip delay, and medical expenses (with a waiver for preexisting conditions).

Without insurance you will lose all or most of your money if you cancel your trip, regardless of the reason. Default insurance covers you if your tour operator, airline, or cruise line goes out of business. Trip-delay covers expenses that arise because of bad weather or mechanical delays. Study the fine print when comparing policies.

If you're traveling internationally, a key component of travel insurance is coverage for medical bills incurred if you get sick on the road. Such expenses are not generally covered by Medicare or private policies. U.K. residents can buy a travel insurance policy valid for most vacations taken during the year in which it's purchased (but check preexisting-condition coverage). British and Australian citizens need extra medical coverage when traveling overseas. Always **buy travel policies directly from the insurance company**; if you buy them from a cruise line, airline, or tour operator that goes out of business, you probably will not be covered for the agency or operator's default, a major risk. Before making any purchase, **review your existing health and home-owner's policies** to find out what they cover away from home.

➤ TRAVEL INSURERS: In the U.S.: **Access America** (✉ 6600 W. Broad St., Richmond, VA 23230, ☎ 804/285–3300 or 800/284–8300, FAX 804/673–1583, www.previewtravel.com), **Travel Guard International** (✉ 1145 Clark St., Stevens Point, WI 54481, ☎ 715/345–0505 or 800/826–1300, FAX 800/955–8785, www.noelgroup. com). In Canada: **Voyager Insurance** (✉ 44 Peel Center Dr., Brampton, Ontario L6T 4M8, ☎ 905/791–8700; 800/668–4342 in Canada).

➤ INSURANCE INFORMATION: In the U.K.: **Association of British Insurers** (✉ 51–55 Gresham St., London EC2V 7HQ, ☎ 020/7600–3333, FAX 020/7696–8999, info@abi.org.uk, www.abi.org.uk). In Australia: **Insurance Council of Australia** (☎ 03/9614–1077, FAX 03/9614–7924).

LANGUAGE

Nearly 70% of the population of Switzerland speaks one dialect or another of German; Swiss German can be a far cry from high German, although standard German is generally understood. French is spoken in the southwest, around Lake Geneva (Lac Léman), and in the cantons of Fribourg, Neuchâtel, Jura, Vaud, and most of the Valais. Italian is spoken in the Ticino. In the Upper and Lower Engadines, in the canton Graubünden, the last gasp of a Romance language called Romansh is still in daily use. There are several dialects of Romansh—five, in fact—so there's not much point in trying to pick up a few phrases. If you want to attempt communicating with the locals there, venture a little Italian. In the areas most frequented by English and American tourists—Zermatt, the Berner Oberland, the Engadine, Luzern—people in the tourist industry usually speak English. Elsewhere, you might not be as lucky. Ask before you plunge into your mother tongue—the person you're addressing may run to fetch a staff member who can converse with you on your own language terms. *See* the Swiss Vocabulary and Menu Guide at the back of the book for helpful words and phrases.

LANGUAGES FOR TRAVELERS

A phrase book and language-tape set can help get you started.

➤ PHRASE BOOKS & LANGUAGE-TAPE SETS: *Fodor's French for Travelers, Fodor's German for Travelers, Fodor's Italian for Travelers* (☎ 800/733–3000 in the U.S.; 800/668–4247 in Canada; $7 for phrasebook, $16.95 for audio set).

LODGING

Switzerland is as famous for its hotels as it is for its mountains, knives, and chocolates; its standards in hospitality are extremely high. Rooms are impeccably clean and well maintained, and they are furnished with comforts ranging from the simplest to the most deluxe. Prices are accordingly high: You will pay more for minimal comforts here than in any other European country. Americans accustomed to spacious motels with two double beds, a color TV, and a bath/shower combination may be disappointed in their first venture into the legendary Swiss hotel: Spaces are small, bathtubs cost extra, and single rooms may have single beds. What you're paying for is service, reliability, cleanliness, and a complex hierarchy of amenities you may not even know you need.

Where no address is provided in the hotel listings, none is necessary: In smaller towns and villages, a postal code is all you need. To find the hotel on arrival, watch for the official street signs pointing the way to every hotel that belongs to the local tourist association.

Some things to bear in mind when you check in: The standard double room in Switzerland has two prim beds built together, with separate linens and, sometimes, sheets tucked firmly down the middle. If you prefer more sociable arrangements, ask for a "French bed," or *lit matrimonial*—that will get you a single-mattress double. Some hotels may offer extra beds—for example, to expand a double room to a triple.

The lodgings we list are the cream of the crop in each price category. We always list the facilities available—but we don't specify whether they cost extra: When pricing accommodations, always ask what's included and what costs extra. In addition, assume that all rooms have a private bath unless otherwise noted. Properties indicated by an ✕🏠 are lodging establishments whose restaurant warrants a special trip (and will accommodate non–hotel guests). In regional chapters price charts appear in the lodging section of Pleasures and Pastimes, which follows each chapter introduction. In chapters devoted to a single city, price charts appear in the introductions to the dining section.

Particularly in ski resorts or in hotels where you'll be staying for three days or more, you may be quoted a room price per person including *demipension* (half board). This means you've opted for breakfast included and to eat either lunch or dinner in the hotel, selecting from a limited, fixed menu. Unless you're holding out for gastronomic adventure, your best bet is to take half board. Most hotels will be flexible if you come in from the slopes craving a steaming pot of fondue, and they will then subtract the day's pension supplement from your room price, charging you à la carte instead. A *garni* hotel is one without a restaurant on the premises.

APARTMENT & VILLA RENTALS

If you want a home base that's roomy enough for a family and comes with cooking facilities, **consider a furnished rental.** These can save you money, especially if you're traveling with a group. Home-exchange directories sometimes list rentals as well as exchanges. Most resort tourist offices have lists of apartments for rent.

➤ INTERNATIONAL AGENTS: **Drawbridge to Europe** (✉ 5456 Adams Rd., Talent, OR 97540, ☎ 541/512–8927 or 888/268–1148, FAX 541/512–0978, requests@drawbridgetoeurope. com, www.drawbridgetoeurope.com). **Hometours International** (✉ Box 11503, Knoxville, TN 37939, ☎ 865/690–8484 or 800/367–4668, hometours@aol.com, thor.he.net/åhometour/). **Interhome** (✉ 1990 N.E. 163rd St., Suite 110, N. Miami Beach, FL 33162, ☎ 305/940–2299 or 800/882–6864, FAX 305/940–2911, interhomeu@aol.com, www. interhome.com). **Villas and Apart-**

ments Abroad (✉ 1270 Avenue of the Americas, 15th floor, New York, NY 10020, ☎ 212/897–5045 or 800/433–3020, FAX 212/897–5039, vaa@altour.com, www.vaanyc.com). **Villas International** (✉ 950 Northgate Dr., Suite 206, San Rafael, CA 94903, ☎ 415/499–9490 or 800/221–2260, FAX 415/499–9491, villas@best.com, www.villasintl.com).

CAMPING

☞ Outdoors & Sports, *below*.

FARM STAYS

An unusual option for families seeking the local experience: Stay on a farm with a Swiss family, complete with children, animals, and the option to work in the fields. Participating farm families register with the Schweizerischer Bauernverband (Swiss Farmers Association), listing the birth dates of their children, rooms and facilities, and types of animals your children can see. Prices are often considerably lower than those of hotels and vacation flats. You should be reasonably fluent in French or German, depending on the region of your stay. Further information is available through Switzerland Tourism (☞ Visitor Information, *below*).

➤ ORGANIZATIONS: **Schweizerischer Bauernverband** (Swiss Farmers Association; ✉ Laurstr. 10, CH-5201 Brugg, ☎ 056/4625111, FAX 056/4415348). **Swiss Travel Fund** (Reka; ✉ Neueng. 15, CH-3001 Bern, ☎ 031/3296633, FAX 031/3296601, www.reka.ch).

HOME EXCHANGES

If you would like to exchange your home for someone else's, **join a home-exchange organization,** which will send you its updated listings of available exchanges for a year and will include your own listing in at least one of them. It's up to you to make specific arrangements.

➤ EXCHANGE CLUBS: **HomeLink International** (✉ Box 650, Key West, FL 33041, ☎ 305/294–7766 or 800/638–3841, FAX 305/294–1448, usa@homelink.org, www.homelink.org; $98 per year).**Intervac U.S.** (✉ Box 590504, San Francisco, CA 94159,

☎ 800/756–4663, FAX 415/435–7440, www.intervac.com; $89 per year includes two catalogs).

HOSTELS

No matter what your age, you can **save on lodging costs by staying at hostels.** In some 5,000 locations in more than 70 countries around the world, Hostelling International (HI), the umbrella group for a number of national youth-hostel associations, offers single-sex, dorm-style beds and, at many hostels, rooms for couples and family accommodations. Membership in any HI national hostel association, open to travelers of all ages, allows you to stay in HI-affiliated hostels at member rates; one-year membership is about $25 for adults (C$26.75 in Canada, £9.30 in the U.K., $30 in Australia, and $30 in New Zealand); hostels run about $10–$25 per night. Members have priority if the hostel has limited availablility; they're also eligible for discounts around the world, even on rail and bus travel in some countries.

➤ ORGANIZATIONS: **Hostelling International—American Youth Hostels** (✉ 733 15th St. NW, Suite 840, Washington, DC 20005, ☎ 202/783–6161, FAX 202/783–6171, www.hiayh.org). **Hostelling International—Canada** (✉ 400–205 Catherine St., Ottawa, Ontario K2P 1C3, ☎ 613/237–7884, FAX 613/237–7868, www.hostellingintl.ca). **Youth Hostel Association of England and Wales** (✉ Trevelyan House, 8 St. Stephen's Hill, St. Albans, Hertfordshire AL1 2DY, ☎ 01727/855215 or 01727/845047, FAX 01727/844126, www.yha.uk). **Australian Youth Hostel Association** (✉ 10 Mallett St., Camperdown, NSW 2050, ☎ 02/9565–1699, FAX 02/9565–1325, www.yha.com.au). **Youth Hostels Association of New Zealand** (✉ Box 436, Christchurch, New Zealand, ☎ 03/379–9970, FAX 03/365–4476, www.yha.org.nz).

HOTELS

When selecting a place to stay, an important resource can be the Swiss Hotel Association (SHA), a rigorous and demanding organization that maintains a specific rating system for lodging standards. Eighty percent of

Swiss hotels belong to this group and take their stars seriously. In contrast to more casual European countries, stars in Switzerland have precise meaning: A five-star hotel is required to have a specific staff-guest ratio, a daily change of bed linens, and extended-hour room service. A two-star hotel must have telephones, soap in the room, and fabric tablecloths in the restaurant. But the SHA standards cannot control the quality of decor and the grace of service. Thus you may find a four-star hotel that meets these technical requirements but has shabby appointments, leaky plumbing, or a rude concierge; a good, family-run two-star may make you feel like royalty.

Some rules of thumb: If you are looking for American-style chain-motel-level comfort—a big bed, color TV, minibar, safe—you will probably be happiest in four-star business-class hotels, many of which cater to Americans through travel agents and tour organizers; a number of four-star hotels in Switzerland are part of the Best Western organization. If you are looking for regional atmosphere, family ownership (and the pride and care for details that implies), and moderate prices, but don't care about a TV or minibar, look for three stars: Nearly all such rooms have showers and toilets. Two stars will get you tidy, minimal comfort with about a third of the rooms having baths. One-star properties are rare: They have no baths in rooms and no phone available in-house and generally fall below the demanding Swiss national standard. Several hotels in the SHA are specially rated *Landgasthof* or *relais de campagne,* meaning "country inn." These generally are rustic-style lodgings typical of the region, but they may range from spare to luxurious and are rarely set apart in deep country, as Americans might expect; some are in the midst of small market towns or resorts. The SHA distinguishes them as offering especially high-quality service, personal attention, and parking.

Many hotels close for a short period during their region's off-season; closing dates often vary from year to year, so be sure to call ahead and check.

➤ TOLL-FREE NUMBERS: **Best Western** (☎ 800/528–1234, www.bestwestern. com). **Choice** (☎ 800/221–2222, www.hotelchoice.com). **Clarion** (☎ 800/252–7466, www.choicehotels. com). **Comfort** (☎ 800/228–5150, www.comfortinn.com). **Holiday Inn** (☎ 800/465–4329, www.holiday-inn. com). **Inter-Continental** (☎ 800/327–0200, www.interconti.com). **Marriott** (☎ 800/228–9290, www.marriott. com). **Le Meridien** (☎ 800/543–4300, www.forte-hotels.com). **Sheraton** (☎ 800/325–3535, www.sheraton.com).

INNS

Travelers on a budget can find help from the *Check-in E & G Hotels* guide (E & G stands for *einfach und gemütlich*: roughly, "simple and cozy"), available through Switzerland Tourism. These comfortable little hotels have banded together to dispel Switzerland's intimidating image as an elite, overpriced vacation spot and offer simple two-star standards in usually very atmospheric inns.

Other organizations can help you find unusual properties: The Relais & Châteaux group seeks out manor houses, historic buildings, and generally atmospheric luxury, with most of its properties falling into the $$$ or $$$$ range. A similar group, Romantik Hotels and Restaurants, combines architectural interest, historic atmosphere, and fine regional food. Relais du Silence hotels are usually isolated in a peaceful, natural setting, with first-class comforts.

MAIL & SHIPPING

POSTAL RATES

Mail rates are divided into first-class "A" (airmail) and second-class "B" (surface). Letters and postcards to North America weighing up to 20 grams cost 1.80 SF first class, 1.40 SF second class; to the United Kingdom, 1.30 SF first class, 1.20 SF second class.

RECEIVING MAIL

If you're uncertain where you'll be staying, you can have your mail, marked "poste restante" or "postlagernd," sent to any post office in Switzerland. It needs the sender's name and address on the back, and you'll need proof of identity to collect

THE GOLD GUIDE / SMART TRAVEL TIPS

it. You can also have your mail sent to American Express for a small fee; if you are a cardholder or have American Express traveler's checks, the service is free. Postal codes precede the names of cities and towns in Swiss addresses.

MONEY MATTERS

Despite increased competition across Europe, the recent decrease in the Swiss franc's value against other currencies, and the negligible inflation rate over the past several years, Switzerland remains one of the most expensive countries on the Continent for travelers, and you may find yourself shocked by the price of a light lunch or a generic hotel room. If you are traveling on a tight budget, avoid staying in well-known resorts and the most sophisticated cities; Geneva, Zürich, Zermatt, Gstaad, and St. Moritz are exceptionally expensive. If you are traveling by car, you have the luxury of seeking out small family hotels in villages, where costs are relatively low. Unless you work hard at finding budget accommodations, you will average more than 150 SF a night for two—more if you stay in business-class hotels, with TV and direct-dial phone.

A cup of coffee or a beer costs about 3 SF in a simple restaurant; ordinary open wines, sold by the deciliter ("deci"), start at about 3 SF. All three beverages cost sometimes double that in resorts, city hotels, and fine restaurants. A plain, one-plate daily lunch special averages 14–18 SF. A city bus ride costs between 1.50 SF and 2.20 SF, a short cab ride 15 SF. Prices throughout this guide are given for adults. Substantially reduced fees are almost always available for children, students, and senior citizens. For information on taxes, *see* Taxes, *below*.

ATMS

You can withdraw money from ATMs in Switzerland as long as your card is properly programmed with your personal identification number (PIN). For use in Switzerland, your PIN number must be four digits long. Banks offer good wholesale exchange rates.

CREDIT CARDS

Throughout this guide the following abbreviations are used: **AE**, American Express; **DC**, Diner's Club; **MC**, Master Card; and **V**, Visa. Note that Master Card is affiliated with Eurocard.

➤ REPORTING LOST CARDS: **American Express** (☎ 800/327–2177; 336/393–1111 call collect). **Diners Club** (☎ 800/234–6377; 702/797–5532 call collect). **Master Card** (☎ 800/307–7309; 0800/897092 toll-free). **Visa** (☎ 800/847–2911; 410/581–9994 call collect).

CURRENCY

The unit of currency in Switzerland is the Swiss franc (SF), available in notes of 10, 20, 50, 100, 200, and 1,000. Francs are divided into centimes (in Suisse Romande) or rappen (in German Switzerland). There are coins for 5, 10, and 20 centimes. Larger coins are the half-, 1-, 2-, and 5-franc pieces.

CURRENCY EXCHANGE

At press time (summer 2000), the Swiss franc stood at 1.67 to the U.S. dollar, 1.12 to the Canadian dollar, and 2.5 to the pound sterling.

For the most favorable rates, **change money through banks.** Although ATM transaction fees may be higher abroad than at home, ATM rates are excellent because they are based on wholesale rates offered only by major banks. You won't do as well at exchange booths in airports or rail and bus stations, in hotels, in restaurants, or in stores. Convenience-wise, train stations have an edge; more than 300 stations have exchange points that are open daily, including lunch hours, when many banks are closed. These booths exchange currency, buy and sell traveler's checks in various currencies, and cash Eurocheques. To avoid lines at airport exchange booths, **get a bit of local currency before you leave home.**

➤ EXCHANGE SERVICES: **International Currency Express** (☎ 888/278–6628 for orders, www.foreignmoney.com). **Thomas Cook Currency Services** (☎ 800/287–7362 for telephone orders and retail locations, www.us.thomas-cook.com).

TRAVELER'S CHECKS

Do you need traveler's checks? It depends on where you're headed. If you're going to rural areas and small towns, go with cash; traveler's checks are best used in cities. Lost or stolen checks can usually be replaced within 24 hours. To ensure a speedy refund, buy your own traveler's checks—don't let someone else pay for them: irregularities like this can cause delays. The person who bought the checks should make the call to request a refund.

Note that there is a limitation (300 SF) on the cashing of Eurocheques drawn on European banks.

OUTDOORS & SPORTS

BICYCLING

☞ Bike Travel, *above*.

CAMPING

Switzerland is ideal for campers, with approximately 450 sites throughout the country. All are classified with one to five stars according to amenities, location, and so on. The rates vary widely but average around 15 SF per night for a family of four, plus car or camper. For further details see the *Swiss Camping Guide*, published by the Swiss Camping Association, available at bookshops for 15 SF or from the **Camping and Caravaning Association** (✉ Box 24, CH-6000 Luzern 4, ☎ 041/2104822, FAX 041/2104822). Listings are also available from the **Touring Club of Switzerland** (✉ Ch. de Blandonnet 4, CH-1214 Vernier, ☎ 022/4172727, FAX 022/4172020) and from the **Swiss Campsite Association** (✉ CH-3800 Interlaken-Thunersee, ☎ 033/8233523, FAX 033/8233523, www.swisscamps.ch).

To stay in most European campsites, you must have an **International Camping Carnet** verifying your status as a camper. This is available from any national camping association within Europe or from the **National Campers and Hikers Association** (✉ 4804 Transit Rd., Bldg. 2, Depew, NY 14043, ☎ 716/668–6242).

GOLF

There are 72 golf courses throughout Switzerland where you can rent clubs and play on a daily greens fee basis. For more information contact the **Swiss Association of Golf** (✉ pl. Croix-Blanche 19, CH-1066 Epalinges-Lausanne, ☎ 021/7843531, FAX 021/7843536 www.asg.ch), which has a directory of all courses. It can also provide specific information, such as course fees and conditions.

HIKING

The Swiss Alps, naturally, are riddled with hiking trails; yellow trail indicators are standard all over the country. Hiking is an especially popular pastime in the German-speaking areas, such as the Berner Oberland. For suggested hiking itineraries, contact regional tourist offices; many bookstores also carry detailed topographical maps with marked trails. You can also contact the **Fédération Suisse de Tourisme Pédestre** (✉ Im Hirsholm 49, CH-4125 Riehen, ☎ 061/6069340, FAX 061/6069345, www.swisshiking.ch).

SKIING

Slope difficulty levels are indicated with color codes. A black slope is the most difficult; blue indicates intermediate levels; red is for beginner slopes. A daily bulletin of ski conditions at 220 locations throughout Switzerland is available by calling 157/120120 (0.86 SF/min.); reports are in the local language. You can also check the Switzerland Tourism Web site (☞ Visitor Information, *below*). Applications to the **Swiss Alpine Club** should be addressed to the club at Sektion Zermatt, Mr. Edmond F. Krieger, Haus Dolomit, CH-3920 Zermatt (☎ FAX 027/9672610). Remember to include a passport-size photo. Excursions involve serious climbing; it's not necessary to be fluent in German. For a **booklet** of mountain-club huts, contact the Swiss Alpine Club (✉ Monbijoustr. 61, Postfach, CH-3000 Bern 23, ☎ 031/3701818 FAX 031/3701800, www.sac-cas.ch). A hut directory, "Hütten der Schweizer Alpen," complete with color photos, can be ordered for 38 SF from **SAC-Buchauslieferung** (✉ Felsenaustr. 5, CH-7000 Chur, ☎ 081/2583335, FAX 081/2502666).

PACKING

Switzerland is essentially sportswear country. City dress is more formal.

Men would be wise to pack a jacket and tie if dining in some of the great restaurants; otherwise, a tie and sweater are standard at night. Women wear skirts more frequently here than in America, especially women over 50, though anything fashionable goes. Except at the most chic hotels in international resorts, you won't need formal evening dress.

Even in July and August the evening air grows chilly in the mountains, so **bring a warm sweater.** And **bring a hat or sunscreen,** as the atmosphere is thinner at high altitudes. Glaciers can be blinding in the sun, so **be sure to bring sunglasses, especially for high-altitude excursions.** Good walking shoes or hiking boots are a must, whether you're tackling medieval cobblestones or mountain trails.

To ensure comfort, **budget travelers should bring their own washcloth and soap,** not always standard equipment in one- and two-star-rated Swiss hotels. If you're planning on shopping and cooking, a tote bag will come in handy: Most groceries do not provide sacks, but sturdy, reusable plastic totes can be bought at checkout. Laundromats are rare, so laundry soap is useful for hand washing.

In your carry-on luggage, **pack an extra pair of eyeglasses or contact lenses** and **enough of any medication you take** to last the entire trip. You may also ask your doctor to write a spare prescription using the drug's generic name, since brand names may vary from country to country. In luggage to be checked, **never pack prescription drugs or valuables.** To avoid customs delays, carry medications in their original packaging. And don't forget to carry with you the addresses of offices that handle refunds of lost traveler's checks.

CHECKING LUGGAGE

How many carry-on bags you can bring with you is up to the airline. Most allow only one, but not always, so make sure that everything you carry aboard will fit under your seat or in the overhead bin, and get to the gate early. Note that if you have a seat at the back of the plane, you'll probably board first, while the overhead bins are still empty.

If you are flying internationally, note that baggage allowances may be determined not by piece but by weight—generally 88 pounds (40 kilograms) in first class, 66 pounds (30 kilograms) in business class, and 44 pounds (20 kilograms) in economy.

Airline liability for baggage is limited to $1,250 per person on flights within the United States. On international flights it amounts to $9.07 per pound or $20 per kilogram for checked baggage (roughly $640 per 70-pound bag) and $400 per passenger for unchecked baggage. You can buy additional coverage at check-in for about $10 per $1,000 of coverage, but it excludes a rather extensive list of items, shown on your airline ticket.

Before departure, **itemize your bags' contents** and their worth, and label the bags with your name, address, and phone number. (If you use your home address, cover it so potential thieves can't see it readily.) Inside each bag, **pack a copy of your itinerary.** At check-in, **make sure that each bag is correctly tagged** with the destination airport's three-letter code. If your bags arrive damaged or fail to arrive at all, file a written report with the airline before leaving the airport.

PASSPORTS & VISAS

When traveling internationally, **carry your passport even if you don't need one** (it's always the best form of I.D.) and **make two photocopies of the data page** (one for someone at home and another for you, carried separately from your passport). If you lose your passport, promptly call the nearest embassy or consulate and the local police.

ENTERING SWITZERLAND

Australian, British, Canadian, New Zealand, and U.S. citizens need only a valid passport to enter Switzerland for stays of up to 90 days.

PASSPORT OFFICES

The best time to apply for a passport or to renew is in fall and winter. Before any trip, check your passport's expiration date and, if necessary, renew it as soon as possible.

➤ AUSTRALIAN CITIZENS: **Australian Passport Office** (☎ 131–232, www.dfat.gov.au/passports).

➤ CANADIAN CITIZENS: **Passport Office** (☎ 819/994–3500 or 800/567–6868, www.dfait-maeci.gc.ca/passport).

➤ NEW ZEALAND CITIZENS: **New Zealand Passport Office** (☎ 04/494–0700, www.passports.govt.nz).

➤ U.K. CITIZENS: **London Passport Office** (☎ 0990/210–410) for fees and documentation requirements and to request an emergency passport.

➤ U.S. CITIZENS: **National Passport Information Center** (☎ 900/225–5674; calls are 35¢ per minute for automated service, $1.05 per minute for operator service).

SAFETY

Use common sense, especially after dark, and particularly in large cities. Walk on well-lighted, busy streets. **Look alert and aware;** a purposeful pace helps deter trouble wherever you go. Store valuables in a hotel safe or, better yet, leave them at home. Keep a sharp eye (and hand) on handbags and backpacks; do not hang them from a chair in restaurants. Carry wallets in inside or front pockets rather than hip pockets. Use ATMs in daylight, preferably in an indoor location with security guards.

SENIOR-CITIZEN TRAVEL

Women over 62 and men over 65 qualify for special seasonal (and in some cases year-round) discounts at a variety of Swiss hotels. With married couples, at least one spouse must fulfill these conditions. Prices include overnight lodging in a single or double room, breakfast, service charges, and taxes. Arrangements can also be made for extended stays. Senior citizens are entitled to discounts on trains, buses, and boats, at all movie theaters in Switzerland, and, where posted, at museums and attractions.

To qualify for age-related discounts, **mention your senior-citizen status up front** when booking hotel reservations (not when checking out) and before

you're seated in restaurants (not when paying the bill). When renting a car, ask about promotional car-rental discounts, which can be cheaper than senior-citizen rates.

A special guide to hotels that offer senior discounts, *Season for Seniors*, is available from the Swiss Hotel Association (✉ Monbijoustr. 130, CH-3001 Bern, ☎ 031/3704111, FAX 031/3704444, www.swisshotels.ch) or from **Switzerland Tourism** (☞ Visitor Information, *below*).

➤ EDUCATIONAL PROGRAMS: **Elderhostel** (✉ 75 Federal St., 3rd floor, Boston, MA 02110, ☎ 877/426–8056, FAX 877/426–2166, www.elderhostel.org). **Interhostel** (✉ University of New Hampshire, 6 Garrison Ave., Durham, NH 03824, ☎ 603/862–1147 or 800/733–9753, FAX 603/862–1113, www.learn.unh.edu).

STUDENTS IN SWITZERLAND

Reduced student fees are often available for individual admission tickets, transportation, and so forth. An International Student Identification Card (ISIC), available through the Council on International Educational Exchange, is generally accepted. The Swiss Museum Passport (☞ Discounts & Deals, *above*) has a reduced student fee, and the Eurail Youth pass (☞ Train Travel, *below*) has a reduced fee for people between ages 12 and 25.

➤ I.D.S & SERVICES: **Council Travel** (CIEE; ✉ 205 E. 42nd St., 14th floor, New York, NY 10017, ☎ 212/822–2700 or 888/268–6245, FAX 212/822–2699, info@councilexchanges.org, www.councilexchanges.org), for mail orders only, in the United States. **Travel Cuts** (✉ 187 College St., Toronto, Ontario M5T 1P7, ☎ 416/979–2406 or 800/667–2887, www.travelcuts.com), in Canada.

TAXES

What you see is what you pay in Switzerland: Restaurant checks and hotel bills include all taxes.

VALUE-ADDED TAX

Switzerland's value-added tax is 7.6%; it can add a significant amount to already pricey bills. (On receipts, the VAT is usually indicated separately.) Theater and movie tickets are some of the few items exempted from this tax.

However, on any one purchase of 550 francs or more from one store, refunds are available to nonresidents for clothes, watches, and souvenirs, but not for meals or hotel rooms. To **get a VAT refund,** pay by credit card; at the time of purchase, the store clerk should fill out and give you a red form and keep a record of your credit card number. When leaving Switzerland, you must hand-deliver the red form to a customs officer at the customs office at the airport or, if leaving by car or train, at the border. Customs will process the form and return it to the store, which will refund the tax by crediting your card. Global Refund is a V.A.T. refund service that makes getting your money back hassle-free. The service is available Europe-wide at 130,000 affiliated stores. In participating stores, **ask for the Global Refund form** (called a Shopping Cheque). Have it stamped like any customs form by customs officials when you leave the European Union. Then take the form to one of the more than 700 Global Refund counters—conveniently located at every major airport and border crossing—and your money will be refunded on the spot in the form of cash, check, or a refund to your credit-card account (minus a small percentage for processing).

➤ VAT REFUNDS: **Global Refund** (✉ 99 Main St., Nyack, NY 10960, ☎ 800/566–9828, ℻ 845/348–1549, taxfree@us.globalrefund.com, www.globalrefund.com).

TELEPHONES

Cellular phones (*natels*) may be rented at either the Geneva or Zürich airports from **Rent@phone** (☎ 022/7178263 in Geneva, ☎ 01/8165063 in Zürich, www.rentaphone.ch). You can arrange for a rentals n a daily, weekly, or monthly basis. The Rent@phone desks are clearly indicated in each airport.

AREA & COUNTRY CODES

The country code for Switzerland is 41. When dialing a Swiss number from abroad, drop the initial 0 from the local area code. The country code is 1 for the United States and Canada, 61 for Australia, 64 for New Zealand, and 44 for the United Kingdom.

DIRECTORY & OPERATOR ASSISTANCE

Dial 111 for information within Switzerland (1.10 SF for two requests on weekdays from 9–5). All telephone operators speak English, and instructions are printed in English in all telephone booths. Precede the area-code number with 0 when dialing long-distance within Switzerland.

Anglo-Phone (☎ 1575014) is an English-language information service giving details on hotels, restaurants, museums, nightlife, skiing, what to do in an emergency, and more. Lines are open weekdays 9–7 and 9–1 on Saturday. Calls cost 2.13 SF per minute.

INTERNATIONAL CALLS

You can dial most international numbers direct from Switzerland, adding 00 before the country code. If you want a number that cannot be reached directly, dial 1141 for a connection. Dial 1159 for international numbers and information. (Neighboring countries have their own information numbers: 1151 for Austria; 1152 for Germany; 1153 for France; and 1154 for Italy.) It's cheapest to use the booths in train stations and post offices: Calls made from your hotel cost a great deal more. Rates for calls to the United States and Canada cost 0.12 SF per minute weekdays and 0.10 SF per minute on weekends and Swiss holidays. Calls to the United Kingdom, Australia, and New Zealand cost 0.25 SF a minute weekdays and 0.20 SF per minute on weekends and Swiss holidays.

LONG-DISTANCE CALLS

On January 1, 1998, the state monopoly on telecommunications ended. Rates have been continually decreasing since the entrance of new companies into the market to compete with the state-owned Swisscom. There is direct dialing to everywhere in Switzerland. For local area codes consult the pink pages and for international country and city codes, consult the green-banded pages at the front of the telephone book.

AT&T, MCI, and Sprint access codes make calling long distance relatively convenient, but you may find the local access number blocked in many hotel rooms. First ask the hotel operator to connect you. If the hotel operator balks, ask for an international operator or dial the international operator yourself. One way to improve your odds of getting connected to your long-distance carrier is to travel with more than one company's calling card (a hotel may block Sprint, for example, but not MCI). If all else fails, call from a pay phone.

➤ ACCESS CODES: **AT&T Direct** (☎ 0800/890011). **MCI WorldPhone** (☎ 800/444–4141). **Sprint International Access** (☎ 800/877–4646 for other areas).

PUBLIC PHONES

To make a local call on a pay phone, pick up the receiver, insert a phone card and dial the number. A local call starts at.60 SF. Swisscom phone cards are available in 5 SF, 10 SF, or 20 SF units; they're sold at post offices, train stations, airports, and kiosks. Slip a card into an adapted public phone, and a continual readout will tell you how much money is left on the card. The cost of the call will be counted against the card, with any remaining value still good for the next time you use it. If you drain the card and still need to talk, the readout will warn you: You can either pop in a new card or make up the difference with coins, although very few phones still accept coins. Many phone booths now also accept Visa, MasterCard, and American Express cards, but be sure to have a four-digit PIN code (☞ Credit Cards *in* Money, *above*).

TIME

Switzerland is six hours ahead of New York, nine hours ahead of Los Angeles, one hour ahead of London, and nine hours behind Sydney.

TIPPING

Despite all protests to the contrary and menus marked *service compris,* the Swiss *do* tip at restaurant meals, giving quantities anywhere from the change from the nearest franc to 10 SF for a world-class meal exquisitely served. Unlike American-style tipping, calculated by a percentage, usually between 10% and 20%, a tip is still a tip here: a nod of approval for a job well done. If, in a café, the waitress settles the bill at the table, fishing the change from her leather purse, give her the change on the spot—or calculate the total, including tip, and tell her the full sum before she counts it onto the tabletop. If you need to take more time to calculate, leave it on the table, though this isn't common practice in outdoor cafés. If you're paying for a meal with a credit card, try to tip with cash instead of filling in the tip slot on the slip: Not all managers are good about doling out the waiters' tips in cash. Tipping porters and doormen is easier: 2 SF per bag is adequate in good hotels, 1 SF per trip in humbler lodgings (unless you travel heavy). A fixed rate of 5 SF per bag applies to porter fees at the Geneva and Zürich airports.

TOURS & PACKAGES

Because everything is prearranged on a prepackaged tour or independent vacation, you'll spend less time planning—and often get it all at a good price.

BOOKING WITH AN AGENT

Travel agents are excellent resources. But it's a good idea to collect brochures from several agencies as some agents' suggestions may be influenced by relationships with tour and package firms that reward them for volume sales. If you have a special interest, **find an agent with expertise in that area**; ASTA (☞ Travel Agencies, *below*) has a database of specialists worldwide.

Make sure your travel agent knows the accommodations and other services of the place they're recommending. Ask about the hotel's location, room size, beds, and whether it has a pool, room service, or programs for children, if you care about these. Has your agent been there in person or sent others whom you can contact?

Do some homework on your own, too: local tourism boards can provide information about lesser-known and small-niche operators, some of which may sell only direct.

BUYER BEWARE

Each year consumers are stranded or lose their money when tour operators—even large ones with excellent reputations—go out of business. So **check out the operator**. Ask several travel agents about its reputation, and try to **book with a company that has a consumer-protection program** (look for information in the company's brochure). In the United States, members of the National Tour Association and the United States Tour Operators Association are required to set aside funds to cover your payments and travel arrangements in the event that the company defaults. It's also a good idea to choose a company that participates in the American Society of Travel Agents' Tour Operator Program (TOP); ASTA will act as mediator in any disputes between you and your tour operator.

Remember that the more your package or tour includes, the better you can predict the ultimate cost of your vacation. Make sure you know exactly what is covered, and **beware of hidden costs**. Are taxes, tips, and transfers included? Entertainment and excursions? These can add up.

➤ TOUR-OPERATOR RECOMMENDATIONS: **American Society of Travel Agents** (☞ Travel Agencies, *below*). **National Tour Association** (NTA; ✉ 546 E. Main St., Lexington, KY 40508, ☎ 606/226–4444 or 800/682–8886, www.ntaonline.com). **United States Tour Operators Association** (USTOA; ✉ 342 Madison Ave., Suite 1522, New York, NY 10173, ☎ 212/599–6599 or 800/468–7862, ℻ 212/599–6744, ustoa@aol.com, www.ustoa.com).

TRAIN TRAVEL

The Swiss Federal Railways, or **SBB/CFF/FFS** (☎ 0900/300300, 1.19 SF/min.), has a very extensive network; trains and stations are clean, and as you'd expect, service is extremely prompt. The cleanliness extends to train-station bathrooms—in most countries these are grim affairs, but in Switzerland's large city stations, look for "McClean" restrooms. They have nothing to do with the red-and-yellow hamburger chain; instead, they're immaculate, sleekly designed spaces, with bathrooms, changing stations, showers, and a toiletries kiosk. Entrance is about 2 SF.

Trains described as Inter-City or Express are the fastest, stopping only in principal towns. *Regionalzug/Train Régional* means a local train. If you're planning to use the trains extensively, get the official timetable ("Kursbuch" or "Horaire") for 16 SF; the portable pocket version is called "Reka" and costs 12 SF.

In addition to the federal rail lines there are some private rail lines, such as the Montreux-Oberland-Bernois line and the Rhätische Bahn. These private lines generally accept discount rail passes (☞ Cutting Costs, *below*) for a surcharge.

Consider a first-class ticket only if the extra comfort is worth the price. The principal difference between first- and second class is more space to yourself; the first-class cars are less crowded. Seat size is the same, upholstery fancier, and you usually will be delivered to the track position closest to the station. **Make seat reservations** for trips during rush hours and in high season, especially on international trains.

If your itinerary requires changing trains, **bear in mind that the average connection time is six to eight minutes.**

CUTTING COSTS

To save money, **look into rail passes.** But be aware that if you don't plan to cover many miles, you may come out ahead by buying individual tickets.

If Switzerland is your only destination in Europe, there are numerous passes available for visitors. The **Swiss Pass** is the best value, offering unlimited travel on Swiss Federal Railways, postbuses (☞ Bus Travel, *above*), lake steamers, and the local bus and tram services of 36 cities. It also gives reductions on many privately owned railways, cable cars, and funiculars. Available from Switzerland Tourism and from travel agents outside Switzerland, the card is valid for four days (160 SF second class; 245 SF first class); eight days (220 second class; 330 SF first class); 15 days (265 SF second class; 400 SF first class), 21 days (305 SF second class; 458 SF first class); or one month (345 SF second class; 525 SF first class). There is also a three-day **Flexipass** (156 SF second class; 234 SF first class), which offers the same unlimited-travel options as a regular Swiss Pass for any three days within a 15-day period. There is a 15% discount on the Swiss Pass and the Flexipass for two or more people. The STS **Family Card** is issued to nonresidents of Switzerland and Liechtenstein, upon request. For information on the **Swiss Boat Pass,** *see* Boat Travel, *above;* for information on the Family Card, *see* Children in Switzerland, *above.*

Within some popular tourist areas, **Regional Holiday Season Tickets** are available. Their discount offers vary; prices vary widely too, depending on the region and period of validity. Passes are available from Switzerland Tourism (☞ Visitor Information, *below*) and local tourist boards, but to be on the safe side, inquire well in advance.

The **Swiss Card,** which can be purchased in the United States through Rail Europe and at train stations at the Zürich and Geneva airports and in Basel, is valid for 30 days and grants full round-trip travel from your arrival point to any destination in the country, plus a half-price reduction on any further excursions during your stay (104 SF second class; 138 SF first class). For more information about train travel in Switzerland, get the free "Swiss Travel System" or "Discover Switzerland" brochures from Switzerland Tourism (☞ Visitor Information, *below*).

Switzerland is one of 17 countries in which you can **use Eurailpasses,** which provide unlimited first-class rail travel, in all of the participating countries, for the duration of the pass. If you plan to rack up the miles, get a standard pass. These are available for 15 days ($554), 21 days ($718), one month ($890), two months ($1,260), and three months ($1,558). If your plans call for only limited train travel, **look into a Europass,** which costs less money than a EurailPass. Unlike with Eurailpasses,

however, you get a limited number of travel days, in a limited number of countries, during a specified time period. For example, a two-month pass allows between 5 and 15 days of rail travel; costs range between $348 and $728. Keep in mind that the basic Europass is good only in France, Germany, Italy, Spain, and Switzerland, though you have the option of adding two "associate countries" (Austria, Hungary, the Netherlands, Belgium, Luxembourg, Greece, or Portugal).

In addition to standard Eurailpasses, **ask about special rail-pass plans.** Among these are the Eurail Youthpass (for those under age 26), the Eurail and Europass Saverpasses (which give a discount for two or more people traveling together), a Eurail Flexipass (which allows a certain number of travel days within a set period), the Euraildrive Pass and the Europass Drive (which combines travel by train and rental car). Whichever pass you choose, remember that you must **purchase your pass before you leave** for Europe.

Many travelers assume that rail passes guarantee them seats on the trains they wish to ride. Not so. You need to **book seats ahead even if you are using a rail pass;** seat reservations are required on some European trains, particularly high-speed trains, and are a good idea on trains that may be crowded—particularly in summer on popular routes. You will also need a reservation if you purchase sleeping accommodations.

FROM THE U.K.

With the Channel Tunnel completing a seamless route, you can leave London around noon on the Eurostar and (thanks to connections via Paris/Lyon on the superb French *train à grande vitesse,* TGV) have a late supper in Geneva.

The *Venice–Simplon–Orient Express* (✉ 20 Upper Ground, London SE1 9PD, ☎ 020/7928–6000) runs from London to Zürich. Information is also available from the tour company Abercrombie & Kent.

➤ TRAIN INFORMATION: **Rail Europe** (✉ 500 Mamaroneck Ave., Harrison, NY 10528, ☎ 914/682–5172 or 800/

438–7245, FAX 800/432–1329; ✉ 2087 Dundas E, Suite 106, Mississauga, Ontario L4X 1M2, ☎ 800/361–7245, FAX 905/602–4198). **DER Travel Services** (✉ 9501 W. Devon Ave., Rosemont, IL 60018, ☎ 800/782–2424, FAX 800/282–7474 for information; 800/860–9944 for brochures). **CIT Tours Corp.** (✉ 15 W. 44th St., 10th floor, New York, NY 10036, ☎ 212/730–2400; 800/248–7245 in the U.S.; 800/387–0711; 800/361–7799 in Canada). **Abercrombie & Kent** (✉ 1520 Kensington Rd., Oak Brook, IL 60521-2141, ☎ 630/954–2944 or 800/323–7308, FAX 630/954–3324).

PAYING

You may pay for rail tickets with either cash or major credit cards.

SCENIC ROUTES

Switzerland makes the most of its Alpine rail engineering, which cuts through the icy granite landscape above 2,000 m (6,560 ft), by offering special trains that run from one tourist destination to another, crossing over spectacular passes with panoramic cars. The *Glacier Express* connects the two glamorous resorts of Zermatt and St. Moritz, crawling over the Oberalp Pass and serving lunch in a burnished-wood period dining car; the *William Tell Express* combines a rail crossing of the Saint Gotthard Pass with a cruise down the length of Lake Luzern. The *Golden Pass/Panoramic Express* climbs from the balmy waterfront of Montreux into the Alpine terrain around Interlaken and rolls on to Luzern via the Brünig Pass. The *Bernina Express* ascends from Chur to St. Moritz, then climbs over the magnificent Bernina Pass into Italy, where visitors can connect by postbus to Lugano. These sightseeing itineraries take 4–11 hours' travel time. For more information, contact Swiss Federal Railways (☞ *above*) or **Railtour Suisse** (✉ Chutzenstr. 24, CH-3000 17 Bern, ☎ 031/3780000, FAX 031/3780222).

TRANSPORTATION AROUND SWITZERLAND

Switzerland offers perhaps the best transit network in Europe: Impeccable autoroutes studded with emergency phones; trams and buses snaking

through city streets; steamers crisscrossing blue lakes; and, of course, the famous trains, whose wheels roll to a stop under the station clock just as the second hand sweeps 12.

It doesn't end there. Once on site, a web of tourist transportation gets you even closer to those spectacular views: Cogwheel trains grind up 45-degree slopes, lifts and gondolas sail silently to vantage points, tiny Alpine Metros bore through granite up to green tundra above 8,000 ft.

Traveling by car is the surest way to penetrate the Swiss landscape, but if you invest in a rail pass (☞ Train Travel, *above*), you will not feel cut off. Most Swiss trains intersect with private excursion networks and allow for comfortable sightseeing itineraries without huge layovers. And there's always a sturdy yellow postbus, following its appointed rounds with mountain-goat efficiency at minimal cost; connections to obscure villages and trails are free to holders of the Swiss Pass.

TRAVEL AGENCIES

A good travel agent puts your needs first. Look for an agency that has been in business at least five years, emphasizes customer service, and has someone on staff who specializes in your destination. In addition, **make sure the agency belongs to a professional trade organization.** The American Society of Travel Agents (ASTA), with 27,000 agents in some 170 countries, is the largest and most influential in the field. Operating under the motto "Integrity in Travel," it maintains and enforces a strict code of ethics and will step in to help mediate any agent-client disputes if necessary. ASTA also maintains a Web site that includes a directory of agents. (If a travel agency is also acting as your tour operator, *see* Buyer Beware *in* Tours & Packages, *above*.)

➤ LOCAL AGENT REFERRALS: **American Society of Travel Agents** (ASTA; ☎ 800/965–2782 24-hr hot line, FAX 703/684–8319, www.astanet. com). **Association of British Travel Agents** (✉ 68–71 Newman St., London W1P 4AH, ☎ 020/7637–2444, FAX 020/7637–0713, abta.co.uk, www. abtanet.com). **Association of Cana-**

dian Travel Agents (⊠ 1729 Bank St., Suite 201, Ottawa, Ontario K1V 7Z5, ☎ 613/521–0474, FAX 613/521–0805, acta.ntl@sympatico.ca). **Australian Federation of Travel Agents** (⊠ Level 3, 309 Pitt St., Sydney 2000, ☎ 02/9264–3299, FAX 02/9264–1085, www.afta.com.au). **Travel Agents' Association of New Zealand** (⊠ Box 1888, Wellington 10033, ☎ 04/499–0104, FAX 04/499–0827, taanz@ tiasnet.co.nz).

VISITOR INFORMATION

➤ TOURIST INFORMATION: **U.S. (nationwide):** (⊠ 608 5th Ave., New York, NY 10002, ☎ 212/757–5944, FAX 212/262–6116). **El Segundo, CA:** (⊠ 222 N. Sepulveda Blvd., Suite 1570, 90245, ☎ 310/335–5980, FAX 310/335–5982). **Chicago:** (⊠ 150 N. Michigan Ave., Suite 2930, 60601, ☎ 312/630–5840, FAX 312/630–5848). **Canada:** (⊠ 926 The East Mall, Etobicoke, Ontario M9B 6KI, ☎ 416/695–2090 or 514/333–9526, FAX 416/695–2774). **U.K.:** (⊠ Swiss Centre, 1 New Coventry St., London W1V 8EE, ☎ 020/7734–1921, FAX 020/7437–4577).

➤ U.S. GOVERNMENT ADVISORIES: **U.S. Department of State** (⊠ Overseas Citizens Services Office, Room 4811 N.S., 2201 C St. NW, Washington, DC 20520, ☎ 202/647–5225 for interactive hot line, 301/946–4400 for computer bulletin board, FAX 202/647–3000 for interactive hot line); enclose a self-addressed, stamped business-size envelope.

WEB SITES

Do check out the World Wide Web when you're planning. You'll find everything from current weather forecasts to virtual tours of famous cities. Fodor's Web site, www.fodors. com, is a great place to start your online travels. When you see a ⬢ in this book, go to www.fodors.com/urls for an up-to-date link to that destination's site.

For more specific information on Switzerland, visit: **Switzerland Tourism** (www.myswitzerland.com), which allows travelers to customize a vacation in Switzerland and even to book it through an interactive travel planner; **Travel.Org** (www.travel.org/

switz.html) for links and information on more than a dozen cities, general travel tips, and more specialized topics like vegetarian restaurants; **Swiss Federal Railways** (www.rail.ch), which broadcasts train schedules and timetables; or **Swiss Post** (www. swisspost.com) for postbus schedules, excursions, and fares.

The **Swissart Network** site (www. swissart.ch) has links to several museums, city art associations, and galleries; some information is in English. **Great Outdoor Recreation Pages** (GORP; www.gorp.com) has pages on trekking and walking in the Alps. **Complete-skier.com** reviews more than 100 Swiss ski resorts.

WHEN TO GO

In July and August Switzerland's best weather coincides with the heaviest crowds. June and September are still pleasant, and hotel prices can be slightly lower, especially in resorts. In May and June the mountains are at their loveliest, with Alpine flowers blooming and the peaks capped with snow; however, as ski season is over and high summer hasn't begun, this is often considered low season, and many resort hotels close down. Those that remain open reduce their prices considerably. Another low-season disadvantage: Some cable-car and cogwheel train operations take a break between the midwinter and midsummer rushes; some must wait for snow to clear before reopening. The most prestigious ski resorts charge top prices during the Christmas–New Year holidays but reduce them slightly in early January. February through Easter is prime time again. Many of the family-run traditional hotels fill up a year ahead, and you'll have to settle for less appealing lodgings. Also, check with the resort for exact dates of high seasons: They vary slightly from region to region. Late autumn—from mid-October through early December—is the least appealing season for visiting the Alps because there's usually little snow, no foliage, and a tendency toward dampness and fog. If you're sticking to the cities to shop and tour museums, you won't notice the doldrums that take over the resorts. The exception to the above rules of thumb: Ticino, the only portion of Switzerland south of the Alps, boasts a Mediterranean climate and declares high season from April through October. Many of its hotels close down altogether from November through March.

CLIMATE

➤ FORECASTS: **Weather Channel Connection** (☎ 900/932–8437), 95¢ per minute from a Touch-Tone phone.

What follow are average daily maximum and minimum temperatures for major cities in Switzerland.

BERN

Jan.	36F	2C	May	65F	18C	Sept.	67F	19C
	25	– 4		47	8		50	10
Feb.	40F	4C	June	70F	21C	Oct.	56F	13C
	27	– 3		52	11		41	5
Mar.	49F	9C	July	74F	23C	Nov.	45F	7C
	34	1		56	13		34	1
Apr.	58F	14C	Aug.	72F	22C	Dec.	38F	3C
	40	4		56	13		29	– 2

GENEVA

Jan.	40F	4C	May	67F	19C	Sept.	70F	21C
	29	– 2		49	9		54	12
Feb.	43F	6C	June	74F	23C	Oct.	58F	14C
	31	– 1		56	13		45	7
Mar.	50F	10C	July	77F	25C	Nov.	47F	8C
	36	2		59	15		38	3
Apr.	59F	15C	Aug.	76F	24C	Dec.	40F	4C
	41	5		58	14		32	0

LUGANO

Jan.	43F	6C	May	70F	21C	Sept.	74F	23C
	29	– 2		50	10		56	13
Feb.	49F	9C	June	77F	25C	Oct.	61F	16C
	31	– 1		58	14		47	8
Mar.	56F	13C	July	81F	27C	Nov.	52F	11C
	38	3		61	16		38	3
Apr.	63F	17C	Aug.	81F	27C	Dec.	45F	7C
	45	7		59	15		32	0

ST. MORITZ

Jan.	29F	– 2C	May	50F	10C	Sept.	58F	14C
	11	–12		32	0		38	13
Feb.	34F	1C	June	59F	15C	Oct.	50F	10C
	13	–11		40	4		31	– 1
Mar.	38F	3C	July	63F	17C	Nov.	38F	3C
	18	– 8		41	5		22	– 6
Apr.	45F	7C	Aug.	61F	16C	Dec.	31F	– 1C
	25	– 4		41	5		14	10

ZÜRICH

Jan.	36F	2C	May	67F	19C	Sept.	68F	20C
	27	– 3		47	8		52	11
Feb.	41F	5C	June	74F	23C	Oct.	58F	14C
	29	– 2		54	12		43	6
Mar.	50F	10C	July	77F	25C	Nov.	45F	7C
	34	1		58	14		36	2
Apr.	59F	15C	Aug.	76F	24C	Dec.	38F	3C
	40	4		56	13		29	– 2

1 DESTINATION: SWITZERLAND

THE GOOD, THE BAD, AND THE TIDY

U P IN THE HOARY windswept heights and black fir forests of the Alps, an electric eye beams open a glistening all-glass door—and reveals the honey-gold glow of wood, the sheen of copper, the burnt-chocolate tones of ancient wooden rafters. Candles flicker; Sterno radiates blue-white flames under russet pots of bubbling fondue. The cheery *boomp-chick boomp-chick* of an accordion filters down from high-tech stereo speakers cleverly concealed behind oversize cowbells. Waitresses in starched black dirndls and waiters in bleached white ties scuttle briskly from kitchen to table, table to kitchen, while platters of gravy-laden veal, sizzling *Rösti* (hash brown potatoes), and rosy entrecôte simmer over steel trivets—preheated, electrically controlled—ready to be proudly, seamlessly served.

Coziness under strict control, anachronism versus state-of-the-art technology: strange bedfellows in a storybook land. Nowhere else in Europe can you find a combination as welcoming and as alien, as comfortable and as remote, as engaging and as disengaged as a glass cable car to the clouds. This is the paradox of the Swiss, whose primary national aesthetic pitches rustic Alpine homeyness against high-tech urban efficiency. Though they're proud, sober, self-contained, independent culturally and politically, disdainful of the shabby and the slipshod, painfully neat, rigorously prompt—the Swiss have a weakness for cuteness, and they indulge in incongruously coy diminutives: A German *Bierstube* becomes a *Stübli*, *Kuchen* (cake) becomes *Küchli*, *Wurst* becomes *Würstli*, *Pastete* (vol-au-vent) becomes *Pastetli*, and a *coupe* (glass) of champagne becomes a *Cüpli*.

It is lucky for tourists, this dichotomy of the folksy and the functional. It means your trains get you to your firelighted lodge on time. It means the shower in your room runs as hot as a Turkish bath. It means the cable car that sweeps you to a mountaintop has been subjected to grueling inspections. It means the handwoven curtains are boiled and starched, and the high-thread-count bed linens are turned back with a chocolate at night. It means the scarlet geraniums that cascade from window boxes on every carved balcony are tended like prize orchids. It means the pipe smoke that builds up in the Stübli (cozy little pubs) at night is aired out daily, as sparkling clean double-glazed windows are thrown open on every floor, every morning, to let sharp, cool mountain air course through hallways, bedrooms, and fresh-bleached baths.

Yet there is a stinginess that peeks around the apron of that rosy-cheeked efficiency. Liquor here is measured with scientific precision into glasses marked for one centiliter or two, and the local wines come in carafes reminiscent of laboratory beakers. Despite the fine linens and puffs of down that adorn each bed, double beds have separate mattresses with sheets tucked primly down the middle, sometimes so tightly you have to lift the mattress to loosen the barrier. And if you wash out your socks and hang them loosely on the shower rod in the morning, you may return at night and find them straightened, spaced, toes pointing the same direction, as orderly as little lead soldiers.

Nevertheless there is an earthiness about these people, as at ease with the soil as they are appalled by dirt. A banker in Zürich may rent a postage-stamp parcel of land in a crowded patchwork outside town, sowing tight rows of cabbages and strawberries, weeding bright borders of marigolds, and on Sunday he may visit his miniature estate, pull a chair out from the tidy toolshed, and simply sit and smoke, like Heidi's Alm-Uncle surveying his Alpine realm. An elderly woman may don knickers and loden hat and board a postbus to the mountains and climb steep, rocky trails at a brisk clip, cheeks glowing, eyes as icy bright as the glaciers above her. A family of farmers—grandparents, schoolgirls, married sons—unites for the hay cutting as if for Christmas dinner, standing shoulder to shoulder in the hip-high gold, swinging scythes from dawn to sunset.

There's a 21st-century counterpoint to this: the high-tech, jet-set glamour that splashes vivid colors across the slopes at St. Moritz, Gstaad, Zermatt, Verbier. Step out of a bulbous steel-and-glass cable car onto a concrete platform at 2,000 m (6,560 ft) and see Switzerland transformed, its workers' blue overalls and good wool suits exchanged for Day-Glo ski suits—mango, chartreuse, swimming-pool blue. Wholesome, healthy faces disappear behind mirrored goggles and war-paint sunblock, and gaudy skis and poles bristle militarily, like the pikes and halberds in the Battle of Sempach.

The contradictions mount: while fur-clad socialites raise jeweled fingers to bid at Sotheby's on Geneva's quai du Mont-Blanc, the women of Appenzell stand beside their husbands on the Landsgemeindeplatz and raise their hands to vote—a right not won until 1991. While digital screens tick off beef futures in Zürich, the crude harmony of cowbells echoes in velvet mountain pastures. While a Mercedes roars down an expressway expertly blasted through solid rock, a horse-drawn plow peels back thin topsoil in an Alpine garden plot, impossibly steep, improbably high.

And on August 1, the Swiss national holiday, while spectacular displays of fireworks explode in sizzling colors over the cities and towns, the mountain folk build the bonfires that glow quietly, splendidly, on every hillside of every Alp, uniting Swiss citizens as they celebrate their proud independence, their cultural wealth, and above all their diversity. It's that diversity and those quirky contradictions that make Switzerland a tourist capital—the folksy, fiercely efficient innkeeper to the world.

— Nancy Coons

NEW AND NOTEWORTHY

The new **ICN (InterCity "Neigezug") tilting trains** are set to begin service in summer or fall 2000; these trains manage higher speeds on winding tracks. The Interregio (two-tier) trains should be in service by 2001.

A new section of the A1 autoroute connecting Yverdon-les-Bains and Payerne is scheduled to open in spring 2001. Completion of the road work between Payerne and Fribourg should also finish that spring.

Zürich West is being reinvented as Zürich's up-and-coming new neighborhood. The industrial area's profile is changing fast, as restaurants, bars, galleries, and clubs move into former factory spaces. Most construction and restoration work should be done early in 2001—stay tuned.

New cultural offerings are developing as well. At press time **La Liberté,** a reconstruction of a 17th-century galley, was being completed in Morges, just west of Lausanne. The ship launched in summer 2001. Fribourg's **Gutenbergmuseum,** which illuminates the history of printing, will open in late fall of 2000.

At the turn of 2000 many areas, such as forests and ports, sustained damage from the violent storm Lothar. Cleanup and repairs are ongoing.

Train stations are now using electronic, touch-pad machines to dispense tickets. Using these machines, you can purchase train tickets at any station for any destination in Switzerland for any day. Instructions are available in English.

As with the train-ticket machines, telephone books for public phones have been converted to electronic listings operated by touch pad. Instructions are given in English.

The Swiss postal service and Western Union have joined forces to expedite money transfers. Look for the yellow Western Union logo at more than 500 Swiss post offices; transfers can now be done in just 10 minutes.

WHAT'S WHERE

Zürich

Known as one of the leading financial centers of the world, Zürich at first sight may appear to be a modest, small-scale city, but the array of luxury shops along its Bahnhofstrasse and its renowned opera reveal its cultural and material riches. Its old center, which straddles the River Limmat, has few high-rise buildings; Gothic guildhalls take the place of imperial palaces. In the distance snow-clad peaks overlook the waters of the lake, dwarfing everything below.

Eastern Switzerland

Near Zürich, the cantons of Glarus, Schaffhausen, Thurgau, St. Gallen, and Appenzell, as well as the independent principality of Liechtenstein, are dominated by the Rhine River. With its obscure backcountry and thriving cities, the German-influenced region has everything from wood-shingle farmhouses to town houses adorned with oriel windows and frescoes. Still, the eastern cantons remain one of the most untouched regions of Switzerland.

Graubünden

Dominated by its trendy resorts—St. Moritz, Davos, Klosters, Arosa, Pontresina—Graubünden is nonetheless Switzerland's most culturally diverse and largest canton. German, Italian, and Romansh—the ancient dialect that is thought to date from 600 BC—are all spoken here. This is also the site of Switzerland's only national park, probably the only place in the country where skiing is forbidden.

The Ticino

Italian in language, culture, and spirit, the Ticino is an irresistible combination of Mediterranean pleasures and Swiss efficiency. With its yacht-filled waterfront promenades of Locarno and Lugano and its constantly sunny climate, the Ticino is a canton set apart.

Luzern and Central Switzerland

Blessed with a sophisticated transportation system that makes it one of the easiest regions to visit, central Switzerland is full of neat little towns, accessible mountains, and modest resorts. Centered around the Vierwaldstättersee, "the lake of the four forest cantons," the region is steeped in history: it is where the Oath of Eternal Alliance is said to have been renewed, and it's also the birthplace of the legend of Wilhelm Tell.

Basel

At the juncture of France and Germany, German-speaking Basel is a cultural capital with a sense of fun. Cultivated and yet down-home, it has more than 30 museums, Switzerland's oldest university, and some of the most diverse shopping in the country. All the same, beer and sausages are the snack of choice, and the annual Fasnacht (Carnival) is observed with a boisterousness that's unparalleled by other Swiss towns.

Fribourg, Neuchâtel, and the Jura

Unself-conscious and largely undiscovered, the cantons of Fribourg, Neuchâtel, and the Jura represent three very different worlds in western Switzerland. Fribourg, part German and part French, is full of medieval villages; Neuchâtel, French in language and culture, is beginning to shift its focus from watchmaking to tourism; and the isolated Jura Mountains, part German and part French, exist in a realm of their own.

Bern

Humble and down-to-earth, Bern is a city of broad medieval streets, farmers' markets, and friendly, slow-spoken people. It is also the federal capital of Switzerland and, more remarkably, a World Cultural Heritage city known for its sandstone arcades, fountains, flowers, and thick, sturdy towers.

Berner Oberland

The Bernese Alps concentrate the very best of rural Switzerland: panoramas of the Eiger, Mönch, and Jungfrau mountains; crystalline lakes, gorges, and waterfalls; and emerald slopes dotted with gingerbread chalets and cows with bells—not to mention world-class skiing. It's no secret, though: the Berner Oberland is among the most popular tourist destinations in Switzerland.

Valais

Alpine villages, famous peaks (the Matterhorn, most notably), and world-class resorts (Zermatt, Saas-Fee, Crans, Verbier) are all reasons to visit the valley of the Rhône. This is the Switzerland of tumbledown huts, raclette eaters, and yodelers.

Vaud

Lausanne, Montreux, and the Alpes Vaudoises comprise one of Switzerland's most diverse regions. Centered around Lac Léman (Lake Geneva), this French-speak-

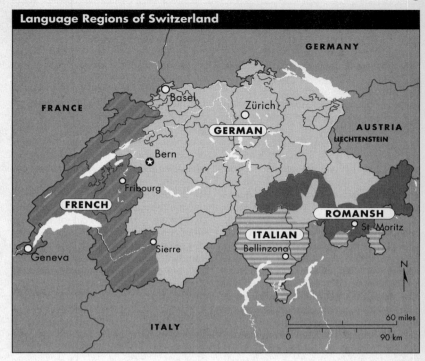

Language Regions of Switzerland

ing canton harbors some of the country's most famous cathedrals and castles, as well as Alpine villages, balmy lake resorts, and above all, its most verdant vineyards.

Geneva

As the European headquarters of the United Nations and birthplace of the International Red Cross, an international mecca for writers and thinkers of every stripe, and a stronghold of luxurious stores and extravagant restaurants, Geneva is Switzerland's most cosmopolitan city.

PLEASURES AND PASTIMES

Dining

If you're looking for diverse dining experiences, you can't do much better than Switzerland, where French, Italian, or German cuisine may dominate, depending on which cantons you visit. In French areas (roughly Vaud, Geneva, Jura, Neuchâtel, and western parts of Fribourg and Valais) the cuisine is clearly Gallic, and wine stews, organ meats, and subtle sausages appear alongside standard *cuisine bourgeoise:* thick, rare beef entrecôte with a choice of rich sauces and *truite meunière* (trout dredged in flour and sizzled in butter). In the Ticino, the Italian canton, Italian cuisine appears virtually unscathed, particularly the Alpine-forest specialties of Piedmont and Lombardy (risotto, gnocchi, polenta, porcini mushrooms). The German cantons serve more pork than their neighbors and favor another standard dish that represents Switzerland though it vanishes in French-speaking or Italian-speaking areas: *Rösti,* a broad patty of hash brown potatoes crisped in a skillet and often flavored with bacon, herbs, or cheese, is as prevalent in the German regions as fondue is in the French. Beyond the obvious cultural differences, Swiss cuisine is also influenced by the terrain: mountain farmers have traditionally subsisted on such basic foods as raclette (cheese melted over boiled potatoes and garnished with pickled vegetables), while cities nurtured wealthy burghers and noblemen with the cream of the crops of outlying lands—milk-fed veal, fruits from low-lying orchards. Though fondue, Rösti, and veal are likely to be on any resort's menu these days, traces of these influences can still be found almost everywhere.

Hiking

When the snow melts and the mountain streams start to flow, Switzerland takes to the hills. That the Swiss Alps are the ultimate in hiking is no secret: on a sunny day in high season in the more popular vacation areas, footpaths can be almost as crowded as a line for World Series tickets. On narrow trails hikers walk in single file, and the more aggressive pass on the left as if on the autobahns of Germany. However, there is an almost infinite quantity of quiet, isolated routes to be explored; if you prefer to hike in peace, head for one of the less inhabited Alpine valleys—in the Valais or Graubünden there are several—and strike out on your own. Each of the regional tourist departments publishes suggested hiking itineraries, and major map publishers distribute excellent topographical maps of wilderness trails. In the German-speaking region especially, hiking is a deeply rooted tradition, and people of all ages and in all physical conditions head for well-beaten paths in jeans as often as knickers, woolen stockings, rucksacks, and hiking boots.

Regional Celebrations

Basel's extravagant pre-Lenten observance of Fasnacht (Carnival)—in which up to 20,000 costumed revelers fill the streets with the sounds of fifes and drums—is only one of the hundreds of festivals that the Swiss celebrate during the year. As if to prove that its spirit is vast despite its small size, almost every Swiss canton hosts its own popular celebration of one event or another. In Geneva the Festival of the Escalade commemorates the town's repulsion of invading Savoyards. Lesser-known festivals range from the frivolous—in the Schlitteda Engiadinaisa, young unmarried men and women ride decorated sleighs through the villages of the Engadine—to the symbolic—in the Landsgemeinde, the citizens of Appenzell pay homage to their country's democratic tradition by conducting a vote by public show of hands.

Shopping

Swiss Army knives, Swiss watches, Swiss chocolate—what could be more. . . Swiss? Though you won't find many bargains in Switzerland anytime soon, you will find some uniquely Swiss treasures. Some of the best souvenirs of this pragmatic country are typically practical, such as watches, clocks, and Swiss Army knives. Others are more luxurious, such as sweet milk chocolate; you'll be on the home turf of major manufacturers Lindt, Nestlé, and Tobler. But you should also try small local chocolate shops, where the candy is made on the premises. Marvelous music boxes from the watchmaking country around Lake Neuchâtel are sold in specialty shops all over the country. Linens and good cottons—dish and tea towels, aprons, sheets—are another Swiss specialty, as are pottery and ceramics—most of them dark-glazed and hand-painted with simple designs. Decoupage is the Swiss art of intricate silhouette paper cutting. It's traditionally done with black paper, but it can also be found in color. Farm or *desalpage* (bringing cows down from mountain pastures) scenes are common motifs.

Skiing

Switzerland is Europe's winter playground, and its facilities are as technically advanced as its slopes are spectacular. As one recent skier put it, "There's just *more*"—more slopes, longer runs, more stunning, crisp scenery than you'll find in U.S. resorts. Any level of skier can find a resort to meet his or her needs, from a cozy family-oriented village with easy and moderate slopes to the world-class challenges at Crans-Montana, Verbier, Wengen, St. Moritz, and Zermatt. Most resorts publish an area map showing their slopes and rating the trails for difficulty. Familiarize yourself with the resort's signs, including those warning of avalanche zones, before you set out. For an analysis of the best ski resorts, *see* Skiing Switzerland *in* Chapter 14.

Spectator Sports

If awards were given to countries with the most unusual sports competitions, Switzerland would win hands down. In the winter the action centers around St. Moritz, where a frozen lake provides a novel setting for golf, polo, dogsled races, and horse races: in the Winter Golf Tournament, red balls on white "greens" are a festive sight. The resort also has the world's only Cresta run; toboggan riders zip head-first down a winding ice channel, accelerating to 90 mph. Another unique sport is *Skikjöring,* which involves skiers being pulled by galloping horses. Cows are the players in another, nonwinter event: in April small towns throughout the Valais hold a *combat de reines,* or cow fight. Female cows head-butt each other (though some contestants have been known to just placidly chew their cud); the winner, *la reine* (the queen), is decorated and awarded with the best grazing ground. *Hornuss* is played in rural areas of the French-speaking cantons, particularly Fribourg and Vaud. Players wield wooden placards on sticks, tossing the placards into the air to stop a ball that is launched by a person wielding an extremely long, flexible implement that looks roughly like a golf club. Wrestling is a popular Swiss tradition: men wear big baggy shorts of burlap and stand in sawdust rings; after the competition, costumed spectators sing and dance. Perhaps most unusual, stone-throwing competitions in Unspunnen (in the canton of Bern) take place every five years; 180-pound stones are used.

GREAT ITINERARIES

In a country as diverse as Switzerland, it makes sense to visit with a theme in mind. Below, we have outlined itineraries for culinary adventures and exploring historic castles. *Bon appétit* and happy exploring.

Swiss Gastronomy

This food-intensive itinerary offers aficionados an opportunity to travel from one great dining experience to another, sampling the very finest *haute gastronomie* at one stop, the most authentic regional classics—even the earthiest peasant cuisines—at another. Incidental pleasures—wandering in the Alps, for example, or strolling through medieval town centers in Switzerland's greatest cities—can be squeezed in between meals. Remember that reservations must be made well in advance.

DURATION➤ Depending on your capacity for stellar meals—one or two per day—you can concentrate the highlights of this trip into nine marathon days or stretch it out over two weeks or more. If you're planning to pack it all into a few days, check opening days carefully. Many restaurants in Geneva close weekends, and many elsewhere close Monday or Tuesday.

GETTING AROUND➤ Each of the stopovers is accessible by train, though some of the restaurants may require cabs or tram rides; a rental car will give you more flexibility for reaching country inns.

THE MAIN ROUTE➤ **1 night: Geneva.** Your first night, indulge in a hearty Lyonnaise bistro meal at the Bistrot du Boeuf Rouge. For lunch the next day, head out to Geneva's wine country for exquisite seasonal cuisine at the Domaine du Château-vieux. Back in Geneva, have a relatively light Ticinese supper at La Favola. Fill the time between meals with a brisk stroll along the quais and visits to one of the world-class museums and the early Christian ruins under the cathedral.

1 night: Lausanne. Testing Phillipe Rochat's mettle at Restaurant de l'Hôtel de Ville in nearby Crissier may be the triumph of the trip—but reserve judgment for after Basel and Zürich. At night, head down to the waterfront at Ouchy and have a chic, light supper at the Café Beau-Rivage.

1 night: Basel. Two hours north, compare Jean-Claude Wicky with Rochat at lunch. Then, after visiting, say, the Münster and the history museum, relax in the downstairs bistro at the Teufelhof: the light specialties are prepared by Michael Baader, who is chef for the top-notch restaurant upstairs as well.

2 nights: Zürich. Have lunch at Petermann's Kunststuben, in the suburb of Küssnacht, where the gastronomy vies for the title "best in Switzerland." Then, after a thorough walking tour of Zürich's Old Town, you can settle in for an atmospheric, Old World evening at the Kronenhalle.

1 night: Luzern. For a total contrast and perhaps the most authentically *Swiss* meal of your tour, head for Galliker and a lunch of real farm food. Having absorbed the Lion Monument, crossed the Kapellbrücke, and toured the history museum, you can think about the evening meal: A light, sophisticated river-fish meal at Rotes Gatter affords waterfront views.

1 night: Saas-Fee. From Luzern allow for a full day's scenic mountain drive south over the Brünigpass, then on over the Grimselpass and down the Rhône Valley to Brig and the spectacular little resort of Saas-Fee. Once there, retreat to the isolated Waldhotel Fletschhorn for a sophisticated dinner and a bare minimum of one night to take in the mountain air.

1 night: Verbier. Following the Rhône back west toward Geneva, take one more Alpine side trip up to this famous ski resort to feast and sleep at Rosalp, the popular rustic-chic inn in the village center.

INFORMATION➤ *See* Chapters 2, 6, 7, and 11–13.

Castles and Cathedrals

Romantics, history buffs, and architecture fans will enjoy a circle tour that takes in some of the best of western Switzerland's medieval and Gothic landmarks.

DURATION➤ Six days.

GETTING AROUND➤ All stops are easily accessible by expressway and connecting roads.

The complete itinerary works by rail, with most sites accessible on foot from the station; Gruyères has bus connections to the elevated castle and the Old Town.

THE MAIN ROUTE➤ **1 night: Geneva.** The Cathédrale St-Pierre, begun during the 12th century, sinks roots into early Christianity: immediately below its current structure, you'll find the *site archéologique,* where excavations have yielded two 4th-century sanctuaries and an 11th-century crypt.

1 night: Montreux. The Château de Chillon, partially surrounded by the waters of Lac Léman (Lake Geneva), may be the most completely and authentically furnished in Switzerland, with tapestries, carved fireplaces, ceramics, and painted wooden ceilings. Lord Byron signed the pillar where his "Prisoner of Chillon" was manacled.

1 night: Gruyères. This craggy castle-village draws crowds to its ancient central street, souvenir shops, quaint inns, and frescoed castle, complete with dungeon and spectacular views.

1 night: Fribourg. This bilingual city is the last Catholic stronghold of western Switzerland, rooted in its single-tower Cathédrale St-Nicolas. The cathedral's Last Judgment tympanum and art nouveau stained-glass windows deserve attention— but leave time to explore the Old Town, with its multilevel fortifications constructed for the ubiquitous Zähringens.

1 night: Thun. If you're driving, cut across the rolling verdure of canton Fribourg toward Thun (by train, connect through Bern), where you'll see the Bernese Alps looming in all their splendor. Schloss Zähringen, which dates from 1191, features a knights' hall, tapestries, local ceramics, and an intimidating collection of weapons.

1 night: Bern. The Zähringens fortified this gooseneck in the River Aare; its 15th-century Münster features an unusually restored (full-color, painted) main portal.

1 night: Basel. In this historic, cosmopolitan city is a Münster with a lovely Romanesque portal and the tomb of the great humanist Erasmus.

INFORMATION➤ *See* Chapters 8–10, 12, and 13.

FODOR'S CHOICE

No two people will agree on what makes a perfect vacation, but it's fun and helpful to know what others think. We hope you'll have a chance to experience some of Fodor's Choices yourself while visiting Switzerland.

Flavors

Enjoy the fruits of Philippe Rochat's work with legendary chef Girardet at **Restaurant de l'Hôtel de Ville.** Rochat spent nearly 20 years with his mentor, and he maintains the restaurant's stellar standards. *$$$$*

You'll have to go off the beaten track to find one of the best chefs in Switzerland; the **Hôtel-Restaurant de la Gare** is in the village of Le Noirmont, practically on the French border. It's well worth the trek, as chef Georges Wenger adapts local Jura ingredients to sophisticated, seasonal cuisine. *$$$$*

Local vintners save their best wines for the cellars of Philippe Chevrier's **Domaine de Châteauvieux,** outside Geneva. Sweeping vineyard views crown a phenomenal French meal. *$$$$*

The 20th-century art collection is as plentiful as the food at Zürich's **Kronenhalle,** where robust cooking in hearty portions draws a genial crowd. *$$$–$$$$*

Inside what was once the Heuberg mansion in Basel, the **Teufelhof** has an excellent restaurant, a chic Weinstube, and a trendy bar—there are even medieval ruins in the basement. The menus are always intriguing. *$$–$$$$*

The restaurant in Locarno's **Hotel Navegna** stands out for its phenomenally delicate homemade pastas. *$$–$$$*

In a 1677 inn at the hub of Chur, **Stern** carries on the age-old tradition of Graubündner culture, complete with waitresses in folk costumes. *$$–$$$*

At **Wirtschaft zum Frieden,** in Schaffhausen, you can opt for a daily plate lunch in an intimate Stübli, a fancier meal in a tile-stove dining room, or selections from either menu in a private garden thick with wisteria. *$$–$$$*

Under a giant boar's head and century-old murals at **Bierhalle Kropf,** businesspeople, workers, and shoppers share crowded tables to feast on hearty Zürich cuisine. *$–$$*

Comforts

Lausanne's **Beau Rivage-Palace** stands apart in neoclassical grandeur, with manicured waterfront grounds and several first-class restaurants. *$$$$*

Giardino, in the small Ticinese village of Ascona, is decidedly decadent, from the pure linen sheets to the chauffeured Bentley. *$$$$*

Overlooking green waterfront grounds on the Murtensee, the turn-of-the-century **Le Vieux Manoir au Lac** offers sumptuously decorated rooms. *$$$$*

A 600-year-old structure on the banks of the Limmat, **Zum Storchen** is one of Zürich's most atmospheric hotels. *$$$*

In Château-d'Oex the 18th-century **Bon Accueil** has low wood-beam ceilings, creaking floors, antiques, and fresh flowers inside and out. *$$–$$$*

A demure little inn on a residential hillside between Chillon and Montreux, **Masson** has offered peace and quiet to weary travelers since 1829. *$$*

With leaded-glass windows, homespun linen, and pewter pitchers, the all-wood chalet **Ruedihus** in Kandersteg re-creates the atmosphere of the 1753 original. *$$*

Basel's **Krafft am Rhein** is a rare find in Swiss cities—it's an elegant little inn sitting directly on the right-bank waterfront, with mosaic floors, elaborate moldings, and a sinuous atrium stairwell. Try for a Rhine-side room. *$–$$*

The **Bel'Espérance** is an especially bright and friendly hotel tucked between Geneva's waterfront and Old Town. *$*

Perfect Moments

★ When the sound of fife-and-drum music drifts from upstairs windows of guild houses in **Basel's Old Town,** you'll think the Middle Ages have dawned once again.

★ Feeding swans and ducks by the **Kapellbrücke** in Luzern is a favorite pastime of locals and tourists alike.

★ Drinking **steaming-fresh milk** in an Alpine barn, you'll understand why Heidi loved Switzerland.

★ Fireworks burst and mountain-farm bonfires smolder on the **Swiss National Holiday** (August 1).

★ For a festive, outdoorsy evening, rent a lap blanket for a summer night's outdoor performance of the *Tellspiel* at Interlaken.

Picturesque Villages and Towns

★ In the Lower Engadine, **Guarda** is a federally protected hamlet of architectural photo-ops, with cobblestone streets and flower boxes filled with red geraniums.

★ An eagle's-nest town set on a precarious 1,000-m (3,280-ft) slope in the Rhône Valley, **Isérables** is full of stone-shingled *mazots* (barns typical of the Valais) and narrow, winding streets.

★ Clinging vertiginously to a hillside, its flower-filled balconies overlooking the lake, tiny **Gandria** retains the ambience of an ancient fishing village.

★ **Morcote,** an old resort village below Lugano, has clay-color Lombard-style houses and arcades that look out on the waterfront.

★ In western Switzerland near Avenches, the ancient town of **Murten** (known in French as Morat) is a popular lake resort with a superbly preserved medieval center.

★ In the vineyard region of Vaud, the scenic **Corniche Road** joins cobblestone villages, such as St-Saphorin, and beckoning vineyards. The lake and mountain views—and the tastings of fruity, local wine—make this a memorable area.

★ On the Rhine River in eastern Switzerland, **Stein-am-Rhein** is a nearly perfectly preserved medieval village, replete with shingled, half-timber town houses boasting ornate oriels and flamboyant frescoes.

Views

★ The terrace café of the Disneyland-like **Château Gütsch** affords an idyllic view of Luzern and the Vierwaldstättersee.

★ In the **Emmental region** near Bern, the gentle hills begin to roll out village after beautiful village, dotted with many impressive examples of the classic Emmental farmstead.

★ From the top of the 3,474-m (11,395-ft) **Jungfraujoch**, the Aletsch Glacier looks like a vast sea of ice.

★ From the summit station of Gornergrat, the snaggle-tooth **Matterhorn** steals the thunder from all surrounding peaks.

★ Up on **Muottas Muragl,** near Pontresina, you can focus on the stunning views or study the Philosophers' Path, three circular walks that are dotted with thoughtful sayings.

★ With its mists, roaring water, jutting rocks, and bushy crags, the **Rheinfall,** from the Neuhausen side, appears truly Wagnerian.

★ Perched high above town, Bern's **Rose Garden** overlooks the entire Old Town.

★ The sunset from the south-facing hilltop resort of **Wengen** is a sublime way to end a day of skiing.

★ From Geneva's Right Bank waterfront, watch **Mont-Blanc** and the snow-capped peaks around it turn pink in a sunset's afterglow.

FESTIVALS AND SEASONAL EVENTS

Top events in Switzerland include Fasnacht (Carnival) celebrations in February and March, the Landsgemeinde open-air vote in Appenzell in April, the Montreux International Jazz Festival in July, the Menuhin Festival in Gstaad in August, Luzern's International Festival of Music from mid-August to mid-September, and the Fête de l'Escalade in Geneva in December. Events are named below as publicized by the host region, usually in the local language.

SPRING

MAR.➤ Villages throughout the Engadine celebrate the **Chalanda Marz** children's festival. Kids in costume parade and sing, ringing bells to chase away winter (despite which, it often snows).

MID-MAR.➤ The **Engadine Ski Marathon** covers the 42 km (26 mi) between Zuoz and Maloja.

LATE MAR.–EARLY APR.➤ During St. Moritz's **Snow & Symphony Music Festival,** top classical and jazz musicians perform in luxury hotels and on mountaintops.

MAR.–MAY➤ The **Primavera Concertistica** music festival takes place in Lugano.

APR.➤ **Sechseläuten,** in Zürich, shows all its medieval guilds on parade and climaxes in the burning of the Böögg, a straw scarecrow representing winter. Small towns throughout the Valais hold a **Combat de Reines,** or cow fight, where female cows are pitted against each other in a head-butting contest. **Good Friday** (April 13) processions take place in several southern villages, including Mendrisio in the Ticino, where the procession derives from a medieval Passion Play that is performed on Maundy Thursday as well. Luzern's **Osterfestspiele** celebrates Easter with sacred music.

LATE APR.➤ **Landsgemeinde** takes place in the town of Appenzell on the last Sunday of the month punctually at noon, with all citizens voting by public show of hands.

APR.–MAY➤ The **International Jazz Festival—Bern** lasts five days in the federal capital.

MID-APR.–MAY➤ The lovely lake town of Morges draws a crowd to its annual **Fête de la Tulipe** (Tulip Festival).

SUMMER

MID-JUNE➤ The **Grindelwald Country-Festival** brings American country-and-western groups to this mountain resort.

LATE JUNE–MID-JULY➤ The **Zürich Festival** hosts dance, opera, theater, and more in several venues throughout the city.

LATE JUNE–MID-SEPT.➤ A **Wilhelm Tell** outdoor theater production, in Interlaken, has an epic-scale cast of locals.

JULY➤ World-class artists perform at the **Montreux International Jazz Festival.**

MID-JULY➤ The **British Classic Car Meeting** brings antique autos to St. Moritz.

JULY–AUG.➤ **Engadiner Concert Weeks** bring outdoor classical music events to resorts throughout the region. The **Festival International de l'Orgue Ancien,** at Valère in Sion, honors the 13th-century instrument within.

LATE JULY➤ During the **Paléo Festival Nyon,** international musicians play a multistage outdoor concert.

LATE JULY–AUG.➤ For more than two weeks the **Verbier Festival and Academy** hosts a classical music festival with an impressive guest roster.

AUG. 1➤ **Swiss National Holiday** celebrates the confederation's birth in 1291 with fireworks and bonfires.

EARLY AUG.➤ The **Fête de Genève** packs Geneva's waterfront for ten days of food and music, plus a techno parade and fireworks.

AUG.➤ Locarno's **International Film Festival** unveils top new movies in the Piazza Grande.

MID-AUG.➤ **Grächen Country Festival** imports American C&W music to the Alps. The Vevey **International Festival of Film Comedy** honors comic classics on the outdoor screen.

LATE AUG.➤ The **International Folklore Festival,** in Fribourg, celebrates its 25th anniversary.

MID-AUG.–MID-SEPT.➤ The world-renowned **Internationale Musikfestwochen,** in Luzern, combines concerts, theater, and art exhibitions. Davos's **Young Artists in Concert** features tomorrow's classical music stars.

AUG.–MID-SEPT.➤ The **Yehudi Menuhin Festival,** in Gstaad, showcases world-class musicians. Lugano's **Blues to Bop Festival** brings authentic blues to the lakefront.

LATE AUG.➤ Zürich's **Theaterspektakel** showcases avant-garde and mainstream playwrights as well as theater troupes from around the world.

LATE AUG.–OCT.➤ The **Vevey-Montreux Music Festival** invites important artists to these twin lake resorts.

AUTUMN

EARLY SEPT.➤ **Knabenschiessen** takes place in Zürich with a folk festival and fair.

MID-SEPT.➤ **Bénichon,** a traditional autumn Fribourg feast, is held during the second week of September.

LATE SEPT.➤ The **Neuchâtel Wine Festival** is the biggest in the country.

LATE SEPT.➤ **Etivaz Cheese Sharing** celebrates the division of spoils from the cheese cooperative with yodeling, wrestling, and

other activities. **Fribourg Braderie** combines a citywide sidewalk sale, folk festival, and onion market.

LATE SEPT.–EARLY OCT.➤ The small Vaud town of St-Cergue has an annual **Fête Desalpe,** a ritual for the cows coming down from the mountains. It lasts all of a Saturday morning, allowing hundreds of cows to parade the streets in amazing floral headgear. Another *desalpe* festival is held in October in Charmey, near Gruyères in Fribourg.

OCT.➤ In Lugano a traditional **Wine Harvest Festival** is held at the Piazza della Riforma and on the lakeside.

LATE OCT.➤ **Olma Schweizer Messe für Land- und Milchwirtschaft** (agricultural and dairy fair), in St. Gallen, gathers representatives of the farming industry from across Switzerland.

LATE NOV.➤ Bern's **Zwiebelemärit** (Onion Market) celebrates the open market established for area farmers in gratitude for aid they gave Bern after the great fire of 1405.

WINTER

EARLY DEC.➤ Geneva's **Fête de l'Escalade** commemorates the defeat of the Duke of Savoy. One local woman fought off the soldiers scaling the walls by dumping hot soup on their heads.

MID-JAN.➤ **Vogel Gryff Volksfest** is a colorful Basel tradition, with a costumed Griffin, a Lion, and a Wild Man of the Woods floating down the Rhine and dancing on the Mittlere Rheinbrücke.

LATE JAN.➤ **Schlittedas Engiadinaisa** is a winter Engadine tradition in which young unmarried men and women ride decorated sleighs from village to village. The **Château-d'Oex Hot-Air Balloon Week** showcases the Vaud resort's specialty.

LATE JAN.–MID-FEB.➤ St. Moritz hosts a blizzard of special events. The **Gourmet Festival** draws top-tier chefs. Several uncommon sports competitions take place on snow, such as the annual **Polo on Snow, Cricket Tournament on Snow,** and the **White Turf** horse race.

EARLY FEB.➤ **Hom Strom,** at Bad Scuol in the Lower Engadine, observes the burning of Old Man Winter.

LATE FEB.–EARLY MAR.➤ **Fasnacht** is observed throughout Switzerland, but nowhere more festively than in Basel, where it begins at 4 AM on the Monday after Ash Wednesday (March 5), with a drumroll and a costume parade. Luzern celebrates on the Thursday before Ash Wednesday (February 22), with a traditional **Fritschi** procession. On the same day Schwyz celebrates **Blätzli** with a mummers' procession of harlequins. Lugano celebrates Carnevale with a **Festa del Risotto,** with risotto and sausages served in the streets.

2 ZÜRICH

Known as one of the leading financial
centers of the world, Zürich is a surprisingly
modest, small-scale city. Its Old Town, which
straddles the Limmat River, has just a handful
of high-rise buildings, and Gothic guildhalls
take the place of imperial palaces. In the
distance, snow-clad peaks overlook the
waters of the lake, a tantalizing promise
of the mountains beyond.

Updated by
Katrin Gygax

WHEN THE POUND STERLING sagged in the 1960s, the English coined the somewhat disparaging term "the gnomes of Zürich," which evoked images of sly little Swiss bankers rubbing their hands and manipulating world currencies behind closed doors. Yet the spirit that moves the Züricher doesn't come out of folkloric forests but rather from the pulpit of the Grossmünster, where the fiery Reformation leader Huldrych Zwingli preached sermons about idle hands and the devil's playthings. It's the Protestant work ethic that has made Zürich one of the world's leading financial centers. One Zwingli lesson stressed the transience of wealth, and Zürichers show native caution in enjoying their fabulous gains. Nor have they turned their backs on their humbler heritage: on a first visit you might be surprised to see a graceful jumble of shuttered Gothic buildings instead of cold chrome-and-glass towers.

Zürich is, in fact, a beautiful city, sitting astride the Limmat River where it emerges from the Zürichsee (Zürich Lake). Its charming Altstadt (Old Town), comprising a substantial part of the city center, is full of beautifully restored historic buildings and narrow, hilly alleys. In the distance, snowy mountains overlook the waters of the lake, and the shores are dominated by turn-of-the-century mansions. Only three high-rise buildings disturb the skyline, and even they are small by U.S. standards. There are not even any dominating castles to haunt the Züricher with memories of imperialism: in keeping with its solid bourgeois character, Zürich has always maintained a human scale.

The earliest known Zürichers lived around 4500 BC in small houses perched on stilts by the lakeside. The remains of 34 Stone Age and Bronze Age settlements are thought to be scattered around the lake. Underwater archaeologists have discovered a wealth of prehistoric artifacts dating back thousands of years, from Stone Age pottery and Bronze Age necklaces to charms made from boar fangs, bear teeth, and animal skulls; many relics are on display at the Schweizerisches Landesmuseum (Swiss National Museum) near the main train station.

In the 1st century BC the Romans, attracted by Zürich's central location, built a customs house on a hill overlooking the Limmat River. In time the customs house became a fortress, the remains of which can be seen on the Lindenhof, a square in the city center. The Romans were also accommodating enough to provide Zürich with its patron saints. Legend has it that the Roman governor beheaded the Christian brother and sister Felix and Regula on a small island in the river. The martyrs then picked up their heads, waded through the water, and walked up a hill before collapsing where the Grossmünster now stands.

When the Germanic Alemanni, ancestors of the present-day Zürichers, drove out the Romans in the 5th century, the region gradually diminished in importance until the Carolingians built an imperial palace on the Limmat four centuries later. Louis the German, grandson of Charlemagne, then founded an abbey here, appointing his daughter the first abbess; it was built on the site of what is now the Fraumünster, near the Bahnhofstrasse.

By the 12th century Zürich had already shown a knack for commerce, with its diligent merchants making fortunes in silk, wool, linen, and leather. By 1336 this merchant class had become too powerful for an up-and-coming band of tradesmen and laborers who, allied with a charismatic aristocrat named Rudolf Brun, overthrew the merchants' town council and established Zürich's famous guilds. Those 13 original guilds never really lost their power until the French Revolution—and have yet to lose their prestige. Every year prominent Zürich businessmen dress up in medieval costumes for the guilds' traditional march through the streets, heading for the magnificent guildhalls.

If the guilds defined Zürich's commerce, it was the Reformation that defined its soul. From his pulpit in the Grossmünster, Zwingli galvanized the region, and he ingrained in Zürichers their devotion to thrift and hard work—so successfully that it ultimately led them into temptation: the temptations of global influence and tremendous wealth. The Zürich stock exchange, fourth-largest in the world, after those of New York, London, and Tokyo, turned over 810 billion Swiss francs in domestic shares in 1999.

However, Zürich is far from a cold-hearted business center. In 1916 the avant-garde Dadaist movement started here, when a group of artists and writers, including Tristan Tzara, Jean Arp, and Hugo Ball, rebelled against traditional artistic expression. Zürich also drew in Irish author James Joyce, who spent years here re-creating his native Dublin in his *Ulysses* and *A Portrait of the Artist as a Young Man*. Now the city's extraordinary museums and galleries and luxurious shops along the Bahnhofstrasse, Zürich's 5th Avenue, attest to its position as Switzerland's cultural—if not political—capital.

The latest addition to the city's profile is Zürich West, an industrial neighborhood that's quickly being reinvented. Amid the cluster of cranes, former factories are being turned into spaces for restaurants, bars, art galleries, and dance clubs. The area is bordered by Hardstrasse, Hardturmstrasse, and Pfingstweidstrasse; to get there by public transportation, take Tram 4 or 13 to Escher Wyss Platz. The bulk of the construction and restoration work should be done early in 2001—stay tuned.

Pleasures and Pastimes

Dining

Over the past few years a crop of new restaurants, both Swiss and international, has sprouted up. The trend is toward lighter, leaner meals served in bright spaces often open to the street. The traditional cuisine, no longer ubiquitous but still easily found, is called *nach Zürcher Art,* meaning "cooked in the style of Zürich." Think meat, mushrooms, potatoes, butter, cream—and heartburn. Zürich's cuisine is extremely rich, perfectly suited to the leaded-glass and burnished-oak guildhalls. The signature dish, which you'll encounter throughout both French and German Switzerland, is *geschnetzeltes Kalbfleisch,* or in French *émincé de veau:* bite-size slices of milky veal (and sometimes veal kidneys) sautéed in butter and swimming in a rich brown sauce thick with cream, white wine, shallots, and mushrooms. Its closest cousin is *geschnetzeltes Kalbsleber* (calves' liver), in similar form. Both are often served in hefty portions; you'll clean your plate only to have a fresh one appear with the second half of your serving. The inevitable accompaniment is *Rösti* (hash brown potatoes), served in portions of equal scale—often the full 8-inch-diameter patty is a serving for one. You may also find *Spätzli,* or "little sparrows": flour-egg dough fingers, either pressed through a sieve or snipped, gnocchi style, and served in butter. Another culinary must is Zürich's favorite portable food, sausage and *Bürli* (a roll). The best are to be had at the Hintere Sterne at Bellevueplatz, an outdoor stand run by gruff men who are a tradition in themselves. *Kalbsbratwurst* (veal) is mild, the smaller *Cervelat* (pork) saltier. Join the locals and munch away while waiting for a tram.

Zürichers also have a definite sweet tooth: refined cafés draw crowds for afternoon pastries, and chocolate shops vie for the unofficial honor of making the best chocolate truffles in town.

Guildhalls

In exploring Zürich's core, you will want to enter at least one of the famous medieval union clubhouses scattered along the riverfront neighborhoods; the best way is to dine in one, as all but the Zunfthaus zur Meisen have been converted to public restaurants. Having polished off a traditionally meat-heavy meal, ask if you can have a peek into the other dining rooms—they are, for the most part, museum-perfect in their leaded-glass and Gothic-wood detail.

Museums

The wealth of Zürich bankers and industrialists gave rise to private art collections that are now part of the public art scene. Among the best is the Kunsthaus, with one of the world's best collections of Swiss art; the Museum Rietberg is famous for its East Asian collections. Many local museums host temporary design exhibitions, since Zürich was one of the centers of the graphic design industry early in the 20th century; the Museum für Gestaltung is devoted to all types of design.

Shopping

Many of Zürich's shopping finds lie hidden along the narrow streets between the Bahnhofstrasse and the Limmat River; these are peppered with designer boutiques. Quirky bookstores and antiques shops lurk in the sloping cobblestone alleyways leading off Niedorfstrasse and Oberdorfstrasse. The fabled Bahnhofstrasse—famous because it's reputedly the most expensive street in the world—is dominated by large department stores and extravagantly priced jewelry.

EXPLORING ZÜRICH

From the northern tip of the Zürichsee, the Limmat River starts its brief journey to the Aare and, ultimately, to the Rhine—and it neatly bisects Zürich at the starting gate. The city is crisscrossed by lovely, low bridges. On the left bank are the Altstadt (Old Town), the grander, genteel section of the old medieval center; the Hauptbahnhof, the main train station; and Bahnhofplatz, a major urban crossroads and the beginning of the world-famous luxury shopping street, Bahnhofstrasse. The right bank constitutes the livelier old section, divided into the Oberdorf (Upper Village) toward Bellevueplatz, and the Niederdorf (Lower Village), from Marktgasse to Central and along Niederdorfstrasse, which fairly throbs on weekends. Most streets around the Rathausbrücke and the Grossmünster are pedestrian-only zones.

Scattered throughout the town are 13 medieval guildhalls, or *Zunft-häuser,* that once formed the backbone of Zürich's commercial society. Today most of these house atmospheric restaurants where high ceilings, leaded-glass windows, and coats of arms evoke the mood of merchants at their trade. Often these restaurants are one floor above street level because in the days before flood control the river would rise and inundate the ground floors.

Numbers in the text correspond to numbers in the margin and on the Zürich map.

Great Itineraries

IF YOU HAVE 1 DAY

Start in the small but luxuriously gentrified Altstadt and window-shop along the Bahnhofstrasse. Wind through the medieval streets toward the pretty Limmat River, looking into the Fraumünster to see the Chagall stained-glass windows. Then cross over to the bustling Oberdorf and Niederdorf areas to see the Grossmünster and the Rathaus. If you're in the mood for a museum, choose from three excellent, varied collections: Asian art at the Museum Rietberg, historic and cultural artifacts at the Swiss National Museum, or paintings at the Kunsthaus.

IF YOU HAVE 3 DAYS

In three days you can take fuller advantage of Zürich's cultural offerings. Start with the introductory walk outlined above; also consider ordering opera or concert tickets on your first day. The next afternoon can be spent visiting another museum or two. In good weather take a boat trip on the Zürichsee. Or, better yet, rent a bicycle, ride downriver, then pick a spot on the wide grassy riverbank to relax and have a picnic (☞ Outdoor Activities and Sports, *below*).

IF YOU HAVE 5 DAYS

For a taste of backcountry Switzerland, drive north through the scenic countryside up to Schaffhausen (☞ Chapter 3), passing the Rhine Falls and a slew of wood-shingle farmhouses. If art is more your interest, visit the Am Römerholz collection in the nearby art town of Winterthur (☞ Off the Beaten Path, *below*).

Bahnhofstrasse and the Altstadt

Zürich's Altstadt (Old Town) is home to several of Zürich's most important landmarks—the Lindenhof, St. Peters, the Fraumünster, and the Stadthaus—as well as its luxury shopping street, the world-famous Bahnhofstrasse.

A Good Walk

Begin at the **Hauptbahnhof** ①, a massive 19th-century edifice. Directly behind the Hauptbahnhof is the **Schweizerisches Landesmuseum** ②, housed in an enormous 19th-century neo-Gothic mansion; behind that is a shady green park. Walk northward to the tip of the park, cross on the left-hand side of the bridge, turn south a bit along Sihlquai, and head up Ausstellungsstrasse to the **Museum für Gestaltung** ③, which holds an impressive collection of 20th-century graphic art. Back at the train station, look across Bahnhofplatz, and you'll see traffic careening around a statue of **Alfred Escher,** the man who brought Zürich into the modern age.

Cross the square to the **Bahnhofstrasse,** Zürich's principal business and shopping boulevard. A quarter of the way up the street—about five blocks—veer left into the Rennweg and left again on Fortunagasse, an atmospheric medieval street well removed from the contemporary elegance of the Bahnhofstrasse. Climb up to the **Lindenhof** ④, a quiet, grassless square with a view of the remains of the city's original Roman customs house and fortress. From here a maze of medieval alleys leads off to your right. Nestled among them is **St. Peters Kirche** ⑤, whose tower has the largest clock face in Europe.

From St. Peters Kirche bear right on Schlüsselgasse and duck into a narrow alley, Thermengasse, which leads left; you'll walk directly over excavated ruins of **Roman baths**. At Weinplatz, turn right on Storchengasse, where some of the most elite boutiques are concentrated, and head toward the delicate spires of the **Fraumünster** ⑥. In the same square, you'll see two of Zürich's finest guildhalls, the **Zunfthaus zur Waag** ⑦ and **Zunfthaus zur Meisen** ⑧.

Wind left up Waaggasse past the Hotel Savoy to the **Paradeplatz** ⑨. Continue south on Bahnhofstrasse, which, as it nears the lake, opens onto a vista of boats, wide waters, and (on a clear day) distant peaks. At the Bürkliplatz, look to your right: those manicured parks are the front lawn of the **Hotel Baur au Lac,** the aristocrat of Swiss hotels. Beyond, you'll see the modern structure of the **Kongresshaus** and the **Ton-**

halle, where the Zürich Tonhalle Orchestra resides. Across General-Guisan-Quai is one of the local swans' favorite hangouts: the boat dock, which is the base for trips around the Zürichsee.

Here you can take General-Guisan-Quai west to Seestrasse to the **Museum Rietberg** (about a 15-minute walk) or turn left and cross the **Quaibrücke** (Quay Bridge) for one of the finest views in town, especially at night, when the floodlighted spires are mirrored in the inky river, whose surface is disturbed only by drifting, sleeping swans.

TIMING

The area is surprisingly compact; half a day is enough time for a cursory visit. If you're planning on museum hopping, the Schweizerisches Landesmuseum and Museum Rietberg merit at least two hours apiece.

Sights to See

🕮 *following the text of a review is your signal that the property has a Web site, where you will find details and, usually, images; for a link, visit www.fodors.com/urls.*

Alfred Escher. Leave it to Zürich to have a statue that honors not a saint, not a poet or artist, but rather the financial wizard who single-handedly dragged Zürich into the modern age back in the mid-19th century. Escher (1819–82) established the city as a major banking center, championed the development of the federal railways and the city's university, and pushed through the construction of the tunnel under the St. Gotthard Pass. ⊠ *In the middle of Bahnhofpl.*

Bahnhofstrasse. Zürich's principal boulevard offers luxury shopping and hulking department stores, while much shifting and hoarding of the world's wealth takes place discreetly behind the banks' upstairs windows. However, the long-standing story of the treasure trove below the Bahnhofstrasse was recently quashed—the subterranean vaults that once stored great piles of gold and silver now lie empty. In mid-1998 a local journalist was allowed access to the vaults; at the end of the dark labyrinths the scribe found nothing but empty rooms, the precious metals having been moved to a site near the airport several years earlier. ⊠ *Runs north–south west of Limmat River.*

★ ❻ **Fraumünster** (Church of Our Lady). Of the church spires that are Zürich's signature, the Fraumünster's is the most delicate, a graceful sweep to a narrow spire. It was added to the Gothic structure in 1732; the remains of Louis the German's original 9th-century abbey are below. Its Romanesque choir is a perfect spot for meditation beneath the ocher, sapphire, and ruby glow of stained-glass windows by the Russian-born Marc Chagall, who loved Zürich. The Graubünden sculptor Alberto Giacometti's cousin, Augusto Giacometti, executed the fine painted window in the north transept. ⊠ *Stadthausquai.* ☉ *May–Sept., Mon.–Sat. 9–6; Oct., Mon.–Sat. 10–5; Nov.–Feb., Mon.–Sat. 10–4; Mar.–Apr., Mon.–Sat. 10–5.*

OFF THE
BEATEN PATH

MUSEUM RIETBERG – A prodigious gathering of art from India, China, Africa, Japan, and Southeast Asia is displayed in the neoclassical Villa Wesendonck, once home to Richard Wagner (it was for the lady of the house that he wrote his *Wesendonck Songs*). The rich collection ranges from Cambodian Khmer sculptures and jade Chinese tomb art to Japanese Nô masks and Tibetan bronzes. From the city center follow Seestrasse south about 1¾ km (1 mi) until you see signs for the museum; or take Tram 7 to the Rietberg Museum stop. ⊠ *Gablerstr. 15,* ☎ *01/2024528.* 🎟 *12 SF.* ☉ *Tues.–Sun. 10–5.*

❶ Hauptbahnhof (Main Railway Station). From the bustling main concourse of this immaculate 19th-century edifice you can watch crowds of people rushing to their famously on-time trains. Beneath lies a shopping mall, open daily from 8 to 8 (an exception to the closed-on-Sunday rule), with everything from grocery stores to clothing boutiques and bookshops. ⊠ *Between Museumstr. and Bahnhofpl.*

❹ Lindenhof (Linden Court). On this quiet square, overlooking both sides of the river, are the remains of the original Roman customs house and fortress and the imperial medieval residence. The fountain was erected in 1912, commemorating the day in 1292 when Zürich's women saved the city from the Habsburgs. As the story goes, the town was on the brink of defeat as the imperial Habsburg aggressors moved in. Determined to avoid this humiliation, the town's women donned armor and marched to the Lindenhof. On seeing them, the enemy thought they were faced with another army and promptly beat a strategic retreat. Today, the scene could hardly be less martial, as locals play boccie and chess under the trees. ⊠ *Bordered by Fortunag. to the west and intersected by Lindenhofstr.*

❸ Museum für Gestaltung (Design Museum). Innovative temporary exhibitions focus on topics such as architecture, poster art, graphic design, and photography. ⊠ *Ausstellungstr. 60,* ☎ *01/4462211.* 🎫 *5 SF.* 🕙 *Tues., Thurs., and Fri. 10–6, Wed. 10–9, weekends 11–6.*

❾ Paradeplatz (Parade Square). The hub of the Bahnhofstrasse and a tram junction, this square is a great place to observe a microcosm of the local upper crust—furrowed-brow bankers striding to work while their fur-trimmed wives struggle with half a dozen bags and the dilemma of where to shop next. While you're at it, spoil your taste buds with incredible chocolate from the Sprüngli café (☞ Shopping, *below*). ⊠ *Intersection of Bahnhofstr. and Poststr.*

★ ❺ St. Peters Kirche. Dating from the early 13th century, Zürich's oldest parish church has the largest clock face in Europe. A church has been on this site since the 9th century. The existing building has been considerably expanded over the years. The tower, for example, was extended in 1534, when the clock was added; the nave was rebuilt in 1705. Keep an eye out for inexpensive or even free classical concerts. ⊠ *St. Peterhofstatt,* ☎ *no phone.* 🕙 *Weekdays 8–6, Sat. 8–4.*

★ ❷ Schweizerisches Landesmuseum (Swiss National Museum). Housed in a gargantuan neo-Gothic building opened in 1889, the Swiss National Museum owns an enormous collection of objects dating from the Stone Age to modern times. There are costumes, furniture, early watches, and a great deal of military history, including thousands of toy soldiers reenacting battle scenes. In the hall of arms there's a splendid mural, painted by the late-19th-century Bernese artist Ferdinand Hodler, *The Retreat of the Swiss Confederates at Marignano*—depicting a defeat in 1515 by the French that set Zürich back considerably after generations of prosperity. ⊠ *Museumstr. 2,* ☎ *01/2186511.* 🎫 *5 SF.* 🕙 *Tues.–Sun. 10:30–5.* 🐾

❽ Zunfthaus zur Meisen. This aristocratic baroque edifice, erected for the city's wine merchants in the 18th century, houses the Swiss National Museum's exquisite ceramics collection; the selection of 18th-century porcelain is particularly strong and includes works by Zürich and Nyon makers. Enter on the Fraumünster side. ⊠ *Münsterhof 20,* ☎ *01/2212807.* 🎫 *5 SF.* 🕙 *Tues.–Sun. 10:30–5.*

20

Zürich

0 — 200 yards

0 — 200 meters

KEY

i Tourist Information

Tram Line

Museum Rietberg

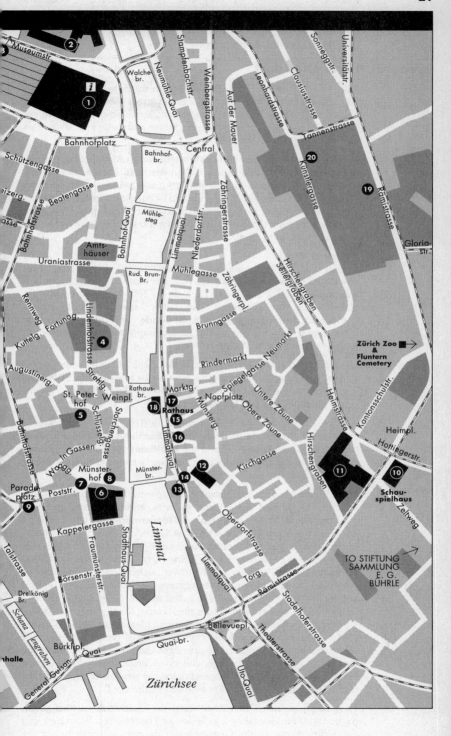

Museumstr

Walche br.

i

Bahnhofplatz

Bahnhof-br.

Central

Schützengasse

Beatengasse

Amts-häuser

Uraniastrasse

Rud. Brun-Br.

Mühle-steg

Mühlegasse

Zähringerpl.

Brunngasse

Rennweg

Fortunag.

Lindenhofstrasse

Kuttelg.

Strehlg.

Augustinerg.

St. Peter-hof

Rindermarkt

Neumarkt

Rathaus-br.

Marktg.

Spiegelgasse

Weinpl.

Münsterg.

Napfplatz

Untere Zäune

Schlüsselg.

Obere Zäune

Storchengasse

In Gassen

Bahnhofstrasse

Wogg

Münster-hof

Münster-br.

Limmatquai

Kirchgasse

Parade platz

Poststr.

Kappelergasse

Fraumünsterstr.

Stadthaus-Quai

Oberdorfstrasse

Börsenstr.

Dreikönig Br.

Schanz

Längraben

Bürkl.pl.

Quai

Quai-br.

Bellevuepl.

Theaterstrasse

Stadelhoferstrasse

General-Guisan

nhalle

Zürichsee

Limmat

Talstrasse

Sonneggstr.

Universitätstr.

Clausiusstrasse

Leonhardstrasse

Auf der Mauer

Tannenstrasse

Künstlergasse

Rämistrasse

Gloria-Str.

Hirschengraben

Seilergraben

Zähringerstrasse

Niederdorfstr.

Limmatquai

Neumühle-Quai

Neumühlebachstr.

Stampfenbachstr.

Weinbergstrasse

Schweizerg.

Bahnhofstrasse

Zürich Zoo →
&
Fluntern
Cemetery

Hirschengraben

Helmstrasse

Kantonschulstr.

Heimpl.

Hottingerstr.

Schau-spielhaus

Zeltweg

TO STIFTUNG
SAMMLUNG
E. G.
BÜHRLE →

Rämistrasse

Torg.

Limmatquai

Rathaus

1 2 4 5 6 7 8 9 10 11 12 13 14 15 16 17 18 19 20

➐ Zunfthaus zur Waag. This circa-1637 guildhall was the meeting place for linen weavers and hat makers. Today it houses a lovely restaurant (☞ Dining, *below*). ⊠ *Münsterhof 8.*

Niederdorf and Oberdorf

As soon as you step off the Quai Bridge on the right bank of the Limmat River, you'll notice a difference: the atmosphere is trendier and more casual. The area is also the center of Zürich's nightlife—both upscale and down, with the city's opera house and its historic theater, as well as plenty of bars and clubs.

As you explore the area along Münstergasse to Marktgasse, parallel to the river, you'll notice a less Calvinistic bent. Each of the narrow streets and alleys that shoot east off Marktgasse (which quickly becomes Niederdorfstrasse) offers its own brand of entertainment. Marktgasse eventually empties onto the Central tram intersection, opposite the main train station; from there it's easy to catch a tram along the Bahnhofstrasse or the Limmatquai.

A Good Walk

Start at the Quai Bridge and head up Rämistrasse to Heimplatz, where you'll find the **Schauspielhaus** ⑩. Across Heimplatz is the important **Kunsthaus** ⑪ museum. Head back down Rämistrasse to Bellevueplatz—where you can catch a tram that will take you to the impressive private **Stiftung Sammlung E. G. Bührle** collection—and follow Limmatquai downstream to the gaunt, imposing **Grossmünster** ⑫, with its distinctive stout twin towers.

Head back down the steps to the bank of the Limmat, where you'll find the 18th-century **Helmhaus** ⑬. Now an art museum, the Helmhaus is attached to the late-15th-century **Wasserkirche** ⑭, one of Switzerland's most delicate late-Gothic structures.

Along the Limmatquai a series of guildhalls today houses popular and atmospheric restaurants, the 13th-century **Zunfthaus zum Rüden** ⑮, **Zunfthaus zur Zimmerleuten** ⑯, and the **Zunfthaus zur Saffran** ⑰ among them. Across the Limmatquai, the striking baroque **Rathaus** ⑱ seems to rise up from the river.

Head back across the Limmatquai and up into the Niederdorf streets, which meander past tiny houses, galleries, antiques shops, and neopunk boutiques. Follow Marktgasse to **Rindermarkt,** site of the historic home of the Swiss poet and novelist Gottfried Keller. The Rindermarkt joins the picturesque Neumarkt and Spiegelgasse streets at a tiny medieval square where you'll see a fine early Gothic tower, the **Grimmenturm.** There's another Gothic tower farther down Spiegelgasse at **Napfplatz,** used during the 14th century by Zürich bankers. Several artistic and political figures have called narrow Spiegelgasse home—Lenin lived at No. 14, just before the Russian Revolution, and at No. 12 the exiled young revolutionary German playwright Georg Büchner (1813–37) wrote *Woyzeck* here before dying of typhoid. At the foot of the street a plaque marks the site of the Cabaret Voltaire, where the Dadaist movement took shape, conceived in Zürich by French exile Hans Arp, who in the 1920s proclaimed the new movement one that could "heal mankind from the madness of the age."

From Napfplatz take Obere Zäune up to the broad medieval **Kirchgasse,** packed with antiques shops, galleries, and bookstores. From here you can either return to the Grossmünster or venture north to see the **Graphische Sammlung** ⑲, with its woodcuts, etchings, and engravings; or head to the **Zoologisches Museum** ⑳.

TIMING

A quick overview of the Niederdorf and Oberdorf won't take more than a half day, but it's the kind of area where there is always something new to find, no matter how often you come back. Leave yourself extra time if you'd like to window-shop or invest a couple of hours in one of the galleries or museums, especially the Kunsthaus.

Sights to See

⑲ Graphische Sammlung. The impressive collection of the Federal Institute of Technology includes a vast library of woodcuts, etchings, and engravings by such European masters as Dürer, Rembrandt, Goya, and Picasso. Pieces from the permanent collection are often arranged in thematic exhibitions. Take Tram 6 or 10 from the Bahnhofplatz or Central stops or Tram 9 from Bellevue toward the ETH stop. ✉ *Rämistr. 101,* ☎ *01/6324046.* ✆ *Free.* ☉ *Mon., Tues., Thurs., and Fri. 10–5, Wed. 10–8.*

★ ⑫ **Grossmünster** (Great Church). This impressive cathedral is affectionately known to English speakers as the "Gross Monster." Executed on the plump twin towers (circa 1781) are classical caricatures of Gothic forms bordering on the comical. The core of the structure was built in the 12th century on the site of a Carolingian church dedicated to the memory of martyrs Felix and Regula, who allegedly carried their severed heads to the spot. Charlemagne is said to have founded the church after his horse stumbled over their burial site. On the side of the south tower an enormous stone Charlemagne sits enthroned; the original statue, carved in the late 15th century, is protected in the crypt. In keeping with what the 16th-century reformer Zwingli preached from the Grossmünster's pulpit, the interior is spare, even forbidding, with all luxurious ornamentation long since stripped away. The only artistic touches are modern: stained-glass windows by Augusto Giacometti, and ornate bronze doors in the north and south portals, dating from the late 1940s. ✉ *Zwinglipl.,* ☎ *01/2513860.* ☉ *Late Mar.–Oct., daily 9–6; Nov.–mid-Mar., daily 10–5.*

⑬ **Helmhaus.** The open court of this museum once served as a linen market. Inside, there are changing exhibitions of contemporary, often experimental, art by Zürich-based artists. In spring the museum hosts an exhibition of works from the city's annual competition for young artists. ✉ *Limmatquai 31,* ☎ *01/2516177.* ✆ *Free.* ☉ *Tues., Wed., and Fri.–Sun. 10–6, Thurs. 10–8.*

Kirchgasse. Antiques, art, and book enthusiasts will delight in the shops on this street. No. 13 was Zwingli's last home before he was killed in battle (1531) while defending the Reformation.

★ ⑪ **Kunsthaus.** With a varied and high-quality permanent collection of paintings—medieval, Dutch and Italian baroque, and Impressionist—the Kunsthaus is possibly Zürich's best art museum. The collection of Swiss art includes some fascinating works; others might be an acquired taste. Besides works by Ferdinand Hodler, with their mix of realism and stylization, there is a superb room full of Johann Heinrich Füssli paintings, which hover between the darkly ethereal and the grotesque. Otherwise, Picasso, Klee, Degas, Matisse, Kandinsky, Chagall, and Munch are all satisfyingly represented. ✉ *Heimpl. 1,* ☎ *01/2516765.* ✆ *Varies with exhibition.* ☉ *Tues.–Thurs. 10–9, Fri.–Sun. 10–5.* ✑

OFF THE BEATEN PATH

STIFTUNG SAMMLUNG E. G. BÜHRLE – One of Switzerland's best private art collections is owned by the E. G. Bührle Foundation. Though it's known especially for its Impressionist and post-Impressionist works, the collection also includes religious sculpture as well as Spanish and Italian paintings from the 16th to 18th centuries. Take Tram 11 from Bellevue-platz, then Bus 77 from Hegibachplatz. ⊠ *Zollikerstr. 172,* ☎ *01/ 4220086.* ▣ *9 SF.* ⊙ *Tues., Fri., and Sun. 2–5, Wed. 5–8.*

★ ⑱ **Rathaus** (Town Hall). Zürich's striking baroque town hall dates from 1694–98, and its interior remains as well preserved as its facade: There's a richly decorated stucco ceiling in the Banquet Hall and a fine ceramic stove in the government council room. ⊠ *Limmatquai 55,* ☎ *no phone.* ▣ *Free.* ⊙ *Tues., Thurs., and Fri. 10–11:30.*

Rindermarkt (Cattle Market). Fans of Gottfried Keller, commonly considered Switzerland's national poet and novelist, will want to visit this street. The 19th-century writer's former home, at No. 9, became famous thanks to his novel *Der Grüne Heinrich* (*Green Henry*). Opposite is the restaurant, **Zur Oepfelchammer** (☞ Dining, *below*), where Keller ate regularly. ⊠ *Street between Marktg. and Neumarkt.*

⑩ **Schauspielhaus.** During World War II this was the only German-language theater in Europe that wasn't muzzled by the Berlin regime, and it attracted some of the Continent's bravest and best artists. It's been presenting literary plays ever since it was built in 1884; today its productions aren't always so risky, but they are stunningly mounted and performed, in German of course. ⊠ *Rämistr. 34,* ☎ *01/2655858.*

⑭ **Wasserkirche** (Water Church). One of Switzerland's most delicate late-Gothic structures, this church displays stained glass by Augusto Giacometti. Both the church and the Helmhaus once stood on the island on which Felix and Regula supposedly lost their heads. ⊠ *Limmatquai 31,* ☎ *no phone.* ⊙ *Wed. 9–11, 2–5.*

🄲 ⑳ **Zoologisches Museum.** Engaging and high-tech, the Zoological Museum allows you a close look in its accessible displays on Swiss insects, birds, and amphibians. You can examine butterflies and living water creatures through microscopes and listen to birdcalls as you compare avian markings. ⊠ *Karl Schmid-Str. 4,* ☎ *01/6343838.* ▣ *Free.* ⊙ *Tues.–Fri. 9–5, weekends 10–4.*

⑮ **Zunfthaus zum Rüden.** Now housing one of Zürich's finest restaurants (☞ Dining, *below*), this 13th-century structure was the noblemen's guildhall. Peek inside at the barrel-vaulted ceiling and 30-ft beams; or better yet, stay for a meal. ⊠ *Limmatquai 42.*

⑰ **Zunfthaus zur Saffran.** Portions of this guildhall for haberdashers date from as early as 1389. It is now a highly acclaimed restaurant, with beautiful old rooms and a facade facing the river. ⊠ *Limmatquai 54.*

⑯ **Zunfthaus zur Zimmerleuten.** Dating from 1708, this was the carpenters' guild. Its main restaurant draws business groups to a number of lovely dark-wood halls; its former storage cave houses a cozy restaurant, too (☞ Dining, *below*). ⊠ *Limmatquai 40.*

OFF THE
BEATEN PATH   **WINTERTHUR –** A wealth of fine art was donated to the textile town Winterthur by prosperous local merchants. One such denizen was Oskar Reinhart, whose splendid home on the hill overlooking the town now contains the huge **Am Römerholz** collection of paintings from five centuries, including works by Rembrandt, Manet, Renoir, and Cézanne. Winterthur is a half hour from Zürich by train, on the main rail route to St. Gallen; fast trains depart daily from the main train station, about every half hour. From the train station, take Bus 10 to Haldengut or Bus 3 to Spital and follow the Römerholz sign up the hill. By car, follow the autobahn signs for Winterthur–St. Gallen. Take the Winterthur-Ohringen exit onto Schaffhauserstrasse into town, then left on Rychenbergstrasse

to Haldenstrasse. ⊠ *Haldenstr. 95, Winterthur,* ☎ *052/2692740.* ⌦ *8 SF.* ⊙ *Tues.–Sun. 10–5*

ZÜRICH ZOO – This is one of Europe's outstanding zoos, with more than 1,500 animals including Asian elephants, black rhinos, seals, and big cats. Set in a tree-filled park, it's just east of the city center and easily reached by Trams 5 and 6. ⊠ *Zürichbergstr. 221,* ☎ *01/2542505.* ⌦ *14 SF.* ⊙ *Nov.–Feb., daily 8–5; Mar.–Oct., daily 8–6.*

JAMES JOYCE'S GRAVE – Joyce, the inimitable Irish author, not only lived and wrote in Zürich, he died here as well. The city's most famous literary resident is buried in the Friedhof Fluntern (Fluntern Cemetery); atop his grave sits a contemplative statue of the writer, complete with cigar. A few steps away is the grave of another renowned author, Nobel Prize winner Elias Canetti. The cemetery is right next to the Tram 6 terminus. ⊙ *Mar.–Apr. and Sept.–Oct., daily 7–7; May–Aug., daily 7 am–8 pm; Nov.–Feb., daily 8–5.*

DINING

Zürich's inflated cost of living is reflected in its restaurants. There is a shortage of truly budget options, but keep in mind that daily prix-fixe menus are considerably cheaper, and even the glossiest places have business-lunch menus at noon—your best bet for sampling Zürich's highest cuisine at cut rates. For tight-budget travel, watch for posted *Tagesteller* listings: cheap menus of the day, with meat, potatoes, and possibly a hot vegetable, can still be found in the Niederdorf for under 20 SF.

CATEGORY	COST*
$$$$	over 90 SF
$$$	50 SF–90 SF
$$	30 SF–50 SF
$	under 30 SF

*Prices are per person for a three-course meal (two-course meal in $ category), including sales tax and 15% service charge.

$$$$ ✕ **Baur au Lac Rive Gauche.** Though it has traded its self-important neo-Gothic decor for a light, Mediterranean look, businesspeople still flock to this traditional clubhouse-style institution. The cuisine is lighter and trendier now, with fresh seafood and salads, but the wine list still taps the Baur's impressive cave. ⊠ *Hotel Baur au Lac, Talstr. 1,* ☎ *01/2205060. Reservations essential. AE, DC, MC, V.*

$$$$ ✕ **La Rotonde.** Even when not illuminated by candlelight, the Dolder
★ Grand's haute-cuisine restaurant is one of Zürich's most grandiose spots. Housed in a great arc of a room, La Rotonde provides sweeping views over the terrace to the lake below. The atmosphere is formal, the staff attentive to a fault, the culinary style traditional French with a fashionably light touch—sweetbreads on a bed of gnocchi with asparagus and truffles, for instance. ⊠ *Kurhausstr. 65,* ☎ *01/2693870. Jacket and tie. AE, DC, MC, V.*

$$$$ ✕ **Petermann's Kunststuben.** Serious and chicly formal, this is one of
★ Switzerland's gastronomic meccas. Though it's south of city center, in Küssnacht on the lake's eastern shore, it's more than worth the investment of time, effort, and travel budget. Chef Horst Petermann never rests on his laurels: the ever-changing menu may include lobster with artichoke and almond oil; rabbit terrine with black truffles; or Tuscan dove with pine nuts and herbs. ⊠ *Seestr. 160, Küssnacht,* ☎ *01/9100715. Reservations essential. AE, DC, MC, V. Closed Sun. and Mon., 2 wks in Feb., and 3 wks in late summer.*

26

Zürich Dining and Lodging

Lagerstrasse
Militärstrasse
Gessner-Allee
Gessner
Br.
Löwen-
pl.
Zeughausstrasse
Kasernenstrasse
Militär
Br.
Gessner-Allee
40
Löwenstrasse
Seidengasse
Rotwandstrasse
Müllerstr.
Bäckerstr.
Stauffacherstr.
Sihl
Schanzengraben
Uraniastrasse
Sihlstrasse
39
38
St. Annag.
Sihl-
Br.
Sihlstrasse
Nüschelerstrasse
Werdstr.
Stauffacher-Quai
Talacker
Pelikanstrasse
Talstrasse
41
Weberstr.
Stauff-
Br.
Selnaustrasse
Selnau-
Br.
Bären
Br.
Bärengasse
Flössergasse
Brandschenkestr.
Tödistrasse
Am Schanzengraben
Sihlhölzli-
Br.
Freigutstrasse
Gartenstrasse
Bleicherweg
Claridenstrasse
Beethovenstrasse
Dreikönigstrasse
Stockerstrasse
Gotthardstrasse
Tödistrasse
28
Alfred Escher
Strasse
29

N

Mutschellenstrasse

KEY

i Tourist Information
— Tram Line

0 . . . . . 200 yards
0 . . . . . 200 meters

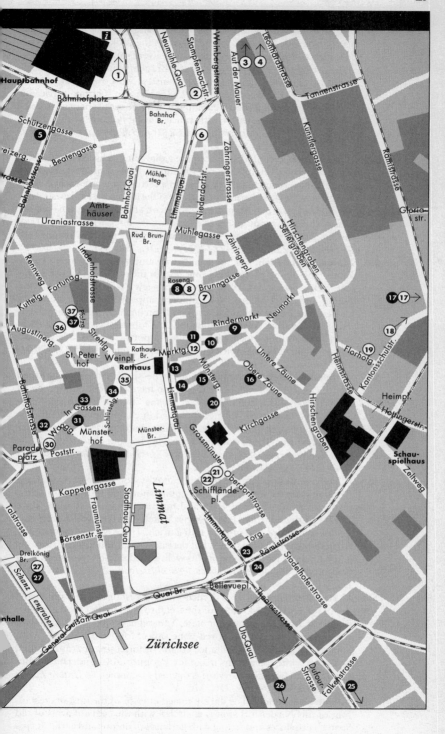

$$$-$$$$ ✕ **Kronenhalle.** From Stravinsky, Brecht, and Joyce to Nureyev,
★ Deneuve, and Saint-Laurent, this beloved landmark has always drawn
a stellar crowd. The atmosphere is genial, the cooking hearty, and the
collection of 20th-century art astonishing. Every panel of gleaming wood
wainscoting frames works by Picasso, Braque, Miró, or Matisse, col-
lected by patroness-hostess Hulda Zumsteg, who owned the restau-
rant from 1921 until her death in 1985. Her son, Gustav, carries on
the tradition, serving robust cooking in hefty portions: herring in dou-
ble cream, tournedos with truffle sauce, duck *à l'orange* with red cab-
bage and Spätzli. ⊠ *Rämistr. 4,* ☎ *01/2516669. Reservations essential.
AE, DC, MC, V.*

$$$ ✕ **Blaue Ente.** Part of a chic shopping gallery in a converted mill south
of the city center, this modern bar-restaurant draws well-dressed crowds
from the advertising and arts scene. In a setting of whitewashed brick
and glass, with jazz filtering through from the adjoining bar, guests sample *Zander* (pike-perch) roasted with bacon and sauerkraut, baked sea
bass with basil-cream sauce, or roast barbary duck with Spätzli. Take
the No. 2 or 4 tram toward Wildbachstrasse. Reservations are advised.
⊠ *Seefeldstr. 223,* ☎ *01/4227706. AE, DC, MC, V.*

$$$ ✕ **Haus zum Rüden.** The most culinarily ambitious of Zürich's many
Zunfthaus dining places, this fine restaurant is also the most archi-
tecturally spectacular, combining river views with a barrel-vaulted
ceiling and 30-ft beams. Slick modern improvements—including a
glassed-in elevator—manage to blend intelligently with the ancient
decor. Innovative entrées might include lobster lasagna in saffron
sauce, veal in lime sauce, or beef fillet in port. It's especially impres-
sive at night; ask for a window table. ⊠ *Limmatquai 42,* ☎ *01/
2619566. AE, DC, MC, V.*

$$$ ✕ **Hummer- und Austernbar.** In a fin de siècle setting of polished
wood, candles, and rich scarlet, you can have your fill of impeccably
fresh lobster and oysters (*Hummer* means "lobster"; *Austern,* "oysters"), such as Brittany lobsters poached in champagne sauce. In August, the city's expatriate Swedes flock here for crayfish, a late-summer
Nordic favorite. There's depth to the wine list, but champagne seems
to be the beverage of choice. ⊠ *Hotel St. Gotthard, Bahnhofstr. 87,*
☎ *01/2118315. AE, DC, MC, V.*

$$$ ✕ **Veltliner Keller.** Though its rich, carved-wood decor borrows from
Graubündner Alpine culture, this dining spot is no tourist-trap trans-
plant: the house, built in 1325 and functioning as a restaurant since
1551, has always stored Italian-Swiss Valtellina wines, which were car-
ried over the Alps and imported to Zürich. There is a definite empha-
sis on the heavy and the meaty, but the kitchen is flexible and reasonably
deft with more modern favorites as well: grilled salmon, veal steak with
Gorgonzola, and dessert mousses. ⊠ *Schlüsselg. 8,* ☎ *01/2254040. AE,
DC, MC, V.*

$$$ ✕ **Zum Grünen Glas.** This French-inclined restaurant in a quiet cor-
★ ner of the Niederdorf is part of the trend toward lighter food and por-
tions that don't overflow your plate. You might try red-lentil soup with
sorrel or an entrecôte with red wine sauce, followed by crepes with
apples, calvados, and vanilla ice cream. Wainscoting, parquet floors,
and crisp white tablecloths make for a comfortable, understated dining room; an outside courtyard is opened in summer. ⊠ *Untere Zäune
15,* ☎ *01/2516504. AE, DC, MC, V.*

$$ ✕ **Bodega Española.** The dark-paneled interior of the upstairs restau-
rant of this Niederdorf spot is encircled with the coats of arms of old
Spanish provinces and strung with garlands of onions and garlic. It spe-
cializes in big steaks, good seafood, omelets, and paella. Be sure to sam-
ple the excellent house Rioja (a Spanish-wine specialty shop adjoins,
so the choice is extensive) and crown your meal with a Cuban cigar.

Downstairs is a smoky bar that serves amazing tapas. ⊠ *Münsterg. 15,* ☎ *01/2512310. AE, DC, MC, V.*

$$ ✕ **Opus.** In this warm, bookish decor, you can enjoy a chic supper of Italian-inspired specialties: olive risotto with shrimp, duck breast with orange and balsamic vinegar sauce. The three-course lunch menu is a good value, especially the vegetarian version. On some winter weekends there's a hip salon or cabaret show between courses, with anything from the Singing Waiters to cigar-smoking evenings. ⊠ *Pfalzg. 1,* ☎ *01/2115917. AE, DC, MC, V.*

$$ ✕ **Zunfthaus zur Schmiden.** The sense of history and the decor alone— a magnificent mix of Gothic wood, leaded glass, and tile stoves—justify a visit to this popular landmark, the guild house of blacksmiths and barbers since 1412. All the Zürich meat classics are available in enormous portions (steaming double portions of Geschnetzeltes, whole skillets of crisp Rösti), and there's a considerable selection of alternatives—fish among them. The guild's own house-label wine is fine. ⊠ *Marktg. 20,* ☎ *01/2505848. AE, DC, MC, V.*

$$ ✕ **Zunfthaus zur Waag.** Another, airier guildhall, its woodwork whitewashed, its leaded-glass windows looking out to the Fraumünster, this lovely dining spot offers generous portions of the local classics: richly sauced veal, butter-crisped salmon, and sizzling potatoes simmered in gleaming skillets and chafing dishes. ⊠ *Münsterhof 8,* ☎ *01/2110730. AE, DC, MC, V.*

$$ ✕ **Zunfthaus zur Zimmerleuten/Küferstube.** Although the pricier Zunft-
★ haus upstairs is often overwhelmed with large banquets, at substreet level a cozy, candlelighted haven called the *Küferstube* (Coopers' Pub) serves atmospheric meals in a dark-beamed Old Zürich setting. Standard dishes have enough novelty to stand apart: duck salad with herb dressing and wild lettuce, roast pork with smoked bacon, homemade cinnamon ice cream with wine-poached pear. ⊠ *Limmatquai 40,* ☎ *01/2520834. AE, DC, MC, V.*

$$ ✕ **Zur Oepfelchammer.** Dating from 1801, this was once the haunt of
★ Zürich's beloved writer Gottfried Keller. One section is a dark and heavily graffitied bar, with sagging timbers and slanting floors; there are also two welcoming little dining rooms with coffered ceilings and plenty of carved oak and damask. Traditional meat dishes—calves' liver, geschnetzeltes Kalbfleisch, tripe in white-wine sauce—come in generous portions; salads are fresh and seasonal. The place is always packed, and service can be slow, so stake out a table and plan to spend the evening. ⊠ *Rindermarkt 12,* ☎ *01/2512336. MC, V. Closed Sun.–Mon.*

$–$$ ✕ **Adler's Swiss Chuchi.** Right on the Niederdorf's main square,
★ Hirschenplatz, this squeaky-clean Swiss-kitsch restaurant has an airy, modern decor, with Alpine-rustic chairs, Big Boy–style plastic menus, and good home-cooked national specialties. Excellent lunch menus are rock-bottom cheap and served double quick; the fondue is reputedly the best in Zürich. ⊠ *Roseng. 10,* ☎ *01/2669696. AE, DC, MC, V.*

$–$$ ✕ **Bierhalle Kropf.** Under the mounted boar's head and restored cen-
★ tury-old murals depicting gallivanting cherubs, businesspeople, workers, and shoppers share crowded tables to feast on generous hot dishes and a great selection of sausages. The *Leberknödli* (liver dumplings) are tasty, the potato croquettes are filled with farmer's cheese and garnished with a generous fresh salad, and the *Apfelküechli* (fried apple slices) are tender and sweet. The bustle and clatter provide a lively, sociable experience, and you'll more than likely get to know your neighbor. ⊠ *In Gassen 16,* ☎ *01/2211805. AE, DC, MC, V. Closed Sun.*

$–$$ ✕ **Mère Catherine.** This popular bistro with a Provençal veneer presents blackboard specials, with the chef turning out onion soup, duck-liver terrine, seafood, and a few meat dishes—even American-raised *steak de cheval* (horse steak). The young, bohemian clientele also enjoys the restaurant's small, hipster-packed Philosoph bar next door. On warm evenings, opt for courtyard seating. ⊠ *Nägelihof 3,* ☎ *01/2505940. AE, MC, V.*

$–$$ ✕ **Zeughauskeller.** Built as an arsenal in 1487, this enormous stone-
★   and-beam hall offers hearty meat platters and a variety of beers and wines in comfortable Germanic chaos. The waitstaff is harried and brisk, especially at lunchtime, when crowds are thick. Unlike the shabbier beer halls in Niederdorf, this is clean and bourgeois, reflecting its Paradeplatz location. They're not unaccustomed to tourists—menus are posted in English, Japanese, and at least 10 other languages—but locals consider this their home away from home. ⊠ *Bahnhofstr. 28, at Paradepl.,* ☎ *01/2112690. AE, DC, MC, V.*

$ ✕ **Hiltl Vegi.** Founded in 1898, when vegetarians were regarded as cranks and "grass eaters," this restaurant has more than proved its staying power. It was taken over in 1904 by Bavarian Ambrosius Hiltl, who married the cook; the current patron, Rolf Hiltl, is their great-grandson. The lunchtime salad bar has plenty of flavorful options; at night there is an all-you-can-eat Indian buffet. ⊠ *Sihlstr. 28,* ☎ *01/2213870. AE, DC, MC, V.*

$ ✕ **Odéon.** This historic café-restaurant was once frequented by the pre-
★   Revolution Lenin, who nursed a coffee and read the house's daily papers. Now the crowd is just as intense, and a tonic air of countercultural chic mixes with the cigarette smoke. You can nurse a coffee, too, or have a plate of pasta, a sandwich, or dessert; there's also a daily lunch menu for under 20 SF. The pharmacy next door used to be part of the café; an ongoing (but slow-motion) campaign aims to reintegrate the two. ⊠ *Limmatquai 2,* ☎ *01/2511650. AE, DC, MC, V.*

$ ✕ **Reithalle.** In a downtown theater complex behind the Bahnhofstrasse,
★   this old military riding stable now does its duty as a noisy and popular restaurant, with candles perched on the mangers and beams and heat ducts exposed. Young locals share long tables arranged mess-hall style to sample French and Italian specialties, many vegetarian, as well as an excellent international list of open wines listed on the blackboard. ⊠ *Gessnerallee 8,* ☎ *01/2120766. AE, MC, V.*

$ ✕ **Rheinfelder Bierhaus.** Dark and smoky, this solid old Niederdorf institution serves a rich *Rindspfeffer* (preserved beef stew) with Spätzli; sausage standbys; and the pride of the Spanish/Romansch owners: an incongruous but freshly homemade paella, served on the last Tuesday of every month. ⊠ *Marktg. 19,* ☎ *01/2512991. No credit cards.*

LODGING

Spending the night in Zürich is as expensive as eating out, though the options are no more outlandishly priced than those in the prestigious ski resorts. Deluxe hotels—the five-star landmarks—average between 450 SF and 600 SF per night for a double, and you'll be lucky to get a shower and toilet in your room for less than 140 SF. Yet a full (if top-heavy) range of choices is available in the city center, so even if you're flying into Zürich-Kloten on your way to a mountain retreat, don't shy away from a stopover of a day or two. Luckily, almost all the hotels that cater to businesspeople during the week offer significantly cheaper weekend rates.

CATEGORY	COST*
$$$$	over 430 SF
$$$	300 SF–430 SF
$$	160 SF–300 SF
$	under 160 SF

Prices are for a standard double room, including breakfast, tax, and service charge.

$$$$ ★ 🏨 **Baur au Lac.** This highbrow patrician of Swiss hotels turns its broad back to the commercial center, while its front rooms overlook the lake, the canal, and the manicured lawns of its own private park. The signature classic room decor gleams with rich fabrics and such ultra-modern comforts as triple-glazed windows and CD players. Lakeside corner junior suites (priced as deluxe doubles) are a relatively good value. In summer, meals (including breakfast) are served in the glassed-in pavilion along the canal; in winter, in the glowing Restaurant Français. ⊠ *Talstr. 1, CH-8022,* ☎ *01/2205020,* FAX *01/2205044. 107 rooms, 18 suites. 2 restaurants, bar, café, beauty salon, exercise room, dance club. AE, DC, MC, V.*

$$$$ ★ 🏨 **Dolder Grand.** Even if you're not staying here, you might wish to indulge in afternoon English tea at this sprawling Victorian-fantasy manse sitting high over Zürich. Its opulence leaves you feeling like you're in a lavish period film—you half expect to see Jeremy Irons and Kate Winslet casting agonized glances at each other across the dining room. The exterior is a picturesque hodgepodge of turrets, cupolas, half-timbering, and mansards, while guest rooms, with Empire-cum–Euro modern decor, are distinguished by their spaciousness and high ceilings. An uncompromisingly modern wing was added in the '60s; for the best experience a room in the old section is a must. La Rotonde, the hotel's restaurant (☞ Dining, *above*), serves excellent traditional French haute cuisine. The funicular (free for guests) runs from the Römerhof. ⊠ *Kurhausstr. 65, CH-8032,* ☎ *01/2693000,* FAX *01/2693001. 149 rooms, 34 suites. Restaurant, bar, café, pool, beauty salon, 9-hole golf course, 5 tennis courts, ice-skating, parking (fee). AE, DC, MC, V.*

$$$$ 🏨 **Savoy Baur en Ville.** The city's oldest hotel perennially improves itself, regularly sprucing up its rooms and amenities to maintain its conservative sleekness. The 35 rooms, with gray-stone bathrooms, walk-in closets, and mixed-period furniture, typify what the hotel calls its "past-modern" decor. It's directly on the Paradeplatz, at the hub of the banking, shopping, and sightseeing districts, and there are two fine restaurants—one French, one Italian—as well as a slick café-bar. ⊠ *Am Paradepl., Poststr. 12, CH-8022,* ☎ *01/2152525,* FAX *01/2152500. 112 rooms, 8 suites. 2 restaurants, bar. AE, DC, MC, V.*

$$$$ ★ 🏨 **Widder.** Zürich's most captivating hotel was created when 10 adjacent medieval houses were gutted and combined—now steel fuses with ancient stone and time-worn wood. Behind every door is a fascinating mix of old and new; a guest room could mix restored 17th-century frescoes and stone floors with a leather bedspread and halogen bell jars. Each room has a private fax, and guests are provided with their own business cards upon check-in. Four suites have private roof terraces, while in the basement you can mosey into the wine cellar to sample and discuss the vintages. ⊠ *Rennweg 7, CH-8001,* ☎ *01/2242526,* FAX *01/2242424. 42 rooms, 7 suites. 2 restaurants, bar. AE, DC, MC, V.*

$$$ 🏨 **Central-Plaza.** Despite its landmark-quality exterior—it was built in 1883—this hotel aims to please a young crowd, with a fresh, if chain-style, decor: brass, bamboo, palms. The bars and theme restaurants all seem contrived to appeal to shopping-mall habitués: the King's Cave, for instance, has faux Gothic stone and "medieval" goblets. It's directly on the Central tram crossroads on the Niederdorf side, and the compact rooms are well protected against the sounds of the busy intersection below. ⊠ *Central 1, CH-8001,* ☎ *01/2515555,* FAX *01/2518535. 100 rooms. 2 restaurants, 2 bars. AE, DC, MC, V.*

$$$ ★ 🏨 **Florhof.** This is an anti-urban hotel, a gentle antidote to the bustle of downtown commerce. In a dreamily quiet residential area by the Kunsthaus, this Romantik property pampers guests with its polished wood, blue-willow fabric, and wisteria-sheltered garden. The restaurant serves light, seasonal, fish-based menus, and meals on the terrace on a summer's night are positively rhapsodical. ⊠ *Florhofg. 4, CH-8001,* ☎ *01/2614470,* FAX *01/2614611. 33 rooms, 2 suites. Restaurant. AE, DC, MC, V.*

$$$ 🏨 **Neues Schloss.** Managed by the Arabella-Sheraton chain, this intimate hotel in the business district, just a few minutes' walk from Paradeplatz, offers a warm welcome, good service, and dark, classic decor. Its Le Jardin restaurant (closed Sunday) is popular with theatergoers for its preperformance menu. ⊠ *Stockerstr. 17, CH-8022,* ☎ *01/2869400,* FAX *01/2869445. 58 rooms. Restaurant. AE, DC, MC, V.*

$$$ 🏨 **Splügenschloss.** Constructed at the turn of the century as luxury apartments, this Relais & Châteaux property maintains its ornate, historic decor. One room has been paneled completely in Graubünden-style pine; others are decorated in warm pastel shades, and many are fitted with antique wardrobes. The restaurant doubles as an exhibition space, with annual shows of artists such as Expressionist painter Gen Paul. The location—in a spare banking district—may be a little out of the way for sightseeing, but if you yearn for atmosphere, you'll find this worth the effort. ⊠ *Splügenstr. 2, CH-8002,* ☎ *01/2899999,* FAX *01/2899998. 50 rooms, 2 suites. Restaurant, bar. AE, DC, MC, V.*

$$$ 🏨 **Wellenberg.** This Niederdorf hotel makes a definite retro statement with its burled wood, black lacquer, art deco travel posters, and Hollywood photos. Guest rooms are relatively spacious, the central location is superb, and if you're somehow feeling cut off from the outside world, you can bring your laptop and modem, get a password at reception, and plug into the Internet. ⊠ *Niederdorfstr. 10, CH-8001,* ☎ *01/2624300,* FAX *01/2513130. 45 rooms. Breakfast room, in-room data ports. AE, DC, MC, V.*

$$$ 🏨 **Zum Storchen.** The central location of this airy 600-year-old struc-
★ ture—tucked between the Fraumünster and St. Peters Kirche on the gull-studded bank of the Limmat River—is stunning, the hotel itself modern, impeccable, and intimately scaled. It has warmly appointed rooms with pretty toile de Jouy fabrics, some with French windows that open over the water. Extensive renovations in 2000 refreshed rather than changed the Storchen's style. The lobby incorporates a "business corner" (a laptop computer, photocopier, fax, etc.). Deluxe corner rooms, with views toward both river and lake, are worth fighting for. ⊠ *Weinpl. 2, CH-8001,* ☎ *01/2272727,* FAX *01/2272700. 73 rooms. Restaurant, bar, café. AE, DC, MC, V.*

$$ 🏨 **Adler.** This once-shabby place, smack in the middle of Niederdorf, has metamorphosed into a smart, state-of-the-art hotel on a modest and affordable scale. From the gleaming lobby to the sleek, modular rooms, the ashwood-and-granite decor makes the most of tight spaces, and hand-painted murals of city landmarks remind you you're in Zürich. The restaurant off the lobby, Adler's Swiss Chuchi (☞ Dining, *above*), is known locally as a great place for fondue. ⊠ *Roseng. 10, CH-8001,* ☎ *01/2669696,* FAX *01/2669669. 52 rooms. Restaurant. AE, DC, MC, V.*

$$ 🏨 **City.** Close to the Bahnhofstrasse and the main train station, this is a hotel in miniature, with small furnishings and baths and a high proportion of single rooms. An antique grandfather clock guards the lounge, and a model cow is stationed on the sun terrace (it was left over from a 1998 exhibition which dotted the entire city with bizarrely colored, life-size model cattle). ⊠ *Löwenstr. 34, CH-8021,* ☎ *01/2171717,* FAX *01/2171818. 73 rooms. AE, DC, MC, V.*

$$ 🏨 **Haus zum Kindli.** This charming little bijou hotel could pass for a 3-D Laura Ashley catalog, with every cushion and bibelot as artfully styled as a magazine ad. The result is welcoming, intimate, and a sight less contrived than many hotels' cookie-cutter decors. Even the Opus restaurant downstairs is filled with English bookcases and floral prints, and guests earn 10% off menu prices to vie with crowds of locals for a seat near the cabaret stage (☞ Dining, *above*). ⊠ *Pfalzg. 1, CH-8001,* ☎ *01/2115917,* FAX *01/2116528. 21 rooms. AE, DC, MC, V.*

$$ ⊞ **Helmhaus.** In an assertively modernized 600-year-old building, this hotel softens its edges with bright florals, white furniture, and some lake views. It makes the most of its limited space, and service is crisply professional. Since it's near the Niederdorf, it's convenient for night crawling. ⊠ *Schifflländepl. 30, CH-8001,* ☎ *01/2518810,* FAX *01/ 2510430. 25 rooms. Breakfast room. AE, DC, MC, V.* ✎

$$ ⊞ **Rex.** Its parking-garage architecture brightened up with assertive colors and jazz posters, this foursquare property has some business-people's necessities (laptop jacks, desks big enough to spread your papers on), without the depth of service offered by more expensive hotels. Its restaurant, the Blauer Apfel, draws a loyal, young-pro lunch clientele to its cool, blue-halogen-lighted tables. It's three stops from the Central heading north on Tram 7 or 15. ⊠ *Weinbergstr. 92, CH-8006,* ☎ *01/3602525,* FAX *01/3602552. 37 rooms. Restaurant. AE, DC, MC, V.*

$$ ⊞ **Rössli.** Ultrasmall but friendly, this hotel is set in the heart of Ober-
★ dorf. The chic white-on-white decor mixes stone and wood textures with bold textiles and mosaic bathrooms, and extras include safes and bathrobes—unusual in this price range. Some singles are tiny, but all have double beds. The suite on the top floor has a roof terrace with a marvelous view of the Limmat and the Altstadt. ⊠ *Rösslig. 7, CH-8001,* ☎ *01/2567050,* FAX *01/2567051. 16 rooms, 1 suite. Breakfast room, bar. AE, DC, MC, V.* ✎

$$ ⊞ **Zürichberg.** This hotel is like the Dolder Grand's stepsister: both hotels share the same view from atop the prestigious hill that gave its name to both the neighborhood and the hotel. However, where the Dolder is flashy, the Zürichberg is down-to-earth—especially in its room rates. Its rooms are minimally but effectively furnished; all have parquet floors. In the Schneckenhaus (Snail House) annex, rooms radiate outward from a central, oval atrium. Run by the Zürich Women's Association, the hotel is alcohol-free. Tram 6 heads straight to the hotel from the Hauptbahnhof. ⊠ *Orellistr. 21, CH-8044,* ☎ *01/2683535,* FAX *01/2683545. 67 rooms. Restaurant, café. AE, DC, MC, V.*

$ ⊞ **Etap.** Working on the principle that cheap should only mean inexpensive, this chain hotel is a dependable pick. Every Etap room around the world is exactly the same: violet and grey pastel walls and carpeting, one double bed, a single bunk set above it, and shower and toilet in separate, immaculate fiberglass modules. The rate is always the same, whether occupied by one, two, or three people. The location gives this branch an edge—it's in the industrial Zurich West neighborhood, which is currently morphing into a hip restaurant and gallery enclave. Take Tram 4 or 13 from the Hauptbahnhof to Escher Wyss Platz; the Etap is within easy walking distance from there. ⊠ *Technoparkstr. 2, CH-8005,* ☎ *01/2762000,* FAX *01/2762001. 160 rooms. Breakfast room. AE, MC, V.* ✎

$ ⊞ **Leoneck.** From the cowhide-covered front desk to the edelweiss-print curtains, this budget hotel wallows in its Swiss roots but balances this indulgence with no-nonsense conveniences: tile baths (albeit with cow-print shower curtains), murals, and built-in pine furniture. There isn't much space to stretch out, though, and the decor sometimes shows its wear. The adjoining restaurant, Crazy Cow, slings out its own Swiss kitsch (Rösti-burgers) in an over-the-top decor of milk cans, miniature Matterhorns, and the ubiquitous black-and-white bovine. ⊠ *Leonhardstr. 1, CH-8001,* ☎ *01/2542222,* FAX *01/2542200. 65 rooms. Restaurant. AE, DC, MC, V.* ✎

$ 🏨 **Limmathof.** This spare but welcoming hotel inhabits a handsome, historic shell and is ideally placed on the Limmatquai, minutes from the Hauptbahnhof and steps from the Limmatquai and Central tram stops. All rooms have tile bathrooms and plump down comforters; TVs are available for an extra 22 SF. There's an old-fashioned wood-paneled Weinstube and a bright vegetarian restaurant that doubles as the breakfast room. ✉ *Limmatquai 142, CH-8023,* ☎ *01/2614220,* FAX *01/2620217. 62 rooms. Restaurant, Weinstube. AE, DC, MC, V.*

$ 🏨 **St. Georges.** This simple former pension drenches its rooms in a milky, all-white look. Seventeen rooms now offer full bathrooms; the rest, each under 100 square ft, share the shower and toilet down the hall. Take Tram 3 or 14 from the station to Stauffacher; it's another five minutes on foot. ✉ *Weberstr. 11, CH-8004,* ☎ *01/2411144,* FAX *01/2411142. 40 rooms. Breakfast room. AE, MC, V.*

$ 🏨 **Zic-Zac Rock Hotel.** Perfectly set at ground zero of the lively Niederdorf, this hotel lets you indulge your inner groupie. All rooms are named after rock personalities, from Bryan Adams to Led Zeppelin, and decorated accordingly. Framed albums, portraits, and gold records hang on the pastel yellow walls. Furnishings are no-frills but comfortable; most rooms share showers and toilets. The American restaurant and bar downstairs draw plenty of nonguests and on weekends the hotel fairly throbs with bass. ✉ *Marketg. 17, CH-8001,* ☎ *01/2612181,* FAX *01/2612175. 34 rooms, 2 suites, 7 with bath. Restaurant, bar, breakfast room, airport shuttle. AE, DC, MC, V.* 🐾

NIGHTLIFE AND THE ARTS

Nightlife

Of all the Swiss cities, Zürich has the liveliest nightlife. The Niederdorf is Zürich's nightlife district, with cut-rate hotels, strip joints, and bars crowding along Marktgasse, which becomes Niederdorfstrasse. On Thursday and weekend nights, the streets flow with a rowdy crowd of club- and bar-hoppers. In winter things wind down between midnight and 2 AM, but come summer most places stay open until 4 AM.

Bars

Barrique (✉ Marktg. 17, ☎ 01/2525941) is a vinotheque featuring a world-renowned wine list. The service may be surly at **Brasserie Federal** (✉ Hauptbahnhof, ☎ 01/2171515), but you'll have the rare luxury of choosing from over 100 Swiss beers. **Café Central Bar,** in the Hotel Central (✉ Central 1, ☎ 01/2515555), is a popular neo–art deco café by day and a piano bar by night. **Cranberry** (✉ Metzgerg. 3, ☎ 01/2612772) stocks broad selections of rum and port; it also has a cigar room. The **James Joyce Pub** (✉ Pelikanstr. 8, off Bahnhofstr., ☎ 01/2211828) is a beautifully tiled and paneled Irish pub where the wood is as dark as the Guinness. The **Jules Verne Panorama Bar** (✉ Uraniastr. 9, ☎ 01/2111155) serves up cocktails with a wraparound view of downtown. The narrow bar at the **Kronenhalle** (✉ Rämistr. 4, ☎ 01/2516669) draws mobs of well-heeled locals and internationals for its prize-winning cocktails. **Malatesta** (✉ Niederdorfstr. 15, ☎ 01/2514274) is a well-established bistro/hangout for locals 20–80. Serving a young, arty set until 4 AM, **Odéon** (☞ Dining, *above*) is a cultural landmark—Mata Hari danced here, Lenin and Trotsky plotted the revolution, and James Joyce scrounged drinks—but watch out for inflated prices after midnight.

Dancing

The medieval-theme **Adagio** (✉ Gotthardstr. 5, ☎ 01/2063666) books classic rock, jazz, and tango for well-dressed thirtysomethings. **Kauf-**

Ieuten (✉ Pelikanstr. 18, ☎ 01/2253300) is a landmark dance club that draws a well-dressed, upwardly mobile crowd. **Mascotte** (✉ Theaterstr. 10, ☎ 01/2524481), blasting funk and soul, is popular with all ages on weeknights and has a gay night on Sunday. **Oxa Dance Hall** (✉ Andreastr. 70, Oerlikon, ☎ 01/3116033) is a legendary techno club that draws thousands of casual young Swiss who dance all night (and to noon Sunday). Take Tram 14 from the Hauptbahnhof to the Oerlikon terminus. **Le Petit Prince** (✉ Bleicherweg 21, ☎ 01/2011739) attracts a chichi set; go ahead and request a tune, from disco to techno.

Jazz Clubs

Casa Bar (✉ Münsterg. 30, ☎ 01/2612002), long the sole bastion of jazz here, now has excellent competition. **Moods** (✉ Schiffbauhalle, ☎ 01/2018140) is due to reopen in fall 2000 at its new location in a converted factory. The popular **Widder Bar** (✉ Widderg. 6, ☎ 01/2242411), in the Widder Hotel (☞ Lodging, *above*), attracts local celebrities with its 800-count "library of spirits" and top-name acts.

The Arts

Despite its small population, Zürich is a big city when it comes to the arts; it supports a top-rank orchestra, an opera company, and a theater. Check *Zürich News*, published weekly in English and German, or "Züritipp," a German-language supplement to the Friday edition of the daily newspaper *Tages Anzeiger*. The city's annual **Züricher Festspiele**—a celebration of opera, ballet, concerts, theater, and art exhibitions—runs from late June through mid-July. You'll need to book well ahead for this— details are available from the tourist office or Info- und Ticketoffice (✉ Postfach, CH-8023, ☎ 01/2154030). Tickets to opera, concert, and theater events can also be bought from the tourist office, while tickets for almost any event can be purchased in advance by telephone from **Fastbox** (☎ 0848/800800) or **Ticketline** (☎ 01/2256060). Depending on the event, **Musik Hug** (✉ Limmatquai 28–30, ☎ 01/2694100) makes reservations. Also try **Jecklin** (✉ Rämistr. 30, ☎ 01/2537676).

Film

Movies in Zürich are serious business, with films presented in the original language. Check newspapers and the ubiquitous posters and watch for the initials *E/d/f,* which means an English-language version with German (Deutsch) and French subtitles.

Music

The Zürich Tonhalle Orchestra, named for its concert hall, the **Tonhalle** (✉ Claridenstr. 7, ☎ 01/2063434), which was inaugurated by Brahms in 1895, enjoys international acclaim. There are also solo recitals and chamber programs here. The season runs from September through July; tickets sell out quickly, so book directly through the Tonhalle.

Opera

The permanent company at the **Opernhaus** (✉ Theaterpl., ☎ 01/2686666) is widely recognized and difficult to drop in on if you haven't booked well ahead, but single seats can often be had at the last minute. Performances are held from September through July.

Theater

The venerable **Schauspielhaus** (☞ Exploring Zürich, *above*) has a long history of cutting-edge performances with a strong inventive streak; during World War II this was the only German-language theater in Europe that remained independent. Nowadays its main stage presents finely tuned productions (in German), while experimental works are given in the Keller (cellar). ✉ *Rämistr. 34,* ☎ *01/2655858.*

During late August and early September the **Theaterspektakel** takes place, with circus tents housing avant-garde theater and experimental performances on the lawns by the lake at Mythenquai.

OUTDOOR ACTIVITIES AND SPORTS

Bicycling

You don't get much for free in Switzerland, but one exception is Zürich's free bike-rental program. For a refundable deposit of 20 SF and your passport you can borrow a bike. More than 300 bikes are available from six pickup points; children's bicycles and child seats are available. The most central pickup points are at Platform 18 of the Hauptbahnhof, the Globus department store on the Bahnhofstrasse (☞ Shopping, *below*), and at Theaterplatz/Stadelhofen. The other pickup points are the Enge railway station, the Altstetten railway station, and the marketplace in the Oerlikon suburb. Bikes are available from the train station year-round; the other locations distribute bikes between early May and the end of October. A great place to bike is the path along the river; it starts at the Hauptbahnhof and runs along the left bank of the Limmat, heading downriver. You can reach Kloster Fahr, the last Catholic monastery in the canton of Zürich, in under an hour. A yellow hiking trail sign will point you in the right direction.

Golf

The nine-hole **Dolder Golf Club** (☎ 01/2615045) is near the Dolder Grand Hotel (☞ Lodging, *above*). **Golf & Country Club Zürich** (☎ 01/9180050), with 18 holes, is near the city center in Zumikon, a suburb of Zürich.

Running

The track closest to the center is at **Allmend Sportplatz** (✉ Take Tram 13 to last stop). The **Dolder Grand** hotel (☞ Lodging, *above*) has a running path that winds through the forest; it's open to nonguests.

SHOPPING

Many city-center stores are open weekdays 9–8, Saturday 8–4. Most close on Sunday, with the exception of the shops at the Hauptbahnhof and the Stadelhofen train station. Many smaller shops, particularly in the Niederdorf area, open later in the morning or the early afternoon and are closed entirely on Monday.

Department Stores

ABM (✉ Bellevuepl., ☎ 01/2614484) is cheap and cheerful. **Globus** (✉ Bahnhofstr. and Löwenpl., ☎ 01/2266060) has a pricey but irresistible delicatessen in the basement, in addition to men's and women's designer clothes and housewares. **Jelmoli** (✉ Bahnhofstr. and Seideng., ☎ 01/2204411) has top-notch merchandise and swarms of staffers. **Manor** (✉ Bahnhofstr. 75, ☎ 01/2295111) is dependable and affordable.

Markets

At **Bürkliplatz** (✉ Lake end of Bahnhofstr.), there's a flea market open Saturday from 6 to 3:30 from May to October. There's a curio market on the **Rosenhof** (✉ At intersection of Niederdorfstr. and Marktg.) every Thursday 10–9 and Saturday 10–4 between April and Christmas.

Shopping Streets

The store-lined **Bahnhofstrasse** concentrates much of Zürich's most expensive (from elegant to gaudy) goods at the Paradeplatz end. There's another pocket of good stores around **Löwenstrasse,** southwest of the Hauptbahnhof. The **Niederdorf** offers less expensive, younger fashions, as well as antiques and antiquarian bookshops. The west bank's **Altstadt,** along Storchengasse near the Münsterhof, is a focal point for high-end designer stores.

Specialty Items

Books

The antiquarian bookshops in the upper streets of the Niederdorf area are rich with discoveries—and most have selections of English books. **Buchhandlung Buchmann** (⊠ Kirchg. 40, ☎ 01/2512368) specializes in art and art history. The **EOS Buchantiquariat Benz** (⊠ Kirchg. 17 and 22, ☎ 01/2615750) is a superb general bookshop spread over two storefronts (both shops sell secondhand books as well as antiquarian tomes). Even more eclectic is **medieval art & vie** (⊠ Spiegelg. 29, ☎ 01/2524720), selling books, music, and replicas of medieval artifacts, including reproduction medieval shoes, jewelry, and water bottles.

Chocolate

Sprüngli (⊠ Paradepl., ☎ 01/2117616; ⊠ Hauptbahnhof, ☎ 01/2118483; ⊠ Löwenpl., ☎ 01/2119612), the landmark chocolatier and café for wealthy Bahnhofstrasse habitués, concocts heavenly truffles and *Luxembourgli,* small cream-filled cookies that require immediate eating. Good, plain hot lunches and salads are also served. **Teuscher** (⊠ Storcheng. 9, ☎ 01/2115153; ⊠ Jelmoli, Bahnhofstr. and Seideng., ☎ 01/2204387; ⊠ Cafe Schober, Napfg. 4, ☎ 01/2518060) specializes in champagne truffles.

Collectibles

In the center of town virtually every street has some kind of antiques or collectibles shop. Especially intriguing are "modern antiques" shops, which carry odds and ends from decades past. **Eselstein** (⊠ Stadelhoferstr. 42, ☎ 01/2611056) stocks items from the 1950s through the 1970s ranging from lamp shades to standing ashtrays, plus finds such as Russian samovars. **Hannibal** (⊠ St. Jakobstr. 39, ☎ 01/2426044) is a delightful lumber room of postwar vases, chairs, pedal-operated trash bins, and rotary-dial telephones (remember them?).

Food

Inhale tempting smells from around the world at **H. Schwarzenbach** (⊠ Münsterg. 19, ☎ 01/2611315), an old-style, open-bin shop with oak shelves lined with coffee, dried fruits, nuts, and grains. Or whet your palate at **Scot & Scotch** (⊠ Wohllebg. 7, ☎ 01/2119060) with any one of 400 whiskeys from around the globe (nosings and tastings on request).

Men's Clothes

The classic, elegant designs of **Giorgio Armani** (⊠ Zinneng. 6, ☎ 01/2212348) are found in the west bank's Altstadt. **Trois Pommes** (⊠ Storcheng. 6/7, ☎ 01/2110239) is the central boutique of a series of designer shops scattered through the Storchengasse area; the racks are heavily stacked with such high-profile international designers as Jil Sander, Versace, Donna Karan, and Dolce & Gabbana.

Toys

AHA (⊠ Spiegelg. 14, ☎ 01/2131020) sells hypnotic optical-illusion gifts in styles and sizes to suit all ages. **Pastorini Spielzeug** (⊠ Weinpl. 3, ☎ 01/2287070) is a four-story mother lode of original and creative playthings, many hand-carved.

Women's Clothes

Beatrice Dreher Presents (✉ In Gassen 14, ☎ 01/2111348) carries Chloë and Krizia. **En Soie** (✉ Strehlg. 26, ☎ 01/2115902) carries gleaming, sometimes raw-textured silks, but although the fabrics are sophisticated, there's still an element of whimsy. You can snag some of last season's fashions at deep discounts at Trois Pommes' bargain-basement **Check Out** (✉ Waldmannstr. 8, ☎ 01/2128318), where DKNY, Calvin Klein, and Dolce & Gabbana are jumbled on the racks. For the absolute latest, go to the main **Trois Pommes** (✉ Storcheng. 6/7, ☎ 01/2110239) for Jil Sander, Alaïa, and Comme des Garçons.

ZÜRICH A TO Z

Arriving and Departing

By Car

The **A2** expressway from Basel to Zürich leads directly into the city. **A1** continues east to St. Gallen. Approaching from the south and the St. Gotthard route, take **A14** from Luzern (Lucerne); after a brief break of highway (**E41**) it feeds into **A3** and approaches the city along the lake's western shore. You can take **A3** all the way up from Chur in Graubünden.

By Plane

AIRPORTS AND AIRLINES

Zürich-Kloten (✉ 11 km [7 mi] north of Zürich, ☎ 1571060) is Switzerland's most important airport and the 10th busiest in the world. It is served by some 60 airlines, including **American, United,** and, of course, **Swissair.** You can also catch domestic and European flights out of Kloten on **Crossair** (☎ 01/8164170), Switzerland's domestic airline.

BETWEEN THE AIRPORT AND THE CENTER

It's easy to take a **Swiss Federal Railways feeder train** directly from the airport to Zürich's **Hauptbahnhof** (main station; ☎ 0900/300300). Tickets cost 6.20 SF one way, and trains run every 10–15 minutes, arriving in 10 minutes. **Taxis** cost dearly in Zürich. A ride into the center costs 50 SF–60 SF and takes around 20 minutes. The **Airport Shuttle** (☎ 01/3001410) costs about 22 SF per person for a one-way trip and runs roughly every half hour to a series of downtown hotels.

By Train

There are straightforward connections and several express routes leading directly into Zürich from Basel, Geneva, Bern, and Lugano. All roads lead to the **Hauptbahnhof** (☎ 0900/300300) in the city center.

Getting Around

By Bus and Tram

VBZ-Züri-Linie, the tram service in Zürich, is swift and timely. It runs from 5:30 AM to midnight, every six minutes at peak hours, every 12 minutes at other times. All-day passes cost 7.20 SF and can be purchased from the same vending machines at the stops that post maps and sell one-ride tickets; you must buy your ticket before you board. Free route plans are available from VBZ offices, located at major crossroads (Paradepl., Bellevue, Central, Kluspl.). Stops are clearly signposted.

By Taxi

Taxis are very expensive, with an 8 SF minimum but no charge for additional passengers. An available taxi is indicated by an illuminated rooftop light. You can order a cab by calling **Züri Taxi** (☎ 01/2222222) or **Alpha Taxi** (☎ 01/7777777).

Contacts and Resources

Embassies and Consulates

Contact the **United States** embassy in Bern (✉ Jubiläumsstr. 93, ☎ 031/3577011). Contact the **Canadian** embassy in Bern (✉ Kirchenfeldstr. 88, ☎ 031/3573200). There is a consulate for the **United Kingdom** (✉ Minervastr. 117, ☎ 01/3833560) in Zürich.

Emergencies

Police (☎ 117). **Ambulance** (☎ 144). **Hospital** (✉ Zürich Universitätsspital, Schmelzbergstr. 8, ☎ 01/2551111). **Doctors and dentists** can be referred in case of emergency by the English-speaking operators who man the *Notfalldienst* (Emergency Service) phones (☎ 01/2616100). **24-hour Pharmacy:** Bellevue Apotheke (✉ Theaterstr. 14, ☎ 01/2525600).

English-Language Bookstores

The Bookshop (✉ Bahnhofstr. 70, ☎ 01/2110444) has a wide selection of new books in English. **Payot** (✉ Bahnhofstr. 9, ☎ 01/2115452) carries a good stock of English fiction despite the store's French focus.

Guided Tours

ORIENTATION

Three introductory **bus tours** with English commentary are offered by the tourist office. **Cityrama**'s daily tour covers the main city sights and then goes on to Rapperswil to see the rose gardens and castle. The trip lasts two hours, leaving at 11 AM; it costs 35 SF. The daily **Sights of Zürich** tour (32 SF) gives a good general idea of the city in two hours; it leaves at 10 AM, noon, and 2 PM, though there is no tour at 10 in winter. **In and Around Zürich** goes farther and includes an aerial cableway trip to Felsenegg. This is also a daily tour, starting at 9:30 AM (9 AM in winter); it takes 2½ hours and costs 39 SF. All tours start from the Hauptbahnhof.

The tourist bureau also offers day trips by coach to Luzern, up the Rigi, Titlis, or Pilatus mountains, and the Jungfrau.

WALKING

Daily from May to October, the tourist office offers two-hour walking tours (18 SF) that start at the Hauptbahnhof. You can join a group with English-language commentary, but the times vary, so call ahead (☞ Visitor Information, *below*).

Travel Agencies

American Express (✉ Uraniastr. 14, ☎ 01/2287777). **Kuoni Travel** (✉ Bahnhofpl. 7, ☎ 01/2243333).

Visitor Information

Tourist service (✉ Hauptbahnhof, CH-8023, ☎ 01/2154000). **Hotel reservations** (☎ 01/2154040, FAX 01/2154044).

3 EASTERN SWITZERLAND

APPENZELL, LIECHTENSTEIN, SCHAFFHAUSEN, ST. GALLEN

Near Zürich, the cantons of Glarus, Schaffhausen, Thurgau, St. Gallen, and Appenzell, as well as Liechtenstein, are dominated by the Rhine River. With its secluded backcountry and thriving cities, the German-influenced region has everything from wood-shingle farmhouses to town houses adorned with oriel windows and frescoes. Still, the eastern cantons remain one of the most untouched regions of Switzerland.

Updated by
Katrin Gygax

DESPITE ITS PROXIMITY TO ZÜRICH, this Germanic region, bordered on the north by Germany and on the east by Austria, maintains a personality apart—a personality that often plays the wallflower when upstaged by more spectacular touristic regions. Lush with orchards and gardens, its north dominated by the romantic Rhine, with a generous share of mountains (including Mt. Säntis, at roughly 2,500 m/8,200 ft) and lovely hidden lakes, as well as the enormous Bodensee (Lake Constance), the region doesn't lack for variety—only tourists. Because the east draws fewer crowds, those who do venture in find a pleasant surprise: this is Switzerland sans kitsch, sans hard sell, where the people live out a natural, graceful combination of past and present. And although it's a prosperous region, with its famous textiles and fruit industry, its inns and restaurants cost noticeably less than those in regions nearby.

The region covers a broad sociological spectrum, from the thriving city of St. Gallen, with its magnificent baroque cathedral, to the obscure Ozark-like backcountry of Appenzell, where women couldn't vote in cantonal elections until the federal court in Lausanne intervened on their behalf in 1990 (federal law had granted women the national vote in 1971). On the last Sunday in April in Appenzell city, you still can witness the *Landsgemeinde,* an open-air election counted by a show of hands.

Architecture along the Rhine resembles that of old Germany and Austria, with half-timbers and rippling red-tile roofs. In cities like Schaffhausen, masterpieces of medieval frescoes decorate town houses, many of which have ornate first-floor bays called oriels. In the country, farmhouses are often covered with fine, feathery wooden shingles as narrow as Popsicle sticks and weathered to chinchilla gray. Appenzell has its own famous architecture: tidy narrow boxes painted cream, with repeated rows of windows and matching wood panels. The very countryside itself—conical green hills, fruit trees, belled cows, neat yellow cottages—resembles the naive art it inspires.

Pleasures and Pastimes

Dining

Your plate will feel the weight of German and Austrian influence in this most Teutonic of Swiss regions: portions are on a Wagnerian scale, and pork appears often. A side of *Spätzli* (little sparrows) or *Knöpfli* (little buttons) adds further heft: these are flour-egg dough fingers, either pressed through a sieve or snipped, gnocchi style, and served in butter. Another favorite side dish is *Hörnli* (little horns), crescent-shape pasta with butter and cheese. You can also can order a full-meal portion of *Käseknöpfli* (cheese dumplings), which come smothered in a pungent cheese sauce.

All across Switzerland you'll find the St. Gallen bratwurst, called *Olmabratwurst* on its home turf (Olma is the name of an annual autumn agricultural exhibition here). In restaurants it's served with thick onion sauce and *Rösti* (hash brown potatoes), but in St. Gallen itself the locals eat it on the hoof, lining up at lunchtime at one of two or three outdoor stands, then holding the thick white-veal sausage in a napkin with one hand and a round, chewy chunk of whole-grain *Bürli* bread in the other.

In the quirky region of Appenzell, the famous Appenzeller cheese deserves its stardom, as among the fine hard cheeses of Switzerland it has the most complex, spicy flavor, with traces of nutmeg. Other Appenzeller treats include a variation of Graubünden's famous air-dried beef, here called *Mostbröckli* and steeped in sweet apple cider before drying. It is served in translucent slices, its moist, mildly sweet flavor countered with bits of pickled onion. *Bauernschüblig* are dark dried-blood sausages. If you've got a sweet tooth, search out two regional specialties: Appenzeller *Biber* (honey cakes filled with almond and stamped with a design) and *Birnebrot* (thick dried-pear puree wrapped in glazed dough). *Chäsemagarone* is a rich, plain dish of large macaroni layered with butter, grated Appenzeller cheese, and butter-fried onions—it's often eaten with *Apfelmus* (applesauce).

Eastern Switzerland is the country's orchard region, especially the Thurgau area. There are several fine fruit juices made here, as well as *Most* (sweet cider) and some good fruit schnapps. Among area wines, Berneck comes from the Rhine Valley, Hallau from near Schaffhausen, and crisp whites from Stein-am-Rhein.

CATEGORY	COST*
$$$$	over 70 SF
$$$	40 SF–70 SF
$$	20 SF–40 SF
$	under 20 SF

Prices are per person for a three-course meal, including sales tax and 15% service charge

Hiking

Uncrowded hiking trails lead through all kinds of terrain, from rolling vineyards along the Rhine to isolated, rugged mountain wilderness above the Toggenburg Valley. This is a region of unspoiled nature, well-preserved villages, and breathtaking scenery.

Lodging

More and more hotels in this region are throwing away their Formica and commissioning hand-painted furniture to complement the beams they've so carefully exposed. However, bargain renovations tend toward the crisp if anonymous look of light tongue-in-groove pine paneling and earth-tone ceramic baths. The prices are somewhat lower on average here, with only slight variations from high to low season. Half board is rarely included. Hotel rates are generally calculated on a per-person basis; be sure to clarify the prices when reserving.

CATEGORY	COST*
$$$$	over 250 SF
$$$	180 SF–250 SF
$$	120 SF–180 SF
$	under 120 SF

Prices are for a standard double room, including breakfast, tax, and service charge.

✎ *following the text of a review is your signal that the property has a Web site, where you will find details and, usually, images; for a link, visit www.fodors.com/urls.*

Exploring Eastern Switzerland

The cantons of Glarus, Schaffhausen, Thurgau, St. Gallen, and Appenzell harbor some of Switzerland's oldest traditions. Although the cities have plenty of energy, the hilly countryside of this region changes little over the years. In the northern part of the region are the old Rhine city of Schaffhausen, the dramatic Rheinfall, and the preserved medieval town of Stein-am-Rhein. The Bodensee occupies the northeastern corner of Switzerland, just below Germany. Farther south are the textile center of St. Gallen, the quirky Appenzell region, and the resort area of the Toggenburg Valley. The tiny principality of Liechtenstein lies just across the eastern border, within easy driving distance.

Numbers in the text correspond to numbers in the margin and on the Eastern Switzerland and Liechtenstein and Schaffhausen maps.

Great Itineraries

Although eastern Switzerland is topographically the country's lowest region, it's still fairly rugged. It will take only a short time to see the major sights, but they are spread throughout the region, so leave time each day to be in transit. Train travel here is more complicated than in neighboring areas, requiring more intercity changes, so plan your itinerary accordingly. If you want to get back into the Appenzell hills, though, you should rent a car. St. Gallen is a good excursion center for visiting the Bodensee, Appenzell, Mt. Säntis, and the principality of Liechtenstein; farther west, Schaffhausen offers easy access to the magnificent Rheinfall, medieval Stein-am-Rhein, and the Bodensee, as well.

IF YOU HAVE 1 OR 2 DAYS

If you are coming from Zürich, enter the region at its northernmost tip and start with the old Rhine city of 🖾 **Schaffhausen** ①–⑩, known for its medieval frescoes and baroque oriel windows. From there it's an easy excursion to the nearby **Neuhausen am Rheinfall** ⑪, the city known for its broad, dramatic series of falls. Just on the other side of Schaffhausen, spend an hour or two in tiny **Stein-am-Rhein** ⑫, a medieval gem situated on the river. Then dip south to 🖾 **St. Gallen** ⑰, a busy textile center with an active Old Town beside its grand baroque cathedral. From St. Gallen you can explore the picture-pretty **Appenzell** ⑱.

IF YOU HAVE 3 OR 4 DAYS

With a little more time, you can spend your first two days in the northernmost areas, visiting 🖾 **Schaffhausen** ①–⑩, **Neuhausen am Rheinfall** ⑪, and **Stein-am-Rhein** ⑫; then make your way south, starting below Germany's Konstanz and following the southern coast of the Bodensee, a popular spot for local resorters. See the twin cities of **Kreuzlingen and Konstanz** ⑮ (the latter is in Germany) and 🖾 **Gottlieben** ⑭. Visit 🖾 **St. Gallen** ⑰ and 🖾 **Appenzell** ⑱, then trace the **Toggenburg Valley** ㉒, which runs in a great curve between Mt. Säntis and Wildhaus and draws Swiss tourists to its resorts and spas. Head to the tiny principality of Liechtenstein to see the royal castle and explore its art and stamp museums. Finally, go west to the Walensee, whose shores are flanked by a series of picturesque villages.

When to Tour Eastern Switzerland

Summers in eastern Switzerland provide the best weather and activities but also the greatest traffic, both on roads and in towns; spring and fall are good alternatives. Though most places in this region are not too terribly crowded even in summer, Stein-am-Rhein is an exception. It receives enough coach tours to virtually paralyze the village with pedestrians during high season; if you go, arrive earlier in the day or come on a weekday when crowds are a bit thinner.

SCHAFFHAUSEN AND THE RHINE

Known to many Swiss as Rheinfallstadt (Rhine Falls City), Schaffhausen is the seat of the country's northernmost canton, which also shares its name. To gaze upon the grand mist-sprayed Rheinfall, arguably the most famous waterfall in Europe, is to look straight into the romantic past of Switzerland. Goethe and Wordsworth were just two of the world's best-known wordsmiths to immortalize the Falls' powerful grandeur.

Eastern Switzerland and Liechtenstein

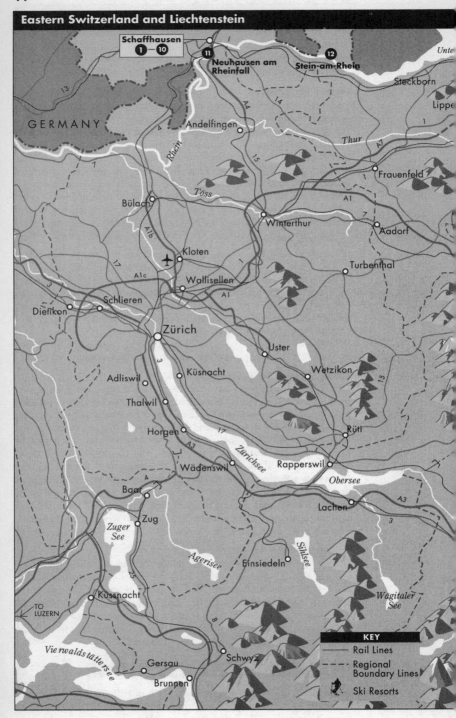

Schaffhausen
1 — 10

11

Neuhausen am Rheinfall

12 Stein-am-Rhein

Unte

Steckborn

Lippe

GERMANY

Andelfingen

Thur

A7

4

Rhein

15

Frauenfeld

7

Toss

1

Bülach

A1

A1b

Winterthur

A1

Aadorf

17

Kloten

7

A1c

1

Turbenthal

3

Wallisellen

A1

Schlieren

Diefikon

Zürich

Uster

Wetzikon

15

Adliswil

Küsnacht

Thalwil

Horgen

17

Rüti

Zürichsee

Wädenswil

A3

Rapperswil

Obersee

Baar

Lachen

A3

Zug

3

Zuger
See

Ägerisee

Einsiedeln

Sihlsee

Wägitaler
See

TO
LUZERN

Küssnacht

8

KEY

Vierwaldstättersee

Rail Lines

Gersau

Schwyz

Regional
Boundary Lines

Brunnen

Ski Resorts

Reichenau
ersee
33
13
Arenenberg **14** **Gottlieben**
15 Konstanz
Kreuzlingen
erswil

GERMANY

SWITZERLAND

Friedrichshafen

Bodensee

31

Lindau

Weinfelden
Thur 14
16 Amriswil
Arbon
Romanshorn

Wil

Rorschach
16
A1 *Rorschacher-*
berg
17
Abtwil St.
St. Gallen Margrethen Lustenau

Gossau
Teufen

Herisau **Stein**
19 Altstätten
Bühler
Gais
18
20 **Appenzell**
Urnäsch
Lienz

ALPSTEIN
Schwägalp **21** **Mt. Säntis**
AUSTRIA

Nesslau Wildhaus Haag
Unterwasser **22** Bendern
Alt **Toggenburg**
St. Johann **Valley** 16 **LIECHTENSTEIN**
CHURFIRSTEN Buchs
Amden
Weesen **23** **Vaduz**
27 **Walensee**
24 **Triesenberg**
Näfels A3 Flums Steg
26 5 **25** **Malbun**
Flumserberg
A3
Sargans

Bad
Ragaz
TO
CHUR Landquart 28

0   6 miles
N
0   9 km

Schaffhausen

★ *48 km (29 mi) northeast of Zürich, 20 km (12 mi) east of Stein-am-Rhein.*

A city of about 35,000, Schaffhausen was, from the early Middle Ages on, an important depot for river cargoes, which—effectively stopped by the rapids and waterfall farther along—had to be unloaded there. The name *Schaffhausen* is probably derived from the skiff houses along the riverbank. The city has a small but beautiful *Altstadt* (Old Town), whose charm lies in its extraordinary preservation; examples of late Gothic, baroque, and rococo architecture line the streets. It doesn't feel like a museum, though; these buildings are very much in use, often as shops or restaurants, and lively crowds of shoppers and strollers throng the streets. Many streets (including Vorstadt, Fronwagplatz, Vordergasse, and Unterstadt) are pedestrians-only, and you can tell which ones are in this zone by the paving—the pedestrian streets are cobblestone.

A Good Walk

Upon entering the Old Town, it becomes obvious why Schaffhausen is also known as the Erkerstadt—the City of Oriel Windows. Begin your walk at the north end of the Old Town at the **Schwabentorturm** ①, where one of the two remaining defense towers houses one of the gates to the town. Continue along Vorstadt, glancing left and right at the oriel windows, many dating from the 17th century. If you cast your gaze up above the houses every now and then, you can see the other tower peek out above the rooftops. The brilliantly painted facade of **Zum Goldenen Ochsen** ② will be on your right—its oriel window is incredible. Vorstadt then leads into **Fronwagplatz** ③, with its clock tower and the Mohrenbrunnen and Metzgerbrunnen fountains at its north and south ends. Then veer right for a quick glance at the second tower, **Obertorturm**, and retrace your steps.

Continue east along the Vordergasse, where on your right you will first admire the **Haus zum Ritter** ④, probably the most famous fresco in Schaffhausen, followed by the **Schmiedstube** ⑤. Farther up the street to your left is the imposing St. Johannkirche. To the right of the church lies the **Haus zum Sittich**, a bright yellow structure with Renaissance oriel windows and relief sculpture. Take a left at the fork in the road up ahead to see the duplex **zur Wasserquelle** and **zur Zieglerburg** ⑥. Across from the duplex stands the Tellenbrunnen fountain.

Double back to the fork in the road and stroll down the tail end of Vordergasse. As you wait at the pedestrian crossing at Bachstrasse, the gray-and-white **Gerberstube** ⑦ welcomes you to this quieter part of town. Farther along the Unterstadt looking north is a group of odd houses with crooked and sharp angles. This is the entrance to the **Munot** ⑧. The meandering steps that lead to the tower are flanked by vineyards. Having enjoyed the view from the tower, double back to the pedestrian crossing at Bachstrasse. Cross the street and take the first left. You will come upon a cluster of large buildings that house the city library and the **Münster zu Allerheiligen** ⑨. Head west on Münsterplatz. This leads you straight to the entrances of the Münster and the **Museum zu Allerheiligen** ⑩. Now head up the hill to the government buildings on your left. The **Altes Zeughaus** (Old Armory), built by Johannes Jacob Meyer, is regarded as a good example of Swiss Renaissance architecture. From here, take any of the streets heading north to get back to the pedestrian zone.

TIMING

The entire walk takes about two hours, including the hike up to the Munot. You may want to linger at the Munot if there is clear weather, when the view is particularly good. A visit at the Museum zu Aller-heiligen will add another hour. Keep in mind that the museum and cathedral are closed on Monday, and from noon to 2 on weekdays.

Sights to See

❸ Fronwagplatz. Lined with shops and cafés, this square is a favorite place for young people to stroll, especially in the evening. A large 16th-century fountain-statue of a prosperous burgher, the **Metzgerbrunnen,** watches over the marketplace. The **clock tower** once held the market scales; its astronomical clock (1564) records not only the time but also eclipses, seasons, and the course of the moon through the zodiac. Across the square, a reproduction of the 1535 **Mohrenbrunnen** (Moor's Fountain) represents Kaspar of the Three Kings. The original fountain is stored in the Museum zu Allerheiligen (☞ *below*).

❼ Gerberstube (Tanners' Guild House). The baroque building is known for its doorway framed by two lions. A two-handled tanner's knife used to stretch between the lions, but it unfortunately collapsed when nearby roadworks shook the neighborhood. Even without the knife, the doorway is still remarkable. A restaurant now occupies the building. ✉ *Bachstr. 8.*

❹ Haus zum Ritter (Knight's House). The city's finest mansion dates from 1492. Its fresco facade was commissioned by the resident knight, Hans von Waldkirch. Tobias Stimmer covered all three stories with paintings on classical themes, which are now displayed in the Museum zu Allerheiligen (☞ *below*); the contemporary replacement was made in the 1930s. ✉ *Vorderg. 65.*

<table>
<tr>
<td>NEED A
BREAK?</td>
<td>Snag an outdoor table at **Restaurant zur Alten Post** (✉ Fronwagpl. 15, ☎ 052/6252255) for a light meal. Besides café standards (mixed salads, schnitzel), there's a lone-wolf dish of yakitori kebabs with mango curry sauce.</td>
</tr>
</table>

❽ Munot. Built between 1564 and 1589 in full circle form based on an idea by Albrecht Dürer, the massive stone ramparts served as a fortress allowing the defense of the city from all sides. From its top are splendid Schaffhausen and Rhine Valley views. ✉ *Munotstieg, Old Town.* 🎫 *Free.* ☉ *May–Sept., daily 8–8; Oct.–Apr., daily 9–5.*

❾ Münster zu Allerheiligen (All Saints Cathedral). This beautiful cathedral, along with its cloister and grounds, dominates the lower city. Founded in 1049, the original cathedral was dedicated in 1064, and the larger one that stands today was built in 1103. Its interior has been restored to Romanesque austerity with a modern aesthetic (hanging architect's lamps, Scandinavian-style pews). The **cloister,** begun in 1050, combines Romanesque and later Gothic elements. Memorial plates on the inside wall honor noblemen and civic leaders buried in the cloister's central garden. The enormous **Schiller Bell** in the courtyard beyond was cast in 1486 and hung in the cathedral tower until 1895. Its inscription, VIVOS—VOCO/MORTUOS—PLANGO/FULGURA—FRANGO ("I call the living, mourn the dead, stop the lightning"), supposedly inspired the German poet Friedrich von Schiller to write his "Lied von der Glocke" ("Song of the Bell"). You'll also pass through the aromatic **herb garden;** it's re-created so effectively in the medieval style that you may feel you've stepped into a tapestry. ✉ *Klosterpl. 1,* ☎ *052/6254377.* 🎫 *Free.* ☉ *Tues.–Fri. 10–noon and 2–5, weekends 10–5. Closed Mon.*

❿ Museum zu Allerheiligen (All Saints Museum). This museum, on the cathedral grounds, houses an extensive collection of ancient and medieval historical artifacts, as well as displays on Schaffhausen indus-

Schaffhausen

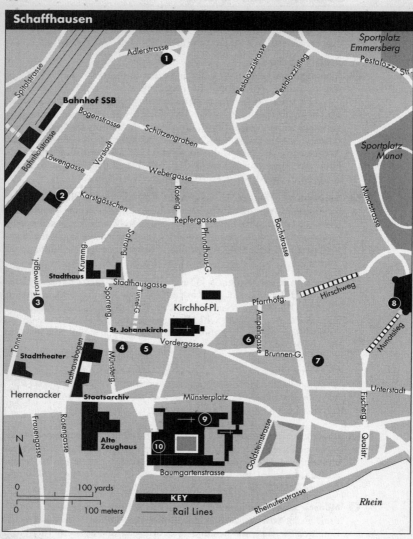

Adlerstrasse
Sportplatz
Emmersberg
Pestalozzi-Str.
Pestalozzistrasse
Pestalozzistieg
Spitalstrasse
Bahnhof SSB
Bogenstrasse
Schützengraben
Sportplatz
Munot
Bahnhofstrasse
Löwengasse
Vorstadt
Webergasse
Roseng.
Munotstrasse
Karstgässchen
Repfergasse
Pfrundhaus-G.
Bachstrasse
Fronwagpl.
Krummg.
Sofrang.
Stadthaus
Stadthausgasse
Tunelg.
Sporreng.
Kirchhof-Pl.
Pfarrhofg.
Hirschweg
St. Johannkirche
Vordergasse
Ampelngasse
Munotstieg
Tanne
Stadttheater
Rathausbogen
Münsterg.
Brunnen-G.
Unterstadt
Herrenacker
Staatsarchiv
Münsterplatz
Fischerg.
Quaistr.
Frauengasse
Rosengasse
Alte
Zeughaus
Goldsteinstrasse
Baumgartenstrasse
N
0   100 yards
0   100 meters
KEY
Rail Lines
Rheinuferstrasse
Rhein

try. The period rooms are definitely worth a look; they cover 15th- to 19th-century interiors. The best of these is the 15th-century refectory, which was rented out and forgotten until its rediscovery in 1924. Temporary exhibitions on various themes reach international caliber. Museum literature is available only in French or German. ⊠ *Klosterpl. 1*, ☎ *052/6330777.* 🎟 *Free.* ☉ *Tues.–Wed. and Fri.–Sun. noon–5, Thurs. noon–8. Closed Mon.*

❺ **Schmiedstube** (Smiths' Guild House). With its spectacular Renaissance portico and oriel dating from 1653, this building is an embodiment of Schaffhausen's state of suspended animation. Framed over the door are the symbols of the tongs and hammer for the smiths and that of a snake for doctors, who depended on smiths for their tools and thus belonged to the guild. ⊠ *Vorderg. 61.*

❶ **Schwabentorturm** (Swabian Gate Tower). Once a part of the city wall, the tower dates from 1370. Inside the arch on the keystone is a relief from 1933 that bears a wise caution for anyone crossing the street: LAPPI TUE D'AUGE UF ("Open your eyes, you idiot!"). The tower's counterpart, the **Obertorturm**, lies just off the Fronwagplatz (☞ *above*).

❷ **Zum Goldenen Ochsen** (At the Golden Ox). This late-Gothic building had a Renaissance-style portico and oriel window added to it in 1608. Flanking the windows are three floors of exterior frescoes depicting historic and mythological figures, most from the Trojan War. ⊠ *Vorstadt 17.*

❻ **Zur Wasserquelle and Zur Zieglerburg** (At the Spring and At the Brick Castle). This rococo duplex dates from 1738; since they're now private residences, you can see them only from the outside. Across the street are the **Tellenbrunnen,** a fountain-statue of Wilhelm Tell copied from the 1522 original, and, farther up Vordergasse, the **St. Johannkirche** (St. John's Church), whose Gothic exterior dates from 1248. ⊠ *Pfarrhofg. 2.*

Dining and Lodging

$$–$$$ ✕ **Theater Restaurant Schaffhausen.** As the name suggests, this bistro and restaurant is connected to Schaffhausen's city theater. The downstairs bistro is decorated with theater paraphernalia; a cozy alcove in the rear has a door leading directly backstage for actors who want a quick snack between scenes. The elegant upstairs restaurant has a view of Herrenacker Square. Choose from a cross section of European cuisine: Swiss sausage salad, Norwegian smoked salmon, Italian ravioli stuffed with ricotta and spinach, and the quintessentially Parisian *entrecôte "Café de Paris."* ⊠ *Herrenacker 23,* ☎ *052/6250558. MC, V. Closed Sun.*

$$–$$$ ✕ **Wirtschaft zum Frieden.** You can choose from a variety of delight-
★ ful settings in this unpretentious, traditional restaurant. There are an intimate (read: tiny) Stübli full of waxed and weathered wood, a graceful tile-stove dining room with antiques, and a small private garden thick with wisteria and luxuriant trees. You can have a cheap, generous Tagesteller (daily special) in the Stübli, an ambitious meal upstairs, or choices from both menus in the garden, where the locals crowd to drink on a summer evening with carafes of local wine. The menu includes home-smoked salmon, homemade Knöpfli, a *Friedentopf* (literally, "peace stew") of fillets of pork, veal, and beef, lamb noisettes, and veal kidneys, with poached plums for dessert. ⊠ *Herrenacker 11,* ☎ *052/6254715. AE, DC, MC, V. Closed Sun.*

$ ✕ **Restaurant Falken.** This busy restaurant caters to crowds with a palate for simple local fare—Rösti, Geschnetzeltes (small pieces of veal in cream sauce), and breaded fish. The Tagesteller is an especially good deal at lunchtime. Though plain, the wooden facade and interior create Gemütlichkeit without the clichés. It is an excellent choice for families; it even houses its own small bowling alley. ⊠ *Vorstadt 5,* ☎ *052/ 6253221. AE, DC, MC, V.*

\$\$\$\$ ✕⊞ **Rheinhotel Fischerzunft.** This modern Relais & Châteaux prop-
★ erty is a bit out of place in such a medieval city. Of its 10 rooms—some in fussy florals, others in sleek jewel-tone solids—seven have river views, but everyone shares the lovely Rhine view at breakfast. The restaurant's mixed nautical and Asian decor reflects the chef's Franco-Chinese leanings: he trained in Hong Kong and has created a brilliant, eclectic cuisine with such dishes as crayfish wrapped in Thai noodles, deep fried and served with lentil sprouts. ⊠ *Rheinquai 8, CH-8200,* ☎ *052/ 6253281,* 𝔽𝔸𝕏 *052/6243285. 6 rooms, 4 suites. Restaurant. AE, DC, MC, V.* 🍴

\$\$\$ ⊞ **Kronenhof.** This fine, quiet city hotel in the heart of Schaffhausen's
★ Old Town has a traditional, shutter- and flower-trimmed facade. Rooms are being redone six at a time; their styles vary slightly, but overall the look is similar: crisp, with birch-wood furniture and abstract prints. The last half dozen are due to be finished in spring 2001. The main restaurant is somewhat drab but serves excellent, refined versions of local dishes, including fresh fish and rich soups. ⊠ *Kirchhofpl. 7, CH-8200,* ☎ *052/6357575,* 𝔽𝔸𝕏 *052/6357565. 38 rooms, 2 suites. Restaurant, bar, café, minibars, in-room safes. AE, DC, MC, V.* 🍴

\$\$–\$\$\$ ⊞ **Park-Villa.** Despite the no-nonsense elevator tacked onto the exterior, this belle epoque–style mansion, built by a local industrialist, has been transformed into a small hotel with surprisingly little disruption to its grand but familial style. Many of the original furnishings—inlaid pieces, chandeliers, Persian rugs—remain. The upper floors are modern but retain their eccentric shapes, and some have Rhine or fortress views. The fine old garden room is luxurious and a steal (the toilet is down the hall); all the other rooms have full baths. The hotel sits slightly apart, and uphill, from the Old Town. ⊠ *Parkstr. 18, CH-8200,* ☎ *052/6252737,* 𝔽𝔸𝕏 *052/6241253. 21 rooms, 4 suites. Restaurant, bar, tennis court. AE, DC, MC, V.*

\$\$ ⊞ **Promenade.** This solid, simple, Edwardian hotel, on the same residential hill as the Park-Villa (☞ *above*), offers spare Formica-and-beige rooms, a garden restaurant, and modest fitness equipment. There's a pretty park walk to the Old Town. ⊠ *Fäsenstaubstr. 43, CH-8200,* ☎ *052/6307777,* 𝔽𝔸𝕏 *052/6307778. 37 rooms. Restaurant, exercise room. AE, DC, MC, V.*

\$ ⊞ **Löwen.** At the edge of suburban Herblingen, where the bedroom community seems to melt back into its origins as a half-timber country town, this quintessential old guest house still draws the locals to its pub and serves regional standards in its restaurant. Rooms, however, are all modern, with ceramic tile and modern pine paneling. ⊠ *Im Höfli 2, CH-8207 Herblingen,* ☎ *052/6432208,* 𝔽𝔸𝕏 *052/6432288. 7 rooms. Restaurant, pub. No credit cards.*

Outdoor Activities and Sports

Bicycles—a popular mode of transportation—can be rented at the train station in Schaffhausen (☎ 0512/234217).

Neuhausen am Rheinfall

★ ⑪ *3 km (1¾ mi) south of Schaffhausen.*

Adjacent to Neuhausen, on the north bank of the Rhine, a series of magnificent waterfalls powers the city's industry (arms, railroad cars, aluminum). The **Rheinfall** is 150 m (492 ft) wide, drops some 25 m (82 ft) in a series of three dramatic leaps, and is split at the center by a bushy crag straight out of a 19th-century landscape painting. The effect—mists, roaring water, jutting rocks—is positively Wagnerian; Goethe saw in the falls the "ocean's source." There is a footpath, Rheinuferweg, that leads from Schaffhausen's Old Town along the river to the falls (a 25- to 35-minute walk). It's marked with the standard yellow hiking-trail signs. From Neuhausen there's a good view toward Schloss Laufen, a 12th-century castle that overlooks the Rheinfall.

Stein-am-Rhein

★ ⑫ *20 km (13 mi) east of Schaffhausen.*

Stein-am-Rhein, a nearly perfectly preserved medieval village and one of Switzerland's most picturesque towns, lies at the point where the Rhine leaves the Bodensee. Crossing the bridge over the river, you see the village spread along the waterfront, its foundations and docks rising directly out of the water. Here, restaurants, hotels, and souvenir stands occupy 16th- and 17th-century buildings, and the Rhine appears to be a narrow mountain stream—nothing like the sprawling industrial trade route it becomes farther downstream.

The **Rathausplatz** (Town Hall Square) and main street, Understadt, are flanked by tight rows of shingled, half-timber town houses, each rivaling the next for the ornateness of its oriels, the flamboyance of its frescoes. The elaborate decor usually illustrates the name of the house: Sonne (Sun), Ochsen (Ox), Weisser Adler (White Eagle), and so on. Most of the artwork dates from the 16th century. The **Rathaus** (Town Hall) itself was built between 1539 and 1542, with the half-timber upper floors added in 1745; look for its fantastical dragon waterspouts, typical of the region.

The Benedictine **Kloster St. Georgen** (Monastery of St. George), a curious half-timber structure built in 1005, houses a small museum of woodwork and local paintings and also shelters a cloister. ⊠ *Edge of Old Town, just upstream from the last bridge over the Rhine before the Bodensee.* ☎ *052/7412142.* ⊙ *Museum: Tues.–Sun. 10–5. Closed Mon.*

Directly above the town atop vineyards and woods stands the 13th-century hilltop castle of **Hohenklingen,** which now houses a restaurant and offers broad views of the Rhine Valley and the lake beyond. ⊠ *Above Schaffhausen.*

Dining and Lodging

$$–$$$$ ✕ **Sonne.** Upstairs, you'll find a formal dining room (ceiling beams,
★ damask, and Biedermeier) where chef Philippe Combe's inventive, contemporary cuisine—Rhine fish, crisp duck with cabbage—commands top prices. Downstairs in the Weinstube, he offers a Tagesteller and simple light lunches, dished up in a spare, chic, gentrified pub: more beams, stone, stucco, parquet, and exposed pipes painted maroon. The Weinstube benefits from the kitchen upstairs; it offers homemade pastas, simple but sophisticated stews, and selections from the fine wine list. ⊠ *Rathauspl.,* ☎ *052/7412128. AE, DC, MC, V. Closed Tues.–Wed.*

$$ ✕ **Der Rote Ochse.** The beautiful frescoed facade invites its admirers into this warm little *Weinstube* (wine parlor), where dark antiques surround a *Kachelofen* (tile stove) and candles glow on the tables. The simple menu is thick with hearty cuisine—a variety of sausages such as *Bauernschüblig* (farmers' sausage), local cheeses, but also delicious homemade pastas. When they say the food is regional, they mean it: all ingredients are obtained from the village and surrounding areas. ⊠ *Rathauspl. 129,* ☎ *052/7412328. No credit cards. Closed Mon.*

$$$$ ▥ **Chlosterhof.** Its brick-and-angled-glass exterior seems utterly misplaced in this medieval setting, but this hotel worked hard to face as

many rooms as possible toward the Rhine. Inside, the look is modern, suburban, and business-class despite token vaulting in the lobby and scattered antiques; indeed, the focus is on entertaining conference groups and their spouses. The rooms have sleek dark-pine cabinetry and some four-poster beds, but the creamy pastels and carpets say up-scale international chain. Suites claim the best Rhine views. ⊠ *Oehningerstr. 201, CH-8260,* ☎ *052/7424242,* ℻ *052/7411337. 44 rooms, 27 suites. 4 restaurants, bar, in-room VCRs, indoor pool, sauna, exercise room, dance club. AE, DC, MC, V.*

$$ ★ **Rheinfels.** Even some of the bathrooms have ceiling beams in this fine old waterfront landmark, which was built between 1508 and 1517. The public spaces have creaking pine-plank floors and suits of armor on display, and every room—modernized in beige and rose tones, with an all-tile bath—has a Rhine view. The hotel's suite is in essence an apartment; it has its own separate entrance, a one-car garage, and a boat jetty. The restaurant specializes in top-quality fresh-water fish at reasonable prices. Both the hotel and the restaurant are closed on Wednesday. ⊠ *Rhig. 8, CH-8260,* ☎ *052/7412144,* ℻ *052/7412522. 16 rooms, 1 suite. Restaurant. MC, V.*

$–$$ ★ **Adler.** With one of the most elaborately frescoed 15th-century fa-cades on the Rathausplatz, this hotel has a split personality. On the outside it's flamboyant, but the interior is no-nonsense. The decor is airy, slick, and immaculate, with gray industrial carpet, white stucco, and blond wood throughout. Double-glazed windows cut the noise from the square. A young local family runs the hotel, so other families will fit right in. The cheerful restaurant serves good regional cooking, along with some French cuisine. ⊠ *Rathauspl. 15, CH-8260,* ☎ *052/7426161,* ℻ *052/7414440. 25 rooms. Restaurant. AE, DC, MC, V.*

$ ★ **Bleiche.** This private farmhouse lodging, on a hill high over the Rhine Valley about a mile from the village center, offers a chance to sleep under deep shingled eaves and wake to the sound of cowbells. The rooms are rock-bottom simple (linoleum, a mix of dormitory and collectible furniture), with showers down the hall, but the setting is surpassingly beautiful. A friendly 80-year-old German-speaking woman runs it. ⊠ *Bleicherhof, CH-8260,* ☎ *052/7412257. 2 rooms. No credit cards.*

$ **Zur Rheingerbe.** Right on the busy waterfront promenade, this small inn has wood-panel ceilings and big furniture reminiscent of Sears (sculptured carpet, spindle beds). Some rooms overlook the Rhine. The first-floor restaurant has a full-length bay window along the riverfront. The hotel and restaurant are closed on Wednesday. ⊠ *Schifflände 5, CH-8260,* ☎ *052/7412991,* ℻ *052/7412166. 7 rooms. Restaurant. AE, DC, MC, V.*

En Route Fourteen kilometers (9 mi) east of Stein-am-Rhein, the town of **Steckborn** has some fine old houses, including the Baronenhaus and the Gerichtshaus. It's also home to **Turmhof Steckborn,** a half-timber wa-terfront castle built in 1342 and now a small local museum contain-ing artifacts from prehistoric times through the Roman and Alemannic settlements. ☎ *052/7612903.* ☉ *Mid-May–mid-Oct., Wed., Thurs., and weekends 3–5; Closed Mon.–Tues. and Fri. and late Oct.–early May.*

Arenenberg

⓭ *20 km (12 mi) east of Stein-am-Rhein, 40 km (25 mi) east of Schaffhausen.*

Just east of Stein-am-Rhein, the Rhine opens up into the Untersee, the lower branch of the Bodensee. In its center lies the German island of Reichenau. Charles the Fat, great-grandson of Charlemagne, was buried here.

The villages on either side of the Untersee are dominated by castles. On the Swiss side, behind the village of Mannenbach (nearly opposite Reichenau), the **castle at Arenenberg** was once home to the future Napoléon III and serves today as a museum with furnishings and artwork from the Second Empire. ⊠ *Behind Mannenbach,* ☎ *071/ 6641866.* ▣ *5 SF.* ☉ *Tues.–Sun. 10–5.*

Gottlieben

⑭ *5 km (3 mi) east of Arenenberg, 45 km (28 mi) east of Schaffhausen.*

The village of Gottlieben has a Dominican monastery-castle, where the Protestant reformers Jan Hus and Jerome of Prague were imprisoned in the 15th century by order of Emperor Sigismund and Pope John XXII. Pope John was himself confined in the same castle a few years later. Today, though the castle can be viewed only from the outside, Gottlieben offers a romantic, half-timber waterfront promenade—and two fine old hotels—before you reach the urban complex of Kreuzlingen and Germany's Konstanz.

Lodging

$$$ ▣ **Drachenburg und Waaghaus.** On the misty bank of the Rhine be-
★ tween the Bodensee and the Zellersee rises this half-timber apparition of onion domes, shutters, and gilt gargoyles. The original house, the early 18th-century Drachenburg, lies across a walk from the second building, the Waaghaus. A third house was added for overflow guests. The Drachenburg has gleaming old staircases, four-poster beds, brocade, chaise lounges, and crystal sconces throughout the labyrinth of rooms and parlors. Rooms in the other buildings follow this elegant lead. The scale is grand but cozy, and Rhine-view rooms are furnished like honeymoon suites. Its three restaurants vary in ambience; the most sophisticated is the one in the original house. ⊠ *Am Schlosspark, CH-8274,* ☎ *071/6667474,* ℻ *071/6691709. 58 rooms, 2 suites. 2 restaurants, bar, minibars, in-room safes. AE, DC, MC, V.* ☙

$$ ▣ **Krone.** Immediately downstream from the Drachenburg und Waaghaus (☞ *above*), this member of the Romantik chain is smaller, cheaper, and a tad more generic than its flamboyant neighbor, though it dates from the same era. Standard doubles are done in mild, classic beiges; the suites are quite baroque and have lake views. Breakfast is served in a beam-and-herringbone-ceiling hall overlooking the Rhine. The glowing dark-wood restaurant offers nouvelle-influenced seafood as well as lake fish. ⊠ *Seestr., CH-8274,* ☎ *071/6698060,* ℻ *071/ 6668069. 22 rooms, 3 suites. Restaurant. AE, DC, MC, V.*

FROM THE BODENSEE TO ST. GALLEN

Along the shores of the Bodensee, orchards stripe rolling hills that slowly rise to meet the foothills of the Alps around St. Gallen. Two thousand years ago this region lay on the northeastern border of the Roman Empire, Arbon (Arbor Felix) being the first stop on the trade route for goods coming into the empire from points east. Today the region is mostly rural, with clusters of farmhouses dotting the grassy slopes. In summer the lake teems with vacationers, but otherwise it's a distinctly tranquil area.

Bodensee

Known in English as Lake Constance, the Bodensee is about 65 km (40 mi) long and 15 km (9 mi) wide, making it second in size in Switzerland only to Lac Léman (Lake Geneva). The strong German flavor of the towns on its Swiss edge is seasoned with a resort-village mellowness; sometimes palm trees fringe the waterfront. This isn't the Mediterranean, though; as the lake is not protected by mountains, it is turbulent in stormy weather and even on fine days is exposed to the wind. Compared with Switzerland's usual crystalline lakes, the Bodensee is gloomy and brooding; nonetheless, it draws European vacationers in summer for swimming, windsurfing, and fishing. Many Swiss have built tidy homes along the lakefront.

Outdoor Activities and Sports

HIKING

As a summer resort destination, the area around the Bodensee is usually thronged with hikers. For timed hiking itineraries, topographical maps, and suggestions on the areas best suited to your style of wandering, consult the **Tourismusverband Ostschweiz** (Tourist Association of Eastern Switzerland; ☞ Visitor Information *in* Eastern Switzerland A to Z, *below*).

SWIMMING

People do swim in the Bodensee; there are several **public beaches**, usually more grass than sand. Most have changing rooms and concession stands. **Arbon** (☎ 071/4461333) has a gravel beach—getting into the water can be a little rough on tender feet. **Kreuzlingen** (☎ 071/6881858) has some sand at the water's edge, though you'll be spreading your towel on the grass. **Romanshorn** (☎ 071/4631147) has a similar setup. **Rorschach** (☎ 071/8411684) has a pocket-size beach.

Kreuzlingen and Konstanz

⑮ *7 km (4 mi) east of Gottlieben, 46 km (28 mi) east of Schaffhausen.*

The big German city of Konstanz, with its Swiss twin of Kreuzlingen, dominates the straits that open into the Bodensee. Though Kreuzlingen itself offers little of interest to travelers, Konstanz has a lovely, concentrated *Altstadt* (Old Town) area. It's easily accessible from the Swiss side, though your passport may be checked even if you pass on foot. Konstanz belonged to Switzerland until 1805; today the two border towns share the dominant German influence.

En Route   About halfway between Kreuzlingen and Rorschach (follow Highway 13 east along the Bodensee), you'll come to the small town of **Romanshorn.** An industrial town and an important ferry port for Friedrichshafen in Germany, this is also a surprisingly enjoyable resort with fine views of the Swiss and Austrian mountains.

Between Romanshorn and Rorschach on Highway 13, **Arbon** (known to the Romans as Arbor Felix) lies on a little promontory jutting out into the Bodensee, surrounded by lovely meadows and orchards. It was a Celtic town before the Romans came in 60 BC and built military fortifications. Evidence of the Romans can be found in an interesting collection of relics in the late-Gothic St. Martinskirche.

Rorschach

⑯ *41 km (25 mi) southeast of Kreuzlingen, 80 km (49 mi) southeast of Schaffhausen.*

The lake resort of Rorschach, a port on the Bodensee, lies on a protected bay at the foot of the Rorschacherberg, an 883-m (2,896-ft) mountain covered with orchards, pine forests, and meadows. For generations, Rorschach has carried on a thriving grain trade with Germany, as the imposing baroque **Kornhaus** (Granary), built in 1746, attests. There's a public beach here, too (☞ Bodensee, *above*).

Outdoor Activities and Sports

SAILING

There are several sailing schools in Goldach, a small town 5 km (3 mi) west of Rorschach, including **Segelschule Rorschach** (☎ 071/8448989).

St. Gallen

⑰ *14 km (9 mi) southwest of Rorschach, 94 km (59 mi) southeast of Schaffhausen.*

Switzerland's largest eastern city, St. Gallen is a bustling city with students dominating its streets during the school year. The narrow streets of the *Altstadt* (Old Town) are flanked by a wonderful variety of boutiques and antiques shops. The city has been known for centuries as both an intellectual center and the source of some of the world's finest textiles. St. Gallus, an Irish missionary, came to the region in 612 to live in a hermit's cell in the Steinach Valley. In 720 an abbey was founded on the site where he died. Soon a major cultural focus in medieval Europe, the abbey built a library of awesome proportions.

★ The abbey was largely destroyed in the Reformation and was closed down in 1805, but its magnificent rococo **Stiftsbibliothek** (Abbey Library), built in 1758–67, still holds a collection of more than 100,000 books and manuscripts. The library hall itself is one of Switzerland's treasures. Visitors enter behind the cathedral. Large, gray carpet slippers are worn to protect the magnificently inlaid wooden flooring. The hall is a gorgeous explosion of gilt, frescoes, and undulating balconies, but the most striking aspect by far is the burnished woodwork, all luminous walnut and cherry. Its contents, including incunabula and illuminated manuscripts that are more than 1,200 years old, comprise one of the world's oldest and finest scholarly collections. Also on display, incongruously, is an Egyptian mummy dating from 700 BC. ⊠ *Klosterhof 6c,* ☎ *071/2273416.* ⌐ *7 SF.* ⊙ *Apr.–Oct., Mon.–Sat. 9–noon and 1:30–5, Sun. 10–noon and 1:30–4; late Nov.–Mar., Mon.–Sat. 9–noon and 1:30–4. Closed first 3 wks in Nov.*

★ The **Kathedrale** (Cathedral) is impressive in its own right. Begun in 1755 and completed in 1766, it is the antithesis of the library, though the nave and rotunda are the work of the same architect, Peter Thumb. The scale is outsize and the decor light, bright, and open despite spectacular excesses of wedding-cake trim. ⊠ *Klosterhof,* ☎ *071/2273415.* ⊙ *Weekdays 9–6:30, Sat. 9–5, Sun. noon–7.*

The grounds of the abbey and the cathedral border the **Old Town,** which demonstrates a healthy symbiosis between scrupulously preserved Renaissance and baroque architecture and a thriving modern shopping scene. The best examples of oriel windows, half-timbering, and frescoes can be seen along Gallusstrasse, Schmiedgasse, Marktgasse, and Spisergasse, all pedestrian streets. For a good picnic spot, head to the **Mühleggbahn,** a self-service funicular that runs up the hillside to a lovely view of St. Gallen and the Bodensee. Once up top, take two immediate right turns to the wooden stairs leading to a paved path with park benches. ⊠ *Off the Abbey end of the Old Town,* ☎ *071/2439595.* ⌐ *1.50 SF.* ⊙ *Daily 6 AM–11:30 PM.*

St. Gallen's history as a textile capital dates from the Middle Ages, when convent workers wove linen toile of such exceptional quality that it was exported throughout Europe. The industry expanded into cotton and embroidery and today dominates the top of the market. To enjoy some marvelously ornate old embroidery, visit the **Textilmuseum** (Textile Museum). Its lighting is dim to protect the delicate fabrics and its captions are all in German, but the work speaks for itself. ⊠ *Vadianstr.*

2, ☎ *071/2221744.* 🎫 *5 SF.* ☉ *Nov.–Mar., weekdays 10–noon and 2–5; Apr.–Oct., Mon.–Sat. 10–noon.*

Dining and Lodging

$$$$ ✕ **Am Gallusplatz.** This is St. Gallen's grandest restaurant for both the cuisine and decor. The menu is based on market-fresh seasonal ingredients and may include saffron perch with new potatoes or spinach crepes with fresh coriander. There's also an enormous wine list. The dining room impresses with its cross-vaulted ceilings and heavy chandeliers. ⊠ *Gallusstr. 24,* ☎ *071/2233330. AE, MC, V. Closed Mon.*

$$–$$$ ✕ **Zum Goldenen Schäfli.** Of the first-floor (second-floor to Americans) restaurants that are St. Gallen's trademark, this is the most popular, and its slanting floors groan under crowds of locals and tourists. The low ceiling and walls are all aged wood. The menu offers hearty regional standards with a special twist: sea trout with lemon foam and brains in butter, for example. ⊠ *Metzgerg. 5,* ☎ *071/2233737. AE, DC, MC, V. Closed Sun. No lunch Sat.*

$$ ✕ **Schlössli.** Tidy, bright, and modern despite its setting in a historic build-
★   ing, this first-floor landmark has a less woody atmosphere than its peers, the Bäumli and the Schäfli, but better cooking. The Käsespätzli are homemade and the salads fresh and good, especially the main-course salad with duck liver. The café draws casual families and locals playing a favorite card game, *Jass,* at lunch; businesspeople choose the only slightly more formal dining room that adjoins it. ⊠ *Am Spisertor, Zeughausg. 17,* ☎ *071/2221256. AE, DC, MC, V. Closed Sun. No lunch Sat.*

$–$$ ✕ **Weinstube zum Bäumli.** All dark, glossy wood and leaded glass, this 500-year-old first-floor (second-floor to Americans) beauty serves classic local fare (veal, bratwurst, Rösti) to tourists, businesspeople, and workers, who share tables comfortably in the midst of the noisy bustle. ⊠ *Schmiedg. 18,* ☎ *071/2221174. MC, V. Closed Sun.–Mon.*

$$$$ 🏨 **Einstein.** Tucked back into a slope at the edge of the Old Town, this former embroidery factory is now a sleek, upscale business-class hotel, with Hilton-like interiors (polished cabinetry, lacquered rattan, subdued florals), a uniformed staff, and a five-star attitude. The generous breakfast buffet, laid out in the skylighted top-floor loft that serves as the à la carte restaurant by night, is not included in the room price. ⊠ *Berneggstr. 2, CH-9001,* ☎ *071/2275555,* ℻ *071/2275577. 62 rooms, 3 suites. Restaurant, bar, minibars, meeting rooms. AE, DC, MC, V.* ❧

$$$ 🏨 **Gallo.** Now a relatively cheap business hotel, this graceful former apartment house is set beside a busy road but has double-glazed windows to shut out the roar. The location is not particularly convenient to the Old Town (Bus 3, named Heiligkreuz, stops at nearby Olma or carries you into the center), but interiors are fresh and attractive, with big tile baths and bright-color lacquer; two lovely attic doubles have beams and dormer windows. There is a great Italian restaurant on the ground floor. ⊠ *St. Jakobstr. 62, CH-9000,* ☎ *071/2452727,* ℻ *071/ 2454593. 24 rooms. Restaurant. AE, DC, MC, V.*

$$$ 🏨 **St. Gallen.** The main building of this Old Town hotel was revamped
★   in 1999, its look updated with blue carpeting and smoked-glass light fixtures. Market watchers head to the coffee room, where a trio of monitors broadcasts stock results. The annex across the street is a step up in comfort: the big, bay-window, half-timber house has been restored and stylishly updated. The rooms combine antiquity (leaded glass, painted woodwork, stone niches) with high tech (halogen and lithographs). ⊠ *Bankg. 12, CH-9000,* ☎ *071/2276100,* ℻ *071/ 2276180. 24 rooms. Restaurant, bar, café, minibars, meeting room. AE, DC, MC, V.* ❧

$$ 🏨 **Elite.** The decor may be functional but the staff is friendly at this Old Town spot. Its style harkens back to 1950s modern deco. Half the rooms have baths; the others have only sinks and thus cost less. The back rooms are quieter. ✉ *Metzgerg. 9/11, CH-9004,* ☎ *071/2221236,* FAX *071/2222177. 26 rooms, 13 with bath. Breakfast room. AE, DC, MC, V.*

$–$$ 🏠 **Vadian.** A narrow town house tucked behind half-timber landmarks in the Old Town, this is a discreet and tidy little place with an alcohol-free policy. Most of its tiny rooms have been updated with beige stucco, knotty pine, and new tile baths. Rooms without bath cost less. ✉ *Gallusstr. 36, CH-9000,* ☎ *071/2236080,* FAX *071/2224748. 13 rooms, 6 with bath. Breakfast room. AE, DC, MC, V.*

Outdoor Activities and Sports

🐾 **Säntispark.** Just outside St. Gallen lies this year-round, family-friendly sports and spa park. There is something to please (and exhaust) everyone—racquet sports, bowling, minigolf, billiards. Children can dive into the wave pool at the water park and enjoy the rides and playgrounds. For relaxing, there's a solarium, sauna, and massage center. Equipment can be rented; most activities cost under 20 SF. ✉ *From main train station in St. Gallen, 15 mins by Bus 7 (Abtwil), or by car along Hwy. N1, exit Winkeln.* ☎ *071/3131555.* 🎫 *Pay per activity.* ⏱ *Daily 9* AM– *11* PM.

Shopping

ANTIQUE PRINTS

An outstanding assortment of antique prints of Swiss landscapes and costumes is sold at a broad range of prices at **Graphica Antiqua** (✉ Oberer Graben 46, near the Einstein Hotel, ☎ 071/2235016). The pictures are cataloged alphabetically by canton for easy browsing.

TEXTILES AND EMBROIDERY

Since the crash of the textile industry in 1918, it's been difficult to find the real thing in this region, although it's still world renowned for its textiles and embroidery. There are a few excellent exceptions, including **Rocco Textil** (✉ Spiserg. 41, ☎ 071/2222407), which has a small but wonderful selection of St. Gallen embroidery, linens, and lace; they're an especially good source for custom work. **Saphir** (✉ Bleichestr. 9, ☎ 071/2236263) carries a high-quality collection of embroidered handkerchiefs, bed and table linens, and bolts of embroidered fabric and lace—all from the St. Gallen region. **Sturzenegger** (✉ St. Leonhardstr. 12, ☎ 071/2224576), the better-known embroidery firm, established in 1883, sells its own line of linens and lingerie, designed and manufactured in the factory a block away.

Appenzell

🔞 *20 km (12 mi) south of St. Gallen, 98 km (60 mi) southeast of Schaffhausen.*

Isolated from St. Gallen by a ridge of green hills, Appenzell is one of Switzerland's most eccentric regions. Fellow Swiss think of its people as hillbillies, citing their quirky sense of humor and old-fashioned costumes. The city of St. Gallen melts away into undulating hills spotted with doe-skin cows, a steep-pastured, isolated verdure reminiscent of West Virginia or the Ozarks. Prim, symmetrical cottages inevitably show rows of windows facing the valley. Named Appenzell after the Latin *abbatis cella* (abbey cell), the region served as a sort of colony to the St. Gallen abbey, and its tradition of fine embroidery dates from those early days. The perfect chance to see this embroidery is during a local festival, such as the Alpfahrten, when cows are herded down the mountains. Women's hair is coiffed in tulle, and their dresses have intricate embroidery and lace, often with an edelweiss motif; men wear embroidered red vests and suspenders decorated with edelweiss or cow figures. These traditional costumes are taken very seriously; they can cost thousands of francs, but in this case, pride supersedes economy. A small highway (No. 3) leads into the hills through Teufen; the quaint Appenzell–Teufen–Gais rail line also serves the region.

The town of Appenzell blends some of the best and worst of the region, offering tourists a concentrated and somewhat self-conscious sampling of the culture. Its streets lined with bright-painted homes, bakeries full of *Birnebrot* (pear bread) and souvenir *Biber* (almond and honey cakes), and shops full of embroidery (which, on close examination, often turns out to have been made in China), Appenzell seems to watch the tourists warily and get on with its life while profiting from the attention. Its **Landsgemeindeplatz** in the town center is the site of the famous open-air elections (until 1991, for men only), which take place the last Sunday in April. Embroidery has become big business here, but it's rare to find handmade examples of the local art; though women still do fine work at home, it's generally reserved for gifts or heirlooms. Instead, large factories have sprung up in Appenzell country, and famous fine-cotton handkerchiefs sold in specialty shops around the world are made by machine here at the Dörig, Alba, and Lehner plants.

The **Museum Appenzell** showcases handicrafts and local traditions, regional history, and an international embroidery collection—it's a good general overview of the area's history and culture. The building itself dates from 1560 and was residential until 1985, when the museum collection was moved here from the Rathaus (town hall) next door. An English-language guide is available. ⊠ *Hauptg. 4*, ☎ *071/7889631*. 🎟 *5 SF.* ⊙ *Apr.–Oct., daily 10–noon and 2–5; Nov.–Mar., Tues.–Sun. 2–4.*

Dining and Lodging

$$ ✕ **Traube.** The understated, traditional interior lacks personality, but in the summer months it opens up onto a terrace overlooking a lovely landscaped garden hidden from major streets. The menu is heavy on pork and potatoes, but the selection is wide enough to please most palates. Fondue and Appenzeller *Chäshörnli* (cheese and macaroni) round off the mostly heavy offerings. The daily special is usually under 20 SF. ⊠ *Marktg. 7*, ☎ *071/7871407. MC, V. Closed Mon.*

$$$ ✕🛏 **Appenzell.** This comfortable lodging has all the gabled
★ Gemütlichkeit of its neighbors, with rows of shuttered windows and a view over the Landsgemeindeplatz. Homey rooms, warmed with polished wood, owe their airiness to the traditional multiple windows. The fine woodwork and antiques in the breakfast room are remnants of the previous house on the property. The restaurant offers fresh interpretations of regional fare, such as the *Hauptgass* (an Appenzeller cheese gratin with pork, prosciutto, and tomato), plus a selection of health and vegetarian dishes, which are rare in these parts. You certainly won't have to squint at your menu; the room is so brightly lighted, it has an almost clinical atmosphere. ⊠ *Landsgemeindepl., CH-9050*, ☎ *071/7874211 or 071/7881515*, 🖷 *071/7874284 or 071/7881551. 16 rooms. Restaurant, breakfast room, café, patisserie, no-smoking rooms. AE, DC, MC, V.* ✎

$–$$ ✕🛏 **Hof.** One of Appenzell's most popular restaurants serves hearty
★ regional meats and cheese specialties, such as *Käseschnitte* (cheese toast) and Käsespätzli, to locals and tourists who crowd elbow to elbow along shared tables and raise their voices to be heard over the clatter from the service bar. The all-modern, rustic-wood decor and ladder-back chairs, the knotty pine, and the display of sports trophies add to the local atmosphere. Upstairs, groups can rent up to 58 beds in cheap summer-camp dormitory lodgings and play skittles after dinner. ⊠ *En-*

gelg. 4, CH-9050, ☎ *071/7872210,* FAX *071/7875883. 10 rooms. AE, DC, MC, V.*

$$$ ⊞ **Löwen.** Wising up to the tourists' quest for "typical" local decor, the owners of this renovated 1780 guest house furnished several rooms in authentic Appenzeller styles, with embroidered linens and built-in woodwork (canopy beds, armoires) painted with bright designs and naive local scenes—some actually reflecting the view from the window. Standard rooms in dormitory-style oak also are available for a slightly lower price. ⊠ *Hauptg. 25, CH-9050,* ☎ *071/7872187,* FAX *071/ 7872579. 17 rooms, 9 suites. Restaurant, bar, sauna. AE, DC, MC, V.*

$$$ ⊞ **Säntis.** A member of the Romantik hotel group, this prestigious hotel has a somewhat new and formal ambience, though the earliest wing has been a hotel-restaurant since 1835. Old-style touches—inlaid wood furnishings, painted beams—mix comfortably with the jewel-tone rooms and gleaming walnut cabinetry; some rooms have four-poster or canopy beds. The main first-floor restaurant serves slightly Frenchified regional specialties in either of two wood-lined dining rooms, one Biedermeier, the other a folksy Appenzeller style. A cherry-wood Stübli at street level attracts locals. Guests can borrow bikes for free. ⊠ *Landsgemeindepl., CH-9050,* ☎ *071/7881111,* FAX *071/7881110. 31 rooms, 6 suites. Restaurant, bar, no-smoking rooms, minibars, in-room safes, sauna. AE, DC, MC, V. Closed early Jan.–early Feb.* 🐾

$ ⊞ **Freudenberg.** This is a cookie-cutter modern chalet, but its vantage point on a velvety green hillside overlooking town is the most scenic and tranquil you'll find here. Built in 1969, it still has dormlike rooms and sculptured carpet in harvest gold, but some rooms have balconies, and the broad, shaded terrace café—festive in the evening with strings of yellow lights—lets you take in the picture-pretty views. ⊠ *Behind the train station, CH-9050,* ☎ FAX *071/7871240. 7 rooms. Restaurant, café. AE.* 🐾

Shopping

CHEESES

Picnickers can sample the different grades of Appenzeller cheese and its unsung mountain rivals at **Mösler** (⊠ Hauptg. 25, ☎ 071/7871317). **Sutter** (⊠ Marktstr. 8, ☎ 071/7871227) also has a good selection of local cheeses.

EMBROIDERY

True, locally made hand embroidery is rare in Appenzell. Many handkerchiefs that beautifully reproduce the blindingly close work that locals no longer pursue have been hand-stitched in Portugal. Though an odd souvenir, they capture the spirit of Appenzell handwork better than much of the pretty, though broad, machine work available in the stores. **Margreiter** (⊠ Hauptg. 29, ☎ 071/7873313) carries a large stock of machine-made handkerchiefs from the local Dörig, Alba, and Lehner factories, many decorated with edelweiss or other Alpine flowers. **Trachtenstube** (⊠ Hauptg. 23, ☎ 071/7871606) offers high-quality local handiwork—lace, embroidery, and crafts.

LIQUEURS

Butchers, bakers, and liquor shops up and down the streets offer souvenir bottles of **Appenzeller Bitter** (Alpenbitter), a very sweet aperitif made in town. A well-balanced **eau-de-vie** called Appenzeller Kräuter, made of blended herbs, is another specialty.

Stein

⑲ *13 km (8 mi) northwest of Appenzell, 94 km (58 mi) southeast of Schaffhausen.*

The quiet village of Stein (not to be confused with Stein-am-Rhein) consists of little more than sturdy old farmhouses and red-roof homes with the obligatory geraniums in window boxes. At the **Schaukäserei** (showcase dairy), modern cheese-making methods are demonstrated. Note that cheese is made 9–2 only. ☎ *071/3685070. ☞ Free. ☉ Mar.–Oct., daily 8–7; Nov.–Feb., daily 9–6.*

The **Appenzeller Volkskunde Museum** (Folklore Museum) displays Appenzell arts and crafts, local costumes, and hand-painted furniture. ☎ *071/3685056. ☞ 7 SF. ☉ Nov.–Mar., Sun. 10–5; Apr.–Oct., Tues.–Sat. 10–noon and 1:30–5, Sun. 10–6.*

Urnäsch

㉓ *10 km (6 mi) west of Appenzell, 110 km (68 mi) southeast of Schaffhausen.*

If you're interested in a traditional festival, you'll want to head to this modest countryside town on December 21 or January 13. New Year's and Old New Year's (according to the Julian calendar) are both celebrated with an early morning parade of *Chläuse,* men done up in amazingly complicated masks, huge headpieces, and costumes made of bark, moss, and branches. Some of the *Chläuse* wear enormous cowbells around their necks as well. It's a good idea to reserve a table for lunch at one of the local restaurants so you don't get left out in the cold—the parade draws crowds of spectators. Contact the Urnäsch tourist office (☞ Visitor Information *in* Eastern Switzerland A to Z, *below*) for more information.

The **Museum für Appenzeller Brauchtum** (Museum of Appenzeller Tradition) displays costumes, cowbells, a cheese wagon, and examples of farmhouse living quarters. ☎ *071/3642322. ☞ 4 SF. ☉ May–Oct., daily 1:30–5; Apr., Wed. and weekends 1:30–5 and by appointment; Nov.–Mar., by appointment only.*

Mt. Säntis

㉑ *11 km (7 mi) south of Urnäsch, 121 km (75 mi) southeast of Schaffhausen.*

A pleasurable high-altitude excursion out of Appenzell takes you west to Urnäsch, then south to the hamlet of Schwägalp, where a cable car carries you up to the peak of Mt. Säntis, at 2,502 m (8,209 ft) the highest in the region and with beautiful views of the Bodensee as well as of the Graubünden and Bernese Alps. The very shape of the summit—an arc of jutting rock that swings up to the jagged peak housing the station—is spectacular. ☎ *071/3656565. ☞ 31 SF round-trip. ☉ July–Aug., daily 7:30–7; May, June, and Sept., daily 7:30–6:30; Oct.–Apr., daily 8:30–5; departures every 30 mins. Closed for 3 wks in Jan.*

Toggenburg Valley

㉒ *Entrance 11 km (7 mi) south of Mt. Säntis, 132 km (82 mi) southeast of Schaffhausen.*

A scenic pre-Alpine resort area popular with locals but relatively unexplored by outsiders, this is an ideal place for skiers and hikers who hate crowds. In the rugged Upper Toggenburg, weather-boarded dwellings surround the neighboring resorts of Wildhaus (birthplace of religious reformer Huldrych Zwingli), Unterwasser, and Alt-St. Johann—all of which draw Swiss families for winter skiing and summer hiking excursions into the Churfirsten and Alpstein mountains. As they lie within shouting distance of each other, the ski facilities can be shared, and the jagged teeth of the mountains behind provide a dramatic backdrop.

If you're interested in the Reformation, you may want to make a pilgrimage to Wildhaus's **Zwinglihaus,** the farmhouse where Huldrych Zwingli was born in 1484. His father was president of the village's political commune, and the house was used as a meeting place for its council. A small museum within displays some restored furniture from his time, though not from his family, and an impressive collection of period Bibles. The fire-and-brimstone preacher celebrated his first mass in the town's Protestant church and went on to lead the Protestant Reformation in Zürich. ✉ Schönenboden, Wildhaus/Lisighaus, ☎ 071/9992178. 🎟 Free. ☉ June–mid-Nov. and Jan.–mid-Apr., Tues.–Sun. 2–4. Closed Mon., late Apr.–May, and late Nov.–Dec.

Skiing

Equally popular with locals, the triplet ski resorts of Wildhaus, Unterwasser, and Alt-St. Johann combine forces to draw visitors into the Churfirsten "paradise" in the Toggenburg Valley. Here you'll find altitudes and drops to suit even jaded skiers, the most challenging starting on the 2,076-m-high (6,809-ft-high) Gamserrugg and winding down 1,000 m (3,280 ft) to Wildhaus itself; a medium-difficult rival winds from Chäserrugg (2,262 m/7,419 ft) all the way down to Unterwasser. A one-day pass for all three resorts costs 43 SF; a five-day pass costs 170 SF; a seven-day pass costs 212 SF. There are ski schools in all three resorts. For more information and reservations, call ☎ 071/9999911, ℻ 071/9992929.

Alt-St. Johann, at 900 m (2,952 ft), has one chairlift and two T-bars. **Unterwasser,** at 910 m (2,985 ft), has one funicular railway, one cable car, four T-bars, 50 km (31 mi) of downhill runs, 45 km (28 mi) of cross-country trails, and 27 km (17 mi) of ski-hiking trails. At 1,098 m (3,601 ft), **Wildhaus** offers skiers four chairlifts, five T-bars, 50 km (31 mi) of downhill runs, 45 km (28 mi) of cross-country trails, and 27 km (17 mi) of ski-hiking trails.

Outdoor Activities and Sports

RACQUET SPORTS

Wildhaus (☎ 071/9991211) has two outdoor courts. **Unterwasser** has three outdoor tennis courts and a tennis and squash center (☎ 071/9993030).

LIECHTENSTEIN AND THE WALENSEE

When you cross the border from Switzerland into the principality of Liechtenstein, you will see license plates marked FL: this stands for Fürstentum Liechtenstein (Principality of Liechtenstein). You are leaving the world's oldest democracy and entering a monarchy that is the last remnant of the Holy Roman Empire—all 157 square km (61 square mi) of it. If you blink, you may miss it entirely.

This postage-stamp principality was created at the end of the 17th century, when a wealthy Austrian prince, Johann Adam von Liechtenstein, bought out two bankrupt counts in the Rhine Valley and united their lands. In 1719 he obtained an imperial deed from Emperor Karl VI, creating the principality of Liechtenstein. The noble family poured generations of wealth into the new country, improving its standard of living, and in 1862 an heir, Prince Johann the Good, helped Liechtenstein introduce its first constitution as a "democratic monarchy" in which the people and the prince share power equally.

Today the principality's 32,000 citizens enjoy one of the world's highest per-capita incomes and pay virtually no taxes. Its prosperous (though discreet) industries range from jam making to the molding of false teeth. Ironically, prosperity has built the lower reaches of Liechtenstein into a modern, comfortable, bourgeois community, full of big, new cream-color bungalows that hardly seem picturesque to tourists seeking traces of the Holy Roman Empire.

Vaduz (Liechtenstein)

㉓ *15 km (9 mi) southeast of the Toggenburg Valley, 159 km (98 mi) southeast of Schaffhausen.*

Arriving in downtown Vaduz (there are exits from the A13 expressway from both the north and the south), a visitor could make the mistake of thinking Liechtenstein's only attraction is its miniature scale. Liechtenstein's small **Briefmarkenmuseum** (Stamp Museum) demonstrates the principality's history as a maker of beautifully designed, limited-edition postage stamps. Have your passport stamped for 2 SF at the **Fremdenverkehrszentrale** (tourist office) (☞ Visitor Information *in* Eastern Switzerland A to Z, *below*) in the same building. ⊠ *Städtle 37,* ☎ *075/2366105.* 🎫 *Free.* ☉ *Apr.–Oct., daily 10–noon and 1:30–5:30; Nov.–Mar., daily 10–noon and 1:30–5.*

The **Liechtensteinische Staatliche Kunstsammlung** (Liechtenstein State Museum of Art) displays an ever-changing fraction of the country's extraordinary art collection, including graphic arts, paintings (with works by Rembrandt and Rubens), and pieces from the world-famous art collection of the prince, which concentrates on Greek and Roman mythological art. ⊠ *Städtle 37,* ☎ *075/2322341.* 🎫 *5 SF.* ☉ *Apr.–Oct., daily 10–noon and 1:30–5:30; Nov.–Mar., daily 10–noon and 1:30–5.*

The **Liechtensteinisches Landesmuseum** (National Museum), in a former tavern and customs house, covers the geology, Roman history, and folklore of the principality. However, it's closed for renovations until approximately 2003. ⊠ *Städtle 43,* ☎ *075/2322310.*

The **Ski Museum Vaduz** is a small shrine to Switzerland's (and the Alps') preferred pastime. Here you'll find numerous variations on the theme, including skis, sleds, ski fashion, and literature. ⊠ *Bangarten 10,* ☎ *075/2321502.* 🎫 *5 SF.* ☉ *Weekdays 2–6. Closed weekends.*

At the top of a well-marked hill road (you can climb the forest footpath behind the Engel hotel) stands **Vaduz Castle.** Here, His Highness Johannes Adam Pius, reigning prince of Liechtenstein, duke of Troppau and Jaegerndorf, reigns in a gratifyingly romantic fortress-home with striped medieval shutters, massive ramparts, and a broad perspective over the Rhine Valley. Originally built in the 12th century, the castle was burned down by troops of the Swiss Confederation in the Swabian Wars of 1499 and partly rebuilt during the following centuries, until a complete overhaul that started in 1905 gave it its present form. It is not open to the public, as Hans-Adam enjoys his privacy. He is the son of the late, beloved Franz Josef II, who died in November 1989 after a more than 50-year reign. Franz Josef's birthday, August 15, is still celebrated as the Liechtenstein national holiday. Hans-Adam—the last living heir to the Holy Roman Empire—has been known to join the crowds below to watch the fireworks while wearing jeans.

Dining and Lodging

$ ✕ **Wirthschaft zum Löwen.** Though there's plenty of French, Swiss, and
★ Austrian influence, Liechtenstein has a cuisine of its own, and this is the place to try it. In a wood-shingle landmark farmhouse on the Aus-

trian border, the friendly Biedermann family serves tender homemade *Schwartenmagen* (the pressed-pork mold unfortunately known as headcheese in English), pungent *Sauerkäse* (sour cheese), and Käseknöpfli, plus lovely meats and the local crusty, chewy bread. Be sure to try the region's wines. When driving here on Route 16, keep an eye out for Schellenberg, posted to the left; if you zip past it, you'll end up in Austria. ⊠ *FL-9488 Schellenberg, 10 km (6 mi) north of Vaduz off Rte. 16,* ☎ *075/3731162. No credit cards.*

$$$–$$$$
★ ✕🏨 **Real.** Here you'll find rich, old-style Austrian-French cuisine in this Relais & Châteaux establishment, prepared these days by Martin Real, son of the unpretentious former chef, Felix Real—who, in his retirement, presides over the 20,000-bottle cellar. There's an abundance of game in season, richly sauced seafood, and soufflés. The extraordinary wine list includes some rare (and excellent) local samplings, some from the family vineyard. Downstairs, the more casual Stübli atmosphere is just right for *Geschnetzeltes mit Rösti* (veal bits in cream sauce with hash brown potatoes); upstairs, the guest rooms are small but airily decorated. ⊠ *Städtle 21, FL-9490,* ☎ *075/2322222,* FAX *075/ 2320891. 11 rooms, 2 suites. Restaurant, Stübli. AE, DC, MC, V.* 🐾

$$
✕🏨 **Engel.** This elegant, centrally located hotel-restaurant has a comfortable local ambience despite the tour-bus crowds. The restaurant downstairs dishes up home cooking, and there's a *Biergarten* (beer garden) where Liechtensteiners meet. Upstairs, the more formal restaurant serves Chinese cuisine. The guest rooms are in fresh colors, with tile bathrooms. ⊠ *Städtle 13, FL-9490,* ☎ *075/2361717,* FAX *075/ 2331159. 20 rooms. Restaurant, pub. AE, DC, MC, V.*

$$$$
🏨 **Park-Hotel Sonnenhof.** A garden oasis—and a Relais & Châteaux property—commanding a superb view over the valley and mountains beyond, this hillside retreat offers understated luxury minutes from downtown Vaduz. Rooms are being renovated one by one; older rooms are decorated in homey pastels, the newer ones in gold and bright colors. Public areas are full of antiques, rugs, woodwork, and familial touches. The excellent French restaurant is exclusively for guests. ⊠ *Mareestr. 29, FL-9490,* ☎ *075/2321192,* FAX *075/2320053. 17 rooms, 12 suites. Restaurant, indoor pool, sauna. AE, DC, MC, V. Closed late Dec.– early Jan.* 🐾

Outdoor Activities and Sports
BICYCLES AND MOTORCYCLES
In Vaduz, bikes and small motorcycles can be rented from **Hans Melliger** (⊠ Kirchstr. 10, ☎ 075/2321606).

TENNIS
Vaduz (☎ 075/2327720) has public covered courts on Schaanerstrasse. Covered courts are also accessible in nearby **Schaan** (☎ 075/2332343). Rental equipment is available.

Shopping
POTTERY
Though shops on the main street of Vaduz carry samples of the local dark-glaze pottery, painted with folksy flowers and figures, the central source is **Schaedler Keramik** (⊠ Nendeln, 8 km [5 mi] north of Vaduz on Rte. 16, ☎ 075/3731414). Simpler household pottery is available for sale as well as the traditional and often ornate hand-painted pieces. Pottery making is demonstrated daily; it's open weekdays 8–noon and 1:30–6.

STAMPS
Liechtenstein is sometimes called the unofficial, per capita world champion of stamp collecting. To buy some of its famous stamps, whether to send a postcard to a philatelist friend or to invest in limited-issue

commemorative sheets, you must line up with the tour-bus crowds at the popular **post office** (⊠ Städtle).

Triesenberg (Liechtenstein)

㉔ *3 km (2 mi) southeast of Vaduz, 162 km (100 mi) southeast of Schaffhausen.*

This cluster of pretty chalets clings to the mountainside, with panoramic views over the Rhine Valley. Triesenberg was settled in the 13th century by immigrants from the Valais in southwestern Switzerland. The **Walser Heimatmuseum** (Valais Heritage Museum) traces the culture of these immigrants. Furnishings and tools from farmers and craftsmen are displayed, and an entertaining 20-minute slide show (in English) illustrates their Alpine roots. ⊠ *Dorfenzentrum,* ☎ *075/2621926.* 🖼 *2 SF.* ☉ *Sept.–May, Tues.–Fri. 1:30–5:30, Sat. 1:30–5; June–Aug., Tues.–Fri. 1:30–5:30, Sat. 1:30–5, Sun. 2–5.*

Malbun (Liechtenstein)

㉕ *5 km (3 mi) southeast of Triesenberg, 167 km (103 mi) southeast of Schaffhausen.*

In winter this 1,600-m-high (5,250-ft-high) mountain resort near the Austrian border draws crowds of local families who come for the varied slopes, many of which are well suited to beginners. England's Prince Charles and Princess Anne learned to ski here while visiting the Liechtenstein royal family in Vaduz. In summer, Malbun becomes a quiet, unpretentious resort with reasonable prices.

Skiing

Malbun is a sunny, natural bowl with low, easy slopes and a couple of difficult runs; you can ride a chairlift to the top of the Sareiserjoch and experience the novelty of skiing from the Austrian border back into Liechtenstein. Facilities are concentrated at the center, including hotels and cafés overlooking the slopes. The resort also has a **ski school** (☎ 075/2639770). One-day lift tickets cost 35 SF; six-day passes cost 143 SF.

Lodging

$ 🏨 **Alpenhotel.** The Vögeli family's welcoming smiles and good food have made this remodeled chalet a Liechtenstein institution. The old rooms are small, with creaky pine trim; the higher-priced new rooms are modern stucco. ⊠ *FL-9490,* ☎ *075/2631181,* 📠 *075/2639646. 21 rooms. Restaurant, café, indoor pool. AE, DC, MC, V.*

Outdoor Activities and Sports

Liechtenstein has a 162-km (100-mi) network of Alpine hiking trails, and another 243 km (150 mi) of valley hiking. **Malbun** and **Steg** are ideal starting points for mountain hikes. You can get trail maps at the tourist office or at magazine kiosks.

Flumserberg

㉖ *25 km (15 mi) west of Malbun, 122 km (75 mi) southeast of Schaffhausen.*

On the windswept, timberless slopes overlooking the Walensee and the Churfirsten Mountains, this resort is the site of one of the world's longest cableways. Over a distance of about 3 km (1¾ mi), a procession of little four-seater cabins reaches up to the rocky summit at **Leist,** 2,056 m (6,743 ft) up.

Skiing

Flumserberg, spanning 1,200 m–2,222 m (3,936 ft–7,288 ft), has five cable cars, 10 chairlifts, four T-bars, 60 km (40 mi) of downhill runs, 21 km (13 mi) of cross-country trails, and 20 km (12 mi) of mountain trails. The runs are suitable for beginner to intermediate skiers. You can also endeavor to skate, skibob, night ski, or snowboard in the Funpark, where snow is molded into jumps and half-pipes. A **ski school** (☎ 081/7333939) provides help for the less proficient. The German-only *Schneebericht* (☎ 081/7201510) gives current information on snow conditions. One-day lift tickets cost 46 SF; six-day passes, 194 SF.

Walensee

 5 km (3 mi) northwest of Flumserberg, 127 km (78 mi) southeast of Schaffhausen.

Between Liechtenstein and Zürich, the spectacular, mirrorlike lake called the Walensee is a deep emerald gash that stretches 16 km (10 mi) through the mountains, reflecting the jagged Churfirsten peaks. At the western end of the lake, **Weesen** is a quiet, shady resort noted for its mild climate and lovely lakeside walkway. Six kilometers (4 miles) north of Weesen on a winding mountain road lies **Amden,** perched 950 m (3,116 ft) above the Walensee in the relatively undiscovered region south of the Churfirsten Mountains.

Skiing

Despite its small size, **Amden** is a major winter sports center, offering modest skiing in a ruggedly beautiful setting. Easy and medium slopes with unspectacular drops and quick, short-lift runs provide good weekend getaways for crowds of local Swiss families. The highest trails start at 1,700 m (5,576 ft); there are a chairlift, three T-bars, one children's lift, 25 km (16 mi) of downhill runs, and 8 km (5 mi) of cross-country trails. You can also take advantage of the **ski school** (☎ 055/6111127), a natural ice rink, and walking paths. One-day lift tickets cost 29 SF; six-day passes cost 125SF.

Outdoor Activities and Sports

For sports enthusiasts, **Amden** also has a public **open-air skating rink,** the heated indoor pool **Hallenbad Amden** (☎ 055/6111588), and an **outdoor tennis court** (☎ 055/6111413).

OFF THE
BEATEN PATH

RAPPERSWIL – Between the Walensee and Zürich, this small town on Zürichsee (Lake Zürich) offers pleasant views and summertime waterfront strolls. Three rose gardens in the town center, including one for people with disabilities, account for Rapperswil's claim as the "Swiss City of Roses." A forbidding 13th-century **castle** looks like part of a gothic novel, with a trio of grave towers. Inside is the small **Polenmuseum** (☎ 055/2101862) which highlights the history of Polish immigrants to Switzerland. It's open on weekends from 1 to 5 in November, December, and March, and daily from 1 to 5 between April and October; admission is 4 SF. The castle's walkway faces a small deer park and affords a view of Zürich; from the terrace you'll see the Glarus Alps. At the **Knie's Kinderzoo** (Children's Zoo, ☎ 055/2206767), there are dolphin shows, 70 types of animals from around the world, elephant and pony rides, and plenty of creatures to feed and pet (elephant rides are not given on rainy days). It's open mid-March through October daily from 9 to 6, and the entrance fee is 8 SF. Follow signs; it's near the train station. ✉ *About 36 km (22 mi) northwest of Weesen and 40 km (24 mi) southeast of Zürich.*

EASTERN SWITZERLAND A TO Z

Arriving and Departing

By Car

The **A1** expressway from Zürich heads for St. Gallen through Winterthur. To reach Schaffhausen from Zürich, take A1 to Winterthur, then head north on the cantonal highway **E41/15.** You also can leave Zürich by way of the **A4** expressway past Kloten Airport, crossing through Germany briefly and entering Schaffhausen through Neuhausen am Rheinfall. From the south, the **A13** expressway, shared with Austria, leads you from Chur along Liechtenstein to the east end of the Bodensee; from there, you take A1 into St. Gallen.

By Plane

Zürich-Kloten Airport (☎ 1571060), just north of Zürich, is about 48 km (30 mi) south of Schaffhausen, about 75 km (46 mi) west of St. Gallen, and 130 km (81 mi) northwest of Liechtenstein.

By Train

A connection by **train** from the Zürich Hauptbahnhof into the SBB **Bahnhof Schaffhausen** (☎ 051/2234500) takes about 40 minutes; into SBB **Bahnhof St. Gallen** (☎ 051/2280233) or Sargans, about an hour. Connections from the south (Graubünden) are more complicated, as both Austria and the Alps intervene.

Getting Around

By Boat

Swiss Federal Railways provides regular year-round service on the Bodensee through **Schweizer Bodensee Schifffahrt Gesellschaft** (Swiss Bodensee Cruiseline Co., ☎ 071/4633435), though fewer boats run in winter (you'll travel free if you have a Swiss Pass). The **Schweizerisches Schifffahrtgesellschaft Untersee und Rhein** ship company (✉ Freierpl. 7, CH-8202 Schaffhausen, ☎ 052/6254282) offers a winning combination of a boat ride on the Rhine with romantic views of storybook castles, citadels, and monasteries. Boats run regularly up- and downstream, docking at Schaffhausen, Stein-am-Rhein, Gottlieben, Konstanz, and Kreuzlingen. Prices vary according to the distance traveled; if you have a Swiss Pass, you travel free. A one-way trip from Schaffhausen to Kreuzlingen takes about 4½ hours.

By Bus

The famous yellow **postbuses** provide much of the public transport in areas not served by trains, particularly smaller towns and, of course, Liechtenstein, which has no rail service. The bus schedules are usually posted outside the town post office, but you can also obtain information from any train station.

By Car

Driving in eastern Switzerland allows you to see the best of this region; highway 13 goes along the south shores of the Untersee and Bodensee and continues up through the hills to Appenzell. Neither St. Gallen nor Schaffhausen is a big enough city to warrant all-out panic, although you'll find it easiest to head directly for the center and abandon the car for the duration of your visit. Try to get into a parking lot, as finding a spot on the street can be difficult. In Schaffhausen, there's a big lot by the Stadttheater on Herrenacker. In St. Gallen, the Old Town is surrounded by underground parking lots. You'll find entrances on Burggraben, Oberergraben, and, most conveniently, on St. Georgenstrasse, right by the abbey.

By Train

Rail connections are somewhat complicated in this area, especially if you want to visit more of Appenzell than its major towns. Schaffhausen and St. Gallen are the main hubs from which regional trains head into the countryside and along the Bodensee. The only railroads into the canton are the narrow-gauge line between St. Gallen and the town of Appenzell, which passes Teufen and Gais, and the Gossau–Appenzell–Wasserauen line. To see more of the territory, you may return to St. Gallen on this same line by way of Herisau.

Although there is no regional rail pass available for eastern Switzerland, the general Swiss Pass (☞ Train Travel *in* Smart Travel Tips A to Z) includes St. Gallen and Schaffhausen city transit as well as over-all rail privileges. You cannot enter Liechtenstein by rail; the international express train that passes between Switzerland and Austria doesn't bother to stop. From the train stations at Buchs or Sargans, you can catch a postbus (☞ By Bus, *above*) into Vaduz.

Contacts and Resources

Emergencies

Police (☎ 117). **Ambulance** (☎ 144). **Doctor, dentist, late-night pharmacies** (☎ 111). **Medical assistance** in St. Gallen (☎ 071/4941111).

Guided Tours

WALKING

The **Schaffhausen tourist office** (☞ Visitor Information, *below*) gives guided walking tours with English commentary of the Old Town, the monastery, and the Munot.

Visitor Information

The tourist office for all of eastern Switzerland is based in St. Gallen: **Tourismusverband Ostschweiz** (Tourist Association of Eastern Switzerland; ⊠ Bahnhofpl. 1a, CH-9001, ☎ 071/2273737, 🖷 071/2273767, ✎). **Liechtenstein**'s office is in its capital (⊠ Städtle 37, FL-9490 Vaduz, ☎ 075/2321443, 🖷 075/3921618).

There are small regional visitor information offices throughout eastern Switzerland. **Appenzellerland** (⊠ Hauptg. 4, CH-9050 Appenzell, ☎ 071/7889641; ⊠ CH-9063 Stein, ☎ 071/3685050). **Schaffhausen** (⊠ Fronwagturm 4, CH-8201, ☎ 052/6255141). **Stein-am-Rhein** (⊠ Oberstadt 9, CH-8260, ☎ 052/7412835). **Thurgau** (⊠ Arbonerstr. 2, CH-8580 Amriswil, ☎ 071/4118181) services the Bodensee. **Urnäsch** (⊠ Dorf 78, CH-9107, ☎ 071/3642640).

4 GRAUBÜNDEN

AROSA, DAVOS, ST. MORITZ

Dominated by its trendy resorts—St. Moritz, Davos, Klosters, Arosa—Graubünden is nonetheless Switzerland's most culturally diverse and largest canton. German, Italian, and Romansh—the ancient dialect that is thought to date from 600 BC—are all spoken here. The true residents, stalwart native farmers, are far outnumbered by short-term visitors.

T HOUGH THE NAMES OF ITS RESORTS—St. Moritz, Davos, Klosters, Arosa—register almost automatic recognition, the region wrapped around them remains surprisingly little known. Resort life in winter contrasts sharply with the everyday existence of the native mountain farmers.

Revised by
Diane Conrad

Graubünden is the largest canton in Switzerland, covering more than one-sixth of the entire country. As it straddles the continental divide, its rains pour off north into the Rhine, eastward with the Inn to the Danube and Black Sea, and south to the River Po. The land is thus riddled with bluff-lined valleys, and its southern half basks in crystalline light: except for the Italian-speaking Ticino, it receives the most sunshine in the country. Its 150 valleys are flanked by dense blue-black wilderness and white peaks, among them Piz Buin (3,313 m/10,867 ft) in the north and Piz Bernina (4,057 m/13,307 ft) in the south, the canton's highest mountain.

Of all the Swiss cantons, Graubünden is the most culturally diverse. To the north it borders Austria and Liechtenstein, and in the east and south it abuts Italy. Swiss-German and Italian dialects are widely spoken. But the obscure and ancient language called Romansh (literally, "Roman") is spoken by almost 20% of the population, harking back to the 1st century BC, when the area was a Roman province called Rhaetia Prima. Some say the tongue predates the Romans and trace its roots back as far as 600 BC, when an Etruscan prince named Rhaetus invaded the region.

Though anyone versed in a Latin language can follow Romansh's simpler signs (*abitaziun da vacanzas* is vacation apartment; *il büro da pulizia*, the police office), it is no easy matter to pick it up by ear. Nor do the Graubündners smooth the way: Rhaetian Romansh is fragmented into five dialects, so that people living in any of the isolated valleys of the region might call the same cup a *coppina*, a *scadiola*, a *scariola*, a *cuppegn*, a *tazza*, or a *cupina*. The name *Graubünden*—Les Grisons (French), I Grigioni (Italian), and Il Grischun (Romansh)—means "gray confederation," referring to the 14th-century rebellion against Habsburg rule. With these dialects and their derivatives cutting one valley culture neatly off from another, it's no wonder the back roads of the region seem removed from the modern mainstream.

Pleasures and Pastimes

Dining
In this relatively exotic region of Switzerland, with its myriad dialects and potent blend of Latin and German blood, the cuisine is as novel and unexpected as its culture. The Graubünden idea of fast food is a *salsiz* (a kind of small, rectangular-shape salami) and a piece of bread. Besides regional specialties like the ubiquitous *Bündnerfleisch* (air-dried beef pressed into rectangular loaves and shaved into translucent slices), the *Bündnerplatte* (a plate of cured meats), *Gerstensuppe* (barley soup), and *Nusstorte* (a kind of shortbread with a chewy walnut-and-caramel filling), you will find a broad range of flavors. Italian influence is strong here, but—unlike the Ticinese to the southwest, who borrow from Italy wholesale—the Graubündners have evolved their own versions and incorporate Germanic styles as well. Takeoffs on gnocchi (potato-based pasta) and *Spätzli* (tiny flour dumplings) coexist here, with relatives of *Rösti* (hash brown potatoes), risotto, and polenta asserting their own local flavors.

Originating in isolated rural areas, the cuisines of Graubünden are earthy and direct, with sausages, potatoes, and cheese as staples and onions, bacon, and dried fruits providing the hearty flavors. You may feel you've stepped back into the Middle Ages when you sit down to *pizzoccheri neri* (buckwheat noodles with greens and potatoes, swimming in garlic butter and melted cheese) or to *maluns* (grated potatoes stirred in pools of butter until they form crisp balls) served with tart applesauce. *Capuns* or *chrutcapuns* are bundles of Swiss chard smothered in butter and cheese and flavored with dried meat, and *Hexenpolenta* is a harmless dish of cornmeal mush sweetened with raisins and apples. These down-to-earth treats are making a comeback in either traditional or more modern interpretations.

In resorts many restaurants close from the end of April to mid-June and October to December; there are variations and exceptions, of course, so if you plan a visit in the off-season, check in advance.

Watch for the annual winter Gourmet Festival in St. Moritz, when world-renowned chefs serve their specialties in host restaurants and hotels. The Grand Gourmet Finale is a gargantuan feast prepared by 30 chefs on the frozen St. Moritz Lake. For reservations call the St. Moritz tourist office (☞ Visitor Information *in* Graubünden A to Z, *below*).

CATEGORY	COST*
$$$$	over 80 SF
$$$	50 SF–80 SF
$$	20 SF–50 SF
$	under 20 SF

Prices are per person for a three-course meal (two-course meal in $ category), including sales tax and 15% service charge

Lodging

Of all the regions in Switzerland—each trading on its homeyness, its quaintness, its own take on a storybook setting—Graubünden delivers the most, as its hoteliers invest fortunes in preserving Alpine coziness inside and out. Unlike other parts of Switzerland, where hotels radiate warmth and history from their shuttered facades but sometimes have interiors as stark as hospital rooms, Graubünden hotels often use wood to soften the interior. The source is often *Arvenholz*, the prized Swiss stone pine (*Pinus cembra*) which grows here. Its wood is thick with knots and rich in natural color, which deepens over the years. This lovely wood, whether carefully preserved or new, plain or elaborately carved, makes for a warm and unmistakably Swiss welcome.

Prices in this popular region are comparatively high. In ski resorts winter prices are higher than summer's—although in the Lower Engadine the reverse can be the case. Even higher prices can be charged for the winter holiday period and in February. Many hotels close between seasons, from April to mid-June and from mid-October to mid-December, but the dates and months vary each year, so be sure to check. In a few winter resorts there are hotels that stay closed all summer; we have not included these in our listings. Hotels publish tariffs in various ways; double-check to see whether you're paying per person or per room, as well as whether you have *demipension* (half board). If you plan to stay in one place for more than a day or two, half board can cut costs. You may also want to ask about guest cards, small booklets given by hotels that provide various deals on local transit or attractions. These are distributed in some resort towns, including Klosters and Davos.

CATEGORY	COST*
$$$$	over 300 SF
$$$	200 SF–300 SF
$$	120 SF–200 SF
$	under 120 SF

Prices are for a standard double room, including breakfast, sales tax, and 15% service charge.

✎ *following the text of a review is your signal that the property has a Web site, where you will find details and, usually, images; for a link, visit www.fodors.com/urls.*

Skiing

With Davos as the site of the first T-bar ski lift in history, St. Moritz as the world's ritziest resort, and a host of other justifiably famous winter wonderlands within its confines, Graubünden easily earns its reputation as the ultimate winter destination. You'll find downhill skiing (including carving and telemark) and snowboarding for all levels, as well as miles of *Langlauf* (cross-country skiing) trails prepared for both the classic and skating techniques. You can participate in moonlight or torchlight skiing in almost all ski centers, usually followed by a get-together with music. Sports shops can outfit you with the necessary equipment; in Davos you can even rent ski clothing.

Trains

The Rhätische Bahn (RhB), with its bright-red cars, feels tailor-made for sightseeing. Along with the legendary, panoramic *Glacier Express* from St. Moritz to Zermatt, trains throughout the region traverse spectacular terrain, crossing bridges built unbelievably high over mountain gorges and cutting through mountainsides by way of tunnels. Lofty little villages, serviced by tiny train stations, show the Swiss affinity for access and for making the impossible seem routine (*See* Getting Around *in* Graubünden A to Z for more details on special trips).

Wines

Although Graubünden produces only a small percentage of Swiss wines, it has its own distinctive kinds: red pinot noir and white Riesling Sylvaner from the Bündnerherrschaft, the sunny region around Maienfeld, Jenins, and Malans. The unique Veltliner, a hearty red Nebbiolo, is actually grown over the border in Valtellina (Veltlin), which was ceded to Italy in 1815, much to the chagrin of some Graubündners. Some Veltliner wine has always been brought in bulk into Graubünden for bottling and can be considered, at least in spirit, as Swiss.

Exploring Graubünden

The region is fairly neatly bisected by a spine of 2,987-m (9,800-ft) peaks into two very different sections connected by the Julier, Albula, and Flüela passes. In the north is the region's capital, Chur. Farther east are the famous ski resorts of Klosters and Davos. The other half of the canton comprises the Engadine, home to mountain-ringed lakes and sophisticated resorts such as St. Moritz—as well as the magnificent Parc Naziunal Svizzer. From here the canton extends south toward Italy from the valleys of Bergell, Müstair, and Puschlav.

Numbers in the text correspond to numbers in the margin and on the Graubünden map.

Great Itineraries

IF YOU HAVE 1 OR 2 DAYS

If you approach Graubünden from the north on A13, begin by exploring the capital, **Chur** ②. Then take the train to 🚠 **Arosa** ③ to ski or hike;

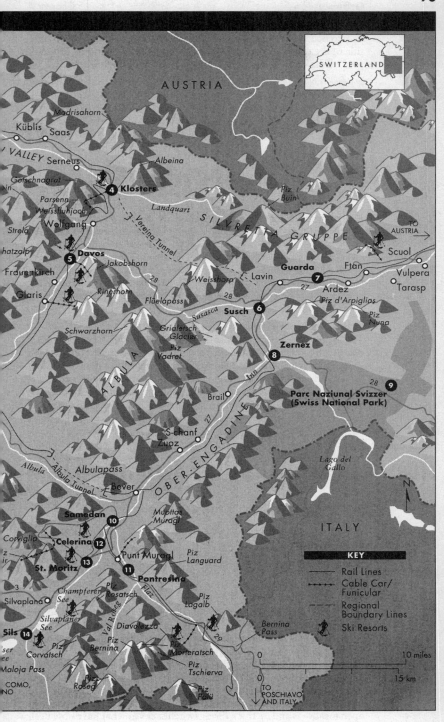

AUSTRIA

Madrisahorn

Küblis — Saas

VALLEY — Serneus

Golschnagrot

Albeina

4 Klosters

ein

Parsenn

Weissfluhjoch

Strela

Wolfgang

Landquart

Vereina Tunnel

SILVRETTA GRUPPE

Piz Buin

TO
AUSTRIA

Scuol

Davos

5

hatzalp

Jakobshorn

Frauenkirch

Glaris

28

Weisshorn

Lavin

Guarda

Ftan

Vulpera

7

Ardez

Tarasp

Rinerhorn

Flüelapass

28

Piz d'Arpiglias

Schwarzhorn

Susasca

Susch

6

Piz
Nuna

Grialetsch
Glacier

Zernez

Piz
Vadret

8

Inn

**Parc Naziunal Svizzer
(Swiss National Park)**

28

9

Brail

27

S-chanf

Zuoz

O B E R - E N G A D I N E

Lago del
Gallo

Albula

Albulapass

Albulapass

Albula Tunnel

Bever

N

ITALY

Samedan

Muottas
Muragl

10

Corviglia

Celerina

12

Punt Muragl

Piz
Languard

13

St. Moritz

11

KEY

Pontresina

Flaz

Piz
Rosatsch

Piz
Lagalb

Rail Lines

Champferer
See

Cable Car/
Funicular

z
ir

3

Silvaplana

Silvaplaner
See

Val Roseg

Diavolezza

Regional
Boundary Lines

Bernina
Pass

Ski Resorts

Sils

14

ser
ee

Piz
Corvátsch

Piz
Bernina

Piz
Morteratsch

29

Maloja Pass

Piz
Roseg

Piz
Tschierva

0   10 miles

COMO,
NO

Piz
Palü

0   15 km

TO
POSCHIAVO
AND ITALY

SWITZERLAND

it's a gorgeous trip in winter or summer. To see the countryside with its perched villages and tiny wooden chalet stations, sit on the right side of the train. To see the engine and first coaches winding ahead of you, take a seat between the middle and back of the train.

IF YOU HAVE 3 OR 4 DAYS

From ⊞ **Chur** ② travel through the Prättigau valley, passing through the canton's wine-producing area around **Maienfeld** ①. Make ⊞ **Klosters** ④ your base if you want peace and quiet, or drive over the Wolfgang Pass to ⊞ **Davos** ⑤ for a busier city-style stay.

IF YOU HAVE 5 OR MORE DAYS

Start from ⊞ **Chur** ②, following the three- or four-day itinerary above. The next part of your itinerary will depend very much on the season. Head into the Lower Engadine; the **Parc Naziunal Svizzer** ⑨ (open June to October only) is a magnificent federally protected preserve of virtually virgin wilderness. If you're traveling by car, detour to visit the pretty village of **Guarda** ⑦. Spend a night in ⊞ **Tarasp, Vulpera,** or **Scuol.** To explore the Upper Engadine, aim for ⊞ **Pontresina** ⑪ or continue on to ⊞ **St. Moritz** ⑬ or ⊞ **Sils** ⑭. You may want to take advantage of the Rhätische Bahn's special trips (open carriages in summer, at the back of a snowplow in winter) over the Bernina Pass to Poschiavo. Or you can loop back to Chur, going over the Julier Pass in winter or the Albula in summer.

When to Tour Graubünden

The tourism industry breathlessly awaits winter, when Graubünden's resorts fill to capacity. Thanks to a score of warm-weather sports such as hiking, cycling, golfing, windsurfing, and even hot-air ballooning, the area is now active in summer as well. In early fall the weather is generally mild, with clear skies. Avoid visiting mountain resorts between mid-October and early December and between mid-April and mid-June; during these off-seasons, most hotels and cable cars close (exact dates vary from year to year, depending on factors such as planned renovations, snowfall, and the Easter holiday).

HEIDI COUNTRY, CHUR, AND AROSA

Outcropped hills, castle ruins, and craggy peaks sloping down to sheltered vineyards highlight the area's topography—and history—as you enter the canton from Sargans or Vaduz. Though it's the gateway to Graubünden, this region has a catchier claim to fame: it was here that the legendary Heidi enjoyed the rustic pleasures of the Alps.

Maienfeld

❶ *17 km (11 mi) north of Chur.*

Above this graceful small town full of fountains, vineyards, and old stucco houses, Zürich author Johanna Spyri set *Heidi,* the much-loved children's story of an orphan growing up with her grandfather on an isolated Alpine farm. Taken away to accompany the invalid Clara in murky Frankfurt, she languishes until returning to her mountain home. Spyri spent time in Maienfeld and nearby Jenins, but it's questionable whether actual people inspired her tale. Nonetheless you can hike from the Heidihof Hotel along the Heidi-Weg (Heidi Path), across steep open meadows and up thick forest switchbacks to what have now been designated **Peter the Goatherd's Hut** and the **Alm-Uncle's Hut.** Here you might meet today's version of that character, a cow and goatherd who enjoys a chat and can answer Heidi-related questions. A few minutes' walk from the Heidihof Hotel is the **Heididorf** (Heidi Village), in reality the hamlet of Oberrofels. Here you can find the "original" house, which was illustrated in the old Heidi books. It's now outfitted to the hilt with Heidi-appropriate furnishings. ☎ *081/3301912.* 🎫 *5 SF.* ☉ *Mar.–Nov., daily 10–5.*

Back in town you can visit wine merchants or have a meal in the Knight's Hall of **Schloss Brandis,** a castle-tower whose earliest portions date from the 10th century. ☎ *081/3022423. Closed mid-July–mid-Aug.*

Chur

② *17 km (11 mi) south of Maienfeld.*

Now a small city (and cantonal capital) of 35,000, with a bustling downtown and a busy rail crossroads, Chur is actually the oldest continuously settled site in Switzerland. Traces of habitation exist here from as far back as 3000 BC–2500 BC. The Romans founded Curia Raetorium on the rocky terrace south of the river; from here, they protected the Alpine routes that led to the Bodensee. By AD 284 it served as the capital of the flourishing Roman colony Rhaetia Prima. Its heyday, evident throughout the Old Town even now, was during the Middle Ages, when it was ruled by bishops and bishop-princes. Narrow streets, cobblestone alleys, hidden courtyards, and ancient shuttered buildings abound; the city's citadel centers on the 12th-century cathedral.

The **Rathaus** (Town Hall) was built as two structures in 1464 and connected in 1540. At ground level, under the arches, is the old marketplace. In the open hall on the second floor is a model of the Old Town, which can help you plan a tour of the city. The **Grosser Ratsaal** (Council Chamber) has a timber ceiling dating from 1493; the **Bürgerratskammer** (Citizens' Council Chamber) has Renaissance wall panels. Both chambers have old ceramic stoves, the one in the Ratsaal depicting the deadly sins and biblical scenes. Embedded in the wall beside the door opening onto Reichsgasse is a rod of iron about a foot long—the standard measure of a foot or shoe before the metric system was introduced. Although both chambers are generally closed to the public, very small groups can contact the tourist office (☞ Visitor Information *in* Graubünden A to Z, *below*) to arrange a visit. ✉ *Poststr.*

The **Kirche St. Martin** (St. Martin's Church) was built in 1491 in the late-Gothic style after a fire destroyed the 8th-century original. Since 1526 it has been Protestant. On your right as you enter are three stained-glass windows created in 1919 by Augusto Giacometti, the father of the Graubünden sculptor Alberto Giacometti. The steeple dates from 1917; with permission from the sacristan, you can climb to the top to see the bells. ✉ *Evangel. Kirchgemeinde, Kirchg. 12,* ☎ *081/ 2522292.*

The **Rätisches Museum** provides a thorough, evocative overview of the canton's development. Displayed in a 1675 mansion, the collection includes not only furnishings and goods from the period, but also archaeological finds from the region, both Roman and prehistoric. ✉ *Hofstr. 1,* ☎ *081/2572889.* 🎫 *5 SF.* ☉ *Tues.–Sun. 10–noon and 2–5.*

Opposite the Rätisches Museum, a stone archway under the **Hof-Torturm** (Citadel Gate Tower) leads into the court of the strong bishop-princes of Chur, once hosts to Holy Roman emperors who passed through on their way between Italy and Germany—sometimes with whole armies in tow. The bishops were repaid for their hospitality by imperial donations to the people. The thick fortifications of the residence demonstrate the disputed powers of the bishops; by the 15th century, irate inhabitants who rebelled again and again were rebuffed and punished with excommunication. By 1526 the Reformation had broken the domination of the Church, although the city remains a Catholic bishopric today. The Hofkellerei Stübli is now at the base of the tower. Head up to the second floor and you can have a drink in the paneled room, dating from 1522, once used for church meetings. There's a good view of the city from this vantage point. ⊠ *Hof 1.*

The **Kathedrale St. Maria Himmelfahrt** (Cathedral of the Assumption), built between 1151 and 1272, is the centerpiece of Chur. Its mix of styles spanned the century and drew on influences from across Europe. The capitals of the columns are carved with fantastical beasts; at their bases are clustered less threatening animals such as sheep and marmots. In the choir is a magnificent 15th-century three-sided altar in gilded wood. The structure built on this site in prehistoric times was supplanted by a Roman castle, a bishop's house in 451, and a Carolingian cathedral during the 8th century. The cathedral treasures can be viewed by appointment. ⊠ *Hof.* ☎ *081/2529250.* ☉ *Daily 8–7.*

Obere Gasse, once the main street through Chur and a major route between Germany and Italy, is now lined with small shops and cafés. At the end stands the 16th-century **Obertor** (Upper Gate), guarding the bridge across the Plessur River. ⊠ *Old Town, between the Obertor and Arcaspl.*

Collections at Graubüunden's art museum, the **Kunsthaus,** include works by well-known artists who lived or worked in the canton, including Angelika Kauffmann, Giovanni Segantini, Giovanni and Alberto Giacometti, and Ernst Kirchner. *Postpl.,* ☎ *081/2572868.* ⊠ *7 SF.* ☉ *Tues.–Wed. and Fri.–Sun. 10–noon and 2–5, Thurs. 10–noon and 2–8.*

☕ At the **Kutschensammlung** (Coach Museum), a collection of turn-of-the-century carriages and sleighs, buffed to a picture-book high sheen, harks back to the era of romance. One 1880 sleigh has a fur blanket and jingle bells straight out of Hans Christian Andersen's *The Ice Queen.* ⊠ *Hotel Stern, Reichg. 11,* ☎ *081/2523555.* ⊠ *Free.* ☉ *Daily by appointment.*

Dining and Lodging

$–$$ ✕ **Controversa.** This modern brasserie-style restaurant offers a wide choice of salads (self-service or made to order) and over a dozen pasta dishes, such as tagliatelle with chicken and mango in a curry sauce. If your appetite isn't up to the heaping servings, you can order half portions. ⊠ *Steinbruchstr. 2,* ☎ *081/2529944. AE, DC, V.*

$$–$$$ ✕🏠 **Stern.** This is a welcome find: a historic inn in the hub of a city
★ with a restaurant that serves moderately priced, authentic regional cooking. Built in 1677, this Romantik hotel has modern, wood-clad rooms, a rooftop terrace, and a fireplace lounge. Don't worry if your room is next to the church; its bells and clock don't ring at night. The elevator goes only to the third floor, with stairs to the fourth. In the pine-lined restaurant, choices on the seasonal menu could include asparagus dishes or *Kalbsleber dolce brusco* (breaded liver in sweet red-wine sauce with raisin polenta). All are served with anise bread and local wine by waitresses in folk costume. If you plan to arrive by train, let the hotel know; staff members will collect you from the station in their 1933 Buick. ⊠ *Reichg. 11, CH-7000,* ☎ *081/2523555,* ℻ *081/2521915. 58 rooms. Restaurant, breakfast room. AE, DC, MC, V.*

$ ✕🏠 **Tom's Räblüta.** This old house was taken over in 2000 by a pair
★ of entrepreneurs (two Toms) who revamped the 15th-century building. The contrast between the carved, dark-wood ceilings and the bright, new furniture takes a bit of getting used to, but the staff's wel-

come is exceptionally warm. Rooms have mass-produced furniture, but all have tiny private baths or showers, a rarity in this price range. Top-floor rooms have sloping rafters and views over the Old Town rooftops (note that there is no elevator). The Zunftstube, one of two restaurants, was once the vintners' guild meeting room; its menu focuses on sea-sonal produce. Be sure to look into the three-course lunch offered at both restaurants on Friday; it's just 10 SF, a remarkable deal. If you're coming by car, remember that the area is traffic-free from afternoon to early morning; you can drop luggage off at the door but will then have to park in a garage. The Zunftstube is closed Sunday and Mon-day. ⊠ *Pfisterpl. 1, CH-7000,* ☎ *081/2571357,* FAX *081/2571358. 11 rooms. 2 restaurants, bar. AE, DC, MC, V.* ✎

$$–$$$ ☎ **ABC Terminus.** This garni business hotel is just yards from the train station. (Luckily, there are no night trains.) It occupies five floors of a corporate metal-and-glass box; the entry is hidden between shops. Amenities and rooms are state-of-the-art. ⊠ *Bahnhofpl., CH-7000,* ☎ *081/2526033,* FAX *081/2525524. 36 rooms. Breakfast room, no-smok-ing floors, sauna. AE, DC, MC, V.* ✎

Nightlife

The futuristic **Giger Bar** (⊠ Comercialstr. 23, ☎ 081/2537506) is as close as you'll come to the flight deck of the *Starship Enterprise*. The strange space was created by 1980 visual effects Oscar winner H. R. Giger, a Chur native who designed the sets for the film *Alien*.

Outdoor Activities and Sports

SWIMMING

Chur has an indoor **swimming pool** (⊠ Sportanlagen Obere Au, ☎ 081/2544288) for the aquatically inclined.

GOLF

The 27-hole **Domat-Ems** (☎ 081/6333212) golf course is 15 minutes by bus or train from Chur.

SKIING

Chur is the only Swiss city to have direct access by cable car from the city center to a ski area. The Brambüesch has 20 km (12½ mi) of easy pistes and a popular 6-km (3.7-mi) sled run. Ski equipment can be hired at **Näf Sport** in town (⊠ Quaderstr. 8, ☎ 081/2571757). Sleds are avail-able on a first come, first served basis at the mountain station. For recorded general information on the ski area, call ☎ 081/2505590; the message is in German only.

Arosa

★ ❸   *29 km (18 mi) east of Chur.*

Although Arosa is one of the best-known Graubünden winter and sum-mer sports centers, its modest size (barely 3,000 year-round residents), isolation, and natural beauty set it apart. There is none of the rush and heavy traffic of Davos or St. Moritz. This is a friendly, down-to-earth, family-oriented spot. On a winter walk through the village you are more likely to be overtaken by sleds and horse-drawn carriages or sleighs than by cars.

Arosa lies at the end of a spectacular, winding 30-km (19-mi) road that cuts through a steep-walled valley and climbs through tiny villages on grades of more than 12%. The road from Chur has no fewer than 360 turns and has a height difference of 1,200 m (3,936 ft) in a distance of only 26 km (16 mi). Taking the *Arosa Express* up from Chur is less nerve-racking than driving and a worthwhile experience in and of it-self (☞ Great Itineraries, *above*). The town is divided into two sections:

Inner-Arosa, at the end of the valley, and Ausser-Arosa, near the train station and the Obersee (Upper Lake). There's a pleasant mix of wooden chalets and flat-roofed blocks—plus the unmissable casino, with its modern art and mosaic facade in screaming colors. The road empties into a sheltered, sunny mountain basin at the end of the Schanfigg Valley. Cars should be left in the lakeside lots when possible, as a convenient free bus shuttles through the town, and traffic is forbidden between midnight and 6 AM.

The town is strung along a narrow shelf with broad southern views, and within moments you can melt into the wilderness on good mountain trails—even in winter. You can take a cable car up the Weisshorn and Hörnli mountains in winter and summer to ski, hike, or take in the scenery. Drop into the **Heimatmuseum** to see a slide show and learn about local history. ⊠ *Poststr., Inner-Arosa,* ☎ *no phone.* 🎦 *3 SF.* ☉ *Winter and summer, Mon., Wed., and Fri. 2:30–4:30.*

Skiing
Open to ski tourism since 1877, Arosa is more remote and less sophisticated than Gstaad and St. Moritz. Closely screened in by mountains, the 5,900-ft-high resort has runs suitable for every level of skier. Its 15 lifts serve 70 km (43 mi) of trails. Although the facilities don't match those of Davos, the not-too-distant neighbor that an unbreachable rock barrier renders light-years away, they are sufficient for the guests that the resort welcomes in high season. The slopes can be accessed directly from the valley at three points: the top of the village; behind the rail station; and Prätschli. Maniacs who want a battering will find an ideal black piste on the **Weisshorn** (2,654 m/8,700 ft), but most of the runs there, as well as on **Hörnli** (2,460 m/8,200 ft) and **Prätschli,** a "feeder" lift to the main ski area, are intermediate to easy. You can get snow-sports instruction at the official **Swiss Ski School** (☎ 081/3771150). Other options are the **ABC Snowsport School** (☎ 081/3565660) and the **Bananas Swiss Snowboard School** (☎ 081/3774008). A one-day lift ticket costs 50 SF; a six-day pass costs 237 SF.

Dining and Lodging
$$$$ ✕ **Zum Wohl!sein.** Chef Beat Caduff is a mastermind of modern Swiss-European cuisine done with a traditional twist—he finds the freshest ingredients and insists on serving only seven-course meals. His specialties include *Wildessenz,* an intense bouillon obtained by simmering pounds of vegetables, plenty of red wine, and choice game for hours. The cellar holds more than 2,000 vintages. Reserve a week in advance and prepare to stay several hours—it's an eating event. ⊠ *Hohe Promenade, in Hotel Anita,* ☎ *081/3771109. Reservations essential. AE, DC, MC, V. Closed Sun.–Tues. No lunch.*

$–$$ ✕ **Hold.** This busy, happy family restaurant sits literally at the foot of the slopes. The menu has traditional fare, including nine different sausage dishes, such as veal sausage with onions and gravy. A trio of advantages make it an especially good place to bring kids: there are children's menu choices for under 10 SF; it's right by the children's ski school; and it has a small playroom behind the restaurant. ⊠ *Poststr.,* ☎ *081/3771408. AE, DC, MC, V. Closed Easter–mid-June and mid-Oct.–early Dec.*

$$$$ ✕🏨 **Waldhotel National.** At this peaceful retreat, set in its own wooded grounds above the village, you can ski or sled home in winter. North-facing rooms look over the forest, south-facing ones over Arosa and the mountains. All are tastefully decorated and have touches of golden pine. The Kachelofastübli serves local and French specialties; you might find pigeon breast with mountain honey and cinnamon–sweet corn blinis or pike fillets with creamed cabbage and Chur chardonnay sauce. Reservations (essential for this popular restaurant) are not just written on paper, but painted on plates. It's closed in Sunday evenings in summer. ⊠ CH-7050 Arosa, ☎ 081/3785555, FAX 081/3785599. 94 rooms. 2 restaurants, Stübli, piano bar, indoor pool, massage, sauna, hairdresser, kindergarten. AE, DC, MC, V. Closed mid-Apr.–mid-June and mid-Sept.–early Dec. ✿

\$\$ ✕▥ **Arve Central.** There are flowers in the window boxes here all year-round—in winter, wooden blooms replace the real thing. The flower theme is carried through the whole hotel, from the deep-pile carpet to the room key rings and the staff's uniforms. All rooms have a fresh wood decor. There are good views on the south side; the back rooms have neither balcony nor view. The wood-clad Arve and the Enzian restaurants offer some of the best food in town with eclectic changing menus. Herbs gathered from their own garden appear in dishes such as frothy herb soup with champagne vinegar and bream baked in a rice crust with coriander sauce and saffron potatoes. The restaurants close on Monday and Tuesday in May. ⊠ Off Poststr., CH-7050, ☎ 081/3785252, FAX 081/3785250. 48 rooms. 2 restaurants, bar, hot tub, sauna, whirlpool, baby-sitting. AE, DC, MC, V. ✿

\$\$\$\$ ▥ **Kulm.** Twenty-eight cowbells hang above the Kulm's reception desk, ★ harking back to the hotel's past as a 19th-century wooden chalet. But any resemblance to a Swiss Alpine hut stops there. The current wood, metal, and glass building, although rather unappealing from the outside, is a refreshingly young and sporty luxury hotel. The huge, light main restaurants are decorated in bright turquoise and yellow. In addition to the three restaurants, a trattoria and a Thai restaurant are open in winter. Rooms have soft furnishings in prints; bathrooms are in tile and stone. The wraparound windows take in acres of green hills or snowy slopes; all south-facing rooms have balconies. Indeed, the hotel's position is its biggest draw, as it stands on the farthest edge of town at the base of the slopes: you can ski home at the end of the day. ⊠ CH-7050 Arosa, ☎ 081/3788888, FAX 081/3788889. 138 rooms, 4 suites. 5 restaurants, bar, piano bar, indoor pool, putting green, 2 tennis courts, bowling, health club, squash, dance club, baby-sitting. AE, DC, MC, V. Closed mid-Sept.–early Dec. and mid-Apr.–mid-June. ✿

\$\$–\$\$\$ ▥ **Alpensonne.** Family owned and run, this hotel is only about 200 yards from the ski lifts of Inner-Arosa. The public spaces are light and bright. Guest rooms have thick carpets, soft colors, tile baths, and lots of wood; those facing south have great views. The café-Stübli serves meat and cheese fondues daily. ⊠ Poststr., CH-7050, ☎ 081/3771547, FAX 081/3773470. 32 rooms. Restaurant, bar, café, Stübli, sauna, recreation room. AE, DC, MC, V. Closed May–June.

\$–\$\$ ▥ **Sonnenhalde.** The automatic heavy pine door that welcomes you to this chalet hotel garni is your first sign of its happy marriage of charm and modern comfort. The sizable rooms are bright, with wall-to-wall wood and rustic decor. Some rooms easily accommodate extra beds (for an additional fee). Bathrooms have showers instead of tubs; the lowest-priced rooms have only sinks and share the other facilities. ⊠ CH-7050 Arosa, ☎ 081/3771531, FAX 081/3774455. 22 rooms, 14 with bath. Sauna, steam room. AE, DC, MC, V. Closed mid-Apr.–late June and mid-Oct.–early Dec.

Nightlife and the Arts

BARS

The Casino has several bars, including the popular **Espresso Bar** (☎ 081/3773940). There's a lively piano bar at **Hotel Carmenna** (☎ 081/3771766).

CASINOS

Arosa's **Kursaal** (Casino; ⊠ Poststr., ☎ 081/3775051) has a roulette wheel with the usual 5 SF gambling limit, 75 slot machines, and video games.

DANCING

The **Kitchen Club** (✉ Hotel Eden, ☎ 081/3787106) is a disco inside an original 1907 kitchen, where a young crowd dances among old pots and pans while the DJ perches above antique aluminum refrigerators. The après-ski crowd here is decidedly city chic—you should change out of your ski bibs first. **Nuts** (✉ Casino, Poststr., ☎ 081/3773940) plays hit-parade tunes for people college age and up; it's open until 3 AM. The tiny **Halli-Galli** (✉ Hotel Obersee, Aussere Poststr., ☎ 081/3771949) manages to squeeze in a live band in front of a '70s-style, rainbow-color backdrop.

MUSIC

There are **organ concerts** in Arosa's Bergkirchli (mountain chapel) from Christmas through mid-April and in summer, Tuesday at 5. An **alphorn and yodeling festival** takes place in July. Check with the tourist office (☞ Visitor Information *in* Graubünden A to Z, *below*) for information on either of these events. Music courses are held from June through October; get the program from **Kulturkreis Arosa** (☎ 081/3538747, FAX 081/3538750).

Outdoor Activities and Sports

CROSS-COUNTRY, SNOWSHOEING, AND SLEDDING

Langlaufschule Geeser (✉ Hof Maran, ☎ 081/3775152) gives lessons and leads cross-country and snowshoeing excursions. If you opt for snowshoeing, the rental equipment is included with your excursion fee. There are three official sled runs: Tschuggen, Prätschli, and Untersee. You can rent sleds at the train station or **S. Schmid**'s shoeshop (✉ Innere Poststr., ☎ 081/3772181).

GOLF

Between 1999 and 2000, Arosa expanded its golf course at **Hof Maran** (☎ 081/3774242) from nine holes to 18 holes.

HIKING AND BIKING

The tourist office organizes tours of one or several days for walkers or cyclists (☞ Guided Tours *in* Graubünden A to Z, *below and* Hiking *in* Davos, *below*).

HORSEBACK RIDING

Call **L. Messner** (☎ 081/3774196) for guided horseback tours and horse-drawn carriage rides in summer or sleigh rides in winter.

PARAGLIDING AND BALLOONING

Ballooning and paragliding season runs from December to March. Contact **The Paragliding Taxi** (☎ 079/4361788), which arranges daily flights in good weather. For a balloon flight over Arosa or the Graubünden Alps, call Walter Vollenweider (☎ 01/3913714). A special ballooning week is held in January.

SKATING AND CURLING

Arosa has several skating rinks. At the indoor **Eissporthalle** you can watch ice hockey as well as take skating or curling lessons; there's an open-air rink alongside (☎ 081/3771745). Another option is the **Inner-Arosa rink** (☎ 081/3772930). **Hof Maran** (☎ 081/3785151), to the north of Arosa, has a rink, too.

SWIMMING

If you can take cold mountain water, you can have a (free) swim in the lakes. Some hotels open their pools to the public; check with the tourist office (☞ Visitor Information *in* Graubünden A to Z, *below*).

TENNIS

There are 15 hotel-owned courts open to the public; contact the tourist office (☞ Visitor Information *in* Graubünden A to Z, *below*) for details. You can rent equipment from the hotels.

PRÄTTIGAU AND DAVOS

The name "Prättigau" means "meadow valley," and it's just that—a lush landscape of alternating orchards, pastures, and pine-covered mountains. The predominant language in the valley is German, though most villages still have Romansch names that date from ancient times. Prättigau's most renowned ski resort is Klosters. Klosters's equally famous neighbor, Davos, lies in the Landwasser Valley, over the Wolfgang Pass. Visitors who like an urban experience head to Davos, while those who prefer a quieter village experience go to Klosters.

Klosters

❹ *26 km (19 mi) southeast of Landquart.*

Once a group of hamlets, Klosters has become a small but chic resort, made up mostly of weathered-wood and white-stucco chalets. The village has two districts: Platz, which is older and busier, and Dorf, which lies on the main road toward Landquart. The church of St. Jacob, in Klosters Platz, dating from 1492, is the only remnant of the medieval monastery from which the village took its name. Klosters is famed for its skiing—British royal family members are faithful visitors—and makes the most of its access to the slopes of the Parsenn, above Davos.

A brief visit to the folk museum **Nutli-Hüschi** will illustrate how far this resort has evolved from its mountain roots: a pretty wood-and-stone chalet, built in 1565, has been restored and fitted with the spare furnishings of its day, including kitchen tools and a children's bed that lengthens as the child grows. ⊠ *Monbielerstr. at Talstr.,* ☎ *081/4102020.* ⊡ *3 SF.* ☉ *Jan.–mid-Apr. and late June–mid Oct., Wed. and Fri. 3–5.*

Skiing

Klosters is known for its vast range of downhill runs which, together with those of Davos (☞ *below*), total 400 km (nearly 250 mi). These are divided nearly equally among easy, moderate, and difficult pistes. From the **Gotschnagrat** (2285 m/7,494 ft), skiers can connect to the **Parsenn** slopes, finishing back in Klosters or in Davos, on the Wolfgang Pass or in the Prättigau villages of Serneus or Küblis. The world's longest ski run is 12.23 km (7½ mi) from the Weissfluhgipfel (2,844 m/9,328 ft) down to Küblis. It is classified as black (difficult) at the top, but for most of its length is red (moderate). The sunny **Madrisa** slopes above Klosters Dorf offer relatively easy skiing and snowboarding. For instruction or to go on a snowshoe trek, contact the **Swiss Ski & Snowboard School** (☎ 081/4102028), which has a branch in both Platz and Dorf. Lift tickets to the combined Davos/Klosters area cost 54 SF for one day and up to 268 SF for six days, depending on how many and in which areas you want to ski. Train or bus transport back to Klosters from other villages within the ski area is included in the price of the regional ski ticket. A cross-country ski pass costs 5 SF for one day or 12 SF for one week. There are 50 km (31 mi) of cross-country tracks and a **cross-country school** (☎ 081/4102020).

Dining and Lodging

$$$ ✕ **Alte Post.** In this warm local favorite, pleasantly cluttered with ceramics and game trophies, choose from a straightforward menu thick with game and salmon (they smoke their own Norwegian salmon). The old-style dishes are a forte: rabbit in thyme, *tête de veau* (veal head) vinaigrette, beef with marsala and risotto, and lots of trout and lamb. If you like salmon, go for the salmon menu, which has salmon in every dish but the sorbet. The restaurant is about a mile out of town but worth the trip. ⊠ *Doggilochstr. 136, Klosters-Aeuja,* ☎ *081/4221716. AE, DC, MC, V. Closed Mon.–Tues. and May and Nov.*

$$ ✕ **Höhwald.** This is a friendly, touristy restaurant up the hill from Klosters in Monbiel, with a large, open terrace that takes in valley and mountain views. Try their special plate of mixed Graubünden specialties, which include Capuns, Prättigauer *Knödlis* (dumplings), and *Chäs-gatschäder* (a mixture of bread, milk, and cheese). ⊠ *Klosters-Monbiel,* ☎ *081/4223045. AE, MC, V. Closed mid-May–mid-June and Nov..*

$$$ ✕⊞ **Walserhof.** Of the high-end hotels in Klosters, this is the most so-
★ phisticated, having struck a smart balance between old and new. It was built in 1981 with the weathered materials from an old farmhouse. Its restaurant and café are paneled with ancient carved wood; stone, stucco, and quarry tile are used elsewhere. The only drawback is its location, on the main road through town; the best views take in either the street or fairly well-developed fields behind. The superb restaurant serves mainly French, Italian, and regional dishes; local specialties could include trout in cider, cabbage dumplings with wild mushrooms, game terrines, or lamb stew with polenta. ⊠ *Landstr., CH-7250 Klosters-Platz,* ☎ *081/4102929,* 𝔽𝔸𝕏 *081/4102939. 11 rooms, 3 suites. Restaurant, café, sauna, exercise room. AE, DC, MC, V. Closed Easter– late June and mid-Oct.–early Dec.* ✍

$$–$$$ ✕⊞ **Rustico.** Good things come in small packages here—guest rooms are on a petite scale but are very attractive. Each has a hand-painted flower on its door. Inside are parquet floors, country cottons, and white tiled showers. The lounge area has a fireplace and leads out to a sum-mer terrace. In the restaurant, hung with original art, a seasonal menu caters to both omnivores and vegetarians with dishes such as venison steaks with elderberry sauce, polenta, and chestnuts and deep-fried mush-rooms on a *mangetout* salad (peas in the pod). The restaurant is closed on Thursday in summer. ⊠ *Landstr., CH-7250 Klosters-Platz,* ☎ *081/ 4221212,* 𝔽𝔸𝕏 *081/4225355. mypage.bluewin.ch/rustico 12 rooms. Restaurant, bar, sauna, billiards. DC, MC, V. Closed June and Nov..*

$$–$$$$ ⊞ **Albeina.** This large and luxurious chalet-style hotel has easy access to the Madrisa slopes. In summer you can join special tennis or horse-back-riding weeks. Rooms are tastefully decorated, with floral details. Rooms in the lowest price category are available only in summer or early December; they're on the north side of the building or in the Chesa Albeina guest house. The popular Dörfji Bar draws regulars. ⊠ *CH-7252 Klosters-Dorf,* ☎ *081/4232100,* 𝔽𝔸𝕏 *081/4232121. www.al-beinahotel.ch 64 rooms. 2 restaurants, bar, indoor pool, 2 tennis courts, boccie, sauna, steam room, billiards, playground. AE, DC, MC, V. Closed mid-Apr.–mid-June and mid-Oct.–mid-Dec.*

$$–$$$$ ⊞ **Chesa Grischuna.** Although it's directly in the town center at the crossroads, this creaky 1890 mountain farmhouse qualifies as a coun-try inn—as well as one of the most popular places to stay. Every room, including those in the nearby annex, is full of old carved wood, and some have balconies. There are antiques throughout, and plenty of pub-lic spaces, as this is a sociable place. Whether you bowl in the vaulted cellar, play cards, or dance to the piano music at happy hour, you'll be surrounded by the coveted social mix of Klosters regulars. ⊠ *Bahn-hofstr., CH-7250 Klosters-Platz,* ☎ *081/4222222,* 𝔽𝔸𝕏 *081/4222225. 25 rooms, 23 with bath. Restaurant, bar, bowling. AE, MC, V. Closed late May–early July and mid-Oct.–mid-Dec.*

\$\$ ★ ⚅ Silvapina. This delightful hotel is family-run and family-welcoming. It is right by the railroad (trains don't run at night) and a few minutes' walk from the Madrisa slopes. The weathered-wood chalet was built in 1931, with a new wing added in 1960. Haus Silvapina, opposite it, has apartments. Rooms are done either all in wood or in white with touches of pine. Bathrooms have showers instead of tubs. A small bar and a sitting area with a fireplace were added in 1999. ⊠ *CH-7252 Klosters-Dorf,* ☎ *081/4221468,* FAX *081/4224078. 15 rooms, 3 apartments. Restaurant, bar, Stübli, sauna, tennis court, Ping-Pong, billiards. AE, MC, V. Closed May and Nov.* ⚅

Nightlife

Revelers dance late into the night at the **Casa Antica** disco (☎ 081/4221621), in a 300-year-old converted barn. **Chesa Bar** (☞ Chesa Grischuna, *above*) is a popular after-dinner spot, with piano music and several intimate bar areas. In the Silvretta Parkhotel there's the **Kir Royal** (☎ 081/4233435) disco and a piano bar.

Outdoor Activities and Sports

HIKING AND BIKING

The Davos/Klosters/Prättigau region has plenty of trails to let you explore the terrain on foot or bicycle. In winter there are 30 km (18½ mi) of prepared walking paths; in summer there are 100 marked walking routes. There are 230 km (142 mi) of cycling and mountain-biking routes. For rental bicycles, try the **Läser Bike Shop** (⊠ Klosters-Dorf, ☎ 081/4223942). Another source is **Andrist Sport** (⊠ Klosters-Platz, ☎ 081/4102080).

HORSEBACK RIDING, CARRIAGE AND SLEIGH RIDES

For summer or winter excursions call **C. Flütsch** (☎ 081/4221873) or **R. Roffler** (☎ 081/4221566). For horseback riding contact **J. Marugg** (☎ 081/4221463).

PARAGLIDING

Grischa Flying School (☎ 081/4222070 or 079/3361919) will sign you up for introductory sessions in winter or summer. Passenger flights start at 160 SF, or you can have a trial day at 90 SF.

RAFTING

River-rafting experiences on the Rhine or Landquart rivers are not just for young adults; in Klosters children and seniors are catered to as well. Contact **Rätikon Adventure** (☎ 081/3252444) or ask for more information at the tourist office (Visitor information, *below*).

SKATING

Klosters's **Sportszentrum** (⊠ Doggilochstr. 11, Klosters-Platz, ☎ 081/4102131) offers rinks for skating, hockey, curling, and ice bowling in season. Skates are available for rent.

SLEDDING

There are three sled runs: Gotschna-Klosters, Alpenrösli, and Mälcheti-Aeuja. You can rent sleds at the **Andrist** (☎ 081/4102080) and **Sport Gotschna** (☎ 081/4221197) sports shops.

SWIMMING

The municipal heated **outdoor swimming pool** (⊠ Doggilochstr., ☎ 081/4221524) is open in summer. The **indoor pools** of the Hotel Pardenn (☎ 081/4221141), Hotel Sport (☎ 081/4222921), and Silvretta Parkhotel (☎ 081/4233435) are open to the public.

TENNIS

There are seven sand courts (five of which are floodlighted) to reserve at the **Sportszentrum** (☞ Skating, *above*). You can rent equipment at the Sportszentrum's **Tennis School Kämpf** (☎ 081/4102141).

Davos

⑤ *11 km (7 mi) south of Klosters.*

Davos, considered to be the highest town in Europe, is one of Switzerland's most esteemed winter resorts, famed for its ice sports and skiing. It also hosts the annual World Economic Forum. The town and its lake lie in the Landwasser Valley, which runs parallel to the Upper Engadine, though they're separated by the vast Albula chain, at some points more than 3,000 m (9,840 ft) high. On the opposite side of the valley stands the Strela chain, dominated by the **Weissfluh.**

Take note: this is a capital for action-oriented sports enthusiasts and not necessarily for anyone seeking a peaceful, rustic mountain retreat. Davos is divided into the Platz and the Dorf (village), which together are one noisier-than-average urban strip (of the two, Dorf is calmer). The town's first visitors came to take cures for lung diseases in the bracing mountain air. Now, except for a few token historic structures and brightly painted buildings, the town is modern and architecturally undistinguished. Yet this Alpine metropolis is surrounded by dramatic mountain passes and farms punctuated by weathered sheds and outbuildings. No matter how densely populated and fast-paced the town becomes, the slopes are still spectacular and the regulars return.

Among the town's few architectural highlights, the late-Gothic **Kirche St. Johann** (Church of St. John the Baptist) stands out by virtue of its windows by Augusto Giacometti. Nearby is the 17th-century **Rathaus** (Town Hall). ⊠ *Rathausstutz 2, Davos-Platz.*

The **Kirchner Museum** houses the world's largest collection of works by Ernst Ludwig Kirchner, the German Expressionist artist who came to Davos in 1917 to cure his failing health and stayed to paint. ⊠ *Promenade 82, Davos-Platz,* ☎ *081/4132202,* 🎫 *7 SF.* ☉ *Easter–Christmas, Tues.–Sun. 2–6; Christmas–Easter, Tues.–Sun. 10–noon and 2–6.*

The **Wintersportmuseum** has a collection of documents and equipment from sleds to ski bindings. ⊠ *Promenade 43, Davos-Platz,* ☎ *081/4132484.* 🎫 *5 SF.* ☉ *Dec.–Apr., Tues., Thurs., and Sat. 4:30–6:30.*

Skiing

Davos (1,560 m/5,116 ft) extends more than 35 km (22 mi) along a relatively sheltered valley floor that opens onto a fantastic panorama at higher elevations. Spanning from Laret (1507 m/4,942 ft) to Monstein (1,626 m/5,333 ft), the commune of Davos is Switzerland's second largest and can accommodate some 24,000 visitors on 325 km (202 mi) of runs.

The steep slopes of the **Parsenn-Gotschna** challenge hordes of experts. These slopes are accessed from the Schatzalp cable car or the Parsenn funicular, both in the town. Lines for the Parsenn can be off-puttingly long in high season. Locals and others in the know often prefer to ski on the **Rinerhorn,** a 15-minute bus or train ride out of town. Here the slopes lead to the hamlet of **Glaris,** 7 km (4½ mi) from Davos. A must for the skilled skier: the descent from **Weissfluhgipfel** (2,844 m/9,330 ft) to Küblis, in the Prättigau (814 m/2,670 ft). This magnificent, 12-km-long (7½-mi-long) piste has a vertical drop of 2,000 m (6,560 ft). **Jakobshorn,** a "fun" ski and snowboard area on the west-facing side, is reached by cable car and lift from Davos-Platz. The **Pischa** ski area, on the Flüela Pass road, and the **Bünda** slope, in Davos-Platz, are especially suitable for children and families. In addition, there are more than 75 km (47 mi) of prepared cross-country ski trails that are free of charge.

Lift tickets to the combined Davos/Klosters area costs up to 54 SF for one day, 228 SF for six days, depending on in which areas you choose to ski. Regional tickets include bus and train transport between the ski areas. Lessons are given by the Swiss **Snowsports School Davos** (☎ 081/4162454) and the **Snowboard School "Bananas"** (☎ 081/4101014). If you need to get completely outfitted for skiing, including clothing, go to **PaarSenn** (✉ Promenade 159, Davos-Dorf, ☎ 081/4101013). The **cross-country ski school** (☎ 081/4164455) is in Davos-Platz.

Dining and Lodging

$$–$$$ ✗ **Vinikus.** If you have had enough Bündner specialties, try this restaurant, which doubles as a store selling wines and spirits, pasta, and honey. Menus (three courses for lunch, four to five for dinner) change every few days depending on what fresh produce is available. You might find venison in a walnut crust with chestnut noodles or a roast with ratatouille. They also offer aperitif and wine evenings. ✉ *Promenade 119, Davos-Platz, ☎ 081/4165979. Reservations essential. AE, DC, MC, V. Closed Sun.–Mon. late Apr.–early July.*

$–$$$$ ✗⊞ **Hubli's Landhaus.** Though on the busy mountain highway between
★ Davos and Klosters, this country inn is quiet as well as comfortable and attractive with its rustic decor. The strong point by far is the food. Chef Felix Hubli prepares sophisticated fare (turbot with fennel and saffron, spring onion soup with truffles) and serves it in two lovely dining rooms: one for visitors, one for demipension guests, who—considering the à la carte prices—are getting a terrific deal. The guest rooms are modestly priced, beginning in the $ category for rooms with a sink and shared bathroom down the hall. ✉ *Kantonstr., CH-7265 Davos-Wolfgang, ☎ 081/4171010, FAX 081/4171011. 20 rooms. 2 restaurants. AE, DC, MC, V. Closed Mon. and late Apr.–early June and mid-Oct.–mid-Dec.* ❧

$$$$ ⊞ **Golfhotel Waldhuus.** Right at the edge of the golf course, this hotel re-creates the feel of a suburban country club on the outskirts of an Alpine town. Solid, sunny, and serene, with plenty of pine and stucco to soften its prefab look, it offers late sun on the terrace, a fireplace in the lobby, and the soothing tunes of a pianist in its bar. The rooms are decorated in country-casual miniature prints and pink linens. The restaurant serves standards with nouvelle twists such as pike quenelles with squid-ink pasta. ✉ *Mattastr. CH-7270 Davos-Platz, ☎ 081/4168131, FAX 081/4163939. 47 rooms. Restaurant, bar, indoor pool, sauna, driving range, 2 tennis courts, exercise room. AE, DC, MC, V.*

$$$$ ⊞ **Steigenberger Belvedere.** With its neoclassical stone fireplace, wedding-cake white plaster, and period details, this is a grand hotel in the full sense of the word. The enormous gray building with south-facing balconies is just above the main street. Rooms are decorated in styles ranging from Arvenholz rustic to classic mahogany; many have hardwood floors. The additional cost of superior-class rooms is worth it, as rooms with north and end views are inferior. ✉ *Promenade 89, CH-7270 Davos-Platz, ☎ 081/4156000, FAX 081/4156001. 133 rooms, 8 suites. 2 restaurants, bar, café, indoor pool, sauna, steam room, massage, hairdresser, kindergarten. AE, DC, MC, V. Closed early Apr.–late May and mid-Oct.–early Dec.* ❧

$$–$$$ ⊞ **Bünda.** This hotel is right by the beginners' ski slope and a ski school branch, as well as on the cross-country ski track. The Parsenn cable car is only a few minutes' walk. Rooms in the main building are smaller, some with showers instead of a full bath. Two share a bathroom. Larger, more expensive rooms are in the Residenz, connected to the hotel by an underground passage. ✉ *Museumstr., CH-7260 Davos-Dorf, ☎ 081/4163757, FAX 081/41664616. 31 rooms, 29 with bath. 2 restaurants, sauna, steam room, fitness room. AE, MC, DC, V. Closed mid-Apr.–early June.* ❧

$$–$$$ ▥ **Ochsen.** An ambitious young team runs this modest hotel. A few
of the hotel's rustic-style rooms take in views of the Jakobshorn (the
Jakobshorn station is just a few minutes' walk). The breakfast room
is wall-to-wall pine; the bar claims to have the biggest selection of
whiskies in Davos. ⊠ *Talstr. 10, CH-7270 Davos-Platz,* ☎ *081/
4154444,* ℻ *081/4154445. 47 rooms. Restaurant, bar, breakfast
room, Stübli. AE, DC, MC, V. Closed Apr. and mid-Oct.–late Nov.* ✎

Nightlife and the Arts

BARS AND CASINO

The **Hotel Europe** (⊠ Promenade 63, ☎ 081/4135921) houses the **EX
Bar,** where hipsters gather for live music and snacks, as well as the **Tonic
Piano Bar** which serves till 3 AM. There's a casino with 133 slot ma-
chines in the same building.

DANCING

The **Cabanna Club** (⊠ Hotel Europe, ☎ 081/4131200) lures an energetic crowd with techno decor and loud music. The **Cava Grischa** (☎
081/4130689) is at the same address; it spins a mix of rock, techno,
and hip hop. **Pöstli Club** (⊠ Promenade 42, ☎ 081/4137676) is a win-
ter-only institution with live bands ranging from rock to folk and pop.
The **Millennium Bar** (⊠ Hotel Seehof, Promenade 15, ☎ 081/4161212)
is a warren of connected vaulted cellars filled with bars, dancing, and
a cigar lounge.

MUSIC

The annual Young Artists in Concert festival is held from mid-July to
early August (dates vary). Young musicians from all over the world
practice and perform in churches and in the Congress Center.

Outdoor Activities and Sports

GOLF

Golf Club Davos (☎ 081/4165634) has 18 holes.

HIKING AND BIKING

Davos is threaded with more than 450 km (280 mi) of marked walks
and mountain trails. You can hike in winter and summer. Rental bikes
are available at the train station or at **Ettinger Sport** (⊠ Promenade 153
and Talstr. 6, ☎ 081/4101212). Through the tourist office (☞ Visitor
Information *in* Graubünden A to Z, *below*), serious walkers and cyclists
can arrange a four-day trip between Davos and Lenzerheide or Arosa.

PARAGLIDING

Delta- und Gleitschirmschule Davos (☎ 081/4136043) gives lessons and
offers tandem flights during Davos's summer and winter seasons.

SAILING AND WINDSURFING

Sailing and windsurfing are popular on Davos Lake. To rent boats or
take a lesson with a sailing school, call **Segelschule Davosersee** (☎ 081/
4161577) or **Hans Heierling** (☎ 081/4165918).

SKATING

Davos has long been reputed as an important ice-sports center, with
its enormous **Sportzentrum Eisbahn** (⊠ Talstr. 41, ☎ 081/4153600)
and speed-skating rink, the biggest natural ice track in Europe. The
Ice Stadium maintains one indoor and two outdoor rinks; rental skates
are available. You might also look into the skating tournament schedule if you'd like to see a competition. Watch for the famous Spengler
Cup international ice-hockey tournament at the end of December.

SPORTS CENTERS

The **Sports & High Altitude Center Davos** (☎ 081/4153600) offers field
facilities for amateurs and Olympians alike.

SWIMMING

Davos has an indoor-outdoor swimming **pool complex** (Hallenbad Davos, ⊠ Promenade 90, ☎ 081/4136463). You can also swim from the **Strandbad** (open beach; ☎ 081/4161505) in Davos Lake.

RACQUET SPORTS

Tennis and Squash Center Davos (⊠ Clavadelerstr., ☎ 081/4133131) has four indoor and five outdoor tennis courts, plus two squash and four badminton courts. Rental equipment is available for all three sports.

En Route The main road from Davos leads into the Engadine by way of the spectacular **Flüelapass** (Flüela Pass, open only in summer). For 16 km (13 mi) you climb southeast over mild grades and modest switchbacks. Dense larch forests give way to pine, then to fir, and finally, above the timberline, to a rocky, desolate waste of boulders and jutting cliffs. Ahead, on the left, are the rocky slopes of the **Weisshorn** 3,086 m/10,119 ft), with the **Schwarzhorn** (3,147 m/10,319 ft) to the right. Toward the summit, even in August, you may drive through snow. You'll pass between two small lakes: the Schottensee and the Schwarzsee. At the summit (2,383 m/7,816 ft), 14 km (9 mi) from Davos, is the **Flüela Hospiz** (☎ 081/4161747), a picturesque wooden chalet with a windmill, where you can get refreshments and a night's lodging at reasonable rates.

The descent from the Flüela Pass into the Romansh region of the Lower Engadine takes you through a narrow valley and across the River Susasca in sight of the 3,229-m (10,600-ft) Piz Vadret to the base of the great **Grialetsch**—a spectacular mass of jagged ice and snow. The road winds, following the increasingly torrential river and its deep, rocky gash, down to Susch, where the Susasca flows into the River Inn, or, in Romansh, En.

Because of the opening of the Vereina Tunnel, which provides train service year-round from Klosters to Sagliains, near Susch/Lavin (☞ Getting Around by Car *in* Graubünden A to Z, *below*), the Flüela Pass is closed in winter.

LOWER ENGADINE

Like Dorothy landing in Oz, you may find your sudden arrival here, in one of Graubünden's most picturesque valleys, something of a shock. You'll hear people talk of Schellenursli, a little boy with a big bell who features in a popular children's story about the festival of Chalanda Marz, held on March 1, which the whole Engadine marks as the end of winter. In an even longer-established folk festival, the children of Scuol make a sort of scarecrow, Hom Strom ("man of straw"), which is burned in February to chase away winter. "*Allegra!*" is the proper greeting on the street, reflecting the Romansh language. The houses typically have deep Etruscan-arch doors, thick walls, and sunken windows. Look for built-in wooden benches at front entrances, a triangular window from which grandparents can watch what is going on in the street, and for the ever-present decorative sgraffiti—the signature of the Engadine. A layer of dark gray stucco is whitewashed, then designs and sometimes sayings are scraped into the paint to reveal the base color. The Lower Engadine—more enclosed than its upper counterpart—shares the region's dry, crisp "champagne" climate.

Susch

❻ *27 km (17 mi) east of Davos.*

Susch guards the entrance to the Lower Engadine, guarded itself by the magnificent Piz d'Arpiglias (3,289 m/9,930 ft). Here the River

Susasca tumbles into the Inn. The two towers of **Kirche St. Jon** (Church of St. John) stand high over the river, one Romanesque, the other—like the body of the church—dating from 1515. During a restoration in 1742, the late-Gothic style of the windows was changed, but in 1933 they were restored to their original form.

Guarda

★ ❼ *7 km (4 mi) east of Susch.*

Between Susch and the resort towns of Scuol and Bad-Tarasp Vulpera, a scenic valley passes through several gorges and then emerges into flow-ered plains and a pleasant chain of hamlets: Lavin, Guarda, Ardez, and Ftan. These are summer-oriented villages in which hotels are normally closed in winter. Each offers a new show of fine sgraffitied homes, but Guarda deserves a leisurely exploration among its steep, patterned-cob-ble streets. The federal government protects the architecture, and row upon row of the vivid dark-on-white etchings, contrasting sharply with the bright red geraniums lined up on the windowsills, draw pedes-trians from one photo stop to another. As its name implies, Guarda ("watch") sits high on a hillside looking out over the valley and the peaks to the south, which reach up to 3,000 m (9,840 ft).

Lodging

$$$ ⊞ **Meisser.** This brightly colored house, family-owned and -run, lives up to its picturesque setting, with sgraffiti and flower boxes outside, antiques and Swiss pine inside. There are a grand Victorian dining hall with pine wainscoting and parquet and a more casual porch restau-rant with spectacular valley views. Some rooms are simple and mod-ern, though you can have a splendid carved-pine room if you pay a little bit more. An adjacent, renovated 17th-century farmhouse has a half-dozen suites. Beginning in December 2000, the hotel will also be open in winter. ⊠ *CH-7545,* ☎ *081/8622132,* 𝖥𝖠𝖷 *081/8622480. 21 rooms, 6 suites. 2 restaurants, playground. AE, DC, MC, V. Closed mid-Apr.–late May and early Nov.–late Dec.* ⊗

Scuol and Bad Tarasp-Vulpera

13 km (8 mi) east of Guarda.

Wedged in a corner of Switzerland, close to the Austrian border, the villages of Scuol and Bad Tarasp-Vulpera effectively form one vaca-tion and health-resort complex. It owes its popularity to the beautiful surroundings of mountains and dense forests; the 20 mineral springs, traditionally used for liver cures; and the proximity of the Parc Nazi-unal Svizzer (☞ *below*). Previously only summer resort areas, today the villages also fill up in winter, thanks to the network of gondolas and ski lifts on the south-facing slopes of Motta Naluns.

Scuol, a small town, has a busy center and a small but exemplary *Alt-stadt* (Old Town), with five functional fountains from which you can do a taste-test comparison of normal tap water against the area's spring water. For the inside-and-out spa experience, head for the **Bogn Engiadina Scuol,** one of Europe's most modern spas. The calming blue interior, fantastic aquatic murals, and shifting reflections from back-lighted pools start relaxing you before your toes even touch the water. Six basins, both indoor and outdoor, are filled from the mineral spring and range in temperature from 60°F to 90°F. There are also saunas, solariums, steam rooms, and a massage section. A special Roman-Irish ritual treatment alternates between moist and dry heat, massage and mineral baths. A therapy center offers mud baths, gymnastics, and elec-trotherapy (if you have a doctor's prescription). If you prefer to drink the water rather than lie in it, four varieties are available. ⊠ *Town center,* ☎ *081/8612000.* 🎟 *23 SF for bathing and sauna area; 54 SF with Roman-Irish baths.* ⊙ *Daily 9 AM–10 PM. Closed May.*

The other two villages are on the opposite side of the river from Scuol. Vulpera consists mainly of a huge Robinson Club complex and other hotels and apartments, plus its mineral spring in the Trinkhalle. The hamlet is truly tiny; its permanent residents number just five. From here you can take a 15-minute bus ride up to Tarasp, a cluster of houses, small farms, and inns grouped around a tiny lake. The village is dominated by the impressive stronghold **Schloss Tarasp,** perched 500 ft above. The main tower and chapel date from the 11th century, when the castle was built by the leading family of Tarasp. Tarasp became part of Austria in 1464; the imperial eagle still can be seen on the castle walls. In the early 1800s, Napoléon gave Tarasp to the canton Graubünden, newly part of the Swiss federation. The castle went through several changes of hands and subsequent neglect before it was acquired in the early 20th century by a German businessman. Today it's owned by Princess Margret von Heessen. You must join a tour to see the interior; the schedule varies quite a bit, so call ahead for tour times. The bus from Vulpera goes roughly every hour. You could walk the route from Scuol, following a yellow-marked path that goes over the Punt'-Ota (Punt Ota Bridge). The walk takes about 1½ hours. ☎ *081/ 8649368.* ⊙ *June–Oct., daily; Christmas–Easter, Tues. and Thurs.*

Skiing and Snowboarding

The region's ski area centers around 16 gondolas and lifts going up Scuol's **Motta Naluns,** at elevations between 1,250 and 2,800 m (4,100 and 9,184 ft). The 80 km (50 mi) of trails include the 12-km (7½-mi) Traumpiste (Dream Run), a good run of medium difficulty, with a few tough areas. Machine-made snow keeps descents to the valley open throughout the season. Lift tickets cost 46 SF for one day, 202 SF for six days; prices drop a bit in January and after mid-March. There's also the Snow Bathing Pass, which includes entry to Bogn Engiadina. This costs 65 SF for one day, 285 SF for six days. Tarasp has one short ski lift for beginners. Bus transport between Scuol/Sent and Scuol/Tarasp-Vulpera is free of charge if you have a ski pass.

Snowboarding is extremely popular on these broad, sunny slopes. Scuol's snowboard school, **The School** (☎ 081/8648220), is the oldest in Europe. You could also sign up with **Schweizer Schneesportschule Scuol** (☎ 081/8641723) for instruction in Alpine and cross-country skiing. There are 60 km (37 mi) of prepared cross-country tracks around Scuol; these cost 5 SF per day, 20 SF per week. Rental equipment is available at sports shops in Scuol and next to the Motta Naluns cable-car station.

Dining and Lodging

$$$ ✕🏠 **Schlosshotel Chastè.** This hidden treasure, now in the Relais and
★   Châteaux association, has been in the Pazeller family's care for 500 years. It started as a farm, then supplied provisions to builders of Tarasp Castle, which looms above. It eventually drew overnight guests—and today it's an impeccable, welcoming inn with every comfort. The Pazellers have preserved the exterior, and behind the magnificently carved wood door, extraordinary effort has been made to match and modernize. Each room varies a bit from the others: a canopy bed here, an antique trunk there, and honey-color Arvenholz everywhere. Rudolf Pazeller himself is the chef and offers a small but sophisticated menu; his fish dishes, such as the fish terrine, are outstanding. ⊠ *CH-7553 Tarasp,* ☎ *081/8641775,* 📠 *081/8649970. 20 rooms. Restaurant, bar, Stübli, sauna, steam room. AE, DC, MC, V. Closed early Apr.– late May and mid-Oct.–mid-Dec.* 🍴

$$$ ⊞ **Guardaval.** This Romantik hotel preserves its original 17th-century wing, with its stucco vaulting and heavy beams, but the rest of the building is up-to-date. The dining/breakfast room shows off mountain views through two stories of windows, and the public areas are dripping with atmosphere (carved and painted antique furniture, hunting trophies). Rooms have spare decor in white and pine. Because the old part of the building is protected by law, a few rooms are almost museumlike. ⊠ *CH-7550 Scuol,* ☎ *081/8641321,* ℻ *081/8649767. 38 rooms. Restaurant, bar, sauna, steam room. DC, MC, V.* 🍽

$$–$$$ ⊞ **Villa Maria.** Family owned and run, this hillside retreat on the road to Tarasp has an elite, genteel air, with flowers on the antique furniture and Oriental rugs on the quarry tile. The rooms are homey but fresh, and some have balconies overlooking the forested valley. The main restaurant has a fireplace and serves food based on fresh market produce; the chef also grows his own vegetables. There's also a small fondue Stübli should you be struck by cheese cravings. ⊠ *CH-7552 Vulpera,* ☎ *081/8641138,* ℻ *081/8649161. 15 rooms. 2 restaurants, bar. AE, DC, MC, V.* 🍽

$$
★ ⊞ **Engiadina.** This typical Engadine house, with sgraffiti, oriels, vaulting, and beams, was built during the 16th century in the lower section of Scuol. Newer guest rooms are done in beige tones touched with bright reds or blues, while four older units surround you with Swiss pine. Spacious, loftlike apartments, which are in a second house, can also be rented. The main restaurant and the Arvenstube have a welcoming, country feel, with light wood, blue linens, and cushions in every corner. ⊠ *Rablüzza, CH-7550 Scuol,* ☎ *081/8641421,* ℻ *081/8641245. 10 rooms, 2 apartments. 2 restaurants. MC, V. Closed late Apr.–mid-June and mid-Oct.–mid-Dec.*

$$ ⊞ **Traube.** This friendly inn reflects the personal touch: the rooms are all wood, the baths are all tile, and the public areas—in parquet or tile and pine, with antiques and a ceramic stove—are pristine. The candlelighted restaurant draws on market-fresh produce; the menu includes hearty risottos and homemade Nusstorte. You can also try water from the hotel's own iron-rich mineral spring in the basement. Although it's in town, a sun terrace with mountain views is available for summer use. ⊠ *CH-7550 Scuol,* ☎ *081/8610700,* ℻ *081/8610777. 19 rooms. Restaurant, Stübli, sauna. AE, DC, MC, V. Closed mid-Apr.–early June and late Oct.–mid-Dec.*

$$ ⊞ **Element Igloos.** Here's an alternative to the usual pine guest room: a night in an igloo on Motta Naluns. The igloos are built at the beginning of the winter season (you can also join a building party). The price excludes the cable-car fare but includes a hot evening meal of soup, fondue, or a barbecue, extra-thick sleeping bags and sheepskins for the night, and a hot breakfast in the morning. You'll beat everyone else to the cable cars. ⊠ *CH-7500 Scuol,* ☎ *081/8600600,* ℻ *081/8600601. AE, DC, MC, V.*

Outdoor Activities and Sports

BIKING

Rental bicycles are available at sport shops and the Motta Naluns cable-car station. For the adventurous, bikes can be taken up the mountain on the cable car; once up, you can bike on your own or go on a guided tour. Contact the tourist office (☞ Visitor Information *in* Graubünden A to Z *below*) for details.

GOLF

There is a **nine-hole course** and driving range (☎ 081/8649688) open in Vulpera from late May to early October. Winter golf is played in Tarasp from late January on for as long as conditions hold. Contact Herr Jäger at the Hotel Villa Maria (☞ *above*).

ICE SPORTS

Open-air ice rinks for hockey, curling, and skating are available in Scuol from early December to early March at **Sportanlage Trü** (☎ 081/8612000). **Eishalle Gurlaina** (☎ 081/8640272), in Scuol, has indoor facilities and skates for rent. There are three main **sled runs,** which are between 2½ and 7 km (1½ and 4½ mi) long; two end in Scuol, while the other ends in the nearby village of Ftan. You can rent a sled at the Motta Naluns mountain station or from **Sport Conradin** (☎ 081/8641410) or **Sport Heinrich** (☎ 081/8641956) in Scuol.

PARAGLIDING AND HANG GLIDING

For paragliding and flyovers (beginners to advanced gliders), contact the tourist office (☞ Visitor Information *in* Graubünden A to Z, *below*).

RAFTING AND CANOEING

Swissraft (⊠ Scuol, ☎ 081/9115250) organizes daily rafting expeditions in rubber dinghies on the River Inn from late May to early October. **Engadin Adventure** (⊠ Motta Naluns, ☎ 081/8611414) runs rafting and canoeing excursions from early June to mid-September.

TENNIS

Reserve sand courts in Scuol through **Tennis Gurlaina** (☎ 081/8640643); the courts are available from mid-May to mid-October, and coaching also is available. **Robinsons Club Schweizerhof** (☎ 081/8611700), in Vulpera, has two indoor courts and two outdoor sand courts. You can also rent equipment.

Zernez

❽ *6 km (4 mi) south of Susch.*

This small town lies at the crossroads of the Lower Engadine and the route over the Ofen Pass to the Val Müstair and Italy. Serious hikers sporting loden hats, knickers, warm kneesocks, and sturdy boots come to stock up on picnic goods, day packs, and topographical maps before setting off for the Swiss National Park (☞ *below*). It's also a good overnight spot for park visits and for winter cross-country skiing. The Alpine skiing areas of the Lower and Upper Engadine are accessible by public transport.

Dining and Lodging

$–$$ ⌘ **Bär-Post.** After a first life as a post stagecoach stop in the late 1800s, this has been a family-run hotel since 1905. The pale yellow, blue-trimmed exterior conceals a rustic, wood-clad interior. All rooms have baths with either tub or shower. The main difference between the higher- and lower-priced rooms is size, but all are very comfortable. There are three restaurants in addition to the high-ceiling, parquet-floor dining room. A pool and tennis court open in summer. ⊠ *CH-7530,* ☎ *081/8515500,* FAX *081/8515599. 46 rooms. 4 restaurants, sauna. AE, DC, V. Closed late Oct.–late Dec.* ⌘

$ ⌘ **Chasa Veglia.** "The old house" with its converted barn is down a
★ quiet side street. The owner's wood-carving skills are on display at every turn, from the doors and chairs to ceilings and fretwork panels over the wall lighting. (There's one intricately carved bed that he did not work on—it dates from 1762.) Rugs on parquet floors and a display of old farm and kitchen implements add to the atmosphere. One room is an exception, decorated in a pink ultramodern "baroque" style. Rooms are small; those without a bathtub have a shower, except for two rooms with only a toilet and sink. ⊠ *CH-7530,* ☎ FAX *081/2844868 or 081/8561351. 11 rooms, 4 with bath. Breakfast room. No credit cards. Closed early May–mid-June and early Nov.–late Dec.* ⌘

$ 🔲 **Piz Terza.** This garni hotel is completely modern behind its traditional facade; its rooms have plain built-in cabinetry and a utilitarian look. Yet the back rooms have balconies, and each has its own box of geraniums—an indication of the management's friendly approach to bargain hotel service. The public pool is across the street; the National Park Information Center is just a block away. ⊠ *CH-7530,* ☎ *081/ 8561414,* FAX *081/8561415. 20 rooms. No credit cards. Closed mid-Mar.–early June and late Oct.–Christmas.*

Parc Naziunal Svizzer

★ ❾ *Access roads from Zernez, Scuol, S-Chanf, and the Ofen Pass.*

The Swiss National Park is a magnificent nature reserve of virtually virgin wilderness. Although its 169 square km (105 square mi) equal only 1% or 2% of the territory of a U.S. or Canadian national park, it has none of the developments that typically hint of "accessibility" and "attraction": no campgrounds, no picnic sites, no residents. It also has few employees: just a handful of staffers run the visitor center, and the rangers live outside the park. This is genuine wilderness. Dead wood is left to rot, insects to multiply, and only carefully screened scholars are allowed to perform preapproved experiments. As a result, the park contains large herds of ibex with their long, curving horns; short-horned chamois; red deer and roe deer; and vast colonies of marmots. Before heading into the park, visit the **Nationalpark-Haus** (National Park House) in Zernez, where you can get the latest information on the likely whereabouts of animals, watch a video in English, get a map, and look at the natural history exhibition. Also, don't forget to rent binoculars; without them you might not see much in the way of fauna.

Remember that the park's animals are not conditioned by human contact. You may feel more privileged at the sight of a group of ibex on a distant hill, or a herd of male red deer, their antlers silhouetted above a snowy ridge, than when snapping close-up pictures of a dozen Yellowstone bison. But if the big game make no appearance, rein in your expectations and try to follow the park's advice: "Appreciate a butterfly or an ant as much as a herd of chamois."

Other signs, flyers, and brochures reiterate the park's philosophy of restriction and conservation, adopting an almost scolding tone in five languages: "Wastepaper and other residues disfigure natural beauty. Take them with you! Don't pick a single flower! Leave your dog at home!" The list of prohibitions includes hunting, fishing, camping, picking berries, taking plants (with or without the roots), grazing cattle, carrying guns, skiing, making commercial movies, even making loud noises. Nonetheless, the wildlife give a wide berth to the 80 km (50 mi) of marked pathways.

Trails start out from small parking lots off the park's only highway (visitors are encouraged to take postbuses back to their starting point), a series of wild, rough, and often steep paths takes off into the coniferous forests. From Parking 7 the Il Fuorn–Stabelchod–Val dal Botsch trail marks botanical and natural phenomena with multilingual information boards and leads to a spectacular barren ridge at 2,340 m (7,672 ft); the round-trip takes about four hours.

A three-hour route, from picturesque S-chanf (pronounced sss-*chanff*) to Trupchun, takes the Höheweg, or High Road, into a deep glacial valley where ibex and chamois often gather; the return, by a riverside trail, passes a handy log snack bar—just across the park border and thus permitted. Visitors are restricted to the trails except at designated resting places, where broad circles are marked for hikers to collapse in and have lunch. ⊠ *Nationalpark–Haus, CH-7530, Zernez, leaving the village toward Ofenpass,* ☎ *081/8561378,* 🅵🅰🆇 *081/8561740.* 🍽 *4 SF.* ☉ *June–Oct., Wed.–Mon. 8:30–6, Tues. 8:30 AM–10 PM.* 🍽

Lodging

$$ 🏨 **Il Fuorn.** This mountain inn was built in 1894 in the middle of what is now the Swiss National Park. It's on the highway, and it makes an ideal base for hikers tackling more than one route. Choose from either old-style rooms without bath (though there are sinks in the rooms) or pine-and-stucco rooms with bath in the new wing, added in 1980. The plain Swiss cooking is augmented by a salad bar. ⊠ *CH-7530,* ☎ *081/8561226,* 🅵🅰🆇 *081/8561801. 32 rooms, 12 with bath. Restaurant, Stübli. AE, DC, MC, V. Closed late Oct.–mid-May.* 🍽

En Route Driving south along the River Inn from the Swiss National Park toward its source in the Upper Engadine Valley, you will pass **Zuoz,** one of the most attractive Upper Engadine villages, with its small, uncrowded ski area and cross-country trails in winter and its fountains and overflowing flower boxes in summer. Neat modern buildings mix with the core of old Engadine houses. It's a peaceful, Romansh-flavored stop before reaching the busier resorts farther up the valley.

UPPER ENGADINE

Stretching from Maloja to Brail and with a gate to the vast Swiss National Park at S-chanf, this is one of the country's highest regions—the highest settlement is at 2,046 m (6,710 ft)—and one of its most dazzling. From mountain peaks, such as Piz Corvatsch or Piz Nair, you can swoosh down world-class slopes or simply take in the dizzying view over the lakes and mountains. Besides summer and winter sports, both seasons are packed tight with cultural and events programs (☞ Festivals and Seasonal Events *in* Chapter 1). Summer is also when the lowland farmers send their cows up, by truck or by train, so they can have a relaxing mountain holiday, too.

Samedan

⑩ *27 km (17 mi) southwest of Zernez, 10 km (6 mi) northeast of St. Moritz.*

This small, if less prestigious, resort is the administrative capital of the Upper Engadine; it was once its largest community. There are magnificent views of the awe-inspiring Bernina chain to the south, including the permanently snowcapped **Piz Bernina** (4,057 m/13,300 ft), Graubünden's highest peak, and **Piz Palü** (3,905 m/12,808 ft). The town has several good sports facilities, from a rollerblading track to a small ski area. Host to the Upper Engadine's airfield, it has a popular gliding center that's open in summer. The 18-hole golf course (☞ St. Moritz, *below*) is the highest in Europe, but with hardly any noticeable gradients. Access to the Upper Engadine's main ski areas is provided by the Engadin Bus service, which is included in the price of a regional ski ticket (☞ St. Moritz, *below*).

Dining

$$–$$$ ✕ **Berghotel Muottas Muragl.** For a meal with a truly spectacular view, ★ reserve a window table here, on a mountainside outside town (☞ En Route, *below*). The menu covers international, Swiss, and regional specialties, such as pizzocheri and capuns with smoked ham. The international wine list is the result of the English manager's worldwide winery visits. There's a "smoker's den," where you can also choose a cigar and a whisky after your meal. Bright, very simple guest rooms are available if you'd like to spend a night in total peace and quiet. ⊠ *CH-7503 Punt Muragl,* ☎ *081/8428232. AE, DC, MC, V. Closed mid-Apr.–late May and mid-Oct.–mid-Dec.*

En Route   At **Punt Muragl,** off the highway between Samedan and Pontresina, you'll
★   find the funicular for **Muottas Muragl** at 2,456 m (8,055 ft). Up here
walkers can take the Philosophers' Path, which is dotted with quota-
tions from famous minds like Socrates and Descartes, as well as ob-
servations about life from present-day "laypeople." Following the
three circular paths takes about 2½ hours. Two lifts give access to limited, easy skiing. These, together with a playground, make Muottas a
good excursion for children. An alternative way back down to the valley is the 4.2 km (2.6 mi) sled run. Sleds can be rented at the valley
station. The funicular fare is 26 SF, 15 SF for an evening round-trip.

Pontresina

⑪   *5 km (3 mi) south of Samedan.*

Pontresina, lying on a south-facing shelf along the Flaz Valley, grew by
converting its farmhouses to pensions and hotels, primarily for use by summer tourists. Today its climbing school is making a name for itself, and
the village is a popular hiking center. From here you can see clear across
to the Roseg Valley, once filled with the Roseg Glacier, which has retreated
to the base of Piz Roseg itself. The Flaz River winds through the moun-
tain-framed valley from its source, the Morteratsch Glacier, which oozes
down from Piz Bernina. Although the main street is built up with restaurants and shops, the resort still has the feel of a balanced vacation retreat.
Every second Thursday in July and August, there's a street market in the
lower part of the village, with local produce and crafts for sale, as well
as live music and long picnic tables—a good place to meet some locals.

The **Museum Alpin** gives some local background and history; be sure
to check out the room full of birds, whose recorded songs can be
heard at the push of a button. ⊠ *Via Maistra,* ☎ *081/8427273.* 🖭 *5*
SF. ☉ *Mid-June–mid-Oct. and late Dec.–mid-Apr., Mon.–Sat. 4–6.*

Skiing
There is a small beginners' slope in the village at San Spiert. The small-
ish ski areas of **Diavolezza** (2,968 m/9,768 ft) and, on the other side
of the road, **Lagalb** (2,959 m/9,705 ft), on the Bernina Pass, complement the much more extensive ones of St. Moritz. All three are about
20 minutes away by bus. Lift tickets cost 58 SF for one day, 274 SF
for a six-day regional ticket. Rides on the Engadin Bus service are included in the price of a regional ski ticket (☞ St. Moritz, *below*). There
is a **Ski and Snowboard School** (☎ 081/8388383), as well as the **To-
lais cross-country ski center** (☎ 081/8426844), below the village, on
the Engadin Marathon trail.

Dining and Lodging
$–$$ ✕ **Steinbock.** Owned by the Walther family (☞ Hotel Walther, *below*),
this 17th-century house has been modernized in keeping with Engadine style—lots of wood and warm colors. The Colani Stübli, named
after a famous Engadine hunter, serves regional and seasonal specialties. Appropriately, the game dishes in autumn are exceptional, such
as *Gemspfeffer* (chamois ragout cooked in wine) with hazelnut *Spätzli* (tiny pasta dumplings) and red cabbage. For dessert you might try
Nusskrapfen, puff pastry with a sticky nut filling. ⊠ *Via Maistra,* ☎
081/8426371. AE, DC, MC, V.

$ ✕ **Café Puntschella.** Either way you look here, you can't go wrong:
★   you'll face either the Roseg Valley or the spread of fresh-made pastries.
The menu can satisfy all kinds of cravings, from bowls of breakfast
muesli to hearty ravioli. Locals know to ask for the beignet-like *Quarki-
nis* with vanilla sauce—as well as a seat on the terrace. ⊠ *Via Mulin,*
☎ *081/8388030. V. Closed Mon. and Tues. in May.*

$$$$ ✕▥ **Kronenhof.** This grand hotel began life as a stop for stagecoaches
★ running Veltliner wine over the Bernina Pass. The building was completed in 1898, and the exterior has changed very little since then. The
views from the lobby bay and the baroque splendor of some ceilings—
with elaborate moldings, pink cherubs, and blushing nymphs—are dazzling. In such surroundings, jacket and tie are expected in the evenings.
Rooms are tastefully done, with Biedermeier furniture. The lawn that
sprawls out toward the Roseg Valley is a social center in summer and
winter, with tennis courts doubling as an ice rink and a pavilion for taking in the sun. The Kronenstübli, all in pine, serves international cuisine du marché—such as millefeuille of monkfish and eggplant or roast
lamb with an olive crust—and the wine may be drawn from the still-
functioning Veltlinerkeller (wine cellar) below. ⊠ CH-7504, ☎ 081/
8303030, ℻ 081/8303031. 93 rooms. 2 restaurants, bar, café, indoor-
outdoor pool, hairdresser, massage, sauna, steam room, 2 tennis courts,
bowling, ice-skating, kindergarten. AE, DC, MC, V. ✅

$$$$ ✕▥ **Walther.** Though built in 1907, this hotel's interior is contempo-
★ rary, save for a few ornate moldings; the look is gracious without being
overly formal. The restaurant serves beautifully presented international dishes; you can also eat at the more casual Steinbock next door
(☞ above). The decor is strictly classical, with discreet blues and yellows in public rooms. Guest rooms have pastel color schemes and modern baths; those with south-facing balconies are most in demand. The
pool is in a pavilion that opens on to a wooded garden. ⊠ CH-7504,
☎ 081/8426471, ℻ 081/8427922. 62 rooms, 9 suites. 2 restaurants,
piano bar, indoor pool, hot tub, massage, sauna, steam room, 3 tennis courts, indoor driving range, health club, bicycles (summer). AE,
DC, MC, V. Closed Easter–mid-June and mid-Oct.–Christmas. ✅

$ ✕▥ **Roseggletscher.** You can reach this isolated, traditional hotel near
★ the base of the Roseg Glacier on foot or by horse-drawn carriage or
sleigh (it's about 7½ km/4½ mi up the ruggedly beautiful Roseg Valley). The restaurant offers simple regional favorites. In fall there is game
from the surrounding countryside; hunting trophies adorn the walls.
This is a very popular lunch spot for hikers, bikers, and cross-country
skiers, who reward themselves with a selection from the massive dessert
buffet. The rooms are spartan but fresh; you pay a little more for a
private shower. ⊠ CH-7504, ☎ 081/8426445, ℻ 081/8426886. 13
rooms, 6 with bath, 3 dorm rooms. Restaurant, cafeteria. AE, V.

$$$ ▥ **Saratz.** The marriage of tradition and innovation is wonderfully ef-
★ fective throughout this revamped 19th-century grand hotel. A spacious
lobby with huge windows and a 60-room wing, built in toast-color tufa
in the spirit of the hotel's original stone portals, extend the building
lengthwise. Interiors are done in warm yellow-greens and orange-reds.
Room decor ranges from gilt-mirror grandeur in the renovated part
of the house to modern design. You can dine in the period à la carte
restaurant or try ethnic specialties in one of the old Stübli of the
Pitschna Scena, where there is regular live music. The hotel is child-
friendly, with family-accommodating suite-style rooms, a kindergarten,
and even special cereals on a kid-size breakfast bar. The views of the
Roseg Valley from the lobby terrace, or from anywhere within the hotel's
extensive grounds, are inspiring. Rates are very reasonable for the
price category, but there is an extra charge for south and south-side
corner rooms. ⊠ CH-7504, ☎ 081/8394000, ℻ 081/8394040. 92
rooms. 2 restaurants, bar, indoor pool, outdoor pool, sauna, massage,
Turkish bath. AE, DC, MC, V. Closed early Apr.–early June and mid-
Oct.–early Dec. ✅

$$$ ▥ **Schweizerhof.** The refreshingly spacious and modern public areas
here have sleek lines and colorful leather furniture. Guest rooms are
more traditional, with Arvenholz accents; rooms with balconies fac-

ing southwest are more expensive. The main restaurant has a verandah extension; there's also a fondue Stübli. There's a grassy summer roof terrace, and the public pool is across the street. ⊠ *CH-7504,* ☎ *081/8420131,* FAX *081/8427988. 70 rooms. 2 restaurants, piano bar, Stübli, hot tub, sauna, hairdresser. AE, DC, MC, V. Closed Easter–late June and mid-Oct.–mid-Dec.* 🍃

$–$$ 🏠 **Bahnhof.** Right next to the entrance to the Roseg Valley, the cross-country skiing center, and (as the name suggests) the train station, the hotel offers dependable, low-key accommodations. Rooms have sinks with bathrooms down the hall; one room in an adjoining house has a shower. The restaurant, with its pink linen and flowers, offers simple fare at reasonable prices. ⊠ *CH-7504,* ☎ *081/8388000,* FAX *081/ 8388009. 22 rooms. Restaurant, café. AE, DC, MC, V.* 🍃

Nightlife and the Arts

BARS AND LOUNGES

Popular nightspots include **Cento Bar** (⊠ Hotel Müller, ☎ 081/8426341), a local hangout with rustic furnishings; **Bar "Pitschna Scena"** (⊠ Hotel Saratz, ☎ 081/8394000), which has live music every Thursday in both summer and winter; **Piano-Bar** (⊠ Sporthotel, ☎ 081/8426331), a cozy, blond-wood bar; and the trendy **Pöstli-Keller** (⊠ Hotel Post, ☎ 081/8426318), geared toward a younger crowd.

DANCING

Sarazena (⊠ Via Maistra, ☎ 081/8426353), in an old Engadine house, starts the night as a moodlighted restaurant serving Far- and Middle Eastern, Spanish, and Italian food. At 11 PM the restaurant makes way for a dance floor with music to a disco beat and occasional live performances. It keeps going until 3 AM.

MUSIC

The **Kurorchester Pontresina** plays chamber concerts daily between mid-June and mid-September at 11 AM in the Taiswald (Tais Forest) free of charge. Other concerts are held at various times in the Rondo Congress, Cultural and Information Center; check with the tourist office (☞ Visitor Information *in* Graubünden A to Z, *below*) for more information.

Outdoor Activities and Sports

BICYCLING

Conventional and mountain bikes can be rented at **Fähndrich-Sport** (☎ 081/8427155), **Flück Sport** (☎ 081/8426262), and **Michel Massé** (☎ 081/8426824).

CARRIAGE AND SLEIGH RIDES

Horse-drawn carriages or, in winter, sleigh rides can be booked through **M. Keiser** (☎ 081/8426620) or **P. Thom** (☎ 081/8426543). The Roseg Valley "horse omnibus" is run by **L. Costa** (☎ 081/8426057) as a scheduled service in summer and winter. The trip is very popular, so be sure to make a reservation.

FISHING

Trout fishing in the Lej Nair and Lej Pitschen mountain lakes is free for Pontresina guests in season, from mid-June to mid-September. For license information, contact the tourist office (☞ Visitor Information *in* Graubünden A to Z, *below*).

HIKING

Pontresina village or the top of the Alp Languard chairlift (open only in summer) are good starting points for hikers. The Diavolezza and Lagalb cable cars operate also in summer; schedules vary. Guided excursions include the Swiss National Park, Languard, or Lagalb for sunrise walks, mushroom hunting in season (usually August–September), and glacier hiking on the Morteratsch Glacier. Call the tourist office (☞ Visitor Information *in* Graubünden A to Z, *below*) for info. If you are staying in Pontresina overnight, the tours are free of charge, though you will have to pay any transport costs; day visitors pay a small fee.

MOUNTAINEERING AND CLIMBING

Bergsteigerschule Pontresina (Pontresina Mountain Climbing School; ⌧ Via Maistra, ☏ 081/8388333) is the biggest in Switzerland and offers rock and ice instruction for both beginners and advanced climbers, plus private guided tours. Along with the tourist office and the ski school, it's in the Rondo Congress, Cultural and Information Center.

RAFTING

For white-water rafting excursions on the Flaz River, call **Michel Massé** (☏ 081/8426824).

SKATING AND CURLING

There's a large natural ice-skating rink off the main street in winter; rental skates are available. Ten curling rinks with instructors are available at **Sportpavilion Roseg** (⌧ Via Maistra, ☏ 081/8426346 or 081/8426349) from December through March.

SWIMMING

In addition to an indoor pool, **Pontresina Hallenbad** (⌧ Via Maistra, ☏ 081/8427341 or 081/8428257) offers a sauna, a solarium, and a sunbathing terrace.

TENNIS

Thirteen public tennis courts are available in Pontresina at different hotels; inquire at the tourist office (☞ Visitor Information *in* Graubünden A to Z, *below*). **Gruber Sport** (⌧ Via Maistra, ☏ 081/8426236) rents racquets.

Celerina

⓬ *2 km (1 mi) south of Samedan, 3 km (1¾ mi) northeast of St. Moritz*

Celerina (Schlarigna in Romansh) lies just below St. Moritz, at the foot of that resort's bobsled and Cresta runs (☞ *below*). Even though it may seem overshadowed by its more famous neighbor, Celerina is a first-rate winter resort in its own right; not only does it share the ski area of Corviglia/Marguns with St. Moritz, but it is reputed to be the sunniest place in the valley. A cluster of Engadine houses characterizes its oldest neighborhood. Its most striking landmark stands just outside the village: the 15th-century church of **San Gian** (St. John), which has a richly painted wooden ceiling. The church lost its spire in a lightning strike in 1682. Many years later an offer to replace the spire was turned down, as it was thought the church looked more impressive without it. ☉ *Mid-June–mid-Oct. Mon. 2–4, Wed. 4–5:30, and Fri. 10:30–noon.*

St. Moritz

★ ⓭ *5 km (3 mi) west of Pontresina, 85 km (53 mi) southeast of Chur.*

St. Moritz is one of the world's best-known winter resorts and is even a registered trademark. It's had longer than most to build its reputation, as winter tourism began here in 1864. The town has been a favorite among celebrities, blue bloods, tycoons, and wanna-bes for generations, though nowadays the winter crowds also include nature lovers and sports enthusiasts. Fur coats mix with anoraks and colorful cross-country ski leggings.

The resort stands at the edge of a lake; the original center around the spa (Bad) is at lake level, with the village (Dorf) above. At the top of the Dorf is St. Moritz's answer to Pisa—its own leaning tower, which is all that's left of a 13th-century church. It can't be denied that it's a small town and not of the picturesque chocolate-box-lid variety. It has its fair share of unattractive buildings and, in the winter, high-season traffic problems. But the latter have improved quite a bit since the creation of a pedestrians-only zone in the village, which hosts a Christmas market and other celebrations.

Some of the top hotels in the world are here, but if you'd rather not splurge on such luxury accommodations, you can see the same beautiful scenery—and enjoy the scene—without digging too deep into your pocket. You can window-shop the designer boutiques from A(rmani) to Z(egna), savor chocolates from a *confiserie,* or relax with coffee and cake on a sunny café terrace.

The resort's events calendar is especially impressive. This is the place to see unique winter sports; some were or still are found only here, such as polo played on snow, bobsledding on natural ice, the Cresta run, and horseracing on snow, including skikjöring. The frozen lake acts as the "white arena" for some events and provides the backdrop for others. A tent village complete with grandstands, palm trees, restaurants, bars, and art exhibitions is installed on the lake during the peak season (late January through February). Other special events range from classic car rallies and a rollerblading marathon to gourmet cuisine and music festivals (☞ Festivals and Seasonal Events *in* Chapter 1).

Besides challenging sports, the town offers relaxation at the **St. Moritz Bad** (spa complex). The local mineral springs have been known for hundreds of years; in 1535 the physician and alchemist Paracelsus praised the water, which is the richest in iron and carbonic acid in Europe. Massages and most treatments are done in individual cabins with private baths. Peat baths and packs need a doctor's prescription, but you can take a mineral bath anytime; try one with natural aromas such as pine or rosemary (30 SF). The decor in the treatment and massage rooms is done in 1970s orange and olive, but you'll probably have your eyes shut most of the time anyway. ☎ 081/8333062. ⊙ *June–Apr., weekdays 8–noon and 2–6:30, Sat. 8–noon.*

Get a glimpse of the old local way of life in the **Engadine Museum,** a reproduction of a traditional, sgraffitied home. It displays furniture, tools, and pottery in rooms restored in different styles. ⊠ *Via dal Bagn 39,* ☎ *081/8334333.* ⊡ *5 SF.* ⊙ *June–Oct., weekdays 9:30–noon and 2–5, Sun. 10–noon; Dec.–Apr., weekdays 10–noon and 2–5, Sun. 10–noon.*

The **Segantini Museum,** renovated and extended in 1999, showcases the work of 19th-century artist Giovanni Segantini. His huge triptych *La Vita, La Natura, La Morte (Life–Nature–Death)* hangs in the domed top floor. Take a seat on the visitors' bench to absorb the paintings' colors and themes. ⊠ *Via Somplaz,* ☎ *081/8334454.* ⊡ *10 SF.* ⊙ *June–mid-Oct. and early Dec.–late Apr., Tues.–Sun. 10–noon and 3–6.*

Skiing

Don't let all the activities, events, and spectator sports make you forget that St. Moritz's raison d'être is skiing. You can reach the **Corviglia-Piz Nair, Suvretta,** and **Marguns** slopes, immediately above St. Moritz, from the Chantarella/Corviglia funicular in Dorf, the Signal cable way in Bad, the Suvretta chairlift, and the Marguns gondolas in Celerina (☞ *above*). There are 80 km (50 mi) of difficult, intermediate, and easy runs, a half-pipe for snowboarders, and 24 transport installations. Altogether the Upper Engadine ski region offers 350 km (217 mi) of prepared trails. The views from Corviglia, Piz Nair, and the Suvretta Paradise run are magnificent.

At the end of the season it may not always be possible to ski down to the village. But with the help of snowmaking equipment, conditions in the areas mentioned above usually remain excellent until late April. Descents behind Piz Nair (3,057 m/10,026 ft) eventually lead down to Marguns; they are often in shadow in early winter but have the best snow up to the end of the season. The sunny Suvretta slopes are usually less crowded but do not benefit from snowmaking equipment. For instruction, contact Switzerland's oldest ski school, **St. Moritz Ski School** (☎ 081/8338090 in town or 081/8335553 on Corviglia), or the **Suvretta Snowsports School** (☎ 081/8333332). You can join a group and go with an instructor on a free "ski safari," which begins in Sils and ends in St. Moritz Bad. Rental equipment is available at the Ski Service Corvatsch shops (☎ 081/8322370) at the Corviglia valley and mountain stations. Ticket prices for St. Moritz alone for one day are between 47 SF and 55 SF; for the whole Upper Engadine region a one-day pass costs costs between 53 SF and 58 SF. Six-day regional passes run between 247 SF and 274 SF. Prices include transportation between ski stations on the Engadin Bus service and free entry to the public swimming pools in St. Moritz and Pontresina (☞ Pontresina *above*; Sils *and* Silvaplana, *below*). For reports on daily snow conditions, call the **hot line** (☎ 0844/844944); the English-language version comes last.

Cross-country skiing has its base in St. Moritz Bad, where the **Langlauf school** (✉ Back of Parkhotel Kurhaus, ☎ 081/8336233) offers lessons and excursions. You can try out the Engadin Marathon track or go into the many side valleys. There's also a floodlighted circular trail of 3 km (almost 2 mi) open from 5 PM to 9:30 PM. The suggested contribution for cross-country skiing is 5 SF per day or 25 SF for the season.

Dining and Lodging

$$$$ ✗ **Jöhri's Talvò.** Roland Jöhri's restaurant, in a 17th-century Engadine house, marries the best of Graubünden tradition with classic French elegance. Both the cooking and decor reflect this philosophy, from the delicate linens softening weathered woodwork to the light sauces that curb the heartiness of local dishes. A popular fish menu combines lobster, bouillabaisse, and other fresh choices; the desserts are elaborate works of art. But be prepared to spend as much on a meal as on a room at a luxury hotel. ✉ *Champfèr, 3 km (2 mi) southwest of St. Moritz,* ☎ *081/8334455. AE, DC, MC, V. Reservations essential. Closed mid-Apr.–mid-June and mid-Oct.–mid-Dec.*

$$ ✗ **Engiadina.** With its plain linoleum and pine, this could pass for a St. Moritz diner, though its raison d'être is fondue; champagne fondue is the house specialty. Other favorites are *steak-frîtes* (steak with french fries) and escargots. It's a popular oddity in this ritzy resort. ✉ *Schulhauspl., Dorf,* ☎ *081/8333265. AE, DC, MC, V.*

$$ ✗ **Meierei.** On a winding, private forest road, this *Landgasthof* (coun-★ try inn) started in the 17th century as a farm where the bishop stopped over when traveling. In fact, there is still a *Meierei* (tenant farm) attached to it. Today its restaurants draw people across the lake for such modern combinations as pumpkin gnocchi with lobster. If you're not up for a full meal, you can have just coffee and cake or Bündnerfleisch and a glass of wine. The sun terrace is a popular meeting spot for walkers, cross-country skiers, and horseback riders. There are also a few rooms available for overnight stays. You can make the trip on foot or by a horse-drawn carriage or sleigh; only overnight guests can drive there. ✉ *Via Dimlej,* ☎ *081/8333242. AE, DC, MC, V. Closed late March–mid-June and mid-Oct.–mid-Dec.*

$$ ✕ **Veltlinerkeller.** This bright, genial restaurant has nothing swanky about
★ it—just lots of wood and a welcoming fire where the meat is roasted
while you and an enormous elk (one of the owner's hunting trophies)
look on. In addition to grilled meats and whole trout, there are good,
varied homemade pastas. ⊠ *Via dal Bagn, Bad,* ☎ *081/8334009. AE,
DC, MC, V.*

$$$$ 🏨 **Badrutt's Palace.** This was the world's first Palace hotel, and although
the property came under the management of Rosewood Hotels & Re-
sorts in 1999, it remains in Badrutt family hands. Major renovations
of the public areas and guest rooms are underway. The lobby is almost
cathedral-like with its huge arches, carved ceilings, leaded glass, and
original artwork. The number of facilities and services is impressive,
with everything from its own ski school to a bridge hostess. A jacket
and tie are required in the main restaurant, and a jacket is required in
public areas after 7:30 PM, except in the informal Trattoria. If you want
to eat away from the main premises, the Badrutt-owned **Chesa Veg-
lia,** one of the oldest houses in St. Moritz, offers three more restau-
rants; in summer you can have lunch on its flowered terrace. Some hotel
facilities are seasonal, such as the disco, open in winter only, or the
summer barbecue. ⊠ *Via Serlas, CH-7500,* ☎ *081/8371000,* ℻ *081/
8372999. 160 rooms, 40 suites. 3 restaurants, 3 bars, indoor pool, out-
door pool, hairdresser, hot tubs, massage, sauna, indoor driving range,
4 tennis courts, exercise room, ice-skating, ski school, sports shop, night-
club, kindergarten. AE, DC, MC, V. Closed mid-Apr.–early July and
early Sept.–mid-Dec.* ⊛

$$$$ 🏨 **Carlton.** If you want luxury without blatant glitz and won't miss
having hotel grounds in exchange for inclusive outdoor activities, con-
sider this hotel, which was built in 1913 for the last czar of Russia.
It's now bright and modern, without a scrap of pine, its white-marble
lobby more like a performing-arts center. Blue runners lead upstairs
to the lounge and to the regal dining room (tie requested). Guest rooms
have every modern amenity; some are are designed along contempo-
rary lines, with leather furniture; others evoke eras gone by with crys-
tal chandeliers. The baths are white marble. The pool and south-facing
rooms have views over the lake. ⊠ *Via J. Badrutt, CH-7500,* ☎ *081/
8367000,* ℻ *081/8367001. 99 rooms, 6 suites. 2 restaurants, bar, in-
door pool, beauty salon, hairdresser, sauna, massage, kindergarten. AE,
DC, MC, V. Closed late Mar.–mid-June and late Sept.–early Dec.* ⊛

$$$$ 🏨 **Kulm.** The Kulm claims some important firsts: it was the first lux-
ury hotel in St. Moritz (1856) *and* the first house in all of Switzerland
to have electricity (1878). Rooms have all been renovated over the last
five years; the most expensive ones have south-facing balconies. The
decor is elegant, if slightly heavy-handed in the lobby and lounge. The
Panorama Healthclub is superlative; it's done in light-gray marble and
has a pool, whirlpool, saunas, steam baths, a saltwater grotto, and tha-
lasso, massage, and beauty treatments, not to mention a fitness area
with a view over the lake. In the grill room (open only in winter) and
the main dining room you'll be expected to wear a jacket and tie; there
are also more casual dining options. A nine-hole golf course should be
open in summer 2001. ⊠ *Via Maistra, CH-7500, Dorf,* ☎ *081/
8368000,* ℻ *081/8368001. 139 rooms, 41 suites. 4 restaurants, 2 bars
(1 winter only), hairdresser, 3 tennis courts, health club, ice-skating,
kindergarten. AE, DC, MC, V. Closed early Apr.–late June and mid-
Sept.–mid-Dec.* ⊛

$$$$ 🏨 **Schweizerhof.** This family-owned, big-city hotel was built in 1896
and is still grand. Public areas are heavy with carved wood and mold-
ings; a lighter touch is the painted ceiling of the guests' dining room,
depicting a glittering birch forest. Guest rooms are slick postmodern,
with burled-wood cabinets and contemporary color schemes. There are

a popular piano bar and a lively Stübli that draw a young après-ski crowd; an extra restaurant opens in summer. The rooftop wellness center offers saunas, steam baths, massages, and superb views over the lake. ⊠ *Via dal Bagn 54, CH-7500, Dorf,* ☎ *081/8370707,* FAX *081/ 8370700. 90 rooms. 2 restaurants, 4 bars, health club, kindergarten (winter only). AE, DC, MC, V.*

$$$$ ⊞ **Steffani.** Built in 1869, the Steffani is owned and run by the third generation of the Märky family; it is a member of the Best Western reservations system. There is a cosmopolitan, lively atmosphere, with young skiers congregating in the Cava bar and the English-speaking Cresta crowd meeting nightly in the first-floor bar. Also on the first floor is the only Chinese restaurant in town; for Swiss/international cuisine try the Lapin Bleu. The hotel's decor has been dubbed by regulars (and accepted with good humor by the management) as "Austrian–yodel–baroque." The Corviglia funicular station and the shops are just a few steps away. The hotel stays open throughout the off-seasons—in fact, it hasn't closed one day since 1930. ⊠ *Via Traunter Plazzas, CH-7500, Dorf,* ☎ *081/8369696,* FAX *081/8369717. 59 rooms, 5 suites. 3 restaurants, 3 bars, Stübli, indoor pool, hot tub, massage, sauna, hairdresser, dance club. AE, DC, MC, V.* ☜

$$$$ ⊞ **Suvretta House.** What makes this hotel special is not only its unique
★ location, outside the village at the foot of the ski slopes, but its welcoming atmosphere, exceptional for a luxury hotel of its size. It has stupendous views of Piz Corvatsch and the Silvaplana Lake. Rooms are discreetly, individually decorated. In the health and fitness complex you can take in the views or relax in a sauna under a night sky reproduced with tiny lights. Access to the Corviglia slopes is just outside the front door, and the hotel has its own ski school. Although jacket and tie are requested after 7 PM in the lobby and main dining room, the more casual Club area downstairs offers English-style lounges and the informal Stube restaurant. There's even a children's restaurant, the Teddy Club. In addition, the hotel runs a couple of mountain restaurants, **Chasellas** and **Trutz,** which serve excellent game and fish dishes. ⊠ *CH-7500 St. Moritz-Suvretta,* ☎ *081/8363636,* FAX *081/8363737. 210 rooms. 4 restaurants, 2 bars, indoor pool, beauty salon, massage, driving range, 3 tennis courts, health club, ski school, ice-skating, shops, kindergarten. AE, DC, MC, V. Closed mid-Apr.–late June and early Sept.–mid-Dec.* ☜

$$$–$$$$ ⊞ **Waldhaus am See.** With a big, sunny terrace, dining rooms with
★ views, and a clientele ranging from family clans to seniors, this hotel is geared to leisurely stays. It's across from the rail station, perched on the edge of the lake, a good walk from the center of town. Rooms are plain with pine trim, and baths have all been renovated with white-and-gray or beige-and-brown tiles. The manager stocks more than 1,700 different wines and, according to Guinness, has the world record for the largest selection of whiskies. ⊠ *Via Dimlej, CH-7500,* ☎ *081/ 8337676,* FAX *081/8338877. 53 rooms, 4 apartments. Restaurant, bar, Stübli, sauna, exercise room. AE, DC, MC, V.* ☜

$$–$$$ ⊞ **Languard.** This small, family-owned garni hotel stands in the town center just below the Kulm (☞ *above*), sharing the lake and mountain views. Details like sgraffiti, carved ceilings, and fine darkened pine in some rooms preserve the best from its earlier days. The big corner rooms deserve the price they command; back rooms are small and look over town, but all have tiled baths. In the small sitting area, check out the collection of skiing trophies and medals won by the owner, who used to run St. Moritz's ski school. ⊠ *Off Via Maistra, CH-7500, Dorf,* ☎ *081/8333137,* FAX *081/8334546. 22 rooms. Breakfast room. AE, DC, MC, V. Closed late Apr.–early June and mid-Oct.–early Dec.*

$-$$$ ☷ **Laudinella.** Here you'll find the facilities of a first-class hotel for a
★   reasonable price—and cultural offerings to boot. The hotel has a spe-
cial role as an arts center, as it hosts more than 50 courses each year,
mostly for writers and music lovers. Your stay might coincide with that
of an orchestra, an alpenhorn group, gospel singers, or a choir. If you're
interested, you can join a course or attend a concert. The hotel is a short
walk from the cross-country trails and from the Signal cable car to the
Corviglia ski area. The good-size rooms are white with pine furniture;
those in the newly renovated wing have soft furnishings in primary col-
ors, while the older rooms are done in pastels. A minibus service to and
from the train station is available. ✉ *CH-7500, Bad,* ☎ *081/8360000,*
FAX *081/8360001. 170 rooms. 3 restaurants, bar, café, massage, sauna,
library, children's playroom. AE, DC, MC, V.* ✍

Nightlife and the Arts

To find out what's happening, check the weekly *Engadin Information*
brochure (it has an English section), available at the tourist office, ho-
tels, and shops.

BARS AND LOUNGES

Choose from the world's biggest selection of whiskies at the **Devil's
Place** (☞ Waldhaus am See, *above*). For elegant but informal sur-
roundings try the **Grischuna** bar (✉ Schulhauspl., ☎ 081/8370404).
A fun-loving, English-speaking crowd hangs out during the winter sea-
son at the Steffani hotel's **Stübli** (☞ *above*). The après-ski clique fa-
vors the Steffani's **Cava** (☞ *above*) and the open-air **Roo** bar (✉ Via
Traunter Plazzas, ☎ 081/8334402) on the Hotel Hauser's terrace.
Many hotels, including the **Schweizerhof** (☞ *above*), also have piano
bars or bars with live music during the winter season.

CASINOS

The casino in **St. Moritz** (✉ Via Veglia 15/Via Maistra 28, ☎ 081/
8321080) supplements its 5 SF roulette with 59 slot machines. It's open
Sunday to Thursday until 2 AM, Friday and Saturday until 3 AM. It closes
in May and November.

DANCING

The winter-only **King's Club,** in Badrutt's Palace (☞ *above*), has a Moor-
ish decor; its cover charge gets steep on weekends. **Vivai** (✉ Via Som-
plaz, ☎ 081/8336939) opens for the winter and summer seasons; the
music tends to house, with occasional live performances and well-known
DJs. For more formal dancing to live music, aimed at the older gen-
eration, try the **Sunny Bar,** in the Kulm (☞ *above*), or **Anton's Bar,** at
the Suvretta (☞ *above*). Both open for the winter season only and re-
quire a jacket and tie.

MUSIC

The musical highlight in St. Moritz is the **Snow & Symphony Music
Festival** (☎ 081/8344646), which takes place over 10 days in early spring.
Prize-winning classical musicians, a symphony orchestra and chamber
orchestras, and jazz musicians, too, give roughly 20 concerts. The per-
formances are held in luxury hotels and on mountaintops. The **Enga-
dine Concert Weeks** (☎ 081/8426573) take place from mid-July to late
August, with smaller-scale performances throughout the Upper Enga-
dine. The **St. Moritz Chamber Orchestra** (☞ Visitor Information *in*
Graubünden A to Z, *below*) gives free daily concerts in summer at 10:30
AM in the spa center's hall or park.

Outdoor Activities and Sports

BICYCLING

The tourist office stocks maps of bicycling routes (3 SF). Mountain bikes
are rented for 30 SF a day from **Corviglia Sport** (✉ Via Maistra 21,

☎ 081/8334477), **Scheuing Sport** (✉ Schulhauspl., ☎ 081/8333170), **Blue Motion** (✉ Via del Bagn, ☎ 081/8330832), and the Corviglia Tennis center (☞ Tennis, *below*). "Country" bikes (more substantial road bikes) can be rented at the **railroad station** (☎ 081/8333125) for 27 SF a day. For a further 7 SF you can take these bikes on a train back to town if you've no pedal power left at the end of the day.

BOBSLEDDING

In 1890–91 the first bobsled races were held on the road between St. Moritz and Celerina. The present-day run, built each year from natural ice, follows roughly the same course; it's the only one of its kind in the world. You can watch the **Olympia Bob Run** (☎ 081/8300200) races for around 5 SF. Or you can tear along the run yourself by riding behind an experienced pilot. The taxi ride costs 220 SF; book well in advance. The bob run is open from late December through early March.

CRESTA

On the world's only Cresta Run, riders on skeletons (a kind of metal toboggan) rush headfirst down a winding ice channel from St. Moritz to Celerina, accelerating to about 90 mph. You can watch the runs every morning from the path or the roof of the Junction Hut. If you'd like to try the run, contact the **St. Moritz Tobogganing Club** (☎ 081/8334609). It's a private club, but they do allow temporary memberships (for a steep fee) for instruction and access to the run. The Cresta is open from late December to the last day of February. Note that the run is not open to women.

GOLF

Samedan's 18-hole **Engadine Golf Course** (☎ 081/8510466) is about 10 minutes by car from St. Moritz (☞ Samedan, *above*). It's open from late May to early October. The **Corviglia Tennis Center** (☞ Tennis, *below*) has an indoor driving range; call ahead to reserve it.

HIKING

There are dozens of hiking and walking routes around St. Moritz, including a popular walk around the lake, all well signposted. Maps are available at the tourist office (☞ Visitor Information *in* Graubünden A to Z, *below*). Most cable cars, funiculars, and some chair lifts run in summer, providing access to higher trails. **S. Lareida** (☎ 081/8334465) leads guided botanical or minerological walks. (Mr. Lareida speaks English.)

HORSEBACK RIDING AND HORSEDRAWN CARRIAGES/SLEIGHS

At the **Riding Resort Seaside stables** just by the lake (✉ Via Ludains, ☎ 081/8335733) you can take a group lesson or go on an excursion for 50 SF an hour. The **Hossmann stables** (✉ Champfèr, 3 km (2 mi) southwest of St. Moritz, ☎ 081/8337125) specialize in Western riding; a group lesson or excursion costs 45 SF.

For horse-drawn sleigh or carriage rides, contact **M. Giovanoli** (☎ 081/8331279); **A. Lampert** (☎ 081/8333235); **A. Melcher** (☎ 081/8337457); or **D. Motti** (☎ 081/8333768). A popular winter route is the ride across the frozen lake.

ICE-SKATING AND CURLING

The lakeside **Ludains skating rink** (✉ St. Moritz-Bad, ☎ 081/8335030), renovated in 2000, is open from mid-July to late April. Rental skates are available. The **Kulm hotel** skating and curling rinks at Chesa al Parc (☎ 081/8334588) are open to the public; rental skates and curling lessons are available.

PARAGLIDING

H. Zwyssig (☎ 081/8332416 or 079/3532159) and **A. Kuhn** (☎ 081/8265400) offer flights with an experienced pilot from the top station of the Corviglia funicular for 220 SF. The views on the way down are spectacular; you land on the lake. The flights are done from mid-December to late March, depending on the weather conditions.

TENNIS

The **Corviglia Tennis Center** (⊠ St. Moritz-Bad, ☎ 081/8331500) has four indoor and four outdoor tennis courts, plus a couple of squash courts. It's open year-round except from late May to early June.

En Route   Between St. Moritz and Sils lies the village of **Silvaplana,** on the lake of the same name. Its main attraction is **Piz Corvatsch** (3,451 m/11,319 ft), whose ski area adjoins that of Furtschellas (☞ Sils, *below*). Together the areas have 45 km (28 mi) of runs. The gorgeous views from the top are worth the trip in summer or winter—on a clear day you can see as far as Monte Rosa, the Jungfrau, and the Austrian Alps.

Sils

⑭   *13 km (8 mi) southwest of St. Moritz.*

The village of Sils (in Romansh, Segl) sits in the meadows between the lakes of Silvaplana and Sils, just by the road leading to Italy over the Maloja Pass. It has two sections: Sils Maria, at the foot of the mountains, and Sils Baselgia. Access to Sils Baselgia is over the Inn River just by the tiny church of St. Lorenz; a barrier prevents through traffic to Sils Maria. If you're driving, you should leave your car in Sils Maria's underground parking lot.

Although the approach to Sils Maria takes you through expanding new housing, the village center and Sils Baselgia are a smooth mix of old and new. There are many examples of Engadine architecture; often the older houses have roofs of slate from the Fex Valley (☞ Hiking, *below*). The awe-inspiring views from Sils Baselgia over the Sils Lake are still a favorite subject for artists. Friedrich Nietzsche, who spent eight years in Sils Maria, called the lakeside and plain "the land of silver colors." The philosopher wrote several works, including *Also Sprach Zarathustra (Thus Spake Zarathustra),* while living in what is now the **Nietzsche Haus** museum. The house displays a collection of his manuscripts next to originals in his own fascinatingly scrawly script. You can also see photos and mementos of other literati who put their thoughts on paper while vacationing in the village—from Thomas Mann to Anne Frank. ☎ *081/8265369.* 🖾 *6 SF.* ⊘ *Tues.–Sun. 4–6 in season.*

Skiing

Sils was a predominantly summer resort, until the Sils Furtschellas cableway opened in 1972. The Furtschellas slopes join those of Corvatsch (☞ Silvaplana, *above*), and skiing on this north side of the Upper Engadine Valley is especially popular at the beginning and end of the winter season. Lessons are available through Sils's **Swiss Ski School** (☎ 081/8385055). One-day passes for Furtschellas/Corvatsch cost 55 SF.

Dining and Lodging

$$$$ ✕🏨 **Margna.** Named after the mountain above Sils, this hotel was originally a private house and has been expanded over the years. Today's Margna still has the atmosphere of an elegant home; the public rooms are full of thick rugs, antiques, original paintings, and flowers. The main restaurant, The Grill, is the place for French and Italian food; lighter pasta or Engadine specialties are served in the Arvenstübli. Rooms are all individually decorated in Engadine style and priced according to

size. Some are done in white with Swiss pine furniture, others are all in Swiss pine. The brightest rooms face the garden. If you want a fully modern bath, request it, as not all have yet been renovated. The hotel has its own short course and driving range, with a resident English pro. ⊠ *CH-7515 Sils Baselgia,* ☎ *081/8384747,* FAX *081/8384748. 78 rooms, 5 suites. 3 restaurants, bar, whirlpool, steam room, sauna, massage, driving range, 6-hole golf course. MC, V. Closed early Apr.–mid-June and early Oct.–mid-Dec.* ✑

$$ ✕☷ **Chesa Marchetta/Pensiun Andreola.** This twin pension and restau-
★ rant run by two sisters is a special regional experience. The guest house is furnished in pine and cotton prints, while the tiny, neighboring restaurant, the Stüva Engiadinaisa, in the Chesa Marchetta, is an Arvenholz gem, perfectly preserved since 1671 (and we do mean tiny—there are only four tables). The menu is limited to one main dish a night—homemade pasta with lamb, perhaps, or polenta with veal, with the permanent option of fondue chinoise (paper-thin sliced meat cooked in bouillon instead of oil). Meals are served evenings only; snacks are served from 3:30 on. Reservations are essential. ⊠ *CH-7514, Sils Maria,* ☎ *081/8265232,* FAX *081/8266260. 10 rooms, 4 with bath. Restaurant, Stübli. MC, V. Closed mid-Apr.–mid-June and mid-Oct.–mid-Dec.*

$$$$ ☷ **Waldhaus.** Approaching Sils from either direction, you'll spot what
★ seems to be a castle perched above the village—this is the Waldhaus, whose guests have included Hermann Hesse, Marc Chagall, Albert Einstein, and Richard Strauss. The hotel has been in the same family hands since it opened in 1908. It's continually updated with an eye to tradition without fuss. For instance, the large bar was renovated for the 1999–2000 winter season, with subtle halogen lighting gleaming over its fireplace and walnut walls. The understated rooms come in a wide range of sizes, some for families; antique fittings shine in the baths. Here price differences are not usually based on scenic views, as every room has one. The Waldhaus stays open longer than other luxury hotels in the valley—over Easter and to the end of October. ⊠ *CH-7514, Sils-Maria,* ☎ *081/ 8385100,* FAX *081/8385198. 140 rooms. 3 restaurants, bar, Stübli, indoor pool, hairdresser, massage, steam room, miniature golf, 3 outdoor tennis courts, l indoor tennis court, kindergarten, chapel. AE, DC, MC, V. Closed late Apr.–early June and late Oct.–mid-Dec.* ✑

$$ ☷ **Chesa Randolina.** This hotel used to be a farm and horse-drawn coach business with a guest house. The rooms are mostly furnished in pine; the best have balconies facing south to the lake. There are a spacious lounge with a stone fireplace and a restaurant done in soft greens and yellows, plus a fondue Stübli (all for hotel guests only). ⊠ *CH-7515 Sils Baselgia,* ☎ *081/8265151,* FAX *081/8265600. 37 rooms. Restaurant, Stübli, bar. No credit cards. Closed mid-Apr.–early June and mid-Oct.–mid-Dec.*

Nightlife and the Arts

Small **chamber ensembles** perform from late June through September at 4 or 4:30 on the Konzertplatz in Sils-Maria; in bad weather, they move to the schoolhouse.

Outdoor Activities and Sports

BOATING AND WINDSURFING

Rowboats can be rented from **Schiffahrtgesellschaft Silsersee** (☎ 081/ 8265343) in Sils Maria. Two **Windsurf Centers,** one in Sils (☎ 081/ 8265786) and one in Silvaplana (☎ 081/8289229), operate on Silvaplana lake. Both give lessons and rent equipment; they're run by a former world champion windsurfer. **E. Gianni** (☎ 081/8265343) runs the only motorboat allowed on the Engadine lakes; you can take it around the lake, stopping in tiny communities like Isola.

Contact **Sämy Stöckli** (☎ 079/4404166) to have a dozen snow-hungry huskies pull you across extraordinary frozen landscapes near Sils.

HIKING AND WALKING

Sils has 90 km (55 mi) of paths, including the popular walk into the Fex Valley, where you can visit a frescoed 16th-century church; the key is at the Hotel Sonne, opposite.

HORSE-DRAWN CARRIAGES

From June to October a scheduled "bus service" goes into the Fex Valley from the Hotel Maria in Sils Maria to the end of the valley for 25 SF round-trip. Private carriages or sleighs go into the valley from the village square in both summer and winter. You can arrange a trip with **Mr. Clalüna** (☎ 081/8265286), **G. Coretti** (☎ 081/8265673), or **C. Klopfstein** (☎ 081/8265225).

ICE-SKATING

The **Muot Marias** (☎ 081/6550207) ice rink is open daily in winter, and on Tuesday and Thursday it's floodlit for evening skating. Rental skates and lessons are available.

TENNIS

Sils has six courts open to the public. Four are at the **Waldhaus Hotel** (☞ *above*), while the other two are outdoor courts which can be booked through the tourist office (☞ Visitor Information *in* Graubünden A to Z, *below*).

GRAUBÜNDEN A TO Z

Arriving and Departing

By Bus

You can take the Swiss postbus system's **Palm Express** (☎ 081/8376764 or 091/8078520) from Lugano in the Ticino to St. Moritz. The 4½-hour trip passes through a corner of Italy and over the Maloja Pass. The bus runs twice daily from mid-June through mid-October; reservations are essential.

By Car

Graubünden is mountainous and thin on major highways. Drivers can enter either by way of the San Bernardino Pass from the Ticino or from the north on **A13**, the region's only expressway. Coming from Austria and München, the **A27** leads into the Lower Engadine; roads over the Ofen and Bernina passes lead into the Engadine from the South Tyrol and Veltline areas of Italy, respectively. From Canton Uri, and the Oberalp Pass, the **A19** passes through the Surselva region to join A13.

By Plane

The **Engadin Airport** (✉ Samedan, 5 km/3 mi from St. Moritz, ☎ 081/8525433) is used mainly by private planes. At 1,707 m (5,600 ft), it's the highest airport in Europe.

By Train

The only **Swiss Federal Railway** (SBB/CFF/FFS; ☎ 0900/300300) trains to enter Graubünden come as far as Chur. From there the fine local **Rhätische Bahn** (RhB) takes over. For information on the RhB, contact Graubünden Holidays (☞ Visitor Information, *below*).

To make the most of the RhB, take famous scenic train routes in or out of the region. The **Bernina Express** runs from Chur to St. Moritz via the Albula route and on to Italy past the spectacular Bernina peaks, lakes, and glaciers. The glamorous **Glacier Express,** "the slowest express in the world," connects St. Moritz with Zermatt via the Oberalp Pass, crossing 291 bridges on its 7½-hour route. The train pulls a burnished-wood period dining car; you can reserve a table through the **Schweizerische Speisewagen Gesellschaft** (✉ CH-7000 Chur, ☎ 081/2521425). Seat reservations for these trains are mandatory and can be made at almost any European rail station. As on the federal railways, there is a variety of reduced-price passes and tickets available (☞ Train Travel *in* Smart Travel Tips A to Z).

Getting Around

By Bus

Postbuses are a good way to wind your way up Alpine switchbacks over the region's great passes—that is, if you're not inclined to motion sickness. You can also use them to make circle tours with some careful study of the schedule. Information is available at all post offices. The main ski resorts have "sport bus" shuttles, which connect the villages and mountain stations. The service is usually included in the price of your ski pass or on presentation of your guest card (☞ Lodging *in* Pleasures and Pastimes, *above*).

By Car

The A13 expressway cuts a swift north–south route through Graubünden. If you want to get back into the deep farmlands, you'll definitely need a car. Fine valley highways connect the rest of the area, though to move from one resort to another you may have to crawl over a mountain pass. If you're traveling in winter, make sure to check on the status of the passes; weather is obviously a major player. The San Bernardino old road and the Oberalp, Albula, and Flüela passes close, but the San Bernardino Tunnel and the Maloja, Bernina, Julier, and Ofen passes are usually open to traffic. Trains through the **Vereina Tunnel** shuttle cars between Klosters and Susch–Lavin in the Lower Engadine. The tunnel cuts the travel time from Zürich from five hours to just 2¾ hours. Cars can also be taken by rail from Thusis to Samedan; the service is limited and reservations are essential (☎ 081/6511113).

By Train

The Rhätische Bahn, or **Rhaetian Railway** (☞ Arriving and Departing, *above*), is very tourism oriented. Its network of narrow-gauge track runs through some of the most spectacular scenery in Switzerland. Without resorting to cogwheels, some of the trains climb stiff mountain grades of up to 7%. Special short trips for rail enthusiasts include excursions with the three remaining RhB steam locomotives and open-carriage trips over the Bernina Pass down to Italy. For information and reservations contact Graubünden Holidays (☞ Visitor Information, *below*). The Swiss Pass is accepted on RhB trains.

Contacts and Resources

Emergencies

A general line is available for the criminal **police** (☎ 117). Local police numbers include: **Arosa** (☎ 081/3771938); **Chur** (☎ 081/2544341); **Davos** (☎ 081/4137622); **Klosters** (☎ 081/4221236); **Pontresina** (☎ 081/8426271); **St. Moritz** (☎ 081/8322727); **Scuol** (☎ 081/8641414); **Zernez** (☎ 081/8561212).

The general number for an **emergency doctor or ambulance** is ☎ 144. Local ambulance contacts include: **Davos** (☎ 081/4101111); **Klosters** (☎ 081/4221713); **Upper Engadine** (☎ 081/8518888). **Hospitals:** **Chur** (☎ 081/2566111); **Davos** (☎ 081/4148888); **Upper Engadine/Samedan** (☎ 081/8518111); **Scuol** (☎ 081/8611000). **Doctors:**

Arosa (☎ 081/3772728); **Chur** (☎ 081/2523636); **Klosters** (☎ 081/3080808); **Pontresina** (☎ 081/8427766 or 081/8426268); **St. Moritz** (☎ 081/8330033); **Zernez** (☎ 081/8561215 or 081/8561616). **Accident clinic:** Klinik Gut (☎ 081/8334141) in St. Moritz. Duty doctors, dentists, and emergency pharmacies are listed in resort tourist periodicals or can be requested by calling **information** (☎ 111).

Guided Tours

HIKING

Arosa, Davos, and Lenzerheide-Valbella offer an unusual **hiking package:** they'll book your hotel and deliver your bags ahead. You can walk from Davos to Arosa one day and from Arosa to Lenzerheide the next. A seven-day program lets you spend more time in each resort. Similar arrangements can be made in the Engadine. Contact local tourist offices or Graubünden Holidays (☞ Visitor Information, *below*).

WALKING

The **Arosa** tourist office (☞ Visitor Information, *below*) offers guided tours and nature walks every morning and afternoon from June through October; you can visit a cheese maker, a regional museum, and a 15th-century chapel. The **Chur** tourist office (☞ Visitor Information, *below*) arranges guided tours from April to October every Wednesday at 2:30. To explore on your own instead, pick up a map and printed information (available in English) and follow the green and red footprints on the pavements. The **Pontresina** tourist office (☞ Visitor Information, *below*) offers guided walking tours of its Old Town, full of typical Engadine houses, from mid-June to mid-October. It also offers guided botanical excursions, sunrise viewings, glacier tours, and hiking trips to the Swiss National Park, plus mushroom-picking outings in season (usually August–September). If you are staying in Pontresina, the tours are free but exclude transport costs; day visitors pay a small fee. Guides for all of the above tours speak English.

Visitor Information

The canton's tourist information center is **Graubünden Holidays** (✉ Alexanderstr. 24, CH-7001 Chur, ☎ 081/3026100, FAX 081/3021414, ✉). There's also a **branch office** at the Heidiland restaurant on the A13 just after you enter Graubünden which is open daily. It can be reached at the same phone number as the main office. **Chur,** the cantonal capital, has its own city tourist office as well (✉ Grabenstr. 5, CH-7002, ☎ 081/2521818, FAX 081/2529076, ✉). For information about the **Rhaetian Railway**'s special trips contact their call center (☎ 0900/552010 or 081/2549499 for steam train information, ✉).

Arosa (✉ CH-7050, ☎ 081/3787020). **Bündner Herrschaft/Maienfeld** (✉ CH-7304 Maienfeld, ☎ 081/3301912 or 081/3025858). **Davos** (✉ Promenade 67, CH-7270, ☎ 081/4152121). **Klosters** (✉ Alte Bahnhofstr. 6, CH-7250, ☎ 081/4102020). **Pontresina** (✉ Rondo Center, CH-7504, ☎ 081/8388300). **St. Moritz** (✉ Via Maistra, CH-7500, ☎ 081/8373333). **Scuol and Bad-Tarasp Vulpera** (✉ CH-7550, ☎ 081/8612222). **Sils** (✉ CH-7514 Sils Maria, ☎ 081/8385050). **Zernez** (✉ CH-7530, ☎ 081/8561300).

5 THE TICINO

LOCARNO, LUGANO

Italian in language, culture, and spirit, the Ticino is an irresistible combination of Mediterranean pleasures and Swiss efficiency. With its yacht-filled waterfront promenades of Locarno and Lugano and its sunny climate, the Ticino is a canton set apart, a happy harbor for Switzerland's Italian-speaking minority.

Updated by
Susan Tuttle-
Laube

NEWCOMERS TO THE OLD WORLD, a little weak on their geography, might hear the names Lugano, Ascona, Locarno, and Bellinzona and assume—quite naturally—they're in Italy. Color photographs of the region might not set them straight: nearly every publicity shot shows palm trees and mimosas, red roofs and loggias, azure waters and indigo skies. Surely this is the Italian Mediterranean or the coast of the Adriatic. But behind the waving date palms are telltale signs: fresh paint, manicured gardens, punctual trains. There's no mistake about it: it's a little bit of Italy, but the canton Ticino is decidedly Swiss.

For the German Swiss, it's a little bit of paradise. They can cross over the Saint Gotthard or San Bernardino passes and emerge in balmy sunshine, eat gnocchi and polenta in shaded *grotti* (rustic outdoor restaurants), drink merlot from ceramic bowls, gaze at the waters of Lago di Maggiore (Lake Maggiore)—and still know their lodging will be strictly controlled by the Swiss Hotel Association. They don't even have to change money. The combination is irresistible, and so in spring, summer, and fall they pour over the Alps to revel in low-risk Latin delights.

And the Ticinese welcome them like rich, distant cousins, to be served and coddled and—perhaps just a bit—despised. For the Italian-speaking natives of the Ticino—a lonely 8% of the Swiss population—are a minority in their own land, dominated politically by the German-speaking Swiss, set apart by their culture as well as by their language. Their blood and their politics are as Mediterranean as their climate: in a battle over obligatory seat belts, the Ticinese consistently voted to reject the federal intrusion. They were voted down by their Germanic neighbors—a 70% majority—and they protested. It was brought to vote again, and again they were defeated. Nowadays the Ticinese defy the federal law—and their policemen, Ticinese themselves, of course, turn a blind and supportive eye.

Their Italian leanings make perfect sense: an enormous mountain chain cuts them off from the north, pushing them inexorably toward their lingual roots. Most of the territory of the Ticino belonged to the pre-Italian city-states of Milan and Como until 1512, when the Swiss Confederation took it over by force. It remained a Swiss conquest—oppressed under the then-tyrannical rule of Uri, Schwyz, and Unterwalden, the very cantons now revered for forming the honorable Confederation of Switzerland—until 1798, when from the confusion of Napoléon's campaigns it emerged a free canton, and in 1803 it joined the confederation for good.

It remains a canton apart nonetheless, graceful, open, laissez-faire. Here you'll instantly notice differences in manner and body language among Ticinese engaged in conversation; you'll also notice fewer English-speaking Swiss. The climate, too, is different: there's an extraordinary amount of sunshine here, more than in central Switzerland and even sunny Italy immediately across the border. Mountain-sports meccas aside, this is the most glamorous of Swiss regions: the waterfront promenades of Lugano, Locarno, and Ascona, lined with pollards, rhododendrons, and bobbing yachts, blend a rich social mix of jet-set resorters. A few miles' drive brings the canton's impoverished past into view—the foothill and mountain villages are still scattered with low-roof stone peasants' cabins, but nowadays those cabins often prove to have been gentrified as chic vacation homes.

Although they're prosperous, with Lugano standing third in banking, after Zürich and Geneva, the Ticinese hold on to their past, a mountain-peasant culture that draws them to hike, hunt, and celebrate with great pots of risotto stirred over open outdoor fires. It's that contrast—contemporary glamour, earthy past—that grants travelers a visit that's as balanced, satisfying, and as unique as a good merlot.

Pleasures and Pastimes

Dining

Of all the Swiss regions, this can be the most pleasurable to eat in, as the stylish and simple cuisine of Italy has been adopted virtually intact. Because the Ticinese were once a poor mountain people, their everyday cooking shares the earthy delights of another once-poor mountain people, the Piedmontese, whose steaming polenta and rib-sticking gnocchi break bread with game and meaty porcini mushrooms. *Manzo brasato* (savory braised beef with vegetables) and osso buco are standards, as are polenta *con carne in umido* (with meat stew), *busecca* (vegetable soup with tripe), and any number of variations on risotto. Game offerings usually include *coniglio* (rabbit), *lepre* (hare), and *capretto* (roast kid).

As in the rest of Switzerland, local cold meats come in a broad variety, from myriad salamis to prosciutto *crudo,* the pearly-pink cured raw ham made famous in Parma. Any food product made locally is called *nostrano,* and the prosciutto crudo nostrano is worth asking for, as you won't find a match for its forthright, gamey flavor back home. Eat it with bread and sweet butter to balance the salt.

Most cooks import Italian cheeses—Parmigiano-Reggiano, sharp pecorino—though there are good, hard, white mountain varieties (Piora, Gesero) in most shops. Tiny *formaggini*—little molds of ultra-fresh goat cheese—taste best with coarsely ground black pepper and olive oil. Or try the *zincarlin,* a fresh cheese mixed with parsley, garlic, and pepper.

The best place to sample these down-to-earth delicacies is in a grotto, one of the scores of traditional country restaurants scattered across the region. Some of them are set deep in the mountains and forests, little more than a few rows of picnic tables and a string of festive lights. Some serve only cold meats, but a few offer a daily hot dish or two. To experience an authentic grotto, avoid the ones with *ristorante* in their names; the categories of eating establishments are carefully regulated, so these will always be pricier—and not the real thing. The local wine is merlot; a warm, generous wine counted as one of the top Swiss reds. The wine is poured into an individual *boccalino,* a traditional ceramic pitcher, or a small ceramic bowl, to be drunk from like a cup. Instead of beer to quench locals' thirsts, a mix of *gazosa* (lemon-lime soda) and *vino nostrano* (the house red wine) is de rigueur. If you want a real Italian-style espresso, one-finger deep and frothing with golden foam, ask for *un liscio.* Otherwise they'll serve it with cream, Swiss style—and might even charge you extra. If you want a shot of grappa (grape brandy) thrown in, ask for it *corretto*—literally, "correct." Or finish off your meal with a shot of *Nocino,* a traditional walnut liqueur also known as *Ratafiá* (from *rata fiat,* meaning "it's done"). Walnuts picked before San Giovanni's day (June 25) are soaked in grappa and mixed with a secret combination of herbs and spices. Most Nocino is produced privately from closely guarded recipes—no two taste alike.

CATEGORY	COST*
$$$$	over 80 SF
$$$	50 SF–80 SF
$$	20 SF–50 SF
$	under 20 SF

Prices are per person for a three-course meal (two-course meal in $ category), including sales tax and 15% service charge

Lodging

The hotel industry of this Mediterranean region of Switzerland capitalizes on its natural assets, with lakeside views of Lago di Lugano and Lake Maggiore, and swimming pools and terraces that pay homage to the omnipresent sun. As the Ticino is at its best in spring and fall, and packed with sunseekers in summer, many hotels close down for the winter. Tourist offices often publish lists of those remaining open, so if you're planning to come in low season—and even in January the lake resorts can be balmy—check carefully. Keep in mind that most hotels are not air-conditioned, in spite of hot spells in July and August. Places that might catch a breeze off the lake, like lakefront or hillside lodgings, are more comfortable in high summer. Although these are vacation resorts, they do not depend on the *demipension* (half board) system as much as their mountain counterparts, but arrangements can be made.

CATEGORY	COST*
$$$$	over 300 SF
$$$	180 SF–300 SF
$$	120 SF–180 SF
$	under 120 SF

Prices are for a standard double room, including breakfast, tax, and service charge.

✍ *following the text of a review is your signal that the property has a Web site, where you will find details and, usually, images; for a link, visit www.fodors.com/urls.*

Mountain Valleys

Valle di Blenio, Valle Maggia, Valle Verzasca, Valle Leventina, and other mountain valleys just a short distance from the major cities are rugged reminders of the region's modest history. Stone peasant homes, called *rustici,* dot the valleys, some cut so deeply into the land that the sun never quite reaches bottom. Driving these valleys can be disorienting, for time seems to have stopped; you'll encounter whole villages perched on craggy mountainsides in apparent defiance of gravity.

Waterfront Promenades

Switzerland's sunniest waterfronts—with boating, swimming, charming cafés, fine dining, and shops of all sorts—are in the Ticino. Palm-lined promenades in Lugano, Locarno, and Ascona offer tremendous views overlooking rugged Italian Alps.

Exploring the Ticino

The canton is divided into two geographic regions by the small mountain range (554 m/1,817 ft) called Monte Ceneri, which rises up south of the valley below Bellinzona. Extending northeast and northwest of Monte Ceneri in the windswept Sopraceneri region are several mountainous valleys, including Valle di Blenio, Valle Maggia, Valle Verzasca, and Valle Leventina. Included in this region north of or, literally, above Monte Ceneri are Locarno and Ascona, which share a peninsula bulging into Lake Maggiore. The more developed southern region, Sottoceneri ("below Ceneri"), is home to business and resort towns, notably Lugano.

Numbers in the text correspond to numbers in the margin and on the Ticino and Lugano maps.

Great Itineraries

Lugano and Locarno alone provide an overview of the region, but completing the picture requires forays to the less touristy waterfront village of Ascona, the mountain stronghold of Bellinzona, and the rural, rugged mountain valleys beyond.

IF YOU HAVE 1 OR 2 DAYS
Concentrate on ⊞ **Lugano** ⑦–⑲, exploring the waterfront shops, venturing east to the Villa Favorita, and riding a funicular up Monte Brè. On the second day, take in the sights of the serene hillside city ⊞ **Locarno** ③ and the former fishing village of **Ascona** ⑥, both on the shore of Lake Maggiore.

IF YOU HAVE 3 OR 4 DAYS
In addition to all of the above, explore the medieval fortifications of **Bellinzona** ①, the canton's capital, and tiny **Campione** ㉑, an Italian enclave on Swiss territory. Also take a drive through the wilds of the Ticino, into any of the numerous rugged valleys, and discover tiny ancient villages perched on the mountainsides. A perfect sample would be a drive through **Valle di Blenio** ②.

When to Tour the Ticino

Lush and Mediterranean, the Ticino is gorgeous in springtime; the season starts as early as mid-March here, making the region a popular late-winter escape. In summertime, lakeside activity surges, and the weather can at times be hot. Warm summer nights are incredibly romantic, particularly on the Lago di Lugano. Crowds fill the promenades at Lugano and Locarno throughout the summer, but neither waterfront becomes unpleasantly jammed—although the road from Bellinzona to Locarno and Lugano is usually packed.

SOPRACENERI

The mountainous valleys of Valle di Blenio, Valle Maggia, Valle Verzasca, and Valle Leventina reach like the fingers of a hand south from the Alps into the basin of Lake Maggiore and Monte Ceneri, in the Sopraceneri. At the tips are the sun-kissed resorts of Locarno and Ascona, both on Italy's Lake Maggiore. Here the true spirit of the canton is still evident in the numerous small valley communities, some with fewer than 100 inhabitants—although each, nonetheless, is politically autonomous. The Sopraceneri reveals a slightly slower-paced, homier side of the Ticino, leaving the flashier offerings to Lugano in the south.

Bellinzona

★ ❶ *128 km (79 mi) south of Luzern, 150 km (93 mi) south of St. Moritz.*

All roads lead to Bellinzona, the fortified valley city that guards the important European crossroads of the St. Gotthard and San Bernardino routes. Its importance through the ages makes itself evident: massive fortified castles—no fewer than three—rise over its ancient center. They were built by the noble Sforza and Visconti families, the dukes of Milan who ruled northern Italy and environs for centuries and held this crucial juncture until 1422, when the Swiss Confederates began a violent century of battling for its control. Bellinzona passed to the Swiss Confederation in 1503. Ironically, the names of the castles built in part to keep the Swiss at bay were then changed to Schwyz, Uri, and Unterwalden—the three core cantons of the Swiss Confederation. Eventually the names were changed again, and the fortresses are known today as Castelgrande, Castello di Montebello, and Castello di Sasso Corbaro.

The three castles have been exceptionally well restored, and each merits a visit, but the city itself should not be overlooked: it is a classic Lombard town, with graceful architecture, red cobblestones, and an easy, authentically Italian ambience. It is relatively free of tourists and thus reveals the Ticino way of life.

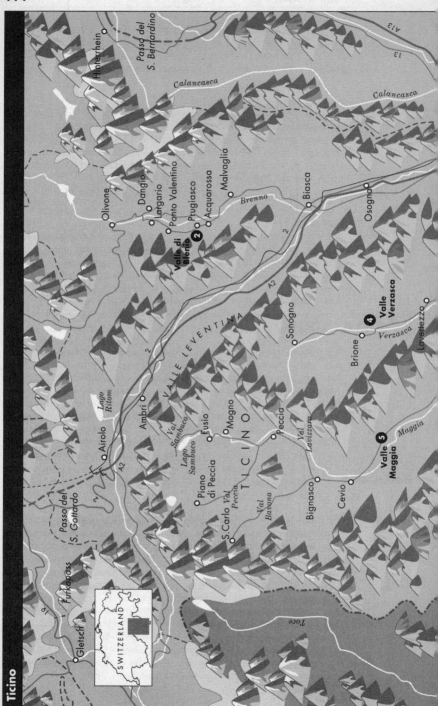

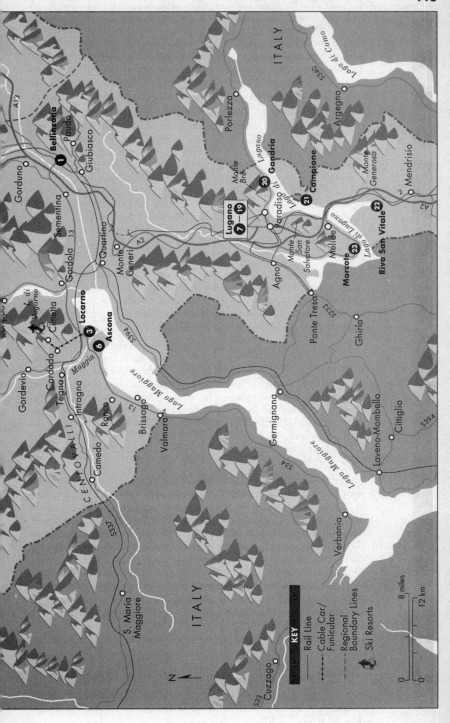

Pick up a map in the tourist office in the **Palazzo Civico** (⊠ Via Cam-
minata, ☎ 091/8252131), a splendid Renaissance structure heavily rebuilt in the 1920s. Its courtyard is framed by two stacked rows of delicate
vaulted arcades, with airy loggias at the top. The **centro storico** (Old
Town), with its heavy-column arcades, wrought-iron balconies, and
shuttered facades, exhibits the direct influence of medieval Lombardy.
It's a small area, distinguished by its red cobblestones.

The **Castelgrande** was begun in the 6th century, though the current structure dates from the 1200s. The massive exterior is dominated by two
heavy, unmatched towers and the remaining portion of a crenellated
wall that once stretched all the way to the river. Renovations and
modern additions have created an elaborate new complex of restaurants (☞ Dining, *below*) and museums, including art and archaeology
exhibitions. The 14th-century ceiling murals, created to embellish the
wooden ceiling of a local villa (now demolished), offer a peek at privately commissioned decorative art. ⊠ *Monte San Michele*, ☎ *091/
8258145.* ▨ *4 SF; 8 SF combination ticket for Castelgrande, Castello
di Montebello, and Castello di Sasso Corbaro.* ☉ *Feb.–Dec., Tues.–
Sun. 10–6.*

The imposing late-Renaissance facade of the **Chiesa Collegiata di San
Pietro e San Stefano** (Church of St. Peter and St. Stephen), begun in
the 16th century, stands across from the Castelgrande. Its interior is
lavishly frescoed in the baroque style by late-18th-century Ticino
artists. ⊠ *Piazza Collegiata*, ☎ *091/8252605.*

The most striking of Bellinzona's three castles is the **Castello di Montebello.** The center portion, its oldest section, dates from the 13th century; there are also a palace and courtyard from the 15th century, with
spectacular walkways around the top of the encircling walls. The center structure houses an attractive, modern **Museo Civico** (Municipal
Museum), with exhibits on local history and architecture, including
an impressive collection of Gothic and Renaissance stone capitals. ⊠
Salita ai Castelli, ☎ *091/8251342.* ▨ *4 SF, 8 SF combination ticket
for Castelgrande, Castello di Montebello, and Castello di Sasso Corbaro.* ☉ *Feb.–Dec., Tues.–Sun. 10–6.*

The lofty **Castello di Sasso Corbaro** is a typical Sforza structure, designed by a Florentine military engineer and built in 1479 for the duke
of Milan, who insisted the work be completed in six months. In the
dungeon there's a branch of the **Museo dell'Arte e delle Tradizioni Popo-
lari del Ticino** (Museum of Traditional Ticino Arts and Crafts), displaying coins, stamps, historic photographs of Bellinzona, and a fine
exhibit of Ticino folk costumes. Ambitious walkers can reach it in about
45 minutes by going uphill from the Castello di Montebello along a
switchback road through woods; if you are driving, follow signs. ☎
091/8255906. ▨ *4 SF, 8 SF combination ticket for Castelgrande,
Castello di Montebello, and Castello di Sasso Corbaro.* ☉ *Feb.–Dec.,
Tues.–Sun. 10–6.*

Chiesa San Biagio (Church of St. Biagio), one of Bellinzona's two Italianate churches, is a spare medieval treasure guarded on the exterior
by an outsize fresco of a soldierly Christ. The 12th-century late-Ro-
manesque structure suggests a transition into Gothic style. Natural alternating redbrick and gray stone complement fragments of exquisitely
colored 14th-century frescoes. ⊠ *Via San Biagio 13, Bellinzona-Ravec-
chia*, ☎ *091/8252505.*

The city's art gallery, **Villa dei Cedri,** sporadically dips into its coffers—
made up of a donated private collection—and hangs worthwhile exhibits. Behind the garden and grounds, the city maintains a tiny vineyard

used to produce its very own merlot, available for sale inside. ⊠ *Piazza San Biagio 9,* ☎ *091/8218520.* ⊠ *4 SF.* ☉ *Mid-Nov.–Mar., Tues.–Sun. 10–noon and 2–5; Apr.–mid-Nov., Tues.–Sat. 10–noon and 2–6, Sun. 10–6.*

Dining and Lodging

$$–$$$
★
✕ **Castelgrande.** Don't expect a quick cafeteria lunch served to shorts-clad tourists here: this chic restaurant is a serious experience, with a daringly cool decor and sophisticated efforts from the Italian chef, such as goose liver with blueberries or pigeon and pearl onions in sweet-and-sour sauce. The wine list flaunts more than 70 Ticino merlots. The terrace has a lighter atmosphere; it's a great spot to soak up views and sunshine. ⊠ *Monte San Michele,* ☎ *091/8262353. AE, DC, MC, V. Closed Mon.*

$$
✕ **Osteria Sasso Corbaro.** From the heights of the ancient Castello di Sasso Corbaro, this atmospheric restaurant serves meals inside a beautifully restored hall or outside, at stone tables, in the shady, walled-in courtyard. The cooking is simple and regional, with cold and grilled meats, trout, and seasonal vegetables. Good local wines toast a holiday air, as the restaurant opens only in high season. ⊠ *Castello Sasso Corbaro,* ☎ *091/8255532. AE, DC, MC, V. Closed Mon. and Nov.–Apr.*

$–$$
✕ **Montebello.** At this spot on a hill above the center in the adjoining suburb of Daro, you can relax under a grape arbor at linen-covered tables and enjoy an authentic meal in true Italian style: easygoing and elegantly simple. From a standing menu and a list of daily specials, sample carpaccio, homemade pasta, and frothy zabaglione. ⊠ *Via alla Chiesa 3, Bellinzona-Daro,* ☎ *091/8258395. AE, DC, MC, V. Closed Sun.*

$
✕ 🖫 **Grotto Paudese.** Immaculate, friendly, and family-run, this grotto-cum-bed-and-breakfast perches high above the town in the tiny hamlet of Paudo. Its handful of rooms are tastefully simple if small; they squeeze in the occasional antique chest of drawers. There's also an unsurpassed view of the twinkling valley and the Alps beyond. The adjoining grotto is warmly traditional, turning out a robust daily meal (homemade pasta, polenta, and the like). The inn is roughly a 15-minute drive from Bellinzona. Going east into the Val Morobbia, follow signs for Pianezzo and then for Paudo. ⊠ *CH-6582 Paudo,* ☎ FAX *091/8571468. 4 rooms. Restaurant, bar. V. Closed mid-Dec.–Apr.*

En Route To see the deep countryside of the Ticino—beyond its resorts and cities—follow the A2 expressway north from Bellinzona toward St. Gotthard; after 17 km (11 mi), exit at **Biasca,** a miniature Bellinzona itself, as it guards two major access roads from the north.

Valle di Blenio

❷ *17 km (11 mi) north of Bellinzona, 80 km (49 mi) north of Lugano.*

North of Biasca toward Olivone is the Valle di Blenio, a characteristic Ticinese valley cutting deeper and higher into wild, rocky country. Its villages mingle tidy suburban cottages with the architectural signature of Ticino life: ancient stone houses, some little more than huts, with ramshackle roofs of odd-size slabs. This is the *rustico* once inhabited by mountain peasants starving under the harsh rule of the Swiss-German confederates. Today the heirs of both those ancient lines happily profit from a new twist: the Ticinese now rent their *rustici* to wealthy tourists—most of them Swiss-German—seeking to escape the pressures of urban prosperity. In these villages—Largario, Ponto Valentino, Prugiasco—you'll see the real, rural Ticino.

Locarno

❸ *21 km (13 mi) west of Bellinzona, 39 km (24 mi) northwest of Lugano.*

Superbly placed on the sheltered curve of the northernmost tip of Lake Maggiore and surrounded on all sides by mountains, Locarno is Switzerland's sunniest town. Subtropical flora flourish here, with date palms and fig trees, bougainvillea, rhododendron, even aloe vera burgeoning on the waterfront. Its fauna are no less colorful: every spring, summer, and fall the arcaded streets and cafés teem with exotic characters in fur coats and T-shirts, lamé, leather—and sunglasses. You don't show your face in Locarno without a stylish set of shades.

In August, Locarno makes worldwide news with its film festival, showcasing the latest cinema on an outdoor screen in the Piazza Grande; it is also host to international artists in concert. Its facilities haven't just drawn culture hounds: here, in 1925, Briand, Stresemann, Mussolini, and Chamberlain initialed the Locarno Pact, securing the peace—albeit temporarily—in Europe.

Locarno's raison d'être is its waterfront, which has a graceful promenade curving around the east flank of the bay and a beach and public pool complex along the west. Its clear lake is often still as glass, reflecting the Ticinese Alps across to the south. Locarno's Lombard-style arcades and historic landmarks continually draw visitors inland as well. There are a few pedestrians-only streets in the heart of the Old Town.

★ The **Piazza Grande** is the heart of the Old Town and its social center, too: from under the crowded arcades shoppers spill onto open ground to lounge in cafés and watch each other drink, smoke, and pose. **Chiesa Nuova** (New Church; ✉ Via Cittadella) is an exuberantly decorated baroque church (1630) with an enormous statue of St. Christopher on the facade. Down the street from the New Church, the **Casa dei Canonici** (House of the Canons; ✉ Via Cittadella) dates from the same period. Note the lovely interior courtyard; it's now a private house.

The 17th-century **Chiesa di Sant'Antonio** (Church of St. Anthony) lies at the end of **Via Sant'Antonio,** a fine, narrow street lined with splendid old houses in both medieval and flamboyant baroque styles. Immediately to the right of the Church of St. Anthony stands the **Casa Rusca,** an 18th-century residence that now serves as the city art gallery. Its permanent collections include the work of Jean Arp, and temporary exhibits highlight both Swiss and international artists. ✉ *Via Sant'Antonio,* ☎ *091/7563170.* ⌨ *7 SF.* ☉ *Tues.–Sun. 10–5.*

The heavy, frescoed **Chiesa di San Francesco** (Church of St. Francis) and its convent date from the mid-15th century; legend has it that it was founded by St. Anthony of Padua. The emblems on its Renaissance facade show Locarno's social distinctions of the era: the eagle represents the aristocrats; a lamb, the country folk; and the ox (unkind, surely), the citizens. In its sanctuary, concerts are performed every spring and fall; contact the tourist office (☞ Visitor Information *in* The Ticino A to Z, *below*) for more information. ✉ *Via S. Francesco.*

Built in 1300 as a stronghold of the dukes of Milan, **Castello Visconteo** was soon virtually destroyed by the invading Swiss Confederates. Today it contains a **Museo Civico e Archeologico** (Municipal and Archaeological Museum), with Roman relics, including a major glass collection, and Romanesque sculpture. ✉ *Piazza Castello 2,* ☎ *091/ 7563180.* ⌨ *5 SF.* ☉ *Apr.–Oct., Tues.–Sun. 10–5.*

★ You can get to the **Santuario Madonna del Sasso** (Sanctuary of the Madonna of the Rock) via a five-minute funicular ride to a high plateau (the funicular is close to the train station). The sprawling church complex is where, in 1480, Brother Bartolomeo da Ivrea saw a vision of the Virgin Mary; the sanctuary was begun seven years later and gradually enlarged to include a convent, a museum, and side galleries. Within the sanctuary, you'll find Bramantino's *The Flight into Egypt* (1520) and *Christ Carried to the Sepulcher,* a dramatic, Caravaggiesque procession scene painted in 1870 by Antonio Ciseri, from nearby Ascona. You'll also see naïve-art votive gifts to the Madonna from peasants who've survived everything from family tragedies to fender benders. ⊠ *Via Santuario 2, Orselina,* ☎ *091/7436265.* ☉ *Sanctuary: daily 6:30 AM–8 PM; church: daily 6:30 AM–7 PM; museum: weekdays 2–4:30, Sun. 10–noon and 2–5.*

OFF THE
BEATEN PATH

CIMETTA – A winter-sports center with views of Monte Rosa, the Swiss Alps, and the Italian Apennines, Cimetta (1,672 m/5,482 ft) can be reached only by chairlift; first you must catch a cable car (near the train station) to Cardada, then a chairlift to the resort. But don't be put off; the ride is part of the fun: as the lake falls away below, you'll sail over meadows and wooded hills. Cimetta is also a hiker's paradise. The trip costs 33 SF. ☎ *091/7353030.* ☉ *Summer and winter, daily 8:30–5:30.*

Dining and Lodging

$$$$
★

✕ **Centenario.** Set back from the waterfront east of the urban tangle, this gracious *ristorante* serves innovative Franco-Italian cuisine that is unashamedly nouvelle and absolutely top quality, from its moderately priced business lunch to the all-out *menu de dégustation* (sampling menu). Specialties include risotto in merlot with crayfish tails, rack of roe deer, and tangy lemon soufflé. You can have an aperitif on the lakefront terrace before sitting down to a meal surrounded by quarry tile, Persian rugs, and gleaming silver. ⊠ *Lungolago 13, Locarno-Muralto,* ☎ *091/7438222. AE, DC, MC, V. Closed Sun. and Mon.*

$-$$

✕ **Casa del Popolo.** Although the politics might lean left at this popular restaurant, the Italian favorites are done just right. Try the amazingly delicate *picatta alla Milanese* (veal cutlets pounded thin, coated in egg, and sautéed), the spicy *penne all'arrabbiata* (pasta with red pepper and tomato sauce), or any of the 20 types of pizza. Red-checked tablecloths and occasional appearances by the local politico round it all out. ⊠ *Piazza Corporazione,* ☎ *091/7511208. No credit cards.*

$$$-$$$$

✕🏨 **Belvedere.** Well above the city, this wonderfully situated hotel has gone all out, with interiors in postmodern beech, lacquer, and marble. All rooms face south; the suites in the wing on the hill offer particularly breathtaking views. The elegant dining hall, with its frescoes, elaborately trimmed vaults, and a massive stone fireplace, is all that remains of the original building, a private home built in 1680. L'Affresco, the formal restaurant, serves upscale Italian specialties; look for the turbot in a potato crust and the homemade pastas. You can reach the Belvedere by funicular from the train station or on foot in a five-minute uphill walk. ⊠ *Via ai Monti della Trinità 44, CH-6601,* ☎ *091/ 7510363,* ℻ *091/7515239. 52 rooms, 12 suites. 3 restaurants, bar, no-smoking rooms, pool, hot tub, sauna, health club, bicycles, playground, business services. AE, DC, MC, V.* 🕭

$$$-$$$$

✕🏨 **Reber au Lac.** This richly landscaped oasis at the end of the waterfront row holds a roomy, comfortable hotel dating from 1886 and continuously run by the Reber family. The interiors exude patrician calm with pleasing touches such as antique Venetian glass lamps, lacy duvet covers, and the occasional bit of gilt or wrought iron. Awning-shaded balconies overlook the lake or pool, and interiors are done in tasteful pastels—no two rooms are alike. The Grill Room has a good reputation among locals for its Franco-Italian cuisine and creative fish menus served in a Spanish setting. ✉ *Viale Verbano 55, CH-6600 Locarno-Muralto,* ☎ *091/7358700,* 𝔽𝔸𝕏 *091/7358701. 60 rooms, 8 suites. Restaurant, bar, no-smoking rooms, pool, sauna, tennis court, beach, business services. AE, DC, MC, V. Closed mid-Nov.–Feb.* ✍

\$\$–\$\$\$ ✕⊡ **Hotel Navegna.** It may not look like much from the outside, but
★   this is a true diamond in the rough, right on the lake farther up the shore from the promenade. The rooms are simply furnished in bright florals, and there's a fireplace in the living room for damp days. But it is the inventive Ticinese cooking that earns raves for gregarious owner Enrico Ravelli. The phenomenally delicate homemade pastas should not be missed. It's easiest to reach the hotel via the Minusio exit from the A13 highway. ✉ *Via alla Riva 2, CH-6648 Locarno-Munusio,* ☎ *091/7432222,* 𝔽𝔸𝕏 *091/7433150. 22 rooms. Restaurant, bicycles. MC, V. Closed Dec.–Feb.* ✍

\$–\$\$\$ ✕⊡ **Cittadella.** This popular dining spot in the Old Town offers inexpensive regional food—pizzas, pastas, simply prepared fish—in its casual downstairs trattoria and fine fish dishes in the more formal restaurant upstairs. The preparation is light, the flavors subtle with oils and herbs. Upstairs are a handful of pleasing rooms, some up under the rafters, all with classic stone-tile floors in cream and red. They may be simple, but they're a great bargain. ✉ *Via Cittadella 18, CH-6600,* ☎ *091/7515885,* 𝔽𝔸𝕏 *091/7517759. 11 rooms. Restaurant. AE, DC, MC, V.*

\$\$–\$\$\$ ⊡ **Du Lac.** A terrific location makes this friendly garni hotel a particularly good base. It's at the east end of the Old Town's nerve center, the Piazza Grande, but as it's in a pedestrians-only zone and across from the public gardens, it's calm and quiet. The rooms are done in refreshing cool greens, yellows, and blues; many have balconies. There's a lovely terrace for breakfast, and public parking is close by. ✉ *Via Ramogna 3, CH-6600,* ☎ *091/7512921,* 𝔽𝔸𝕏 *091/7516071. 30 rooms. Breakfast room. AE, DC, MC, V.* ✍

Nightlife and the Arts

BARS

The piano bar/jazz club **La Bussola** (✉ Lungolago, Locarno-Muralto, ☎ 091/7436095) is a favorite among locals; it's closed on Tuesday. **Palm'Arte** (✉ Hotel La Palma au Lac, Viale Verbano 29, Locarno-Muralto, ☎ 091/7353636) is a good piano bar; it's closed Tuesday during the high season and from December to February. **Simba Bar** (✉ Lungolago Motta 3a, ☎ 091/7523388) is very popular with a young crowd of locals and Italians.

CASINO

The **Casinò di Locarno** (✉ Via Largo Zorzi 1, Piazza Grande, ☎ 091/7511535) has 195 slot machines and *boule* (a type of roulette), with a federally imposed 5 SF limit. It's open every day from noon to 2 AM, until 4 AM on Friday and Saturday nights.

FILM

The **Locarno International Film Festival,** gaining ground from Cannes on the prestige front because of the caliber of the films it premieres, takes place every August in the Piazza Grande. The 2001 festival will run August 8–18. For information contact: Festival Internazionale del Film Locarno (✉ Via B. Luini 3/a, CH-6601 Locarno, ☎ 091/7562121).

MUSIC

The **I Feel Good Funk Festival,** a new, annual open-air event staged in the Piazza Grande, hosts local and international funk artists. It's slated to run in mid-June 2001. The **Back Home Again–American Music Festival Locarno** is scheduled for late May 2001. The musical menu has a little of everything, from Cajun and country to bluegrass and blues.

Valle Verzasca

④ *12 km (7 mi) north of Locarno, 25 km (15½ mi) north of Lugano.*

A short drive along the A13 highway through the wild and rugged mountain gorge of the Valle Verzasca leads to **Corippo,** where a painterly composition of stone houses and a 17th-century church are all protected as architectural landmarks.

About 12 km (7 mi) north of Corippo, in the town of **Lavertezzo,** you'll find a graceful double-arch stone bridge, the **Ponte dei Salti,** dating from 1700. The mountain village of Sonogno lies at the end of the 26-km (16-mi) valley.

Valle Maggia

⑤ *4 km (2 mi) northwest of Locarno, 30 km (19 mi) northwest of Lugano.*

A drive through this rugged agricultural valley that stretches northwest from Locarno will give you a sense of the tough living conditions endured for centuries by Ticinese farmers, who today mine granite. The valley is cut so far into the earth that sunlight in winter never seems to reach bottom—a stark contrast to sunny Locarno, only a short distance south. Until the 1920s, many Valle Maggia natives immigrated to the United States; some returned, bringing with them several English phrases that still pepper the local dialect. As you pass through Gordevio, Maggia, Someo, and Cevio—the latter, the valley's main village—you'll feel as if you're in a time capsule. There's little commercialization, and the mostly 17th-century houses call to mind a movie set. Bignasco, just beyond Cevio, is the last village before the valley splits in two continuing north.

OFF THE
BEATEN PATH

MOGNO – Beyond Bignasco, to the east, lies the Val Lavizzara. At Peccia the road splits again, with Val Sambuco to the east. Nearly at the end of this valley, in tiny Mogno, stands a beautiful modernist chapel built in 1994 by world-renowned Ticinese architect Mario Botta, who designed the San Francisco Museum of Modern Art.

Ascona

⑥ *3 km (1¾ mi) west of Locarno.*

Though it's only a few minutes from Locarno, tiny Ascona has a life of its own. Little more than a fishing village until the turn of the century, the town was adopted by a high-minded group of northerners who arrived to develop a utopian, vegetarian artists' colony on **Monte Verità,** the hillside park behind the waterfront center. Influenced by Eastern and Western religions as well as the new realms of psychology, its ideals attracted thousands of sojourners, including dancer Isadora Duncan and psychologist C. G. Jung. You can visit the group of Monte Verità buildings, including the unusual flat-roof, wooden **Casa Anatta,** and view papers and relics of the group's works. ☎ *091/7910327 or 091/7910181 (Monte Verità Foundation).* ⊡ *6 SF.* ⊙ *Apr.–June and Sept.–Oct., Tues.–Sun. 2:30–6; July and Aug., Tues.–Sun. 3–7.*

Monte Verità's influence spread and its reputation grew throughout the world. Today the still-small village of 5,000 attracts artists, art restorers, and traditional bookbinders to its ancient, narrow streets. On ★ the waterfront, however, it's a sun-and-fun scene, with the **Piazza Motta** (isolated from traffic as a pedestrian zone) crowded with sidewalk cafés and the promenade on the water's edge swarming with boats.

Behind Piazza Motta, a charming labyrinth of lanes leads uphill past artisan galleries (not all showing gallery-quality work) to **Via Borgo,** lined with contemporary shops and galleries.

OFF THE
BEATEN PATH

BRISSAGO ISLANDS – From Ascona, an easy excursion by car or bus leads to Brissago, a flowery lakefront resort at the lowest elevation in Switzerland. The main attraction, however, lies offshore: the Brissago Islands have been federally preserved as botanical gardens, with more than 1,000 species of subtropical plants. Plaques identify the flora in Italian, German, and French; an English guide to the plants is for sale at the gate (5 SF). You may have lunch or drinks at the islands' restaurant, in a beautifully restored 1929 villa that now doubles as a seminar center and offers lodging to groups. Individuals must leave with the last boat back to the mainland—usually around 5:45—so check schedules carefully when you plan your excursion. You can buy tickets at the entrance or with the boat ticket; group and Swiss Boat Pass (☞ Boat Travel in Smart Travel Tips A to Z) discounts apply. ⊠ *Boats depart regularly from Brissago, Porto Ronco, Ascona, and Locarno,* ☎ *091/7511865.* 🚢 *Boat: 11 SF round-trip from Ascona, 20 SF round-trip from Locarno; island: 5 SF.*

Dining and Lodging

$$–$$$ ✕ **San Pietro.** Tucked away in a maze of tiny streets, this little gem offers creative Italian-influenced pasta and fish dishes. Sample its wolf fish in a salt crust, champagne risotto with shrimp, pumpkin gnocchi with walnuts and sage, or any of the grilled specialties. The most romantic tables are in the intimate garden, slipped between the walls of neighboring houses. ⊠ *Passagio S. Pietro,* ☎ *091/7913976. AE, DC, MC, V. Closed Mon. and Jan..*

$–$$ ✕ **Osteria Nostrana.** The tables of this bustling restaurant spill out into the piazza overlooking the lake. Inside, rough wooden ceilings, marbletop tables, chandeliers, and a hodgepodge of photos and posters add to its charm. The menu includes spaghetti Enzo (with porcini mushrooms, bacon, and cream) as well as daily and seasonal specials. The wine list deserves consideration; it has more than 100 Italian and Swiss vintages. ⊠ *Piazza Motta,* ☎ *091/7915158. AE, DC, MC, V.*

$$$$ ✕🏨 **Giardino.** Glamorous, atmospheric, cosmopolitan—this hotel
★   feels like the kissing cousin of a Mediterranean villa. Portuguese ceramics, Florentine floor tiles, Veronese marble, ceramic room-number plaques in della Robbia style, and even a Swiss-baroque carved-wood conference chamber from Zürich's Bierhalle Kropf have been imported. The luxury of this Relais & Châteaux property borders on decadence: the sheets are pure linen, ground-floor rooms have small private gardens, and there's a landscaped pool, not to mention a chauffeured Bentley, an antique-bus shuttle service, and pink bicycles for guest use. The staff is extraordinary—all young, warm, and professional. The restaurants are excellent: Aphrodite, with modern Italian and vegetarian cuisine, rates among the best in Switzerland. The Osteria runs close behind with its regional and Italian specialties. Varied weekly programs include a sunrise mountaintop breakfast, lunch on the hotel's boat, simple hikes and bike-and-picnic excursions. On Sunday there's Teatro Giardino: dinner theater including ballet one week, singing waiters, jazz, or opera the next. Prepare to be spoiled. ⊠ *Via Segnale 10, CH-6612,* ☎ *091/7858888,* 🖷 *091/7858899. 54 rooms, 18 suites, 5 apartments. 3 restaurants, bar, pool, beauty salon, hot tub, steam room, bicycles, baby-sitting. AE, DC, MC, V. Closed mid-Nov.–mid-Mar.* 🍽

$$$$ 🏨 **Casa Berno.** This Relais du Silence hotel manages absolute isolation; it's on a forest road tucked into a hillside far above the town and lake. Self-contained and calm, the hotel appeals to relaxed vacation-

ers who want to laze by the big pool overlooking the lake, have drinks and lunch on the broad roof terrace, and get away from it all—completely. The bar and lounge, both with breathtaking views, were redone in spring 2000 in lapis blue brightened with pastels. Multilevel terraces catch the best views, from the Brissago Islands to Bellinzona. Room decor ranges from polished, dark wood to white wood with red or blue accents. Request a room on one of the top floors for the most sweeping views. Demipension is encouraged, but menus can be modified. ⊠ CH-6612, ☎ 091/7913232, FAX 091/7921114. 65 rooms. 2 restaurants, bar, pool, beauty salon, sauna, health club, bicycles. AE, DC, MC, V. Closed Nov.–mid-Mar. ✍

$$$–$$$$ ⊞ **Castello Seeschloss.** Dating from 1250, though completely rebuilt
★ within, this Romantik property is a romantic enough hotel as is—not even taking into account its garden setting and position across from the waterfront. Its interior is rich with frescoes, beams, vaults, and heavy masonry, lightened with a contemporary touch. Each room is different: a wrought-iron bed in the back tower, a blue wooden canopy bed in Room 205, or the loft in the lavish front tower room. Most impressive are the lakeside rooms, which have original 16th- to 18th-century frescoes. There are a private courtyard for summer-night dining and an isolated pool. Honeymooners, take note: deluxe rooms in the towers start at prices not much higher than standard doubles. ⊠ Piazza Motta, CH-6612, ☎ 091/7910161, FAX 091/7911804. 45 rooms. 2 restaurants, bar, no-smoking rooms, pool. AE, DC, MC, V. Closed mid-Nov.–mid-Mar. ✍

$$–$$$ ⊞ **Schiff.** You're assured of a good view at this family owned and -run hotel; the front rooms face the bustling piazza and the placid lake, while back rooms look over the rooftops. All are pretty and bright, with spring-green decor and white-tile baths. Look into the excellent low- and off-season deals here. ⊠ Lungolago G. Motta 21, CH-6612, ☎ 091/7912533, FAX 091/7921315. 16 rooms. Restaurant, café, bicycles, parking (fee). AE, DC, MC, V. Closed mid-Dec.–mid-Feb. ✍

$–$$$ ⊞ **Tamaro.** The shuttered windows of this 18th-century patrician house look out on the waterfront; inside, you can lounge in sitting rooms richly furnished with antiques, books, and even a grand piano. The rooms range from lavish corner doubles with lake views and repro antiques to tiny quarters overlooking the courtyard that are an excellent value. There's a private sun terrace high over the street with fine lake views. ⊠ Piazza G. Motta 35, CH-6612, ☎ 091/854848, FAX 091/7912928. 51 rooms. 3 restaurants, café, pool, bicycles, meeting room. AE, MC, DC, V. Closed mid-Nov.–Feb. ✍

Nightlife and the Arts

The ideals that brought Isadora Duncan here still bring culture to Ascona: Every year it hosts Ascona New Orleans Jazz and the Settimane Musicali di Ascona series of world-class classical music concerts (☞ Music, below). The lakefront piazza serves as an open-air stage for almost daily summer entertainment, with mime, theater, and live pop bands. Locarno's August film festival is only a cab ride away across the peninsula.

BARS AND DANCING

Very popular, but not too wild, dancing can be found at the **Lello Bar** (⊠ Via Aerodromo 3, ☎ 091/7911374). **La Tana** (⊠ Via Locarno 110, ☎ 091/7911381) has live music and striptease acts. Note that most bars and clubs are open only during the tourist season (Easter–late October), but La Tana is open year-round.

MUSIC

Ascona New Orleans Jazz (☎ 091/7910090) seeks out performers a cut above standard Dixieland and swing groups and brings an amazing international selection of them to its open-air bandstands; in 2001 the festival will run from late June to early July. The **Settimane Musicali** (Musical Weeks; ☎ 091/7851943) bring in full orchestras, chamber groups, and top-ranking soloists to Ascona and Locarno; in 2001 they will run from August 27 to October 16.

THEATER

The **Teatro di Locarno** (✉ Palazzo Kursaal, Via Largo Zorzi 1, ☎ 091/7566151) hosts international theatrical companies from October through May. For tickets contact the tourist office (☞ Visitor Information *in* The Ticino A to Z, *below*).

SOTTOCENERI

Although Monte Ceneri is no Everest, it marks the borderline between the Sopraceneri with its vastly different southern cousin "below" the Ceneri. The Sottoceneri is the Ticino with attitude, where culture and natural beauty join forces with business and cash. The resort town of Lugano is an international glamour magnet, but even there the incredible scenery and native Ticinese warmth haven't been completely upstaged.

Lugano

45 km (28 mi) southeast of Ascona, 39 km (24 mi) southeast of Locarno.

Strung around a sparkling bay like Venetian glass beads, with dark, conical mountains rising primordially out of its waters and icy peaks framing the scene, Lugano earns its nickname as the Rio of the Old World. Of the three world-class waterfront resorts, Lugano tops Ascona and Locarno for architectural style, sophistication, and natural beauty. This is not to say that it has avoided the pitfalls of a successful modern resort: there's thick traffic right up to the waterfront, much of it manic Italian style, and it has more than its share of concrete waterfront high-rise hotels with balconies skewed to produce "a room with a view" regardless of aesthetic cost. Yet the sacred *passeggiata*—the afternoon stroll to see and be seen that winds down every Italian day—asserts the city's true personality as a graceful, sophisticated resort. It's not Swiss, not Italian. . . just Lugano.

A Good Walk

Begin at the **Piazza della Riforma** ⑦, which is dominated by the **Palazzo Civico** ⑧, or town hall. Look up to the gable above the clock to see the city's coat of arms. (The building also houses the tourist office, entrance on the lake side.) On the western side of the square the Piazza della Riforma bleeds into the **Piazza Rezzonico**, which contains a large fountain by Otto Maraini (1895).

Heading out of the Piazza della Riforma on the north side, onto the Via Luvini, you come to the **Piazza Dante**, which is dominated by a large department store and a bank. From here, if you pop over one street east to the busy Via Pretorio, you can get a look at Lugano's oldest building, the **Pretorio** (1425), at No. 7. Back at Piazza Dante, turn left down Via Pessina, which will lead you into the **Piazza Cioccaro**, on your right. Here the funicular from the train station terminates and the typical **Old Town** begins, its narrow streets lined with chic clothing shops and small markets offering pungent local cheeses and porcini mushrooms.

From the Piazza Cioccaro walk up the shop-lined staircase street of Via Cattedrale. The street curves left, ending at the **Cattedrale di San Lorenzo** ⑨. Take a moment to enjoy the view from the church square.

Continue up to the right of the church on Via Paolo Ragazonni to the Hotel Federale; there you can leave the road and take the footpath through the gardens on the slope below the train station. Go up the steps but don't cross over to the station. Turn left and follow the Via Maraini south to the end of the parking lot. Cross over the tracks at the marked crossing and turn onto the path that will lead you to **Parco del Tassino** ⑩.

Retrace your steps back to the station and on the way down just near the cathedral, explore the Salita Chiattone, another street of steps and shops parallel to Via Cattedrale. Before reaching the bottom, turn right to connect with Piazza Cioccaro and the funicular. Turn right onto the Via Pessina and follow it into the lively **Piazza Maraini**. Here you can start a leisurely stroll down the **Via Nassa**, which runs between the Piazza della Riforma and the Piazza Luini. It's characterized by a long row of porticos, many housing chic designer clothing shops. Nestled among the medieval and modern buildings on the right, between Piazza San Carlo and Piazza Battaglini, is the 17th-century baroque church **San Carlo Borromeo.** The street ends at the **Chiesa di Santa Maria degli Angioli** ⑪, facing the lake at the Piazza Luini.

Across the road, spreading south along the lakefront promenade, is the **Giardino Belvedere** ⑫. At the southwest end of the gardens, an incongruous **bust of George Washington** stands on the lake promenade in its own little gazebo. "Georgio" Washington never visited Lugano; this image was erected in 1859 by a grateful Swiss engineer who had made his fortune in America. A little farther south, directly across the Riva Antonio Caccia, is the **Museo d'Arte Moderna** ⑬.

Head back northeast along the waterfront promenade, and at the Imbarcadero Centrale (Central Wharf) take the underpass to cross the road, coming back up at the Piazza della Riforma. Leave the piazza at the northeast side through a portico onto the Via Canova. After crossing over the Via della Posta/Via Albrizzi, you'll come to the **Museo Cantonale d'Arte** ⑮, on your right. Continue straight ahead to the 17th-century church of San Rocco, with its neobaroque facade. Turn left onto Via Carducci (before the church), and you'll find a small orange-tile pedestrian entranceway into the **Quartiere Maghetti**—a town within a town. It's a tangle of streets full of porticoes, little squares, shops, and offices, a modern take on old forms, created in the early 1980s by the architects Camazind, Brocchi, and Sennhauser. Exit the Quartiere Maghetti onto Via Canova (you'll be behind the church now) and continue east, crossing Via Stauffacher. On your left is the open Piazza dell'Independenza. Cross over the wide Corso Elvezia to enter the **Parco Civico** ⑯. Inside the grounds, in addition to the 60,000 square m (nearly 15 acres) of greenery, you'll find the **Museo Civico di Belle Arti** ⑰ and **Museo Cantonale di Storia Naturale** ⑱. From here you can opt to spend the afternoon at the **Lido** ⑲, the city's public beach and pool, just east of the park across the River Cassarate. Or you can head back to town along the waterfront promenade, known as **Il Lungolago** ⑭, and take in the stunning mountain views: straight ahead, the rocky top of Monte Generoso (1,702 m/5,579 ft), and flanking the bay at right and left, respectively, Monte San Salvatore and Monte Brè.

TIMING

It is best to walk through the city in the morning, before it gets too hot. A quick overview, without much time in the museums or parks, would take a couple of hours. Or make a day of it, taking in the main sights in the morning, stopping for lunch, and then spending the afternoon in the museums or on the Lido. Remember that the museums are closed on Monday.

Sights to See

⑨ Cattedrale di San Lorenzo (Cathedral of St. Lawrence). Behind this church's early Renaissance facade is a richly frescoed baroque interior with a baptismal font dating from 1430. The church has pre-medieval origins: it became a collegiate church in 1078. Eight hundred years later it became a cathedral. ⊠ *Via Cattedrale.*

★ **⑪ Chiesa di Santa Maria degli Angioli** (Church of St. Mary of the Angels). The simple facade doesn't prepare you for the riches within. Begun in the late 15th century, the church contains a magnificent fresco of the *Passion and Crucifixion,* as well as *The Last Supper* and *Madonna with the Infant Jesus,* all by Bernardino Luini (1475–1532). ⊠ *Piazza Luini.*

⑫ Giardino Belvedere (Belvedere Gardens). This lakefront sculpture garden frames a dozen modern sculptures with palms, camellias, oleanders, and magnolias. At the far west end there's a public swimming area. ⊠ *On lake side of Quai Riva Antonio Caccia near Piazza Luini.* 🎟 *Free.* ⊙ *Daily, 24 hrs.*

⑲ Lido. The city's public beach has two swimming pools and a restaurant. To reach it, you'll have to cross the Cassarate River, heading east from the Parco Civico; follow the riverbank left to the main street, Viale Castagnola, and then turn right. The main swimming-area entrance is just ahead on the right. Everyone from families to scenesters comes here to cool off. ☎ *091/9714041.* 🎟 *7 SF; changing cabins 3 SF.* ⊙ *May, June, and Sept., daily 9:30–6; July and Aug., daily 9–7.*

★ **⑭ Il Lungolago** (waterfront promenade). This 2-km (1-mi) lakefront path lined with pollarded lime trees, funereal cypresses, and palm trees stretches from the Lido all the way to the Paradiso neighborhood and is the place to see and be seen, while taking in the views, of course. At night luminous fountains turn the lake near the Parco Civico into a special attraction.

⑬ Museo d'Arte Moderna (Museum of Modern Art). In addition to interesting temporary exhibitions, such as shows of Kirchner or Munch, this museum displays an enormous permanent collection of works by international artists such as Henri Rousseau, Monet, Pissarro, and Futurist artist Umberto Boccioni. Ticinese artists are represented as well. Museum literature is available in English. ⊠ *Villa Malpensata, Riva Antonio Caccia 5,* ☎ *091/9944370.* 🎟 *10 SF.* ⊙ *Tues.–Sun. 9–7.*

⑮ Museo Cantonale d'Arte (Cantonal Art Museum). A group of three palaces dating from the 15th to the 19th centuries was adapted for this museum. Its permanent and temporary exhibits span paintings, sculpture, and photography, including some important avant-garde works. The permanent collection holds works by Klee, Turner, Degas, Renoir, and Hodler as well as contemporary Ticinese artists. Descriptive material is available in English. ⊠ *Via Canova 10,* ☎ *091/9104780.* 🎟 *Permanent collection: 7 SF; temporary exhibits: 10 SF.* ⊙ *Wed.–Sun. 10–5, Tues. 2–5.*

⑱ Museo Cantonale di Storia Naturale (Cantonal Museum of Natural History). A museum since 1854, it contains exhibits on fossils, animals, and plants (there's a large section on mushrooms), mostly those typical of the region. ⊠ *Viale Cattaneo 4, in the Parco Civico,* ☎ *091/9115380.* 🎟 *Free.* ⊙ *Tues.–Sat. 9–noon and 2–5.*

⑰ Museo Civico di Belle Arti (Muncipal Art Museum). The restored Villa Ciani, with its lofty vaulted ceilings and tile floors, displays hundreds of works by Swiss and European artists from the 15th to the 20th centuries. Especially noteworthy is the extensive collection of paintings by Futurist Umberto Boccioni, Cesare Tallone, and other late 19th and early 20th-century artists. English-language museum literature is available. ⊠ *Villa Ciani, in Parco Civico,* ☎ *091/8007196.* ⊡ *5 SF.* ☉ *Tues.–Fri. 10–noon and 2–6.*

⑧ Palazzo Civico (Town Hall). This neoclassical Lombard structure dates from 1844. Inside there is a large inner yard surrounded by a four-sided arcade, with a wide vestibule on the piazza side. It houses the town council and tourist office. ⊠ *Piazza della Riforma.*

⑯ Parco Civico (City Park). A green oasis in the city center, the park has cacti, exotic shrubs, and more than 1,000 varieties of roses, as well as an aviary, a tiny deer zoo, and a fine view of the bay from its peninsula. ⊠ *Area south of Viale Carlo Cattaneo, east of Piazza Castello.* ⊡ *Free.* ☉ *Daily, 24 hrs.*

☞ ⑩ Parco del Tassino (Tassino Park). On a plateau just behind and south of the train station, this park offers lovely bay views from among its rose gardens. A small deer park and playground make it very child-friendly. ⊠ *Take Bus 2 east to San Domenico stop in Castagnola, or use funicular from Old Town to train station.* ⊡ *Free.*

★ ⑦ Piazza della Riforma (Reformation Square). In the early 19th century, several buildings were removed in order to enlarge the square—providing more room for the 20th-century café tables. Commonly referred to simply as "la Piazza," it's the social and cultural heart of the city and the site of markets and open-air music performances. ⊠ *Just north of Imbarcadero Centrale (main boat wharf).*

OFF THE BEATEN PATH

VILLA FAVORITA – This splendid 16th-century mansion in Castagnola houses a portion of the extraordinary private art collection of the Baron von Thyssen-Bornemisza. Although, after a scandalous international divorce battle, portions of the collection were transferred to Spain, a significant display of 19th- and 20th-century paintings and watercolors from Europe and America remains. Artists represented include Giorgio de Chirico, Frederick Church, Lucien Freud, Edward Hopper, Jackson Pollock, and Andrew Wyeth. The villa gardens are also worth a stroll; they're planted with native and exotic flora. Take Bus 1 in the direction of Castagnola (ask to be let off at the Villa as the bus only stops on demand), or take the 40-minute walk from town, heading east along the lake on Viale Castagnola, which turns into Via Riviera past the Castagnola Wharf. You may want to call ahead, as opening hours and entrance fees can change during special exhibitions. ⊠ *Strada Castagnola, Via Rivera 14,* ☎ *091/9716152.* ⊡ *10 SF.* ☉ *Easter–Oct., Fri.–Sun. 10–5.*

CASTAGNOLA PARKS – For an idyllic daytime excursion, combine a trip to the Villa Favorita (☞ *above*) with one or both of the parks adjacent to it. The **Parco degli Ulivi** (Olive Park) spreads over the lower slopes of Monte Brè and offers a romantic landscape of silvery olive trees mixed with cypress, laurel, and wild rosemary; you enter it from the Gandria Footpath (Sentiero di Gandria). **Parco San Michele** (St. Michael Park), also on Monte Brè, has a public chapel and a broad terrace that overlooks the city, the lake, and, beyond, the Alps. From Cassarate, walk up the steps by the lower terminus of the Monte Brè funicular.

MONTE BRÈ, MONTE SAN SALVATORE, MONTE GENEROSO – The serious view hound may want to reach the top of one of the three peaks that define the landscape around Lugano. **Monte Brè** has a funicular that takes you up from the east end of Lugano in Cassarate, although it's also possible to drive, cycle, or hike to the crest. At the top are several well-marked hiking trails, and there is an "art trail" in the summit village of

128

Lugano

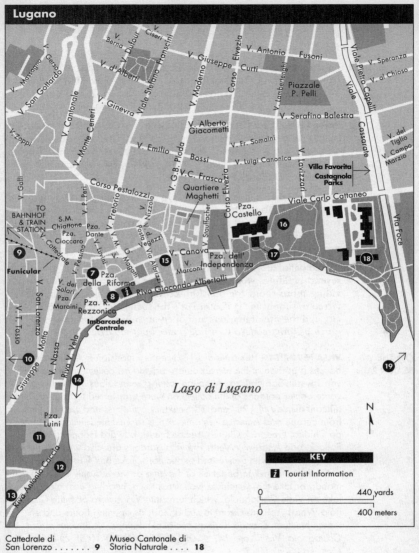

Brè, a path studded with pieces of sculpture. A guided tour can be booked for the art trail at the funicular station. **Monte San Salvatore** can be reached via the funicular in Paradiso. At the top are a huge relief model of the entire Sottoceneri region, marked "nature itinerary" paths, which have signs pointing out flower and tree specimens, and other marked hikes down and around the area. For yet more spectacular views take a boat from Lugano across to Capolago, where you can take the 40-minute cogwheel train up **Monte Generoso.** At the top are a restaurant, café, and lots of marked hiking trails. *Monte Brè:* ☎ 091/ 9713171. 🚠 *19 SF round-trip.* ⊘ *Feb.–Dec., daily 9:10–noon and 12:45–6:30. Monte San Salvatore:* ☎ 091/9852828. 🚠 *18 SF round-trip.* ⊘ *Mid-Mar.–mid-Nov., daily 8:30–7. Monte Generoso:* ☎ 091/ 6481105. 🚠 *49 SF round-trip.* ⊘ *Dec.–Oct., trains up at 10, 11, noon, 2, and 3:30, trains down at 1:45, 4:15, and 5:15.*

HERMANN HESSE MUSEUM – In the tower of the Casa Camuzzi, a fabulous jumble of old houses on a hilltop in Montagnola, is this tiny but impressive museum dedicated to Hermann Hesse. Though born in Germany, the Nobel Prize–winning author became a Swiss citizen and lived here the last 43 years of his life, writing most of his important works, including *Siddhartha* and *Steppenwolf.* The rooms in which he lived and worked have been preserved; you can see his papers, books, desk, glasses, even his straw hat. Take the postbus marked Agra-Montagnola from Lugano's train station for the 10-minute ride to Montagnola. Once there, walk down past the parking lot, going straight between the old houses (and sometimes actually through them, via passageways) to the Casa Camuzzi. ⊠ *Montagnola,* ☎ 091/9933770. 🚠 *5 SF.* ⊘ *Mar.–Oct., Tues.–Sun. 10–12:30 and 2–6:30; Nov.–Feb., weekends 10–12:30 and 2–6:30.*

Dining and Lodging

$$$$ ✕ **Al Portone.** Silver and lace dress up the stucco and stone here, but
★   the ambience is strictly easy. Chef Roberto Galizzi pursues *nuova cucina* (contemporary Italian cuisine) with ambition and flair. You might choose duck liver with mango chutney and pears, spaghetti with fresh tomatoes and lobster in squid-ink sauce, or Scottish rack of lamb with a sweet red pepper confit. Or you could *lascia fare a Roberto* (leave it to Robert)—as he calls his menu *de dégustation.* ⊠ *Viale Cassarate 3, Lugano/Cassarate,* ☎ *091/9235511. AE, DC, MC, V. Closed Sun.– Mon.*

$$$ ✕ **Locanda del Boschetto.** The grill is the first thing you see in this no-
★   nonsense, grotto-style ristorante, a specialist in pure and simple seafood *alla griglia* (grilled). The decor is a study in linen and rustic wood, and the service is helpful and down to earth. ⊠ *Via Boschetto 8,* ☎ *091/ 9942493. AE, DC, MC, V. Closed Mon. and 1st 2 wks of Nov.*

$$$ ✕ **Santabbondio.** Ancient stone and terra-cotta blend with pristine pas-
★   tels in this upgraded grotto, where subtle, imaginative, new Franco-Italian cuisine *du marché* (menus based on fresh market produce) is served in intimate, formal little dining rooms and on a shady terrace. Watch for lobster risotto, scallops in orange-basil sauce, or eggplant ravioli to confirm what locals assert: chef Martin Dalsass is the canton's best. There's a good selection of open wines. You'll need a cab to get here, but it's worth the trip. ⊠ *Via Fomelino 10, Lugano/Sorengo,* ☎ *091/9932388. AE, DC, MC, V. Closed Mon., 1st wk of Jan., last wk of Feb. No lunch Sat., no dinner Sun.*

$–$$ ✕ **Al Lago.** A short drive into the countryside north of Lugano, you'll
★   find this soothing, sunny lakeside spot in the wooded wetland of a nature preserve on Origlio Lake. Calabrian chef Francesco Ferraro re-creates a Mediterranean cuisine; the extensive antipasto buffet is

delightful, but don't overlook the fresh fish and pasta dishes from various regions in Italy. ⊠ *Origlio,* ☎ *091/9451333. AE, DC, MC, V. Closed Tues., Jan., and 1st 2 wks of Nov.*

$–$$ ✕ **Da Raffaelle.** Having a meal in this family-run Italian restaurant feels like being let in on a neighborhood secret. Start with a pasta, like their marvelous homemade *orecchiette* (ear-shape pasta) with seasonal vegetables, then try something from the grill, like *gamberoni all griglia* (grilled shrimp). The staff does not speak English, but their warmth needs no translation. The restaurant is just outside the city in a residential neighborhood but is easily reached by car or bus (take Bus 8 or 9 from the train station to the last stop, Viganello). ⊠ *Contrada dei Patrizi 8/Via Pazzalino, Viganello,* ☎ *091/9716614. AE, MC, V. Closed Sun., last wk of July, and 1st 2 wks of Aug. No lunch Sat.*

$ ✕ **Grotto Figini.** Absolutely authentic, this grotto pulls in a rowdy local crowd for a *boccalino* of good merlot and a satisfying, rib-sticking meal of polenta and grilled meats. Don't expect English or other tourists, and don't take too personally the stares you'll receive when you first walk in. It's in a short stretch of woods on a hill in Gentilino, above Lugano-Paradiso. After your meal you can stroll down the shady road to see old *grotti* hidden in the overgrown hillside. ⊠ *Via ai Grotti, Gentilino,* ☎ *091/9946497. V. Closed Mon., mid-Dec.–Feb.*

$ ✕ **La Tinera.** Tucked down an alley off Via Pessina in the Old Town,
★ this cozy basement taverna squeezes loyal locals and tourists onto wooden benches for authentic regional specialties, hearty meats, and pastas. Regional wine is served in traditional ceramic bowls. ⊠ *Via dei Gorini 2,* ☎ *091/9235219. AE, DC, MC, V. Closed Sun., Aug.*

$$$$ ✕🏠 **Ticino.** In this 500-year-old former monastery (protected as a his-
★ torical monument) in the heart of the Old Town, shuttered windows look out from every room onto a glassed-in garden. The vaulted halls are lined with art and antiques, and the rooms are unpretentious yet elegant, with pleasing details such as embroidered towels and special mattresses. The formal restaurant, one of the few elegant dining establishments left in Lugano, is full of dark-wood wainscoting and leather banquettes. The menu blends Ticinese and French cuisine; it's famous for its rack of lamb with herbs and fresh seafood. The hotel is only steps from the funicular to the train station. There's a two-night minimum stay. ⊠ *Piazza Cioccaro 1, CH-6901,* ☎ *091/9227772,* 🏠 *091/9236278. 18 rooms, 2 suites. Restaurant, bar, no-smoking rooms, library. AE, DC, MC, V. No lunch on weekends. Closed Jan.* ✎

$$$$ ✕🏠 **Villa Principe Leopoldo and Residence.** This extravagantly furnished
★ garden mansion, on a hillside high over the lake (Collina d'Oro, or Golden Hill), offers Old World service with splendor to match. The villa was built in 1868 on behalf of Prince Leopold of Hohenzollern. There's a stunningly arranged pool-and-terrace complex encircled by a double staircase—a slightly baroque touch of Bel Air. The rooms in both the villa and the adjacent Residence are gracefully lush in muted tones and marble. Fabulous creations from chef Dario Ranza, such as lobster risotto or sea bass baked in a salt crust, make dining here a notable experience. ⊠ *Via Montalbano 5, CH-6900,* ☎ *091/9858855,* 🏠 *091/9858825. 70 rooms, 4 suites. 3 restaurants, bar, no-smoking rooms, pool, hot tub, massage, sauna, indoor golf, tennis court, health club, business services, meeting rooms. AE, DC, MC, V.* ✎

$$$$ 🏠 **Splendide Royale.** This landmark was first converted from a villa
★ to a hotel in 1887, and much of the Victorian luster of its public spaces—with their marble, pillars, terrazzo, and antiques—has been respectfully preserved. Since a wing was added in the '80s, you can choose between sleek rooms decorated in beech, beige, and gold or more florid period rooms in the original wing. All rooms are air-conditioned and have heated floors in the bathrooms; they offer lake or garden views

from their balconies or terraces. There's also an attractive S-shape indoor pool. ✉ *Riva A. Caccia 7, CH-6900,* ☎ *091/9857711,* FAX *091/9722. 86 rooms, 10 suites. Restaurant, piano bar, indoor pool, massage, sauna, business services, meeting rooms. AE, DC, MC, V.* ✉

$$$ **Du Lac.** This comfortable, bright hotel offers more lakefront luxury than do some glossier hotels farther down the same beach. Owned by one family since it was founded in 1920, Du Lac was completely rebuilt in 1962 and has since been regularly renovated. Huge, impressive needlework tapestry art reproductions, handmade by the owner's father, cover the walls of the open lobby and restaurant. The rooms are all spacious and face the lake; those on the sixth floor are the quietest. The hotel has a private swimming area on the lake. ✉ *Riva Paradiso 3, CH-6902 Lugano/Paradiso,* ☎ *091/9941921,* FAX *091/9941122. 52 rooms, 1 suite. Restaurant, bar, no-smoking rooms, pool, whirlpool bath, massage, sauna, exercise room, beach, waterskiing, meeting room. AE, DC, MC, V. Closed Jan.–mid-Mar.* ✉

$$$ 🏨 **International au Lac.** Just a stone's throw from the lake and next to the Church of St. Mary of the Angels, this big, old-fashioned, friendly hotel offers many lake-view rooms. The interiors are floridly decorated, with many paintings and antiques and with heavy plush furniture. The large garden and pool in the back make you forget you're downtown. Side rooms are quieter, and half the rooms are air-conditioned. ✉ *Via Nassa 68, CH-6901,* ☎ *091/9227541,* FAX *091/9227544. 80 rooms. Restaurant, bar, pool, garden, parking (fee). AE, DC, MC, V. Closed Nov.–Easter.* ✉

$$$ 🏨 **Park-Hotel Nizza.** Tucked into the dense tropical foliage of the
★ lower slopes of Monte San Salvatore and well above the lake, this former villa is an attractive combination of luxurious parlors and modern comforts. Most rooms are small, with a hodgepodge mix of old and new furnishings, but all are quiet and comfortable; lake panoramic views don't cost extra. The hotel has its own farm and vineyards on the hill behind—the source of organic produce for the restaurant. They even make their own wine, with some very original labels designed by the owner. Summer meals are served in the garden; there's a special farmer's breakfast on Tuesday and a weekend evening cocktail party. ✉ *Via Guidino 14, CH-6902 Lugano-Paradiso,* ☎ *091/9941771,* FAX *091/9941773. 29 rooms. Restaurant, bar, no-smoking rooms, pool, whirlpool bath, playground, free parking. AE, MC, V. Closed Nov.–Mar.* ✉

$$ 🏨 **San Carlo.** Ideally located on the main shopping street, a block from the waterfront, and only 150 yards from the funicular, this friendly hotel is one of the best deals in town. At press time floor-by-floor renovations were underway; these should be finished by 2001. Clever carpentry makes the most out of small spaces, creating niches for a mirror, a television, or a hideaway bed. The breakfast room is small, so breakfast in bed is encouraged. ✉ *Via Nassa 28, CH-6900,* ☎ *091/9227107,* FAX *091/9228022. 22 rooms. Breakfast room. AE, DC, MC, V.*

$$ 🏨 **Cristina.** Part of this pleasant, well-managed hotel is in a 100-year-old villa, evidence of which can be seen in the dining area where original Jugendstil doorways frame the otherwise 1970s decor. They offer nicely maintained rooms in a mix of patterns and light wood, all with a view of either town or the lake. The best views are from the fifth through the seventh floors. ✉ *Via Zorzi 28, CH-6902,* ☎ *091/9943312,* FAX *091/9931568. 60 rooms. Restaurant, bar, pool, laundry service, playground, free parking. AE, DC, MC, V. Closed Nov.–mid-Mar.*

$ 🏨 **Dischma.** The welcoming owners of this hotel, the Abgottspons, make it a bargain worth seeking out. The rooms are clean and bright, and the flowers on the balconies have won the owners awards. The public rooms are a riot of colors, souvenirs, and knickknacks; there's a mynah bird to talk to near the elevator. The restaurant is nonsmoking (rare in these parts), and they even have a coin-op washer and dryer for guests. ⊠ *Vicolo Geretta 6, CH-6902 Lugano Paradiso,* ☎ *091/9942131,* FAX *091/9941503. 35 rooms. Restaurant, room, coin laundry. AE, MC, V. Closed Dec.–Feb.* ☜

$ 🏨 **Zurigo.** Handy to parks, shopping, and the waterfront, this spartan hotel offers quiet comfort. Its rates are affordable, high season, and its rooms are consistently well maintained. the Via Pioda side are quieter. ⊠ *Corso Pestalozzi 13, CH-6* 091/9234343, FAX *091/9239268. 28 rooms. Breakfast room. AE, MC, V. Closed Nov.–mid-Mar.*

Nightlife and the Arts

BARS
Hotel Eden (⊠ Riva Paradiso 1, ☎ 091/9859200) has a popular piano bar. The piano player strikes up a tune nightly, sometimes with a singer, at **Principe Leopoldo** (⊠ Via Montalbano 5, ☎ 091/9858855). Another nice place for drinks is the **Splendide Royale** (☞ *above*).

CASINO
The **Casinò Kursaal** (⊠ Via Stauffacher 1, ☎ 091/9233281) has a restaurant, disco, bar, slot machines, movie theater, and gaming room.

DANCING
For a true nightclub experience with live music, cabaret, and shows in a plush setting, try **Cecil** (⊠ Riva Paradiso 3, ☎ 091/9949724). **La Piccionaia Club** (⊠ Corso Pestalozzi 21, ☎ 091/9234546) is a classy spot for adults. **Titanic** (⊠ Via Cantonale, Pambio-Noranco, off the A2 exit for Lugano-Sud, ☎ 091/9856010), is the Ticino's biggest disco, with three dance floors.

MUSIC
There is a free **Blues to Bop Festival** in the Piazza della Riforma scheduled for the first weekend in September 2001. The **Estival Jazz** (second weekend in July 2001) offers free outdoor concerts in the Piazza della Riforma. From April to June the city hosts its **Primavera Concertistica di Lugano,** with top-level orchestras and conductors.

Shopping

You'll find all the glossy-magazine designers in the beautiful shops along the car-free **Via Nassa** in the Old Town. Cute novelty shops and antiques stores line the staircase street of **Via Cattedrale.** If it's Italian and international designer clothing bargains you're after, you could explore the factory outlet store called **Fox Town** (⊠ Via Angelo Maspoli, Mendrisio, ☎ 091/6462111), in nearby Mendrisio—it's open every day, including Sunday.

Gandria

⓴ *7 km (4 mi) east of Lugano.*

Although today its narrow waterfront streets are crowded with tourists, the tiny historic village of Gandria merits a visit, either by boat from Lugano (☞ Getting Around by Boat *in* The Ticino A to Z, *below*) or by car, as parking is available just above the town. It clings vertiginously to the steep hillside; a labyrinth of stairways and passageways and flower-filled balconies hangs directly over open water. Souvenir and crafts shops now fill its backstreet nooks, but the ambience of an ancient fishing village remains.

OFF THE BEATEN PATH **CANTINE DI GANDRIA –** Across Lake Lugano from Gandria—almost in Italy—this tiny village has a small **Museo Doganale** (Customs Museum;

☎ 091/9104811 or 9239843), casually known as the Smugglers' Museum. Here you'll learn the romantic history of clandestine trade through displays of ingenious containers, weapons, and contraband. You can catch a boat from the jetty. ☎ 091/9239843 or 091/9104811. ✉ Free. ⊙ Apr.–Oct., daily 1:30–5:30.

Campione

㉑ *18 km (11 mi) south of Gandria, 12 km (7 mi) south of Lugano.*

In the heart of Swiss Italy lies Campione. Here, in this southernmost of regions, the police cars have Swiss license plates but the policemen inside are Italian; the inhabitants pay their taxes to Italy but do it in Swiss francs. Its narrow streets are saturated with history and the surrounding landscape is a series of stunning views of Lake Lugano and Monte San Salvatore.

In the 8th century, the lord of Campione gave the tiny scrap of land, less than a square kilometer (½ square mi) in area, to the monastery of St. Ambrosius of Milan. Despite all the wars that passed it by, Campione remained Italian until the end of the 18th century, when it was incorporated into the Cisalpine Republic. When Italy unified in 1861, Campione became part of the new Kingdom of Italy—and remained so. There are no frontiers between Campione and Switzerland, and it benefits from the comforts of Swiss currency, customs laws, and postal and telephone services. Despite its miniature scale, it has exercised disproportionate influence on the art world: in the Middle Ages, a school of stonemasons, sculptors, and architects from Campione and the surrounding region worked on the cathedrals of Milan, Verona, Cremona, Trento, and Modena—even Hagia Sophia in Istanbul.

Nightlife and the Arts

Today, Campione is a magnet for gamblers, as its large, glittering **Casino** (⊠ Piazza Milano 1, ☎ 091/6401111) offers visitors to conservative Switzerland a chance to play for higher stakes than the usual 5 SF: following Italian law, the sky's the limit here. The casino has a restaurant, dancing, and a show; this is jacket-and-tie territory.

Riva San Vitale

㉒ *9 km (5½ mi) south of Campione, 13 km (8 mi) south of Lugano.*

At the south end of Lake Lugano sits Riva San Vitale, which rivals Campione for its odd history: in 1798 its people objected to new boundaries and declared themselves an independent republic. Their glory lasted 14 days before a small cantonal army marched in and convinced them to rejoin Switzerland. A 5th-century **Battistèro** (baptistery) remains, still containing its original stone immersion font.

Four kilometers (2 miles) south of Riva San Vitale is little **Mendrisio,** cradle of the Ticinese wine industry. It's known for its medieval processions, which take place on the Thursday and Friday before Easter.

Morcote

★ ㉓ *6 km (4 mi) northwest of Riva San Vitale, 10 km (6 mi) south of Lugano.*

At the southernmost tip of the glorious Ceresio Peninsula waterfront is the atmospheric, old resort-village of Morcote, its clay-color Lombard-style houses and arcades looking directly over the waterfront. A steep and picturesque climb leads up to the **Chiesa di Madonna del Sasso** (Church of the Madonna of the Rock), with its well-preserved 16th-century frescoes; its elevated setting affords wonderful views.

Dining and Lodging

★ ✕⏢ **Bella Vista.** High above Lake Lugano, surrounded by vineyards, lies this outstanding getaway. A handful of superb rooms occupy two restored 17th-century Ticinese houses; the decor is a mix of antique and ultramodern. One sleek room has the original fireplace; the tower suite's bathroom is done in granite and glass. All have beautiful views. The restaurant is an equally luxe experience. The menu includes several lobster dishes (the lobsters are flown in from Maine!), homemade pastas, and a heavenly potato gratin. In fine weather you'll be served on the outdoor terrace, which has a truly spectacular view. Vico Morcote is about 2 km (1 ¼ mi) south of Melide; from the main road a sign will point the way. The road up is steep and winding; Vico Morcote is the first cluster of houses you'll come to. ⊠ *CH-6921 Vico Morcote*, ☎ *091/9961143*, ℻ *091/9961288. 9 rooms, 2 suites. Restaurant, bar, garden. AE, DC, MC, V. Closed mid.-Dec.–Jan.*

THE TICINO A TO Z

Arriving and Departing

By Bus

The **Palm Express** scenic postbus route carries visitors from St. Moritz to Lugano via the Maloja Pass and Italy; reservations are strongly recommended. It takes about four hours and can be arranged at any train station or tourist office (☞ Visitor Information, *below*). You can also contact **Railtour Suisse** (☎ 031/3780000).

By Car

There are two major gateways into the Ticino: the St. **Gotthard Pass**, in the northwest, and the **San Bernardino Pass**, to the northeast. From the St. Gotthard Pass, the swift **A2** expressway leads down the Valle Leventina to Bellinzona, where it joins with **A13**, which cuts south from the San Bernardino. A2 directs the mingled traffic flow southward past Lugano to Chiasso and the Italian border, where the expressway heads directly to Como and Milan. As an alternative, there's the St. Gotthard Tunnel—17 km (11 mi) of dense air and darkness speeding you through the Alps rather than over them. If traffic is light, it can cut an hour off your travel time, but if the passes are closed and it's holiday migration time, tunnel traffic can be nasty.

By Plane

The nearest international airport is in Italy. **Malpensa** (⊠ About 50/31 mi northwest of Milan) is one of the biggest hubs in southern Europe. Some flights from the international **Linate** (⊠ Less than 10 km/6 mi east of Milan) will be transferred to Malpensa. For air-traffic **information** for both airports and information on connections with Milan, call 0039/2/74852200. You can continue into the Ticino via rail, car, or taxi. **Crossair** (☎ 084/8852000 for central reservations), Switzerland's domestic airline, connects directly into the domestic **Aeroporto Lugano-Agno** (⊠ 7 km/4½ mi west of Lugano, Agno, ☎ 091/6051226 or 091/6101212) from **Zürich**'s Kloten Airport (☎ 1571060) and from **Geneva**'s Cointrin (☎ 1571500), as well as from other European destinations. There's a **shuttle bus** connecting Agno airport with Lugano, which operates on request (☎ 079/2214243). Call upon arrival.

By Train

The St. Gotthard route connects south from Zürich, cuts through the pass tunnel, and heads into Bellinzona and Lugano. Side connections lead into Locarno from Brig, crossing the Simplon Pass and cutting through Italy. Swiss Pass (☞ Train Travel *in* Smart Travel Tips A to Z) travelers do not have to pay Italian rail fares to cross from Brig to Locarno via Domodossola. Trains connect out of Zürich's airport and take about three hours; from Geneva, catch the Milan express, changing at Domodossola, Locarno, and Bellinzona. Trains do not go directly into Ascona but stop at Locarno: you must connect by taxi or local bus. For train information from Lugano, call the Swiss federal railway, here called the **Ferrovie Federali Svizzere (FFS),** at 0900/300300 (1.19 SF/min).

Getting Around

By Boat

Lake Lugano and northern Lake Maggiore are plied by graceful steamers that carry passengers from one waterfront resort to another, offering excellent views of the mountains. Steamer travel on Lake Lugano is included in the Swiss Pass (☞ Train Travel *in* Smart Travel Tips A to Z); tickets can be purchased near the docks before departure. On Lake Lugano, the **Navigazione Lago di Lugano** (Navigation Company of Lake Lugano, ✉ Casella Postale 56, CH-6900 Lugano, ☎ 091/9715223 or 091/9234610) offers cruise-boat excursions around the bay to Gandria and toward the Villa Favorita.

Boats owned by **Navigazione Lago Maggiore-Bacino Svizzero** (Swiss Navigation Company of Lake Maggiore, ✉ Lungolago Motta, CH-6600 Locarno, ☎ 091/7511865) cruise Lake Maggiore. Discounts are given for Swiss and Swiss Boat passes (☞ Train Travel *and* Boat Travel *in* Smart Travel Tips A to Z).

By Bus

There is a convenient postbus sightseeing system here that tourists can use to get around the region, even into the backcountry. La Posta (post and telegraph office) publishes illustrated booklets with suggested itineraries and prices; you can get them through the **Autopostale Ticino-Moesano** (✉ Via S. Balestra, CH-6900 Lugano, ☎ 091/8078520) or through local tourist and post offices. Postbus excursion prices are reduced with the Locarno or Lugano Holiday Passes (☞ By Train, *below*) and are free with the Swiss Pass (☞ Train Travel *in* Smart Travel Tips A to Z).

By Car

A car is a real asset here if you intend to see the mountain valleys—and a hindrance in the congested, urban lakeside resorts. Lugano is particularly difficult to drive through, and the parking garages are usually packed. Traffic between Bellinzona and Locarno can move at a crawl during high season. There's a handful of basic main roads between towns, but secondary roads peter out. Wherever you are in the Ticino, the Italian (read: fast and risky) driving style dominates.

By Train

Secondary rail connections here are minimal and can make all but the most mainstream rail sightseeing a complicated venture; most excursions will require some postbus connections. Nevertheless, there is a regional discount pass called the **Holiday Pass FART.** The pass is valid for the Lugano and Locarno areas and gives you unlimited free travel for three or seven consecutive days on many transit routes and a 30% to 50% discount on others. Besides train travel, it covers buses, cable cars, funiculars, and chairlifts. A three-day pass costs 46 SF; a weekly pass costs 66 SF. It's available from the tourist office (☞ Visitor Information, *below*).

Contacts and Resources

Emergencies
Police: (☎ 117). **Medical assistance/ambulance:** (☎ 144). Lugano civic **hospital** (☎ 091/8056111). Lugano **dental clinic** (☎ 091/9350180).

Guided Tours
ORIENTATION

The *Wilhelm Tell Express* carries you by paddle steamer and rail from Luzern over the St. Gotthard Pass and into Locarno and Lugano with a guide and running commentary in English. Inquire at any rail station for details. The *Bernina Express,* Europe's highest Alp-crossing railway, takes you from Chur to St. Moritz in the *Glacier Express;* then you cross the Alps over the Bernina Pass into Italy (in summer it's even possible in an open-air train car) and continue into Lugano. Several variations are possible. Both offer discounts for Swiss Pass and Swiss Boat Pass holders (☞ Train Travel *and* Boat Travel *in* Smart Travel Tips A to Z). Inquire at any railway station for information and reservations.

Guided walks are available in all areas covering cultural, historical, architectural, and natural interests. Wonderfully detailed English-language brochures with maps are available from local tourist offices for both guided and self-guided tours.

Visitor Information
The principal tourist authority for the Ticino is **Ticino Turismo** (✉ Villa Turrita, Via Lugano 12, CP 1441, CH-6501 Bellinzona, ☎ 091/8257056, FAX 091/8253614, ✆).

Local offices: Ascona (✉ Casa Serodine, Box 449, CH-6612, ☎ 091/7910090). **Bellinzona** (✉ Palazzo Civico, Box 1419, CH-6500, ☎ 091/8252131). **Biasca** (✉ CH-6710, ☎ 091/8623327). **Blenio** (✉ CH-6716 Acquarossa, ☎ 091/8711765). **Brissago Islands** (✉ CH-6614 Brissago, ☎ 091/7931170). **Locarno** (✉ Via Largo Zorzi, CH-6600, ☎ 091/7510333). **Lugano** (✉ Palazzo Civico, CH-6901, ☎ 091/9133232). **Mendrisiotto e Basso Ceresio** (✉ Via Angelo Maspoli 25, CH-6850 Mendrisio, ☎ 091/6465761).

6 LUZERN AND CENTRAL SWITZERLAND

LUZERN, ENGELBERG, WEGGIS, SCHWYZ, ZUG

Blessed with a sophisticated transportation system that makes it one of the easiest regions to visit, central Switzerland is full of neat little towns, accessible mountains, and modest resorts. Centered around the Vierwaldstättersee, the Lake of the Four Forest Cantons, the region is steeped in history: it is where the Oath of Eternal Alliance is said to have been renewed, and it's also the birthplace of the legend of Wilhelm Tell.

Updated by
Katrin Gygax

A S YOU CRUISE DOWN THE LEISURELY sprawl of the Vierwaldstättersee (Lake Luzern), mist rising off the gray waves, mountains—great loaflike masses of forest and stone—looming above
the clouds, it's easy to understand how Wagner could have composed
his *Siegfried Idyll* in his mansion beside this lake. This is inspiring terrain, romantic and evocative. When the waters roil up, you can hear the
whistling chromatics and cymbal clashes of Gioacchino Rossini's thun-
derstorm from his 1829 opera, *Guillaume Tell*. It was on this lake, after
all, that Wilhelm Tell—the beloved, if legendary, Swiss national hero—
supposedly leapt from the tyrant Gessler's boat to freedom. And it was
in a meadow nearby that three furtive rebels and their cohorts swore an
oath by firelight and planted the seed of the Swiss Confederation.

The Rütli Meadow, a national landmark on the western shore of Lake
Luzern, is the very spot where the Confederates of Schwyz, Unterwald,
and Uri are said to have met on the night of November 7, 1307, to renew
the 1291 Oath of Eternal Alliance—Switzerland's equivalent of the
U.S. Declaration of Independence. With this oath, the world's oldest
still-extant democracy was formed, as the proud charter territories
swore their commitment to self-rule in the face of the oppressive Habsburgs and the Holy Roman Empire. Every August 1, the Swiss national
holiday, citizens gather in the meadow in remembrance of the oath, and
the sky glows with the light of hundreds of mountaintop bonfires.

Wilhelm Tell played an important role in that early rebellion, and his
story, especially as told by German poet and playwright Friedrich von
Schiller in his play *Wilhelm Tell* (1805), continues to stir those with a
weakness for civil resistance. Though there are no valid records to prove
his existence, and versions of the legend conflict with historical fact,
no one denies the reality of his times, when central Switzerland—then
a feudal dependent of Austria but by its own independent will not yet
absorbed into the Holy Roman Empire—suffered brutal pressures and
indignities under its local rulers. The mythical Gessler was one of
those rulers, and his legendary edict—that the proud Swiss should bow
before his hat suspended from a pole in the village square at Altdorf—
symbolizes much crueler oppressions of the time. Schiller's Tell was a
hero through and through: brisk, decisive, a highly skilled helmsman
as well as marksman, and not one for diplomatic negotiations—he refused to kneel. Tell's famous punishment: to shoot an apple off his young
son's head before a crowd of fellow townsmen; if he refused, both would
be killed. Tell quietly tucked an arrow in his shirt bosom, loaded another into his crossbow, and shot the apple clean through. When
Gessler asked what the second arrow was for, Tell replied that if the
first arrow had struck his child, the second arrow would have been for
Gessler and would not have missed.

For this impolitic remark, Tell was sentenced to prison. While de-
porting him across Lake Luzern, the Austrians (including the ruthless
Gessler) were caught in a violent storm (remember your Rossini) and
turned to Tell, the only man on board who knew the waters, to take
the helm. Unmanacled, he steered the boat to a rocky ridge, leapt free,
and pushed the boat back into the storm. Later he lay in wait in the
woods near Küssnacht and, as Gessler threatened to ride down a
woman begging mercy for her imprisoned husband, shot him in the
heart. This act of justified violence inspired the people to overthrow
their oppressors and swear the Oath of Eternal Alliance around a
roaring bonfire, laying the groundwork for the Swiss Confederation.

Pretty romantic stuff. Yet for all its potential for drama, central Switzerland and the area surrounding Lake Luzern are tame enough turf: neat little towns, accessible mountains, smooth roads, resorts virtually glamour-free—and modest, graceful Luzern (Lucerne) astride the River Reuss much as it has been since the Middle Ages.

An eminently civilized region, Zentralschweiz (Central Switzerland) lacks the rustic unruliness of the Valais, the spectacular extremes of the Berner Oberland, the eccentricity of Graubünden. Nor does it have the sophistication and snob appeal of jet-set resorts or the cosmopolitan mix of Geneva, Basel, and Zürich. Instead, the area radiates tradition. Villages range neatly around their medieval centers; houses are tidy, pastel, picture-book cottages, deep-roofed and symmetrical, each rank of windows underscored with flowers. Luzern, the capital, hosts arts festivals and great shopping but little native industry. Serene and steady as the Reuss that laps at the piers of its ancient wooden bridges, it's an approachable city in an accessible region.

Central Switzerland's popularity with tourists has spawned an infrastructure of hotels, restaurants, museums, excursions, and transportation that makes it one of the easiest places in Switzerland to visit, either by car or by rail—and one of the most rewarding. As Wagner exclaimed, perhaps carried away a bit by his own waterfront idyll: "I do not know of a more beautiful spot in this world!"

Pleasures and Pastimes

Dining

Rooted in the German territory of Switzerland and the surrounding farmlands, central Switzerland's cuisine is down-home and hearty, though its specialties offer some variety from the veal-and-*Rösti* (hash brown potatoes) found everywhere else. In the heights, there are Alpine cheese specialties (*Aelpler Magrone*—pasta, butter, cheese, and fried onions); in the orchard country around Zug, there are such cherry specialties as *Zuger Kirschtorte,* a rich white cake soaked with cherry schnapps. Pears from the local orchards are dried, then spiced and poached in sweetened red *Dole* (wine). Luzern takes pride in its *Kügeli-paschtetli,* puff-pastry nests filled with tiny veal meatballs, chicken, or sweetbreads; mushrooms; cream sauce; and occasionally raisins.

But here the real *cuisine du marché,* based on fresh market ingredients, focuses on lake fish. Lake Luzern and its neighboring Zugersee (Lake Zug) produce an abundance of *Egli* (perch), *Hecht* (pike), *Forellen* (trout), and *Felchen* (whitefish); Zug produces its own exclusive *Röteln,* a red-bellied relative of the trout. Restaurants—especially along waterfronts—trade heavily in these freshwater products, whether they come from the region or not. Ask, and you may get an honest answer: the sources vary, but the style of preparation remains local. In Zug, whole fish may be baked with sage, bay leaves, shallots, cloves, and plenty of white wine and butter; a Luzern tradition has them sautéed and sauced with tomatoes, mushrooms, and capers.

CATEGORY	COST*
$$$$	over 70 SF
$$$	40 SF–70 SF
$$	20 SF–40 SF
$	under 20 SF

Prices are per person for a three-course meal (two-course meal in $ category), including sales tax and 15% service charge.

Hiking

Since Switzerland's 1991 septicentennial, celebrating the 700-year anniversary of its confederation, central Switzerland has marked and developed a historic foot trail, the Swiss Path, which covers 35 km (21½ mi) of lakefront lore along the southernmost branch of Lake Luzern. You'll trace the mythical steps of Wilhelm Tell and the genuine steps of medieval forerunners, climb through steep forests and isolated villages, and visit the holiday resort of Brunnen. Complete information and maps can be requested through Central Switzerland Tourism (☞ Visitor Information *in* Luzern and Central Switzerland A to Z, *below*). The videocassette *Hiking the Swiss Path* is available through branches of Switzerland Tourism.

Lodging

Luzern provides a convenient home base for excursions all over the region, though villages are peppered with small, shuttered guest houses, and you may easily find an overnight spot as you drive through the countryside. As the terrain and climate vary radically between balmy lakefronts and icy heights, check carefully for high and low seasons before booking ahead. Such water-sport resorts as Weggis and Vitznau cut back service considerably in winter, just when Engelberg comes alive. Luzern, unlike most Swiss urban areas, has high and low seasons, and prices drop by as much as 25% in the winter, approximately November through March. Rates are usually calculated on a per-person basis, so it is wise to confirm the rates, particularly if you're traveling as anything other than a couple.

CATEGORY	COST*
$$$$	over 350 SF
$$$	250 SF–350 SF
$$	120 SF–250 SF
$	under 120 SF

Prices are for a standard double room, including breakfast, tax, and service charge.

✎ *following the text of a review is your signal that the property has a Web site, where you will find details and, usually, images; for a link, visit www.fodors.com/urls.*

Shopping

Although Luzern no longer produces embroidery or lace, you can find a wide variety of Swiss handiwork of the highest quality, crafts, and watches in all price categories. High-end watch dealers Gübelin and Bucherer offer inexpensive souvenirs to lure shoppers into their luxurious showrooms; smaller shops carry Tissot, Rado, Corum, and others—but prices are controlled by the manufacturers. Watch for closeouts on out-of-date models.

Exploring Luzern and Central Switzerland

Though called the Lake of the Four Forest Cantons, Lake Luzern and its environs take in not only the four cantons that abut the lake—Luzern, Uri, Schwyz, and Unterwalden—but the canton of Zug as well. Unterwalden itself is divided politically into two half-cantons: Obwalden (upper) and Nidwalden (lower). It was the canton of Schwyz that gave Switzerland its name.

The narrow, twisting lake flows from Flüelen, where the Reuss opens into the Urnersee, its southernmost leg. This is the wildest end of the lake, where much of the Tell story was set. The north end of the lake is flanked by the region's highest points, Mt. Pilatus (2,121 m/6,953 ft) and Mt. Rigi (1,798 m/5,894 ft). Luzern lies in a deep bay at the lake's northwest extreme and at the point where the rivers Reuss and Emme part ways. Zug stands apart, on the northern shore of its own Lake Zug, which is divided from Lake Luzern by the mass of Mt. Rigi.

Numbers in the text correspond to numbers in the margin and on the Central Switzerland and Luzern (Lucerne) maps.

Great Itineraries

When visiting this multiterrain area, you must change modes of transit frequently to see it all; part of the region's interest is the variety of boat trips, train rides, and drives you'll take to reach the sights. On any given day, you may walk through the lovely Old Town of Luzern, ascend Mt. Pilatus by cable car and descend by cogwheel train, take a lake steamer, or drive through the Rütli Meadow.

IF YOU HAVE 1 OR 2 DAYS

Take in the Old Town sights of ☷ **Luzern** ①–⑮, then consider a half-day boat trip on the Vierwaldstättersee, which gives you the opportunity to see the sights of the region from the lake itself. **Mt. Pilatus** ⑯ offers central Switzerland's best mountaintop panoramas. Allow yourself a half day to ascend the mountain.

3 OR MORE DAYS

In addition to all of the above, take a trip to **Einsiedeln** ㉗, with its 9th-century Benedictine monastery. A combined train and cable-car trip from ☷ **Weggis** ⑳ will take you to the summit of **Mt. Rigi,** where you can see as far as the Black Forest and Mt. Säntis and even spend the night in the hotel at the top. If you're traveling by car, you can follow the course of a lake steamer from Luzern, driving to the St. Gotthard Pass along the lakefront highway (A2).

When to Tour Luzern and Central Switzerland

If you don't mind negotiating heavy traffic, particularly in Luzern, summer is the ideal season for boat excursions and great views from the tops of Mt. Pilatus and Mt. Rigi. In fall, when the crowds thin, you'll find crisp weather around the mountains and the lake. This isn't a big ski area, so wintertime tends to be quiet, even in Luzern.

LUZERN

57 km (36 mi) southwest of Zürich.

Luzern city is a convenient home base for excursions all over central Switzerland. The countryside here is tame, and the vast Vierwaldstättersee (Lake Luzern) offers a prime opportunity for a lake steamer cruise.

Where the River Reuss flows out of Lake Luzern, Luzern's Old Town straddles the narrowed waters. The right (north) bank is generally livelier than the left. There are a couple of passes available for discounts for museums and sights in the city. One is a museum pass that costs 25 SF and grants free entry to all museums for one month. If you are staying in a hotel, you may also want to pick up a special visitor's card; once stamped by the hotel, it entitles you to discounts at most museums and other tourist-oriented businesses as well. Both are available at the tourist office (☞ Visitor Information *in* Luzern and Central Switzerland A to Z, *below*).

Old Town and Beyond

A Good Walk

Start at the new **Kultur- und Kongresszentrum** ①, by the train station, which gives you a beautiful view of all the places you'll see in Luzern. Walk down Bahnhofstrasse to the modern bridge, the **Rathaus-Steg,**

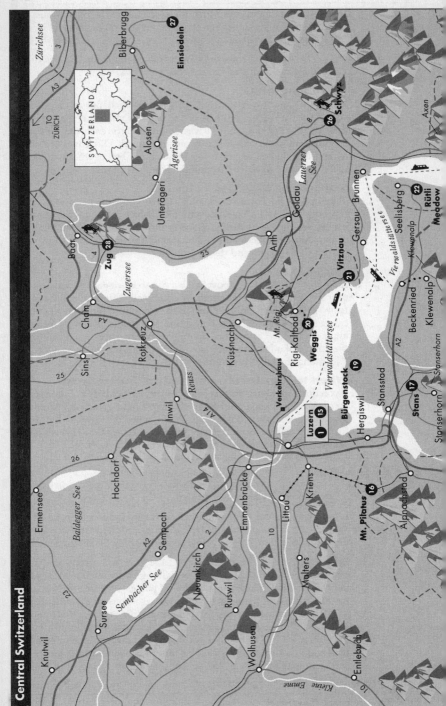

Zürichsee

Biberbrugg

27 Einsiedeln

TO ZÜRICH

SWITZERLAND

A3

3

8

Schwyz **26**

Axen

Alosen

Ägerisee

Unterägeri

Goldau

Lauerzer See

Arth

Brunnen

Gersau

Seelisberg

22 Rütli Meadow

Klewenalp

Baar

28 Zug

Zugersee

Cham

Rotkreuz

Sins

25

4

25

Mt. Rigi

Rigi-Kaltbad

Weggis **20**

Vitznau **21**

Vierwaldstättersee

Seelisberg

Beckenried

Klewenalp

Küssnacht

Vierwaldstättersee

19

Stansstad

17 Stans

Stanserhorn

Stanserhorn

Inwil

Reuss

A14

Verkehrshaus ■

Bürgenstock

19

Hergiswil

Luzern **1** – **15**

Hochdorf

26

Baldegger See

Emmenbrücke

Littau

Kriens

Mt. Pilatus **16**

Alpnachstad

Ermensee

Sempach

Sursee

23

Neuenkirch

2

A2

Ruswil

10

Malters

Knutwil

Wolhusen

Entlebuch

Kleine Emme

10

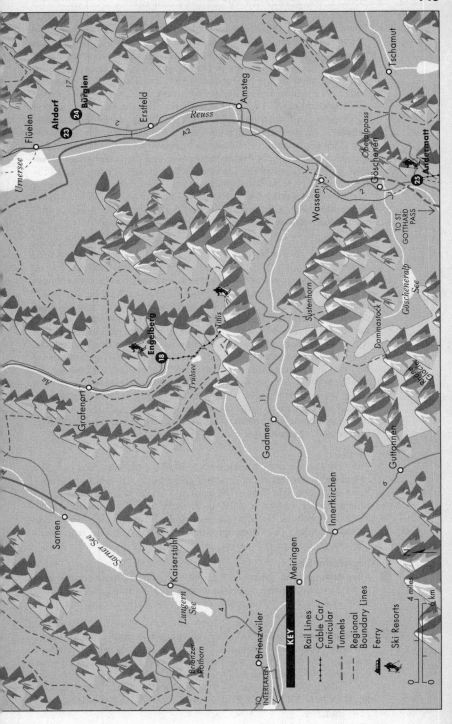

and head north to the **Altes Rathaus** ②, across the bridge. (This late-Renaissance style building is on **Rathausquai**, the city's main avenue.) Just to the right of the Rathaus is the **Am Rhyn-Haus** ③, now a Picasso museum. Turn left and climb the stairs past the ornately frescoed Zunfthaus zur Pfistern (☞ Pfistern *in* Dining and Lodging, *below*), a guildhall dating from the late 15th and early 16th centuries, to the **Kornmarkt**, where the grinding din of the grain market was once heard. Cut left to the **Weinmarkt** ④. Leave the square from its west end, turn right on Kramgasse, and head west across the Mühlenplatz to the **Spreuerbrücke** ⑤, an unlikely exhibition space for dark paintings of the medieval plague epidemic. Crossing the bridge to the left bank, you'll find a pair of museums, the **Natur-Museum** ⑥ and the **Historisches Museum** ⑦. From the end of the Spreuerbrücke, cut back upriver along Pfistergasse, veer left on Bahnhofstrasse, and turn right into Münzgasse to the **Franziskanerkirche** ⑧. Return to Bahnhofstrasse and head to the **Jesuitenkirche** ⑨. Continuing east past the Rathaus-Steg Bridge, you'll see the **Kapellbrücke** ⑩, the oldest of its kind in Europe.

After crossing the Kapellbrücke, break away from Old Town through thick pedestrian and bus traffic at Schwanenplatz to Schweizerhofquai. Double back and take the first right, St. Leodegarstrasse, to the **Hofkirche** ⑪ (you may have to be content with the exterior, as the church is closed for renovations until spring 2001). Go back down the church steps, doubling back on St. Leodegarstrasse, turn right, and continue on to Löwenstrasse. Turn right and walk up to Löwenplatz and the **Bourbaki-Panorama** ⑫, which dominates the square with its mix of Victorian and modern architecture. Beyond the plaza, up Denkmalstrasse, is the **Löwendenkmal** ⑬, called by Mark Twain "the most mournful and moving piece of stone in the world." Immediately adjoining the small park that shades the lion lies the **Gletschergarten** ⑭. Return down Denkmalstrasse and, at Löwenplatz, turn right on Museggstrasse, which cuts through an original city gate and runs parallel to the watchtowers and crenellated walls of Luzern, constructed around 1400. The fifth tower is **Zytturm** ⑮.

TIMING

The Old Town is easy to navigate and ideal for walking. You can take in the sights on this route in about three hours; to this add another hour each to see the Natur-Museum and Historisches Museum, and time to linger awhile at the Kapellbrücke and the Löwendenkmal. Note that both the Natur-Museum and the Historisches Museum are closed Monday; the Gletschergarten is closed Monday from mid-November through February.

Sights to See

❷ **Altes Rathaus** (Old Town Hall). In 1606, the Luzern town council held its first meeting in this late-Renaissance style building, built between 1599 and 1606. It still meets here today. ✉ *Rathausquai, facing the north end of Rathaus-Steg.*

❸ **Am Rhyn-Haus** (Am Rhyn House). Also known as the Picasso Museum, this spot contrasts a beautiful, 17th-century building with its modern holdings. The collection consists mainly of works from the last 20 years of Picasso's life, including his *Déjeuner sur l'Herbe* and giant iron sculptures, along with more than 100 photos of the artist. ✉ *Furreng. 21,* ☎ *041/4101773.* ✉ *6 SF.* ☉ *Apr.–Oct., daily 10–6; Nov.–Mar., daily 11–1 and 2–4.*

★ ⑫ **Bourbaki-Panorama.** The panorama was the IMAX theater of the 19th century; its sweeping, wraparound paintings brought to life scenes of epic proportions. The Bourbaki is one of only 30 remaining in the world. Painted by Édouard Castres between 1876 and 1878 (who was aided by many uncredited artists, including Ferdinand Hodler), it depicts the French Army of the East retreating into Switzerland at Verrières, a famous episode in the Franco-Prussian War. As you walk around the circle, the imagery seems to pop into three dimensions; in fact, with the help of a few strategically placed models, it does. There's a recorded commentary in English. The panorama was renovated in 1999, and now its conical wooden structure is surrounded by a modern glass cube filled with shops, movie theaters, and restaurants. ⊠ *Löwenpl.,* ☎ *041/4123030.* ☒ *6 SF.* ☾ *Daily 9–6.* ⌘

⑧ Franziskanerkirche (Franciscan Church). Since its construction in the 13th century, this church has been persistently remodeled. It still retains its 17th-century choir stalls and carved wooden pulpit. The barefoot Franciscans once held a prominent social and cultural position in Luzern, which took a firm Counter-Reformation stance and remains more than 70% Roman Catholic today. ⊠ *Franziskanerpl., just off Münzg.*

⑭ Gletschergarten (Glacier Garden). The bedrock of this 19th-century tourist attraction was excavated between 1872 and 1875 and has been dramatically pocked and polished by Ice Age glaciers. A private museum on the site displays impressive relief maps of Switzerland. ⊠ *Denkmalstr. 4,* ☎ *041/4104340.* ☒ *8 SF.* ☾ *May–Oct., daily 9–6; Mar.– Apr., daily 10–5; Nov.–Feb., Tues.–Sun. 10–5.*

⑦ Historisches Museum (Historical Museum). Housed in the late-Gothic armory dating from 1567, this stylish institution exhibits city sculptures, Swiss arms, and flags. Reconstructed rooms depict rural and urban life; it also has the original Gothic fountain from the Weinmarkt (☞ *below).* ⊠ *Pfisterg. 24,* ☎ *041/2285424.* ☒ *5 SF.* ☾ *Tues.–Fri. 10– noon and 2–5, weekends 10–5.*

⑪ Hofkirche. This sanctuary of St. Leodegar was first part of a monastery founded in 750. Its Gothic structure was mostly destroyed by fire in 1633 and rebuilt in late-Renaissance style, so only the towers of its predecessor were preserved. The carved pulpit and choir stalls date from the 17th century, and the 80-rank organ (1650) is one of Switzerland's finest. Outside, Italianate loggias shelter a cemetery for patrician families of old Luzern. At press time, the church was closed for renovations until spring 2001. ⊠ *St. Leodegarstr. 6,* ☎ *041/4105241.* ☾ *Call for hrs after reopening.*

OFF THE BEATEN PATH

VERKEHRSHAUS – Easily reached by steamer, car, or Bus 2, the Swiss Transport Museum is almost a world's fair in itself, with a complex of buildings and exhibitions both indoors and out, including dioramas, live demonstrations, and a "Swissorama" (360-degree screen) film about Switzerland. Every mode of transit is discussed, from stagecoaches and bicycles to jumbo jets and space capsules. The museum also has Switzerland's first IMAX theater. If you're driving, head east on Haldenstrasse at the waterfront and make a right on Lidostrasse (it's also signposted). ⊠ *Lidostr. 5,* ☎ *041/3704444.* ☒ *18 SF.* ☾ *Apr.–Nov. 1, daily 9–6; Nov. 2–Mar., daily 10–5.*

★ ⑨ Jesuitenkirche (Jesuit Church). Constructed in 1666–77, this baroque church with a symmetrical entrance is flanked by two onion-dome towers, added in 1893. Go inside: its vast interior, restored to mint condition, is a rococo explosion of gilt, marble, and epic frescoes. Nearby is the Renaissance **Regierungsgebäude** (Government Building), seat of the cantonal government. ⊠ *Bahnhofstr., just west of Rathaus-Steg,* ☎ *041/2100756.* ☾ *Daily 6 AM–6:15 PM.*

Luzern (Lucerne)

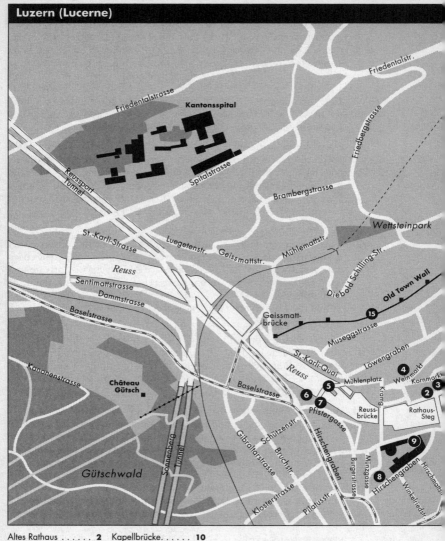

Landschaustrasse

Abendweg

Dreilindenstr.

Zürichstrasse

Denkmalstr.

Fluhmattstrasse

Kapuzinerweg

Dreilindenstr.

Hitzlisbergstr.

Bergstrasse

14

13

Weystrasse

Adligenswilerstr.

12

Löwen-
platz

Löwenstr.

Museggstrasse

11

Zinggentorstr.

Haldenstrasse

St. Leodegar-Str.

Haldenstrasse

**Kursaal
(Casino)**

Carl Spittelerquai

Hertensteinstr.

Nationalquai

Schweizerhofquai

N

Schwanen-
Platz

Vierwaldstättersee

urrengasse

Rathausquai

Seebrücke

10

Kapell-
brücke

Europa-
platz

KEY

—— Rail Lines

•–•–• Funicular

▨▨▨ Tramway

Bahnhofstrasse

Bahnhof-
platz
Bahnhof

1

Theaterstr.

Pilatusstrasse

Frankenstrasse

Zentralstrasse

Inselquai

0   200 yards

0   200 meters

★ ⑩ **Kapellbrücke** (Chapel Bridge). The oldest wooden bridge in Europe snakes diagonally across the Reuss. When built in the early 14th century, it served as the division between the lake and the river. Its shingle roof and grand stone water tower are to Luzern what the Matterhorn is to Zermatt, but considerably more vulnerable, as a 1993 fire proved. Almost 80% of this fragile monument was destroyed, including many of the 17th-century paintings inside; restorations are still underway. However, a walk through this dark, creaky landmark will take you past polychrome copies of the 112 gable panels, painted by Heinrich Wägmann in the 17th century and depicting Luzern and Swiss history, stories of St. Leodegar and St. Mauritius, Luzern's patron saints, and coats of arms of local patrician families. ⊠ *Between Seebrücke and Rathaus-Steg, connecting Rathausquai and Bahnhofstr.*

★ ❶ **Kultur- und Kongresszentrum** (Culture and Congress Center). Architect Jean Nouvel's stunning glass-and-steel building manages to both jolt and yet seem to fuse with its ancient milieu. The lakeside center's roof is an oversized, cantilevered, flat plane; shallow water channels thread inside, and immense glass plates mirror the surrounding views. The main magnet is the concert hall, opened in 1998. Although the lobbies are rich in blue, red, and stained wood, the hall itself is refreshingly pale, with acoustics so perfect you can hear the proverbial pin drop. Among the annual music events is the renowned International Music Festival (☞ Nightlife and the Arts, *below*). A museum with both permanent and rotating exhibits was slated to open in summer 2000. ⊠ *Europapl.,* ☎ *041/2207070.* 🏵

★ ⑬ **Löwendenkmal** (Lion Monument). The Swiss officers and 760 guards officers who died defending Louis XVI of France at the Tuileries in Paris in 1792 are commemorated here. Designed by Danish sculptor Berthel Thorwaldsen and carved out of a sheer sandstone face by Lucas Ahorn of Konstanz, this 19th-century wonder is a simple, stirring image of a dying lion. The Latin inscription translates: "To the bravery and fidelity of the Swiss." ⊠ *Denkmalstr.*

🖐 ❻ **Natur-Museum** (Natural History Museum). Unusually modern display techniques bring nature lessons to life. The museum focuses on local natural history, with model panoramas of early Luzern settlers and live animals for children to meet. ⊠ *Kasernenpl. 6,* ☎ *041/2285411.* 🎟 *5 SF.* ☉ *Tues.–Sat. 10–noon and 2–5, Sun. 10–5.*

❺ **Spreuerbrücke.** This narrow, weathered, all-wood covered bridge dates from 1408. Its interior gables hold a series of eerie, well-preserved 17th-century paintings by Kaspar Meglinger of the *Dance of Death.* Medieval in style and inspiration, they chronicle the plague that devastated all of Europe in the 14th century. ⊠ *Between Geissmattbrücke and Reussbrücke, connecting Zeughaus Reuss-Steg and Mühlenpl.*

❹ **Weinmarkt** (Wine Market). What is now the loveliest of Luzern's several fountain squares drew visitors from all across Europe in the 15th to 17th centuries with its passion plays. Its Gothic central fountain depicts St. Mauritius (patron saint of warriors), and its surrounding buildings are flamboyantly frescoed in 16th-century style. ⊠ *Square just west of Kornmarkt, north of Metzgerainli.*

⑮ **Zytturm.** The clock in this fifth watchtower was made in Basel in 1385 and still keeps time. ⊠ *North of and parallel to Museggstr.*

Dining and Lodging

$$$ ✕ **Old Swiss House.** Conceived as self-consciously as its name implies— no doubt to satisfy the romantic expectations of the flood of English

tourists heading for the Lion Monument—this popular establishment pleases crowds with its beautifully contrived collection of 17th-century antiques, its leaded glass, and an old-world style now pleasantly burnished by more than 130 years of service. The standing menu includes specialties from around the country: cheese croquettes, veal and Rösti, lake fish, and Swiss chocolate mousse. ⊠ *Löwenpl. 4,* ☎ *041/ 4106171. AE, DC, MC, V. Closed Mon. and Feb.*

$$$ ✕ **Rotes Gatter.** This chic restaurant in the Des Balances hotel (☞ *below*)
★ has a combination as desirable as it is rare: soigné decor, shimmering river views, and a sophisticated menu with fish dishes such as seasonal salad with salmon, or the house specialty, meat and fish fondue. There's a more casual, less expensive bistro area as well. ⊠ *Weinmarkt,* ☎ *041/ 4103010. AE, DC, MC, V.*

$$ ✕ **Galliker.** Step past the ancient facade into a room roaring with local
★ action, where Luzerners drink, smoke, and wish each other "*Guten Appetit.*" Brisk, motherly waitresses serve up the dishes *Mutti* used to make: fresh *Kutteln* (tripe) in rich white wine sauce with cumin seeds; real *Kalbskopf* (chopped fresh veal head) served with heaps of green onions and warm vinaigrette; and authentic Luzerner Kügelipaschtetli. Desserts may include dried pears steeped in pinot noir. Occasional experiments in a more modern mode—such as ginger ice cream—prove that Peter Galliker's kitchen is no museum. ⊠ *Schützenstr. 1,* ☎ *041/ 2401002. AE, DC, MC, V. Closed Sun., Mon., and 3 wks in Aug.*

$$ ✕ **Rebstock/Hofstube.** At the opposite end of the culinary spectrum from Galliker (☞ *above*), this up-to-date kitchen offers modern, international fare, including rabbit and ostrich, as well as East Asian and vegetarian specialties. But you're still in Switzerland: the chewy breads, baked up the street, are so beautiful that they're displayed as objets d'art. The lively bentwood brasserie hums with locals lunching by the bar, while the more formal old-style restaurant glows with wood and brass under a low-beamed parquetry ceiling. ⊠ *St. Leodegarpl. 3,* ☎ *041/4103581. AE, DC, MC, V.*

$ ✕ **Pfistern.** One of the architectural focal points of the Old Town waterfront, this floridly decorated old guild house—the guild's origins can be traced back to 1341—offers a good selection of moderate meals in addition to higher-price standards. Lake fish and *pastetli* (meat pies with puff pastry) are worthy local options. Inside, it's woody and publike, if slightly down-at-the-heels, but in summer the small first-floor balcony may provide the best seat in town. ⊠ *Kornmarkt 4,* ☎ *041/ 4103650. AE, DC, MC, V.*

$$$$ ✕▥ **Palace Hotel.** This waterfront hotel drinks in the broadest pos-
★ sible lake views. Built in 1906, it's been brilliantly refurbished so that its classical look has a touch of postmodernism. Rooms are large enough for a game of badminton, and picture windows afford sweeping views of Lake Luzern and Mt. Pilatus. The hotel's elegance seeps into its restaurant, Mignon, as well. The contemporary cuisine—rosemary beef tenderloin in olive oil and black pepper jus, for example— is faultlessly prepared and formally presented. Reservations are essential. ⊠ *Haldenstr. 10, CH-6002,* ☎ *041/4161616,* FAX *041/4161000. 178 rooms, 45 suites. 2 restaurants, bar, in-room dataports, in-room safes, massage, 2 saunas, steam room, health club, laundry, meeting rooms, parking (fee). AE, DC, MC, V.* ✎

$$$ ✕▥ **Wilden Mann.** The city's best-known hotel offers its guests a gra-
★ cious and authentic experience of old Luzern, with stone, beams, brass, hand-painted tiles, and burnished wood everywhere. (Even the street is atmospheric—across the way is a 16th-century pharmacy.) Standard rooms have a prim 19th-century look. The hotel's reputation extends to its restaurants; the Burgerstube, which began in 1517, is cozy with its dark beams and family crests, while vaulting and candlelight give

the Liedertafel restaurant a more formal atmosphere. On either side, young chef Andreas Stübi strikes a fine balance between old-style local cooking and savvy French cuisine: vegetable gratin with scallops and hollandaise; duck breast with dandelion honey and balsamic vinegar. ✉ *Bahnhofstr. 30, CH-6003,* ☎ *041/2101666,* FAX *041/2101629. 35 rooms, 8 suites. 2 restaurants, minibars, library. AE, DC, MC, V.* 🐾

$$$$ 🏨 **Château Gütsch Kempinski.** This "castle," built in 1888, is not exactly authentic, but honeymooners, gullible romantics, and other neophytes seeking out storybook Europe enjoy the Disneyland-like experience: the turrets and towers worthy of a mad Ludwig of Bavaria; the cellars, crypts, and corridors lined with a hodgepodge of relics; not to mention the magnificent hilltop site above Luzern. Fantasy-style rooms are decked out for romance, some with four-poster canopy beds, all with grand baths. The restaurant is known for its dramatic views of Luzern, and there are wine tastings in the atmospheric cellar. You can get a funicular up to the hotel (2 SF); catch it where Pfistergasse meets Baselstrasse. ✉ *Kanonenstr., CH-6003,* ☎ *041/2494100,* FAX *041/2494191. 28 rooms, 3 suites. 2 restaurants, pool, free parking. AE, DC, MC, V.* 🐾

$$$$ 🏨 **National Hotel.** In this monumental landmark, founded in 1870 and once home base to Cesar Ritz, the inner sanctums have been restored to florid splendor, down to the last cupola, crown molding, and Corinthian column. The hotel's mansarded facade stretches the length of two city blocks, dominating the lakeside promenade. Rooms are French provincial with brass beds, the domed bar is decked with mahogany and aglitter with crystal, and the marble-columned breakfast hall may be the most splendid in Switzerland—even without the lake view. ✉ *Haldenstr. 4, CH-6003,* ☎ *41/4190909,* FAX *041/4190910. 78 rooms, 10 suites. 4 restaurants, breakfast room, café, piano bar, in-room safes, indoor pool, massage, sauna, health club, baby-sitting, parking (fee). AE, DC, MC, V.* 🐾

$$$$ 🏨 **Schweizerhof.** Built in 1844 and expanded in the 1860s, this imposing structure has hosted Napoléon III, Leo Tolstoy, and Mark Twain—and Richard Wagner lived here while his lakefront home at Tribschen was being completed. The rooms, all with sweeping views of the lake and mountains, were renovated in 1999. Their period style has a modern twist; gilt mirrors, richly colored carpets, and marble-and-tile bathrooms cover the luxury bases, while Internet access and voice mail keep you connected. Peripheral construction (a parking garage and a building next door) was scheduled for completion in fall 2000. ✉ *Schweizerhofquai 3, CH-6002,* ☎ *041/4100410,* FAX *041/ 4102971. 101 rooms, 6 suites. Restaurant, café, bar, minibars, in-room dataports, in-room safes, exercise room, meeting rooms, free parking. AE, DC, MC, V.* 🐾

$$$ 🏨 **Des Balances.** This riverfront property, built in the 19th century on
★   the site of an ancient guildhall, gleams with style. State-of-the-art tile baths, up-to-date pastel decor, and one of the best sites in Luzern (in the heart of the Old Town) make this the slickest in its price class. Rear rooms look toward the Weinmarkt. The restaurant Rotes Gatter (☞ *above*) is so good that you may want to eat every meal in the hotel. ✉ *Weinmarkt, CH-6000,* ☎ *041/4103010,* FAX *041/4106451. 50 rooms, 7 suites. Restaurant, minibars, meeting rooms. AE, DC, MC, V.* 🐾

$$$ 🏨 **Hofgarten.** This gracious 12th-century house reflects the creative mind of owner Claudia Moser. The rooms are an eclectic mix of colors and themes. One contains a 5-ft-tall antique stove (still operable), while another is called the Ship Room and resembles the interior of a clipper ship. The Hofgarten also offers Luzern's only all-vegetarian restaurant, whose dishes could satisfy even a meat lover. ✉ *Stadthofdstr. 14, CH-6006,* ☎ *041/4108888,* FAX *041/4108333. 18 rooms. Restaurant, parking (fee). AE, DC, MC, V.* 🐾

$$$ **Montana.** This 1910 palace glows with beeswaxed beauty, its luxurious original woodwork, parquet, and terrazzo in superb condition. The public rooms flank the ground floor's south side and on a clear day offer a magnificent view of the lake and the Alps. The guest rooms echo art deco, with bold patterns and funky furniture. Those in back overlook a hillside, while the front doubles (slightly costlier) have balconies overlooking the city and lake. The building is perched on a slope above town, accessible by funicular from the lakeshore Haldenstrasse or by car. TV is available by request only. Renovations are in the works but will maintain the Deco style; they're scheduled for completion in spring 2000. ⊠ *Adligenswilerstr. 22, CH-6002,* ☎ *041/4106565,* FAX *041/4106676. 55 rooms, 10 suites. Restaurant, bar, free parking. AE, DC, MC, V.* ✏

$$ **Des Alpes.** This historic hotel, with a terrific riverfront location in the bustling heart of the Old Town, has an interior resembling a laminate-and-vinyl chain motel. The rooms, however, are generously proportioned, tidy, and even sleek; front doubles, five with balconies, overlook the water and promenade. Cheaper back rooms face the Old Town; those on higher floors have rooftop views and plenty of light. ⊠ *Rathausquai 5, CH-6003,* ☎ *041/4105825,* FAX *041/4107451. 45 rooms. Restaurant, café. AE, DC, MC, V.* ✏

$$ **Diana.** This is a city hotel, on the south bank and off the main shopping street, but it's reached through a quiet park. Newly decorated rooms may have built-in fixtures in sleek beech or warm knotty pine; some have French windows that open onto balconies. In the oldest rooms, a bleak Formica look, a holdover from the '60s, prevails. Jugendstil touches remain in the corridors, and the public areas are modern but worn. ⊠ *Sempacherstr. 16, CH-6003,* ☎ *041/2102623,* FAX *041/2100205. 38 rooms. Breakfast room. AE, DC, MC, V.*

$$ **Krone.** Spotless and modern, this hotel softens its edges with pastel linens and walls; look in one of the interior walls for a stone prayer shrine retained from the original structure. The rooms facing the Weinmarkt have high ceilings and tall windows that let in floods of sunshine. Rooms to the back have no direct sunlight but are still bright and a little larger. The restaurant's menu is devoted to chicken—outside the dessert list, that is (there's also a no-alcohol policy). Tables sprawl out onto the Weinmarkt in the summer. ⊠ *Weinmarkt 12, CH-6004,* ☎ *041/4194400,* FAX *041/4194490. 25 rooms. Restaurant, outdoor café. AE, DC, MC, V.* ✏

$–$$ **Goldener Stern.** This plain and pleasant former wine cellar has restored its fine 17th-century exterior to present a scrubbed face to the world. Pristine linens soften the modern rooms; windows, some looking over the Franciscan Church, are double-glazed. The Stübli is popular with locals. ⊠ *Burgerstr. 35, CH-6003,* ☎ *041/2275060,* FAX *041/2275061. 18 rooms. Restaurant. AE, MC, V.*

$ **Schlüssel.** This spare, no-nonsense lodging on the Franziskanerplatz attracts young bargain hunters; several of its rooms overlook the square's Franciscan church and fountain (be prepared for morning church bells). It's a pleasant combination of tidy new touches (quarry tile, white paint) and antiquity: you can have breakfast or a simple hot meal in a low, cross-vaulted "crypt" and admire the fine old beams in the lobby. ⊠ *Franziskanerpl. 12, CH-6003,* ☎ *041/2101061,* FAX *041/2101021. 11 rooms. Breakfast room. AE, MC, V.*

$
★   **Tourist.** Despite its friendly, collegiate atmosphere, this cheery dorm-like spot is anything but a backpackers' flophouse. It has a terrific setting on the Reuss around the corner from the Old Town. Its spare modern architecture is brightened with fresh, trendy colors and framed prints, and rooms that don't have the river view face Mt. Pilatus instead. The staff is young and helpful, and the coed four-bed dorms (sex-segregated

in high season) draw sociable travelers with their rock-bottom prices. There are also seven private-bath doubles. Shared baths are well maintained. ⊠ *St. Karli Quai 12, CH-6004,* ☎ *041/4102474,* FAX *041/4108414. 35 dormitory rooms. Coin laundry. AE, DC, MC, V.* ✍

Nightlife and the Arts

For information on goings-on around town, get a copy of the *Luzern City Guide,* published seasonally by the city; it's available at the tourist office (☞ Visitor Information *in* Luzern and Central Switzerland A to Z, *below*). It's bilingual (German/English).

Nightlife

BARS AND LOUNGES

Château Gütsch Kempinski (⊠ Kanonenstr., ☎ 041/2494141) draws a sedate dinner-and-dancing crowd. **Mr. Pickwick** (⊠ Rathausquai 6, ☎ 041/4105927) serves up pints. The **National Hotel** (☞ Dining and Lodging, *above*) mixes drinks in both its glossy bar and its imposing lobby lounge. The **Palace Hotel** bar (☞ Dining and Lodging, *above*) has a similarly clubby look—leather chairs, brass fixtures, and a long oak bar.

CASINOS

The most sophisticated nightlife in Luzern is found in the **Casino** (⊠ Haldenstr. 6, ☎ 041/4185656), a turn-of-the-century building on the northern shore by the grand hotels. You can play *boule* (a type of roulette) in the Gambling Room (5 SF limit, federally imposed); dance in its club, **Vegas;** watch the cabaret in the **Red Rose;** or have a Swiss meal in **Le Chalet** while watching a folklore display.

The Arts

FILM

Movie theaters, concentrated on the south bank along Pilatusstrasse and Bahnhofstrasse, usually present films in their original language. You can also catch a show in the new Bourbaki-Panorama development.

FOLKLORE

The *Night Boat* (☎ 041/3194978), which sails from the Landungsbrücke every evening from May through September, offers meals, drinks, and a folklore show during a pleasant lake cruise. Performances at the **Stadtkeller** (⊠ Sternpl. 3, ☎ 041/4104733) come with Valais-cheese specialties, yodelers, dirndled dancers, and more.

MUSIC

Luzern, the cultural hub of central Switzerland, annually hosts the **International Music Festival** for three weeks in August. The festival is now held in the Kultur- und Kongresszentrum (☞ Exploring, *above*). Outstanding performers come from all over the world; guests scheduled for 2000 included conductor Zubin Mehta with the Vienna Symphony, clarinetist Sabine Meyer, and the Berlin Philharmonic Orchestra. For further information on the festival, contact **International Musikfestwochen** (⊠ Hirschmattstr. 13, CH-6002, ☎ 041/2264400, FAX 041/2264460). The **Luzerner Symphonieorchester** (LSO), the local orchestra in residence, offers a season of concerts from October through June at the Kultur- und Kongresszentrum (⊠ Europapl., ☎ 041/2105050).

THEATER

The **Luzerner Theater** (⊠ Theaterstr. 2, ☎ 041/2106618), directly on the waterfront on the Bahnhof side of town, is home to Luzern's principal theater group, which stages plays in German and operas, usually in the original language.

Outdoor Activities and Sports

Bicycling

The standard Swiss practice of renting bicycles from the **train station** (☎ 051/2273261) comes in handy here, as the lake-level terrain offers smooth riding.

Boating

Pedal-, motor-, and sailboats are available in Luzern through **Bucher & Co.** (✉ Luzernerhof, ☎ 041/4102055). **SNG Luzern** (✉ Alpenquai 11, ☎ 041/3680808), open weekdays only, offers fair-weather boat rentals from April through October and year-round hour-long boat tours for 15 SF. **Werft Herzog AG** (☎ 041/4104333) specializes in exclusive yacht excursions for as many as 12 passengers.

Golf

Golfplatz Dietschiberg (✉ Just above Luzern, near city center, ☎ 041/4209787) has an 18-hole course open to visitors.

Swimming

At the **Lido** (✉ Lidostr., ☎ 041/3703806), past the casino and near the Verkehrshaus, you can swim in Lake Luzern.

Windsurfing

Contact **Kempf Sport AG** (✉ Bahnhofstr. 24, ☎ 041/2101057).

Shopping

The best shopping in the region is concentrated in Luzern, which, although it no longer produces embroidery or lace, still offers a wide variety of Swiss handiwork as well as the luxury goods appropriate to its high profile. During the summer most shops remain open in the evening until 9 and open on Sunday morning after 11. On Thursday night year-round, shops stay open until 9.

Department Stores

The main department store in town is **Globus** (✉ Pilatusstr. 4, ☎ 041/2270707); it's a good place to hunt for souvenirs. **Migros** (✉ Hertensteinstr. 44, ☎ 041/4106363; ✉ Letzihof mall, Hirschengraben 41, ☎ 041/2405571) specializes in groceries and also has inexpensive stationery and office supplies.

Embroidery

For fine handcrafted lace and embroidery, visit **Neff** (✉ Löwenstr. 10, ☎ 041/4101965), if not to buy then just to browse. The main producer of Swiss embroidery is **Sturzenegger** (✉ Schwanenpl. 7, ☎ 041/4101958) of St. Gallen, which sells its own machine-made lace and embroidered goods as well as Hanro and Calida underwear. The store also stocks a conservative line of women's dresses and blouses.

Handicrafts and Gifts

Aux Arts du Feu (✉ Schweizerhofquai 2, ☎ 041/4101401) offers high-end china and crystal. **Ordning & Reda** (✉ Hertensteinstr. 3, ☎ 041/4109506), an upscale Swedish stationer, stocks precision writing instruments and brightly colored, handmade recycled-paper products. **Schmid-Linder** (✉ Denkmalstr. 9, ☎ 041/4104346) carries an extensive line of Swiss embroidery and linen as well as cuckoo clocks, cowbells, and a large stock of wood carvings from Brienz, in the Berner Oberland.

Markets

A **flea market** takes place every Saturday from 8 to 4 at Untere Burgerstrasse. For locally made crafts, there's a **Handwerksmarkt** on the Weinmarkt on the first Saturday of every month.

Watches

Competition is fierce, and the two enormous patriarchs of the watch business advertise heavily and offer inexpensive souvenirs to lure shoppers into their luxurious showrooms. **Bucherer** (⊠ Schwanenpl., ☎ 041/3697700) represents Piaget and Rolex. **Gübelin** (⊠ Schweizerhofquai 1, ☎ 041/4105142) is the exclusive source for Audemars Piguet, Patek Philippe, and its own house brand.

Women's Clothing

The czarina of women's fashion in Luzern is **Christina De Boer,** who runs a group of designer boutiques: De Boer (⊠ Weggisg. 29, ☎ 041/4102022), De Boer Rive Gauche (⊠ Pilatusstr. 14, ☎ 041/2108916), and Christina De Boer (⊠ Weggisg. 29, Werchlaube, ☎ 041/4106239). **McStore/Maglia Poletti** (⊠ Furreng. 7, ☎ 041/4102115) stocks such hip Euro designers as Apropos, Annex, Pink Flamingo (all Swiss designers), and Paul Smith, as well as Poletti's own line of knits in wool, silk, and cotton.

LUZERN ENVIRONS

Since Luzern doesn't have the sprawling suburbs associated with most cities, bucolic landscapes are just a short day-trip away. Craggy mountain tops, lush hills dotted with grazing cows, and peaceful lakeside villages are easily reached by boat, train, or car.

Mt. Pilatus

⑯ *10 km (6 mi) southwest of Luzern.*

This 2,121-m (6,953-ft) mountain was named either from the Latin *pileatus* (wearing a cap), to refer to its frequent cloud covering, or, more colorfully, for the ghost of Pontius Pilate, who supposedly haunts the summit: his body, it was said, was brought here by the devil. For centuries it was forbidden to climb the mountain and enrage the ghost, who was said to unleash deadly storms. Unlike Queen Victoria, who rode to the summit by mule in 1868, you can now reach it by cable car for a hefty 78 SF in summer, 43 SF in winter.

Take a bus from the train station in Luzern to the suburb of Kriens, where you catch a tiny, four-seat cable car that flies silently up to Fräkmüntegg (1,403 m/4,600 ft); then change to the 40-seat cable car that sails through open air up the rock cliff to the summit station (1,696 m/5,560 ft). From here a 10-minute walk takes you to the **Esel,** at the center of Pilatus's multiple peaks, where views unfold over the Alps and the sprawling, crooked Lake Luzern.

A pleasant variation for the return trip to Luzern from Mt. Pilatus involves riding a steep cogwheel train, often down gradients inclined nearly 48%, through four tunnels that pierce sheer rock, to Alpnachstad. From there take the train or the ferry, which leaves from the jetty across from the train station, back to Luzern. To go on to Engelberg, get off the Luzern-bound train at Hergiswil, where you can cross the track and climb aboard the small, private Stans-Engelberg train that heads up the Engelbergertal (Engelberg Valley).

Stans

⑰ *10 km (6 mi) east of Mt. Pilatus, 10 km (6 mi) south of Luzern.*

In the heart of lush valley terrain and mossy meadows, Stans is an old village whose appealing Old Town center is dotted with the deep-roof houses typical of central Switzerland. This was the home of the beloved

Heinrich Pestalozzi, the father of modern education. When the French army invaded the village in 1798, slaughtering nearly 2,000 citizens, it was Pestalozzi who gathered the orphaned children into a school, where he applied his progressive theories in the budding science of psychology to the practice of education. Instead of rote memorization and harsh discipline, Pestalozzi's teaching methods emphasized concrete examples (using plant specimens to teach botany, for example) and moral as well as intellectual development—quite a liberal education. He also championed the idea of children's individuality.

The bell tower of Stans's **Pfarrkirche St. Peter und St. Paul** (Church of Sts. Peter and Paul) is in Italian Romanesque style (with increasing numbers of arched windows as the tower rises), though the incongruous steeple was added in the 16th century; the church as it stands dates from the Renaissance period. ✉ *Knirig. 1*, ☏ *no phone*.

On the town square stands a 19th-century **monument to Arnold von Winkelried,** a native of Stans who martyred himself to lead the Swiss Confederates to victory over the Austrians at the battle of Sempach in 1386. The Austrians, armed with long spears, formed a Roman square so that the Swiss, wielding axes and halberds, couldn't get in close enough to do any damage. Shouting, "Forward, confederates, I will open a path!" von Winkelried threw himself on the spears, clasping as many of them as he could to his breast—creating an opening for his comrades. ✉ *Knirig., in front of Church of Sts. Peter and Paul*.

Another native son, from the neighboring village of Flüeli, is Niklaus von Flüe, who saved the Confederation again, nearly 100 years after von Winkelried, with his wise council at the Diet of Stans in 1481. He was canonized in 1947.

En Route   A two-part journey on a nostalgic 1893 funicular and an ultramodern cable car takes you to the **Stanserhorn** (1,891 m/6,200 ft), from whose peak you can see the lakes; the Titlis, at 3,050 m (10,000 ft) the highest point in central Switzerland; and even the Jungfrau.

Engelberg

⑱   *12 km (8 mi) south of Stans, 27 km (17 mi) south of Luzern.*

At the top of the village of Obermatt, Engelberg (1,000 m/3,280 ft) is a popular resort for skiers from nearby Zürich, but its slopes are limited in comparison to those of St. Moritz, Wengen, and Zermatt. Engelberg clusters at the foot of its Benedictine **Kloster** (monastery), founded in 1120; inside there's one of the largest organs in the country. Until the French invaded in 1798, massacring thousands, this monastery ruled the valley. ✉ *Signposted*, ☏ *041/6371143*. ☉ *Mon.–Sat. 10–4*.

If you are coming straight from Luzern, you can take one of the hourly trains to Engelberg.

OFF THE
BEATEN PATH
TITLIS – This is perhaps the most impressive of the many rocky peaks that surround the Obermatt's long, wide bowl. Thanks to a sophisticated transportation system that benefits skiers, hikers, climbers, and tourists alike, it's possible to ride a small cable car up to the tiny mountain lake (and famous ski area) called **Trübsee** (1,801 m/5,904 ft). From there change to a larger cable car, which rotates to give 360-degree panoramas, and ascend to Stand and ultimately to the summit station on the Titlis. There are an ice grotto (serving drinks from a solid-ice bar) and a panorama restaurant: views take in the Jura Mountains, the Graubünden and Bernese Alps, and what seems from this perspective like the puny Pilatus. ✉ *45 SF round-trip*.

Skiing

At the base of the 3,021-m-high (9,906-ft-high) **Titlis,** Engelberg has two funicular railways, seven cable cars, 13 lifts, 45 km (28 mi) of downhill runs, 34 km (21 mi) of cross-country trails, 3½ km (2 mi) of toboggan runs, and ice-skating. About half the runs are intermediate level, and there are plenty of easy slopes as well; advanced skiers will have relatively slim pickings. A **ski school** (☎ 041/6373040) and **snowboard school** (☎ 041/6374050) are in the **Tourist Center** (☞ Visitor Information *in* Luzern and Central Switzerland A to Z, *below*).

Dining and Lodging

$$–$$$ ✕ **Bierlialp.** The pizzas at this trattoria are incredible: delicious 18-
  ★   inch stone-oven-baked extravaganzas—and that's a single serving! The modern decor is softened by warm candlelight and an even warmer welcome. For a more elaborate entrée try *tagliatelle nere* (black noodles, fish, and shrimp with a pepper-cream sauce) or the truffle ravioli. ⊠ *Dorfstr. 21,* ☎ *041/6371717. AE, MC, V.*

$$ ✕☲ **Spannort.** Regular renovations keep this 1970s version of a traditional hotel looking sharp. Light stained wood is everywhere, from the beamed ceilings to the heavy chalet-style furniture. An emphasis on light and innovative cuisine makes the restaurant a favorite of guests and locals alike; look for fresh choices such as butter lettuce salad with shrimp and saffron vinaigrette. ⊠ *Dorfstr. 26, CH-6390,* ☎ *041/6372626,* FAX *041/6374477. 14 rooms, 4 suites. Restaurant, bar, sauna. AE, DC, MC, V.*

$ ✕☲ **Alpenclub.** This is the real McCoy: an old-fashioned chalet, built
  ★   in 1856, with every square inch pine-paneled and dark-timbered. It's got all the requisites, such as down-quilted beds, a glowing fondue Stübli, and a quiet sun terrace looking out on snowy peaks. It's lively, casual, and, above all, cheap. It draws mobs of young skiers to its disco-bar and pizzeria, and families to its firelighted restaurant (all serve à la carte only). Though it stands slightly beyond the urbanized center, it's not for quiet retreats, at least in ski season. ⊠ *Dorfstr. 5, CH-6390,* ☎ *041/6371243,* FAX *041/6374477. 8 rooms. Restaurant, bar, pizzeria, Stübli. AE, DC, MC, V. Closed May–June.* ✧

$$$ ☲ **Edelweiss.** Walk a few minutes uphill from the center of town to
  ★   find this 1903 hotel. It's perfect if you're looking for organized activities: skiing, snowman-building, or sleigh-rides in winter; biking, river-rafting, or wellness courses in summer. Rooms are outfitted with modern, Scandinavian-style wood furniture, some with beautiful old bathroom fixtures. A fixed, four-course dinner is served nightly, although special needs (vegetarian, low sodium) can be accommodated. Children have a supervised playroom. ⊠ *Terracestr., CH-6390,* ☎ *041/6370737,* FAX *041/6373900. 50 rooms. Restaurant, bar, sauna, free parking. AE, DC, MC, V.* ✧

$$$ ☲ **Treff Regina Titlis.** In a resort haunted by fading grand hotels from a bygone Victorian boom, this central high-rise, a little bit of Dallas in the Alps, strikes a jarring note. Built in 1983 on the ashes of its predecessor, it has fresh, solid rooms with warm wood accents, balconies with views, and generous facilities. If you're looking for quiet, reserve a room at the back of the hotel, away from the street. ⊠ *Dorfstr. 33, CH-6390,* ☎ *041/6372828,* FAX *041/6372392. 96 rooms, 28 suites. 2 restaurants, bar, café, minibars, indoor pool, sauna, exercise room, parking (fee). AE, DC, MC, V.* ✧

$$ ☲ **Europe.** Built in 1908, this Jugendstil beauty offers modern amenities in a bright, elegant setting. Some of the rooms are simple to the point of being bland, but others have small chandeliers and beautifully detailed, mirrored wardrobes. Step onto the wrought-iron balconies and gaze up at the Titlis or down at the neighboring park; if you score

one of the rooms over the front entrance, you'll have especially incredible views. The restaurant, for hotel guests only, serves contemporary cuisine and traditional Swiss favorites. The hotel also houses a hotel management school, so you might find yourself being practiced on every now and then. ✉ *Dorfstr. 40, CH-6390,* ☎ *041/6370094,* FAX *041/ 6372255. 59 rooms, 7 suites. Restaurant, bar. AE, DC, MC, V.*

$$ ⌂ **Schweizerhof.** Though the exterior suggests a once–grande dame, this lovely old fin de siècle structure has been attentively remodeled inside to combine a fresh, light, new knotty-pine look with plush Edwardian comforts. Guest rooms are modern and airy. Bay-window corner doubles are worth asking for. Four family suites with separate bed- and living rooms make this a perfect option for families and small groups. ✉ *Dorfstr. 42, CH-6390,* ☎ *041/6371105,* FAX *041/6374147. 30 rooms, 10 suites. Restaurant, sauna, steam room, exercise room. AE, DC, MC, V.* ✪

Outdoor Activities and Sports
MOUNTAIN BIKING

Mountain biking is very popular here; there's a well-traveled path from the Jochpass to the Trübsee. Free biking maps are available at the tourist office. You can rent bikes from **Amstutz** (✉ Dorfstr. 39, ☎ 041/6371178). Also try **Bike 'n' Roll** (✉ Dorfstr. 31, ☎ 041/6380255).

TENNIS

The **Sportcenter Erlen** (✉ Engelbergstr. 11, ☎ 041/6373494) has two indoor courts and six outdoor courts; they also rent equipment.

VIERWALDSTÄTTERSEE TO ST. GOTTHARD AND EINSIEDELN

From Luzern you can take a lake steamer all the way down to the Urnersee, the southern leg of Vierwaldstättersee (Lake Luzern), or you can drive the same route along the northern lakefront highway to Brunnen, then head north for 30 km to the historic pilgrimage town of Einsiedeln. If you want to climb to Rigi Kulm, the summit of Mt. Rigi, the trip will involve switching to train or cable car. To visit the St. Gotthard Pass you'll need a car. Drive Route 2 all the way up the Reuss Valley to the pass and you'll be rewarded with a fabulous view of the Leventina Valley on the other side. Hannibal's elephants never had it so easy.

If you choose to take a lake cruise, depart at any convenient time (schedules are available at the ticket and tourist offices; *see* Visitor Information *in* Luzern and Central Switzerland A to Z, *below*) from the main docks by the train station; the boat will be marked for Flüelen. First-class seats are on top; each level has a restaurant-café. The exterior seats are only slightly sheltered; if you want to sit inside, you may feel obligated to order a drink. Take advantage of the boat's many stops— you can get on and off at will.

Bürgenstock

⑲ *20 km (13 mi) southeast of Luzern.*

Most Flüelen-bound boats go to the base of the Bürgenstock, where visitors can take a funicular to the isolated resort at the top of a ridge. Though the plateau isn't terribly high—only 458 m/1,500 ft—it rises dramatically above the water and offers striking views over the lake region; that's why a small colony of luxury hotels has mushroomed here, most of them owned by the Frey family. Bürgenstock also can be approached by car, up a narrow, steep road, from Stansstad, on the road between Luzern and Stans.

Weggis

★ ⑳ *25 km (15 mi) northeast and across the lake from Bürgenstock, 20 km (12 mi) northeast of Luzern.*

Weggis is a summer resort town known for its mild, almost subtropical climate. There's a pretty waterfront park and promenade; and as it's far from the auto route and accessible only by the secondary road, you get a pleasant sense of isolation. The famed **Mt. Rigi** (1,800 m/5,900 ft) is just a cable-car ride away from Weggis: follow signs for the Rigibahn, a station high above the resort (a 15-minute walk). From here you can ride a large cable car to **Rigi-Kaltbad**, a small resort on a spectacular plateau; walk across to the electric rack-and-pinion railway station and ride the steep tracks of the Vitznau–Rigi line to the summit of the mountain. Take an elevator to the Hotel **Rigi-Kulm** (☞ *below*) to enjoy the views indoors or walk to the crest (45 minutes) to see as far as the Black Forest in one direction and Mt. Säntis in the other. Or consider climbing to the top, staying in the hotel, and getting up early to see the sun rise over the Alps—a view that astounded both Victor Hugo and Mark Twain. With Lake Luzern on one side and Lake Zug on the other, Mt. Rigi can seem like an island.

You have the option of returning to Luzern from Weggis by taking a different railway down, from Rigi to Arth-Goldau; the two lines were built by competing companies in the 1870s in a race to reach the top and capture the lion's share of the tourist business. The line rising out of the lakefront resort of Vitznau won, but the Arth-Goldau line gets plenty of business, as its base terminal lies on the mainstream St. Gotthard route. The round-trip fare from Vitznau or Arth-Goldau to Rigi-Kulm is 56 SF.

Skiing
Mt. Rigi, at 1,798 m (5,900 ft), has two funicular railways, three cable cars, seven lifts, 30 km (19 mi) of downhill runs, 14 km (9 mi) of cross-country trails, 14 km (9 mi) of ski-hiking trails, and curling.

Dining and Lodging
$$$ ✕ **Renggli's.** This restaurant is ideally located on the waterfront, with its own private dock and a terrace overlooking the lake. The eclectic cuisine ranges from refined vegetarian dishes to more exotic fare, such as poached guinea fowl with a mango-curry sauce. Standards are jazzed up, too: steamed whitefish with apple cider–herb sauce, for instance. ✉ *Seestr. 21,* ☏ *041/3900170. AE, DC, MC, V.*

$$$ 🏨 **Albana.** From this lush art nouveau hotel you can drink in fabulous lake and mountain views. The grand public areas are its best features. These three magnificent rooms have 15-ft ceilings, with one painted with cherubs and clouds and trimmed in gold leaf. A pair of 100-year-old Venetian chandeliers glistens; under the original period furniture shine buffed parquet floors. The dusty-pink-and-white rooms, however, are outfitted with modern furniture; white-tile bathrooms have tubs with room to stretch out. Eight rooms have the original parquet floors—these are the ones to ask for. The restaurant's menu is imaginative, with choices such as "herb cappuccino" (soup) and lamb enveloped in Rösti with a white-bean ragout. The hotel is a short walk uphill from the boat landing. ✉ *Luzernerstr. 26, CH-6353,* ☏ *041/3902141,* 🖷 *041/3902959. 57 rooms. Restaurant, bar, sauna, steam room, meeting rooms. AE, DC, MC, V.* ⍟

$$–$$$ 🏨 **Beau-Rivage.** Built in 1908 but much modernized, this attractive
★ business-class resort concentrates its comforts on a small but luxurious waterfront site, with a restaurant above the manicured lawn, a small swimming pool with mountain views, and lounge chairs at the lake's

edge. Its rooms glow with rosy wood, brass, and pastel fabrics. It's at the center of town, near the boat landing. ✉ *Gotthardstr. 6, CH-6353,* ☎ *041/3907900,* ☏ *041/3901981. 40 rooms. Restaurant, bar, pool. AE, DC, MC, V. Closed Nov.–Mar.*

$$ ⌕ **Rigi-Kulm.** If you find the novelty of mountaintop stopovers appealing, this high-altitude hotel is for you; built in 1950 and rather generic, it still has the air of a rugged but genteel lodge. Southern rooms have rustic decor and great views. (Be warned, however: mountainside transportation makes this an awkward home base for excursions, and if it's raining during your stay, the views disappear.) A short walk from the summit, at 1,800 m (5,900 ft), it is accessible by cable car from Weggis to Rigi-Kaltbad, then by cogwheel rail; or by cogwheel from Vitznau or Arth-Goldau. Or you can climb up from Weggis, allowing either three hours or, as Mark Twain required, three days, depending on your penchant for resting. If you'd like to follow an old romantic tradition, get up at the crack of dawn to see the sun rise over the Alps. ✉ *CH-6410,* ☎ *041/8550303,* ☏ *041/8550055. 40 rooms. Restaurant, café. AE, DC, MC, V.* ✍

Outdoor Activities and Sports

The tourist office at Weggis (☞ Visitor Information *in* Luzern and Central Switzerland A to Z, *below*) rents **bicycles.** Weggis maintains several public **tennis** courts; call the tourist office for information. Windsurfing lessons and rentals in Weggis are available through the **Hotel Hertenstein** (☎ 041/3901444).

Vitznau

㉑ *4 km (2½ mi) southeast of Weggis, 26 km (16 mi) east of Luzern.*

For a quintessentially scenic, quiet spot, stop over in Vitznau, a tiny waterfront resort that competes with Weggis in balmy weather, although its main claim to fame is the palatial Park Hotel, built in 1902.

Lodging

$$$$ ⌕ **Park Hotel.** This isolated but lavish retreat dominates the tiny lake-
★ front village of Vitznau. Constructed in 1902 and enlarged in 1985, it's a vaulted and beamed Edwardian dream in impeccable modern form. Even the corridors are grand, with massive oak triple doors and Persian runners stretching over quarry tile. Rooms have timeless pastels, and lakefront rooms command dreamy Alpine views. The back rooms overlook the slopes of the Rigi, dotted with grazing cows. With the hotel's restaurants and all the activities available, you could easily find yourself not wanting to budge. ✉ *Kantonstr., CH-6354,* ☎ *041/3996060,* ☏ *041/3996070. 97 rooms, 7 suites. 2 restaurants, bar, café, indoor pool, pool, in-room safes, miniature golf, 2 tennis courts, health club, beach, dock, waterskiing, bicycles, playground, meeting rooms, free parking. AE, DC, MC, V. Closed Nov.–Mar.* ✍

$$ ⌕ **Rigi.** Less than half the price of the grandiose Park (☞ *above*), this solid lodging has modernized interiors and a welcoming Stübli atmosphere in its public areas. Corner rooms have balconies with a lake view; four rooms have small kitchenettes. The hotel is just one block from the boat landing and close to the Rigibahn (which means there's some traffic noise during the day). Both the restaurant and the less formal Stübli serve good, simple fish dishes, and there's a pleasant garden terrace. ✉ *Hauptstr., CH-6354,* ☎ *041/3972121,* ☏ *041/3971825. 36 rooms. Restaurant, Stübli. AE, DC, MC, V.* ✍

$ ⌕ **Schiff.** Commanding much the same view as the Park (though the
★ Park itself clouds some of its lakefront beauty), this plain old road-house perches on the hill across the street and offers cheap, no-bath rooms in '50s summer-cottage styles. The vine-trellised terrace restau-

rant, wide open to the water and mountain skyline, serves inexpensive lake-fish dishes. It's down-to-earth here and decidedly friendly. ⊠ *Kantonstr., CH-6354,* ☎ *041/3971357,* 𝖥𝖠𝖷 *041/3972498. 6 rooms. Restaurant. AE, DC, MC, V. Closed Oct.–Nov.*

Outdoor Activities and Sports

TENNIS

The **Park hotel** (⊠ Hertensteinstr. 34, ☎ 041/3901313) in Weggis, 4 km (2½ mi) away, rents court time to nonguests for 18 SF an hour. Equipment can also be rented. The **Seehotel Vitznauerhof** (⊠ Seestr., ☎ 041/3997777) has a court and equipment to rent at 20 SF per hour.

WATER SPORTS

Motorboats and paddleboats are for rent through **Anker Travel** (⊠ Zihlstr. ☎ 041/3971707). You can swim in the bay, which is naturally warmer than Luzern's Lido.

En Route From Vitznau a boat tour will take you across Lake Luzern to **Beck-**
★ **enried,** from which a cable car leads up to **Klewenalp** (1,601 m/5,250 ft), a small winter-sports and summer resort overlooking the lake. The area is excellent for hiking, with breathtakingly panoramic views of the lake and mountains on clear days. You can get a hiking trail map from newsstands or from local tourist offices (☞ Visitor Information *in* Luzern and Central Switzerland A to Z, *below*). If you're driving, you could also follow the north shore to **Gersau,** a tiny lake resort that was an independent republic—the world's smallest—from 1332 to 1798. From Gersau the boat snakes around the sharp peninsula of the Seelisberg; the 1980 completion of a 9¼-km (6-mi) tunnel across the peninsula, south of the lake, opened the way for even swifter north–south travel between Luzern and points north and the St. Gotthard route and points south.

At the south end of Lake Luzern, past the Seelisberg Peninsula, the narrow, majestic **Urnersee** is the wildest and most beautiful leg of the lake. Along its shores lie some of the most historic—or, at least, romantic—landmarks in the region. The **Schillerstein,** on the right as you cruise past the peninsula, is a natural rock obelisk extending nearly 26 m (85 ft) up out of the lake; it bears the simple dedication: TO THE AUTHOR OF *WILHELM TELL,* FRIEDRICH VON SCHILLER. 1859.

Rütli Meadow

★ ㉒ *15 km (10 mi) northwest of Altdorf on Urnersee, 35 km (22 mi) south-east of Luzern.*

Perhaps the most historically significant site in central Switzerland, the Rütli Meadow, just above the Rütli dock, is where the confederates of Schwyz, Unterwald, and Uri are said to have met in 1307 to renew the 1291 Oath of Eternal Alliance. The **Tellsplatte,** on the east side of the lake, at the foot of the Axen Mountain, is the rocky ledge onto which Tell, the legendary rebellious archer, leapt to escape from Gessler's boat, pushing the boat back into the stormy waves as he jumped. There is a small chapel here, built around 1500 and restored in 1881; it contains four frescoes of the Tell legend, painted at the time of restoration.

Another monumental event took place here centuries later: amid threats of a 1940 German invasion, General Guisan, Swiss army commander-in-chief, summoned hundreds of officers to the meadow to reaffirm their commitment to the Swiss Confederation in a secret, stirring ceremony.

Altdorf

ⓓ *20 km (12 mi) south of Rütli Meadow, 35 km (22 mi) southeast of Luzern.*

Schiller's play *Wilhelm Tell* sums up the tale for the Swiss, who perform his play religiously in venues all over the country—including the town of Altdorf, just up the road from the Rütli Meadow. Leave the steamer at Flüelen, the farthest point of the boat ride around the lake, and connect by postbus to Altdorf, the capital of the canton Uri and, by popular if not scholarly consensus, the setting for Tell's famous appleshooting scene. There is a much-reproduced **Tell monument** in the village center, showing a proud father with crossbow on one shoulder, the other hand grasping his son's hand; it was sculpted by Richard Kissling in 1895.

Outdoor Activities and Sports

BIKING

You can rent bikes at the **train station** (☎ 041/8701093) in Flüelen. Mountain bikes and motorbikes can be rented and serviced in Altdorf through **Zweirad Affentranger** (✉ Gotthardstr. 53, ☎ 041/8701315).

WATER SPORTS

You can rent pedal boats and motorboats in Flüelen at **Herr F. Kaufmann** (✉ Seestr. 1, Flüelen, ☎ 041/8701575).

Bürglen

ⓓ *3 km (1¼ mi) southeast of Altdorf, 40 km (25 mi) southeast of Luzern.*

Tell was supposedly from the tiny town of Bürglen, just up the road from Altdorf. The **Tell Museum** devoted to him displays documents and art on the legend. ✉ Postpl., ☎ 041/8704155. 🎫 4 SF. 🕐 May–Oct., daily 10–11:30 and 2–5; July and Aug., daily 10–5.

Andermatt

ⓓ *25 km (15 mi) south of Bürglen (exit the A2 expressway at Göschenen), 67 km (41 mi) southeast of Luzern.*

Andermatt serves as a crossroads for traffic arriving from the Furka Pass, the Oberalp Pass, and the St. Gotthard Pass. It's a relaxing little backwater (no tracts of condos here), with lovely valley hiking and, thanks to its level terrain, fine cross-country skiing. It's much more of a local spot than a sunglasses-and-celebrities resort. From the top of **Gemsstock,** approached by cable car from the town, it is said you can see 600 Alpine peaks.

Skiing

A high, sheltered plateau at the crossroads of three passes—the Gotthard, the Furka, and the Oberalp—**Andermatt** (1,449 m/4,750 ft) is easily accessible from all directions. It has five cable cars, 10 lifts, 55 km (34 mi) of downhill runs, and 20 km (12 mi) of cross-country trails and a snowboard fun park. The ski runs are especially suited for intermediate to advanced skiers. The German-language **snow hot line** (☎ 041/8870181) reports on the latest conditions.

Outdoor Activities and Sports

MOUNTAIN BIKING

Mountain biking is popular here; to rent bikes, call **Christen Sport** (✉ Gotthardstr. 55, CH-6490, ☎ 041/8871251), which stocks summer-sports and snow equipment.

OFF THE
BEATEN PATH

ST. GOTTHARD PASS – This ancient passage started as a narrow path in the 13th century; a railway tunnel was not completed until 1882, and the new road tunnel was finished in 1980. In these bleak and icy heights, the watershed of both the Rhine and the Rhône, you may spot eerie, partially concealed military facilities dug deep into the rock and see soldiers drilling in the snow: it's the Swiss army, refining its Alpine defense skills. The pass closes in winter, but in summer it's a great mountain-biking destination. Take the old road that's closed to traffic; it's known as Alte Gotthardstrasse and runs alongside the main road. There's a hotel at the top; you can gaze at the breathtaking views and have a simple meal at its terrace restaurant.

Schwyz

㉖ *30 km (20 mi) north of Andermatt (via Hwy. 8 or the A2 expressway—exit just past Altdorf), 44 km (27 mi) east of Luzern.*

This historic town is the capital of the canton Schwyz, root of the name Switzerland, and source of the nation's flag. Switzerland's most precious archives are stored here as well. Traces of an independent settlement at Schwyz have been found from as far back as the Bronze Age (2500 BC–800 BC), but it was its inhabitants' aid in the 1291 Oath of Allegiance that put Schwyz on the map. You can see the beautifully scripted and sealed original document as well as battle flags and paintings of the period in Schwyz's **Bundesbriefmuseum** (Federal Charters Museum). ⊠ *Bahnhofstr. 20,* ☎ *041/8192064.* 🎫 *4 SF.* ☉ *May–Oct., Tues.–Fri. 9:30–11:30 and 1:30–5, weekends 9–5; Nov.–Apr., Tues.–Fri. 9:30–11:30 and 1:30–5, weekends 1:30–5. Closed Mon.*

Schwyz has several notable baroque churches and a large number of fine old patrician homes dating from the 17th and 18th centuries, not least being the **Ital-Redinghaus** with its magnificent interior, antique stoves, and fine stained glass. A visit to this grand house includes a peek inside the neighboring **Bethlehemhaus,** the oldest wooden house in Switzerland, dating from 1287. ⊠ *Rickenbachstr. 24,* ☎ *041/8114505.* 🎫 *4 SF.* ☉ *May–Oct., Tues.–Fri. 2–5, weekends 10–noon and 2–5. Closed Mon. and Nov.–Apr.*

Curiously, many of Schwyz's splendid houses owe their origin to the battlefield. The men of Schwyz had a reputation as fine soldiers and were in demand in other countries as mercenaries during the 16th and 17th centuries. They built many of the houses you can see today with their military pay. Schwyz's most famous landmark is the **Rathaus** (Town Hall); its richly frescoed exterior (1891) depicts the Battle of Morgarten, where the Austrian army was defeated by the Swiss. The building is still used as the Town Hall. ⊠ *Hauptpl. 1.*

Einsiedeln

㉗ *27 km (18 mi) northeast of Schwyz, 69 km (43 mi) northeast of Luzern.*

A minor summer and winter resort, Einsiedeln has been a pilgrimage site since AD 946. It is also the home of the **Black Madonna,** still on display in the **Benedictine monastery** after more than a thousand years. The monastery was founded in Charlemagne's time, when Meinrad, a Hohenzollern count and monk, chose the remote site to pursue his devotions in solitude. The abbess of Zürich gave him an image of the Virgin Mary, for which he built a little chapel, and Meinrad lived in peace, fed—the story goes—by two ravens who brought him supplies.

When he was murdered by brigands seeking treasure, the ravens followed the thieves to Zürich and shrieked over their heads until they were arrested. A monastery was built over Meinrad's grave. When it was completed, the bishop of Konstanz was invited to consecrate it, but as he began the ceremony, a voice was heard crying out in the chapel three times, "Brother, desist: God himself has consecrated this building." A papal bull acknowledged the miracle and promised a special indulgence to pilgrims.

Through the ages the monastery of Einsiedeln has been destroyed many times by fire, but the Black Madonna has always been saved. When Napoléon's armies plundered the church, hoping to carry off the sacred image, it had already been taken to the Tirol in Austria for safekeeping. Today the Black Madonna is housed in a black-marble chapel just inside the west entrance to the church. When seen from a distance, its color appears to be a rich bronze, not black, and there is something quaint and gentle about the figure despite its jeweled splendor. The present abbey structure was built by Caspar Moosbrugger in 1735 and decorated by the famous brothers Egid Quirid and Cosmos Damian Asam; it is one of the finest late-baroque churches of its kind, the impressive simplicity and grace of the exterior contrasting vividly with the exuberance of its ornate interior. In front of the church, a grand square surrounds a golden statue of the Virgin Mary with a large gilt crown. Around the base, water trickles from 14 spouts, and pilgrims, to be sure of good luck, traditionally drink from each one in turn.

Einsiedeln is just off the A3 autobahn that connects Zürich with eastern Switzerland. You can take this autobahn to return to Luzern, but a more interesting route is via Alosen and Unterägeri by the Ägerisee, to Zug (☞ *below*), famous for its Old Town.

The Arts
Einsiedeln remains a center for religious pomp and ceremony and celebrates a Festival of the Miraculous Dedication every September 14. Every five years some 700 citizens, coached by the monks, perform *Das Grosse Welttheater* (*the Great World Drama*) before the abbey church. A religious drama on life and the problems of humankind, it was first performed before the Court of Spain in 1685. The next performance of this historic pageant takes place in summer 2003.

Zug

28   *27 km (17 mi) north of Einsiedeln, 28 km (18 mi) northeast of Luzern (via A14 and A4).*

On arriving at the train station in Zug, you may be surprised to find that the town is bustling, modern, and full of multinational corporations. Its contemporary life unfurls around the remnants of ancient ramparts, and its lakefront neighborhood seems frozen in another century. From the train station area on Alpenstrasse you can head straight for the waterfront of the **Zugersee** (Lake Zug). This landscaped promenade and park has fine views of the Pilatus, Rigi, and the Bernese Alps—including the Eiger, the Mönch, and the Jungfrau.

Zug's Old Town is dominated by the **Rathaus** (Town Hall), which was completed in the early 16th century. Inside, there are exhibits of gold and silver work as well as embroideries, wood carvings, stained glass, and the flag Peter Kolin held until he perished in the Battle of Arbedo (1422), when 3,000 Swiss tried valiantly to hold off 24,000 Milanese soldiers. Unfortunately, you'll see these fine furnishings only if you dine in the **Rathauskeller** (☞ Dining and Lodging, *below*), one of the best—

but most expensive—restaurants in central Switzerland. ⊠ *Oberaltstadt 1. Closed to the public.*

By passing through a gate under the Zytturm (Clock Tower), you'll come upon the waterfront **Kolinplatz,** dedicated to the prominent local Kolin family and decorated with a fountain topped by a statue of Wolfgang Kolin. South of the Kolinplatz, up a small hill, is the **Kirche St. Oswald** (Church of St. Oswald), built in the 15th and 16th centuries; its delicate spires rise high above the town.

The Burg, a former Habsburg residence, has a half-timber exterior so heavily restored it looks like a Disney set for *Snow White*. It now houses the **Burg-Museum,** focusing on archaeology, art, and the history of Zug. ⊠ *Kirchenstr. 11,* ☎ *041/7283297.* 🎫 *5 SF, free Sun.* ☉ *Tues.–Fri. 2– 5, weekends 10–noon and 2–5. Closed Mon.*

NEED A BREAK?	Stop at the patisserie-café **Meier** (⊠ Alpenstr. 16, ☎ 041/7111049) for coffee and a slice of the famous Zug Kirschtorte—though called cherry cake, the only cherry you'll find is the heavily alcoholic essence that soaks the delicate yellow cake and butter cream. (The café shares its space with the tourist office.)

The most atmospheric streets of Zug are the **Oberaltstadt** and the **Unteraltstadt,** tight lanes closed in on each side by narrow, shuttered 16th-century town houses now in the beginning throes of gentrification: the storefronts are full of arts and crafts, ceramics, and jewelry.

Dining and Lodging

$$$$ ✕ **Rathauskeller.** Upstairs in this historic landmark you are surrounded by a museumlike collection of medieval regional treasures but are served nothing but cutting-edge cuisine. The emphasis is on fish (scallops marinated in olive oil and lemon juice), meats (tender rabbit fillet with wild-mushroom risotto), and a minimum of visual fuss. Downstairs, in the traditional, dark little Stübli you can order simpler, cheaper dishes from the same kitchen. ⊠ *Oberaltstadt 1,* ☎ *041/ 7110058. AE, V. Closed Sun. and Mon.*

$–$$ ✕ **Aklin.** This 500-year-old Altstadt landmark offers *Grossmutters Küche* (Grandmother's cooking)—*Kalbskopf* (chopped veal head), *Siedfleisch* (boiled beef), and lake fish—on candlelit wooden tables by a ceramic-tile stove in the upstairs restaurant or in the atmospheric, casual bistro downstairs. ⊠ *Kolinpl. 10,* ☎ *041/7111866. AE, DC, MC, V. Closed Sun.*

$$–$$$ 🏨 **Ochsen.** Although the notch-gabled facade has been preserved at this 16th-century landmark on the imposing Kolinplatz in Zug's Old Town, the interior is strictly upscale-chain. Hints of architectural detail have been sanded away, and the buffed wood of the restaurant looks more Scandi-sleek teak now than Swiss; it's hard to believe that Goethe was once a guest here. The rooms are high-tech chic; the best are at the far back (above a tiny courtyard) and—of course—looking over the Kolinplatz fountain toward the lake. The restaurant deserves its good reputation for fine local dishes: meats, Rösti, and its specialty, lake fish. ⊠ *Kolinpl. 11, CH-6301,* ☎ *041/7293232,* 𝔽𝔸𝕏 *041/7293222. 46 rooms. Restaurant. AE, DC, MC, V.* 🕊

Outdoor Activities and Sports

At 436 m (1,430 ft), Zug has 9 km (6 mi) of **cross-country ski** trails, 17 km (11 mi) of **ski-hiking** trails, and **curling.** You can rent bicycles from the **train station** (☎ 041/7113988).

LUZERN AND CENTRAL SWITZERLAND A TO Z

Arriving and Departing

By Car

It's easy to reach Luzern from Zürich by road, approaching from national expressway **A3** south, connecting to **A4** via the secondary **E41** in the direction of Zug, and continuing on A4, which turns into the **A14**, to the city. A convenient all-expressway connection between the two cities won't be open for more than a decade. Approaching from the southern, St. Gotthard Pass route (**A2**) or after cutting through the Furka Pass by rail ferry, you descend below Andermatt to Altdorf, where a tunnel sweeps you through to the shores of the lake. If you're heading for resorts on the north shore, leave the expressway at Flüelen and follow the scenic secondary route. From Basel in the northwest, it's a clean sweep by the **A2** to Luzern.

By Plane

The nearest international airport is **Zürich-Kloten** (✉ Approximately 54 km/33 mi northeast of Luzern, ☎ 1571060). **Swissair** (☎ 800/221–4750 in the U.S.; 0171/434–7300 in the U.K.) flies in most often from the United States and the United Kingdom.

By Train

Luzern functions as a rail crossroads, with express trains connecting hourly from Zürich, a 49-minute trip, and every two hours from Geneva, a 3½- to 4-hour trip changing at Bern. Trains enter from the south via the St. Gotthard Pass from the Ticino and via the Furka Pass from the Valais. For rail information, call the **Bahnhof** (train station; ✉ Bahnhofpl., ☎ 0900/300300).

The **Wilhelm Tell Express,** a cooperative effort of Swiss Federal Railways and lake steamers, operates daily from May through October; a boat ride takes you from Luzern to Flüelen, then a train zips to Lugano. The journey, without stopovers, takes six hours. For information contact the Luzern tourist office (☞ Visitor Information, *below*).

Getting Around

By Boat

It would be a shame to see this historic region only from the shore; some of its most impressive landscapes are framed along the waterfront, as seen from the decks of one of the cruise ships that ply the lake. Rides on these are included in a **Swiss Pass** (☞ Train Travel *in* the Gold Guide) or a **Swiss Boat Pass** (☞ Boat Travel *in* the Gold Guide). Individual tickets can be purchased at Luzern's departure **docks** (✉ Near the train station, ☎ 041/3676767); the fee is based on the length of your ride. Any combination of transportation can be arranged, such as a leisurely cruise from Luzern to Flüelen at the lake's southernmost point, lasting about 3½ hours and costing 42 SF for second class, 64 SF for first class. The return train trip, via the Arth–Goldau line, takes little more than an hour. The **Tell Pass** (☞ By Train, *below*) gives you free boat rides.

By Bus

The postbus network carries travelers faithfully, if slowly, to the farthest corners of the region. It also climbs the St. Gotthard and the Furka passes (remember, these are closed in winter). For schedules and prices, check at the post office nearest your home base or pick up a copy of the *Vierwaldstättersee Fahrplan,* a booklet (50 rappen) that covers cruise ships and private railways as well as postbuses, available at the local tourist office (☞ Visitor Information, *below*). If you're staying in a Luzern hotel, you will be eligible for the special **Guest-Ticket,** offering unlimited rides for three days for a minimal fee of 8 SF. The **Tell Pass** (☞ By Train, *below*) includes postbus discounts.

By Car

Although Mt. Rigi and Mt. Pilatus are not accessible by car, nearly everything else in this region is. The descent from Andermatt past the Devil's Bridge, which once carried medieval pilgrims from the Saint Gotthard and drew thrill seekers during the 19th century, now exemplifies awe-inspiring Swiss mountain engineering: from Göschenen, at 1,106 m (3,627 ft), to the waterfront, it's a four-lane expressway.

By Train

Swiss National Railways is enhanced here by a few private lines (to Engelberg, Pilatus, the Rigi Kulm) that make it possible to get to most sights. If you don't have a Swiss Pass, there's a central Switzerland regional discount pass, called the **Tell Pass.** The 15-day pass grants you five days of unlimited free travel on main routes, 10 days at half fare. The seven-day pass gives you two days free, five at half fare. (Besides the SBB lines, most private rail lines will also accept the pass.) The ticket can be bought at rail or boat ticket offices, on a cruise boat, from travel agencies, or from the tourist office (☞ Visitor Information, *below*). The 15-day pass costs 179 SF second class, 201 SF first class; the seven-day pass costs 131 SF second class, 143 SF first class. Plan your itinerary carefully to take full advantage of all discount rates, and before you buy a regional pass, add up your excursions à la carte. Remember that many routes always charge half price. All boat trips and the private excursions to Rigi and Pilatus are free to holders of regional passes—but getting to the starting point may cost you half price. If you plan to cover a lot of ground, however, you may save considerably. Choose your free days in advance: you must confirm them *all* with the first inspector who checks your pass.

Contacts and Resources

Emergencies

Police (☎ 117). **Medical, dental, and pharmacy referral** (☎ 111). **Auto breakdown:** Touring Club of Switzerland (☎ 140); **Swiss Automobile Club** (☎ 041/2100155).

Guided Tours

The **Luzern tourist office** (☞ Visitor Information, *below*) offers a guided walking tour of Luzern with English commentary. It takes about two hours and cost 16 SF, including a drink. **Schiffahrtsgesellschaft des Vierwaldstättersees** (✉ Werftestr. 5, CH-6002 Luzern, ☎ 041/3676767) offers historic and Alpine theme cruises with English commentary.

Visitor Information

The principal tourist office for the whole of central Switzerland, including the lake region, is **Zentralschweiz Tourismus** (Central Switzerland Tourism; ✉ Alpenstr. 1, CH-6002 Luzern, ☎ 041/4184080, FAX 041/4107260, ✆). The main tourist office for the city of **Luzern** (✉ Zentralstr. 5, ☎ 041/2271717,✆) is in the Bahnhof, off Track 3. There's also an accommodations service.

Local offices: **Altdorf** (✉ Rathauspl., CH-6460, ☎ 041/8720450). **Andermatt** (✉ Offizieles Verkehrsbüro, Gotthardstr. 2, CH-6490, ☎ 041/8871454). **Einsiedeln** (✉ Hauptstr. 85, ☎ 055/4184488). **Engelberg** (✉ Klosterstr., CH-6390, ☎ 041/6373737). **Schwyz** (✉ Obersteisteg 14, CH-6430, ☎ 041/8101991). **Stans** (✉ Bahnhofpl. 4, CH-6370, ☎ 041/6108833). **Vitznau** (✉ Seestr., CH-6354, ☎ 041/3980035). **Weggis** (✉ Seestr. 5, CH-6353, ☎ 041/3901155). **Zug** (✉ Alpenstr. 14, CH-6300, ☎ 041/7110078).

7   BASEL

At the juncture of France and Germany is German-speaking Basel, a cultural capital with a sense of fun. Cultivated and yet down-home, it has more than 30 museums, Switzerland's oldest university, and some of the most diverse shopping in the country. All the same, beer and bratwursts are the snack of choice, and the annual Carnival is observed with a boisterousness that's unparalleled in other Swiss towns.

Updated by
Kara
Misenheimer

THOUGH IT LACKS THE GILT AND GLITTER of Zürich and the Latin grace of Geneva, in many ways quiet, genteel Basel (Bâle in French) is the most sophisticated of Swiss cities. At the frontier between two of Europe's most assertive personalities, France and Germany, and tapped directly into the artery of the Rhein (Rhine), it has flourished on the lifeblood of two cultures and grown surprisingly urbane, cosmopolitan, worldly wise. It is also delightfully eccentric, its imagination fed by centuries of intellectual input: Basel has been host to Switzerland's oldest university (1460) and patron to some of the country's—and the world's—finest minds. A northern center of humanist thought and art, it nurtured the painters Konrad Witz and Hans Holbein the Younger as well as the great Dutch scholar Erasmus. And it was Basel's visionary lord mayor Johann Rudolf Wettstein who, at the end of the Thirty Years' War, negotiated Switzerland's groundbreaking—and lasting—neutrality.

Every day 27,500 French and German commuters cross into Basel. Banking activity here is surpassed only by that of Zürich and Geneva, and every month representatives of the world's leading central banks meet behind closed doors in the city center at the Bank for International Settlements, the world's central bank clearinghouse. Enormous international pharmaceutical firms—Novartis and Roche—crowd the riverbanks. Yet Basel's population hovers around a modest 200,000; its urban center lies gracefully along the Rhine, no building so tall as to block another's view of the cathedral's twin spires. Two blocks from the heart of the thriving shopping district you can walk 17th-century residential streets cloaked in perfect, otherworldly silence.

The disproportionate number of museums per capita is a reflection of Basel's priorities: the city has more than 30, including the world-class Kunstmuseum (Museum of Fine Arts), the Tinguely Museum, and the Beyeler Foundation. As high culture breeds good taste, Basel has some of the most varied, even quirky, shopping in Switzerland; antiquarian bookstores, calligraphers, and artisans do business next to sophisticated designer shops and famous jewelers. But you can still get a beer and a bratwurst here: Baslers almost exclusively speak German or their own local version of *Schwyzerdütsch,* called *Baseldütsch*. On Freiestrasse, the main shopping street, dense crowds of shoppers stand outside a local butcher's, holding bare *Wienerli* (hot dogs) and dipping the pink tips into thick golden mustard. They also indulge in *Kaffe und Kuchen*—the late-afternoon coffee break Germans live for—but Baslers do it differently. Instead of the large slices of creamy cake, they select tiny sweet gems—two or three to a saucer, but petite nonetheless—and may opt for a delicate Chinese tea.

The Celts were the first to settle here, some 2,000 years ago, on the site of the Münster (cathedral). During the 1st century BC the Romans established a town at Augst, then called Colonia Augusta Raurica; the ruins and the theater can be visited today, 10 minutes by car outside town. By the 3rd century, the Romans had taken the present cathedral site in Basel proper, naming the town Basilia (royal stronghold). Germanic invaders banished them in 401, and it was not until the Holy Roman emperor Henry II took Basel under his wing in the 11th century that stability returned. His image and that of his wife, Kunegunde, adorn the cathedral and the Rathaus (Town Hall). Henry built the original cathedral—on the site of a church destroyed by a raiding band of Hungarian horsemen in 916—and established Basel as one of the centers of his court. In 1006 the bishop of Basel was made ruler of the town, and throughout the Middle Ages these prince-bishops gained and exerted enormous temporal and spiritual powers. Though the prince-bishops are no more, Basel still uses one of their symbols in its coat of arms—a striking black staff.

Yet Basel is first and foremost a Renaissance city in the literal sense of the word: a city of intellectual and artistic rebirth, its flourishing river commerce bringing with it a flow of ideas. In 1431 the Council of Basel, an ecumenical conference on church reform, was convened here, bringing in—over a period of 17 years—the great sacred and secular princes of the age. One of them, who later became Pope Pius II, granted permission for the founding of the university and established Basel as the cultural capital it remains today.

Art and academia over the ages haven't made Basel stuffy, however. The Baslers' Lenten celebration of Fasnacht (related to Mardi Gras, or Carnival) turns the city on its ear. The streets are filled with grotesquely costumed revelers bearing huge homemade lanterns scrawled with comments and caricatures relating to local current events. Although the festivities last only three days, you'll see masks, drums, and fifes displayed and sold everywhere all year long, and you'll hear strains of fife-and-drum marches wafting from the guild houses' upper windows; they're rehearsing for Fasnacht. Like confetti lodged between the cobblestones, there always seems to be a hint of Fasnacht, age-old and unpredictable, even in Basel's most sedate and cultivated corners.

Pleasures and Pastimes

Dining
When the Alemanni hordes sent the Romans packing, they brought their Germanic cuisine as well, and for the most part the German style stuck. When Baslers eat home style, it's inevitably sausage, schnitzel, *Spätzli* (tiny flour dumplings), and beer. The city is full of comfortable haunts lined with carved wood and thick with the mingled odors of cooking meat and cigar smoke.

Yet the proximity of the Rhine has given Basel a taste for river fish, too, and if Basel could claim a regional specialty, it would be salmon. Salmon became so commonplace in Basel's golden age that some cooks refused to prepare it more than twice a week. Basel's better restaurants often feature the meaty pink fish (though it's likely imported, as the Rhine has suffered from pollution), served in a white-wine marinade with fried onions on top—*nach Basler-Art* (Basel style). Try it with a bottle of the fruity local Riesling-Sylvaner.

Fasnacht
Dating from the Middle Ages, Switzerland's best-known Carnival is a must-see if Basel is on your early-spring travel itinerary. Beginning at 4 AM the morning after Ash Wednesday, the Morgenstraich opens the event with a blast of fifes and drums loud enough to wake the living, the dead, and the hard-of-hearing too. As it happens, no one's sleeping at all: they're waiting for the start of colorful masked processions that traverse the Old Town until dawn and continue for several days. Nearby Liestal stages its own spectacular and more primitive ceremony the night before, when burning stacks of wood are paraded through the town and heaped together. Crackling torches are carried on participants' backs, while increasingly larger blazing log piles are pulled behind on wagons. The flames flare splendidly against the town's medieval *Tor* (gate) as each passing group rushes through.

Museums
With a renowned gallerist's handpicked paintings (the Fondation Beyeler), an homage to unique mechanized art (the Tinguely Museum),

and one of the world's oldest public art collections (the Kunstmuseum), Basel easily earns high rank in the art world. But the city goes even farther, with additional museums of astounding variety—from collections featuring design and caricature to paper, printing, and pharmaceutical history. The larger museums, such as the Historisches Museum, publish guides in English. Also, the tourist office sells the BaselCard, which provides admission to the city's museums for a flat fee.

EXPLORING BASEL

The Rhine divides the city of Basel into two distinct sections: the whole of the Old Town lies in Grossbasel (Greater Basel), the commercial, cultural, and academic center. The opposite bank, to the northeast, is Kleinbasel (Little Basel), a Swiss enclave on the "German" side of the Rhine that is the industrial quarter of the city. Unless you are visiting on business and meeting at the convention center east of the river, your time on the right bank will probably be limited to a waterfront stroll and possibly a good night's sleep, as it does have some hotels.

Numbers in the text correspond to numbers in the margin and on the Basel map.

Great Itineraries

IF YOU HAVE 1 OR 2 DAYS

Begin with a stroll through Basel's Old Town, making sure to see the Münster and the sweeping views from the church's Rhine terrace, the Pfalz. Art enthusiasts could decide to circle from here directly to the Kunstmuseum, while shoppers may want to head down one of the winding alleyways into the Freiestrasse or the Marktplatz. A leisurely late-afternoon walk across the Mittlere Rheinbrücke and upstream along the sunny Kleinbasel riverside promenade (Oberer Rheinweg) is a good way to see the town in its best light.

On the following day take in some of the city's smaller museums, perhaps in the picturesque St. Alban quarter. From here take a ferry boat across the river and head east to the Tinguely Museum. Or organize your day around a trip to Riehen; the Fondation Beyeler's stunningly well-rounded (and beautifully presented) collection of 20th-century art can be reached in a mere 20 minutes by tram.

IF YOU HAVE 3 TO 5 DAYS

Given the luxury of several days, you can explore even more of Basel's museums. In season you might opt to take a boat trip to the Roman ruins of Augusta Raurica, east of Basel. You could also take a driving tour of the small villages scattered south of Basel: Balsthal, Holderbank, Oberer Hauenstein, Langenbruck, and Liestal.

Old Town

Standing in the middle of the Marktplatz or even watching river traffic from the Mittlere Rheinbrücke, it's easy to envision the Basel of centuries ago. On a bend of the Rhine, Basel's Old Town is full of majestic Gothic spires and side streets that have remained largely unchanged since the 1600s. Still, much of the delicately preserved architecture of the Old Town incorporates impressive, state-of-the-art museums and miles of shop-lined pedestrian zones.

A Good Walk

Six bridges link the two halves of the city; the most historic and picturesque is the **Mittlere Rheinbrücke** ①. Start at its Grossbasel end, near the tourist office. On the corner of what is now a chain restaurant (Churrasco) at Schifflände, you can see a facsimile of the infamous

Lällekönig ②, a 15th-century gargoyle once mechanized to stick out his tongue and roll his eyes at his rivals across the river.

Walking across the bridge, you'll see Basel's peculiar, gondolalike ferry boats, attached to a high wire and angling silently from shore to shore, powered only by the swift current of the river (you can ride one for 1.20 SF). Across the Rhine, pause at the seated **statue of Helvetia,** one of Basel's many tongue-in-cheek sculptures.

Back across the Mittlere Rheinbrücke in Grossbasel, turn left up a steep alley called the **Rheinsprung,** banked with 15th- and 16th-century houses. Turn right at Archivgässlein, and you'll come to the **Martins-kirche** ③, the city's oldest parish church, dating from 1288.

Continue along Martinsgasse, on your left, to the elegant neighboring courtyards of the **Blaues und Weisses Haus** ④, meeting place of kings. Just beyond, turn left and head toward the fountain adorned by a myth-ical green basilisk into the Augustinergasse. At No. 2 is the entrance to the **Naturhistorisches Museum** ⑤ and the **Schweizerisches Museum der Kulturen** ⑥. Under one roof you will find one of the world's fore-most natural history and prehistory collections.

Augustinergasse leads into the Münsterplatz, dominated by the strik-ing red-sandstone 12th-century **Münster** ⑦, burial place of Erasmus and Queen Anna of Hapsburg. Walk around to the church's riverside to a terrace called the **Pfalz,** which affords wide views of the river, the Old Town, and, on a clear day, the Black Forest.

From the Münsterplatz, head down Rittergasse, past its elegant villas and courtyards, to the first busy cross street. Ahead of you is St. Alban-Vorstadt, which leads to the **St. Alban-Tor** ⑧, one of the original 13th-century medieval city gates. St. Alban-Tal leads from St. Alban-Vorstadt down to St. Alban-Rheinweg on the Rhine to the **Basler Papier-mühle/Schweizer Papiermuseum und Museum für Schrift und Druck** ⑨ and **Museum für Gegenwartskunst** ⑩.

Leaving the museums by way of the St. Alban-Rheinweg along the river-side, ascend the Wettstein Bridge stairs and head left onto St. Alban-Graben. Here is the imposing **Kunstmuseum** ⑪, home of one of Europe's oldest public collections.

Continue down St. Alban-Graben to the intersection of Steinenberg. A few blocks straight ahead into Elisabethenstrasse will take you to the **Haus zum Kirschgarten** ⑬, which has parts of the Basel Historical Museum's collections. To circle back into the Old Town, however, veer right on Steinenberg, which goes by the **Kunsthalle** ⑫. Just beyond the art gallery, the whimsical Tinguely-Brunnen, or **Fasnacht-Brunnen,** puts on a show on the Theaterplatz. (A Richard Serra sculpture, nor-mally covered in graffiti, also punctuates the square.) Zoo enthusiasts may want to take advantage of tram service along Steinentorstrasse to reach the **Zoologischer Garten** ⑭, west of the SBB train station.

Continue on Steinenberg until it opens out onto the bustling Bar-füsserplatz. Here the **Puppenhaus Museum** ⑮ displays toys from the 18th and 19th centuries, while the **Historisches Museum** ⑯ exhibits an-nals and objects out of Basel's proud past in the mid-14th-century Fran-ciscan **Barfüsserkirche,** or Church of the Discalced Friars.

Behind the tram concourse on Barfüsserplatz, follow the pedestrian zone to Leonhardsberg, which leads left up the stairs to the late-Gothic **Leon-hardskirche** ⑰. Continue along the church walk into Heuberg street, the spine of one of the loveliest sections of old Basel. A network of small streets threads through the quarter, lined with graceful old houses from many periods: Gothic, Renaissance, baroque, Biedermeier. Heuberg feeds into Spalenvorstadt, which will take you ahead two blocks to the **Holbeinbrunnen,** styled from a drawing by Hans Holbein.

The Spalenvorstadt stretches on to the impressive 14th-century **Spalentor** ⑱, another of Basel's medieval city gates. Spalengraben curves north from here past the buildings of the Universität, one of the six oldest universities in German-speaking Europe. Nearby Petersplatz is the site of the 13th-century **Peterskirche** ⑲.

Petersgasse, behind the Peterskirche, presents an exemplary row of houses, some only a single window wide. Several small streets scale downhill from here, among them the Totengässlein, which leads past the **Pharmazie-Historisches Museum** ⑳. The steep stairs wind on in the direction of the **Marktplatz** ㉑, the historic and modern heart of Basel, with its towering **Rathaus** ㉒.

Leading off the south end of the Marktplatz, main shopping streets Freiestrasse and Gerbergasse are lined with international shops and department stores. The north end heads toward **Fischmarkt** ㉓. Marktgasse leads past the historic **Drei Könige Hotel** ㉔. If you're feeling energetic, walk to the **Tinguely Museum** ㉕ by crossing over the Mittlere Rheinbrücke and heading east toward Solitude Park on Kleinbasel's sunny waterfront promenade Oberer Rheinweg. Or take a tram (No. 6 from Barfüsserplatz, Marktplatz, or Schifflände; No. 2 from Bankverein or Munstermesse in the direction of Riehen-Grenze) to the **Fondation Beyeler** ㉖, with its modern-art collection and green park.

TIMING

Moving at a rapid clip you can see the major sights, as well as a cross section of the cultural and artistic collections, in three to five hours. A more leisurely itinerary, including strolling, Old Town shopping along the Spalenburg, and museums on the Kleinbasel side, will while away the better part of at least one day, if not two. Keep in mind that many museums are closed Monday.

Sights to See

✑ *following the text of a review is your signal that the property has a Web site, where you will find details and, usually, images; for a link, visit www.fodors.com/urls.*

👆 ❾ **Basler Papiermühle/Schweizer Papiermuseum und Museum für Schrift und Druck** (Basel Paper Mill/Swiss Museum of Paper, Writing, and Printing). Though its name sounds esoteric, this museum, in a beautifully restored medieval waterfront mill house, is surprisingly accessible. A functioning waterwheel and demonstrations of papermaking, typesetting, and bookbinding show how the site still practices the ancient craft. You can participate in a 12-step papermaking process, beginning with the pulpy raw material simmering in the "Visitors' Vat." Kids can try out quills and ink or spell their names in pieces of type for printing. Most descriptions have an English translation, but some special exhibits are in German only. ⊠ *St. Alban-Tal 35/37,* ☎ *061/2729652.* 🎫 *9 SF.* ☉ *Tues.–Sun. 2–5.*

❹ **Blaues und Weisses Haus** (Blue House and White House). Built between 1762 and 1768 for two of the city's most successful silk merchants, these were the residences of the brothers Lukas and Jakob Sarasin. In 1777 the emperor Joseph II of Austria was a guest in the Blue House and subsequent visitors, including Czar Alexander of Russia, Emperor Francis of Austria, and King Friedrich Wilhelm III of Prussia, who met for dinner here in 1814, take this historical site's guest book over the top. The restored twinlike houses are both white with blue trim, but they're distinguished by their gates: one is intricate iron (Blue House) and the other stately wood. ✉ *Martinsg.*

㉔ Drei Könige Hotel (Three Kings Hotel). The statues on the facade depict three wise men who visited here nearly a millennium ago, in 1032 to be precise. Rodolphe II, king of Burgundy; Holy Roman emperor Konrad II; and the latter's son, the future Heinrich III, held a meeting here that joined Burgundy to the Holy Roman Empire. The young general Napoléon Bonaparte stayed here in 1797 (the suite has been named for him and redecorated in opulent Empire style), followed by other stellar guests: the kings of Italy, Princess Victoria, Charles Dickens, and Picasso (who once spent the night on the balcony admiring the view). In 1887 the great Hungarian-born Jewish writer Theodor Herzl stayed here during the first Zionist Congress, which laid the groundwork for the founding of the state of Israel. ✉ *Blumenrain 8.*

Fasnacht-Brunnen (Carnival Fountain). Created by the internationally famous Swiss artist Jean Tinguely, known for his work in mechanized media, this witty, animated construction was commissioned by the city in 1977. Its nine busy metal figures, in Tinguely's trademark whimsical style, churn, lash, and spray with unending energy. ✉ *Theaterpl.*

㉓ Fischmarkt (Fish Market). Fishmongers once kept the catch fresh for the market on this square, whose fountain basin served as a sort of communal cooler. The fountain itself dates from 1390 and upholds figures of the Virgin Mary, St. Peter, and John the Baptist. ✉ *Marktg., northwest of Marktpl.*

★ **㉖ Fondation Beyeler** (Beyeler Foundation). In the Basel suburb of Riehen, art dealers Ernst and Hedy Beyeler established a permanent public home for their astonishingly well-rounded collection of 20th-century art. Architect Renzo Piano's building uses simple, introverted lines to direct attention to the 175 paintings and objects. Rightly so, as the collection's catalog reads like a who's who of modern artists—Cézanne, Matisse, Lichtenstein, Rauschenberg.

In this limpid setting of natural light and openness, Giacometti's wiry sculptures stretch toward the ceiling while Monet's water lilies seem to spill from the canvas into an outdoor reflecting pool. Indigenous carved figures from New Guinea and Nigeria stare into faces on canvases by Klee and Dubuffet. And a stellar selection of Picassos is juxtaposed with views of blue skies and neighboring fields.

The harmony of the collection notwithstanding, personal preference is a perceivable theme, and there is a strong sensation of being invited into an intimate space. The tram trip from Schifflände takes about 20 minutes. Although there isn't much museum literature in English, an English-language tour is offered. ✉ *Baselstr. 101, Riehen,* ☎ *061/6459700.* 🎟 *8 SF.* ☉ *Thurs.–Tues. 10–5, Wed. 10–8.* ✑

⑬ Haus zum Kirschgarten (Kirschgarten House). This 18th-century home was built as a palace for a young silk-ribbon manufacturer. Nowadays it contains the 18th- and 19th-century collections of the city's Historical Museum, displayed as furnishings in its period rooms. The timepieces, porcelain, and faience are especially outstanding. ✉ *Elisabethenstr. 27,* ☎ *061/2711333.* 🎟 *5 SF, 1st Sun. of month free.* ☉ *Tues.–Sun. 10–5.*

★ **⑯ Historisches Museum** (Historical Museum). Housed within the **Barfüsserkirche** (Church of the Discalced Friars), which was founded by the barefoot Franciscans in 1250 and rebuilt during the mid-14th century, the museum has an extensive collection of tapestries, wooden sculptures, coins, armor, and other vestiges of Basel's past. An underground gallery

174

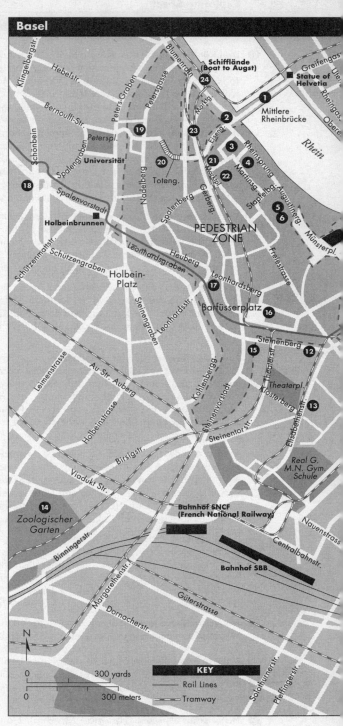

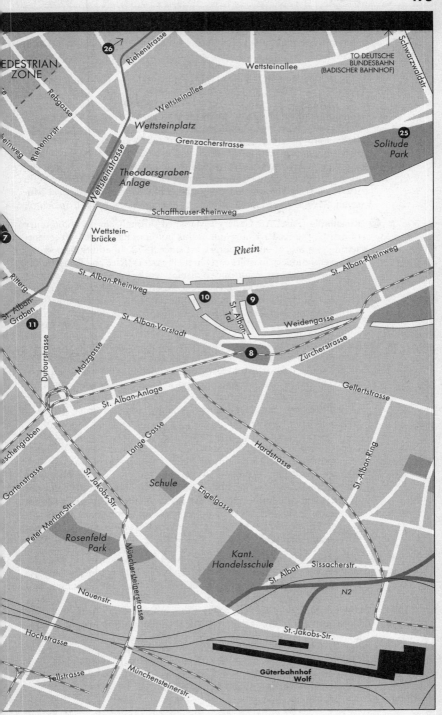

PEDESTRIAN ZONE

26

Riehenstrasse

Wettsteinallee

TO DEUTSCHE BUNDESBAHN (BADISCHER BAHNHOF)

Schwarzwaldstr.

Rebgasse

Wettsteinallee

Riehentorstr.

Rheinweg

Wettsteinstrasse

Wettsteinplatz

Grenzacherstrasse

25

Solitude Park

Theodorsgraben-Anlage

Schaffhauser-Rheinweg

7

Wettstein-brücke

Rhein

St. Alban-Rheinweg

St. Alban-Rheinweg

Ritterg.

St. Alban-Graben

10

St. Alban-Vorstadt

9

St. Alban Tal

Weidengasse

11

Dufourstrasse

Malzgasse

8

Zürcherstrasse

St. Alban-Anlage

Gellertstrasse

eschengraben

Lange Gasse

Hardstrasse

St. Alban-Ring

Gartenstrasse

St. Jakobs-Str.

Schule

Engelgasse

Peter Merian-Str.

Rosenfeld Park

Münchensteinerstrasse

Kant. Handelsschule

St. Alban

Sissacherstr.

Nauenstr.

N2

Hochstrasse

St. Jakobs-Str.

Tellstrasse

Münchensteinerstr.

Güterbahnhof Wolf

displays fully reconstructed **medieval and Renaissance guild rooms**, complete with stained glass, ceramic stoves, and richly carved wood. Downstairs, in the back of the church, the **Münster Treasury** contains priceless reliquaries in gold. Despite its status as one of the finest examples of Franciscan architecture north of the Alps, the church was deconsecrated in the 19th century and turned into a warehouse until it was rescued in 1894 and converted to the present-day museum. Most museum descriptions are in German only. ⊠ *Barfüsserpl., Steinenberg 4,* ☎ *061/2058600.* 🎟 *5 SF, 1st Sun. of month free.* ☉ *Wed.–Mon. 10–5.* 🐾

Holbeinbrunnen (Holbein Fountain). Created by an unknown 16th-century stonemason, this fanciful fountain is a bundle of copies. It depicts a group of dancing farmers, copied from a drawing by Hans Holbein; above stands a bagpiper, copied from a Dürer engraving. The fountain itself is a copy, the original having been moved to the Historical Museum. ⊠ *Spalenvorstadt, 2 blocks up the tram tracks toward Spalentor.*

★ ⑫ **Kunsthalle** (Basel Art Gallery). Managed through Basel's community of artists, the Basler Kunstverein, this museum has hosted precedent-setting exhibits of contemporary art since 1872. In addition to showing several modern masters early in their careers (Klee and Picasso), the gallery was the first in Europe to display works by American Abstract Expressionists. Recent exhibits have featured Christopher Wool and the sculpture of Cy Twombly. An on-site theater shows video installations, performances, and local and foreign films. ⊠ *Steinenberg 7,* ☎ *061/2069900.* 🎟 *9 SF.* ☉ *Tues. and Thurs.–Sun. 11–5, Wed. 11–8:30.* 🐾

★ ⑪ **Kunstmuseum** (Museum of Fine Arts). In a city known for its museums, the Kunstmuseum is Basel's heirloom jewel. It was built in 1932–36 to house one of the oldest public collections of art in Europe, owned by the city since 1661; the imposing facade gives way to an inner courtyard studded with statues. Inside is the world's largest assemblage of paintings by Hans Holbein the Younger, an exceptional group of works by Konrad Witz, and, in fact, such a thorough gathering of the works of their contemporaries that the development of painting in the Upper Rhine is strikingly illuminated. Other Swiss artists are well represented: from the 18th-century Alpine landscapes of Caspar Wolf through Klimt-like Ferdinand Hodler. The museum's other forte is its international 20th-century collection, from Georges Braque to Jasper Johns. Most museum materials are in German only, but English descriptions are sometimes provided for special exhibits. ⊠ *St. Alban-Graben 16,* ☎ *061/2066262.* 🎟 *7 SF includes admission to Museum für Gegenwartskunst; 1st Sun. of month free.* ☉ *Tues.–Sun. 10–5.* 🐾

★ ② **Lällekönig.** When a famous gate tower on the Grossbasel side was destroyed, with it went the notorious Lällekönig, a 15th-century gargoyle of a king once mechanized by clockwork to stick out his tongue and roll his eyes at the "lesser" citizens across the river. Kleinbasel residents seek symbolic revenge even today, though. Every year during the Vogel Gryff festival, a birdlike figure dances to the midpoint of the bridge, gives the Lällekönig a flash of his backside, and takes the party back to Kleinbasel. You can see a facsimile of the Lällekönig on the corner of what is now a chain restaurant (Churrasco) at Schifflände 1. The mechanized original still ticks and taunts away in the nether regions of the Historical Museum. ⊠ *Schifflände.*

⑰ **Leonhardskirche** (St. Leonard's Church). Like virtually all of Basel's churches, this one was destroyed in the 1356 quake and rebuilt in the Gothic style, although its Romanesque crypt remains. Its High Gothic wooden pulpit is distinctive. Free organ concerts are held on Friday evening. ⊠ *Heuberg.* ☉ *Daily 10–5.*

㉑ Marktplatz. Fruits, flowers, and vegetables are sold most mornings from open stands in this central square, Basel's historic and modern heart. In fall and winter passersby purchase bags of hot roasted chestnuts, the savory smoke of which fills the square. ✉ *Tram crossroads at the foot of Rathaus, south of Marktg.* ☉ *Market: Mon., Wed., and Fri. 6 AM–6:30 PM; Tues., Thurs., and Sat. 6 AM–1:30 PM.*

❸ Martinskirche (St. Martin's Church). The acoustics inside make this church popular for concerts, although it's rarely used for services. The lower portions of the tower date from 1288, making it the oldest parish church in town; the greater part was rebuilt after the earthquake of 1356. The fountain outside, with the statue of a warrior dressed for battle, dates from the 16th century. ✉ *Martinsg.*

★ **❶ Mittlere Rheinbrücke** (Middle Rhine Bridge). Basel's most historic bridge is a good metaphor for the city's successful mix of custom and commerce. It's used as a catwalk for many of Basel's centuries-old celebrations; bright banners seem to anticipate a passing parade. But underneath it's practical—processions of barges glide through its low-slung arches. First built around 1225, the bridge made possible the development of an autonomous Kleinbasel and the consequent rivalry that grew between the two half-towns. The wooden bridge was replaced in stone at the turn of the 20th century, its 1478 chapel reconstructed at the center of the new bridge. ✉ *Schifflände.*

★ **❼ Münster** (Cathedral). Basel's cathedral evolved into its current form through a chance shift of nature and the changing whims of architects. The site started as a 9th-century Carolingian church, then became a cathedral, which was consecrated by Henry II in 1019. Additions, alterations, and reconstructions in late Romanesque/early Gothic style continued through the 12th and 13th centuries. When Basel's devastating earthquake destroyed much of the building in 1356, subsequent reconstruction, which lasted about a century, took on the dominant Gothic style. The facade of the north transept, the **Galluspforte** (St. Gall's Door), is a surviving remnant of the original Romanesque stucture. It is one of the oldest carved portals in German-speaking Europe—and one of the loveliest. Slender, fine-tooled columns and rich high-relief and freestanding sculptures frame the door. Each of the Evangelists is represented by his symbol: an angel for Matthew, an ox for Luke, a bulbous-chested eagle for John, a slim-limbed lion for Mark. Above, around the window, a wheel of fortune flings little men off to their fates.

Inside on the left, following a series of tombs of medieval noblemen whose effigies recline with their feet resting on their loyal dogs, stands the strikingly simple **tomb of Erasmus.** Below the choir, you can see the delicately rendered death portraits on the double **tomb of Queen Anna of Habsburg** and her young son Charles, from around 1285. The vaulted **crypt** was part of the original structure and still bears fragments of murals from 1202.

The Münsterplatz square itself is one of the most satisfying architectural ensembles in Europe, its fine town houses set well back from the cathedral, the center filled with pollarded trees. ✉ *Münsterpl.* ☉ *Easter–mid-Oct., weekdays 10–6, Sat. 10–noon and 2–5, Sun. 1–5; mid-Oct.–Easter, Mon.–Sat. 10–noon and 2–4, Sun. 2–4.*

NEED A BREAK?	It's hard to beat the plaza tables of **Café zum Issak** (✉ Münsterpl. 16, ☎ 061/2617711) for scenic value; you look straight up at the cathedral's towers. The house favorite, *gaggocino,* is an elaborate, semisweet hot chocolate with alpine peaks of white froth. They're closed Monday; no credit cards accepted.

⓾ **Museum für Gegenwartskunst** (Museum of Contemporary Art). Carrying Basel's art collections up to the present, this museum focuses on works from the 1970s on. The fittingly modern building looks as though it has shouldered its way in between the street's half-timber houses. Inside are selections by artists such as Frank Stella, Bruce Naumann, and photographer Cindy Sherman. The language of the exhibition materials typically corresponds to the nationality of the artists. ⊠ *St. Alban-Rheinweg 60,* ☎ *061/2728183.* ⊡ *7 SF includes admission to Kunstmuseum; 1st Sun. of month free.* ☉ *Tues.–Sun. 11–5.*

ⓒ ➎ **Naturhistorisches Museum** (Natural History Museum). Under the same monumental roof as the Schweizerisches Museum der Kulturen (☞ *below*), this museum outlines the history of the earth and its current and onetime inhabitants, from mammoths to insects. There is also a focus on local fossil finds and indigenous minerals from the Alps and Jura regions. Most descriptive materials are in German only. ⊠ *Augustinerg. 2,* ☎ *061/2665500.* ⊡ *6 SF includes admission to Schweizerisches Museum der Kulturen; 1st Sun. of month free.* ☉ *Tues.–Sun. 10–5.*

⓳ **Peterskirche** (St. Peter's Church). Evidence of Basel's late-Gothic heyday, the 13th-century St. Peter's Church sits across from **Petersplatz,** a lovely park next to the **Universität** (University). In the rose-lighted chapel are some interesting 15th-century frescoes. Call for information about services. ⊠ *Just across Peters-Graben from Peterspl.,* ☎ *061/ 2618724.*

⓴ **Pharmazie-Historisches Museum** (Museum of Pharmaceutical History). Although pharmaceuticals as the topic of an entire museum may seem like too much of a necessary thing, this collection showcases Basel's roots in the industry that dominates the banks of the Rhine today. There are original and re-created pharmacy counters and all kinds of beakers, flacons, and ceramic measures. The old remedies on display now seem like candidates for a witches' brew: insects, adders, even poisonous plants. The museum is housed in Zum Vorderen Sessel, a home once frequented by Erasmus. You can request an English-language information sheet. ⊠ *Totengässlein 3,* ☎ *061/2617940.* ⊡ *Free.* ☉ *Weekdays 9–noon and 2–5.*

ⓒ ⓯ **Puppenhaus Museum** (Doll House Museum). Bordering on the Barfüsserplatz, this museum has several floors stuffed with 18th- and 19th-century toys and classic miniature toy furnishings. The main stars here are stuffed themselves; more than 2,000 teddy bears are exhibited in perhaps the world's most complete collection representing major manufacturers. The museum's collections are organized not by toy type but by themes—don't be surprised to see a Steiff sitting in a model Formula 1 racecar. ⊠ *Steinenvorstadt 1,* ☎ *061/2259595.* ⊡ *7 SF.* ☉ *Fri.–Wed. 11–5, Thurs. 11–8.*

★ ㉒ **Rathaus** (Town Hall). This late-Gothic edifice, built to honor the city's entry into the Swiss Confederation in 1501, towers over the Marktplatz. Only the middle portion actually dates from the 16th century; pseudo-Gothic work was added in 1900. A massive clock with figures of the Madonna, the emperor Henry II, and his wife, Kunegunde, adorns the center of the facade, and all around is a series of colorful frescoes, painted in 1608. Step into the courtyard, where the frescoes continue. ⊠ *Marktpl.*

....

NEED A   Choose a few jewel-like pastries and order loose-leaf-brewed tea in the
BREAK?   carved-wood, clubby upstairs tearoom of the **Café Schiesser** (⊠ Marktpl.
                19, ☎ 061/2616077), steeping since 1870.

....

Rheinsprung. Fifteenth- and 16th-century houses and a handful of ink makers' shops line this steep little alley in Grossbasel. No. 11 housed Basel's university when it was first founded, in 1460. ⊠ *Grossbasel, parallel to and south of Rhine, between Eiseng. and Stapfelbg.*

⑧ St. Alban-Tor. This original medieval city gate is set amid a lovely garden near remnants of the town's ramparts. Parts of the gate date from the 13th century. ⊠ *St. Alban-Berg.*

⑥ Schweizerisches Museum der Kulturen (Swiss Museum of World Cultures). You'll experience a moment of extreme cultural contrast here—walk in from the cobblestone street, and you'll suddenly find yourself at a woven-palm "culthouse" from Papua, New Guinea. This is one of the world's foremost ethnographic collections, with 32,000 non-European pieces from the far corners of the globe. The extensive ground-floor exhibits on Oceania and Melanesia include standing pole figures, dance staffs, and bristling headdresses. The museum shares its space with the Natural History Museum (☞ *above*). Key elements of the collection have English-language information sheets. ⊠ *Augustinerg. 2,* ☎ *061/2665500.* ▢ *6 SF includes admission to Natural History Museum; 1st Sun. of month free.* ◷ *Tues.–Sun. 10–5.*

⑱ Spalentor. Like the St. Alban-Tor (☞ *above*), the Spalentor served as one of Basel's medieval city gates beginning in the 14th century. More imposing than graceful, it has a toothy wooden portcullis; also note Basel's coat of arms atop the gate. ⊠ *Spalenvorstadt.*

Statue of Helvetia. What would the woman pictured on most Swiss coins do if freed from the confines of currency? With spear and shield set aside (and suitcase already packed!) this humanistic interpretation shows her seemingly contemplating the possibilities from a perch not far from the border of her homeland and the wide world beyond. ⊠ *Kleinbasel, right bank of Rhine, near Mittlere Rheinbrücke.*

★ ㉕ Tinguely Museum. Stay alert and be ready to get involved—the fascinating mechanized artworks of 20th-century master Jean Tinguely invite close inspection and interaction. As you circle the installations, some a story high, you may wonder: how do they work? what do they mean? and where did he find this stuff? Born in Fribourg, Tinguely is best known for his whimsical *métamécaniques* (mechanical sculptures), which transform machinery, appliances, and items straight from the taxidermy shop into ironic and often macabre statements. For instance, *Le Ballet des Pauvres,* from 1961, suspends a hinged leg with a moth-eaten sock, a horse tail and fox pelt, a cafeteria tray, and a blood-soaked nightgown, all of which dangle and dance on command. The Barca, a wing projecting over the Rhine, has a splendid river view of Basel. Many of the museum's "sculptures" play on timers, typically every 5–15 minutes, and it pays to wait and see them in action. Schedules are listed on each work's nameplate, and information sheets are available in English. ⊠ *Grenzacherstr. 210,* ☎ *061/6819320.* ▢ *7 SF.* ◷ *Wed.–Sun. 11–7.* ✑

☙ ⑭ Zoologischer Garten (Zoological Garden). Famed for its armored rhinoceroses (it has had great luck breeding them) as well as its pygmy hippopotamuses, gorillas, and Javanese monkeys, this is no ordinary zoo. It's very child-friendly, and the enormous restaurant-pavilion in the center of the zoo serves kid-size meals. Buy a booklet with a map to find your way, or you may end up wandering in circles. ⊠ *Binningerstr. 40,* ☎ *061/2953535.* ▢ *12 SF.* ◷ *May–Aug., daily 8–6:30; Mar.–Apr. and Sept.–Oct., daily 8–6; Nov.–Feb., daily 8–5:30.*

OFF THE
BEATEN PATH **LANGENBRUCK AND ENVIRONS –** In the German-speaking countryside south of Basel, known as the Baselbiet, is a handful of stately little villages with sturdy old guest houses and a range—from medieval to Roman—of historic sites to explore. Take the winding forest road (A12) west of the freeway between Liestal and Oensingen, watching for Balsthal, Holderbank, Oberer Hauenstein, and Langenbruck; the industrial stretch just south of Liestal is less attractive. Landgasthof Bären (☎ 062/3901414) in Langenbruck offers superb regional cooking, inexpensive prix-fixe menus, and locally brewed beer.

VITRA DESIGN MUSEUM – Ten kilometers (6 miles) across the border in the German town of Weil am Rhein, this museum is a startling white geometric jumble designed by American architect Frank Gehry as part of an avant-garde building complex associated with the Vitra furniture manufacturer. The Gehry section generally hosts traveling architectural exhibits. The permanent collection, including the soaring Wall of Chairs (just what it sounds like), is displayed in the nearby Vitra Fire Station, accessible only on the guided tour. To get here by car, take A5/E35 north from Basel toward Karlsruhe; turn right just after German customs onto Route 532, parallel to the parking lot, and turn left after exiting at Weil am Rhein. The museum is 1½ km (about 1 mi) ahead on the right. Or from the Deutscher Bahnhof in Basel (also known as the Badischer Bahnhof), take Bus 5 toward Kandern to the Vitra stop. Bring your passport and call ahead to arrange for an English-speaking tour guide. Tours are given Wednesday through Friday at 2. ✉ *Charles-Eames-Str. 1, Weil am Rhein, Germany,* ☎ *49/7621/7023200.* 🎫 *DM 10.* ☉ *Tues.–Sun. 11–6.*

Colonia Augusta Raurica (Augst)

Founded in 44–43 BC, Augst is the oldest Roman establishment on the Rhine. The site is reachable by car from Basel in 10 minutes or, from mid-May to mid-October, via a leisurely boat trip up the river. To view the restoration areas scattered around the almost suburban neighborhood, be prepared to do some walking.

A Good Tour

A scenic 1½-hour boat ride will take you to Kaiseraugst, known for its thermal spas. From there walk uphill, following the signs to the ruins of **Augusta Raurica,** a 2,000-year-old Roman settlement that's been almost entirely rebuilt. Stop in for a map and a peek at the excavated treasures in the **Römermuseum.** Boats (Basler Personenschiffahrts-Gesellschaft, ✉ Depart from the Schifflände, behind the Drei Könige hotel, ☎ 061/6399500) to Augst leave up to three times a day in high season. For a round-trip fare of about 35 SF, you'll cruise slowly up the Rhine, passing the Old Town and the cathedral.

TIMING

Augst merits at least a half day, slightly more if you go by boat. Drinks and cold snacks are available on all cruises, hot meals on some. The last boat returning to Basel each day leaves Augst around 5 PM.

Sights to See

★ **Augusta Raurica.** The remains of this 2,000-year-old Roman settlement have been extensively rebuilt (one suspects the Swiss might have done the same with Rome's Colosseum if they had gotten their hands on it), with substantial portions of the ancient town walls and gates, streets, water pipes, and heating systems all in evidence. The 2nd-century theater has been restored for modern use, and open-air plays and concerts are staged in summer; contact the Römermuseum for details.

Römermuseum (Roman Museum). Roman daily life is vividly depicted in this rebuilt ocher-hue home. Everything—from the thermal baths to the ancient board games in the sitting room—has been completely re-created. The museum also exhibits a treasure trove of Roman-era coins and silver unearthed in 1962. The objects, dating mostly from the 4th century, are believed to have been buried by the Romans in 350 to protect them from the ravages of the Alemanni, the German tribes who drove the Romans out of Switzerland. Another exhibit, running through 2001, demonstrates how a typical day, even 2,000 years ago, revolved around religion, money, and pleasures of the palate. Trilingual (English/French/German) brochures are available. ⊠ *Giebenacherstr. 17, Augst,* ☎ *061/8162222.* 🖭 *5 SF.* ⊙ *Mar.–Oct., Mon. 1–5, Tues.–Sun. 10–5; Nov.–Feb., Mon. 1–4, Tues.–Sun. 10–noon and 1:30–4:30.* 🐾

DINING

Of course, Basel can't help but show the sophistication of generations of cosmopolitan influence, and it has a surprising number of innovative French and international restaurants—some of them world-class (and priced accordingly). In fact, dining in Basel is a pricey venture, whether your sausage is stuffed with lobster and truffles or merely pork scraps. To keep expenses down, stick to beer-hall fare or watch posted menus for lunch specials (*Tagesmenu*).

CATEGORY	COST*
$$$$	over 70 SF
$$$	40 SF–70 SF
$$	20 SF–40 SF
$	under 20 SF

Prices are per person for a three-course meal (two-course meal in $ category), including sales tax and 15% service charge.

$$$$
★ ✕ **Stucki.** Chef Jean-Claude Wicky continues in the vein of the late master chef Hans Stucki at what is still one of Basel's best spots. Classics include pigeon in truffle coulis (liquid puree of cooked vegetables), duck à l'orange, and grilled lobster in tarragon sabayon. The service at this restaurant, in the leafy residential neighborhood of Bruderholz, is formal and the seating competitive: reserve as far ahead as possible. ⊠ *Bruderholzallee 42,* ☎ *061/3618222. Reservations essential. AE, DC, MC, V. Closed Sun.–Mon.*

$$–$$$$
★ ✕ **Teufelhof.** Owners Monica and Dominique Thommy have transformed a grand old Heuberg mansion into a top gastronomic restaurant, a chic Weinstube, a trendy bar, two theaters, and guest rooms (☞ Lodging, *below*); there are even medieval ruins in the basement. The formal restaurant Bel Étage's decor is almost minimalist, showcasing a few artworks and a star-pattern parquet floor. Michael Baader's masterly guidance might result in such inventions as grouper in oyster sauce with *spaghettini* and glazed celery or beef in Stilton and balsamic vinegar with polenta soufflé. Wines by the glass come in astonishing variety, and you can buy by the bottle in the house wine shop. The casual, high-tech, and warm-wood Weinstube serves a crowd of low-key, upscale bohemians. The café-bar is tiny and usually crowded with new-wave artists. ⊠ *Leonhardsgraben 47/Heuberg 30,* ☎ *061/2611010. AE, MC, V. Restaurant closed Sun.–Mon. No lunch Sat.*

$$$
✕ **Chez Donati.** Success(or) at last—early in 2000 local restaurateurs Peter Wyss and Romano Villa took over this much-loved family establishment. The new managers won't be messing with a good thing; though some updates to the decor and menu are in store, much will remain the same. Loyal followers can still indulge in the long-stand-

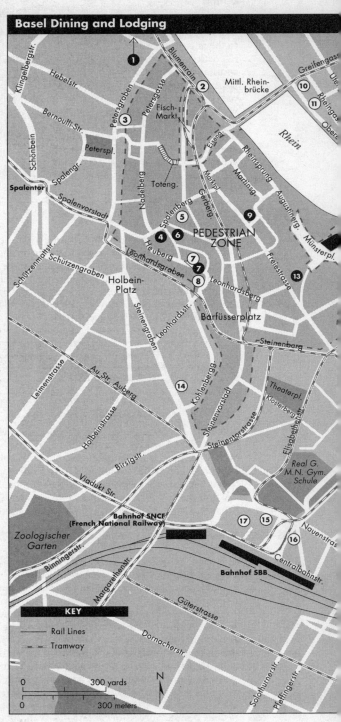

Basel Dining and Lodging

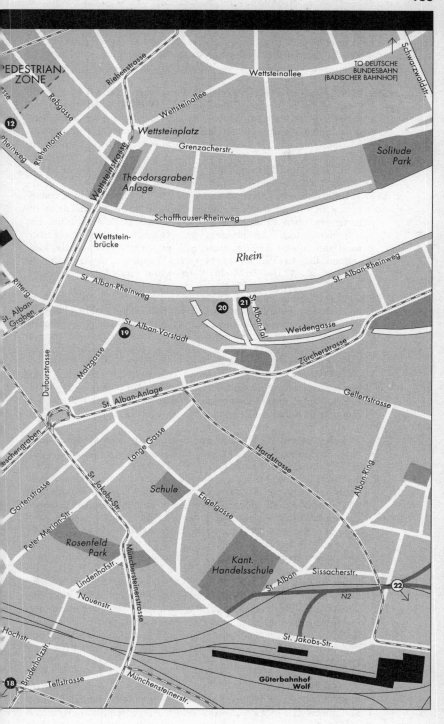

PEDESTRIAN ZONE

Rebgasse

Riehenstrasse

Riehenstrasse

Rheinweg

Riehenhofstr.

Wettsteinallee

Wettsteinallee

Wettsteinplatz

Grenzacherstr.

To Deutsche Bundesbahn (Badischer Bahnhof)

Schwarzwaldstr.

Solitude Park

Theodorsgraben-Anlage

Wettsteinstrasse

Schaffhauser-Rheinweg

Wettstein-brücke

Rhein

St. Alban-Rheinweg

St. Alban-Rheinweg

Ritterg.

St. Alban-Graben

St. Alban-Vorstadt

St. Alban-Tal

Weidengasse

Zürcherstrasse

Dufourstrasse

Malzgasse

St. Alban-Anlage

Gellertstrasse

Nonnengraben

Lange Gasse

Hardstrasse

Alban-Ring

Gartenstrasse

St. Jakobs-Str.

Schule

Engelgasse

Peter Merian-Str.

Rosenfeld Park

Lindenhofstr.

Münchensteinerstrasse

Kant. Handelsschule

St. Alban-

Sissacherstr.

N2

Nauenstr.

Hochstr.

Brudeholzstr.

Tellstrasse

Münchensteinerstr.

St. Jakobs-Str.

Güterbahnhof Wolf

12

19

20

21

22

18

ing selection of Italian standards, like Parma ham with truffles, but can also try new specialties such as oven-baked sole. The traditional, gilt-framed Venetian paintings will be supplemented with modern art, but you can still get that white-draped table looking out on the Rhine. ⊠ *St. Johanns-Vorstadt 48,* ☎ *061/3220919. AE, DC, MC, V. Closed Sun.– Mon.*

\$\$\$ ✕ **St. Alban-Eck.** This café, a five-minute walk behind the Kunstmuseum, shows a glimpse of Basel's French blood. In a half-timber historic home, it's a real *petit coin sympa* (friendly little corner), with plank wainscoting in natural wood, framed historic prints, and net curtains. The cuisine gracefully mixes German and French favorites: grilled entrecôte, sole, salmon, and *foie de veau à la Riehen* (liver with onion, apple, and smoked bacon). ⊠ *St. Alban-Vorstadt 60,* ☎ *061/2710320. AE, DC, MC, V. Closed Sun. No lunch Sat.*

\$\$\$ ✕ **Schlüsselzunft.** This historic guildhall holds an elegant little restaurant with a ceramic stove and rustic appointments, as well as an inexpensive, open-atrium courtyard café called the Schlüsselhöfli. The restaurant, which draws business-lunch crowds, serves well-bred French food and cuisine *Bâloise,* meaning liver with onions and the local salmon dish; the café serves shoppers cheap international plates. ⊠ *Freiestr. 25,* ☎ *061/2612046. Reservations essential in restaurant. AE, DC, MC, V. Closed Sun.*

\$\$ ✕ **Zum Goldenen Sternen.** Dating from 1506, this *Gasthof* claims to be the oldest restaurant in Switzerland, though the building has been moved from town center to its current Rhine-side site. The impeccable restoration retains the antique beams, stenciled ceilings, and unvarnished planks, yet without seeming contrived. Though it could easily play a secondary role, the food almost lives up to the setting: it's classic French, only slightly updated. Game and fish are strong suits; one favorite is the *Fisch Harmonie,* a sampling of six kinds of fish with saffron sauce. There's also a seven-course tasting menu that changes monthly. ⊠ *St. Alban-Rheinweg 70,* ☎ *061/2721666. AE, DC, MC, V.*

\$–\$\$ ✕ **Café Papiermühle.** With the splashing of the paper mill's waterwheel
★ in the background, this is a comfortable local spot for lunch or a coffee break (they're open only until 6 PM). The hand-scrawled chalkboard and printed menus are not translated but most often include two multicourse meals in the 15- to 20-SF range, brunch favorites (vegetable quiche, *Birchermüsli,* granola mixed with yogurt and fruit), salads, soups, and pasta dishes. Hand signals, however, are all you'll need to point out one of the homemade cakes. ⊠ *St. Alban-Tal 35,* ☎ *061/2724848. No credit cards. Closed Mon.*

\$ ✕ **Brauerei Fischerstube.** If you're serious about local color, venture
★ beyond the tourist pale and try a home brew here. The Fischerstube brews its own lagers and ales in the deep, frothing copper tanks behind the bar. The house label is Ueli Bier, named for a jesterlike Fasnacht clown; the timid can taste it at the upscale Teufelhof (☞ *above*). Pretzels hang on wooden racks on the sanded wooden tables, and the menu includes such local dishes as *Fleischkäse* (sausage loaf) with eggs and *frites* (french fries), rump steak, and just plain *Würstli* (sausage) from the grill. There's a beer garden in back. ⊠ *Rheing. 45,* ☎ *061/ 6926635. Reservations not accepted. AE, DC, MC, V.*

\$ ✕ **Café Pfalz.** This bookish little self-service café, down a narrow street below the cathedral, dishes out veggie plates, muesli, sausage, and quiche in a trim beech-wood-and-black contemporary setting. A salad bar, juicer, and one hot daily special add to the options. ⊠ *Münsterberg 11,* ☎ *061/2726511. No credit cards.*

$ ✕ **Löwenzorn.** This is a classic, comfortable gathering place for plain Germanic food. Though the menu is a hodgepodge of fondues, fish, and Italian dishes as well as standard local fare, regulars come here for beer, a full plate, and some laughs with the friendly staff. With stained-glass lamps resembling Fasnacht lanterns, woodwork, ceramic stoves, and a roof garden, it's a nice mix of bistro and beer hall. ⊠ *Gemsberg 2,* ☎ *061/2614213. AE, DC, MC, V. Closed Sun.*

$ ✕ **Zum Schnabel.** This dark-green and aged-wood *Wirtshaus* (inn) has a clubby, unpretentious feel, with multiple variations on Basel-brewed beer. Sausage, pork, steak, and, of course, *Rösti* (hash brown potatoes) reign. If you're in the mood for linens, candles, and a more serious meal, climb up to the lovely wood-lined dining area. ⊠ *Trillengässlein 2,* ☎ *061/2614909. AE, DC, MC, V. Closed Sun.*

LODGING

With its industry, its banking, and its conference center, this is a business city first. As a result, hotel prices tend to be steep, bargains in short supply, and comforts—TV, minibar, phone—more important than atmosphere in the all-out competition for expense-account travelers. When there's a conference in town, every bed for miles can be filled; book well ahead. Hotel reservations can be made through the **Basel Hotel Reservation Service** at the City Information office and at the tourist office (☞ Visitor Information *in* Basel A to Z, *below*).

CATEGORY	COST*
$$$$	over 300 SF
$$$	200 SF–300 SF
$$	140 SF–200 SF
$	under 140 SF

Prices are for a standard double room, including breakfast, tax, and service charge.

$$$$ ▥ **Drei Könige.** An integral part of Basel history even before the first
★ bridges drew the distant banks of the Rhine together, this riverside hotel began in the 11th century as a small inn; it later became a coach stop, and today it's a landmark of the modern city. Expanded to its present form in 1835, it was bought by the family du Boisrouvray in 1976; corridors are lined with a fascinating variety of their portraits. The furnishings have regained their 19th-century grandeur, with ravishing colors of cream, gilt, and powder blue; ornate woodwork, paintings, and tapestries nudge the opulence factor even higher. All rooms have big, tile baths with recessed lighting and modern fixtures; balconied rooms and rooms with river views cost more. The formal French restaurant serves haute cuisine on the broad, awning-shaded Rhine terrace, which is heated well into fall. ⊠ *Blumenrain 8, CH-4001,* ☎ *061/ 2605050,* FAX *061/2605060. 80 rooms, 7 suites. 3 restaurants, bar. AE, DC, MC, V.* ✆

$$$$ ▥ **Euler.** An archetypal little Old World luxury hotel, this landmark
★ draws a loyal business clientele, which mingles with local and international bankers over a *Cüpli* (glass of champagne) in the famous leather-and-red-velvet bar. Duvets billow like baking bread out of the bed frames in some of the cushier rooms and suites; standard rooms are furnished in a classic but spare style, with reproduction antique furnishings. All have triple-glazed windows to cut out tram-traffic noise. ⊠ *Central-bahnpl. 14, CH-4002,* ☎ *061/2758000,* FAX *061/2758050. 59 rooms, 7 suites. 2 restaurants, bar, no-smoking rooms, conference rooms, parking (fee). AE, DC, MC, V.* ✆

$$$ 🏨 **Basel.** This all-modern hotel built in 1975 has become part of the Old Town neighborhood, its bars and restaurants filling with locals after work. The wood-walled rooms are accented with contemporary leather furniture and chrome; polished marble adds luster to the baths. There are two no-smoking floors. The clientele is almost exclusively businesspeople, but there's plenty of room on weekends. ⊠ *Münzg. 12, CH-4001,* ☎ *061/2646800,* FAX *061/2646811. 69 rooms, 3 suites. 2 restaurants, café. AE, DC, MC, V.* 🏨

$$$ 🏨 **Merian am Rhein.** Built in 1972 to blend with the neighboring landmark Café Spitz, this has a modern, airy look, with touches of gray wood, russet leather, le Corbusier chairs, and live plants. Café Spitz has been a meeting place since the early 13th century, but you wouldn't guess it to look at it; now it's done in light wood, linens, and halogen, with fish dominating the wall decor and the menu. ⊠ *Rheing. 2, CH-4005,* ☎ *061/6851111,* FAX *061/6851101. 65 rooms. Restaurant, café, minibars, in-room VCRs, conference rooms. AE, DC, MC, V.* 🏨

$$$ 🏨 **Schweizerhof.** This bastion of the station area, once a luxury hotel, now bestows on business travelers the proud personal service once lavished on such musical stars as Toscanini. Built in 1864 and in the same family since 1896, it is filled with antiques and faience, though its marble floors and wing chairs mingle with faded updates from the '50s and '60s. The most recently modernized rooms mix Biedermeier with beech and pine, though the big front bays are done in rose plush and rosewood. Staff cuts have cost this landmark its official fifth star, if not its five-star style. ⊠ *Centralbahnpl. 1, CH-4002,* ☎ *061/2712833,* FAX *061/2712919. 75 rooms. Restaurant, bar. AE, DC, MC, V.*

$$$ 🏨 **Teufelhof.** In addition to its bars, theaters, medieval ruins, and
★ restaurants (☞ Dining, *above*), this Basel bastion of style and gourmandise have a small guest house whose eight rooms are works of art in their own right: each is decorated by a different artist and redesigned by another artist every other year. By contrast, the serenely simple 25 rooms of the adjoining Galerie Hotel function collectively as a canvas for one particular artist; these are also redecorated by another artist annually. There's a food and wine shop in the archaeological cellar, and there's even a pair of small theaters that put on various performances (cabaret, satire) from mid-September to early May. In-room TVs are available upon request. ⊠ *Leonhardsgraben 49/Heuberg 30, CH-4051,* ☎ *061/2611010,* FAX *061/2611004. 29 rooms, 4 suites. 2 restaurants, bar, café, 2 theaters. AE, MC, V.* 🏨

$$ 🏨 **Bad Schauenburg.** Ten kilometers (6 miles) southeast of Basel, this charming country inn has suites done in Biedermeier-period antiques and a restaurant serving *cuisine de marché.* Take the main road to Liestal, then follow the signs after the turnoff in Frenkendorf. ⊠ *Schauenburgerstr., CH-4410 Liestal,* ☎ *061/9062727,* FAX *061/9062700. 31 rooms, 3 suites. Restaurant, conference rooms. AE, DC, MC, V. Closed mid-Dec.–mid-Jan.* 🏨

$$ 🏨 **Central.** If you hadn't just picked up your key from the reception
★ desk of a five-star hotel, you might have reservations about your reservation in an economical *garni* down an alleyway near the train station. But this hotel is under the same management as the nearby Euler (☞ *above*), and the larger hotel's care and professionalism carry over. Rooms can be on the small side but are tasteful and cheerful, with hardwood floors and dashes of strong color—tangerine bedspreads, bouquet-pattern drapes, and poppy-red baths. Check in at the Euler's main entrance on Centralbahnhofplatz. ⊠ *Kücheng. 7, CH-4002,* ☎ *061/2724500,* FAX *061/2715000. 23 rooms. Bar. AE, DC, MC, V.* 🏨

$$ 🏨 **Rochat.** Location is this modest but roomy property's main asset; it was built in 1898 across from the university. The main brownstone building and the adjacent annex offer plain, mildly institutional comforts. The brownstone has a dorm-like feel, while the white-washed annex, with its twisting hallways, comes across as a scaled-down inn. Some rooms have spacious bathrooms with either a shower or a tub. The three rooms without a private bath cost less. The restaurant is alcohol-free. ⊠ *Petersgraben 23, CH-4051,* ☎ *061/2618140,* FAX *061/2616492. 50 rooms, 47 with bath. Restaurant, café. AE, DC, MC, V.*

$$ 🏨 **Steinenschanze.** Despite its awkward, isolated position above the busy highway and behind the nightlife district, this hotel is clean, welcoming, and bright, with good-size rooms, blue-and-white-tile baths, and tasteful Scandinavian furniture. The harsh parking-garage lines have been softened by recessed lighting and a scattering of plants, posters, and knickknacks. Back rooms are quiet; there are a garden behind and a breakfast buffet with fresh cheeses (included in the rate). ⊠ *Steinengraben 69, CH-4051,* ☎ *061/2725353,* FAX *061/2724573. 54 rooms. Breakfast room. AE, DC, MC, V.*✎

$–$$ 🏨 **Hotel Brasserie Au-Violon.** The former "guests" here—priests and
★ prisoners—never had it so good. Housed in what was once a 12th-century cloister, then until the 1990s a prison, the Au-Violon now captivates its clientele with subdued elegance, a peaceful location, and a terrific restaurant. There are some reminders of the building's austere past; rooms overlooking the Lohnhof courtyard still conform to cellblock arrangements, with uniformly tight square footage. Rooms facing the Old Town offer more spacious salons with TVs. All include baths with showers and individual appointments: murals, breezy curtains, tiny bedside lamps. The brasserie, with its mirrored bar, deco fixtures, and iron-leg tables, serves French classics. ⊠ *Im Lohnhof, CH-4051,* ☎ *061/2698711,* FAX *061/2698712. 14 rooms, 6 suites. Restaurant. AE, DC, MC, V.*✎

$–$$ 🏨 **Krafft am Rhein.** A rare find in Swiss cities, this is an elegant little man-
★ sion of an inn directly on the right-bank waterfront, with mosaic floors, elaborate moldings, chandeliers, and a sinuous atrium stairwell. The accommodating management more than makes up for any wear and tear. Some higher-price Rhine-side rooms have polished wood floors, Biedermeier beds, and Oriental runners; others still have '50s mix-and-match. Those without bath fall into the $ category. There's a traditional dining room with Rhine views for breakfast and dinner, but the downstairs Zem Schnooggeloch (Mosquito's Den) is where everyone gathers for German-style food. The waterfront terrace café is justifiably popular. ⊠ *Rheing. 12, CH-4058,* ☎ *061/6909130,* FAX *061/6909131. 52 rooms, 45 with bath. Restaurant, Stübli. AE, DC, MC, V.*✎

NIGHTLIFE AND THE ARTS

For a complete listing of events in Basel, pick up a copy of *Basel Live,* a booklet published every two weeks. It is written partially in English. *Basel,* another listings publication, comes out every three months and is fully bilingual (German/English). Both are available at the tourist office and usually at hotel desks. If you'd like to play it by ear, the Steinenvorstadt is crowded with cinemas, bars, and young people, while on the Kleinbasel side, there are more late-night bars along the Oberer Rheinweg.

Nightlife

Bars and Lounges

Brauner Mutz (⊠ Barfüsserpl., ☎ 061/2613369) is a big, landmark beer hall with long wooden tables and a beer in every hand. **Campari Bar** (⊠ Steinenberg 7, ☎ 061/2728383), behind the Basel Art Gallery and the Tinguely Fountain, pulls in an artsy crowd to its pop-art interior or tree-canopied terrace. The **Euler** Bar (✉ Centralbahnpl. 14, ☎ 061/2724500), inside the Hotel Euler, draws a conservative business crowd after work. Outside peak mealtimes nondiners may snag a seat in the casual section of the **Kunsthalle Restaurant** (✉ Steinenberg 7, ☎ 061/2724233); it's a lovely (if smoke-filled) muraled room. **Zum Sperber** (✉ Münzg. 12, ☎ 061/2646800), behind the Hotel Basel, fills tables and bar stools with well-heeled workers at happy hour; there's live music some evenings.

Dancing and Nightclubs
Atlantis (✉ Klosterberg 13, ☎ 061/2289696) hosts a regular roster of live blues, rock, and alternative bands in a loftlike setting. **Casper's** (✉ Blumenrain 10, ☎ 061/2613050) is an upscale discotheque with a cover charge. At **Le Plaza Club** (✉ Am Messepl., ☎ 061/6923206) the DJ spins pop hits. **Singerhaus** (✉ Marktpl., ☎ 061/2616466) is a traditional nightclub with a show; the bar opens at 7, and dancing starts at 9.

The Arts

Film
Movies in Basel are usually shown in the original language with subtitles. Newspaper listings can be deciphered, but most houses are along Steinenvorstadt in the Old Town, and times are prominently posted. Prices vary depending on how close to the screen you choose to sit.

Music
Stadtcasino (✉ Steinenberg 14, ☎ 061/2726658), along with its restaurants and piano bar, hosts the Basel Symphony Orchestra, the Basel Chamber Orchestra, and visiting performers. Tickets are sold at the theater box office one hour before performance. Advance bookings can be made at Musikhaus au Concert (✉ Aeschenvorstadt 24, ☎ 061/2721176) or Musik Hug (✉ Freiestr. 70, ☎ 061/2723396). The **Musik-Akademie der Stadt Basel** (✉ Leonhardsgraben 4–6, ☎ 061/2645757) is an important academy with top-quality international performers. Book as for the Stadtcasino (☞ *above*).

Theater
Basel Stadttheater (✉ Theaterstr. 7, ☎ 061/2951133), hosts opera, operetta, and dance, as well as drama (usually in German). Book in advance weekdays 10–1 and 3:30–6:45, Saturday 10–6:45. The box office opens one hour before the performance. The **Komödie** (✉ Steinenvorstadt 63, ☎ 061/2951133) performs light German-language theater in an intimate atmosphere. Book through the Stadttheater (☞ *above*) or at the box office one hour before the curtain.

OUTDOOR ACTIVITIES AND SPORTS

Golf
Golf and Country Club Basel (✉ Hagenthal-le-Bas in France, ☎ 03/89685091) is one of the most beautiful golf courses in Europe, with attractive views of the Jura, Black Forest, and Vosges mountains. It is open to visitors; bring your passport.

Squash
Sportcenter Paradies (✉ Bettenstr. 73, ☎ 061/4859580) has good squash facilities (try to make a reservation if you're going during the week); there are eight courts, and you can rent equipment there.

SHOPPING

Though first impressions here may suggest yet another modern pedestrian shopping district, it's worth a closer look. There are still a lot of lone-wolf, quirky shops that contain extraordinary treasures.

Department Stores

Whether you're in need of socks, toothpaste, or chocolate on the cheap, department store chains **Manor** (✉ Greifeng. 22, ☎ 061/6959511) and **EPA** (✉ Gerberg. 4, ☎ 061/2699250) have items to get by on, plus groceries in the basement. **Globus** (✉ Marktpl. 2, ☎ 061/2614411) is a nicer version, with gourmet edibles and sleeker clothes. In what can often be a somewhat barren area, **Migros** (✉ Centralbahnpl., ☎ 061/2799745), open at its SBB train station location until 10 PM, is a good place to buy provisions.

Shopping Streets

The major, central shopping district stretches along **Freiestrasse** and **Gerbergasse**, though lower-price shops along **Steinenvorstadt** cater to a younger crowd. Streets radiating left, uphill from the Gerbergasse area, feature more one-of-a-kind boutiques. Most antiquarian bookshops concentrate their business on **Klosterberg** through Elisabethenstrasse to Aeschengraben.

Specialty Stores

Antique Books

Among many fine competitors, **Erasmushaus/Haus der Bücher** (✉ Bäumleing. 18, ☎ 061/2723088) has one of the largest collections of fine old and used books, mostly in German but including some multilingual art publications.

Calligraphic Paraphernalia

Abraxas (✉ Rheinsprung 6, ☎ 061/2616070) is a great source for fine writing tools and paraphernalia, from thick papers and delicate fountain pens to luxurious sealing waxes and reproductions of antique silver seals. **Scriptorium am Rhysprung** (✉ Rheinsprung 2, ☎ 061/2613900) mixes its own ink and carries calligraphy pens.

Coins

Münzen und Medaillen AG (✉ Malzg. 25, ☎ 061/2727544) is a good place to find coins and medals dating from antiquity to the mid-19th century.

Crafts and Gifts

Though primarily specializing in home furnishings, **Atelier Baumgartner** (✉ Spalenberg 8, ☎ 061/2610843) also stocks Swiss and European handicrafts, including music boxes and nutcrackers from the Erzgebirge region of Germany. **Heimatwerk** (✉ Schneiderg. 2, ☎ 061/2619178) sells Swiss crafts from traditional ceramics to Basel-made embroidered silk ribbons. Highly specialized handiwork comes from **Johann Wanner** (✉ Spalenberg 14, ☎ 061/2614826), which sells Christmas goods year-round, including hand-blown, hand-painted, and hand-molded ornaments, tin Victorian miniatures, Advent cards, tartan ribbons, cards, and candles. **Zem Baselstab** (✉ Schnabelg. 8, ☎ 061/2611016) has Fasnacht figurines and other Basel paraphernalia.

Food Specialties

The famous **Läckerli-Huus** (✉ Gerberg. 57, ☎ 061/2612322) sells a variety of sweets but highlights the local specialty—*Leckerli,* a chewy

spiced cookie of almonds, honey, dried fruit, and kirsch. A large selection of gift canisters and a shipping service make getting gifts home
a cinch. **Bachmann** (⊠ Gerberg. 51, ☎ 061/2613583; ⊠ Blumenrain
1, ☎ 061/2614152; and ⊠ Centralbahnpl. 7, ☎ 061/2712627) also
carries the primly packaged lovely little sweets that set Basel apart.
Glausi's (⊠ Spalenberg 12, ☎ 061/2618008) ages its own cheeses, which
are sold alongside myriad fresh Swiss specialties. **Schiesser** (⊠ Marktpl., ☎ 061/2616077), a convivial tearoom opened in 1870, sells carefully crafted (and costly) confections in its downstairs shop.

Linens
Caraco (⊠ Gerberg. 77, Falknerstr. entrance, ☎ 061/2613577) sells
handmade Swiss lace and embroidered goods as well as imports. **Langenthal** (⊠ Gerberg. 26, ☎ 061/2610900) offers mostly Swiss products: tea towels, tablecloths, and folk-style aprons. **Sturzenegger** (⊠
Freiestr. 62, ☎ 061/2616867) specializes in household linens made in
St. Gallen, the Swiss textile capital.

Lingerie
Beldona (⊠ Freiestr. 103, ☎ 061/2731170) stocks Swiss cotton lingerie. **Fogal** sells its famous Swiss hosiery at two locations (⊠ Freiestr.
44, ☎ 061/2617461; ⊠ Freiestr. 4, ☎ 061/2611220); both branches
set out trays of clearance goods. **Sturzenegger** (☞ Linens, *above*) also
carries an extensive line of Hanro and Calida underwear.

Men's Clothes
K. Aeschbacher (⊠ Schnabelg. 4, ☎ 061/2615058) carries unique
Swiss silk ties, scarves, robes, and pajamas. For the smoking-jacket set,
Renz (⊠ Freiestr. 2a, ☎ 061/2612991) has a small but impeccable se-
lection of fine Swiss-cotton pajamas, Hanro underwear, and classic Scot-
tish cashmeres.

Shoes
Kropart (⊠ Schneiderg. 16, ☎ 061/2615133) specializes in trendy, com-
fort-oriented styles. **Müki** (⊠ Münsterberg 14, ☎ 061/2712436) focuses on functional yet stylish European-made kids' shoes, from
patent-leather loafers to fun-colored fleece house slippers. **Rive Gauche**
(⊠ Schneiderg. 1, ☎ 061/2611080) carries high-end designer shoes—
the place to get a Prada fix.

Toys
Bercher & Sternlicht (⊠ Spalenberg 45, ☎ 061/2612550) has miniature trains and accessories. **Spielegge** (⊠ Rümelinspl. 7, ☎ 061/
2614488) places an emphasis on wood, with chisel-carved puppets and
whimsical Decor puzzles watercolored with fairy-tale scenes. Slightly
less folksy than Heimatwerk (☞ Crafts and Gifts, *above*), **Spielhuus**
(⊠ Eiseng. 8, ☎ 061/2649898) is a good source for board games and
reasonably priced children's toys, as well as Fasnacht costumes.

Women's Clothes
Trois Pommes (⊠ Freiestr. 74, ☎ 061/2729255) dominates the high
end, with Jil Sander, Versace, Armani, and Valentino. **S.T.O.C.K. Fashion** (⊠ Eiseng. 6, ☎ 061/2620007) sounds the siren call of a bargain;
you'll find mostly cut-rate French and Italian styles.

BASEL A TO Z

Arriving and Departing

By Car
The German autobahn **A5** enters Basel from the north and leads directly to the Rhine and the city center. From France, the auto route

A35 (E9) peters out at the frontier, and secondary urban roads lead to the center. The **A2** autobahn leads off to the rest of Switzerland. As the most interesting and scenic portions of Basel are riddled with pedestrians-only streets, it is advisable to park your car for the duration of your visit (☞ Getting Around, *below*).

By Plane

EuroAirport (⊠ Just across the border in France, ☎ 061/3252511) is shared by Basel, Mulhouse, and Freiburg in Germany. Direct flights link Basel to most major European cities. The nearest intercontinental airport is **Kloten** outside **Zürich** (⊠ Approximately 80 km/50 mi southeast of Basel, ☎ 1571060). There are connecting flights from Zürich into Basel's airport on **Crossair** (☎ 061/3252525 for reservations; 084/8852000 within Switzerland), Switzerland's domestic airline.

BETWEEN THE AIRPORT AND THE CITY CENTER

By Bus. Regular bus service runs between the airport and the train station in the city center. The trip takes about 15 minutes and costs 2.80 SF per person; call 061/3252511 for schedules and information.

By Taxi. One-way fare from the airport to the Basel center is approximately 35 SF; it takes about 15 minutes in light traffic and up to 30 minutes at rush hours (around noon, 2 PM, and between 5 PM and 7 PM). There are normally cabs at the taxi stand, but if you do need to call one from the airport (in France), you must dial two prefixes: 19 to get out of the country, then 4161, then the number; the cost is negligible. Taxi companies: **Mini Cab** (☎ 061/2711111); **33er Taxi** (☎ 061/6333333); **Taxi-Zentrale** (☎ 061/2712222).

By Train

There are two main rail stations in Basel. The **SBB** (Schweizerische Bundesbahnen; ⊠ Centralbahnstr., ☎ 0900/300300, 1.19 SF/min) connects to Swiss destinations as well as to France and its trains. The **DB** (Deutsche Bundesbahn, locally known as the Badischer Bahnhof; ⊠ North of Rhine in Kleinbasel, Schwarzwalderstr. and Riehenstr., ☎ 061/6901111) connects to Germany and to the SBB. Arriving in Basel from France, you get off on the French side of the border; carry your bags through a small customs station, where your passport will be checked; then either continue into the open track area to find your connection or exit left into the city center. Arriving from Germany at the DB station, you walk through a customs and passport check as well.

Getting Around

The best way to see Basel by far is on foot or by tram, as the landmarks, museums, and even the zoo radiate from the Old Town center on the Rhine, and the network of rails covers the territory thoroughly. Taxis are costly, less efficient, and less available than the ubiquitous tram. Parking in the city center is competitive and in some areas nonexistent. If you've driven in by car, you'll save time and hassle by heading straight for an all-day garage, such as the Parkhaus Elisabethen, on Heuwaage near the SBB train station. Rates run from 10 to 20 SF per day.

By Tram and Bus

Most trams run every six minutes all day, every 12 minutes in the evening. Tickets must be bought at the automatic machines at every stop (most give change). Stops are marked with green-and-white signs; generally the trams run from 5:30 or 6 in the morning until midnight or shortly thereafter. As long as you travel within the central Zone 10, which includes even the airport, you pay 2.80 SF per ticket. If you are making a short trip—four stops or fewer—you pay 1.80 SF. *Mehrfahrtenkarten* (multijourney cards) allow you 12 trips for the price of 10 and can be purchased from the ticket office at Barfüsserplatz. *Tageskarten* (day cards) allow unlimited travel all day within the central zone and cost 7.20 SF. Guests at hotels in Basel receive a complimentary Basel Mobility Ticket for free use of all public transportation for the duration of their stay; ask at the reception desk of your hotel. Holders of the Swiss Pass (☞ Train Travel *in* Smart Travel Tips A to Z) travel free on all Basel public transport systems.

Contacts and Resources

Emergencies
Police (☎ 117). **Hospital** (⊠ Kantonsspital, Petersgraben 2, ☎ 061/2652525). **Medical emergencies and late-night pharmacy** referral (☎ 061/2611515).

English-Language Bookstores
Bider & Tanner (⊠ Aeschenvorstadt 2, at Bankverein, ☎ 061/2069999) has a good range of fiction and nonfiction, plus travel-focused and intercultural publications. **Jäggi** (⊠ Freiestr. 32, ☎ 061/2615200) shelves plenty of best-sellers.

Guided Tours
Basel Tourismus (☞ Visitor Information, *below*) organizes daily tours of the city by bus, departing at 10 AM from the Euler hotel by the SBB. The tours last about 1¾ hours and cost 20 SF. Commentary is in English. They also lead two-hour walking tours from Schifflände in German, French, and English on Monday, Wednesday, and Saturday afternoons from May to October for 15 SF. Sunday afternoon guided tours of the Roman Museum in Augst are held from May to October.

Travel Agencies
American Express (⊠ Steinenvorstadt 33, ☎ 061/2813380).

Visitor Information
Basel Tourismus (Basel Tourism; ⊠ Schifflände 5, ☎ 061/2686868, FAX 061/2686870, ✍) is on the Rhine just left of the Mittlere Brücke, at the Schifflände tram stop. The Basel Tourism branch at the **SBB center** (⊠ Bahnhof, ☎ 0900/300300) will help you with hotel reservations. **City Information** (⊠ Bahnhof, SBB, ☎ 061/2713684) also provides hotel and museum information.

8 FRIBOURG, NEUCHÂTEL, AND THE JURA

Unpretentious and largely undiscovered, the regions of Fribourg, Neuchâtel, and Jura represent three very different worlds. Fribourg, two-thirds French and one-third German, is full of medieval villages and rolling farmland; Neuchâtel, French in language and culture, sparkles from the shores of its glittering lakes to the precision time pieces of its watchmaking industry; and the Jura is a realm of sunny, high plateaus and deeply cleft valleys, of horses and hidden streams.

Updated by
Susan Rose

S HOULDERED BY THE MORE PROMINENT CANTONS of Bern and Vaud, the cantons of Fribourg, Neuchâtel, and Jura are easily overlooked by hurried visitors. If they do stop, it is usually for a quick dip into Fribourg and Gruyères. That leaves the rest of this largely untouched area to the Swiss, who enjoy its relatively unspoiled nature and relaxed approach to life: a hiker stops to enjoy the view while sipping a crisp Fendant wine; a family shares homemade sausage and crusty bread at a riverside picnic.

Although the strict cantonal borders are a messy reflection of historic power struggles, the regional boundaries are unmistakable, even to an outsider. Fribourg starts in the pre-Alpine foothills above Charmey and rolls down across green hills, tidy farms, and ancient towns until it reaches the silty shores of the Murten, Neuchâtel, and Biel lakes. The region of Neuchâtel begins in these silt-rich fields (which grow everything from lettuce to tobacco), sweeps across the lake to the chateaux- and vineyard-lined western shore of Lake Neuchâtel and rises up to the craggy valleys of the Jura Mountains. The Jura is a deceptive region: its smoky, forested slopes, sheltering the "arc" of the Jurassian watchmaking industry, suddenly flatten out onto open, sunny plateaus, gentle pastures, and low-roofed farmhouses. Each of the cantons meanders along a porous line where French meets German; it's not unusual in certain towns to walk into a *boulangerie* selling dark *Vollkornbrot* (wholegrain bread) or to find a family named Neuenschwand that hasn't spoken German for generations. If you're looking for an untouristy experience, this is an excellent place for exploring.

Pleasures and Pastimes

Bicycling

Each region has miles of bicycle routes from which to choose, and route maps can be picked up in most tourist offices. Swiss Federal Railways (CFF/SBB) offers reasonably priced rentals, including mountain bikes and children's bikes, at many train stations throughout the three cantons. Bicycles must be reserved at least one day in advance; in summer you should call at least three days in advance. Call the local tourist office or train station for details. In addition, tourist offices in Fribourg run a unique program called Bike Broye. They've charted 20 different biking itineraries (a vineyard or abbey tour, for example) each of which can be paired with an overnight package. Contact local tourist boards for more information. To reserve an overnight package, contact the Avenches Tourist Office (☞ Visitor Information *in* Fribourg, Neuchâtel, and the Jura A to Z, *below*) at least three weeks in advance (if you plan to do the tour in July, book at least two months in advance).

Cheese

The name *Fribourg* immediately brings to mind *fondue fribourgeoise,* as the canton combines its two greatest cheeses—Gruyère and Vacherin— for a creamy *moitié-moitié* (half-and-half) blend. The Vacherin can be melted alone for an even creamier fondue; potatoes can be dipped instead of bread. From the Jura comes the Vacherin Mont d'Or—woodringed cheese so creamy you can spoon it out—or the Tête de Moine, the "monk's head" cheese, which is stuck on a metal post and shaved off in nutty-flavored ruffles.

You can find many places to view cheese being made; but those familiar cows that relieve the saturation of green in the Fribourg countryside yield more than cheese: we owe them an additional debt of gratitude for producing *crème-double,* a Gruyères specialty that rivals Devonshire cream. A rich, extra-thick, high-fat cream that—without whipping—almost supports a standing spoon, it is served in tiny carved-wood *baquets* (vats), to be spooned over a bowl of berries or a giant meringue, another regional specialty. When the crème-double is not pasteurized, you'll get a whiff of green meadows and new-mown hay.

Dining

In these three regions you'll reap the benefits of a great palette of tastes. Each region enjoys robust, seasonal food: perch from the lakes, game and mushrooms from the forested highlands, and, of course, the dairy products of Fribourg and Gruyères. In the lake towns menus are thick with *perche* (perch), *sandre* (a large cousin of the perch), *bondelle* (a pearly fleshed trout found exclusively in Lake Neuchâtel), or *silure* (catfish). Mushrooms are another strong suit, from the delicate *Schwämli* to the delicacy of the Jura—the *bolets,* fat, fleshy mushrooms with a meaty texture and taste. These are particularly wonderful when served with local rabbit or venison, along with a glass of red Neuchâtel pinot noir.

The traditional autumn Fribourg feast, called Bénichon (Kilbi in Swiss German), embodies the region's love of fundamental food. Like the American Thanksgiving, it is a harvest feast that fetes not only the return of the cattle from the high pastures to the plains but also the season's final yield: chimney-smoked ham, served hot with *moutarde de Bénichon* (sweet mustard); mutton stew with plump raisins and potato puree; and tart *poires-à-Botzi* (pears poached and lightly caramelized). The main feast takes place during the second week of September, but restaurants across the region serve versions of Bénichon all fall.

CATEGORY	COST*
$$$$	over 70 SF
$$$	40 SF–70 SF
$$	20 SF–40 SF
$	under 20 SF

Prices are per person for a three-course meal (two-course meal in $ category), including tax and 15% service charge.

Hiking and Walking

Fribourg is ideal hiking and walking country for every level of difficulty, with its rugged pre-Alps and flat lake lands. Hiking in the Jura offers open terrain and thick forest. All trails are well marked by yellow signs, and hiking maps are available at local tourist offices. If city wandering is more your style, the city of Neuchâtel has one of the country's largest pedestrian zones, the first Swiss city to designate such a zone. The winding streets of Fribourg are a tougher workout.

Lodging

As relatively untouristed cantons, Fribourg, Neuchâtel, and Jura have a less developed hotel infrastructure, which means fewer lodging choices but also more authentically homey hotels. Fribourg is by far the best equipped, though there's only a handful of choices in the city itself. In Neuchâtel most lodgings are along the lake; as you venture inland, there are fewer available. Not all towns in the Jura have hotels; you may prefer to make excursions from Neuchâtel or contact the tourist offices for recommendations.

CATEGORY	COST*
$$$$	over 250 SF
$$$	180 SF–250 SF
$$	120 SF–180 SF
$	under 120 SF

Prices are for a standard double room, including breakfast, tax, and service charge.

🐌 *following the text of a review is your signal that the property has a Web site, where you will find details and, usually, images; for a link, visit www.fodors.com/urls.*

Snowshoeing

This newly updated winter sport, involving lightweight plastic *raquettes de neige* that allow snow hikers to leave the trail, was revived in the Jura resort of St-Cergue a few years ago. You'll find hook-sole snowshoes in many Swiss sports shops and good company on the relatively gentle Jura Mountain slopes.

Exploring Fribourg, Neuchâtel, and the Jura

These three regions are roughly organized like a hand. At the wrist are the Alpine foothills of Fribourg; these curve gently down to the palm of flatter Neuchâtel, with the long ellipse of Lake Neuchâtel. The Jura's rugged fingers form valleys in the Jura Mountains and finally rest on the plateaus. The formal cantonal borders defy the Swiss penchant for neatness since they're based on medieval landholdings. For instance, the present-day cantonal borders of Fribourg still surround odd bits belonging to other cantons, such as the town of Avenches, which technically belongs to Vaud.

Numbers in the text correspond to numbers in the margin and on the Fribourg, Neuchâtel, and the Jura map.

Great Itineraries

Though the major sights themselves don't require too much time, they are scattered throughout the region so it takes time to get to them. You can easily explore much of this area by train, but renting a car will save you some time and allow you to go at your own pace (though many places are connected by two-lane roads often used by tractors).

IF YOU HAVE 1 OR 2 DAYS

Plan your itinerary according to your starting point. If you're coming from the east (Bern, Basel, or Zürich), start with the Old Town and lakefront promenade of ⊞ **Neuchâtel** ⑩; go on to the medieval lakeside town of **Murten** ⑨, then continue to ⊞ **Fribourg** ①. Make a side trip to **Gruyères** ③ on your way to Lausanne or Geneva. If you're coming from the south (Geneva or Lausanne), reverse the order.

IF YOU HAVE 3 OR MORE DAYS

More time allows you to leisurely crawl over ancient ramparts, wander through a medieval town, and visit a 17th-century château. Visit ⊞ **Fribourg** ①, then cut south to the castle at **Gruyères** ③; from there circle northwest through the ancient towns of **Bulle** ④, **Romont** ⑤, **Payerne** ⑥, **Avenches** ⑧, and **Murten** ⑨. From Murten go on to ⊞ **Neuchâtel** ⑩, then head south along the Route du Vignoble (Vineyard Road) to the château town of **Grandson** ⑪ and the spa town of **Yverdon-les-Bains** ⑫. Or you can go northwest from Neuchâtel through watchmaking country to **La Chaux-de-Fonds** ⑬; then go on to enjoy the natural beauty of the Jura, perhaps stopping at **Saignelégier** ⑭ to go horseback riding or cross-country skiing.

When to Tour Fribourg, Neuchâtel, and the Jura

Throughout the year you'll encounter lighter tourist traffic here than in any other region. Summer is a lovely time in the Jura, when forest glades become ripe with the smells of the woods. Fribourg is also pleasant in summer, but crowds tend to pick up, especially in Gruyères. Spring and fall are beautiful times to visit anywhere in this region.

FRIBOURG

With its landscape of green, rolling hills against the craggy peaks of the pre-Alps, Fribourg is one of Switzerland's most rural cantons; its famous Fribourgeois cows—the Holsteins (black and white, the colors of the cantonal coat of arms)—provide the canton with its main income, although light industry is replacing the cows. Fondue was invented here; Gruyère cheese and Switzerland's famous double cream both originated here.

Fribourg

★ ❶ *34 km (21 mi) southwest of Bern.*

Between the rich pasturelands of the Swiss plateau and the Alpine foothills, the Sarine River twists in an S-curve, its sandstone cliffs joined by webs of arching bridges. In one of the curves of the river is the old (nearly 1,000 years behind it) city of Fribourg. The city grew in overlapping layers; it's an astonishing place of hills and cobblestones, medieval passageways and worn wooden stairs, red-orange rooftops and sudden views. Only on foot can you discover its secret medieval charm.

Fribourg is a stronghold of Catholicism; it remained staunchly Catholic even during the Reformation. The evidence is everywhere, from the numerous chapels and religious orders to the brown-robed novitiates walking the sidewalks. Fribourg University, founded in 1889, remains the only Catholic university in Switzerland. It is also the only bilingual institution of its kind and reflects the region's peculiar linguistic agility. Two-thirds of the people of Canton Fribourg are native French speakers, one-third are native German speakers, and many switch easily between the two. In the *Basse-Ville* neighborhood, old-timers still speak a unique mixture of the two languages called Boltz. The city is officially bilingual, although French predominates.

At its very core, and a good place to start a walk, is the **Basse-Ville** (Lower City), tucked into a crook of the river, where you'll find the 11th- through 16th-century homes of the original village. The Bernese would come here for the lucrative Sunday business since the extremely Catholic Fribourgeois were not allowed to work. It's now a lively café and cellar-theater scene. The oldest bridge in this city of bridges is the **Pont de Berne** (Bern Bridge), so called because it was then the only access to the territory of Bern. It's made entirely of wood. All Fribourg's bridges were once like this but were modernized; in the 19th century, engineers even built a series of spectacular suspension bridges strung high across the valley. Those bridges have been replaced by the solid, concrete arches you see today.

As the town expanded from the Basse-Ville, it crossed the river over the **Pont du Milieu** (Middle Bridge) to a narrow but nevertheless inhabitable bank, the **Planche-Inférieure,** a row of tightly packed houses. As the town prospered, it spread to the more stately 16th- and 17th-century **Planche-Supérieure,** a large, sloping, open triangular *place* (square) that was once the busy livestock market; it is now lined with several upscale restaurants and cafés. From here you can make a small detour to the **Chapelle de Lorette** (Loreto Chapel), once a favored pilgrimage site, at the far end of the square.

When the **Pont St-Jean** was built in the 17th century, making the northern bank of the river readily accessible, the merchant houses and walled cloisters of the **Neuve-Ville** (New Town) popped up. From the steep, cobbled rue Grand-Fontaine, you can spy narrow passageways

Fribourg, Neuchâtel, and the Jura

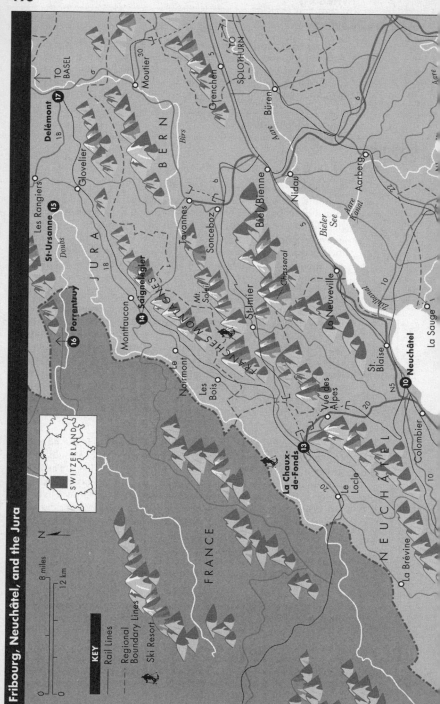

KEY

Rail Lines
Regional
Boundary Lines
Ski Resort

SWITZERLAND

0   8 miles
0   12 km

N

FRANCE

JURA

FRANCHES MONTAGNES

BERN

NEUCHÂTEL

TO BASEL

Delémont
18

17

Glovelier

Les Rangiers

St-Ursanne **15**

Doubs

16 Porrentruy

Saignelégier **14**

Montfaucon

Le Noirmont

Les Bois

Moutier 30

Grenchen

5

TO SOLOTHURN

Aare Büren

Birs

Aare

Tavannes

Sonceboz

6

Biel/Bienne

Nidau

Aare Aarberg

Aare Kanal

12

Bieler See

Mt. Soleil

St-Imier

Chasseral

La Neuveville

10

Zihlkanal

5

La Sauge

St. Blaise

Vue des Alpes

La Chaux-de-Fonds

13

20

N5

Neuchâtel **10**

Le Locle

20

La Brévine

Colombier

10

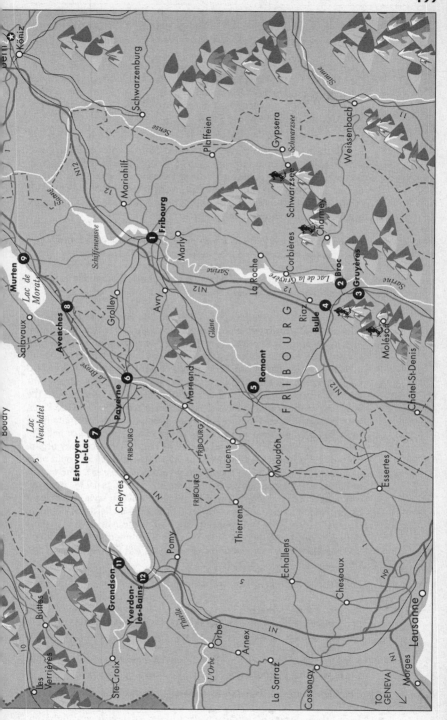

and hidden courtyards; or you can take the *funiculare* up and walk down the route des Alpes to the **Hôtel de Ville,** or Rathaus (Town Hall). This is the seat of the cantonal parliament; it was built on the foundations of the château of Berthold IV of Zähringen, who founded the town of Fribourg in 1157. The symmetrical stairways were added in the 17th century, as were the clockworks in the 16th-century clock tower. The place de Tilleul (Linden Square) has its own dramatic history (☞ Murten, *below*); nowadays it buzzes with a busy local market every Saturday morning. ⊠ *pl. de Tilleul.*

From the Place de Tilleul, the shop-lined rue de Lausanne and rue des Alpes climb upwards, their tightly spaced 18th-century buildings hiding terraced gardens of surprising size. The 19th- and 20th-century section of the city begins at the top of rue de Lausanne. Here an 18th-century facade screens a McDonald's and part of the ancient stone city wall can be seen in the grocery section of the Placette department store. Nearby are the main buildings of the university.

NEED A BREAK?	Belonging to the old Perriard family and sometimes still called that by townspeople, the **Confiserie Bürgisser** (⊠ 61 rue de Lausanne, ☎ 026/ 3223489) has the best chocolate around. Stop for a *ristrette* (espresso) or a *renversée* (coffee with milk) and a slice of rich black-truffle torte or caramelly nut torte. It's closed Monday.

A block away from the Hôtel de Ville is the **Cathédrale St-Nicolas** (St. Nicholas Cathedral), which rears up from the gray 18th-century buildings in striking Gothic unity. Its massive tower was built in the 15th century, three centuries after construction of the cathedral was begun in 1283. It draws the Catholic powers of not only Fribourg but also Geneva and Lausanne, whose cathedrals now serve the Protestant faith. Above the main portal, a beautifully restored tympanum of the Last Judgment shows the blessed being gently herded left toward Peter, who holds the key to the heavenly gates; those not so fortunate head right, led by pig-face demons, into the jaws and cauldrons of hell. Inside the enormous structure you can see its famous 18th-century organ, built by Fribourger Aloys Mooser, as well as the rare 1657 organ built by Sebald Manderscheidt (completely restored in 1998). The exceptional stained-glass windows, dating from 1895 through 1936, are beautifully executed in a pre-Raphaelite and art nouveau style reminiscent of America's Louis Comfort Tiffany. In the **Chapelle du St-Sépulcre** (Chapel of the Holy Sepulcher) a group of 13 polished-wood figures dating from 1433 movingly portrays the entombment of Christ. If you can handle the stairs, climb up the tower. ⊠ *rue St-Nicolas.* ☜ *Free.* ☺ *Mon.–Sat. 7:30–7, Sun. 9–7.*

From the cathedral slip through the rue des Épouses (Street of the Married) to the Grand-Rue, lined with 18th-century patrician homes. At the end of this street is the Sarine-spanning **Pont de Zaehringen** (Zähringen Bridge), with views over the Pont de Berne, the Pont de Gottéron, and the wooden remains of the ancient towers that once guarded the entrance to the city. You're now in the area where Duke Berthold IV first established his residence and founded the city in 1157—or so claims the Hotel Duc Berthold (☞ Dining and Lodging *below*).

The 13th-century **Église des Cordeliers** (Church of the Franciscan Friars), north of the Cathédrale St-Nicolas, is attached to a Franciscan friary; the lightness of its white walls and the rose-, gray, and alabaster-color ceiling contrast with the Gothic darkness of the cathedral. A 16th-century polytych by the anonymous Nelkenmeister, or Maîtres à l'Oeillet (who signed their works only with red and white carnations) hangs over the high altar. A carved wood triptych, believed to be Alsatian, and a 15th-century retable by the Fribourg artist Hans Fries depicting the temptation of St. Anthony adorn the side walls. At the entrance to the *Kreuzgang/Cloître* (cloister) leading to the friary is a 13th-century five-paneled fresco depicting the birth of the Virgin Mary. ⊠ *6 rue de Morat,* ☎ *026/3471160.* ⊡ *Free.* ⊙ *Mon.–Sat. 9–6, Sun. noon–6.*

Near the Church of the Franciscan Friars, on rue de Morat, are a couple of fascinating museums. The **Musée d'Art et d'Histoire de Fribourg** (Fribourg Museum of Art and History) occupies a Renaissance mansion and, incongruously, an old slaughterhouse connected to it by an underground passage. The graceful gray-stone Ratzé mansion, built in 1581–84, displays a concentration of local art from the 11th to 18th centuries as well as a strong collection on Fribourg archaeology. The museum's most striking aspect, however, is the 19th-century slaughterhouse, a stark stone structure modernized with steel-and-glass blocks to display a provocative mix of sacred sculptures (many from the cathedral) and the black whimsy of Jean Tinguely. The sun-washed attic gallery displays 19th- and 20th-century paintings from Delacroix and Courbet to Ferdinand Hodler. Cool your heels in the museum sculpture garden next to one of Niki de Saint Phalle's voluptuous figures. Some descriptive material in English is available upon request. ⊠ *12 rue de Morat,* ☎ *026/3055140.* ⊡ *Permanent collection free; temporary expositions 5 SF–10 SF.* ⊙ *Tues.–Wed. and Fri.–Sun. 11–6, Thurs. 11–8.*

Espace Jean Tinguely–Niki de Saint Phalle was once the city's tram terminal. The kinetic metallic sculptures of Jean Tinguely (1925–91), a native Fribourgeois and an "ethnologist of the modern age," are paired with the oversize, joyously colorful works of his then-wife, Niki de Saint Phalle. Some descriptive material in English is available upon request. ⊠ *2 rue de Morat,* ☎ *026/3055140.* ⊡ *5 SF.* ⊙ *Wed. and Fri.–Sun. 11–6, Thurs. 11–8.*

The **Gutenbergmuseum** (Gutenberg Museum), behind the Espace Jean Tinguely, lets you discover the history of printing in five ways—including hands-on workshops in setting type or bookbinding—as you travel its five floors. Wax models illustrate key points; you'll pass by figures of monks copying manuscripts as well as Johannes Gutenberg, the inventor of printing from movable type. Displays explain technological advances; finally, a multimedia show discusses what the future may hold for printing. The museum opened in late fall of 2000; at press time, it did not have its own phone number, so call the Museum of Art and History (☞ *above*) for information. ⊠ *pl. de Notre Dame, off rue de Morat.* ⊡ *5 SF.* ⊙ *Wed.–Sun. 11–6.*

Skiing

Winter sports in the *Alpes fribourgeoises* are popular; there are a variety of areas and possibilities for skiing, snowboarding, and sledding. Many major ski lifts also run in summer, shuttling hikers instead of skiers.

Schwarzsee (Lac Noir in French), a popular family resort in the Fribourg Alps, lies at the end of a valley, only 26 km (16 mi) southeast of Fribourg, nestled below several 2,000-m (6,560-ft) peaks. Its lifts operate in both summer and winter, and go up to 1,750 m (5,740 ft), for runs with spectacular views. There are three ski areas with eight lifts, a 4.5-km (2¾-mi) cross-country trail, and a reputable skiing and snowboarding school. Parking can be difficult on weekends, but the postbus runs here from Fribourg. For the ski report in German, call ☎ 026/4121660.

Dining and Lodging

\$\$–\$\$\$ ✕ **L'Aigle Noir.** The views of the Alps and the Old Town make this a worthwhile stop—especially if you can get a seat in the enclosed winter garden. The 17th-century building, on a narrow, cobbled street, was a nobleman's house, and the richly painted knights' hall is still used for groups. The food is a step above *cuisine bourgeoise*—beef with béarnaise sauce comes with touches of ginger and mint and delicate waffle chips. ✉ *10 rue des Alpes,* ☎ *026/3224977. AE, DC, MC, V. Closed Sun.–Mon.*

\$–\$\$ ✕ **Café du Midi.** This 17th-century low-ceilinged, wood-paneled restau-
★   rant—the air thick with the smell of melting cheese—serves the best fondue in Fribourg. You can stick to the traditional *moitié-moitié* or try something different like the garlicky, herb-scented *fondue marseillaise.* Reservations recommended on weekends. ✉ *25 rue Romont,* ☎ *026/3223133. AE, DC, MC, V.*

\$\$\$\$ ✕🏨 **Auberge de Zaehringen.** The oldest private house in Fribourg, now
★   a lovely auberge, has been owned by only three families during its 700 years. The restaurant offers gracious service and elegant dishes such as roasted pigeon or duck breast on a plum crust—and a view little changed for nearly eight centuries. A gleaming suit of armor greets you in the warmly lighted brasserie, where you can choose less expensive specialties such as wild mushrooms with crisp cabbage served on puff pastry with a delicate thyme sauce, or a saffron fish soup. The two guest rooms are vast and luxurious, furnished with antiques, lush fabrics, and marble baths. Free cab service to the hotel is offered from the train station if you telephone in advance. Reservations are essential at the restaurant on weekends. ✉ *13 rue de Zaehringen, CH-1700,* ☎ *026/ 3224236,* 🕿 *026/3226908. 2 suites. 2 restaurants, bar. DC, MC, V. Closed Mon. No dinner Sun.*

\$\$\$ ✕🏨 **Au Sauvage.** The Sauvage began in the 1600s as a cloister, became an inn during the cattle-market days in the 18th and 19th centuries, evolved into a café, and is now a sophisticated auberge with a striking blend of minimalism and medieval details. In the guest rooms, the thick, white-washed stone walls cover TVs and minibars; the sleek bathrooms include elegant walnut vanities. The small dining room under the original vaulted ceiling serves French-influenced cuisine, such as beef fillet with Gorgonzola or fish in a delicate ginger-lime sauce. The restaurant is closed on Sunday and Monday. ✉ *12 Planche-Supérieure, CH-1700,* ☎ *026/3473060,* 🕿 *026/3473061. 17 rooms. Restaurant, bar. AE, DC, MC, V.*

\$\$\$\$ 🏨 **Golden Tulip.** Conveniently near the train station (and unfortunately the downtown reconstruction project too), this modern, multistory box sits next to a small park with a spouting Tinguely fountain and overlooks the New Town. The blue-and-gold decor is perfectly comfortable; stop for a drink in the club-style bar. The spacious rooms have modem hookups. ✉ *14 Grand-Places, CH-1700,* ☎ *026/3519191,* 🕿 *026/3519192. 130 rooms. Restaurant, bar, no-smoking floors, free parking. AE, DC, MC, V.*

\$\$\$ 🏨 **Hotel Duc Berthold.** Berthold IV himself is said to have lived in this ancient building in the 12th century. The narrow rooms have a comfortable, old-fashioned air with their delicate florals and reproduction antique furniture. Triple-glazed windows keep out traffic noise. ✉ *5 rue des Bouchers, CH-1700,* ☎ *026/3508100,* 🕿 *026/3508181. 37 rooms. 2 restaurants, bar, coffee shop. AE, DC, MC, V.*

\$\$–\$\$\$ 🏨 **Auberge aux 4 Vents.** Imaginative is the only word to describe this hotel at the edge of town. Every room in this 200-year old villa has its own quirky decor, a unique mix of kitsch, high tech, and antiques left over from the villa's heyday. A bathtub that wheels out on tracks for *un bain sous les étoiles* (a bath under the stars) is the pièce de résistance in one, for example. The circular café is painted a rich red and looks out onto a gravel terrace and a lush park with rare trees, a knot garden, and a stone swimming pool. ⊠ *rte. Grandfey 124, Grange Paccot, CH-1700,* ☎ *026/3473600* FAX *026/3473610. 8 rooms. Restaurant, bar, outdoor pool. MC, V. Closed 1st 2 wks of Nov.* ⊗

Nightlife

An 18th-century inn, seemingly in the middle of nowhere, has been turned into **Planet Edelweiss,** a lively *restaurant de nuit* and disco. The crowd is wonderfully diverse; don't be surprised to spot a hefty farmer next to a Bernese banker. Cordon bleu cooking is served under strings of colored lights and papier mâché farm animals. It stays open until 2 AM from Sunday to Tuesday, until 3 AM on Wednesday and Thursday, and until 4 AM on Friday and Saturday. It's about a five-minute drive northeast of town; a taxi from the train station would cost about 20 SF. ⊠ *Mariahilf, Düdingen,* ☎ *026/4920505. AE, MC, V.*

Broc

② *33 km (20 mi) south of Fribourg.*

This otherwise unassuming town has a tantalizing draw for chocoholics. The **Nestlé chocolaterie** (chocolate factory), founded by Alexandre Cailler in 1889 and bought by Nestlé in 1929, offers a 40-minute tour with a video showing how the mundane and the exotic team up to make something irresistible the world over. Following the tour—fairly enough—is a chocolate tasting. Chocolate-brown signs along the road from Gruyères (☞ *below*) indicate the way. ☎ *026/9215151.* ✆ *Free.* ☉ *May–Oct., weekdays 9–11 and 1:30–4. Reservations essential.*

Gruyères

★ **③** *5 km (3 mi) south of Broc, 35 km (21 mi) south of Fribourg.*

The castle village of Gruyères rises above the plain on a rocky crag, its single, cobbled main street lined with medieval houses in perfect condition. With its traditional crest bearing a crane (*grue* in French), Gruyères is a perfect specimen of a medieval stronghold: It was once the capital of the idyllic Alpine estates of the Burgundian counts of Gruyères. The town is entirely car-free, so if you're driving, you'll need to park in one of three lots outside town and walk in (a short distance); arrive early to beat the crowds.

Between 1080 and 1554, 19 counts held political power over this region; the last was Michael I of Gruyères, a lover of luxury and a big spender who expanded the estates and then fled his creditors, leaving vast holdings to Fribourg and Bern. In 1848 a wealthy Geneva family bought the old **château.** As patrons of the arts, family members hosted the artist Corot; some of his panels grace the castle's drawing room. In a tour of the castle, you can also see the 13th-century dungeon and the living quarters, decorated in 16th- and 17th-century styles with tapestries, frescoes, and grand fireplaces. ☎ *026/9212102.* ✆ *5 SF.* ☉ *June–Sept., daily 9–7; Mar.–May and Oct., daily 9:30–noon and 1–5; Nov.–Feb., daily 9:30–noon and 1–4:30.*

Gruyères is known for its blue-and-white or dark-red-and-white pottery decorated with the *grue,* and for carved wooden spoons, creamy, nutty cheeses (Vacherin and Gruyère, spelled without the town's *s*), and the 48%-butterfat crème-double, which is dipped from a wooden *barque* and served with a bowl of berries or crumbly, sweet meringues. Before going up the hill to Gruyères, you can visit the demonstration **fromagerie** (cheese dairy), where the famous cheese is produced with fully modernized equipment. ☎ 026/9211410. 🎫 5 SF. ☉ Apr.–Sept., daily 8–7; Oct.–Mar., daily 8–6. Demonstrations at 9:15, 10:15, 2:30, and 3:30.

For a more historical look at cheese making, visit the Magnin family's **fromagerie d'alpage,** in nearby Moléson-sur-Gruyères. Here you can see firsthand how the true Gruyère cheese, called *Gruyère d'alpage,* gets its delicate, complex flavor. The family still makes cheese over an open fire in their low-roofed chalet. An exhibit explains the development of cheese making since the 17th century; a 40-minute video in English describes the process. If all this gets your appetite going, there is also a small restaurant serving raclette and fondue. ⊠ Signposted. ☎ 026/9211044. 🎫 3 SF. ☉ Daily 9:30–7; demonstrations May–mid-Oct. at 10 and 3.

<table>
<tr><td>OFF THE
BEATEN PATH</td><td>CHARMEY, CRÉSUZ, LA VALSAINTE – If you're traveling by car from Gruyères, take the old Fribourg road (before you enter Bulle) and head north through Broc; soon after Broc the road splits, and the right-hand branch heads into a valley toward Charmey/Jaun. Once you've passed Crésuz, but before reaching Charmey, cut left and take the narrow, winding road into La Valsainte. Peaceful and green, with few villages, the valley runs its way upward along a stream, past the austere and impressive Chartreux Monastery (founded by followers of St. Bruno at the end of the 13th century).</td></tr>
</table>

Skiing

Gruyères/Moléson, at 1,100 m (3,609 ft), offers skiing up to 2,002 m (6,568 ft), with wraparound views of the pre-Alps and on to Lake Geneva. It has three cable cars, four lifts, 20 km (12 mi) of downhill ski runs, and 8 km (5 mi) of cross-country trails. **Charmey,** at 900 m (2,953 ft), lies in a bowl surrounded by forested peaks with one ski area between Vounetz, at 1,627 m (5,337 ft), and the village itself. Slopes are of medium difficulty at best. The resort's charms lie in its family-friendly atmosphere and its preservation of Alpine farming traditions such as October's *fête de la désalpe,* the procession of the cows coming down from the mountains. Charmey has seven lifts including a gondola, 35 km (22 mi) of downhill runs, and 20 km (12 ½ mi) of cross-country trails.

Dining and Lodging

$$$$ ✕ **Pinte des Mossettes.** Overlooking a steep valley at the end of a wind-
★   ing road, this lace-curtained, rough-hewn restaurant offers up some of the most intriguing menus in Switzerland. Owner-chef Judith Baumann bases her dishes on wild herbs and locally grown ingredients. In choices such as wild greens with bean mousse or Andalusian ham with black olive and Xeres vinegar sauce, flavors often contrast or surprise. Reservations are highly recommended. ⊠ Road between Gruyères and La Valsainte, Cerniat, ☎ FAX 026/9272097. AE, DC, MC, V. Closed Mon.–Tues. and Nov.–mid-Mar.

$$ ✕ **Auberge de la Halle à Pied Cheval.** The unfussy interior of this medieval house, with its massive raftered ceiling and smooth stone floor, welcomes you like a 16th-century burgher's home. Choose a terraced room according to its view: for people-watching, choose the front; for the town ramparts and the mountains, the back. Then savor traditional Gruyères dishes, such as fondue with potatoes. ⊠ Main street, ☎ 026/9212178. AE, DC, MC, V.

$$ ✕🏨 **Le Vieux Chalet.** Although self-consciously designed, this carefully reconstructed "chalet," built in 1959, has tried to be as authentic as possible; the setting, the fabulous view from the large terrace, and the filling, traditional food make it worth the stop. Try the cheese dishes, such as Rösti with Vacherin. The bedrooms are all done in knotty pine. The restaurant is closed Tuesday. ⊠ *Road from Gruyères to Charmey, in direction of Jaun Pass, CH-1653 Crésuz,* ☎ *026/9271286. 5 rooms. Restaurant, café. AE, MC, V. Closed Jan.–mid-Feb.*

$$$ 🏨 **De Ville.** Directly on the picturesque main street, with back rooms overlooking the valley, this old family inn harbors a warmly traditional interior. Rooms are airy and filled with massive, polished wood furniture. Fittingly, the large dining room serves spruced-up Swiss classics. ⊠ *CH-1663,* ☎ *026/9212424,* FAX *026/9213628. 8 rooms. Restaurant. AE, DC, MC, V. Closed Jan.*

$$–$$$ 🏨 **Hostellerie des Chevaliers.** Step off the main tourist drag at this tra-
★ dition-bound hotel, which stands slightly aloof at the edge of the valley. Though it's outside the main gates of Gruyères, it shares the same views of the castle and the mountains as hotels within the town. The decor is a warm regional mix of antiques, handsome woodwork, and ceramic stoves, which sometimes gets a little eccentric, such as the teal- or pumpkin-tile baths. ⊠ *CH-1663,* ☎ *026/9211933,* FAX *026/9212552. 32 rooms. Restaurant. AE, DC, MC, V. Closed Jan.–mid-Feb.*

$$ 🏨 **Fleur de Lys.** From its vaulted, stenciled reception area to its pine-
★ and-beam restaurant, this is a welcoming little hotel. It has pretty wood-paneled rooms and a hidden rear terrace and garden with a flawless view of the mountains and the castle. ⊠ *CH-1663,* ☎ *026/ 9212108,* FAX *026/9213605. 10 rooms. Restaurant, café, bar. AE, DC, MC, V. Closed Feb.*

Bulle

❹ *5 km (3 mi) northwest of Gruyères, 31 km (19 mi) southwest of Fribourg.*

A small town of fewer than 10,000 people, Bulle condenses the attractions of a larger town: a castle (not open to the public), three-storied patrician houses lining the cobblestone main street, and a scenic backdrop so perfect you might think it's been painted. You can learn about Gruyères traditions at the **Musée Gruérien,** with its displays of folk costumes, handicrafts, and farm tools—it even has a full reproduction of a flagstone farmhouse kitchen and dining room. ⊠ *pl. du Cabalet,* ☎ *026/9127260.* 🎫 *5 SF.* ☉ *Tues.–Sat. 10–noon and 2–5, Sun. 2–5.*

Romont

❺ *15 km (9 mi) northwest of Bulle, 49 km (30 mi) southwest of Fribourg.*

The best way to approach this 13th-century town of two broad streets is to leave the highway and drive up to its castle terrace. The fortress's 13th-century ramparts surround the town, forming a belvedere from which you can see the Alps—from Mont Blanc to the Berner Oberland—as well as other notable buildings: the 12th-century **Cistercian convent,** the 17th-century **Capuchin monastery,** and the lovely 13th-century *Collégiale,* one of the purest examples of a Gothic church in Switzerland, with period windows, sculptures, choir stalls, a screen, and an altarpiece. Inside the castle, the **Musée du Vitrail** (Stained-Glass Museum) shimmers with crisscrossing shafts of colored light from its glass panels, both ancient and contemporary. A slide presentation traces the development of the craft, while a workshop area demonstrates current techniques. ⊠ *Château,* ☎ *026/6521095.* 🎫 *6 SF.* ☉ *Apr.–Oct., Tues.–Sun. 10–1 and 2–7; Nov.–Mar., weekends 10–noon and 2–6.*

Payerne

❻ *15 km (9 mi) north of Romont, 18 km (11 mi) southwest of Fribourg.*

The meandering streets in this market town are filled with pastel-painted 18th-century buildings, now shops and restaurants. Above them stands a magnificent 11th-century *église abbatiale* (abbey church), one of the finest examples of Romanesque art in Switzerland. You can visit its restored austere abbey, with a grand barrel-vaulted sanctuary and primitive capital carvings on the pillars. ☎ *026/6626704.* ✆ *3 SF.* ☉ *May–Oct., Mon.–Sat. 9–noon and 2–6; Nov.–Apr., Tues.–Sat. 9–noon and 2–6.*

Estavayer-le-Lac

★ ❼ *7 km (4 mi) northwest of Payerne, 51 km (32 mi) southwest of Neuchâtel.*

On the shore of Lake Neuchâtel, this modest but charming lake town can still be navigated using a map drawn in 1599. It has retained much of its medieval architecture, from the arcades of the town center to the gracious, multitowered medieval **Château de Chenaux,** which now houses city government offices. But change is waiting in the wings, as a freeway is slated to be built through town; there are only a couple of years left to enjoy Estavayer's special character.

The humorous and quirky **Musée de Grenouilles** (Frog Museum) displays 108 embalmed frogs posed like people in scenes of daily life from the 19th century up through the mid-1900s. Other exhibits include an authentic 17th-century kitchen, various military and household artifacts dredged from Lake Neuchâtel, and more than 200 Swiss railroad lanterns, some up to 100 years old. ✉ *rue des Musées,* ☎ *026/6632448.* ✆ *3 SF.* ☉ *Mar.–June and Sept.–Oct., Tues.–Sun. 9–11 and 2–5; July–Aug., daily 9–11 and 2–5; Nov.–Feb., weekends 2–5.*

Lodging

$ 🏠 **My Lady's Manor.** Set in a gracious park, this 19th-century manor
★ with balconies and mansards on every side is now a very personal bed-and-breakfast. There are plenty of opportunities for conversation, whether at the breakfast table in the chandeliered dining room or outdoors on the lawn. The decor is an eclectic mix of Italian mosaic flooring, turn-of-the-20th-century-style wallpaper, and unmatched linens; shared bathrooms are on each floor. The reasonable price and easy-going, family-friendly atmosphere fills the place up quickly, so make reservations well ahead of time. It's within walking distance of the lake and train station. ✉ *rte. de la Gare, CH-1410,* ☎ *026/6632316,* 𝔽𝔸𝕏 *026/66631993. 5 rooms. Kitchenette. No credit cards. Closed Nov.–Feb.*

Avenches

❽ *5 km (3 mi) northeast of Estavayer-le-Lac, 13 km (8 mi) northeast of Fribourg.*

Avenches (technically in Canton Vaud) is the old capital of the Helvetians, which, as Aventicum, grew into an important city that reached its peak in the 2nd century AD. In its prime, the Roman stronghold was surrounded by some 6 km (4 mi) of 2-m-high (6-ft-high) stone walls. The Alemanni destroyed it in the 3rd century. The town's **castle** was built at the end of the 13th century by the bishops of Lausanne and has belonged to the town since 1804. Aside from its Renaissance-style facade and portal, you'll find a tiny museum dedicated to Swiss aviators (open on weekends 2–4) and a small art gallery (open Wednesday through Sunday 2–6). *Closed Dec.–Mar.*

You can still see the remains of a Roman forum, a bathhouse, and an amphitheater—today the **Musée et Théâtre Romains** (Roman Museum and Theater)—where bloodthirsty spectators once watched the games. Now opera lovers gather here for an annual July evening spectacle; contact the tourist office well in advance for tickets. The collection of Roman antiquities at the museum is noteworthy, including an excellent copy of a gold bust of Marcus Aurelius, unearthed at Avenches in the 1920s, the original of which is in Lausanne. ☎ 026/6751730. ☞ 2 SF. ☉ Apr.– Sept., Tues.–Sun. 10–noon and 1–5; Oct.–Mar., Tues.–Sun. 2–5.

Murten

★ ❾ 6 km (4 mi) northeast of Avenches, 17 km (11 mi) north of Fribourg.

The ancient town of Murten, known in French as Morat, is a popular resort on Lac de Morat (Murten Lake), with a boat-lined waterfront, windsurfer rentals, grassy picnic areas, and a promenade. It was here, on June 22, 1476, that the Swiss Confederates—already a fearsomely efficient military machine—attacked with surprising ferocity and won a significant victory over the Burgundians, who were threatening Fribourg under the leadership of Duke Charles the Bold. Begun as a siege 12 days earlier, the battle cost the Swiss 410 men, the Burgundians 12,000. The defeat at Murten prevented the establishment of a large Lothringian kingdom and left Switzerland's autonomy unchallenged for decades. Legend has it that a Swiss runner, carrying a linden branch, ran from Murten to Fribourg to carry the news of victory. He expired by the town hall, and a linden tree grew from the branch he carried. Today, to commemorate his dramatic sacrifice, some 15,000 runners participate annually on the first Sunday in October in a 17-km (11-mi) race up the steep hill from Murten to Fribourg. As for the linden tree, it flourished in Fribourg for some 500 years, until 1983, when it was ingloriously felled by a car and replaced with a steel sculpture.

Bilingual Murten/Morat has a superbly preserved medieval center. Leave your car in the parking area in front of the 13th century gates and stroll the fountain-studded cobblestone streets; you can even climb up the worn wooden steps of the town ramparts. The **Musée Historique** (Historical Museum) is in the town's old mill, complete with two water-powered mill wheels; on view are prehistoric finds, military items, and trophies from the Burgundian Wars. ⊠ Historic center, ☎ 026/6703100. ☞ 4 SF. ☉ Oct.–Dec. and Mar.–Apr., Tues.–Sun. 2–5; May–Sept., Tues.–Sun. 10–noon and 2–5; Jan.–Feb., weekends 2–5.

Dining and Lodging

$$$$ ✕▥ **Le Vieux Manoir au Lac.** Just 1 km (½ mi) south of Murten on Lake
★ Murten, this stately mansion in a manicured park is a graceful mix of half-timbering and turrets under a deep roofline. The decor is an eclectic mix of parquet and Persian rugs, wing chairs, Biedermeier, and country prints; rooms are a rich blend of chintz, gingham, and toile de Jouy. The restaurant offers a choice of seasonal sampling menus, each with a French/Continental bent; options might include roast lamb with mustard sauce or a lasagna of asparagus with truffle butter. A winter garden allows you to dine in a room bathed with light, just yards from the shore of the lake. ⊠ rue de Lausanne, CH-3280 Meyriez, ☎ 026/ 6786161, ℻ 026/6786162. 30 rooms. Restaurant. AE, DC, MC, V. Closed mid-Dec.–mid-Feb. ✎

$$$ ✕▥ **Schiff am See.** This low white-front building below the town nabbed an ideal setting; its sheltered terrace gives onto a shady park and the waterfront promenade. Inside you'll find an eclectic collection of heavy wood furniture and antiques. The restaurant, Lord Nelson, wraps around the garden and serves ambitious French cuisine on the terrace or in a room with a nautical theme, both with lake views. Specialties may include risotto with porcini mushrooms or local fish (the restaurant is closed on Wednesday and Thursday). The Schiff is a "velo-hotel;" bicycles are welcome, and they can help you rent one in town. ⊠ *Ryf 53, CH-3280,* ☎ *026/6702701,* ℻ *026/6703531. 15 rooms. Restaurant, bar, café. AE, DC, MC, V. Closed Jan.–Feb.*

$$–$$$ ✕▥ **Weisses Kreuz.** Though it shares great lake views with other ho-
★	tels in town, this lodging has more to offer: the devotion—even obsession—of its owners (it has been in one family since 1921) There are two buildings, and though you might be tempted by lakeside panoramas, consider the wing with Old Town views across the street. It's furnished in extraordinary style with complete antique bedroom sets—Biedermeier, art nouveau, Louis XVI, empire. Simpler rooms, in Scandinavian pine or high-tech style, cost less. The lovely formal dining room is known for its broad array of fish specialties: whitefish with chanterelles and cucumbers, timbale of three lake fish, pike braised in dill. ⊠ *Rathausg. 31, CH-3280,* ☎ *026/6702641,* ℻ *026/6702866. 27 rooms. Restaurant, café. AE, DC, MC, V. Closed mid-Dec.–mid-Feb.* 🐾

$$ ▥ **Krone.** The quirky Krone has its own following, and what it lacks in tidiness it makes up for in character (and characters, including the owner, a self-styled cowboy). Rooms are small and veer toward shabbiness, but the views of the lake from the back rooms are terrific. ⊠ *5 Rathausg., CH-3280,* ☎ *026/6705252,* ℻ *026/6703610. 33 rooms. Restaurant, bar, 2 cafés. AE, DC, MC, V.*

LAC NEUCHÂTEL

The region of Neuchâtel belonged to Prussia from 1707 to 1857, with a brief interruption caused by Napoléon and a period of double loyalty to Prussia and the Swiss Confederation between 1815 and 1857. Yet its French culture remains untouched by Germanic language, diet, or culture. Some boast that the inhabitants speak "the best French in Switzerland," which is partly why so many summer language courses are taught here.

Neuchâtel

★ ⑩ *28 km (17 mi) north of Murten, 48 km (30 mi) northwest of Fribourg.*

The city of Neuchâtel, at the foot of the Jura Mountains, flanked by vineyards and facing southeast, enjoys remarkable views across Lac Neuchâtel and the whole crowded range of the middle Alps, from the majestic mass of Mont Blanc to the Bernese Oberland (Lac Neuchâtel, at 38 km [24 mi] long and 8 km [5 mi] wide, is the largest in the country). A prosperous city, Neuchâtel has a reputation for precision work, beginning with watchmaking in the early 18th century. It possesses an air of almost tangible dignity; in the lower part of town, bordering the placid lake, broad avenues are lined with imposing yellow-sandstone buildings that inspired author Alexandre Dumas to call Neuchâtel "a city with the appearance of an immense *joujou* dressed in butter." The overall effect is of unruffled but compact grandeur—the castle and cathedral look gracefully down on the city's bustling Old Town and marketplace, which throng with lively, urban street life.

The extent of French influence in Neuchâtel is revealed in its monuments and architecture, most notably at the **Église Collégiale** (Collegiate Church), a handsome Romanesque and Burgundian Gothic structure dating from the 12th century, with a colorful tile roof. (For anyone not wanting to climb steep streets, the church may be reached from the Prom-

enade Noire off the place des Halles by an inconspicuous elevator—
Ascenseur publique.) The church contains a strikingly realistic and
well-preserved grouping of life-size painted figures called *le cénotaphe,*
or monument to the counts of Neuchâtel. Dating from the 14th and
15th centuries, this is considered one of Europe's finest examples of medieval art. Its two-year restoration was completed in 1999. Grouped
around the church are the ramparts and cloisters of the 12th-century
château, which today houses the cantonal government. A tour of the
château (available in English) is the only way to see the cantonal high
courtroom, a fascinating display of every family crest that ever married
into the governing dynasty of Neuchâtel. ⊠ *12 rue de la Collégiale,* ☎
032/8896000. ☜ *Free.* ⊘ *Weekdays 8–noon and 1:30–5.*

The **Tour des Prisons** (Prison Tower), which adjoins the Collegiate
Church, affords panoramic views from its turret. On your way up, stop
in one of the original wooden prison cells; on the landings you can see
models of the city as it evolved from the 15th through the 18th centuries. ⊠ *rue Jeanne de Hochberg,* ☎ *no phone.* ☜ *50 centimes.* ⊘
Daily 8–6.

The **architecture of the Old Town** demonstrates a full range of French
styles, far beyond the Gothic. Along rue des Moulins are two perfect
specimens of the Louis XIII period, and—at its opposite end—a fine
Louis XIV house anchors the place des Halles (market square), also
notable for its turreted 16th-century **Maison des Halles.** The **Hôtel de
Ville** (⊠ rue de l'Hôtel de Ville), opened in 1790 east of the Old Town,
is by Pierre-Adrien Paris, Louis XVI's architect. There are also several
fine patrician houses, such as the magnificent **Hôtel DuPeyrou** (⊠ 1
av. DuPeyrou, east of Old Town), home of the friend, protector, and
publisher of Jean-Jacques Rousseau, who studied botany in the nearby
Val-de-Travers. Most of the Old Town is a pedestrians-only zone,
though public buses do run through it.

★ For connoisseurs not only of art but of art museums, the **Musée d'Art
et d'Histoire** (Museum of Art and History) merits a pilgrimage. Thanks
to a remarkably unprovincial curator, it displays a deep collection of
paintings gathered under broad themes—nature, civilization—and
mounted in a radical, evocative way. Fifteenth-century allegories, early
Impressionism, and contemporary abstractions pack the walls from floor
to ceiling: interacting, conflicting, demanding comparison. You may
climb a platform (itself plastered with paintings) to view the higher works.
This aggressive series of displays is framed by the architectural deco-
rations of Neuchâtel resident Clement Heaton, whose murals and
stained glass make the building itself a work of art.

This novel museum also has the honor of hosting three of this watchmaking capital's most exceptional guests: the **automates Jaquet-Droz,**
three astounding little androids, created between 1768 and 1774, that
once toured the courts of Europe like young mechanical Mozarts.
Pierre Jaquet-Droz and his son Henri-Louis created them, and they are
moving manifestations of the stellar degree to which watchmaking had
evolved by the 18th century. One automaton is called **Le Dessinateur**
(the Draughtsman). A dandy in satin knee pants, he draws graphite
images of a dog, the god Eros in a chariot pulled by a butterfly, and a
profile of Louis XV. **La Musicienne** (the Musician) is a soulful young
woman who plays the organ, moving and breathing subtly with the
music, and actually striking the keys that produce the organ notes.
L'Écrivain (the Writer) dips a real feather in real ink and writes 40 different letters, capital and lowercase; like a primitive computer, he can
be programmed to write any message simply by changing a steel disk.
The automates are viewable only on the first Sunday of the month, at

2, 3, or 4, or by appointment, but an audio-visual show and a close-up view of them is enough to re-create the thrill. ⊠ *quai Léopold-Robert,* ☎ *032/7177925.* 🎫 *7 SF; free Thurs.* ⊙ *Tues.–Sun. 10–5.*

The **Papiliorama and Nocturama** literally crawl with life; two separate domes contain two completely different tropical biospheres. The **Papiliorama** pulses with humid tropical plants, lily ponds, more than a thousand living butterflies, dwarf caimans (*crocodilians*), tortoises, birds, fish, and gigantic tropical insects—the latter, fortunately, in cages. The **Nocturama** is filled with bats, opossums, raccoons, skunks, and other nocturnal creatures. Just 5 km (3 mi) from Neuchâtel, you can get there by car or train. ⊠ *Marin,* ☎ *032/7534344.* 🎫 *Both domes: 11 SF.* ⊙ *Apr.–Sept., daily 9–6; Oct.–Mar., daily 10–5.*

Dining and Lodging

$$–$$$ ✕ **Du Banneret.** This popular restaurant, in a late-Renaissance building at the foot of the rue du Château, is especially welcoming. In the brasserie the chef often emerges to greet his guests. The dishes are mostly regional fare, such as homemade pasta with fresh wild mushrooms or lake trout. In the upstairs dining room, the food takes a strong Italian twist. ⊠ *1 rue Fleury,* ☎ *032/7252861. AE, DC, MC, V. Closed Sun.*

$ ✕ **Le Cardinal Brasserie.** At one of the most authentic cafés in the Old Town, stop and have a perfect café crème or a light meal along with the Neuchâteloise. The interior has some striking art nouveau elements; the molded ceiling, etched windows, and blue and green decorative tile all date from 1905. Daily specials might include a plate of smoked salmon, trout, or leg of rabbit. ⊠ *9 rue du Seyon,* ☎ *032/7251286. AE, MC, V.*

$$$ ✕🏠 **Auberge de l'Aubier.** Just a 10-minute drive west from Neuchâtel you'll find this small eco-retreat complete with its own organic farm. There are solar panels on the barn, rainwater is used in the washing machines, and the rooms are tranquilly pale and unfussy. The restaurant emphasizes fresh, local ingredients, turning out dishes such as red-pepper terrine or fish with red onions and a carrot-cream sauce. It's a good idea to make reservations. ⊠ *CH-2205 Montézillon,* ☎ *032/7303010,* 📠 *032/7303016. 15 rooms. Restaurant, shop, meeting rooms. AE, DC, MC, V. No smoking. Closed Jan.* 🍴

$ ✕🏠 **Du Marché.** Opening directly onto the place des Halles, this is a delightful place for a hearty plat du jour or a carafe of local wine. Inside, pass through the lively bar-café to the steamy, old-wood brasserie for a bowl of tripe in Neuchâtel wine or salt pork with lentils. Upstairs, a pretty little dining room serves more sophisticated fare. Plain, functional rooms with tidy tile bathrooms down the hall are an excellent value. ⊠ *4 pl. des Halles, CH-2000,* ☎ *032/7245800,* 📠 *032/7214742. 10 rooms. Restaurant, café. AE, DC, MC, V.*

$$$$ 🏠 **Beau-Rivage.** This thoroughly elegant restored 19th-century hotel ★ sits gracefully on the lakeshore; on a clear day there's a splendid view of the Alps. Its warmly lighted interior, with high ceilings and wild-cherry wood, exudes calm. Each of the spacious rooms has an extra line for faxing and modems; bathrobes hang in the white tile bathrooms. Two-thirds of the rooms have lake views. The sophisticated dining room, done in pale green, offers a fine selection of wines, after-dinner cigars, and brandies. ⊠ *1 esplanade du Mont Blanc, CH-2001,* ☎ *032/7231515,* 📠 *032/7231616. 65 rooms. Restaurant, bar. AE, DC, MC, V.* 🍴

$$$–$$$$ 🏠 **La Maison du Prussien.** Ten minutes from the bustle of Neuchâtel in the gorge of Vauseyon, this 18th-century restored mill, part of the Romantik chain, nestles alongside a roaring woodland stream. The polished beams, stone walls, terra-cotta floors, and lush views are undeniably atmospheric. Every room or suite has a unique decor; three have fireplaces. Take the tunnels under Neuchâtel toward La Chaux-de-Fonds, exit toward Pontarlier-Vauseyon, and then watch for the hotel's signs. ⊠ *Au Gor du Vauseyon, CH-2006,* ☎ *032/7305454,* ℻ *032/7302143. 6 rooms, 4 suites. Restaurant, brasserie, café. AE, DC, MC, V.*

$$ 🖫 **Alpes et Lac.** This modest hotel across from the train station overlooks tile rooftops, the sparkling lake, and the white-capped Alps. The building's renovation preserved the ancient parquet floors and stone steps; along the pale yellow corridors, fresh flowers hide in niches. The gold-and-red-checked bedspreads in the guest rooms, all medium-size, echo the colors found throughout this sunny hotel. A lovely park surrounds the terrace. ⊠ *2 pl. de la Gare, CH-2002,* ☎ *032/7231919,* ℻ *032/7231920. 30 rooms. 2 restaurants. AE, DC, MC, V.*

Outdoor Activities and Sports

BIKING

Neuchâtel has about 400 km (248 mi) of marked mountain-bike trails. You can rent mountain bikes through the train station. Free trail maps are available at the tourist office (☞ Visitor Information *in* Fribourg, Neuchâtel, and the Jura A to Z, *below*).

GOLF

There's an 18-hole golf course at **Voëns sur St-Blaise** (☎ 032/7535550) open to anyone with proof of membership in another club.

SWIMMING

There are **public beaches** at nearly every village and resort around Lake Neuchâtel and Lake Murten, plus a **municipal complex** (⊠ Nid du Crô, Rte. des Falaises 30, ☎ 032/7214848) with outdoor and indoor pools, open daily, in Neuchâtel.

Nightlife

For night owls, Neuchâtel has an ever-changing selection of *restaurants de nuit* and *bars musicaux,* establishments that pulse with disco music till the wee hours of the morning and sometimes serve food (along the lines of *steak frites*) to keep you going. If you want to try the one best known for food, and don't mind loud music and smoke, check out the techno-metallic **Garbo Café** (⊠ 5–7 rue des Chavannes, ☎ 032/7243181). **Casa d'Italia** offers a more varied menu without the disco (⊠ 1 rue de Prebarreau, off rue de l'Ecluse, ☎ 032/7250858). **La Rotonde** (⊠ 14 Faubourg du Lac, ☎ 032/7244848) squeezes in four different discos under one roof but does not serve food. Eurotechno groups play at **Le Black Jack et Le Bronx** (⊠ 3 av. de la Gare, ☎ 032/7240022); Le Bronx also offers jazz and a late-night menu. **Le Shakespeare** (⊠ 7 rue des Terreaux, ☎ 032/7258588), a bar/pub, remains the most conservative.

En Route   Reaching north from Neuchâtel into the Jura Mountains, the A20 highway climbs 13 km (8 mi) from Neuchâtel to the **Vue des Alpes,** a parking area on a high ridge that affords, as the name implies, spectacular views of the Alps, including Mont Blanc.

Just a few miles west of Neuchâtel lie some of Switzerland's best **vineyards,** their grapes producing chiefly white and rosé wines that are light and slightly sparkling. The wines are bottled before the second fermentation, so they have a rather high carbonic-acid content. The tourist office has a map of the *route du vignoble* (Vineyard Road). Three of the larger vintners are **Cave Jungo et Fellerman,** in Cressier (☎ 032/7571162); **Caves de Cortaillod,** in Cortaillod (☎ 032/8412064); and **Château Boudry,** in Tour de Pierre (☎ 032/8421098). If you'd like to arrange a tasting, your best bet would be to call and set up an appointment. Neuchâtel's biggest annual festival is the winemakers' three-day celebration of the grape harvest, the *fête des vendanges.* It's celebrated the last weekend of September with parades and fanfare throughout the city.

Grandson

⓫ *29 km (18 mi) southwest of Neuchâtel.*

This lakeside village in Canton Vaud has a long history. It is said that in 1066 a member of the Grandson family accompanied William of Normandy (better known as the Conqueror) to England, where he founded the English barony of Grandison. Otto I of Grandson took part in the Crusades. When the Burgundian Wars broke out in the late 15th century, the **Château de Grandson** (Grandson Castle), built in the 11th century and much rebuilt during the 13th and 15th centuries, was in the hands of Charles the Bold of Burgundy. In 1475 the Swiss won it by siege, but early the next year their garrison was surprised by Charles, and 418 of their men were captured and hanged from the apple trees in the castle orchard. A few days later the Swiss returned to Grandson and, after crushing the Burgundians, retaliated by stringing their prisoners from the same apple trees. After being used for three centuries as a residence by the Bernese bailiffs, the castle was bought in 1875 by the de Blonay family, which restored it to its current impressive state, with high, massive walls and five cone turrets. Inside, you can see a reproduction of a Burgundian war tent, *oubliettes* (dungeon pits for prisoners held *in perpetua*), torture chambers, and a model of the Battle of Grandson, complete with 20-minute slide show. Cassette-guided tours of the town are available at the castle reception desk. ☎ *024/4452926.* ✎ *8 SF.* ☉ *Apr.–Oct., daily 9–6; Nov.–Jan., Sat. 1–5 and Sun. 9–5 or by request; Feb.–Mar., Mon.–Sat. 8:30–11:30 and 1:30–5, Sun. 9–5.*

Yverdon-les-Bains

⓬ *6 km (4 mi) southwest of Grandson, 36 km (22 mi) southwest of Neuchâtel.*

This pastel-color lakefront town at the southernmost tip of Lake Neuchâtel has been appreciated for its thermal waters and sandy, willow-lined shoreline since the Romans first invaded and set up thermal baths here. In the 18th century its fame spread across Europe; today the **Thermal Center** is completely up-to-date, offering medicinal as well as recreational pools. ✉ *22 av. des Bains,* ☎ *024/4230232.* ✎ *13 SF.* ☉ *Weekdays 8 AM–9:30 PM; weekends 9–7:30.*

On a point of land jutting into the lake sits the turreted, mid-13th-century **Château de Yverdon-les-Bains.** Most of the castle is now a museum, with exhibits on locally found prehistoric and Roman artifacts, Egyptian art, natural history, and of course, local history. A special room is dedicated to the famous Swiss educator Johann Heinrich Pestalozzi (1746–1827), who spent 20 years here. His influential ideas on education led to school reforms at home and in Germany and England. ☎ *024/4259310.* ✎ *6 SF.* ☉ *June–Sept., Tues.–Sun. 10–noon and 2–5; Oct.–May, Tues.–Sun. 2–5.*

In front of Yverdon's Hôtel de Ville (Town Hall)—notable for its Louis XV facade—stands a bronze monument of Pestalozzi, grouped with two children. The charming, bustling town center is closed to traffic. Along the waterfront you'll find parks, promenades, a shady campground, and a 5 km (3 mi) stretch of little beaches.

THE JURA

Straddling the French frontier from Geneva to Basel is a range of low-riding mountains (few peaks exceed 1,500 m/4,920 ft) that fall steeply down to the mysterious River Doubs to the north and to the lakes to the south. The secret of this region, known as the Jura, is the sunny plateau atop the mountains, especially in the Montagnes Neuchâteloise and the Franches-Montagnes in the Jura canton. These lush pastures and gentle woods have excellent hiking, biking, horseback-riding, and cross-country-skiing opportunities—perfectly organized yet unspoiled. (La Brévine, between Le Locle and Les Verrières, is known as the Swiss Siberia.) Administratively, the Jura region is shared by four cantons: Jura, Vaud, Neuchâtel, and Basel. Culturally, it is unified by language (French, except for Basel), economy, and spirit. Watchmaking concentrates around Le Locle and La Chaux-de-Fonds, while horse breeding and tourism flourish in the Franches-Montagnes.

La Chaux-de-Fonds

⑬ *22 km (14 mi) north of Neuchâtel.*

In the early 18th century, watchmaking was introduced in La-Chaux-de-Fonds (called "Tschaux" by locals) as a cottage industry to create income for an area otherwise completely dependent on farming. Over the years the town became the watchmaking capital of Switzerland. Destroyed by fire at the end of the 18th century, the city was rebuilt on a grid plan around the central, broad, tree-lined avenue Léopold-Robert. It is a city of incongruities: pastel-painted town houses and stone villas, working-class cafés and cultural institutions.

Famed architect Charles-Édouard Jeanneret, otherwise known as Le Corbusier, was born here. His birthplace can be seen, although not toured, along with the École d'Art, where he taught, and several villas he worked on between 1906 and 1917. Only one of his buildings is open to the public: the **Villa Turque,** north of the main avenue. It has a glowing terra-cotta-brick facade, rounded wings, and curved edges. The tourist office has a brochure outlining a walk that passes by his buildings. ✉ *147 rue du Doubs,* ☎ *032/9123131.* 🎟 *Free.* ۞ *By appointment only; call weekdays 9–11 and 2–5.*

The **Musée des Beaux-Arts** (Museum of Fine Arts), a striking neoclassical structure, was designed by Le Corbusier's teacher, L'Éplattenier. It contains three of Le Corbusier's works: a furniture set, an oil painting (*Seated Woman*), and a tapestry (*Les Musiciens*). There are also works by such other Swiss artists as Léopold Robert and Ferdinand Hodler. ✉ *33 rue des Musées,* ☎ *032/9130444.* 🎟 *6 SF, Sun. free 10–noon.* ۞ *Tues.–Sun. 10–noon and 2–5.*

★ The **Musée International d'Horlogerie** (International Timepiece Museum) displays a fascinating collection of clocks and watches that traces the development of timekeeping and the expansion of watchmaking as an art form. You can see audiovisual presentations on the history and science of the craft, observe current repairs on pieces from the collection in an open work area, and browse the gift shop, which sells replicas as well as the latest timepieces by stellar local watchmaking firms (Corum, Girard-Perregaux, Ebel, and so on). ✉ *29 rue des Musées,* ☎ *032/9676861.* 🎟 *8 SF.* ۞ *Oct.–May, Tues.–Sun. 10–noon and 2–5; June–Sept., Tues.–Sun. 10–5.*

Dining and Lodging

$$$ ✕ **Au Capucin Gourmand.** A local secret, this restaurant at the edge of town offers a hard-to-beat combination: simplicity, sincerity, and sophisticated cooking. Look for refined entrées such as grilled mountain perch with lightly steamed fennel. ✉ *125 rue de la Charrière,* ☎ *032/9681591. AE, DC, MC, V. Closed Mon. and late July–early Aug. No dinner Sun.*

$$–$$$ ⊞ **Fleur-de-Lys.** This low-key hotel offers comfortable rooms in muted mauves and aquas; there are a few extra perks, such as the fresh fruit and snacks waiting for you on top of the minibar. Though the hotel sits on the main thoroughfare, the rooms are quiet except for two weeks a year when the hotel hosts musicians for the annual music festival. ⊠ *13 av. Léopold-Robert, CH-2300,* ☎ *032/9133731,* ℻ *032/9135851. 28 rooms. Restaurant, bar, meeting room. AE, DC, MC, V.*

$ ⊞ **Du Cheval Blanc.** Behind the spring-green front of this warm, hospitable 18th-century *routier* are clean, comfortable rooms with dormer windows. It's within easy walking distance of the museums and train station. ⊠ *16 rue Hôtel-de-Ville, CH-2300,* ☎ *032/9684098,* ℻ *032/ 9684055. 13 rooms. Restaurant. V.*

Skiing

La Chaux-de-Fonds is very close to cross-country ski areas and some modest downhill runs as well. The **Tête-de-Ran,** beyond Vue des Alpes, tops 1,400 m (4,592 ft) and allows skiers to take in panoramic views toward the Bernese Alps. Together, **Vue des Alpes, Tête-de-Ran, La Corbatière,** and **Le Locle** count 31 lifts, 27 km (16 mi) of downhill runs, and 400 km (nearly 250 mi) of cross-country trails.

OFF THE
BEATEN PATH
★

LE NOIRMONT – One of Switzerland's top gourmet restaurants, Hôtel-Restaurant de la Gare, is just 20 minutes by car or train from La Chaux-de-Fonds in the direction of Saignelégier. Chef Georges Wenger creates elegant, savory dishes with both a regional and seasonal bent. A fall menu, for instance, might include roasted duck with marsala paired with pumpkin with almonds and borlotti beans. An excellent selection of cheeses and a fine wine cellar round out the experience. If you feel you can't tear yourself away, you can spend the night; upstairs are a handful of luxurious, individually decorated rooms. The hotel is very near hiking and skiing trails and an 18-hole golf course. ⊠ *2 rue de la Gare, CH-2340,* ☎ *032/9531110,* ℻ *032/951059. 5 rooms. Restaurant. AE, DC, MC, V. Closed Mon., Tues., and late Dec.–mid-Jan.* ☙

Saignelégier

⑭ *26 km (16 mi) northwest of La Chaux-de-Fonds, 36 km (22 mi) southwest of Delémont.*

A small, fairly modern town set in rolling pastures, Saignelégier is known mostly for its lush surroundings, horseback riding, and cross-country skiing. The Marché-Concours National de Chevaux (National Horse Fair), held since 1897, takes place on the second Sunday in August and draws crowds from throughout Switzerland and France, as does the Fête des Montgolfières (Hot-Air Balloon Festival) the second weekend of October.

Lodging

$ ⊞ **Café Du Soleil.** For the bohemian at heart, the Soleil is a great gathering place. Artists, writers, musicians, and passersby come for the artwork, live music (classical or jazz), and fresh vegetarian food. Rooms are spartan but clean; all have writing desks. It's just across from the town's equestrian center. The restaurant is closed on Monday. ⊠ *CH-2350,* ☎ *032/9511688,* ℻ *032/9512295. 7 rooms, 1 dormitory. Restaurant, café, terrace. MC, V.*

Outdoor Activities and Sports

BICYCLING

As soon as the snow melts, cyclists hit the cross-country tails. The Chemin de Fer du Jura (Jura Railway) offers special "Rent-a-Bike" packages;

call the local train station or the **central office** in Saignelégier (☎ 032/95118252). Call at least three days in advance.

HORSEBACK RIDING

This is terrific horseback-riding country. Many individual farms offer riding packages that include accommodations and are geared for families. Contact the tourist office for information (☞ Visitor Information *in* Fribourg, Neuchâtel, and the Jura A to Z, *below*). You can also rent horses at the **Manège de Saignelégier** (☎ 032/9511755).

SPORTS CENTER

The modern **Centre de Loisirs** (☎ 032/9512474) has an impressive array of facilities: a covered 25-m swimming pool, indoor ice rink, gymnasium, weight room, even conference rooms and a restaurant. There are cross-country ski tracks nearby. A map in front of the sports center displays a network of nearby trails for biking or hiking; trails are clearly indicated with yellow markers.

St-Ursanne

⑮ *22 km (14 mi) west of Delémont, 27 km (17 mi) from Saignelégier.*

This lovely, quiet medieval town in a valley carved by the River Doubs is best known to outdoors enthusiasts—fishermen, bicyclists, canoeists, and kayakers. The 12th-century church, **la Collégiale**, is a mixture of Romanesque and early Gothic architecture; the large cloisters are Gothic. The old stone bridge over the River Doubs, with its statue of St. John of Nepomuk, the patron saint of bridges, best catches the romantic spirit of St-Ursanne. Local restaurants often serve perch and trout from the Doubs.

Porrentruy

⑯ *13.5 km (8 mi) northwest of St-Ursanne, 28 km (mi) from Delémont.*

A small detour toward the French border brings you to the center of the Ajoie region and to this city that has an excellently preserved medieval town center. It is worth the journey just to view the impressive **Château de Porrentruy** towering over the Old Town; it is now used by cantonal offices. This was once the seat of the prince-bishops of Basel; the 13th-century Tour Réfouse (refuge tower), next to the castle, provides a beautiful view and is always open to the public. The Porte de France, a remnant of the walls of the city, and the old stone houses alongside it dramatically reflect a medieval character.

Delémont

⑰ *81 km (50 mi) northeast of Neuchâtel.*

Nestled in a wide, picturesque valley, this is the administrative seat of the Jura Canton; though it's on the French-German language divide, the official language is French. In the 11th century Delémont was annexed by the bishop-princes of Basel, who often used it as a summer residence; it remained an annex until the 18th century. The town center is still atmospheric, with its cobblestone streets and splashing 17th-century fountains. A mile northeast of town is the pilgrimage church **Chapelle du Vorbourg,** perched on a wooded outcropping. The door is usually open; masses are held Sunday and holidays at 9:30 AM.

Dining and Lodging

$$–$$$ ✕🏨 **Hotel du Midi.** This unassuming, charming hotel may be off the tourist-trammeled path, but it hasn't gone undiscovered. Reservations are essential on weekends if you want to savor delicacies such as frog-

leg soup or a simmering beef pot-au-feu. The warmly decorated rooms are tucked under the roof on the third floor; all have a view over the town. ⊠ *10 pl. de la Gare, CH-2800, ☎ 032/4221777, ﬂĀﾮ 032/ 4231989. 4 rooms. Restaurant. DC, MC, V. Closed Wed.*

En Route   Between La Chaux-de-Fonds and Delémont (just 11 mi [6½ mi] south of Delémont), the medieval town of **Moutier** produces the creamy, piquant Vacherin Mont d'Or and the smooth-texture Tête de Moine (monk's head) cheese eaten in finely shaved ruffles, the only reminder of the town's once-renowned monastery of Bellelay.

FRIBOURG, NEUCHÂTEL, AND THE JURA A TO Z

Arriving and Departing

By Car

An important and scenic trans-Swiss artery, the **A12** expressway, cuts from Bern to Lausanne, passing directly above Fribourg; a parallel northwestern route approaches from Basel by expressway (**A1**) to Solothurn, then changes to a secondary highway and follows the northwestern shore of Lake Neuchâtel, with brief sections of expressway at Neuchâtel itself and from Yverdon on down to Lac Léman. A slow but scenic route along A18 cuts from Basel through the Jura by way of Delémont.

By Plane

Geneva's **Cointrin** Airport (⊠ 138 km/86 mi southwest of Fribourg, ☎ 022/7177111) is the second-busiest international airport in Switzerland. Frequent flights from the United States and the United Kingdom arrive on **Swissair** and other international carriers via Cointrin. Bern's small airport, **Belp** (⊠ 34 km/21 mi northeast of Fribourg, ☎ 031/ 9613411), services **Crossair** and **KLM-Alps** (☎ 084/8852000).

By Train

The main train route between Basel, Zürich, and Geneva passes through the **Fribourg station** (⊠ av. de la Gare, ☎ 0900/300300, 1.19 SF/min) between Bern and Lausanne. Trains generally arrive twice an hour.

Getting Around

By Boat

There are boat trips on the lakes of Neuchâtel, Murten (Morat), and Biel (Bienne), as well as on the Aare River and the Broye Canal, a natural wildlife sanctuary. Schedules vary seasonally but in summer are frequent and include evening trips. Contact **Compagnie de la Navigation** (☎ 032/7534012) for more information.

By Bus

Postbus connections, except in the principal urban areas, can be few and far between; plan excursions carefully using the bus schedules available at the train station.

By Car

The charms of this varied region can be seen best by car, and there are scenic secondary highways throughout. Keep in mind that some towns, like Gruyères, are car-free or have pedestrians-only centers; in these cases, parking lots are easy to find.

By Train

Secondary connections are thin, but they allow visits to most towns. To visit Gruyères, you must take a bus out of Broc.

Contacts and Resources

Emergencies

Police: (☎ 117). Fribourg (☎ 117 or 026/3051818). Neuchâtel (☎ 117 or 032/7222222). **Ambulance or medical emergency:** (☎ 026/4225500). Fribourg and Neuchâtel (☎ 117). **Medical and dental referrals:** Fribourg (☎ 026/3223343). Neuchâtel (☎ 032/7222222).

Guided Tours

Guided walks of Neuchâtel with English commentary can be arranged for parties of up to 25 persons. They last about two hours and cost 100 SF per person. Contact the tourist office (☞ *below*) for information.

Visitor Information

The regional office for Canton Fribourg is based in **Fribourg** (✉ 1107 rue de la Glâne, CH-1700, ☎ 026/4025644, FAX 026/4023119, ✍). The regional office for Canton Neuchâtel (as well as its city tourist office) is based in **Neuchâtel** (✉ Hôtel des Postes, CH-2000, ☎ 032/8896890, FAX 032/8896291, ✍). The Jura's regional office is found in **Saignelégier** (✉ 1 rue de la Gruere, CH-2350, ☎ 032/9521952, FAX 032/9521955, ✍).

Local tourist offices: **Avenches** (✉ 3 pl. de l'Église, CH-1580, ☎ 026/6769922). **Charmey** (✉ CH-1637, ☎ 026/92721498). **Estavayer-le-Lac** (✉ pl. du Midi, CH-1470, ☎ 026/6631237). **Fribourg** (✉ 1 av. de la Gare, CH-1700, ☎ 026/3213175, FAX 026/3223527). **Gruyères** (✉ CH-1663, ☎ 026/9211030). **La Chaux-de-Fonds** (✉ 1 Espacité, CH-2302, ☎ 032/9196895). **Murten** (✉ 6 Franz-Kirchg., CH-3280, ☎ 026/6705112). **Porrentruy** (✉ 5 Grand Rue, CH-2900, ☎ 032/4665959). **St-Ursanne** (✉ CH-2882, ☎ 032/4613716). **Yverdon-les-Bains** (✉ 1 pl. Pestalozzi, CH-1400, ☎ 024/4236290).

9 BERN

WITH AN EXCURSION
TO THE EMMENTAL

Humble and down-to-earth, Bern is a city of
broad medieval streets, farmers' markets,
and friendly, slow-spoken people. It is also
the federal capital of Switzerland and, more
remarkably, a World Cultural Heritage city
known for its sandstone arcades, fountains,
and thick, sturdy towers. A short drive
outside the city will take you to the farm-
sprinkled lowlands of the Emmental region.

Updated by
Susan
Tuttle-Laube

T HOUGH BERN IS THE SWISS CAPITAL, you won't find much cosmopolitan nonsense here: the *cuisine du marché,* based on the freshest ingredients available in the local market, features fatback and sauerkraut; the annual fair fetes the humble onion; and the president of the Swiss Confederation often takes the tram to work. It's fitting, too, that a former Swiss patent-office clerk, Albert Einstein, began developing his theory of relativity in Bern. Warm, friendly, down-to-earth, the Bernese are notoriously slow-spoken; ask a question and then pull up a chair while they formulate a judicious response. Their mascot is a common bear; they keep some as pets in the center of town. Walking down broad medieval streets past squares crowded with farmers' markets and cafés full of shirt-sleeve politicos, you might forget that Bern is the geographic and political hub of a sophisticated, modern, and prosperous nation.

Although Bern is full of patrician houses and palatial hotels, there is no official presidential residence: the seven members of the coalition government, each of whom serves a year as president, have to find their own places to live when in Bern.

Bern wasn't always so self-effacing. It earned its pivotal position through a history of power and influence that dates from the 12th century, when Berchtold V, duke of Zähringen and one of the countless rulers within the Holy Roman Empire, established a fortress on this gooseneck in the River Aare. A descendent of the German Alemanni tribes, whose penetration into Switzerland can roughly be measured by the areas where Swiss German is spoken today, he chose Bern not only for its impregnable location—it's a steep promontory of rock girded on three sides by the river—but also for its proximity to the great kingdom of Burgundy, which spread across France and much of present-day French-speaking Switzerland.

By the 14th century Bern had grown into a strong urban republic. When the last Zähringens died, the people of Bern defeated their would-be replacements and, shedding the Holy Roman Empire, became the eighth canton to join the rapidly growing Swiss Confederation. It was an unlikely union: aristocratic, urban Bern allied with the strongly democratic farming communities of central Switzerland. But it provided the Bernese with enough security against the Habsburg Holy Roman Empire to continue westward expansion.

Despite a devastating fire that laid waste to the city in 1405, by the late 15th century the Bernese had become a power of European stature—a stature enhanced exponentially by three decisive victories over the duke of Burgundy in 1476 and 1477. Aided by the other cantons and prompted by Louis XI, king of France and bitter enemy of the Burgundians, the Bernese crushed Charles the Bold and drove him out of his Swiss lands. Not only did the Bernese expand their territories all the way west to Geneva, but they also acquired immense wealth—great treasures of gold, silver, and precious textiles—and assumed the leading role in Switzerland and Swiss affairs.

Bern stayed on top. Through the 17th and 18th centuries, the city's considerable prosperity was built not so much on commerce as on the export of troops and military know-how. The city and her territories functioned essentially as a patrician state, ruled by an aristocracy that saw its raison d'être in politics, foreign policy, the acquisition of new lands, and the forging of alliances. At the same time, her landed gentry continued to grow fat on the fruits of the city's rich agricultural lands. Napoléon seized the lands briefly from 1798 until his defeat in

1815, but by the 1830s the Bernese were back in charge, and when the Swiss Confederation took its contemporary, democratic form in 1848, Bern was a natural choice for its capital.

Yet today it's not the massive Bundeshaus (Houses of Parliament) that dominates the city but instead its perfectly preserved arcades, fountains, and thick, stalwart towers—all remnants of its heyday as a medieval power. They're the reason UNESCO granted Bern World Cultural Heritage status, along with the Egyptian pyramids, Rome, Florence, and the Taj Mahal.

Pleasures and Pastimes

Arcades

Like a giant cloister, Bern is crisscrossed by *Lauben* (arcades) that shelter stores of every kind and quality. Stout 15th-century pillars support the low vaulted roofs, which extend to the edge of the pavement below. At the base of many arcades, nearly horizontal cellar doors lead down into interesting underground eateries and businesses. Combined with Bern's sturdy towers and narrow cobbled streets, the arcades distinguish the city as one of the country's best-preserved medieval towns.

Flowers

Geranium-filled window boxes are as common a sight in Bern as ruins are in Rome. In 1897 Bern formed a preservation society to encourage citizens to decorate their houses with flowers. In 1902 this society began to decorate the public fountains and then, a few years later, the windows of buildings in the Old Town. In 1984 Bern won the title of Europe's most floral city, and the geranium is the city's official flower. The hillside Rosengarten (Rose Garden) and the city's flower market have added to Bern's renown as a blossoming city.

Fountains

Throughout Bern, scores of brilliantly colored and skillfully carved fountains—their bases surrounded by flowers—provide relief from the structural severity of the medieval houses that form their backdrop. Like the stelae of Athens, these fountains remind the Bernese of their virtuous forbears: witness the Anna Seilerbrunnen, an ode to temperance and moderation, and the Gerechtigkeitsbrunnen, with a personification of Justice standing over several severed heads. Most are the work of Hans Gieng, who created them between 1539 and 1546.

Markets

In the Middle Ages, Bern was a great marketing center, and markets today—with stands hawking everything from geraniums to meats—are still an integral part of daily life. The lone surviving market from medieval Bern is the Zwibelemärit (Onion Market), which takes place on the fourth Monday in November. Draped from scores of stalls are long strips of onions woven into the shapes of dolls, animals, and even alarm clocks. The Onion Market dates from the 1405 fire: in gratitude for assistance given by Fribourg, Bern granted farmers the right to sell their onions in the city's market square.

Museums

As the nation's capital, Bern offers a satisfying concentration of museums, including the stellar Kunstmuseum, full of fine art, and its massive Historisches Museum, displaying war trophies and church treasures. All uniquely Swiss are the original Museum für Kommunikation; the Schweizerisches Alpines Museum, exploring the Alps and their conquest; and the Schweizerisches Schützenmuseum, about the innately Swiss love of sharpshooting.

EXPLORING BERN

Because Bern stands on a high, narrow peninsula formed by a goose-neck in the Aare, its streets seem to follow the river's flow, running in long parallels to its oldest, easternmost point; from afar, its uniform red-tile roofs seem to ooze like glowing lava down the length of the promontory. The Old Town was founded on the farthest tip and grew westward; its towers mark those stages of growth like rings on a tree.

Numbers in the text correspond to numbers in the margin and on the Bern map.

Great Itineraries

IF YOU HAVE 1 OR 2 DAYS

You can visit Bern's Old Town in a single day; but two days will allow you a more leisurely pace, with plenty of time for museums and shopping. Starting at the main train station, the Hauptbahnhof, you can move eastward through the towers, fountains, and arcades of the Old Town to the site of Bern's founding at Nydeggkirche. Across the Aare are more museums, the Rosengarten, and the embassy row of Thunstrasse. Back on the north side of the river, the Münster and the Bundeshaus are not to be missed.

IF YOU HAVE 3 TO 5 DAYS

If you're making an extended stay in Bern, spend the first few days as above, exploring the town. To help round out the city's history, visit the Historisches Museum, or try the Naturhistorisches Museum, which is considered one Europe's best natural history museums. Then escape for a half- or full-day drive through the Emmental to experience a landscape that has been left virtually untouched since the 19th century (☞ Excursion to the Emmental, *below*). If you're anxious to get an even closer look at the mountains, head into the Berner Oberland, one hour away. You can visit the Jungfrau region by train, taking the Interlaken–Grindelwald–Klein Scheidegg–Jungfraujoch route (and, weather permitting, Wengen) in a single long day (☞ Chapter 10).

Old Town

Now a pedestrian zone, the old city center west of the river retains a distinctly medieval appeal—thanks to the 1405 fire that destroyed its predominantly wooden structures. The city was rebuilt in sandstone, with arcades stretching on for some 6 km (4 mi).

As medieval as it may look, this old city is decidedly modern, with countless shops concentrated between the Hauptbahnhof (main train station) and the Zytgloggeturm (Clock Tower)—especially on Spitalgasse and Marktgasse. Beyond, along Kramgasse and Gerechtigkeitsgasse and, parallel to them on the north, Postgasse, there are quirkier, bohemian spots and excellent antiques stores. You may hear the Bernese calling the area east of the clock tower the *Altstadt* (Old Town), as its 800 years of commerce give it seniority over the mere 15th-century upstarts to the west.

A Good Walk

Start on the busy Bahnhofplatz in front of the grand old Schweizerhof Hotel, facing the Hauptbahnhof. To your left is the **Heiliggeistkirche** ①. If you turn right down the Bollwerk, away from the church, and veer right down Genfergasse, you'll reach the **Kunstmuseum** ②, on the right at Hodlerstrasse. If you turn left and go back up Bollwerk just past the church, you'll come to the beginning of Spitalgasse on your left. Head down this wide street and walk *outside* the arcades (keeping an eye out for trams) to see some of the city's stunning architecture; if you walk inside the sheltered walkways, you'll be seduced by modern shops and cafés.

Head for the **Pfeiferbrunnen,** or Bagpiper Fountain. At the edge of the Bärenplatz stands the **Käfigturm** ③, once a medieval city gate. Continue down Marktgasse past the **Anna Seilerbrunnen,** an allegory on moderation, and the **Schützenbrunnen,** or Marksman Fountain, a tribute to a troop commander from 1543. Just beyond and spreading to your left lie the Kornhausplatz and the imposing 18th-century **Kornhaus** ④, now a popular restaurant (☞ Dining, *below*). In the Kornhausplatz, the ogre depicted in the **Kindlifresserbrunnen** is worth a second look: he's munching on a meal of small children.

Dominating town center, the mighty **Zytgloggeturm** ⑤ entertains with its hourly mechanical puppet performance. Continue down Kramgasse, a lovely old street with many guild houses, some fine 18th-century residences, more arcades, and, of course, more fountains: first the **Zähringerbrunnen,** or Zähringen Fountain, a monument to Bern's founder, Berchtold V; then the powerful depiction of Samson on the **Simsonbrunnen.** Between the fountains on your right at No. 49 is the **Einsteinhaus** ⑥, once Albert Einstein's apartment and workplace.

Turn left at the next opening (Kreuzgasse) and make a brief diversion to the Rathausplatz and, at its north end, the **Rathaus** ⑦ itself. Across from it stands the **Vennerbrunnen,** or Ensign Fountain, with the figure of a Bernese standard-bearer.

Return as you came and turn left on the main thoroughfare, now called Gerechtigkeitsgasse. You'll pass the **Gerechtigkeitsbrunnen,** or Justice Fountain. Beyond are some lovely 18th-century houses. At No. 7 is the Gasthaus zum Goldenen Adler (☞ Lodging, *below*). Built between 1764 and 1766, it has a particularly captivating coat of arms by locksmith Samuel Rüetschi.

A left turn at the bottom of Gerechtigkeitsgasse will take you steeply down Nydegg Stalden through one of the oldest parts of the city; the **Nydeggkirche** ⑧ is on your right. The sudden quiet of this ancient neighborhood is magical. Down the hill stands the **Läuferbrunnen,** the image of a city herald. Take the Untertorbrücke, or Lower Gate Bridge, across the Aare.

From here, it's a short, steep climb to the east end of the high Nydeggbrücke. If you're feeling energetic, it's well worth crossing the road and either climbing a small path to the left, turning right at the top; or turning right and then left to walk up the broader Alter Aargauerstalden, where you'll turn left. Either will bring you to the **Rosengarten** ⑨, its roses in spectacular bloom from June to October.

Head back down to the Nydeggbrücke but don't cross it yet: on your left, facing the Old Town, you'll find the famous **Bärengraben** ⑩, home to the city's mascots.

Cross the bridge and turn left up Junkerngasse, notable for its fine old houses. Number 59 is the elegant 15th-century **Béatrice von Wattenwyl House,** where the Swiss government gives receptions. In contrast, No. 51 has a gorgeous, unrestored, painted facade that stands out in its dilapidated grandeur. At the top of Junkerngasse, you come to the pride of the city: the magnificent Gothic **Münster** ⑪. On leaving the cathedral, head left to the terrace on its south side. Many of the square's chestnut trees are from the original 18th-century planting. Look east, in the direction you just came from, for a view of the impressive south-side facades of the patrician houses and their gardens leading down to the **Matte** neighborhood.

Bureau de change

Cambio

外国為替

I n this city, you can find money
on almost any street.

NO-FEE FOREIGN EXCHANGE

The Chase Manhattan Bank has over 80 convenient
locations near New York City destinations such as:
Times Square
Rockefeller Center
Empire State Building
2 World Trade Center
United Nations Plaza
Exchange any of 75 foreign currencies

 CHASE

THE RIGHT RELATIONSHIP IS EVERYTHING.®

Cross the Münsterplatz, passing by the **Mosesbrunnen**. Follow Münstergasse, taking a moment to check out No. 62 (the Mayhaus)—the huge, enclosed 1895 balcony connecting two 16th-century houses is held up by a muscled figure whose facial expression is worth a double take. At the street's end turn left into Casinoplatz, where you'll find the so-called **Casino** (actually a restaurant and concert locale). At this point, by crossing the river on the panoramic Kirchenfeldbrücke to Helvetiaplatz, you can visit six major museums that are conveniently grouped together. Just across the bridge, immediately on your left, you'll see the contemporary **Kunsthalle** ⑫. On your right is the **Schweizerisches Alpines Museum** ⑬, for armchair climbers and real ones, too. Across the square behind the massive fountain of Mother Helvetica is the **Historisches Museum** ⑭, where armor and arms, tapestries, and church treasures illustrate Bern's 15th-century victory over Burgundy.

Leaving the history museum, turn left and follow Bernastrasse a half block down. Adjoining the museum at the back is the **Schweizerisches Schützenmuseum** ⑮. Continue down Bernastrasse to the **Naturhistorisches Museum** ⑯. On leaving the museum, head left and then turn left onto Hallylerstrasse, then left again onto Helvetiastrasse, where you'll find the **Museum für Kommunikation** ⑰, tracing the evolution of the Swiss mail system. When you are done with the museums, you can nip down the Thunstrasse for a look at the impressive buildings that make up Embassy Row.

Head back over the Kirchenfeldbrücke, toward Casinoplatz, but turn left into the little alley just after crossing the bridge and stroll along the terrace behind the **Bundeshaus** ⑱. This spot affords another fine view across the river and, in good weather, to the distant Alps; at the bridge end of the parapet is a diagram to help you pick out the principal peaks. You can walk around the Bundeshaus into the Bundesplatz and then into the traffic-free (and bear-free) Bärenplatz. On Tuesday and Saturday mornings, a lively market spills into surrounding streets.

TIMING

You can tour the Old Town in a single day, leaving extra time for the Bärengraben, Münster, and Rosengarten (in clear weather). If you'll be in Bern longer, leave an afternoon for at least one of the many museums, or indulge your whims in the arcade shops. Arrive at the Zytgloggeturm five minutes before the hour at the very latest: the mechanical figures spring into action at precisely four minutes to, and it's best to leave time to claim a spot on the street.

Sights to See

☙ *following the text of a review is your signal that the property has a Web site, where you will find details and, usually, images; for a link, visit www.fodors.com/urls.*

★ ☕ ⑩ **Bärengraben** (Bear Pits). Since the late 1400s, the Bear Pits have been digs for the city's mascots: fat brown bears that clown and beg for carrots, which vendors provide for tourists and loyal townsfolk. According to legend, Berchtold V announced that he would name the new city for the first animal he killed. It was a bear, of course; in those days the woods were full of them. The German plural for bears is *Bären*, and you'll see their images everywhere in Bern: on flags, the city coat of arms, buildings, statues, chocolates, and umbrellas, and—of course—as stuffed toys. Note that, in spite of its name, you won't find the real critters at Bärenplatz, but rather at the east end of the peninsula just across the river. ✉ *South side of Nydeggbrücke.* ☉ *Daily, summer 8–6, winter 9–4.*

224

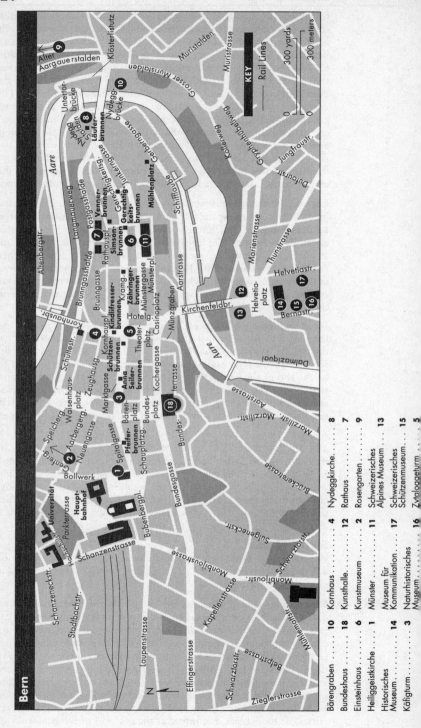

Bern

KEY

—— Rail Lines

0   300 yards
0   300 meters

⑱ Bundeshaus (Houses of Parliament). This hulking, domed building is the beating heart of the Swiss Confederation and meeting place of the Swiss National Council. Free guided tours (in English) include entry to the parliamentary chambers, where there's a spectacular mural of Lake Luzern, considered the cradle of the Confederation. ✉ *Bundespl.,* ☎ *031/3228522.* ⊙ *Tours Mon.–Sat. at 9, 10, 11, 2, 3, and 4, Sun. at 10, 11, 2, and 3. Can vary according to Parliament sessions.*

⑥ Einsteinhaus (Einstein's House). For a bit of recent history, you can visit the apartment and workplace of Albert Einstein. It was during his stay here that, at the age of 26, he published his *Special Theory of Relativity.* ✉ *Kramg. 49,* ☎ *031/3120091.* ▦ *3 SF.* ⊙ *Feb.–Nov., Tues.–Fri. 10–5 and Sat. 10–4. Closed Dec.–Jan.*

❶ Heiliggeistkirche (Church of the Holy Ghost). Completed in 1729, the sanctuary adds a bit of baroque flamboyance to the otherwise medieval Old Town. Like a fly caught in a web, the building is surrounded by tram and bus electrical lines; its ornateness contrasts with the neighborhood—not exactly Bern's nicest. ✉ *Spitalg. 44, across from Hauptbahnhof.* ⊙ *Tues.–Fri. 11–7.*

★ **⑭ Historisches Museum** (Historical Museum). Much of this enormous, enlightening collection is booty from victories over Burgundy, including magnificent tapestries "acquired" in 1476–77, when the Bernese pushed Charles the Bold back into France. There are armor and arms, lavish church treasures (including 15th- and 16th-century stained-glass windows), and the original Last Judgment sculptures from the cathedral's portal. Don't miss the novel three-way portrait of Calvin, Zwingli, and Luther. Among the important exhibitions about the outside world is an exceptional Islamic collection. ✉ *Helvetiapl. 5,* ☎ *031/3507711.* ▦ *5 SF.* ⊙ *Tues.–Sun. 10–5.*

❸ Käfigturm (Prison Tower). A city entrance from the 13th and 14th centuries (later restored in the 18th century), when the limits of Bern extended only this far west, the Käfigturm served as a prison until 1897. ✉ *Marktg. 67.*

❹ Kornhaus (Granary). The imposing 18th-century Kornhaus has a magnificent cellar, now a popular Bernese restaurant (☞ Dining, *below*), which once held wine brought to town by farmers as a tribute to the patrician city government. The upper stories house the **Forum für Media und Gestaltung** (Forum for Media and Design), which hosts exhibitions and events devoted to design, architecture, contemporary media, video, photography, and applied art. ✉ *Kornhauspl. 18.* ☎ *031/3129110.* ▦ *Varies with exhibition/event.* ⊙ *Tues.– Wed., Fri. 10–7, Thurs. 10–9, weekends 10–5.*

⑫ Kunsthalle (Art Gallery). Not to be confused with the traditional Kunstmuseum, this ground-breaking contemporary art venue has no permanent collection, but displays temporary exhibits of living artists, usually before you've heard of them. Built in 1918 in heroic classical style to boost local artists—Kirchner, Klee, Hodler—it grew to attract the young Kandinsky, Miró, Sol LeWitt, Richard Long, Cy Twombly—and a parade of newcomers of strong potential. ✉ *Helvetiapl. 1,* ☎ *031/3510031.* ▦ *6 SF.* ⊙ *Tues. 10–9, Wed.–Sun. 10–5.*

★ **❷ Kunstmuseum** (Art Museum). Just down the hill and three blocks from the Hauptbahnhof, this important museum displays the third-largest art collection in Switzerland—and the largest gathering of works by Paul Klee in the world, with more than 2,000 examples of this native son's skills. From another Bern native, the symbolist Ferdinand Hodler, there are striking allegories (some enormous), landscapes, and portraits;

works by Swiss artists Stauffer, Anker, and Böcklin are also shown. But the Kunstmuseum's concentration is not entirely Swiss, with masterworks ranging from Fra Angelico to Cézanne, Rouault, and Picasso. It also has a cafeteria and a cinema. ✉ *Hodlerstr. 8–12,* ☎ *031/ 3110944.* 🎟 *6 SF.* ⏱ *Tues. 10–9, Wed.–Sun. 10–5.* ✎

Matte. In the narrow row houses below the patrician residences of Junkerngasse, laborers once lived along the banks of the Aare. In those days, as today, the neighborhood was called *Matte,* and was the most sociable, raucous part of town. In the same tradition that produced Cockney rhyming slang, there developed a bizarre dialect—*Mattenenglisch*—that can still be heard today, though it has grown so rare that its proponents have formed a club to keep it alive. Spotted with Yiddish and Gypsy terms, the dialect derives its name from *Matten* (lowland or meadow) and *Englisch* (unintelligible). Even if you don't hear the local tongue, Matte is a lovely old neighborhood to wander, with tiny shops tucked here and there. From the cathedral terrace, take the 183 steps or ride the funky little outdoor elevator (1 SF) down to the river. There's a flea market here on Mühleplatz every third Saturday from May through October. ✉ *Off Gerbeng. and below Junkerng.*

★ ⑪ **Münster** (Cathedral). Started in 1421 by master mason Matthäus Ensinger, Bern's famous cathedral was planned on lines so spacious that half the population could worship in it at one time. The smaller church on the site was kept intact and functioning during construction. Only later was it demolished and removed piece by piece through the main portal of the new cathedral, whose construction went on for centuries. Even the Reformation, the impact of which converted it from a Catholic to a Protestant church, did not halt the work. Daniel Heinz directed construction for 25 years (from 1573 to 1598), completing the nave and the tower. The finishing touch, the tip of the 100-m (328-ft) steeple (the highest in Switzerland), was added only in 1893. Today you can ascend it by a dizzying 254-step spiral staircase to enjoy a panorama of red roofs, the Aare, and if the weather is clear, the Bernese Alps.

The cathedral has two outstanding features, one outside and one in. Outside is the **main portal,** with a magnificent representation of the Last Judgment (1490) composed of 234 carved figures—heaven is on the left, hell on the right. This work was completed immediately before the Reformation, but it escaped destruction by the iconoclasts who emptied the niches of the side portals. The main portal was recently restored and painted in vivid—some may say jarring—colors. Green demons with gaping red maws and ivory-skin angels with gilt hair appear with Technicolor intensity.

Inside the church, while the elaborately carved pews and choir stalls are worth attention, note the **stained glass,** especially the 15th-century windows of the choir, dealing as much with local heraldry as with Christian iconography. ✉ *Münsterpl. 1,* ☎ *031/3110572.* ⏱ *Easter Sun.– Oct. 31, Tues.–Sat. 10–5, Sun. 11:30–5; Nov.–Easter, Sun., Tues.–Fri. 10–noon and 2–4, Sat. 10–noon and 2–5, Sun. 11:30–2.*

⑰ **Museum für Kommunikation** (Communications Museum). Housed in a modern building behind the Historical Museum, this high-concept interactive museum has detailed documents, art, and artifacts of early technology relating to the history of the mails in Switzerland. There's a magnificent stamp and postmark collection, one of the largest and most valuable in the world, exhibited in sleek sliding-glass trays. ✉ *Helvetiastr. 16,* ☎ *031/3575555.* 🎟 *5 SF.* ⏱ *Tues.–Sun. 10–5.*

★ ☙ ⑯ **Naturhistorisches Museum** (Museum of Natural History). Considered one of Europe's finest museums of natural history, this beloved institution has a huge display area with a slick, skylighted four-story wing. It has enormous, evocative wildlife dioramas, as well as row upon row of Victorian oak-and-beveled-glass cases mounting varied species of mammals like so many butterflies. Its quirkiest trophy: the stuffed body of Barry, a St. Bernard that saved more than 40 people in the Alps in the last century. There's also a splendid collection of Alpine minerals. ⊠ *Bernastr. 15,* ☎ *031/3507111.* ⊠ *5 SF.* ⊙ *Mon. 2–5, Tues., Thurs.– Fri. 9–5, Wed. 9–8, weekends 10–5.*

OFF THE BEATEN PATH

☞ **TIERPARK DÄHLHÖLZLI –** Here is a zoo with a difference: parts of the animal habitats are in a densely forested natural woodland park along the Aare river and can be visited anytime day or night. Come by at the right moment, and you'll get a peek at the animals behind the trees. The proper zoo part has some exotic species and a vivarium full of reptiles and fish. The majority of the zoo's creatures are European: wolves, chamois, lynx, seals, and—of course—bears. The zoo is an easy trip south on Bus 18. ⊠ *Tierparkweg 1,* ☎ *031/3571515. Habitats:* ⊠ *Free.* ⊙ *Daily 24 hours. Zoo, Vivarium, Petting Zoo:* ⊠ *7 SF.* ⊙ *Apr.– Sept., daily 8–6:30; Oct.–Mar., daily 9–5.*

❽ Nydeggkirche (Nydegg Church). Built in 1341–46, the Nydegg Church stands on the ruins of Berchtold V's first fortress (destroyed about 1260–70), the site of Bern's founding. You can see parts of the original foundation below the chancel; there's also a wooden pulpit from 1566. ⊠ *Nydegg.,* ☎ *031/3116102.* ⊙ *Mon.–Sat. 10–noon and 2–5:30, Sun. 10–noon.*

❼ Rathaus (Town Hall). Bern's stately Town Hall is the seat of the cantonal government. Along with the city's arcades, it was built after the great fire of 1405 and still retains its simple Gothic lines. It's not open to the public. ⊠ *Rathauspl. 2.*

★ **❾ Rosengarten** (Rose Garden). In this splendidly arranged and well-maintained garden, some 160 varieties of roses bloom from June to October. One of Bern's most popular gathering places, this is a great vantage point from which to admire the Jungfrau, Eiger, and Mönch—on clear days only. ⊠ *Alter Aargauerstalden.* ⊠ *Free.* ⊙ *Daily sunrise–sunset.*

⑬ Schweizerisches Alpines Museum (Swiss Alpine Museum). This arcane but eye-opening museum of the Alps has topographical maps and reliefs and displays illustrating the history of mountain climbing, alongside epic art and fine old photos. There's an enormous model of the Berner Oberland (indispensable for getting your bearings if you're headed for that region) under a magnificent Hodler mural of the tragic conquest of the Matterhorn. ⊠ *Helvetiapl. 4,* ☎ *031/3510434.* ⊠ *5 SF.* ⊙ *Late Feb.–mid-Oct., Mon. 2–5, Tues.–Sun. 10–5; mid-Oct.–late Feb., Mon. 2–5, Tues.–Sun. 10–noon and 2–5.*

⑮ Schweizerisches Schützenmuseum (Swiss Rifle Museum). Run by the Swiss Marksmen's Association, the institution pays homage to this very Swiss art. With a large collection of guns in every imaginable form, the museum traces the evolution of firearms from 1817; with trophies, it celebrates centuries of straight shooting, as Swiss sharpshooters have always measured themselves against the apple-splitting accuracy of archer Wilhelm Tell. ⊠ *Bernastr. 5,* ☎ *031/3510127.* ⊠ *Free.* ⊙ *Tues.–Sat. 2–4, Sun. 10–noon and 2–4.*

★ **❺ Zytgloggeturm** (Clock Tower). Bern's oldest building, the mighty Clock Tower, was built in 1191 as the western gate to the then-smaller city. Today it dominates the town center with its high copper spire and a massive astronomical clock and calendar, built on its east side in 1530.

As an added attraction, a delightful group of mechanical figures performs every hour. To see the show, it's best to take up a position at the corner of Kramgasse and Hotelgasse at least five minutes before the hour: you won't be the only one there.

At four minutes to the hour, heralded by a jester nodding his head and ringing two small bells, the show begins. From a small arch on the left appear a couple of musically inclined bears—a drummer and a piper—leading a procession made up of a horseman with a sword, a bear wearing a crown, and lesser bears, each carrying a gun, a sword, or a spear. When the procession ends, a cockerel on the left crows and flaps his wings, a knight in golden armor above hammers out the hour, and Father Time, on a throne in the middle, beats time with a scepter in one hand and an hourglass in the other. ⊠ *Kramg.*

DINING

Although Bern strikes a diplomatic balance in heading French-Swiss and German-Swiss politics, its Teutonic nature conquers Gaul when it comes to cuisine. Dining in Bern is usually a down-to-earth affair, with Italian home cooking running a close popular second to the local standard fare: German-style meat and potatoes. The most widespread specialty is the famous *Bernerplatte*, a meaty version of Alsatian *choucroûte*—great slabs of salt pork, beef tongue, smoky bacon, pork ribs, and mild, pink pork sausages cooked down in broth and heaped on a broad platter over juniper-scented sauerkraut, green beans, and boiled potatoes. When a waitress eases this wide load onto the table before you, you may glance around to see who's sharing: one serving can seem enough for four. Another meaty classic is the Berner version of *Ratsherrtopf*, traditionally enjoyed by the town councillors: veal shank cooked in white wine, butter, and sage.

CATEGORY	COST*
$$$$	over 80 SF
$$$	50 SF–80 SF
$$	20 SF–50 SF
$	under 20 SF

Prices are per person for a three-course meal (two-course meal in $ category), including sales tax and 15% service charge

$$$$ ★ ✕ **Bellevue-Grill.** When Parliament is in session, this haute-cuisine landmark in the Bellevue Palace (☞ Lodging, *below*) is transformed from a local gourmet mecca to a political clubhouse where movers and shakers confer over unusual dishes such as roast breast of duck in a sauce with a hint of coffee or beef fillet with truffle noodles. The ambience is one of pure luxury. ⊠ *Kocherg. 3–5,* ☎ *031/3204545. Reservations essential. Jacket. AE, DC, MC, V.*

$$$$ ★ ✕ **Schultheissenstube.** The intimate, rustic dining room, with a club-like bar and an adjoining, even more rustic all-wood *Stübli* (tavern-café), looks less like a gastronomic haven than a country pub, but this is formal dining at its best. The cooking is sophisticated, international, and imaginative—consider salmon fillet with a coulis of tomato and black truffles—and the wine list, encyclopedic. ⊠ *Hotel Schweizerhof (☞ Lodging, below), Bahnhofpl. 11,* ☎ *031/3268080. Reservations essential. Jacket in dining room. AE, DC, MC, V. Closed Sun. and July.*

$$$ ✕ **Jack's Brasserie.** This dining room at street level, with high ceilings, wainscoting, and roomy banquettes is airy, bustling, and cosmopolitan. Enjoy a drink here by day at bare-top tables or settle in at mealtime for smartly served Swiss standards (don't miss the Wiener schnitzel), French bistro classics, or a great Sunday breakfast buffet.

⊠ *Hotel Schweizerhof (☞ Lodging, below), Bahnhofpl. 11, ☎ 031/ 3268080. AE, DC, MC, V.*

$$$ ✕ **Verdi.** Named for the Italian opera composer, this restaurant is nothing if not theatrical. There are framed pieces of opera memorabilia, carved wood ceilings, chandeliers, velvet drapes, and occasionally even opera singers to entertain guests between courses. Amazingly, it isn't the least bit kitschy. Chef Giovanni D'Ambrogio even cooks specialties from Verdi's hometown region of Emilia-Romagna. Try his spaghetti Scarpara, with an excellent, garlicky tomato sauce, or the sliced steak on a bed of arugula with Parmesan. Reservations are essential if you want to even get near this popular spot on weekends. ⊠ *Gerechtigkeitsg. 5, ☎ 031/3126368. AE, DC, MC, V.*

$$$ ✕ **Zimmermania.** This deceptively simple bistro has been in business
★ for more than 150 years and is a local favorite for authentic French-bourgeois cooking. The owner visits Paris regularly to update his exceptional seasonal menu. Try their cheese soufflé or veal kidneys in mustard sauce or any of their ocean fish specialties. For a special vintage, ask for the separate French wine list. ⊠ *Brunng. 19, ☎ 031/ 3111542. AE, MC, V. Closed Sun.–Mon.*

$$–$$$ ✕ **Kornhauskeller.** Extensive renovations carefully and reverently lifted this historic spot from beer hall to high society. The vaulted ceilings and frescoes in the old city wine cellar below the Granary are nothing short of spectacular. The menu covers all bases, from local fare to French, Italian, and even Asian dishes; the wine list is extensive. Besides the dining room there are a whiskey lounge and a humidor. An offshoot at street level, the Kornhaus Café, makes a good stop for a light lunch, supper, or cocktail. A reservation is a good idea. ⊠ *Kornhauspl. 18, ☎ 031/3277272. AE, DC, MC, V.*

$$–$$$ ✕ **Zum Zähringer.** For a quiet meal out of range of the city's bustle, head down to the river to this restaurant in the Matte neighborhood. The emphasis here is on fresh and local ingredients. The staff will even tell you the name of the farmer who provides the pork. The menu changes according to the season and the whims of the chef—you might find delicate pumpkin ravioli, a meaty veal shank with a subtle wine sauce, or an original vegetarian dish. One constant: the daily fish special is always a hit. ⊠ *Badg. 1, ☎ 031/3113270. MC, V. Closed Sun.*

$$ ✕ **Brasserie zum Bärengraben.** Directly across from the Bear Pits, this popular, easygoing little local institution is a place to settle in with a newspaper and a *Dezi* (deciliter) of wine. You'll find old-style basics— *Kalbskopf* (chopped veal head) in vinaigrette, pigs' feet, stuffed cabbage—as well as French-accented brasserie fare and wonderful pastries. Stick to daily specials and one-plate meals; dining à la carte can be expensive. ⊠ *Muristalden 1, ☎ 031/3314218. AE, DC, MC, V.*

$$ ✕ **Della Casa.** Affectionately nicknamed "Delli," this favorite has been
★ serving generous platters of local specialties such as oxtail stew with fried macaroni or calves' liver with herbs for more than 100 years. The waitresses are "wonderfully prickly dragons," according to one Swiss food magazine, but no one seems to mind. The yellowed downstairs Stübli and the wood-paneled upstairs rooms are unofficial Parliament headquarters; they buzz during lunch. ⊠ *Schauplatzg. 16, ☎ 031/ 3112142. AE, DC, MC, V. Closed Sun. No dinner Sat.*

$$ ✕ **Harmonie.** Run by the same family since 1900, this lively leaded-glass and old-wood café-restaurant is pleasantly dingy and very friendly. Expect the basics: sausage and *Rösti* (hash brown potatoes), *Käseschnitte* (cheese toast), *Bauern* omelets (farm style, with bacon, potatoes, onions, and herbs), and fondue. ⊠ *Hotelg. 3, ☎ 031/3113840. AE, DC, MC, V. Closed Sun. No dinner Sat., no lunch Mon.*

$$ ✕ **Il Grissino.** In a busy Bernese square, this very popular haunt specializes in pizzas cooked in a wood-fired oven—26 colorful varieties—

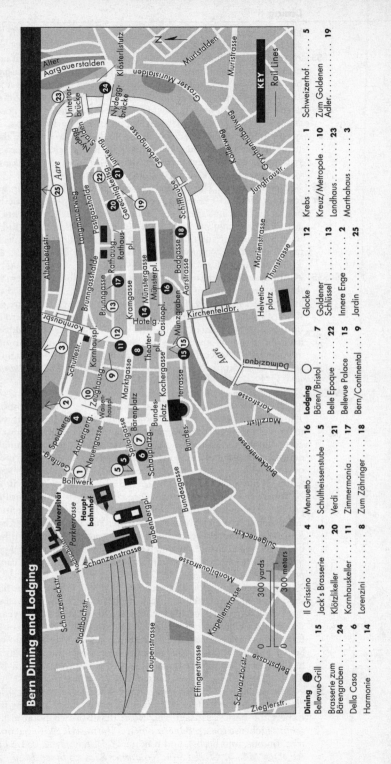

Bern Dining and Lodging

KEY
— Rail Lines

Dining
Bellevue-Grill **15**
Brasserie zum
Bärengraben **24**
Della Casa **6**
Harmonie **14**
Il Grissino **4**
Jack's Brasserie **5**
Klötzlikeller **20**
Kornhauskeller **11**
Lorenzini **8**
Menuetto **16**
Schultheissenstube **5**
Verdi **21**
Zimmermania **17**
Zum Zähringer **18**
Glocke **12**
Goldener
Schlüssel **22**
Innere Enge **15**
Jardin **9**
Krebs **1**
Kreuz/Metropole .. **10**
Landhaus **23**
Marthahaus **3**
Schweizerhof **5**
Zum Goldenen
Adler. **19**

Lodging ○
Bären/Bristol **7**
Belle Epoque **22**
Bellevue Palace **15**
Bern/Continental **9**

and such traditional pastas as fettuccine *nere Stefano* (black noodles with salmon and broccoli). Run by a Swiss-Italian family, it has a bright, contemporary interior with curious ceiling lamps dressed up with glass beads and metallic leaves. The wine list is all Italian. ⊠ *Waisenhauspl. 28,* ☎ *031/3110059. AE, DC, MC, V.*

$$ ✕ **Lorenzini.** After a few days of Bern's rib-sticking cooking, authen-
★ tic Italian food may sound more appealing than ever. Delicious home-
made pastas and seasonal specialties representing various Italian
regions, such as fish carpaccio and ravioli filled with fish and herbs,
jostle for attention with the very trendy patrons crowding the coffee
bar. ⊠ *Theaterpl. 5/Hotelg. 8,* ☎ *031/3117850. AE, DC, MC, V.
Closed Sun.*

$$ ✕ **Menuetto.** A reaction against meaty Bern cuisine, this refreshing veg-
★ etarian oasis creates sophisticated, imaginative cooking—*rouladen*
(roulades) of spinach and feta with tamari beer sauce, raspberry sorbet with thick almond milk and chunks of fresh fruit. The sleek, chic,
white-on-white decor is warmed with parquet floors and hanging
greens. ⊠ *Münsterg. 47 and Herreng. 22 (2 entrances),* ☎ *031/
3111448. AE, DC, MC, V. Closed Sun.*

$–$$ ✕ **Klötzlikeller.** This cozy wine cellar dates from 1635 and is the old-
★ est in Bern. Since 1885 only unmarried women have been permitted
to own and run the place—a tradition begun by the daughters of Mr.
Klötzli himself. Monthly musical-theater dinner programs and a changing menu featuring foods and wine from selected regions make this place
unique. Or try their satisfying traditional Bernese dishes on the standard menu, like tripe and Rösti. ⊠ *Gerechtigkeitsg. 62,* ☎ *031/
3117456. AE, MC, V. Closed Sun.–Mon.*

LODGING

As a frequent host to conventioneers, tourists, and visiting members of Parliament, Bern is well equipped with hotels in all price ranges. Rooms are hard to find when Parliament is in session; this is one town where you need to book well ahead. All but the bargain hotels are concentrated in the Old Town.

CATEGORY	COST*
$$$$	over 300 SF
$$$	200 SF–300 SF
$$	120 SF–200 SF
$	under 120 SF

Prices are for a standard double room, including breakfast, sales tax, and 15% service charge.

$$$$ 🏨 **Bellevue Palace.** At press time, the guest rooms of this 1865 landmark were undergoing extensive renovations, which should be completed by the end of 2001. Half the rooms will be available during the
face-lift. The excellent Bellevue-Grill (☞ Dining, *above*), will also remain open. ⊠ *Kocherg. 3–5, CH-3001,* ☎ *031/3204545,* FAX *031/
3114743. Number of rooms not available at press time. 3 restaurants,
bar. AE, DC, MC, V.* ✆

$$$$ 🏨 **Schweizerhof.** This landmark just across from the Hauptbahnhof
is decidedly nonpalatial: the lobby is deluxe but on a human scale, and
the broad corridors are lined with the antiques and objets d'art of the
Gauers, the hotel's founding family. Lush greens and golds dominate
the freshly refurbished rooms; original artwork adds an individual touch.
Although this hotel is well equipped for business meetings, it's the details—the next day's weather report on your pillow beside the requi-
site truffle—that keep it welcoming, not just efficient. And you won't
go hungry; there's the Schultheissenstube (they say the peephole in the

door was installed for a local politician) and Jack's Brasserie (☞ Dining, *above*). ✉ *Bahnhofpl. 11, CH-3001,* ☎ *031/3268080,* ℻ *031/3268090. 70 rooms, 14 suites. 2 restaurants, bar. AE, DC, MC, V.* ❧

$$$ ⊞ **Bären/Bristol.** These connected Best Western properties are the hotel equivalent of Siamese twins; both are dependable business-class hotels, with fresh, modern rooms in blues and yellows and with tile baths. Top-floor rooms on the court side are quietest. ✉ *Bären: Schauplatzg. 4–10, CH-3011,* ☎ *031/3113367; 800/528–1234 in the U.S. (both hotels),* ℻ *031/3116983, www.baerenbern.ch, 57 rooms; Bristol:* ☎ *031/3110101,* ℻ *031/3119479, www.bristolbern.ch, 92 rooms. Both hotels: Snack bar, sauna, solarium, bicycles, coin laundry. AE, DC, MC, V.*

$$$ ⊞ **Belle Epoque.** Although it's stationed along a medieval Old Town
★   street, this hotel draws from a different inspiration. Every inch of the arcaded row house has been filled with authentic art nouveau (Jugendstil) antiques, from the stylized wooden vines on the reception desk to the stunning light fixtures. The style is suggestive of Gay Paree, but the amenities are up to date, with electric blinds and a no-smoking floor. The glowing, snug hotel bar is one of the most beautiful in the city; look for the photo of Henri de Toulouse-Lautrec over the door. ✉ *Gerechtigkeitsg. 18, CH-3011,* ☎ *031/3114336,* ℻ *031/3113936. 15 rooms, 2 suites. Restaurant, breakfast room, bar. AE, DC, MC, V.*

$$$ ⊞ **Innere Enge.** Eighteenth-century origins and Jugendstil updates are discreetly discernible in this quiet hotel just outside the city center. The rooms are spacious, light, and airy; generous windows face the Bernese Alps. You'll find exposed wood beams and lots of angles in the top-floor rooms and soothing colors with hints of the Jazz Age throughout. The real thing music-wise is to be found downstairs in Marian's Jazzroom, which features top jazz acts Tuesday through Saturday (☞ Nightlife, *below*). Take Bus 21 (marked BREMGARTEN) from the train station. ✉ *Engestr. 54, CH-3012,* ☎ *031/3096111,* ℻ *031/3096112. 13 rooms, 15 suites. Restaurant, bar, café. AE, DC, MC, V.*

$$$ ⊞ **Kreuz/Metropole.** Though facing each other across Zeughausgasse, these two standard hotels have joined forces. The Kreuz is the brighter of the two, with clean, simple rose-hued rooms. Rooms on the upper floors are significantly quieter. The Metropole is slowly shedding a dark '70s decor, but it's worth a look; at press time the rooms varied greatly in quality but not in price, so you could snag a comfortable bargain. Manager Mr. Schüpbach offers a special rate to Fodor's users, which bumps the price back into the 2$ category—ask about it when making reservations. ✉ *Kreuz: Zeughausg. 41, CH-3011,* ☎ *031/3299595,* ℻ *031/3299596, www.culinareum.ch/BE/Hotel-Kreuz-Bern.htm. 103 rooms. Bar, restaurant. Metropole: Zeughausg. 28, CH-3011,* ☎ *031/3115021,* ℻ *031/3121153. 103 rooms. Both hotels: AE, DC, MC, V.* ❧

$$–$$$ ⊞ **Bern/Continental.** Behind a severe and imposing neoclassical facade, a former theater and once-modest hotel has been transformed into the slick, business-class Bern, with air-shaft gardens supplying light to the inner rooms. All the rooms are a bit heavy on the wine-red color scheme, so for the most light, ask for one on the top floors, either facing the back or the traffic-free street. A few doors down is the Bern's less expensive sister lodging, the Continental. Its quiet rooms have much the same decor; guests get discounts at the Bern hotel restaurants. ✉ *Bern: Zeughausg. 9, CH-3011,* ☎ *031/3292222,* ℻ *031/3292299. 98 rooms, 1 suite. 2 restaurants. Continental: Zeughausg. 27, CH-3011,* ☎ *031/3292121,* ℻ *031/3292199. 40 rooms. Both hotels: AE, DC, MC, V.* ❧

$$ ⊞ **Krebs.** A small, scrupulously maintained hotel, the Krebs is solid
★   and impeccable, thanks to the ownership's eye for detail. The rooms are gradually being renovated floor by floor; the older rooms are spare but pristine, while the newer, no-smoking rooms are crisp and bright, with light-wood accents, pastels, and polished granite. The self-service

laundry facilities (rare in Switzerland) and Internet access in the rooms prove they've got your interest at heart. ✉ *Genferg. 8, CH-3001,* ☎ *031/3114942,* FAX *031/3111035. 46 rooms, 41 with bath. Breakfast room, café, laundry. AE, DC, MC, V.*

$$ 🔲 **Zum Goldenen Adler.** Built in a magnificent patrician town house ★ in the Old Town, this guest house has been lodging travelers since 1489, though the current structure dates from 1764. One family has run it for 100-odd years. Despite the striking exterior with its coat of arms, the interiors are modest and modern, with linoleum baths and severe Formica furniture, but the ambience is comfortable and welcoming nonetheless. ✉ *Gerechtigkeitsg. 7, CH-3011,* ☎ *031/3111725,* FAX *031/3113761. 16 rooms. Restaurant. AE, DC, MC, V.*

$ 🔲 **Glocke.** Although it's very plain, there's a young, friendly management here, and the spic-and-span rooms are a bargain. Top-floor rooms with views of the rooftops are best. Downstairs there's Quasimodo, a popular spot with oldies playing in the background. The upstairs Bistrorant is a friendly and affordable restaurant. ✉ *Rathausg. 75, CH-3011,* ☎ *031/3113771,* FAX *031/3111008. 26 rooms, 7 with bath. Restaurant, bar. AE, DC, MC, V.*

$ 🔲 **Goldener Schlüssel.** This bright, tidy little hotel in the heart of the Old Town has standard-issue rooms with fresh linens and tile baths. As the building looks over the Rathausgasse, you'll find the back rooms quieter. The good, inexpensive restaurant serves home-cooked meat-and-Rösti favorites. The seven rooms without bath are a bargain. ✉ *Rathausg. 72, CH-3011,* ☎ *031/3110216,* FAX *031/3115688. 29 rooms, 22 with bath. Restaurant, Stübli. AE, MC, V.* ✎

$ 🔲 **Jardin.** In a commercial neighborhood far above the Old Town, this is an efficient, straightforward hotel with a welcoming management. The decor in the guest rooms is a bit drab, but their spaciousness makes up for it. It's easily reached by Tram 9 to Breitenrainplatz. ✉ *Militärstr. 38, CH-3014,* ☎ *031/3330117,* FAX *031/3330943. 20 rooms. Restaurant, bowling, free parking. AE, DC, MC, V.* ✎

$ 🔲 **Landhaus.** Just across the river from the Old Town, this 90-year-★ old apartment building has been freshly renovated into a simple, clean, and bright hotel/hostel, with natural-wood floors, soothing pastel walls, and modern metal-frame beds. Pick anything from a dorm-style cubicle to a double room with shower; value-for-money-wise, it's a great bargain. Cook for yourself in the community kitchen or dine at the hotel's trendy restaurant. You can get a modem connection at the front desk; there's live jazz at the bar on Thursday. ✉ *Altenbergstr. 46, CH-3013,* ☎ *031/3314166,* FAX *031/3326904. 4 rooms, plus 3 4- or 6-bed dormitories. Restaurant, 2 bars, food shop, bicycles, coin laundry. AE, DC, MC, V.* ✎

$ 🔲 **Marthahaus.** This cheap, cheery pension, originally a hotel for ★ young women, stands at the end of a quiet cul-de-sac in a residential neighborhood north of the Old Town. The comfortable, superclean rooms are done in white and light wood. Fourteen have just a toilet and shower. The hotel's easily reached on Bus 20; it's by the second stop after the Lorrainebrücke Bridge. ✉ *Wyttenbachstr. 22a, CH-3013,* ☎ *031/3324135,* FAX *031/3333386. 38 rooms. Breakfast room. MC, V.*

NIGHTLIFE AND THE ARTS

This Week in Bern carries listings of concerts, museums, and nightlife; it's available at the tourist office (☞ Visitor Information *in* Bern A to Z, *below*) and hotels. *Bern Aktuell,* published every two weeks and also distributed by the tourist office, has listings in English.

Nightlife

Bars

The **Arcady,** at the Schweizerhof (☞ Lodging, *above*), is a mellow piano bar. **Arlequin** (✉ Gerechtigkeitsg. 51, ☎ 031/3113946) is a cozy wine bar where you can also get a small meal. On the ground floor of the little hotel **Belle Epoque** (☞ Lodging, *above*) there's a lovely small bar where you can drink surrounded by art nouveau treasures. For a night-cap in a formal hotel venue, go to the **Bellevue Palace** (☞ Lodging, *above*). The chic bar **CoCo** (✉ Genferg. 10, ☎ 031/3111551) has Gau-guin-esque murals on the walls. For history, head for **Klötzlikeller,** said to be the oldest wine bar in Bern (☞ Dining, *above*).

Casino

Bern's **Kursaal** (✉ Schänzlistr. 71–77, ☎ 031/3331010) has a disco with live music as well as gambling in the **Jackpot Casino,** which stays within the federally mandated 5 SF bet limit.

Dancing

Babalu (✉ Gurteng. 3, ☎ 031/3110808) draws a very young crowd for dancing with live music. One of the hottest spots in town is **Toni's the Club** (✉ Aarbergerg. 35, ☎ 031/3115011), which has two bars and two dance floors. Do keep in mind that places for dancing often also have a separate "cabaret" that is actually a strip club.

Jazz Club

Marian's Jazzroom (✉ Engestr. 54, ☎ 031/3096111), an intimate red-velvet club in the cellar of the hotel Innere Enge (☞ Lodging, *above*), offers top live acts nightly. There are shows from Tuesday to Saturday at 7:30 PM and 10:30 PM; Sunday there's a jazz brunch from 10–2. It's closed June through August.

The Arts

Film

Bern's 26 movie theaters show films in their original languages. Cur-rent listings can be found in hotels, the daily newspapers *Der Bund* (weekly events supplement "Die Berner Woche") and *Die Berner Zeitung* (weekly events supplement "Die Berner Agende"), and the tourist office (☞ Visitor Information *in* Bern A to Z, *below*).

Music

The **Bern Symphony Orchestra** (☎ 031/3114242 for tickets) is the city's most notable musical institution. Concerts take place at the **Casino** (✉ Casinopl.) and the **Stadttheater** (✉ Kornhauspl. 20). There is also a five-day **International Jazz Festival** every April or May, with tickets avail-able at Ticket Corner, at the Schweizerischer Bankverein (Swiss Bank Corporation; ✉ Bärenpl., ☎ 031/3362539).

Opera

Bern's resident company is famous for its adventurous productions. Performances are at the **Stadttheater** (✉ Kornhauspl. 20, ☎ 031/3295151); tickets are sold next door (✉ Kornhauspl. 18) weekdays 10–6:30, Saturday 10–4, and Sunday 10–12:30.

Theater

Although you can see traditional and modern plays at the **Stadtthe-ater** (✉ Kornhauspl. 20, ☎ 031/3110777), a characteristic of Bern is its range of little theaters, mostly found in cellars in the Old Town.

The **Berner Puppentheater** (✉ Gerechtigkeitsg. 31, ☎ 031/3119585) produces funny, action-packed puppet shows—enjoyable even if you don't speak the language. **Kleintheater** (✉ Kramg. 6, ☎ 031/3113080) has a modern repertoire; buy tickets at the **Müller & Schade** store (✉ Kramg. 52, ☎ 031/3202626). Avant-garde plays, satires, and burlesques (in Swiss-German), plus pantomime and modern dance, are performed at **Theater am Käfigturm** (✉ Marktg. 67, ☎ 031/3116100).

OUTDOOR ACTIVITIES AND SPORTS

Bicycling

There are about 300 km (185 mi) of marked trails around Bern; ask for routes at the tourist office. Bikes can be rented at the Hauptbahnhof, the main train station.

Golf

The **Golf and Country Club Blumisberg** (✉ 18 km/11 mi west of town, ☎ 026/4963438) has 18 holes and a clubhouse with a restaurant, bar, showers, and swimming pool. The club admits visitors weekdays, provided they are members of any golf club with handicaps. Only local members and their guests are admitted on weekends.

Swimming

The beach at **Aarebad Lorraine** (✉ Uferweg, ☎ 031/3322950) is on the right bank northwest of the Kursaal. Below the Parliament building you can swim in the river at the **Aarebad Marzili** waterfront (✉ Marzilistr. 29, ☎ 031/3110046). **Hallenbad Hirschengraben** (✉ Maulbeerstr. 14, ☎ 031/3813656) is an indoor swimming pool.

SHOPPING

Shop hours are usually Monday–Wednesday and Friday 8:15–6:30, Thursday 8:15 AM–9 PM, and Saturday 8:15–4; Sunday most stores are closed, and many remain closed Monday morning.

Department Stores

Globus (✉ Spitalg. 17–21, ☎ 031/3118811), one of the city's largest department stores, has a wide variety of designer labels. **Loeb** (✉ Spitalg. 47–57, ☎ 031/3207111) is the good old-fashioned kind of department store where the owner, Mr. Loeb himself, can sometimes be found greeting his customers.

Markets

Every Tuesday and Saturday mornings colorful farmers' markets (fruits, vegetables, and flowers) take place on the **Bärenplatz,** where buskers perform pantomime and music. There's a meat-and-dairy market on **Münstergasse.** A general market is held on **Waisenhausplatz.** Both are held on Tuesday and Saturday. From May through October a flea market sets up shop every third Saturday on **Mühleplatz,** behind the cathedral. On the first Saturday of the month, the **Münsterplatz** is the site of an arts-and-crafts fair. Mid-May brings the geranium market (morning only) to the **Münsterplatz.**

Shopping Streets

The **Old Town** is one big shopping center, and its 6 km (4 mi) of arcades shelter stores of every kind and quality. Many modern, mainstream shops are concentrated between the Bahnhof and the Clock Tower, especially on **Spitalgasse** and **Marktgasse.** Beyond, along **Kramgasse** and **Gerechtigkeitsgasse** and, parallel to them on the north, **Postgasse,** are quirkier, artsy spots and excellent antiques stores. Don't overlook the unusual variety of cellar shops, accessible from the street outside the arcades. Good shopping can be had at **Junkerngasse** and **Münstergasse,** especially in art galleries and avant-garde fashion boutiques.

Specialty Stores

Antiques

The best antiques shops line Gerechtigkeitsgasse and Postgasse; their wares range from cluttery *brocante* (collectibles) to good antiques from all over Europe. The **Puppenklinik** (⊠ Gerechtigkeitsg. 36, ☎ 031/3120771) is just this side of a museum, with its shelves and window densely packed with lovely—if slightly eerie—old dolls and toys.

Chocolate

Abegglen (⊠ Spitalg. 36, ☎ 031/3112111) has great chocolate-covered almonds. Don't leave **Beeler's** (⊠ Spitalg. 29, ☎ 031/3112808) without trying its champagne chocolates. **Eichenberger** (⊠ Bahnhofpl. 5, ☎ 031/3113325) is known for its hazelnut *Lebkuchen* (a flat spice cake). **Tschirren** (⊠ Kramg. 73, ☎ 031/3111717) has been making sweets for more than 80 years. The mandarin chocolates are divine.

Souvenirs/Gifts

Heimatwerk Bern (⊠ Kramg. 61, ☎ 031/3113000) offers a broad, high-quality range of Swiss-made handicrafts, textiles, and ceramics. **Langenthal** (⊠ Marktg. 15, ☎ 031/3118786) is where you'll find fine Swiss embroidery and linens.

EXCURSION TO THE EMMENTAL

The great city of Bern stands alone in a large and lovely region tourists usually overlook: the Berner Mittelland, the rural lowlands of the enormous canton Bern. These mist-wrapped green-velvet foothills lap the base of the Bernese Alps. Driving on back roads, you will see neat, prosperous old towns and farms, a handful of castles, and—most of all—verdant, undulating patchwork countryside.

Its most famous—though as yet unspoiled—region is the **Emmental,** the valley of the River Emme, where Switzerland's trademark cheese is made: Emmentaler, the one with the holes. Here you can visit a cheese factory and admire some of Switzerland's most beautiful farmhouses—plump, broad boxes topped with deep-curving roofs that slope nearly to the ground. In the 19th century, Swiss clergyman Jeremias Gotthelf found the virtues of family life and Christian beliefs in this breathtaking valley to be so inspiring that he turned to writing novels and short stories about the Emmentalers. His efforts revealed a prodigious literary talent, making him one of Switzerland's most famous writers.

Not much has changed in the Emmental since Gotthelf's time. Here the canton is at its slowest. It isn't rudeness that silences the regulars of a local restaurant and directs their stares when an outsider walks in—it's an age-old wariness of strangers, a take-your-time-to-size-'em-up attitude. Service will be friendly but impossibly slow, so leave your schedules behind and enjoy. Within a half hour of leaving the city of Bern on Highway 10 going toward Worb/Langnau, bedroom communities give way to small farm villages with picturesque curved-roof country inns, their emblems suspended from wrought-iron brackets. After about 10 km (6 mi) you'll be in **Zäziwil.** Follow the signs heading to Langnau, then turn left at Bowil for the small road up the hill to the summit of **Chuderhüsi** (6 km/4 mi). At the top (1,103 m/3,650 ft), the road opens to a panorama of the Bernese Alps in all their glory. There is a restaurant, but its only claim to fame is the view; save your appetite for another local spot.

Heading down on the other side of Chuderhüsi, you'll come to the the Würzbrunnen Church, featured in films made about Jeremias Gotthelf and his stories. Take the road down into the valley at Rothenbach and then follow the signs for Eggiwil, where the road meets up with and then follows the Emme, the river from which the valley takes its name. You'll cross or pass seven covered bridges by the time you reach the village of Schüpbach (about 11 km/6½ mi), where you can turn left for a stop in the pretty little village of Signau (2 km/1 mi), a good place to see examples of the local architecture, or head right for a side trip to Langnau (about 10 km/6 mi) and on to Trubschachen (7 km/4½ mi), where you can visit some small local museums and a demonstration pottery studio. From Langnau and Trubschachen double back to the village of Emmenmat and continue north, following the signs to Sumiswald. Take your time—the scenery is nothing short of spectacular.

Here the gentle hills begin to roll out village after beautiful village. The scenery is dotted with many impressive examples of the classic Emmental farmstead. The enormous *Bauernhaus* (main building) shelters the living quarters of the farmer and his family; at the back of the house, built into the central plan, is the cowshed; and grains and feed are stored upstairs, under the deep roof. Next door, in a separate house, lives the older generation: when a farmer retires, he passes the entire farm on to his youngest son and moves into the *Stöckli,* a kind of guest house, conceding the home to the new family. The third building, standing apart, is the *Spycher,* for storing the harvest of food, grains, and in olden days, the family's savings. If the farm caught fire, this building would be saved over the main house.

Continue north in the direction of Huttwil, turning left at Weier (7 mi/4½ mi) to visit the cheese museum in Affoltern. Follow signs to Burgdorf to complete the circuit, where you can pick up the highway back to Bern (20 mi/13 mi).

TIMING

If you are based in Bern and have a car, a 90-km (56-mi) round-trip begun late morning with lots of stops for photos and lunch can get you back in time for dinner in the city. If you plan to spend some time visiting the cheese factory and museums, get an earlier start.

Numbers in the margin correspond to points of interest on the Emmental map.

Signau

❶ *24 km (15 mi) east of Bern.*

Signau is a pretty village typical of the region. There are some impressive examples of the classic Emmental farmstead.

Dining and Lodging

$ ✕ **Zum Wysse Rössli.** In Zäziwil (9 km/6 mi southwest of Signau), this grand old Emmental inn, its roof spreading out like the wings of a mother hen, shelters innumerable halls for local sports clubs and family events, but its main pub and restaurant serve the natives daily. Read a newspaper, meet your card-playing neighbors, and tackle a little local dialect—the menu is in Swiss-German. Rösti, mixed salads, and smoked farm ham are outstanding; heavier meat dishes and meringue with ice cream may do you in (pleasantly). ✉ *Thunstr. 10, Zäziwil,* ☎ *031/7111532. AE, DC, MC, V. Closed Tues.*

$ ✕▥ **Bären.** Look for the enormous bear jutting out above the entrance of this inn on Signau's main street. The restaurant keeps the locals happy with classic Emmental cooking: fluffy cheese tarts, golden Rösti, enor-

Emmental

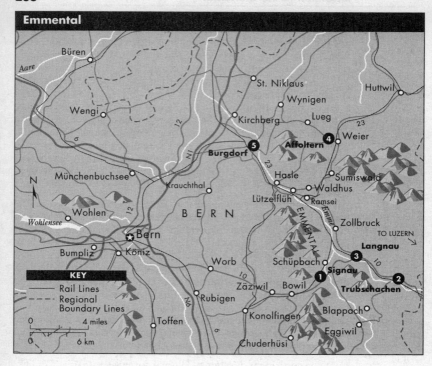

mous mixed salads, local game, and silky wild mushrooms in season. The rooms upstairs offer impeccable modern comfort. ✉ *Dorfstr. 48, CH-3534,* ☎ FAX *034/4971364. 4 rooms. MC, V. Closed Mon.*

Trubschachen

❷ *13 km (8 mi) east of Schüpbach, 37 km (23 mi) east of Bern.*

Trubschachen, a center for the region's folk-style ceramics, sits in the shadow of the 1,195-m (3,920-ft) ridge Blappach. (If you brave the narrow farm road up the ridge, you'll find more good views toward the Bernese Alps.) There's a **Heimatmuseum** (Local Museum) arranged in the three traditional buildings of a farm, with crafts and household antiques displayed in the Spycher and Stöckli. If you plan to visit by appointment, call a few days in advance. ☎ *034/4956038.* 🎫 *4 SF.* 🕐 *Apr.–Nov., Sun. 2–4, or by request. Closed Dec.–Mar.*

For a chance to watch local craftspeople at work, visit the **Schautöpferei** (demonstration pottery studio) in the Bauernhaus building of the Heimatmuseum. There you'll also find a shop full of local ceramics and a cozy upstairs café. ✉ ☎ *034/4956029.* 🎫 *Free.* 🕐 *Weekdays 8–noon and 1:30–5:30, Sat. 9–noon and 1:30–5:30.*

Langnau

❸ *7 km (4 mi) west of Trubschachen, 30 km (19 mi) east of Bern.*

This graceful old market town serves as capital of the region and clearinghouse for its cheese. Here you will find the **Heimatmuseum Langnau,** a museum of traditional crafts, tools, and furniture as well as military paraphernalia, all in an enormous chalet. ✉ *Bärenpl. 2a,* ☎ *034/ 4021819.* 🎫 *3 SF.* 🕐 *Apr.–Nov., Tues.–Sun. 1:30–6. Closed Dec.–Mar.*

Affoltern

❹ *30 km (19 mi) northwest of Langnau, 35 km (22 mi) northeast of Bern.*

Affoltern, another small traditional village, has some strong examples of Emmental architecture. The main attraction is the **Schaukäserei** (demonstration dairy), which allows you to see Swiss cheese in the making. From a glassed-in balcony, you can watch gallons of milk being stirred in copper cauldrons, its curd being separated from its whey in great sieves, with the heavy solids eased into molds to be brine-soaked and then stored. Try to be here between 9 and 11 or between 2 and 4, when the most active stages of cheese making take place. In a restored Stöckli from 1741, old-fashioned ways of cheese making over a wood fire are sometimes demonstrated. ☎ *034/4351611.* ⊠ *Free.* ☉ *Daily 8:30–6:30.*

Dining and Lodging

$ ✕ **Emmentaler Schaukäserei.** After you've toured the factory and exhibits on cheese making, you can sate your appetite at the factory's simple restaurant, where the menu covers cheese dishes—fondue, *Käseschnitte*—as well as local cold meats. Special cheese breakfasts are served daily until 11:30. In fine weather, picnic on the self-service terrace. ⊠ *Affoltern,* ☎ *034/4351611. AE, DC, MC, V.*

$$ ✕🏨 **Sonne.** This is an archetypal Emmental guest house: weathered but pristine, steeped in tradition but airy and bright, and serving rich, hearty cooking based on ingredients straight off the farm. There are satiny soups, flaky *Pastetli* (puff pastry filled with creamed veal), unusually well-executed veal dishes, and freshwater fish. Make a heroic effort to leave room for the meringue, fluffed to enormous proportions with farm-fresh Emmental egg whites. It's set on a sunny hill with valley views, not far from the demonstration cheese dairy. There are a few simple bedrooms upstairs. The restaurant is closed to nonguests on Thursday and serves no lunch on Friday. ⊠ *CH-3416 Affoltern,* ☎ *034/4358000,* 𝔽𝔸𝕏 *034/4358019. 12 rooms. AE, DC, MC, V. Closed Jan.*

OFF THE
BEATEN PATH

Lueg. From Affoltern make a side trip northwest to Lueg (887 m/2,909 ft) for views toward the Alps: It's a brief walk uphill to the crest to take in the great panorama and to catch the Alps in a different light from the one seen earlier in the day from Chuderhüsi.

Burgdorf

❺ *12 km (7 mi) west of Affoltern and 25 km (15 mi) north of Bern.*

In Burgdorf there's a sizable Gothic castle built in the 12th century by the Zähringens, the family responsible for the founding of the cities of Bern, Fribourg, Murten, and Burgdorf. The castle was turned into a museum more than 100 years ago: the **Schlossmuseum Burgdorf** (Burgdorf Castle Museum). A walk through the Knights' Hall and the various rooms, towers, and battlements of the original castle introduces you to the history and culture of Burgdorf and the Emmental. Regional costumes, ceramics, and period furniture are displayed along with alternating exhibitions. ☎ *034/4230214.* ⊠ *5 SF.* ☉ *Apr. 1–Nov. 1, Mon.–Sat. 2–5, Sun. 11–5. Closed early Nov.–Mar.*

The **Kornhaus,** a former granary, now houses the Swiss Center for Folk Culture, a collection of Swiss costumes, phonographs, musical instruments, and a yodeling hall. ⊠ *Kornhausg. 16,* ☎ *034/4231010.* ⊠ *10 SF.* ☉ *Tues.–Fri. 10–12:30 and 1:30–5, weekends 10–5.*

Emmental A to Z

Getting Around

BY CAR

Driving is by far the best way to experience this rural region because good, small highways carry you from town to town through country-side often untouched by modern architecture. Highway 10 from Bern is the best way into the region. Small rural roads are indicated by the names of the towns they connect.

BY TRAIN AND BUS

If you plan your itinerary carefully, you can arrange a comfortable though limited tour of the region combining trains from Bern into Burgdorf, connecting to Hasle; from there you can take a postbus to Affoltern, for instance, to visit the cheese factory. Or stay on the train all the way to Langnau and enjoy the countryside as you travel.

Guided Tours

Badertscher (⊠ Freiburgstr. 430, CH-3018 Bern, ☎ 031/9919100) offers coach excursions through the region. **Emmental Tours** (⊠ CH-3454 Sumiswald, ☎ 034/4312161) is another resource. Some tours are available in English, but they must be arranged through Pro Emmental (☞ Visitor Information, *below*).

One of the most novel and effective ways to experience the region is by plodding down its back roads behind a team of horses in a Gypsy wagon and lodging in typical Emmentaler inns. You can pack a pic-nic or stop for lunch at a guest house along the way. Contact **Eurotrek/Unitours** (⊠ Freischutzg. 3, CH-8004 Zürich, ☎ 01/2955555).

Visitor Information

Pro Emmental (⊠ Schlossstr. 3, CH-3550 Langnau, ☎ 034/4024252, FAX 034/4025667, ✍) is extremely helpful; they can supply you with maps and routes for hikes in the region.

BERN A TO Z

Arriving and Departing

By Car

Bern is connected conveniently by expressway to Basel via **A1**, to the Berner Oberland via **A6**, and to Lac Léman and thus Lausanne, Geneva, and the Valais via **A12**.

By Plane

The small airport **Belp** (⊠ Belpmoos, 9 km/6 mi south of Bern, ☎ 031/9602111) has flights to Amsterdam, Brussels, Frankfurt, and most other major European airports connecting through **Crossair** (☎ 031/9602121 for reservations), Switzerland's domestic airline. **KLM-Alps** (☎ 0848/848328) offers direct flight connections with Munich and Vienna.

BETWEEN THE AIRPORT AND THE CENTER

A city **bus** runs regularly between Belp and the city's Hauptbahnhof (main train station). The fare each way is 14 SF. A **taxi** from the air-port to the Hauptbahnhof costs about 35 SF.

By Train

Bern is a major link between Geneva, Zürich, and Basel, and **fast trains** run almost every hour from the enormous central station, the **Hauptbahnhof** (☎ 0900/300300, 1.19 SF per min.). Bern is the only European capital to have three **high-speed trains**: the ICE, the TGV, and the **Pendolino**. The ICE from Berlin takes nine hours; the TGV from Paris takes 4½ hours; the Pendolino from Milan takes 3–4 hours.

Getting Around

The best of Bern is concentrated in a relatively small area, and it's easy to get around on foot.

By Bus and Tram

Bus and tram services are excellent, with fares ranging from 1.50 SF to 2.40 SF. Buy individual tickets from the dispenser at the tram or bus stop: find the name of the stop closest to your destination on the map, then check to see the fare on the list of stops. There is an unlimited-travel Visitor's Card available—6 SF for 24 hours, 9 SF for 48 hours, and 12 SF for 72 hours—at the tourist office in the Hauptbahnhof (☞ Visitor Information, *below*) or at the public-transportation ticket office in the passageway leading down to the Hauptbahnhof (take the escalator in front of Loeb's department store and turn right through the Christoffel Tower). A Swiss Pass (☞ Train Travel *in* Smart Travel Tips A to Z) includes free travel in Bern.

By Taxi

Taxis are actually a cumbersome alternative to walking, especially when streets are dominated by trams. It costs between 12 SF and 15 SF to cross town. Cabs line up at the train station; you can also call ☎ 031/3111818 to order a taxi.

Contacts and Resources

Embassies

Canada (✉ Kirchenfeldstr. 88, ☎ 031/3573200). **United Kingdom** (✉ Thunstr. 50, ☎ 031/3525021). **United States** (✉ Jubiläumsstr. 93, ☎ 031/3577011).

Emergencies

Police (☎ 117). **Ambulance** (☎ 144). **Hospital** (✉ Insel Spital, Freiburgstr., ☎ 031/6322111). **Medical and dental referrals** (☎ 031/3112211). **All-night pharmacy referrals** (☎ 031/3112211).

English-Language Bookstore

Stauffacher (✉ Neueng. 25, ☎ 031/3112411) has the broadest selection of books in English, plus a great café-bookshop.

Guided Tours

ORIENTATION TOURS

A two-hour English-commentary bus tour around the Old Town covering all the principal sights is offered for 23 SF by the tourist office, where you meet.

PERSONAL GUIDES

To arrange for a private guide, contact the tourist office (☞ *below*).

Travel Agency

Carlson Wagonlit Travel (✉ Von Werdt-Passage 5, ☎ 031/3282828).

Visitor Information

Berne Tourismus (✉ Bahnhofpl., at main train station, CH-3001, ☎ 031/3281212, FAX 031/3121233, ✍) has several special services, including Clock Tower visits, walking tours, and even a city tour by raft on the Aare.

10 BERNER OBERLAND

GSTAAD, INTERLAKEN, WENGEN

The Bernese Alps concentrate the very best of rural Switzerland: panoramas of the treble peaks of the Eiger, Mönch, and Jungfrau mountains; crystalline lakes, gorges, and waterfalls; and emerald slopes dotted with gingerbread chalets and cows with bells— not to mention world-class skiing. It's no secret, though: the Berner Oberland is the most touristic canton in Switzerland.

Updated by
Susan
Tuttle-Laube

THERE ARE TIMES WHEN THE REALITY OF Switzerland puts postcard idealization to shame, surpassing tinted-indigo skies and advertising-image peaks with its own astonishing vividness. Those times happen often in the Berner Oberland. Though the Valais and Graubünden areas offer stiff competition, this rugged region concentrates the very best of rural Switzerland: mountain panoramas that can't be overrated, massive glaciers, crystalline lakes, gorges and waterfalls, chic ski resorts, and emerald slopes scattered with gingerbread chalets.

After contemplating the Staubbach Falls in 1779, the great German writer Johann Wolfgang von Goethe was moved to write one of his most celebrated poems, "Gesang der Geister über den Wassern" ("Song of the Spirits over the Waters"). Rousseau spread word of the region's astounding natural phenomena to Paris society. Then the Romantics began to beat a path to this awe-inspiring area. Lord Byron came to investigate; it's said he conceived his *Manfred* in barren, windswept Wengernalp. Shelley followed, then William Thackeray, John Ruskin, and Mark Twain; the master landscape painter J. M. W. Turner and the composer Johannes Brahms took in the views; finally, Queen Victoria herself came, beginning a flood of tourism that changed the Berner Oberland's—and Switzerland's—profile forever.

Before the onslaught of visitors inspired the locals to switch from farming to innkeeping, agriculture was the prime industry—and is still much in evidence today. As if hired as props to style a photo opportunity, brown cows pepper the hillsides wherever rock gives way to grass, and the mountains echo with their bells. The houses of the Berner Oberland are classics, the definitive Swiss chalets: the broad, low, deep-eaved roofs cover gables that are scalloped, carved, and painted with the family dedication; the wood weathers to dark sienna after generations of harsh cold and clear sun. From early spring through autumn, every window box spills torrents of well-tended scarlet geraniums, and adjacent woodpiles are stacked with mosaiclike precision.

The region is arranged tidily enough for even a brief visit. Its main resort city, Interlaken, lies in green lowlands between the gleaming twin pools of the Brienzersee and the Thunersee, linked by the River Aare. Behind them to the south loom craggy, forested foothills with excellent views, and behind those foothills stand some of Europe's noblest peaks, most notably the snowy crowns of the Eiger (3,970 m/13,022 ft), the Mönch (4,099 m/13,445 ft), and the fiercely beautiful Jungfrau (4,158 m/13,638 ft). Because nature laid it out so conveniently, the region has become far and away the most popular for tourism, with its excursion and transportation systems carrying enormous numbers of visitors to its myriad viewpoints, overlooks, and wonders. The railroad to the Jungfraujoch transports masses of tour groups to its high-altitude attractions, and on a peak-season day its station can resemble the Sistine Chapel in August or the Chicago Board of Trade. But the tourist industry can handle the onslaught, offering such an efficient network of boats, trains, and funiculars, such a variety of activities and attractions, and such a wide range of accommodations, from posh city hotels to rustic mountain lodges, that every visitor can find the most suitable way to take in the marvels of the Bernese Alps.

Pleasures and Pastimes

Dining

Meals in the Berner Oberland tend to be down-to-earth, starting with hearty soup or mixed slawlike salads, followed by lake fish or meat and potatoes, and then a sizable dessert. Fried or broiled *Egli* (perch) and *Felchen* (whitefish) are frequently local and lake-fresh; such waterfront resorts as Spiez, Brienz, and Iseltwald specialize in fish. Meat dishes represent Bernese and Zürich cuisines: *Ratsherrentopf* is a mixed grill, *geschnetzeltes Kalbsfleisch* is veal in cream sauce. Colorful mixed salads include crisp shredded celery root, beet, carrot, and cabbage. Because the Alpine experience demands it, the Oberland has adopted the French territories' cheese fondue and raclette (a dish of melted cheese served with potatoes and pickles) as winter-night staples.

The valley town of Meiringen claims to have invented meringue; whether or not this is true, its region consumes enough to corner the culinary market. Enormous, crisp, ivory meringue puffs may be served with or without vanilla ice cream; regardless, they are buried under mounds of heavy piped whipped cream.

CATEGORY	COST*
$$$$	over 70 SF
$$$	40 SF–70 SF
$$	20 SF–40 SF
$	under 20 SF

Prices are per person for a three-course meal (two-course meal in $ category), including sales tax and 15% service charge

Hiking

Partly because of its spectacular ski-transport network woven throughout the region, the Berner Oberland offers a wealth of highly developed walking and hiking options. The scenery is magnificent—what can surpass the views from the Mürren plateau toward the Jungfrau, Eiger, and Mönch?—and the options varied, from rough trails toward glaciers to smooth postbus roads. From May through October you'll be unlikely to find yourself alone for long on any given trail; you'll even find company on a snowy trail since nearly one-third of the region's visitors come for winter hiking. A wide variety of topographical maps and suggested itineraries is available at local tourist offices, especially the Jungfrau region central office on the Höheweg in Interlaken.

Lake Cruises

Steamers crisscross the lakes of Brienz and Thun, trailing leisurely across crystal waters past rolling panoramas of forested hills and craggy, snow-capped peaks. They provide an alternative to high-speed car cruises and limited train runs and, with their buslike schedule, allow passengers to step off at any port for a visit; you need only choose the best boat to catch next.

Lodging

Berner Oberland tradition mandates charming chalet-style exteriors replete with scalloped-wood balconies, steeply sloped roofs, and cascades of scarlet geraniums, no matter what architectural era a hotel dates from. But many hotels in the region have interiors that reflect their roots in the '60s ski boom, with their no-nonsense, Scandinavian-spare, avocado-beige and walnut-grain Formica furnishings. Some of the most recently renovated have softened the '60s edge with such folksy touches as carved knotty pine. A few landmarks have preserved interiors that reflect their lovely facades. Although a vast majority of the hotels are still family owned and run, big businesses are creeping in, scooping up properties that private families can no longer carry and creating competition that forces even more family-run places to go under, a sad scenario that is actively being fought in some communities. Small towns may not have street addresses; in those cases, hotels large and small are clearly signposted. Prices below are average for the Berner Oberland; note that such car-free resorts as Wengen and Mürren run well above this curve, especially during ski season. Half-board, or *demipension* (breakfast and one hot meal), and full-board (three meals) plans are often the thrust of regional hotels. Remember that many properties post rates on a per-person basis.

CATEGORY	COST*
$$$$	over 250 SF
$$$	200 SF–250 SF
$$	120 SF–200 SF
$	under 120 SF

Prices are for a standard double room, including breakfast, tax, and service charge.

✍ *following the text of a review is your signal that the property has a Web site, where you will find details and, usually, images; for a link, visit www.fodors.com/urls.*

Skiing

As one of Switzerland's winter-sports capitals, the Berner Oberland provides a dazzling variety of choices to skiers. Each resort offers its own style of transit and its own peculiar terrain, from nursery slopes to the deadly narrow pistes of the Schilthorn. The lift lines are a fair bit more tolerable here, although the region as a whole is not as snow-sure as is, for example, the Engadine.

Exploring Berner Oberland

The central, urban-Victorian resort of Interlaken makes a good base for excursions for visitors who want to experience the entire Jungfrau region, which includes the craggy, bluff-lined Lauterbrunnen Valley and the opposing resorts that perch high above it: Mürren and Wengen. Both busy, sporty Grindelwald, famous for scenic rides and sports, and isolated Kandersteg, ideal for hiking and cross-country skiing, can be visited out of Interlaken, but they also make good home bases themselves; they both lie at the dead end of gorge roads that climb into the heights. Spreading east and west of Interlaken are the Brienz and Thun lakes, both broad, crystalline, and surrounded by forests, castles, and picturesque waterfront resorts, including Brienz and Thun. From Spiez on the Thunersee, you can head west through the forest gorge of the Simmental to the Saanenland and glamorous Gstaad. Connections by rail or car keep most highlights within easy reach.

Numbers in the text correspond to numbers in the margin and on the Berner Oberland map.

Great Itineraries

Ten days in the Berner Oberland gives you the luxury of exploring each of the valleys and lakes of this varied region, but you can experience it *en passage* as well, depending on your travel pace.

IF YOU HAVE 3 DAYS

Base yourself in busy 🏨 **Interlaken** ① or the quieter **Bönigen** ②, one day taking a boat trip across the Thunersee to **Thun** ⑫, the next day a driving tour around the Brienzersee to **Brienz** ⑨ and the Freilichtmuseum Ballenberg. The third day (or best-weather day) head up the Lauterbrunnen Valley and take the famous rail trip from **Wengen** ⑥ to the **Jungfraujoch** ⑤, returning via **Grindelwald** ⑦.

IF YOU HAVE 5 DAYS

Follow the tours above, and while in the Lauterbrunnen Valley, take the cable cars or cogwheel rail up to **Mürren** ④ and the Schilthorn. On day five, drive up to **Kandersteg** ⑬ to hike to the Oeschinensee, or wind through the forest to visit famous 🏨 **Gstaad** ⑭.

Berner Oberland

TO BERN

TO LUZERN

Wiggen

Flühli

SWITZERLAND

TO LUZERN

Kleinteil

Marbach

Glaubenbüelenpass

Lungern

4

Brienzer-Rothorn

erei

warzenegg

6-11 **Brienz** ❾

Freilichtmuseum Ballenberg

Brienzersee

■ Giessbach

Meiringen ❿

Niederhorn

Harder Kulm

renberg

St. Beatus-höhlen

❽ **Iseltwald**

ersee

Unterseen

❷

Bönigen

First

Heimwehfluh

❶ **Interlaken**
Matten

Wilderswil

Sohynige Platte

Grindelwald ❼

Zweilütschinen

Gundlischwand

OBERER GRINDELWALD GLETSCHER

❻ **Wengen**

Lauberhorn

Lauterbrunnen ❸

Staubbachfälle ■

Kleine Scheidegg

Eiger

Schilthorn

Mürren ❹

■ **Trümmelbachfälle**

Mönch

❺ **Jungfraujoch**

Mürrenbachfälle

Jungfrau

ALETSCH GLACIER

LÜMLISALP

Breithorn

KEY

——— Rail Lines
•••••• Funicular/ Cable Car
- - - Regional Boundary Line
🎿 Ski Resort

N

0 _____ miles

0 _____ 9 km

Rent an apartment or settle in on a half-board (breakfast and one hot meal) or full-board (three meals) plan in one of the cozier hotels of Interlaken or any crossroads resort (Grindelwald and Lauterbrunnen also offer easy access to sights), taking in the lesser sights as you cruise around the varied region. Visit the Trümmelbach Falls in the Lauterbrunnen Valley, see the castles at Hilterfingen and Oberhofen on the Thunersee, and take another high-altitude excursion out of Interlaken to Harder Kulm, Heimwehfluh, or Schynige Platte. You might even hop on a train and make a day trip into the capital city of Bern, only an hour away (☞ Chapter 9).

When to Tour Berner Oberland

In high summer the Berner Oberland is the most popular tourist area in Switzerland and can feel overrun, so aim for the cusp—mid-June, late September—when the weather still holds but the crowds thin. Ski season begins in mid-December and runs through Easter vacation. May and November are low season, with November being the lowest of the low. Some towns all but roll up their sidewalks; many hotels and cable cars shut down for maintenance, and, depending on snow conditions, some excursions may be closed into June or may shut down mid-October. But fear not: the Jungfraujoch rail trip (☞ *below*) runs 365 days a year, even in pea-soup fog.

JUNGFRAU REGION

The thriving resort town of Interlaken lies between two spectacularly sited lakes, the Brienzersee (Lake Brienz) and the Thunersee (Lake Thun), and is the gateway to two magnificent mountain valleys, one leading up to the popular sports resort of Grindelwald, the other into Lauterbrunnen and the famous car-free resorts of Wengen and Mürren. Rearing over both valleys, the Jungfrau and its partner peaks, the Eiger and Mönch, can be viewed from various high-altitude overviews.

Interlaken

❶ *58 km (36 mi) southeast of Bern.*

The name *Interlaken* has a Latin source: *interlacus* (between lakes). As a gateway to the Berner Oberland, this bustling Victorian resort town is the obvious home base for travelers planning to visit the region's two lakes and the mountains towering behind them. At 570 m (1,870 ft), Interlaken dominates the Bödeli, the branch of lowland between the lakes that Interlaken shares with the adjoining towns of Unterseen, Wilderswil, Bönigen, and Matten. The town's two train stations, Interlaken East and Interlaken West, are good orientation points; most sights are just a few minutes' walk from one of the stations. There are unlimited excursion options, and it's a pleasant, if urban, place to stay put as well, as its setting is spectacular and its ambience genteel.

The **Höheweg** is the city's main promenade, its tree- and flower-lined walkways cutting through the edge of the broad green parklands of the **Höhematte**. This 35-acre park once pastured the herds of the Augustinian monastery that dominated medieval Interlaken. Cows are still pastured there in fenced-off areas.

Mark Twain once sojourned at the **Grand Hotel Victoria-Jungfrau** (☞ Dining and Lodging, *below*), on the Höheweg, conceived to take in the view of the snowy Jungfrau that towers above town. The hotel originated as two humbler inns, the Jungfrau (1864) and the Chalet Victoria (1865); these were merged and expanded in 1895, and the facade redesigned and landmark tower added in 1899.

Between the Höheweg and the River Aare, you'll find the landscaped **Kursaal** (Casino) grounds, complete with a floral clock. Built in 1859 in a dramatic combination of Oberland-chalet and Victorian styles, the Kursaal was renovated in 1968 and has become once again a social focal point for the city. Plays and concerts are presented here, mostly during the high season, and there are folklore evenings in the adjoining *Spycher* (the Swiss name for a farm storage barn). The **casino** here has gambling nightly (☞ Nightlife and the Arts, *below*). ⊠ *Off Höheweg*, ☎ *033/8276100.*

The **Schlosskirche** (Castle Church) was once the chapel for the Augustinian monastery. Though founded in 1133, the monastery and the convent that shared its grounds in the 13th century have left only a 14th-century chancel and a wing of the cloister. The rest of the convent was built into a private castle in 1745, which, attached behind the church, is now used as office space. ⊠ *At the end of the Höhematte, south of the Hotel du Nord.*

On the north side of the River Aare is the tiny town of **Unterseen,** with its picturesque Old Town and Marktplatz (Marketplace). Founded in 1279 on land rented from the Augustinians, Unterseen retains some of the region's oldest buildings, including the 17th-century **Stadthaus** (city hall) and the 14th-century **church,** its steeple dating from 1471. The **Schloss Unterseen** (Unterseen Castle), built in 1656 for the reigning Bernese nobleman, stands at the opposite end of the square, near a medieval arched gateway. You can get here via a short (10-minute) bus ride from Interlaken's center, or even by walking; it's near the Interlaken West train station.

Fronting on the Unterseen Marktplatz is the **Touristik-Museum der Jungfrau Region** (Museum of Tourism of the Jungfrau Region), which traces the history of tourism in the area over the last 200 years. Exhibits include models of early transportation and examples of primitive mountain-climbing and skiing equipment. ⊠ *Obereg. 26*, ☎ *033/8229839.* ☞ *5 SF.* ⊙ *May–mid-Oct., Tues.–Sun. 2–5.*

OFF THE
BEATEN PATH

HARDER KULM – Take the 12-minute funicular ride up Harder Kulm (1,310 m/4,297 ft); from there, hike uphill to views south over the city, the lakes, and the whole panorama of snowy peaks. A turreted Gothic chalet-style restaurant offers Friday-evening visitors more than food: from mid-June through September, there are folk music and dancing, and you're free to join in. The funicular runs every 20 to 30 minutes. ⊠ *Funicular station north of the River Aare near Interlaken East, across the Beaurivagebrücke*, ☎ *033/8287339.* ☞ *Funicular round-trip: 20 SF; music: 4 SF.* ⊙ *Funicular: June–Oct., daily 9:10–6:30. Music: departures every 30 minutes 7–8:30, returns at 11, 11:20, and midnight.*

HEIMWEHFLUH – An old-fashioned, red funicular railway leads to the top of this 669-m (2,194-ft) mountain, where you will get views over both lakes and an elevated peek at the Jungfrau, the Eiger, and the Mönch. A restaurant and playground have been built at the top, complete with a 300-m (985-ft) bob-run, and there's a show of model trains every 30 minutes. The funicular station is a five-minute walk from the Interlaken West station down the Rugenparkstrasse. There's a departure every 15 minutes. If you hike to the top, the train show costs just 6 SF. ☎ *033/8223453.* ☞ *12 SF (includes model train show).* ⊙ *Easter and Apr., weekends; May–Oct, daily 9:30–5:30.*

SCHYNIGE PLATTE – For the most splendid overview in the region, make the ambitious trip to this 1,965-m (6,445-ft) peak for a picnic, a wander down any of numerous footpaths, or a visit to the Alpine Botanical Garden, where more than 500 varieties of mountain flowers grow. You may opt to walk either up or (more comfortably) down: specify when you buy your ticket. Train service runs from approximately 7:40 AM to 6 PM. ⊠ *Take 6-min ride on Bernese Oberland Railway from Interlaken East to Wilderswil; take 50-min cogwheel train ride to peak,* ☎ *033/ 8287233.* 🚞 *Round-trip 54 SF; one-way 32 SF.* ☉ *Late May or early June–late Oct., daily, depending on snow conditions.*

Dining and Lodging

$$$–$$$$ ✕ **Alpenblick.** Just 2 km (1 mi) south of Interlaken, in Wilderswil, this
★   hotel restaurant is one of the best in the Berner Oberland (competing with Grindelwald's Fiescherblick). It is a carved-wood-and-shingle 17th-century landmark in the quiet old Oberdorf (Upper Village) and serves a varied clientele, among them loyal gastronomes who make a pilgrimage to try chef Richard Stöckli's international cuisine. Locals dine here regularly, too, seeking out old-style classics (Rösti with wild mushrooms) and upscale bistro fare (marinated lake fish tartare, duck-liver pâté with onion confit). ⊠ *Wilderswil,* ☎ *033/8220707. AE, DC, MC, V.*

$$–$$$ ✕ **Schuh.** With a luxurious shady terrace spilling into the Höhematte in summer and cocktail piano enhancing the dated elegance inside, this sweet shop and café-restaurant serves everything from tea to rich, hot meals. Leave room for the pastries, like the glossy strawberry tarts, which you'll find in the adjoining shop. ⊠ *Höheweg 56,* ☎ *033/8229441. AE, DC, MC, V.*

$$–$$$ ✕ **Stellambiente.** For something nicely out of the ordinary, try this restau-
★   rant in the Stella Hotel (☞ *below*). The modern, highly flavored cuisine includes several vegetarian options, with locally grown ingredients and an extraordinary variety of salads. Order the "surprise" menu in advance, and you'll be served five courses of unexpected delights on beautiful, individually selected pieces of china. An attractive terrace, complete with fountain, turns summer dining into a garden idyll. Though it's not absolutely required, try to make reservations in advance. ⊠ *Waldeggstr. 10,* ☎ *033/8228871. AE, DC, MC, V.*

$$–$$$ ✕ **Zum Bären.** Walk into this restaurant just across the river in Unterseen, and you'll feel as though you've entered a model-chalet souvenir piggybank. The building has been a restaurant since 1674 and run by the same family for more than 150 years. Standard Swiss dishes are perfectly prepared; for instance, the Rösti are done just right, crisp on the outside and tender within. Piped-in country music (in German) and the occasional yodel from the kitchen round out the experience. ⊠ *Seestr. 2, Unterseen,* ☎ *033/8227526. AE, MC, V.*

$$ ✕ **Im Gade.** This welcoming hybrid of carved-wood coziness and sleek
★   formality fills up with appreciative locals who recognize fresh, fine cooking and alert service. Details count here: even that dab of smoky sauerkraut in your crisp mixed salad is homemade. Seasonal specialties (game, mushrooms) stand out. Fondues are available but are not the restaurant's forte: stick to the hearty veal dishes, the lake fish, or the generous daily specials. ⊠ *Höheweg 70, Hotel du Nord,* ☎ *033/ 8222631. AE, DC, MC, V. Closed mid-Nov.–mid-Dec.*

$$ ✕ **Krebs.** The sunny front-porch serving area looks over the street, but head for the more formal dining room, glassed-in yet still opening onto the main promenade. You may feel you've forgotten your parasol: this is a classic Old World resort spot and serves its upscale Swiss classics and homey daily plates (look for the fish dishes) with starched-collar style. It has been in Interlaken—and the Krebs family—since 1875. ⊠ *Bahnhofstr. 4,* ☎ *033/8227161. AE, DC, MC, V. Closed Nov.–Apr.*

$–$$ ✕ **Laterne.** You'll find this unpretentious local favorite a bit off the tourist
★   track, east of the center near the A8 ring road (a 10-minute walk from

Interlaken West). There's a sports-bar ambience, complete with piles of photo albums chronicling what seems to be every party ever held there, and a rustic, woodsy setting. Besides the big meat dinners there are good Swiss specialties: seven kinds of Rösti served in iron skillets, vegetarian meals, and eight kinds of cheese fondue at reasonable prices. There's also live Swiss folk music every second Friday. ⊠ *Obere Bönigstr. 18,* ☎ *033/8221141. AE, DC, MC, V.*

$$–$$$ ✕▥ **Zum Hirschen.** This 17th-century, dark-beam guest house, in one
★ family since 1666, has old deep-shingle eaves and rooms with fresh knotty-pine walls and built-in furniture. The Stübli, paneled in aged pine, and the highly acclaimed restaurant, scattered with antiques, serve local specialties; veal, beef, cheese, vegetables, and even honey come from the owner's farm. The mixed grill and the Rösti with porcini mushrooms are worth the calories. The hotel's location at an outskirts crossroads makes it convenient for drivers who are covering the region rather than staying in town. ⊠ *Hauptstr. 11, CH-3800,* ☎ *033/8221545,* FAX *033/8233745. 24 rooms, 1 suite. Restaurant, Stübli. AE, DC, MC, V. Closed Nov.–mid-Dec. Restaurant closed Tues.*

$$$$ ▥ **Beau Rivage.** Its atmosphere harkening back more than a few
★ decades, this Interlaken old-timer is steeped in intimate, quiet luxury. Rich in brocades, muted tones, and patterned carpets, the rooms have views of either the mountains or the quiet Aare, and the hotel is just a stone's throw from the Interlaken East train station. Set well back from the road and surrounded by gardens, it maintains an unruffled calm. Delicate *cuisine du marché* (based on the freshest ingredients available) is served in the very highly rated, hearth-warmed restaurant La Bonne Fourchette. ⊠ *Höheweg 211, CH-3800,* ☎ *033/8216272,* FAX *033/8232847. 99 rooms. 2 restaurants, 2 bars, indoor pool, sauna, health club, bicycles. AE, DC, MC, V. Closed mid-Nov.–mid-Dec.* ✤

$$$$ ▥ **Grand Hotel Victoria-Jungfrau.** Grand says it all. Mark Twain may
★ have slept in this 1865 landmark, but its restoration has taken it firmly into the 21st century, with a glitzy postmodern black-and-burled-wood entry and plenty of facilities, including indoor master golf. The rooms are gorgeous, with styles shifting from elegant fabric-covered walls and marble columns to fresh yellow gingham and waxed wood floors. Nearly all take in the obligatory view. The flashy formal restaurant, La Terrasse, is a vision of marble and glass overlooking the promenade and the Höhematte. A jacket and tie are required at the restaurant. ⊠ *Höheweg 41, CH-3800,* ☎ *033/8282828,* FAX *033/8282880. 212 rooms. 3 restaurants, 2 bars, indoor pool, outdoor pool, beauty salon, spa, 7 tennis courts, billiards. AE, DC, MC, V.* ✤

$$$$ ▥ **Hotel Metropole.** As Berner Oberland's only skyscraper, this 18-story concrete high-rise gobbles up the scenery and ruins everyone's view but its own—which is spectacular. The rooms have dark furniture, floral drapes, and enormous closets, but nothing can beat those views. The modern decor continues through the green-and-cream atrium lobby. In the rooftop restaurant you can feast your eyes on more staggering views while having a light lunch or snack. ⊠ *Höheweg 37, CH-3800,* ☎ *033/8286666,* FAX *033/8286633. 97 rooms. 2 restaurants, indoor pool, massage, sauna. AE, DC, MC, V.* ✤

$$$–$$$$ ▥ **Royal–St. Georges.** If you are a fan of Victoriana, this impeccably restored gem is a dream come true, with original moldings, built-in furnishings, and fantastical art nouveau bath fixtures. A few rooms were done in ho-hum modern, as some guests object to bathtubs with feet, but you can ask for a period version. The street-side rooms—the ones with Jungfrau views—are noisier. ⊠ *Höheweg 139, CH-3800,* ☎ *033/8227575,* FAX *033/8233075. 89 rooms, 6 suites. Restaurant, bar, hot tub, sauna, steam rooms. AE, DC, MC, V. Closed Nov.–Jan.* ✤

\$\$\$ ⊡ **Du Lac.** The riverboat docks behind this dependable hotel, with its lovely location across from a wide, woodsy bank of the Aare, near the Interlaken East train station. In spite of hourly trains until 11:30 PM, nights are comparatively quiet, especially on the river side, since the hotel is just outside downtown. Managed by a single family for more than 100 years, it has been carefully maintained and the high-ceiling rooms remain styled in their traditional vein, with touches of French classical and Queen Anne styles. ⊠ *Höheweg 225, CH-3800,* ☎ *033/8222922,* FAX *033/8222915. 40 rooms. Restaurant, bar, Stübli, no-smoking rooms, baby-sitting, free parking. AE, DC, MC, V. Closed mid-Nov.–mid-Mar.* ✎

\$\$\$ ⊡ **Stella.** This small, family-run gem defies its outdated '60s exterior
★   and residential neighborhood setting. Inside you'll find marvelous, friendly service; innovative, cozy rooms; and special, personal touches such as rose petals strewn across your duvet in welcome. This is a small hotel that truly does try harder—and does so successfully. The personal touch carries over to their restaurant, the Stellambiente (☞ *above*). ⊠ *Waldeggstr. 10 CH-3800,* ☎ *033/8228871,* FAX *033/8226671. 30 rooms. Restaurant, indoor pool. AE, DC, MC, V.* ✎

\$\$ ⊡ **Chalet Oberland.** A vacation-intensive combination of rustic decor and city-crossroads position, this downtown lodge occupies both sides of the street and keeps expanding. The newest rooms (in the building pierced by a life-size cow model) are chic, with warm wood tones and funkily designed bathrooms. The rooms in the older wing have a heavy-on-the-browns decor. ⊠ *Postg. 1, CH-3800,* ☎ *033/8278787,* FAX *033/8278770. 137 rooms, 23 suites. Bar, coffee shop, pizzeria. AE, DC, MC, V.* ✎

\$\$ ⊡ **Splendid.** Location is key here: you can't get more central to shopping and nightlife. It's a modest, family-run Victorian palace with some woodsy rooms and the occasional spindle bed breaking with the standard beige decor. The back rooms overlook a quiet backstreet; the corner bays are prettiest. The proprietor is a hunter, so game in season is fresh and local. ⊠ *Höheweg 33, CH-3800,* ☎ *033/8227612,* FAX *033/8227679. 35 rooms. Restaurant, pub. AE, MC, V. Closed late Oct.–Christmas.* ✎

\$\$ ⊡ **Toscana.** Well situated in the pedestrian zone, this lodging emphasizes technical perfection: intercom, elevators, cable TVs, indoor parking, angled mountain views. Rooms are spacious if bland, but the restaurant stands out with its good Tuscan cooking, prepared by the Italian owners. ⊠ *Jungfraustr. 19, CH-3800,* ☎ *033/8233033,* FAX *033/8233551. 23 rooms. Restaurant, café, free parking. AE, MC, V. Closed Jan.–Feb.*

\$–\$\$ ⊡ **Alphorn.** Comfortably old-fashioned, this lovely family-run Victo-
★   rian bed-and-breakfast sits on a quiet side street between Interlaken West and the Heimwehfluh. Some rooms have tapestry wallpaper, waxed parquet floors, and original plaster moldings; florals and other patterns abound. The service is notably warm and welcoming. ⊠ *Rugenaustr. 8, CH-3800,* ☎ *033/8223051,* FAX *033/8233069. 20 rooms. Breakfast room, bar, parking. AE, DC, MC, V.* ✎

\$ ⊡ **Balmer's.** This popular private youth hostel offers families and
★   young travelers bare-bones bedrooms at rock-bottom prices. Kitchen access, washers and dryers, videos, two fireplaces, a convenience store, and self-service suppers make you feel at home in this lively, collegiate party atmosphere. The English-speaking staff is especially helpful in finding you the cheapest deals in skiing and other outdoor activities. Rooms are available with one to five beds, all with sinks. There's even a massive group tent pitched at the edge of town roughly from June through September. Check-in is required by 5 PM, checkout by 10 AM; there are no lockers or day storage. It's a quick bus ride from either rail station; they even offer a free shuttle bus May–September. ⊠

Hauptstr. 23–25, CH-3800, ☎ *033/8221961,* FAX *033/8233261. 50 rooms. Bar, library, coin laundry. AE, MC, V.* 🏊

$ 🖫 **Happy Inn Lodge.** Smack in the middle of town, this low-budget dorm-style hotel under young management is clean, simple, safe, and very friendly. The basic rooms have bunk beds, doubles, or twins. The Brasserie 17 (☞ Nightlife, *below*) downstairs is an incredibly popular nightspot—but since it closes at 12:30 AM you'll still get some sleep. ✉ *Rosenstr. 17, CH-3800,* ☎ *033/8223225,* FAX *033/8223268. 15 rooms. AE, MC, V.*

Nightlife and the Arts

BARS

There's a lively, mixed crowd at **Brasserie 17** (✉ Happy Inn Lodge, Rosenstr. 17, ☎ 033/8223225). **Buddy's Pub** (✉ Hotel Splendid, ☎ 033/8227612) is a popular conversation spot where locals and visitors actually mingle. **Jones' Blues Bar** (✉ Bahnhofstr. 22, ☎ 033/8234863) buzzes with canned blues and clever drinks.

CASINOS

The **Kursaal** (☎ 033/8276140) has *boule* (a type of roulette) and 120 slot machines; it's open from 8 PM till 2:30 AM daily. It's not exactly Vegas, but there's a friendly atmosphere. Remember there's a 5 SF gambling limit.

DANCING

The disco **Black and White,** in the Hotel Metropole (☎ 033/8236633), attracts an upscale crowd. **High-life** (✉ Rugenparkstr. 2, ☎ 033/8221550), near Interlaken West, brings back easygoing oldies. **Hollywood** (✉ Hotel Central, ☎ 033/8231033) draws a painfully young crowd. **Johnny's Club** (✉ Hotel Carlton, ☎ 033/8223821) has been the definitive after-hours club for years—it comes alive at midnight.

FOLKLORE

Folklore shows—yodeling and all—are presented at Interlaken's **Folklore-Spycher,** in the Kursaal (✉ Off Höheweg, ☎ 033/8276100), with admission including meals (44 SF to 54 SF) or not (16 SF), as space allows. Priority is given to diners. Meals are at 7:30, shows at 9. At the restaurant at **Harder Kulm** (☎ 033/8225171), reached by funicular, on Friday only from June through September you can hear typical *Ländler* (traditional dance) music and try a little regional dancing.

THEATER

For a real introduction to the local experience, don't miss the **Tellfreilichtspiele,** an outdoor pageant play presented in Interlaken every summer by a cast of Swiss amateurs. Wrapped in a rented blanket—which you'll need, since evenings can be chilly and the show goes on regardless of weather June through September—and seated in a 2,200-seat sheltered amphitheater that opens onto illuminated woods and a permanent village-set, you'll see 250 players in splendid costume acting out the epic tale of Swiss hero Wilhelm Tell. The text is Schiller's famous play, performed in German with the guttural singsong of a Schwyzerdütsch accent—but don't worry; with galloping horses, flower-decked cows, bonfires, parades, and, of course, the famous apple-shooting climax, the operatic story tells itself. Tickets are available through the **Tellbüro** (✉ Bahnhofstr. 5A, ☎ 033/8223722), travel agents, and some hotel concierges; prices range from 14 SF to 34 SF.

Outdoor Activities and Sports

HORSEBACK RIDING

The area between Lake Thun and Lake Brienz offers a number of scenic marked bridle paths through woods, over fields, and by streams. Guided rides and classes are available from **E. Voegeli** (✉ Scheidg. 66, Unterseen, ☎ 033/8227416 or 079/079/3545289).

MOUNTAIN CLIMBING

Contact **Alpin Center Interlaken** (⊠ CH-3812 Wilderswil, ☎ 033/ 8235523) for placement with accredited mountain guides.

SAILING

Lake Thun provides the area's most beautiful sailing. From April through mid-October, Interlaken's **Swiss Sailing School** (☎ 033/ 8228330) offers courses and boat rental.

TENNIS

The **Victoria-Jungfrau Spa Tennis Center** (☎ 033/8282855) has three outdoor and four indoor courts; rental equipment is available.

Bönigen

❷ *2 km (1 mi) east of Interlaken.*

With Interlaken so close, Bönigen never got a fair chance to develop into a resort town. All the better for the tourist who wants to be near the action but not exactly in it. This quiet, charming lakeside village is a leisurely half-hour stroll or five-minute car or bus ride from Interlaken. Somehow Bönigen escaped major fires in its 750-year history, so there remains a group of *beschnitzten Häuser,* original wooden houses dating from the 16th to the 18th centuries. The homes are covered with elaborate carvings—curling along posts and window frames, dripping off balconies and underscoring the eaves. Arrowed signs lead you past 18 of the nicest. Many of the sightseeing boats on the **Brienzersee** start or stop here, and the open expanse of lake is a welcome sight after all the narrow valleys.

Dining and Lodging

$$$$ ✕🏨 **Seiler au Lac.** Give this hotel a point for trying harder. With some
★   heavy competition down the road in Interlaken, this cheerful lakefront hotel makes up for its less prestigious address with wonderful views of the lake and mountains, a genuinely friendly ambience, and individually designed rooms reflecting the rather novel tastes of the owners. A bathroom could have decorative tiles or perhaps a triangular mirror, or draperies could swag the head of your bed. In the same family for more than 100 years, it has kept up with the times while retaining a conservative streak. The rustic pizzeria is very popular and reasonably priced. The classier restaurant specializes in lake fish dishes. ⊠ *Am Quai 3, CH-3806,* ☎ *033/8223021,* 🖷 *033/8223001. 45 rooms. Restaurant, bar, grill, pizzeria. AE, DC, MC, V. Closed late Oct.– Christmas and mid-Jan.–late Feb.* 🍴

$ 🏨 **Hotel Oberländerhof.** Comfortably worn at the edges, this century-old family-run hotel next door to the Seiler au Lac (☞ *above*) is worth a second look. Ignore the need for fresh paint and the worn red linoleum. Instead, notice the carved gargoyles making faces from the woodwork, the angels looking down from the plaster ceilings, the dusty red-velvet curtains, and the central atrium, all recalling a glamorous past. The rooms are clean and up to par, some with lake views; although they don't have bathtubs, they all have showers and toilets. The service is friendly, and the café is filled with locals. ⊠ *Am Quai 1, CH-3806,* ☎ *033/8221725.* 🖷 *033/8232866. 18 rooms. Breakfast room, café. MC, V.*

Lauterbrunnen

★ ❸ *10 km (6 mi) south of Interlaken.*

Below Interlaken the mountains seem to part like the Red Sea into the awesome, bluff-lined Lauterbrunnen Valley. Around the village of Lauterbrunnen, grassy meadows often lie in shadow, as 460-m (1,508-

ft) rocky shoulders rise on either side. This tidy town of weathered chalets serves as a starting point for the region's two most spectacular excursions: to the Schilthorn and to the Jungfraujoch. Lauterbrunnen's airportlike, superefficient parking and rail terminal allows long- and short-term parking for visitors heading for Wengen, Mürren, the Jungfraujoch, or the Schilthorn. Consider choosing this valley as a home base for day trips by train, funicular, or cable, thereby saving considerably on hotel rates. But don't ignore its own wealth of hiking options through awe-inspiring scenery.

Magnificent **waterfalls** adorn the length of the Lauterbrunnen Valley, the most famous being the 300-m (984-ft) **Staubbachfälle** (Staubbach Falls), which are illuminated at night and visible from town. Just beyond are the spectacular **Trümmelbachfälle** (Trümmelbach Falls), a series of seven cascades hidden deep inside rock walls at the base of the Jungfrau, which you can access by underground funicular. Approach the departure point via a pretty, creek-side walkway and brace yourself for some steep stair climbing. Be sure to bring along a light jacket—the spray can be more than refreshing in the cool Alpine air. ⊠ *Follow signs and walkway,* ☎ *033/8553232.* ⌘ *10 SF.* ⊙ *Apr.–June and Sept.–Nov., daily 9–5; July–Aug., daily 8–6. Closed Dec.–Mar.*

Dining and Lodging

$$ ✕⌂ **Silberhorn.** Though it's across from the train station and next to the cogwheel train to Mürren, this family-owned and -run hotel is surprisingly quiet. Knotty *Arvenholz* (pine) panels the spic-and-span rooms. On clear days you may want to chill out in one of the wicker chairs on the sun porch. The dependable restaurant offers satisfying meals of Rösti and veal favorites. ⊠ *CH-3822,* ☎ *033/8551471,* 🅵🅰🆇 *033/8554213. 30 rooms. Restaurant, bar, sauna, free parking. AE, DC, MC, V.* 🕾

$ ✕⌂ **Stechelberg.** At the very end of the valley, where the road peters out into a beautiful foot trail, this isolated old lodging offers comforts with a hard-core local touch: heavy smoke, muddy boots, and yodeling on Saturday night. Rooms upstairs are creaky, cozy, and all wood, with balconies that open to the sound of the roaring river. In the restaurant, stick to simple sausage-and-Rösti specials; more ambitious attempts fall short. ⊠ *CH-3824,* ☎ *033/8552921,* 🅵🅰🆇 *033/8554438. 16 rooms. Restaurant, café. AE, DC, MC, V. Closed mid-Nov.–mid-Dec.*

$ ⌂ **Staubbach.** At the far end of town on a big plot of land lies the perhaps the best deal in the valley. Young owners have turned this old landmark into a clean, straightforward, simple hotel. Although the emphasis is on low budget, owners Craig and Corinne Rochin don't skimp on personal warmth and charm. And the views are astounding. ⊠ *CH-3822,* ☎ *033/8555454,* 🅵🅰🆇 *033/8555484. 31 rooms. Breakfast room, coin laundry. MC, V. Closed Nov.–mid-Dec.* 🕾

Shopping

A good source of Lauterbrunnen *torchon* lace is **Handwärch Lädeli** (⊠ Near old schoolhouse, ☎ 033/8553551).

Mürren

★ ❹ *7 km (4 mi) southwest of Lauterbrunnen, 16 km (10 mi) south of Interlaken, plus a 5-min cable-car ride from Stechelberg.*

This lofty sports mecca (elevation 1,650 m/5,413 ft) offers panoramic hiking trails in summer and unrivaled views toward the Jungfrau, the Mönch, and the Eiger. Skiers may want to settle here for daredevil year-round skiing at the top; hikers may combine staggering views and bluff-top trails with extraordinarily peaceful mountain nights. Remember that this is a car-free resort.

Mürren is one of the stops along the popular cable-car ride up the south side of the **Schilthorn** (2,970 m/9,742 ft), famed for its role in the James Bond thriller *On Her Majesty's Secret Service*. The peak of this icy Goliath is accessed by a four-stage cable-lift ride past bare rock cliffs and stunning slopes. At each level, you step off the cable car, walk across the station, and wait briefly for the next cable car up. At the top is a revolving restaurant, Piz Gloria. The cable-car station that accesses the Schilthorn actually has its base in nearby Stechelberg, near the site of the **Mürrenbachfälle** (Mürrenbach Falls), which at 250 m (820 ft) are among the tallest in Europe. ☎ *033/8562141.* ☞ *Round-trip cable car Stechelberg–Schilthorn 87 SF (66 SF 7:25–8:55 or after 3:25 in May and in mid-Oct.–mid-Nov.).* ☉ *Departures daily year-round, twice hourly 6:25 AM–4:25 PM; last departure from the top 6:03 PM in summer, 5:03 PM in winter.*

Mürren is the second stop on the cable car up from Stechelberg—the bulk of the hefty price is for the Mürren–Schilthorn segment of the ride. Another, more affordable way to Mürren is by funicular (across the street from Lauterbrunnen's train station), then connecting to the cogwheel rail from Grütschalp, which runs along the cliff with magnificent views of the Big Three. The whole trip takes about 30 minutes and drops you at the Mürren rail station, at the opposite end of town from the cable-car stop. The trains run every 15–20 minutes. If you're not settling in to stay in a Mürren hotel, this is an ideal takeoff point for a day hike along the bluff top. Point your binoculars at the gleaming dome on the Jungfraujoch across the valley: you can almost hear the winds howling off the Aletsch Glacier.

Skiing

Mürren provides access to the **Schilthorn** (2,970 m/9,742 ft)—the start of a 15-km (9-mi) run that drops all the way through Mürren to Lauterbrunnen. At 1,650 m (5,413 ft), the resort has one funicular railway, two cable cars, seven lifts, and 65 km (40 mi) of downhill runs. A one-day pass covering the Schilthorn region costs 52 SF; a seven-day pass costs 227 SF.

Lodging

$$ ⊞ **Alpenblick.** This simple, comfortable, modern pension is in a spectacular setting and has balconies with astonishing views. Friendly owners (and their good home cooking) round out the experience. It's just beyond the center, near the train (not the cable-car) station, so you may choose to take the funicular up if you have loads of luggage. ⊠ *CH-3825,* ☎ *033/8551327,* ℻ *033/8551391. 14 rooms. Restaurant, café. AE, MC, V. Closed mid-Apr.–June and mid-Oct.–mid-Dec.* ☜

$$ ⊞ **Bellevue-Crystal.** Distinguished from surrounding chalets by its sturdy, yellow-brick-and-shutter construction, this older landmark, with welcoming new owners, presents itself as a traditional ski lodge with full modern comforts. Each room has a tiny balcony with fine views, and the decor is fresh pine and gingham. ⊠ *CH-3825,* ☎ *033/8551401,* ℻ *033/8551490. 17 rooms. Restaurant, café, sauna. MC, V. Closed Easter–early June.* ☜

Jungfraujoch

★ ⑤ *½-day cog-railway excursion out of Interlaken, Lauterbrunnen, or Grindelwald.*

The granddaddy of all high-altitude excursions, the famous journey to the Jungfraujoch, site of the highest railroad station in the world, is one of the most popular tourist goals in Switzerland. From the station at Lauterbrunnen you take the green, cogwheel Wengernalp Railway nearly straight up the wooded mountainside as the valley and the village shrink below. From the hilltop resort of **Wengen** (☞ *below*) the train climbs up steep grassy slopes past the timberline to **Kleine Scheidegg,** a tiny, isolated resort settlement surrounded by vertiginous scenery. Here you change to the **Jungfraubahn,** which tunnels straight into the rock of the Eiger, stopping briefly for views out enormous picture windows blasted through its stony face.

The **Jungfraujoch terminus** stands at an elevation of 3,475 m (11,400 ft); you may feel a bit light-headed from the altitude. Follow signs to the **Top of Europe** restaurant, a gleaming white glass-and-steel pavilion. The expanse of rock and ice you see from here is simply blinding.

If you're not sated with the staggering views from the Jungfraujoch terminus, you can reach yet another height by riding a high-tech 90-second elevator up 111 m (364 ft) to the **Sphinx Terrace:** to the south crawls the vast Aletsch Glacier, to the northeast stand the Mönch and the Eiger, and to the southwest—almost close enough to touch—towers the tip of the Jungfrau herself. Note: even in low season, you may have to wait in long lines for the elevator up.

More than views are offered to the hordes that mount the Jungfraujoch daily. You can take a beginner's **ski lesson** or a **dogsled ride,** or tour the chill blue depths of the **Ice Palace,** a novelty attraction on the order of a wax museum, full of incongruous and slightly soggy ice sculptures. Admission is included in the price of the excursion (the ski lessons and dogsled rides cost extra).

A few things to keep in mind for the Jungfraujoch trip: take sunglasses, warm clothes, and sturdy shoes; even the interior halls can be cold and slippery at the top. Some sensitive individuals may experience sleepiness or a headache while at the top from the high altitude, which usually disappears on the train ride down. Return trains, especially toward the end of the day, can be standing-room only. To save money, take the 6:35 AM train. Guided tours with escort and English commentary (called Jungfrau Tour as opposed to *Jungfrau individuell*) also cost less; these leave once a day from Interlaken East. You can get to Lauterbrunnen or Grindelwald (☞ *below*) on your own steam (or using your Swiss Pass; ☞ Train Travel *in* Smart Travel Tips A to Z) and then buy a ticket to the top; if you've driven, of course, you'll have to return the way you came and miss the full round-trip tour. ☎ *033/8287233; 033/8551022 for Jungfraujoch weather information.* ▨ *Round-trip Interlaken East–Lauterbrunnen–Wengen–Jungfraujoch (back via Grindelwald) 159 SF; 6:35 AM 120 SF.* ☉ *Daily June–Sept. 6:35 (first train up)–6:10 (last train down).*

Wengen

❻ *½-hr cog-railway ride from Lauterbrunnen.*

This south-facing hilltop resort perched on a sunny plateau over the Lauterbrunnen Valley has magnificent panoramas down the valley. It rivals Mürren for its quiet, chic, and challenging skiing, which connects with the trail network at Grindelwald; loyalists prefer Wengen for its memorable sunsets. In summer it is a wonderful place to hike. You can aim for central, upscale hotels, near resort shopping and active bars, or head downhill to pleasant, more isolated lodgings, all artfully skewed toward the view. Most hotels encourage longer stays with reduced rates, and half-board is just short of obligatory. (There are only a few restaurants that are not attached to a hotel.) It's a car-free town; most hotels have porters meeting the trains.

Skiing

Just over the ridge from Grindelwald, the sunny resort of **Wengen** (1,300 m–3,450 m/4,265 ft–11,316 ft) nestles on a sheltered plateau high above the Lauterbrunnen Valley; from there, a complex lift system connects to Grindelwald, Kleine Scheidegg, and Männlichen. Wengen has six funicular railways, one cable car, 31 lifts, and 250 km (155 mi) of downhill runs. The Lauberhorn run is tough; it's used for the World Cup Ski Races in January. One-day lift tickets for Kleine Scheidegg/Männlichen cost 52 SF. A two-day pass costs 95 SF. Lift passes for the Jungfrau/Top-Ski-Region are only available for two days or more; a two-day ticket costs 105 SF, a six-day ticket 244 SF. For lessons contact the Swiss Ski and Snowboard School (☎ 033/8552022).

Dining and Lodging

$$$$ ✕🏨 **Regina.** It's all about atmosphere in this genteel Victorian hotel. Between the loyal clientele and the gracious owners, a genuinely familial mood is palpable. Most large rooms have balconies and are done in mauve and rose; rooms under the eaves have loft beds and a green color scheme with wood accents. Paintings and local antiques (such as a huge wooden sled) are scattered throughout. The emphasis is on half-board, and it's a treat; the dining room shares the chef with the hotel's intimate à la carte restaurant, Chez Meyer's. There you'll find dark, polished-wood wainscoting and old family photos on soothing yellow walls—plus an exceptionally creative seasonal menu that might include lobster ravioli with ginger sauce or veal fillet with chanterelles. Reservations are essential, as are a jacket and tie. ⊠ CH-3823, ☎ 033/8551512, FAX 033/8551574. 96 rooms. Restaurant, bar, beauty salon, sauna, steam room, exercise room. AE, DC, MC, V. Closed Nov. ✪

$$$$ 🏨 **Park Hotel Beausite.** Grandly situated on the hill above Wengen, this hotel encourages pampering; you can relax with a massage or sauna. Rooms are spacious, some with elegant brass beds, others in a more traditional, rustic style. For a leisurely look at the view, sink into one of the couches in the front lounge off the lobby. The hotel is near the cable-car station, a 10-minute walk from the village. ⊠ CH-3823, ☎ 033/8565161, FAX 033/8553010. 46 rooms, 7 apartments. Restaurant, piano bar, indoor pool, massage, sauna. AE, DC, MC, V. ✪

$$$$ 🏨 **Silberhorn.** Its 19th-century origins evident only in the roofline, this all-modern resort lodge just across from the cogwheel train station has a young, lively staff and ambience. Bright, generously sized rooms are full of pine and chintz, some with delicate floral and striped wallpaper. The heated floors in the bathrooms are a nice touch. ⊠ CH-3823, ☎ 033/8565131, FAX 033/8552244. 68 rooms. Restaurant, bar, hot tub, sauna, dance club, children's playroom. AE, DC, MC, V. ✪

$$–$$$ 🏨 **Alpenrose.** Wengen's first hotel, this welcoming inn has been run
★ by the same family for more a century—in tried and true fashion, the owners are there to greet you. The decor is homey, with knotty pine, painted wood, and skirted lampshades. Rooms with south-facing balconies are only slightly more expensive and worth it. It's downhill and away from the center, with an emphasis on good half-board food. The restaurant is for guests only. ⊠ CH-3823, ☎ 033/8553216, FAX 033/8551518. 50 rooms. Restaurant. AE, DC, MC, V. Closed Easter–mid-May and early Oct.–Christmas.

$–$$ 🏨 **Eden/Eddy's Hostel.** A shingled Victorian jewel box joins forces with an unpretentious crash pad—the Eden Hotel providing marvelous southern views, very comfy rooms with or without bathrooms, and pretty gardens, and Eddy's Hostel providing a no-frills bed, a shower, and a breakfast buffet across the street at the Eden. The proprietress is terrific: she'll help you organize hikes. There are plenty of occasions to mix at barbecues, over aperitifs on the terrace, or at one of many sum-

mertime live music events. ⊠ CH-3823, ☎ 033/8551634, FAX 033/
8553950. 18 rooms, 6 dorms. Restaurant, café. AE, DC, MC, V.
Closed Nov.–mid-Dec.

$–$$ 🏠 **Schweizerheim.** It's worth the hike to this old-fashioned family-run
★ pension nestled well below the beaten path: the full-valley views are
flawless, the gardens pristine, and the terrace picnic tables balance pre-
cariously over the Lauterbrunnen Valley. The rooms are a dated mix
of wood paneling, Formica, linoleum, and carpet, but the experience
is welcoming and fun—and the owner is a Swiss hand-organ celebrity.
The restaurant serves pension guests only. ⊠ CH-3823, ☎ 033/
8551112, FAX 033/8552327. 24 rooms. Restaurant, bar. MC, V. 🐾

$–$$ 🏠 **Zum Bären.** This lodging just below the center is straightforward
and bright, with good views and low rates. The rooms are freshly done
in blues, yellows, and pale wood; the watercolors are painted by the
owner's mother. For extracheap sleeps (about 35 SF, including breakfast), you can stay in one of the two scout-camp-style dorm rooms, each
with 10 beds. ⊠ CH-3823, ☎ 033/8551419, FAX 033/8551525. 14
rooms. Restaurant, café. AE, DC, MC, V. Closed mid-Oct.–mid-Dec.
and for 2 wks after Easter. 🐾

Outdoor Activities and Sports
SKATING
Wengen has a natural **rink** (Natureisbahn) and a partially sheltered indoor rink (Kunsteisbahn); for hours contact the tourist office (☎ 033/
8551414).

Nightlife and the Arts
DANCING
Hit **Tiffany** (⊠ Hotel Silberhorn, ☎ 033/8565131) for a good mix of
locals and tourists.

Grindelwald

❼ 27 km (17 mi) east of Interlaken.

Strung along a mountain highway with two convenient train stations,
Grindelwald (1,050 m/3,445 ft) is the most easily accessible of the region's high resorts. It makes an excellent base for skiing and hiking,
shopping and dining—if you don't mind a little traffic.

From Grindelwald you can drive, take a postbus, or hike up to the
★ **Oberergletscher,** a craggy, steel blue glacier. You can approach its base
along wooded trails, where there's an instrument to measure the glacier's
daily movement. Better yet, travel down into the valley to Grund, below
Grindelwald, and visit the **Gletscherschlucht** (Glacier Gorge). There you
can walk along a trail through tunnels and over bridges about 1 km (½
mi) into the gorge itself. Although you can't see the glacier itself while
walking along the edges of the spectacular gorge it sculpted, you'll get
a powerful sense of its slow-motion, inexorable force. ⊠ Trail: 🎫 5 SF.
🕑 Late May–mid-Oct.

Also out of Grindelwald, you can take the **Firstbahn,** a 30-minute gondola ride to the lovely views and pistes of the First ski area (2,163 m/7,095
ft). The **Alpine garden** flourishes within easy walking distance (it's even
wheelchair accessible) of the first cable car. Without hiking into the
heights, you can see gentians, edelweiss, anemones, and Alpine asters.

Skiing
An ideal base for the Jungfrau ski area, Grindelwald (1,050 m/3,445
ft) provides access to the varied trails of Grindelwald First and Kleine
Scheidegg/Männlichen. Grindelwald has eight funicular railways, three
cable cars, 22 lifts, and 165 km (103 mi) of downhill runs. Some long

runs go right down to the village; there are special areas for snowboarders and beginning skiers. One-day lift tickets for Kleine Scheidegg/ Männlichen and First each cost 52 SF. A two-day pass costs 95 SF.

Dining and Lodging

$$ ✕ **Memory.** A welcoming, no-fuss, family-style chalet restaurant, Memory is well known for its cheese and potato dishes, which extend beyond the seven kinds of Rösti to include gratins with meat and potato-garlic soup. Sunday nights are burger nights. ⊠ *Eiger Hotel,* ☎ *033/8532121. AE, DC, MC, V.*

$ ✕ **Onkel Tom's Hütte.** This tiny, smoke-free pizza parlor, set in a rus-★ tic A-frame cabin on the main drag, is as cozy as they come. Rough wooden floors accommodate ski boots, and eight wooden tables share space with a huge iron cookstove, where the young owner produces fresh pizzas in three sizes (the smallest of which is plenty!). There are also generous salads, homemade desserts, and a surprisingly large international wine list. Its popularity outstrips its size, so enjoy the good kitchen smells while you wait. ⊠ *Across from Firstbahn,* ☎ *033/ 8535239. MC, V. Closed Mon. and Nov. and June.*

$$$$ ✕▥ **Belvedere.** As you wind your way into Grindelwald, this large, ★ pink structure, precariously perched above the road, comes into view. Rustic styling has given way to tastefully designed interiors; the Salon Louis Philippe is a particularly pleasant place to relax, with its period furniture and wood-inlay games tables. There are drop-dead views of the Eiger and surrounding peaks from almost every room. The staff and management radiate genuine warmth and absolute professionalism; the owner takes groups of guests skiing, hiking, and golfing weekly. The restaurant offers fresh, creative menus that change according to the delicious whims of their trusted chef. Ask about the terms of their special rates for Fodor's guide users when making reservations. ⊠ *CH-3818,* ☎ *033/8545454,* ℻ *033/8535323. 51 rooms. Restaurant, Stübli, piano bar, indoor pool, hot tub, 2 saunas, exercise room, playroom. AE, DC, MC, V. Closed late Oct.–mid-Dec.* ✍

$$$$ ✕▥ **Schweizerhof.** Behind a dark-wood, Victorian-chalet facade dat-★ ing from 1892, this big, comfortable hotel attracts a loyal clientele. Wingbacks and bookcases in the lobby lounge and dining rooms—of scrubbed pine and hand-painted (and carved) trim—are inviting on rainy days. Rooms are decorated in carved pine and have tile baths, along with luxurious bathrobes. The service is attentive, unhurried, flexible, and extremely friendly. They emphasize half-board, and the menu looks beyond Switzerland—try the duck breast with black currant–fig sauce and whole-meal noodles or something from their vegetarian selections. The breakfasts are generously portioned and offered until 11:30 AM (this late schedule is a rarity). In the Stübli you can enjoy fondue *Chinoise* (meat cut into paper-thin slices and quickly cooked in a pot of boiling bouillon). ⊠ *CH-3818,* ☎ *033/8532202,* ℻ *033/8532004. 53 rooms. Restaurant, Stübli, indoor pool, beauty salon, sauna, bowling, health club. Closed Easter–late May and Oct.– late Dec.* ✍

$$–$$$ ✕▥ **Fiescherblick.** This is the place to eat in Grindelwald, whether as ★ a pension hotel guest or day-tripper: the serious cuisine in the intimate restaurant continues to draw kudos and devoted food lovers, and the lower-priced Swiss Bistro in the adjoining bar allows casual lunchers to enjoy the talents of the same chef. The seasonal menu might include wild-garlic sausage in fall, freshwater crayfish for a few weeks in spring, or roast lobster with pistachio oil in winter. As for the rooms, try to nab one of the "superior" rooms, which are bright and spacious, if more expensive. The standard rooms tend to be on the unexciting functional-brown-decor side. ⊠ *CH-3818,* ☎ *033/8534453,* ℻ *033/*

8534457. 25 rooms. Restaurant, Stübli. AE, DC, MC, V. Closed Easter–mid-May and mid-Oct.–mid-Dec. ✍

$–$$ ✕▣ **Hotel Wetterhorn.** Overlooking the magnificent ice-blue upper glacier—as well as the sprawling parking lot where hikers leave their cars—this modest inn offers generous lunches outdoors, with full glacier views, and good regional dining inside its comfortable restaurant. Portions of veal favorites are large and delicious, and there is a good selection of Swiss wines. Everything is homemade, right down to the jam and cheese. The adjoining Gletscherstübli attracts locals as well as the hordes of tourists and hikers who come to marvel at its namesake. Up the creaky old stairs, there are simple, tidy aged-pine rooms—some have glacier views—with sink and shared bath. They have renovated the neighboring farmhouse and chalet into four vacation apartments. ⊠ *CH-3818,* ☎ *033/8531218,* ℻ *033/8535818. 9 rooms, 4 apartments. Restaurant, café, Stübli. AE, DC, MC, V.*

$$$$ ▣ **Grand Hotel Regina.** The turreted exterior dates from the turn of the century, but this pricey hotel is hardly a museum. Touches from the past, such as antiques and elaborate chairs from the founder's collection, individualize the rooms; a luxurious strain runs throughout, with parquet floors, gold-ceiling baths, and white-leather furnishings. The views are flawless, the location central, and the tennis courts may be some of the most spectacularly sited in the world. ⊠ *CH-3818,* ☎ *033/8548600; 800/223–6800 in the U.S.,* ℻ *033/8548666. 100 rooms. Restaurant, indoor pool, pool, beauty salon, massage, sauna, 2 tennis courts, nightclub. AE, DC, MC, V.* ✍

$$$ ▣ **Gletschergarten.** In the same family for three generations, this atmospheric pension radiates welcome, from the heirloom furniture and paintings (by the grandfather) to the tea roses cut from the owner's garden. There's heraldry in the leaded-glass windows, a ceramic stove with built-in seat warmer, and a cozy lounge paneled in wood taken from an old Grindelwald farmhouse. All rooms have balconies, some with glacier views, others overlooking the emerald green hills. Ask for a corner room, as their angles and view are especially pleasing. ⊠ *CH-3818,* ☎ *033/8531721,* ℻ *033/8532957. 26 rooms. Restaurant, bar, sauna, steam room, Ping-Pong, billiards, coin laundry. AE, MC, V.* ✍

$$–$$$ ▣ **Alpina.** This chalet has a lofty perch, making for sensational views from its front balconies—and though it's a cement building, the edges are softened inside and out by light-wood decor, geraniums below every window, and warm, personal service. The slightly more expensive front rooms are especially cheerful and bright, with lovely new bathrooms. The back rooms saw their heyday in the days of dark wood-grain Formica. It's a five-minute walk up from the station. ⊠ *CH-3818,* ☎ *033/8533333,* ℻ *033/8533376. 30 rooms. Restaurant. AE, DC, MC, V. Closed just after Easter–early May.* ✍

$$ ▣ **Gletscherschlucht.** Down below Grindelwald at the entrance to the glacier gorge in Talgrund is this neat, spic-and-span, family-friendly hotel. Bright, sizable new pine rooms have stained-wood furnishings and shiny tile baths. Its quiet valley location is just 2 km (1 mi) below the tourist hubbub. ⊠ *CH-3818,* ☎ *033/8536050,* ℻ *033/8536051. 5 rooms. Restaurant. V.*

$ ▣ **Mountain Hostel.** It's all uphill from here—this welcoming hostel sits at the foot of the Eiger in Grund, 2 km (1¼ mi) from Grindelwald. The beds, with or without covers, are set up in bunk-bed rooms for from two to six people. Showers and toilets are down the hall. The owners take groups out on hikes, and there are grill parties in summer. It's just a couple of minutes on foot from the Grund train station. ⊠ *CH-3818,* ☎ *033/8533900,* ℻ *033/8534730. 20 rooms. Restaurant. MC, V.* ✍

Nightlife and the Arts

DANCING

Challi Bar (⊠ Hotel Kreuz, ☎ 033/8545492) has a DJ who plays requests. The **Gepsi-Bar** (⊠ Eiger Hotel, ☎ 033/8532121) is open late; there are a fun crowd and weekly live music. The **Plaza Club** (⊠ Sunstar Hotel, ☎ 033/8534240) is a Swiss self-styled "ethno disco" (decorated with cows and alphorns), although the music is strictly modern (no yodeling here). There's also the **Regina Bar-Dancing** with live music nightly (⊠ Grand Hotel Regina, ☎ 033/8545455).

Outdoor Activities and Sports

HIKING

Grindelwald is a hiker's paradise, both in summer and winter. Detailed trail maps are available at the tourist office (☞ Visitor Information *in* Berner Oberland A to Z, *below*).

MOUNTAIN CLIMBING

The **Bergsteigerzentrum** (⊠ Grindelwald center, ☎ 033/8535200) offers daily and weekly courses to mountain and glacier hikers.

SKATING

The **Sportzentrum Grindelwald** (☎ 033/8541230) has indoor and natural rinks. You can rent skates at the indoor rink.

TENNIS

Grindelwald has six **public courts** (☎ 033/8531912).

BRIENZERSEE

Reputedly the cleanest lake in Switzerland—which surely means one of the cleanest in the world—this magnificent bowl of crystal-clear water mirrors the mountain-scape and forests, cliffs, and waterfalls that surround it. You can cruise alongside Lake Brienz at high speed on the A8 freeway or crawl along its edge on secondary waterfront roads; or you can cut a wake across it on a steamer, exploring each stop on foot, then cruising to your next destination.

Iseltwald

❽ *9 km (6 mi) northeast of Interlaken.*

This isolated peninsula juts out into the lake, its small hotels, cafés, and rental chalets clustered at the water's edge. Every restaurant prides itself on its lake fish, of course. From the village edge you may want to take off on foot; a lovely forest walk of about 1½ hours brings you to the falls of the **Giessbach** (Giess Brook), which tumbles in several stages down rocky cliffs to the lake. The most scenic route to Iseltwald from Interlaken is via the south-shore road; follow the black-and-white ISELTWALD signs. You can also take the A8 expressway, following the autoroute signs for Meiringen.

Brienz

★ **❾** *12 km (7 mi) northeast of Iseltwald, 21 km (13 mi) northeast of Interlaken.*

The romantic waterfront village of Brienz, world renowned as a wood-carving center, is a favorite stop for boat tourists as well as drivers. Several artisan shops display the local wares, which range in quality from the ubiquitous, winningly simple figures of spotted cows to finely modeled nativity figures and Hummel-like portraits of Wilhelm Tell. Brienz is also a showcase of traditional Oberland architecture, with some of its loveliest houses (at the west end of town, near the church) dating from the 17th century. Once an important stage stop, Brienz hosted Goethe and Byron at its landmark Hotel Weisses Kreuz (☞ Dining and Lodging, *below*); their names, along with the 1688 date of construction, are proudly displayed on the gable.

Switzerland's last steam-driven cogwheel train runs from the center of Brienz, at the waterfront, up to the summit of **Brienzer-Rothorn,** 2,346 m (7,700 ft) above the town. The ride takes one hour. Trains run at least every hour, but to avoid long waits at peak times, purchase your ticket for a particular train in advance on the day you will make the trip; they do not accept reservations. ☎ *033/9522222.* 🖃 *66 SF roundtrip.* ☉ *June–Oct., daily; 1st train up Mon.–Sat. 8:30, Sun. 7:30, last train up 4:15, last train down 5:40.*

At Brienz you may want to try your own hand at **wood carving**: in one lesson at the atelier of Paul Fuchs you can learn to carve the typical Brienzer cow. Make a reservation through the tourist office in Brienz or directly with Mr. Fuchs. You'll be put in a class of a dozen or more. ⊠ *Scheidweg 19D, in Hofstetten, between Brienz and Ballenberg,* ☎ *033/9511418.* 🖃 *22 SF per person.* ☉ *2-hr workshops Apr.–Oct.*

OFF THE BEATEN PATH ☺	**FREILICHTMUSEUM BALLENBERG –** Just east of Brienz, a small road leads to this child-friendly outdoor museum-park, where 80 characteristic Swiss houses from 18 cantons have been carefully reconstructed after being disassembled and moved here. Even the gardens and farm animals are true to type. Old handicrafts and trades like spinning, forging, and lace making are demonstrated using original tools. ☎ *033/ 9511123.* 🖃 *14 SF.* ☉ *Mid-Apr.–Oct., daily 10–5.*

Dining and Lodging

$–$$
★
✕ **Steinbock.** Whether you dine on the broad flower-lined terrace or inside the wonderful, old (1787) carved-wood-and-homespun chalet, you'll feel the atmosphere of this proud local institution. Choose from no fewer than 11 interpretations of Lake Brienz whitefish and perch, regional dishes, or veal classics. ⊠ *Hauptstr. 123,* ☎ *033/9514055. AE, DC, MC, V. Closed Tues. and Feb.*

$$
✕ **Weisses Kreuz.** Generic modern improvements have erased some of the fine origins of this structure, built in 1688 and host to Goethe and Byron, but if you are a history buff, the idea of its antiquity and the hallowed names on the gable may be allure enough. The pine-lined restaurant offers omelets and *Käseschnitte* (cheese and bread baked in its own whey) as well as lake fish, steaks, and strudel. The sunny lake-view terrace café draws locals as well as tourists fresh off the boat. ⊠ *Hauptstr. 143,* ☎ *033/9522020. AE, DC, MC, V.*

$$
★
✕🏨 **Lindenhof.** In a 1787 lodge high above the touristy lakefront, German and Austrian families settle in for a week or two of evenings by the vast stone fireplace, dinners in the panoramic winter garden (or on the spectacular terrace), and nights in dressed-up theme rooms with such evocative names as Marmot Cave, Venus Room, and Hunter's Hut. The grounds are vast and beautifully manicured, the atmosphere familial and formal at once. Families with small children dine together by the fire, apart from other guests. ⊠ *Lindenhofweg 15, CH-3855,* ☎ *033/9511072,* 🖷 *033/9514072. 40 rooms, 4 suites. Restaurant, bar, café, kitchenettes, indoor pool, sauna. AE, MC, V. Closed Jan.–Feb.*

$$
★
🏨 **Schönegg und Spycher.** Clinging to a steep, garden-covered hillside over town, this snug pension is run by house-proud Christine Mathyer, who sees to it that all three small lodgings maintain their old-fashioned charm. There are a 1950s fireplace lounge, with flagstone floors and wood carvings, and rooms with rustic painted furniture, flower-sprigged duvets, and chocolates on the pillow at night. Guests can relax

in the sunny garden overlooking the lake, and it's an easy walk up to the Lindenhof or down to the Steinbock (☞ *above*) for dinner. ⊠ *Talstr. 8, CH-3855,* ☎ *033/9511113.* ℻ *033/9513813. 16 rooms. Bar, breakfast room, Ping-Pong. AE, MC, V. Closed Jan.–Feb.*

$$ 🏨 **Seehotel Bären.** The modern construction and 1960s room decor are upstaged by the gracious dining room, flower-framed terrace café, and private waterfront promenade. Lakeside rooms are considerably pricier in high season; back rooms open over the main road. ⊠ *Hauptstr. 72, CH-3855,* ☎ *033/9512412,* ℻ *033/9514022. 32 rooms. Restaurant, café. AE, DC, MC, V. Closed Dec.–Easter.*

$ 🏨 **Chalet Rothorn.** Family photos, knickknacks, and a doll collection make this private bed-and-breakfast remarkably homey—not to mention Mrs. Jobin's warm welcome. Its perch above town gives it great lake views. One of the rooms makes a particularly nice getaway: it's in a tiny chalet in the garden and has its own balcony. The other guest rooms are distributed between the family's home and another small house in the garden. ⊠ *Talstr. 15, CH-3855,* ☎ ℻ *033/9512374. 6 rooms. No credit cards.*

Shopping

Brienz is the place for good selections of local wood carvings—everything from cows to plates to nativity figures. Check out the wares and get a tour to boot at **Ed Jobin** (⊠ Hauptstr. 111, ☎ 033/9511414) and **Walter Stäheli** (⊠ Hauptstr. 41, ☎ 033/9511471). **H. Huggler-Wyss** (⊠ Fischerbrunnenpl., ☎ 033/9521000) is another worthwhile source.

Meiringen

⑩ *12 km (7 mi) east of Brienz, 35 km (22 mi) northeast of Interlaken.*

Set apart from the twin lakes and saddled between the roads to the Sustenpass and the Brünigpass, Meiringen is a resort town with 300 km (186 mi) of marked hiking trails and 60 km (37 mi) of ski slopes. Its real claim to fame, though, is the **Reichenbachfälle** (Reichenbach Falls), where fictional detective Sherlock Holmes and his archenemy, Professor Moriarty, plunged into the "cauldron of swirling water and seething foam in that bottomless abyss above Meiringen." Visitors can now view the dramatic fall where Conan Doyle intended to end his series of mysteries. A nearby hotel bears the detective's name, and in the center of town the **Sherlock Holmes Museum** has created an "authentic" replica of Holmes's front room at 221b Baker Street. ⊠ *Bahnhofstr. 26,* ☎ *033/9714221.* 🎫 *3.80 SF.* ☉ *May–Sept., Tues.–Sun. 1:30–6; Oct.–Apr., Wed.–Sun. 4:30–6:30.*

Dining and Lodging

$$ 🏨 **Sporthotel Sherlock Holmes.** This sports-oriented hotel is ideal for families, hikers, and skiers. Though the building is modern and unspectacular, most rooms look out on Reichenbach Falls. Rooms are simple, but a meringue on your pillow adds a nice touch. The indoor pool, on the top floor, has a phenomenal view. ⊠ *Alpbachallee 3, CH-3860,* ☎ *033/9729889,* ℻ *033/9729888. 55 rooms. Restaurant, bar, indoor pool, sauna, health club, Ping-Pong, billiards. AE, DC, MC, V.* 🍽

Outdoor Activities and Sports

HIKING

The private, 20-km (12½-mi) **road to Grindelwald** permits no cars but provides a beautiful, seven-hour Alpine hike. For maps of other local hiking trails, hit the tourist office (☞ Visitor Information *in* Berner Oberland A to Z, *below*).

THUNERSEE

If you like your mountains as a picturesque backdrop and prefer a relaxing waterfront sojourn, take a drive around the Thunersee (Lake Thun) or crisscross it on a leisurely cruise boat. More populous than Lake Brienz, its allures include the marina town of Spiez and the large market town of Thun, spread at the feet of the spectacular Schloss Zähringen (Zähringen Castle). There are more castles along the lake, and yet another high-altitude excursion for rising above the waterfront to take in Alpine panoramas—a trip up the Niederhorn.

Spiez

⑪ *19 km (11¼ mi) west of Interlaken.*

The town of Spiez is a summer lake resort with marinas for water-sports enthusiasts. Its enormous waterfront castle, **Schloss Spiez,** was home to the family Strättligen and, in the 13th century, its great troubadour, Heinrich. The structure spans four architectural epochs, starting with the 11th-century tower; its halls contain beautiful period furnishings, some from as long ago as Gothic times. The early Norman church on the grounds is more than 1,000 years old. ☎ *033/6541506.* ☞ *4 SF.* ☉ *Mid-Apr.–June and Sept.–mid-Oct., Mon. 2–5, Tues.–Sun. 10–5; July–Aug., Mon. 2–6, Tues.–Sun. 10–6. Closed late Oct.–early Apr.*

Dining and Lodging

$$–$$$ ✕▥ **Seegarten Hotel Marina.** With a pizzeria corner in one wing and two dining rooms that stretch comfortably along the marina front, this is a pleasant, modern family restaurant, and its lake fish specialties are excellent. Spiez Castle looms directly behind you, unfortunately out of sight. The rooms upstairs are spare and modern. ⌂ *Schachenstr. 3, CH-3700,* ☎ *033/6556767,* ℻ *033/6556765. 42 rooms. Restaurant, bar, café, pizzeria. AE, DC, MC, V.* ☜

$$$$ ▥ **Strandhotel Belvedere.** A member of the Hotel Suisse Silence chain, this graceful, old mansion-hotel has beautiful lawns and gardens, and its manicured waterfront on Lake Thun offers secluded swimming. The decor harkens back a few decades; rooms are done in blue and old rose, with canopy beds. Corner and lakeside rooms are worth the higher price. Guests have free access to the city's heated outdoor pool, 100 m (328 ft) away. ⌂ *Schachenstr. 39, CH-3700,* ☎ *033/6543333,* ℻ *033/6546633. 30 rooms. Restaurant, beach. AE, DC, MC, V. Closed Oct.–Mar.* ☜

Outdoor Activities and Sports

Spiez has municipal tennis courts at the bay, by the **municipal pool** (☎ 033/6544917).

Thun

⑫ *10 km (6 mi) north of Spiez, 29 km (18 mi) northwest of Interlaken.*

Built along an island on the River Aare as it leaves Lake Thun, the picturesque market town of Thun is laced with rushing streams crossed by wooden bridges, and its streets are lined with arcades. The main shopping thoroughfare of the Old Town may be unique in the world: pedestrians stroll along flowered terrace sidewalks built on the roofs of the stores' first floors and climb down stone stairs to visit the "sunken" street-level shops.

From the charming medieval Rathausplatz (Town Hall Square), a cov-
★ ered stair leads up to the great **Schloss Zähringen** (Zähringen Castle), its broad donjon cornered by four stout turrets. Built in 1191 by Berch-

told V, Duke of Zähringen, it houses the fine **Schlossmuseum Thun** (Thun Castle Museum) and provides magnificent views from its towers. In the **Knights' Hall** are a grand fireplace, an intimidating assortment of medieval weapons, and tapestries, one from the tent of Charles the Bold. Other floors display local Steffisburg and Heimberg ceramics, 19th-century uniforms and arms, and Swiss household objects, including charming Victorian toys. Though it's generally closed from November through January, it does open daily from 1 to 4 during the holiday season. ⊠ *Rathauspl.,* ☎ *033/2232001.* 🖃 *5 SF.* ☉ *Apr.–May and Oct., daily 10–5; June–Sept., daily 10–6; Feb.–Mar., daily 1–4.*

Dining and Lodging

$$–$$$ ✕🖃 **Krone.** Positioned directly on the lovely Rathausplatz in the Old Town, this landmark has some fine bay-window tower rooms and river views. Despite its historic setting and classic exterior, the interior is generally tile-and-wood modern. The two tower rooms, however, are special; they're round, with marble and gilt-edged decor. The Chinese restaurant, Wong-Kun, has a cross-cultural menu, and an upscale bistro whips up chic versions of regional dishes. ⊠ *Obere Hauptg. 2, CH-3600,* ☎ *033/2278888,* 🖾 *033/2278890. 27 rooms. 2 restaurants. AE, DC, MC, V.* 🍽

$ ✕🖃 **Zu Metzgern.** This grand, old shuttered and arcaded *Zunfthaus* (guildhall), at the base of the castle hill, provides fresh pastel rooms (bathrooms and toilets down the hall) with Rathausplatz views. There's atmospheric dining, too, whether in the wood-and-linen restaurant or on the intimate little terrace, tucked behind an ivy-covered trellis. They're strong on the traditional Swiss dishes, such as tripe. ⊠ *Untere Hauptg. 2, CH-3600,* ☎ *033/2222141,* 🖾 *033/2222182. 10 rooms. Restaurant, café. MC, V.*

OFF THE
BEATEN PATH

HILTERFINGEN AND OBERHOFEN – These two small towns, just a few kilometers southeast of Thun, are each dominated by a castle. Hilterfingen's castle, **Schloss Hünegg** (Hünegg Castle; ⊠ Staatsstr. 52, ☎ 033/2431982), was built in 1861 and furnished over the years with a bent toward Jugendstil and art nouveau. The stunning interiors have remained unchanged since 1900. It's open from mid-May to mid-October, Monday through Saturday from 2 to 5 and on Sunday from 10 to noon and 2 to 5. Admission is 8 SF. Oberhofen is topped with its own **Schloss Oberhofen** (Oberhofen Castle, ☎ 033/2431235), this one a hodge-podge of towers and spires on the waterfront. Begun during the 12th century, it was repeatedly altered over a span of 700 years. Inside, a historical museum has a display on the lifestyles of Bernese nobility. It's open from mid-May through mid-October, Monday from 2 to 5 and Tuesday to Sunday from 10 to noon and 2 to 5. Admission is 7 SF.

NIEDERHORN – Thirteen kilometers (8 miles) east of Oberhofen, the town of Beatenbucht has a shore terminal that sends funiculars to Beatenberg daily in high season. From there you can either walk up a trail or catch a chairlift to the Niederhorn (1,919 m/6,294 ft), from which an astonishing panorama unfolds: Lake Thun and Lake Brienz, the Jungfrau, and even, on a fine day, Mont Blanc.

ST-BEATUSHÖHLEN – Just west of Beatenberg, the illuminated St-Beatus-höhlen caves have been heavily developed, complete with a wax figure of Irish missionary St. Beatus himself, isolated in his cell as he was in the 6th century. This is less a center for pilgrimage than a simple cave tour with stalactites and stalagmites in dripping grottoes. It's open between April and October daily from 9:30 to 5:30. Guided tours are given every half hour.

Shopping

A good spot for traditional and artisan pottery in Thun is **Töpferhaus** (✉ Obere Hauptg. 3, ☎ 033/2227065). Just outside Thun in Heimberg, the **Museum Hänn** (Bahnhofstr. 4, ☎ 033/4381242) demonstrates and displays its traditional ceramic work, as it has since 1731.

KANDER VALLEY

Easily reached by car or the Lötschberg rail line from Interlaken via Spiez, the spectacular, high-altitude Kander Valley leads up from Lake Thun toward Kandersteg, an isolated resort strewn across a level plateau. From Kandersteg, you can make a hiker's pilgrimage to the silty blue Oeschinensee. En route to the lakes below, you may want to visit the touristy but pleasant Blausee.

Kandersteg

⑬ *45 km (28 mi) southwest of Interlaken.*

At 1,176 m (3,858 ft), Kandersteg stands alone, a quiet resort spread across a surprisingly broad, level—and thus walkable—plateau. Lofty bluffs, waterfalls, and peaks—including the **Blümlisalp**, at 3,664 m (12,018 ft), and the **Doldenhorn**, at 3,643 m (11,949 ft)—surround the plateau, and at the end of its 4-km (2½-mi) stretch, the valley road ends abruptly.

Exploration above Kandersteg must be accomplished by cable car or on foot, unless (depending on Swiss army training schedules and weather) you find the tiny paved road into the magnificent **Gastern Valley** open: carved into raw rock, portions of the road are so narrow that cars must take turns coming and going. Usually the local tourist office (☞ Visitor Information *in* Berner Oberland A to Z, *below*) knows if the road is passable.

Don't miss the **Oeschinensee,** an isolated, austere bowl of glacial silt at 1,578 m (5,176 ft). From Kandersteg you can walk there in about 1½ hours, and it's also accessible by chairlift to the Oeschinen station, with a downhill walk of approximately 30 minutes through peak-ringed meadowlands. You also may choose to hike back down to Kandersteg from the Oeschinensee, but be prepared for the severe downhill grade. Less ambitious hikers can circle back to the chairlift at the end of a relatively level walk.

Although it's a dead-end valley for cars confining themselves to Berner Oberland, Kandersteg is the source of one of Switzerland's more novel modes of transit: the rail-ferry tunnel through the **Lötschenberg.** After driving your car onto a low-slung railcar, you will be swept along piggyback through a dark and airless tunnel to Goppenstein, at the east end of the Valais region (☞ Chapter 11). Travel time is 15 minutes; the cost is 25 SF.

Dining and Lodging

$$ ✕🈯 **Ruedihus.** This beautifully, painstakingly restored all-wood chalet
★ is set in a meadow beyond the village center. With bulging leaded-glass windows, authentically low ceilings and doors (watch your head), and raw, aged woodwork throughout, it re-creates the atmosphere of the 1753 original. Antique beds with bleached homespun linens are counterbalanced by modern baths, and every corner has its waxed cradle, pewter pitcher, or crockery bowl. Upstairs, the Biedermeier restaurant offers excellent meat specialties, but eat downstairs at least once: the Käse- und Wystuben serves nothing but Swiss products—Vaud and Valais wines, greens, and sausages, and a variety of fondues. (No credit cards

are accepted in the restaurants.) ✉ *CH-3718,* ☎ *033/6758182,* FAX *033/6758185. 9 rooms. 2 restaurants, café. AE, DC, MC, V.*

$$–$$$ 🏨 **Waldhotel Doldenhorn.** Nestled into a forest hillside far from the
★   road through the center, this Relais du Silence retreat offers several options: large rooms with balconies and mountain views, smaller rooms opening onto the woods, or a separate budget chalet. The rooms gracefully combine modern and rustic styles. A cross-country ski trail starts at the hotel's door. There's a formal Swiss-French restaurant and a casual Stübli, too. For those with a do-it-yourself approach, one apartment has a kitchenette. ✉ *CH-3718,* ☎ *033/6758181,* FAX *033/6758185. 33 rooms, 1 apartment. Restaurant, Stübli. AE, DC, MC, V.*

$ 🏨 **Edelweiss.** Built in 1903, this inn has sleek, impeccable rooms and an old-fashioned atmosphere, complete with low ceilings and burnished wood. There's a comfortable checkered-cloth Stübli for drinks only. The pretty garden makes you forget you're on the main road, five minutes from the train station. ✉ *CH-3718,* ☎ *033/6751194. 8 rooms. Breakfast room, Stübli. No credit cards.*

OFF THE   **BLAUSEE (Blue Lake)** – If you're traveling with a family, you may want to
BEATEN PATH   visit the much-vaunted Blausee, a naturally blue pool above Frutigen. Be
              warned: it's privately owned and so developed, with a restaurant, boat
              rides, and a shop, that you may think the lake itself is artificial. The sum-
              mer admission price includes a boat ride, a visit to the trout nursery, and
              use of the picnic grounds. In winter you're free to park and roam the
              area. ✉ *4 km (2½ mi) north of Kandersteg, above Frutigen,* ☎ *033/6711641.* 🎫 *4.50 SF (May–early Nov. only).* ☉ *Daily 9–6.*

SIMMENTAL AND GSTAAD

Separate in spirit and terrain from the rest of the Berner Oberland, this craggy forest gorge follows the Lower Simme into a region as closely allied with French-speaking Vaud as it is with its Germanic brothers. Here the world-famous winter resort of Gstaad has flexed the muscle of its famous name to link up with a handful of neighboring ski resorts, creating the almost limitless sports opportunities of the Gstaad "Super-Ski" region. From Gstaad, it's an easy day trip into the contrasting culture of Lac Léman (Lake Geneva) and the waterfront towns of Montreux and Lausanne (☞ Chapter 12).

From Interlaken, take A8 toward Spiez, then cut west on A11 toward Gstaad. The forest gorges of the Simmental Valley lead you through Zweisimmen, the area's principal sporting center, to the Saanenland.

Gstaad

⑭ *49 km (30 mi) southwest of Spiez, 67 km (42 mi) southwest of Inter-laken.*

The peak-ringed valley called the Saanenland is anchored by this, the Oberland's most glamorous resort. Linking the Berner Oberland with the French-accented territory of the Pays-d'Enhaut (Highlands) of canton Vaud, Gstaad blends the two regions' natural beauty and their cultures as well, upholding Pays-d'Enhaut folk-art traditions such as *papier découpé* (paper cutouts) as well as decidedly Germanic ones (cowbells, wood carvings). Even Rösti and fondue cohabit comfortably.

But in Gstaad, neither local culture wins the upper hand: the folksy Gemütlichkeit (homeyness) of the region gives way to jet-set international style, and although the architecture still tends toward weathered-wood chalets, the main street is lined with designer boutiques that seem oddly out of context. Prince Rainier of Monaco, Julie Andrews, Roger

Moore, and Elizabeth Taylor have all owned chalets in Gstaad, rubbing elbows at local watering holes, and the late Yehudi Menuhin founded his annual summer music festival here as well. (The Menuhin festival takes place every August, and hotels fill quickly then—as they do for the Swiss Open Tennis tournament, held here every July.)

This is a see-and-be-seen spot, with less emphasis on its plentiful but moderate skiing than on the scene—après-ski, après-concert, or après-match. The Christmas–New Year's season brings a stampede of glittering socialites to rounds of dinner parties, balls, and elite soirees. Occasionally, the jet-setters even hit the slopes. Despite a few family-style hotels, the number of deluxe lodgings is disproportionate, and prices tend to be high. (The village has few street names, but hotels are clearly signposted.) Yet Gstaad's setting defies its socialite pretensions: richly forested slopes, scenic year-round trails, and, for the most part, stubbornly authentic chalet architecture keep it firmly anchored in tradition. The village is car-free. You can leave your car at one of the two parking facilities at either end of the village.

Skiing

Gstaad does not hesitate to call itself a "Super-Ski" region, and the claim is not far from the truth. It has become increasingly popular since the beginning of the century, both for its ideal situation at the confluence of several valleys and for the warmth of its slopes, which, at 1,100 m (3,608 ft), stay relatively toasty compared to those of other resorts.

Skiing in Gstaad is, in terms of numbers, the equivalent of Zermatt: 69 lifts can transport more than 50,000 skiers per hour to its network of 250 km (155 mi) of marked runs. In fact, these lifts are spread across an immense territory, 20 km (12 mi) as the crow flies, from Zweisimmen and St-Stefan in the east (where German is spoken, as in Gstaad) to Château-d'Oex, a Vaud town where French is spoken. To understand one another, people sometimes use English.

Gstaad's expansive area means that most of its lifts are not reachable on foot: Since parking is in short supply, public transport is the best option. The flip side is that except in very high seasons (Christmas, February, Easter) and in certain places, such as the lift for the Diablerets Glacier, or the Pillon, the crowds are not heavy, and lift-line waits are tolerable. A one-day ticket costs between 24 SF and 49 SF, depending on the sector; a six-day pass costs 233 SF. The **Gstaad Ski School** (☎ 033/7441865) gives lessons in downhill and cross-country skiing and snowboarding.

Dining and Lodging

$$$$ ✕ **Chesery.** This lively late-night dining scene, complete with piano bar, manages to combine the height of upscale chic with summits of culinary excellence—all at 1,100 m (3,608 ft). Chef Robert Speth marries exotic flavors, such as ginger or mango, with market-fresh ingredients: watch for veal and salmon in pastry with spinach, or duck in kumquat sauce. Crowds pack in, ordering dinner until 11:30 PM, so book well ahead in high season. ⊠ *Lauenenstr.,* ☎ *033/7442451. AE, DC, MC, V. Closed Mon.*

$$$$ ✕▥ **Palace.** Towering over tiny Gstaad like one of Mad King Ludwig's
★ castles, this landmark of luxury packs a wallet wallop. An indoor swimming pool with underwater music, water-jet massage, chauffeured Rolls-Royces, and oxygen cures are just a few of the compelling amenities. The Grill and Sans Cravate restaurants practically require indulgence: how does reindeer fillet with goose liver and truffle sauce sound? The rooms have rustic touches but are undeniably lavish; for instance, you may find a hand-painted wooden wardrobe in a room

rich with heavy brocades. ✉ *CH-3780,* ☎ *033/7485000; 800/223–6800 in the U.S.,* FAX *033/7485001. 76 rooms, 31 suites. 4 restaurants, piano bar, indoor pool, outdoor pool, 2 saunas, steam room, 4 tennis courts, health club, squash, ice-skating, nightclub. AE, DC, MC, V.* ✪

$$–$$$ ✕⌂ **Posthotel Rössli.** This comfy, modest pension-style inn, the oldest ★ inn in town, combines down-home knotty-pine decor with soigné style. Despite the mountain-cabin look, the clientele is young and chic, and the café, a local-landmark watering hole, draws crowds. The restaurant, full of linens and candlelight, serves simple daily menus at reasonable prices. ✉ *CH-3780,* ☎ *033/7484242,* FAX *033/7484243. 18 rooms. Restaurant, café. AE, DC, MC, V.* ✪

$–$$ ✕⌂ **Gasthof Alte Post/Weissenburg.** This graceful, isolated old coach ★ stop is on the magnificent forested Simmen Valley road, about halfway between Spiez and Gstaad (roughly a 40-minute drive to Gstaad). Dating from 1808, it has been lovingly restored; you'll find much carved and painted wood, many antiques, and good home cooking. The back rooms look over the Simmen River. The kitchen deftly handles the usual standards (veal, Rösti). ✉ *CH-3764 Weissenburg,* ☎ *033/7831515,* FAX *033/7831578. 10 rooms. Restaurant. AE, MC, V. Closed Nov. Restaurant closed Wed., Thurs.*

$$$$ ⌂ **Grand Hotel Park.** A little bit of Vail comes to the Alps in this spa- ★ cious, modern hotel, opened in 1990 to cater to health-conscious so-cialites unwilling to pay Palace (☞ *above*) prices. The facilities are state of the art, right down to the antistress program and indoor saltwater pool; treatment weeks offer an irresistible mix of glamour and virtue. The rooms keep it down to earth, with flowered wallpaper, waxed wooden furniture, and wardrobes painted with Swiss folk-art scenes. Rooms on the north side face wooded slopes. ✉ *CH-3780,* ☎ *033/ 7489800,* FAX *033/7489808. 88 rooms, 11 suites. 3 restaurants, 2 bars, indoor pool, pool, beauty salon, tennis court, sauna, steam room. AE, DC, MC, V. Closed late Sept.–mid-Dec. and Apr.–early June.* ✪

$$$–$$$$ ⌂ **Bernerhof.** The crowds of young people who came during this chalet-style inn's opening season in 1979 are still returning and stay in touch by means of the hotel's newsletter. It's simple, solid, and sur-prisingly cozy, with tile baths, lots of natural pine, and a balcony for every room. There are good play facilities for children. Though con-siderably lower than those at some nearby hotels, prices remain very expensive by Berner Oberland standards. It's in the center of town, a half block from the station. ✉ *CH-3780,* ☎ *033/7488844,* FAX *033/ 7488840. rooms, 12 suites. 3 restaurants, indoor pool, massage, sauna. AE, DC, MC, V.* ✪

$$$–$$$$ ⌂ **Olden.** In the middle of downtown, this charming Victorian inn has ★ carefully re-created artisan woodwork in every niche. The rooms, done in greens or reds, are folksy and atmospheric. Bathrooms have free-standing tubs mounted on wooden frames; some even come with their own steam bath/shower combination. And they keep up with details such as lighted wardrobes and sound insulation. You can scope out the titled and would-bes from the sidewalk café. ✉ *CH-3780,* ☎ *033/ 7443444, 033/7446164. 15 rooms. 2 restaurants, café. AE, DC, MC, V. Closed late Apr.–mid-May and late Oct.–mid-Nov.*

Outdoor Activities and Sports

GOLF

Gstaad-Saanenland (☎ 033/7484030), in Saanenmöser, a little past Schönried on Route 11, has 18 holes in an idyllic setting.

HORSEBACK RIDING

In Gstaad, the **Reitzentrum Gstaad** (☎ 033/7442460) offers guided out-ings for experienced riders only.

MOUNTAIN CLIMBING

Great day climbs can be had from Gstaad. **Alpinzentrum Gstaad** (☎ 033/7446001) can supply you with mountain guides and snow-sports teachers. **Beats Adventure** (☎ 033/7441521) aims its tough sports excursions at very fit people. **Experience Gstaad** (☎ 033/7448800) is the place to go for guides for off-trail skiing, ice climbing, and snowshoe trekking.

TENNIS

Pro Tennis Gstaad (☎ 033/7441090) has three indoor and two outdoor courts. Rental equipment is available.

Nightlife and the Arts

CONCERTS

The **Menuhin Festival Gstaad** (✉ Postfach 65, CH-3780, ☎ 033/7488338, FAX 033/7488339) hosts a series of world-class concerts throughout the summer. Information on the next summer's programs is generally available in December.

DANCING

The **Club 95** disco (☎ 033/7484422) is in the Sporthotel Victoria.

BERNER OBERLAND A TO Z

Arriving and Departing

By Car

There are swift and scenic roads from both Bern and Zürich to Interlaken. From Bern, the autoroute **A6** leads to Spiez, then **A8** continues as the highway to Interlaken. From Zürich, the planned autoroute link with Luzern (Lucerne) is incomplete; travel by Highway **E41** south, then pick up the autoroutes **A4** and **A14** in the direction of Luzern. South of Luzern, pick up the A4 again in the direction of Interlaken. From Geneva, the autoroute leads through Lausanne and Fribourg to Bern, where you catch **A6** south, toward Thun. A long, leisurely, scenic alternative: leave the autoroute after Montreux, and head northeast on the autoroute **A11** from Aigle through Château-d'Oex to Gstaad and the Simmental.

By Plane

Belpmoos Airport (Belp, ☎ 0848/848328) in Bern brings you within an hour via train of Interlaken, the hub of the Berner Oberland. **EuroAirport** (✉ Just across border from Basel in France, ☎ 061/3252511), shared by Basel, Mulhouse, and Freiburg in Germany, is within 2¼ hours by train. The **Zürich-Kloten** (☎ 1571060) airport is within 2½ hours. Geneva's **Cointrin** (☎ 1571500) is just under three hours away.

By Train

Trains from **Bern** to Interlaken run once an hour between 6 AM and 11 PM, some requiring a change at Spiez. From **Zürich**, a direct line leads through Bern to Interlaken and takes about 2½ hours, departing hourly; a more scenic trip over the Golden Pass route via Luzern takes about two hours. From **Basel** trains run twice an hour via Olten (approximately a 2½-hour trip). Trains run hourly from **Geneva** (a 2¾-hour ride). Trains stop at the **Interlaken West** (☎ 033/8264750) station first. Next stop is **Interlaken East** (☎ 033/8287333). West is the more central, but check with your hotel if you've booked in advance: some of the town's fine hotels are clustered nearer the East station, and all Brienzersee boat excursions leave from the docks nearby. For **train information** in Interlaken, ask at Interlaken West.

Getting Around

By Boat

Round-trip boat cruises around Lake Thun and Lake Brienz provide an ever-changing view of the craggy foothills and peaks. The round-trip from Interlaken to Thun takes about four hours; the trip to Spiez takes about two hours and includes stopovers for visits to the castles of Oberhofen, Spiez, and Thun. A round-trip from Interlaken to Brienz takes around 2½ hours, to Iseltwald about 1¼ hours. These boats are public transportation as well as pleasure cruisers; just disembark whenever you feel like it and check timetables when you want to catch another. Tickets are flexible and coordinate neatly with surface transit: you can cruise across to Thun and then take a train home for variety. Buy tickets and catch boats for Lake Thun at Interlaken West station. For Lake Brienz, go to Interlaken East. The official boat company for both lakes is **Schiffsbetrieb BLS Thuner- und Brienzersee** (☎ 033/ 3345211).

By Bus

Postbuses travel into much of the area not served by trains, including many smaller mountain towns. In addition, a number of private motorcoach tours cover points of interest. Schedules are available from tourist offices or post, telephone, and telegraph offices.

By Cable Car

More than 30 major cableway and lift systems climb Bernese Oberland peaks, including one of the largest cableways in the world, which stretches up to the Schilthorn above Mürren.

By Car

Driving in the Berner Oberland allows you the freedom to find your own views and to park at the very edges of civilization before taking off on foot or by train. If you are confining yourself to the lakefronts, valleys, and lower resorts, a car is an asset. But several lovely resorts are beyond the reach of traffic, and train, funicular, and cable-car excursions take you to places ordinary tires can't tread; sooner or later, you'll leave the car behind and resort to public transportation. Remember that Wengen, Mürren, and Gstaad are all car-free. For maximum flexibility, rent a car in Bern if you fly into Belp.

By Train

The Berner Oberland is riddled with federal and private railways, funiculars, cogwheel trains, and cable lifts designed with the sole purpose of getting you closer to its spectacular views. A **Swiss Pass** lets you travel free on federal trains and lake steamers, and it gives reductions on many private excursions (☞ Train Travel *in* Smart Travel Tips A to Z). If you're concentrating only on the Berner Oberland, consider a 15-day **Regional Pass,** which offers 450 km (279 mi) of free rail, bus, and boat travel for any five days of your visit, with half fare for the remaining 10 days, as well as discounts on some of the most spectacular (and pricey) private excursions into the heights. For adults, the price is 235 SF (first class) and 190 SF (second class); children's fares are half those amounts. A seven-day pass allows you three free travel days for 185 SF (first class) and 150 SF (second class) for adults, halfprice for children. These regional passes also grant a 50% discount for travel to Luzern, Zermatt, and Brig. With a **Family Card** (20 SF; ☞ Children & Travel *in* Smart Travel Tips A to Z), children who are under 16 and accompanied by at least one parent travel free. Discount passes pay for themselves only if you're a high-energy traveler; before you buy, compare the price à la carte for the itinerary you have in mind.

On Foot

You can cover a lot of ground without wheels, as this region (like most others in Switzerland) has highly developed, well-groomed walking trails leading away from nearly every intersection. Most are comfortably surfaced and are marked with distances and estimated walking times. Several itineraries are available from the Berner Oberland tourist office; these combine hikes with lodging along the way. The less ambitious walker may take advantage of postbus rides uphill and a leisurely stroll back down—though descents prove more taxing for calf muscles and knees than novice hikers imagine.

Contacts and Resources

Car Rental

Avis (⊠ Waldeggstr. 34a, Interlaken, ☎ 033/8221939). **Hertz** (⊠ Harderstr. 25, Interlaken, ☎ 033/8226172).

Emergencies

Police (☎ 117). **Hospital** (☎ 033/8262626). **Doctor referral** (☎ 033/8232323). **Dentist and pharmacist referral** (☎ 111).

Guided Tours

Auto AG Interlaken offers guided coach tours and escorted excursions within the Berner Oberland. There are **bus** tours to Mürren and the Schilthorn (including **cable car**), to Grindelwald and Trümmelbach Falls, to Kandersteg and the Blausee, and to Ballenberg. Guests are picked up at either the Interlaken West or East stations or at the Metropole or Interlaken hotels (☎ 033/8281717 for reservations). Some tours are available with English commentary. The tourist office (☞ Visitor Information, *below*) is the best source of information.

If you're traveling without either a Swiss Pass or a Regional Pass (☞ Getting Around By Train, *above*), note that guided tours to the Jungfraujoch or to the Schilthorn, arranged through the railway and cable companies themselves, cost less than independent round-trip tickets.

For a nostalgic tour of the streets of greater Interlaken by **horse-drawn carriage,** line up by the Interlaken West station (⊠ Ernst Voegeli Kutschenbetrieb, ☎ 033/8227416).

Travel Agencies

Kuoni (⊠ Höheweg 3, Interlaken, ☎ 033/8283636). **Jungfrau Tours** (⊠ Strandbadstr. 3, Interlaken, ☎ 033/8283232). **Vaglio** (⊠ Höheweg 72, Interlaken, ☎ 033/8270722).

Visitor Information

Berner Oberland Tourismus dispenses tourist information for the entire region, though it's not oriented toward walk-ins, so write or call (⊠ Jungfraustr. 38, CH-3800 Interlaken, ☎ 033/8230303, FAX 033/8230330, ☜). The **Interlaken Tourist Office,** at the foot of the Hotel Metropole (⊠ Höheweg 37, ☎ 033/8222121, FAX 033/8225221), provides information on Interlaken and the Jungfrau region. Arrange your excursions here.

Other tourist offices: **Brienz** (⊠ CH-3855, ☎ 033/9528080). **Grindelwald** (⊠ CH-3818, ☎ 033/8541212). **Gstaad** (⊠ CH-3780, ☎ 033/7488181). **Kandersteg** (⊠ CH-3718, ☎ 033/6758080). **Meiringen** (⊠ Bahnhofstr. 22, CH-3860, ☎ 033/9725050). **Spiez** (⊠ CH-3700, ☎ 033/6542020). **Thun** (⊠ Bahnhof, CH-3600, ☎ 033/2222340). **Wengen-Mürren-Lauterbrunnen** (⊠ CH-3822, Lauterbrunnen, ☎ 033/8568568).

11 VALAIS

CRANS, VERBIER, ZERMATT

Alpine villages, verdant vineyards, world-class resorts, and that rocky celebrity the Matterhorn—all are good reasons to visit the valley (*valais*) of the Rhône. This is wilderness country, where tumbledown huts and state-of-the-art sports facilities share steep green hillsides and forests. Long isolated from the world by mountains, it remains a land apart.

Updated by
Susan Rose

T HIS IS THE VALLEY OF THE MIGHTY Rhône, a river born in the heights above Gletsch (Glacier), channeled into a broad westward stream between the Bernese and the Valais Alps, lost in the depths of Lac Léman (Lake Geneva), and then diverted into France, where it ultimately dissolves in the marshes of the Camargue. Its broad upper valley forms a region of Switzerland that is still wild, remote, beautiful, and slightly unruly, its *mazots* (barns balanced on stone columns to keep mice out of winter food stores) romantically tumbledown, its highest slopes peopled by nimble farmers who live at vertiginous angles.

The birthplace of Christianity in Switzerland, Valais was never reformed by Calvin or Zwingli, nor conquered by the ubiquitous Bernese—one reason, perhaps, that the west end of Valais seems the most intensely French of the regions of the Suisse Romande.

Its romance appeals to the Swiss, who, longing for rustic atmosphere, build nostalgic Valais-style huts in their modern city centers in order to eat raclette under mounted pitchforks, pewter pitchers, and grape pickers' baskets. For vacations, the Swiss come here to escape, to hike, and, above all, to ski. The renowned resorts of Zermatt, Saas-Fee, Crans-Montana, and Verbier are all in the Valais, some within yodeling distance of villages barely touched by modern technology.

Pleasures and Pastimes

Dining
Though the French influence in the western portion of this region means a steady diet of cuisine *bourgeoise,* leading newcomers to think entrecôte with peppercorn sauce is a native dish, the elemental cuisine of Valais is much simpler. In a word: cheese.

Fondue, of course, is omnipresent. Often it is made with the local Bagnes or Orsières, mild cheeses from near Martigny. But the best application for these regional products is raclette (melted cheese with potatoes and pickles), an exclusive invention of this mountain canton (though the French of Haute-Savoie embrace it as their own). Ideally, the fresh-cut face of a half wheel of Orsières is melted before an open wood fire, the softened cheese scraped onto a plate and eaten with potatoes (always in their skins), pickled onions, and tiny gherkins. Nowadays, even mountain *carnotzets* (cellar pubs) with roaring fires depend on electric raclette heaters that grip the cheese in a vise before toasterlike elements. The beverage: a crisp, bubbly, fruity Fendant.

Valais rivals Graubünden in its production of *viande séchée* (air-dried beef), a block of meat marinated in herbs, pressed between planks until it takes on its signature bricklike form, and then dried in the open air. Shaved into thin, translucent slices, it can be as tender as a good prosciutto *crudo*—or as tough as leather. The flavor is concentrated, the flesh virtually fat-free.

CATEGORY	COST*
$$$$	over 70 SF
$$$	40 SF–70 SF
$$	20 SF–40 SF
$	under 20 SF

Prices are per person for a three-course meal (two-course in $ category), including sales tax and 15% service charge

Hiking

As skiing is to winter, hiking is to summer in Valais, and the network of valleys that radiate north and south of the Rhône provides almost infinite possibilities. Sociable hikers can join the crowds on trails out of the big resorts—especially outside Saas-Fee and Zermatt, where the mountain peaks and glaciers are within tackling distance—but don't overlook wilder, more isolated alternatives in the less developed Val d'Hérens and Val d'Anniviers. Good maps and suggested itineraries are available through the Valais regional tourist office in Sion (☞ Visitor Information *in* Valais A to Z, *below*).

Lodging

The most appealing hotels in Valais seem to be old. That is, historic sites have maintained their fine Victorian ambience; postwar inns, their lodgelike feel. Most of those built after about 1960 popped up in generic, concrete-slab, balconied rows to accommodate the 1960s ski boom. They are solid enough but, for the most part, anonymous, depending on the personality and dedication of their owners.

Valais is home to some of Switzerland's most famous resorts, and prices vary widely between top-level Zermatt lodgings and those in humbler towns. To indicate the relationship between resort prices and simple, wayside auberges (inns), the price categories below have been equally applied, so remember: the standards in a $$$-rated hotel in expensive Zermatt may be moderate compared to ones in nonresort towns. When you write for information, check prices carefully. *Demipension,* or half board (includes breakfast and a hot meal, either lunch or dinner), is often included in the price, and rates may be listed per person. And when planning a vacation in fall or spring, research your itinerary carefully: many of the resorts shut down altogether during the lulls in May and from November to mid-December and schedule their renovations and construction projects for these periods. That means that while some places offer low-season savings, others simply close their doors. The broad price-category spectrum indicated—sometimes from $ to $$$—shows the sometimes enormous differences between high- and low-season prices.

CATEGORY	COST*
$$$$	over 250 SF
$$$	180 SF–250 SF
$$	120 SF–180 SF
$	under 120 SF

*Prices are for a standard double room, including breakfast, tax, and service charge.

✑ *following the text of a review is your signal that the property has a Web site, where you will find details and, usually, images; for a link, visit www.fodors.com/urls.*

Skiing

With plateaus and cavernous gorges branching out from the valley, Valais has nurtured ski resorts for centuries. Zermatt, with its rustic, historic atmosphere, contrasts sharply with its high-tech peers to the west: Verbier, Crans-Montana, and Anzères are virtually purpose-built, with every amenity and connection—and considerably less focus on charm. You can find all ranges of difficulty and all kinds of snow—even, above Crans, in July.

Exploring Valais

Valais is an L-shape valley with Martigny at its angle; the eastern, or long, leg of the L is the most characteristic and imposing. This wide, fertile riverbed is flanked by bluffs and fed from the north and south by remote, narrow valleys that snake into the mountains. Some of these valleys peter out in desolate Alpine wilderness; some lead to its most famous landmarks—including that Swiss superstar, the Matterhorn. Not all of Valais covers Alpine terrain, however: the western stretch—between Martigny and Sierre—comprises one of the two chief sources of wine in Switzerland (the other is in Vaud, along Lake Geneva; *see* Chapter 12). Valais wines, dominated by round, fruity Fendant and light or ruby Dôle, come from verdant vineyards that stripe the hillsides flanking the Rhône.

The Val d'Entremont leads southward down an ancient route from Lake Geneva to the Col du Grand St-Bernard (Great St. Bernard Pass), traversing the key Roman crossroads at Martigny. Up the valley, past the isolated eagle's-nest village of Isérables, two magnificent castle-churches loom above the historic Old Town at Sion. From Sion, the Val d'Hérens winds up into the isolated wilderness past the stone Pyramides d'Euseigne and the Brigadoon-like resorts of Évolène and, even more obscure, Les Haudères. The Val d'Anniviers, the valley winding south from Sierre, leads to tiny, isolated skiing and hiking resorts such as Grimentz. The most famous southbound valley, the Mattertal, leads from Visp to the stellar resort of Zermatt and its mascot mountain, the Matterhorn. A fork off that same valley leads to spectacular Saas-Fee, another car-free resort in a magnificent glacier bowl. Back at the Rhône, the valley mounts southward from Brig to the Simplon Pass and Italy or northeastward to the glacier-source Gletsch and the Furka Pass out of the region.

Numbers in the text correspond to numbers in the margin and on the Valais map.

Great Itineraries

It's not necessary to explore every wild valley that ribs out from the Rhône in order to experience Valais; better to choose one region and spend a few days hiking, driving, or skiing. However, you will want to see the sights of the main river valley: Martigny, Sion, and at least one of the great Alpine passes, depending on your next travel goal.

IF YOU HAVE 2 DAYS

If you're using the Rhône Valley highway as a means to cover ground scenically, enter from Lac Léman and cruise directly to **Sion** ⑦, where you'll walk through the Old Town and climb up to the church fortress of Valére. Although you won't have time to cut north or south into a valley, any pass you use to exit the region will cover magnificent terrain: either the climb from **Martigny** ② to the **Col du Grand St-Bernard** ⑤ into Piedmont in Italy, the dramatic ascent from Brig over the **Simplon Pass** ⑰, or the slow, isolated approach to **Gletsch** ⑲ and the **Furka Pass** ⑳. Whenever time and road conditions permit, opt for the slow switchback crawl over the mountain passes rather than more efficient tunnels.

IF YOU HAVE 5 DAYS

Enter from Lac Léman and visit the museums of **Martigny** ②. Spend the night and next day exploring **Sion** ⑦, then make your selection: if you have never seen the Matterhorn, head directly for **Zermatt** ⑬ and spend three nights shutter-snapping, riding cable cars for better views, and stuffing yourself with fondue. Other Alpine resort options— **Saas-Fee** ⑮, **Verbier** ③, and **Crans-Montana** ⑩—are magnificently sited. If you prefer wilderness and old-fashioned retreat, shun the famous spots and head up the Val d'Hérens to pretty little **Évolène** ⑧, up the Val d'Anniviers to **Grimentz** ⑪, or up the Mattertal to charming **Grächen** ⑭, teetering on a high plateau.

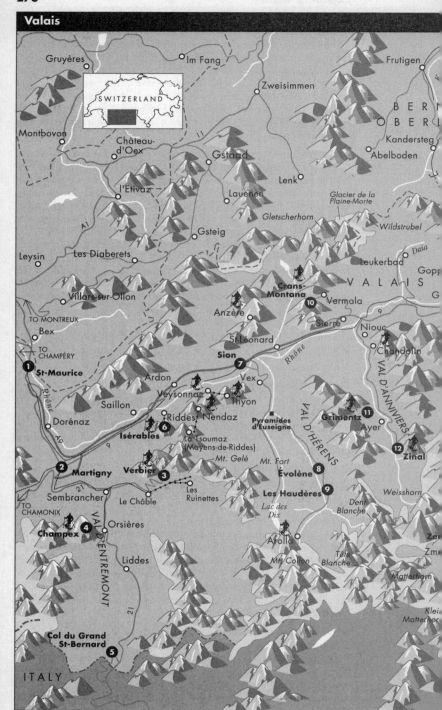

SWITZERLAND

Gruyères
Im Fang
Frutigen

Montbovon
Zweisimmen
BERN
OBERL

Château-
d'Oex
Gstaad
Kandersteg

l'Etivaz
Lauenen
Lenk
Abelboden

Glacier de la
Plaine-Morte

Gsteig
Gletscherhorn
Wildstrubel

Leysin
Les Diablerets
Daia

Leukerbad
Gopp

Crans-
Montana
VALAIS
G

Villars-sur-Ollon
10 Vermala

Anzère
Vermala

TO MONTREUX
Bex
Sierre
Niouc

TO
CHAMPÉRY
St-Léonard
Chandolin

1 St-Maurice
Sion **7**
Rhône

Ardon
Vex

Saillon
Veysonnaz
Thyon

Dorénaz
Riddes Nendaz
Pyramides
d'Euseigne
VAL D'HÉRENS
Grimentz **11**

Isérables **6**
Ayer

La Tsoumaz
(Mayens-de-Riddes)
12 Zinal

Mt. Gelé
Mt. Fort

Martigny **2**
Verbier **3**
Évolène **8**

Sembrancher
Le Châble
Les
Ruinettes
Les Haudères **9**
Weisshorn

TO
CHAMONIX
Orsières
Lac des
Dix
Dent
Blanche

Champex **4**
Liddes
Arolla

VAL D'ENTREMONT
Mt Collon
Tête
Blanche
Matterhorn

Col du Grand
St-Bernard **5**
Klei
Matterhor

ITALY

VAL D'ANNIVIERS

Rhône

Grindelwald

Lauterbrunnen
Mönch

Schilthorn
Jungfrau

Handegg

*Grimsel
Pass*

Gletsch **19** **Furka
Pass** **20**

Rhonegletscher

R
N D

Breithorn

Aletschhorn

Oberwald

Münster

19

Rhône

Val de Conches

*Grosser
Aletschgletscher*

19

Lonza
ein

18 **Riederalp**

Mörel

l

Rhône

Brig

16

Turtmann *9*

Visp

Simplon Tunnel

Stalden

VISPERTAL

Simplon Pass **17**

Gondo

St-Niklaus

14
Grächen

Gstein-Gabi

SAASTAL

MATTERTAL

Saas-Grund

Längfluh

15 **Saas-Fee**

Alphübel

Mittelallalin

Allalinhorn

Domodossola

Täsch

Unterrothorn

13

Gornergrat

ITALY

*Trockener
Steg*

MONTE

KEY

Dufourspitze

Rail Lines

Cable Car/
Funicular

Breithorn

ROSA

Regional
Boundary Lines

Ski Resort

N

0   6 miles

0   9 km

IF YOU HAVE 10 DAYS

En route to the mountains, take time to visit **St-Maurice** ① and **Martigny** ②, then head up to ⚏ **Verbier** ③ for a couple of days' worth of hiking or skiing. For backcountry exploring spend a day or two wandering up the Val Hérens to **Évolène** ⑧, with side trips to see the Grande Dixence Dam and the Pyramides d'Euseigne and time for wilderness walks or cross-country skiing. Set aside a full day for the monuments and museums of ⚏ **Sion** ⑦ before heading back into the heights. You'll feel the contrast when you reach highly developed, Germanic ⚏ **Zermatt** ⑬, where another four nights will give you time to exploit its facilities. From Zermatt, you can exit Valais via the **Simplon Pass** ⑰ or the **Furka Pass** ⑳.

When to Tour Valais

Valais is at its sunny best in high summer and mid-winter, with foggy dampness overwhelming the region in late autumn (its low season). Mid-December to Easter is peak ski season in the resorts. As Europeans vacation here for weeks at a time, book well ahead if you want to compete for lodging in August, at Easter time, and at Christmas and New Year's. And remember: May and November to mid-December are renovation and repair time, with many facilities closed.

VAL D'ENTREMONT TO THE COL DU GRAND ST-BERNARD

The Rhône River at Villeneuve broadens deltalike into a flat valley that pours into Lake Geneva. But heading south, up the valley, the mountains already begin to crowd in on either side. Once you cross the Rhône and officially enter the canton of Valais, leaving Vaud behind, the valley and the river begin to change character. The mountains—the Dents du Midi in the west and the Dents de Morcles to the east—come closer; the Rhône no longer flows placidly but gives a foretaste of the mountain torrent it will become as you approach its source. This most ancient of Alpine routes leaves the Rhône at the Martigny elbow and ascends due south to 2,469 m (8,098 ft) at the St. Bernard Pass before descending into Italy's Valle d'Aosta.

St-Maurice

❶ *46 km (28 mi) west of Sion, 56 km (35 mi) southeast of Lausanne.*

Pushed up against a stern, gray rock face, this village is quiet and peaceful, with patrician homes lining its Grand Rue. Once a customs station along the Roman route over the St. Bernard Pass, in the 3rd century it witnessed the massacre of a band of Christian soldiers, the Theban Legion, and their chief, Maurice, who had refused to worship the Roman deities. At the end of the 4th century the first bishop of the Valais built a sanctuary over Maurice's tomb. In 515 the **Abbaye Saint-Maurice** (St. Maurice Abbey) was founded. Its treasury contains a stellar collection of religious offerings, with precious Romanesque and Gothic objects given in honor of the martyrs. Excavations near the baroque **église abbatiale** (abbey church) have revealed the foundations of the original building. ☎ *024/4860404.* ⚏ *Free.* ☉ *Guided tours July–Aug., Tues.–Sat. at 10:30, 2, 3:15, and 4:30, Sun. at 2, 3:15, and 4:30; May–June and Sept.–Oct., Tues.–Sat. at 10:30, 3, and 4:30, Sun. at 3 and 4:30; Nov.–Apr., Tues.–Sun. at 3.*

Martigny

❷ *17 km (11 mi) south of St-Maurice, 23 km (14 mi) southwest of Sion.*

At the foot of the Grand St. Bernard Pass, Martigny has long been a commercial crossroads. Testimony to this past are the Gallo-Roman ruins discovered in 1976 by engineer Leonard Gianadda. When Gianadda's brother Pierre died in a plane crash, Leonard created a cultural center in his memory. The **Foundation Pierre Gianadda** now rises in bold geometric shapes around the ruins; inside are three separate collections. The Foundation itself sponsors noteworthy themed art exhibits. Recent temporary exhibitions have included "Kandinsky and Russia"; "Picasso and Mythology" is scheduled for 2001. Its permanent collection includes works by van Gogh, Cézanne, and Picasso. The **Musée Gallo-Romain** (Gallo-Roman Museum) displays relics excavated from a 1st-century temple: striking bronzes, statuary, pottery, and coins. A marked path leads you through the antique village, baths, drainage systems, and foundations to the fully restored 5,000-seat amphitheater, which dates from the 2nd century. There's also a sizable **Musée de l'Automobile** (Automobile Museum), which contains some 50 antique cars, all in working order. They include an 1897 Benz, the Delauneay-Belleville of Czar Nicholas II of Russia, and a handful of Swiss-made models, three of which have horns shaped like menacing serpents' heads. And don't be surprised if you see posters for a concert by an international classical star—the Foundation moonlights as a concert hall. ✉ *59 rue de Forum,* ☎ *027/7223978.* 🎫 *14 SF.* ☉ *Mid-June–Oct., daily 9–7; Feb.–June, daily 10–6; Nov.–Jan., daily 10–noon and 1:30–6.*

In the gracefully landscaped garden surrounding the Foundation Pierre Gianadda, a wonderful **Parc de Sculptures** (Sculpture Park) displays works by Rodin, Brancusi, Miró, Calder, Moore, Dubuffet, and Max Ernst.

Lodging

$$$–$$$$ 🏨 **Hotel du Forum.** Martigny is something of a one-street town, but if it suits your itinerary to stop over, then this is a convenient choice. The comfortable rooms are done in pine. Asian influences leaven the restaurant's regional cuisine; you might start a five-course meal with curried lobster, for instance. The brasserie offers simpler fare. Take Bus 13 from the railway station to the Le Bourg stop. ✉ *74 av. de Grand-Saint-Bernard CH-1920,* ☎ *027/7221841,* 📠 *027/7227925. 29 rooms. Restaurant. AE, DC, MC, V.*

Verbier

❸ *29 km (18 mi) east of Martigny (exit at Sembrancher), 58 km (36 mi) southwest of Sion.*

It's the skiing, not the social life, that draws committed sports lovers to Verbier, a high-tech, state-of-the-art sports complex that connects to several nearby resorts (including Thyon and Nendaz). Verbier has the biggest aerial cableway in Europe, with two cabins accommodating 150, and some 86 smaller transportation installations. Summer sports are equally serious: hang gliding and its variations compete with golf as the principal sports. Though it's perched on a sunny shelf high above the Val de Bagnes, with the 3,023-m (9,915-ft) Mont Gelé towering behind and wraparound views, Verbier itself is too modern to be picturesque, but thanks to its compact layout and easygoing locals, the town has a friendlier feel than the traffic-snarled sprawl of Crans-Montana or hotel-packed Zermatt. You won't have any trouble finding your way around; all hotels are clearly signposted.

Skiing

At 1,500 m (4,921 ft), Verbier is the center of Switzerland's most famous transit network, **Televerbier**—which consists of 12 gondolas, eight cable cars, 35 chairlifts, and 47 ski lifts giving access to 410 km (253 mi) of marked pistes. From this resort an immense complex of resorts has developed—some more modest, others more exclusive—covering four valleys in an extended ski area whose extremities are 15 km (9 mi) or so apart as the crow flies and several dozen kilometers apart by way of winding mountain roads.

Les Ruinettes gives access to Verbier's entire upper ski area, which culminates at **Mont-Fort,** at 3,300 m (10,825 ft). This is reached by an aerial tram, *Le Jumbo,* equipped with a cab that accommodates 150. This entire sector is crisscrossed by a dense network of astonishingly varied pistes. There are several strategic passes, including **Les Attelas, Mont-Gelé, Col des Gentianes, Lac des Vaux,** and **Tortin.** One-day lift tickets cost 56 SF; six-day passes cost 282 SF.

Dining and Lodging

$$-$$$$ ✕ **La Grange.** To eat cheese or not to eat cheese will be the question here. In keeping with the traditional decor, you can sample regional specialties, such as fondue or dried beef, or you can go for the more ambitious (and expensive) choices, such as mushroom *cassolette* or liver pâté with plum sauce. The wine list includes an excellent selection of local vintages. ☎ *027/7716431. AE, DC, MC, V. Closed Mon.–Tues. and June.*

$$-$$$ ✕ **Le Bouchon Gourmand.** Away from the main drag of generic fondue cabins and no-surprise pizza houses, this warmly decorated spot serves an excellent range of French-influenced poultry dishes (including gizzard pâté) and tongue-melting desserts. Especially worth sampling are the succulent duck in red-wine sauce and for dessert the brandy-inflamed apple tart. ⊠ *rue de la Poste,* ☎ *027/7717296. AE, DC, MC, V.*

$$$$ ✕🖬 **Rosalp.** The honey-gold-pine rustic-chic decor of the main restau-
★   rant makes a surprisingly warm and comfortable setting for one of Switzerland's great meals. Chef Roland Pierroz continues to earn the highest gastronomic kudos and an international following for his prawn bisque, squab with truffles, and apple tarts, as well as for the variety of fine local cheeses he presents. For simpler, less pricey, but equally creative food, try La Pinte; the bar is the perfect place to settle into a leather sofa with a cognac. If you plan to stay overnight, ask for one of the newer rooms, which have marble baths. The upper rooms are smaller but quieter, with better views. Reservations are essential at Pierroz's restaurant. ⊠ *rte. de Médran, CH-1936,* ☎ *027/7716323,* 🖷 *027/7711059. 18 rooms, 3 apartments. 2 restaurants, bar, hot tub, exercise room, sauna. AE, DC, MC, V.* 🕾

$$$$ 🖬 **Hotel Vanessa.** This comfortable, quiet, centrally located hotel offers mainly southern views and spacious, pine-decorated rooms complete with balcony, kitchenette (even including a dishwasher), as well as a large number of two- and three-room suites. The questionably decorated but convivial bar features a regular in-house pianist. ⊠ *pl. Centrale, CH-1936,* ☎ *027/7752800,* 🖷 *027/7752828. 35 rooms, 21 suites. Restaurant, bar, sauna. AE, DC, MC, V.*

$$$-$$$$ 🖬 **Golf Hotel.** As modern and central as most other Verbier hotels, the Golf is a bit softer; the rooms are lightened with pale pine. Downstairs is the dusky Jacky's Piano Bar, with live piano three nights a week; in summertime, barbecues and raclette dinners promote mingling. The 18-

hole golf course nearby offers magnificent views, although even guests will have to pay for the privilege of a round. The hotel runs a private bus to the cable cars. ⊠ *rue de Verbier, CH-1936,* ☎ *027/7716515,* FAX *027/7711488. 30 rooms. Restaurant, bar, sauna, steam room, exercise room. AE, DC, MC, V.*

$$ ⊞ **Ermitage.** The rooms may not quite allow you the space for a vigorous pre-ski stretch, but they are quite comfortable. The hotel is conveniently central; the south-facing rooms are quieter and have better views, though you'll have to gaze over the parking lot and other hotels to the mountains. ⊠ *pl. Centrale, CH-1936,* ☎ *027/7716477,* FAX *027/7715264. 25 rooms. Restaurant. AE, DC, MC, V.*

$ ⊞ **Les Touristes.** If you're here for the world-class skiing and want to pass on the pricier comforts, head for this old-style pension. Built in the 1940s in a dark-wood roadhouse style, it's in the village below the main resort, where a few traditional chalets are still evident. The rooms are spare, and the bare-bones shower and toilet are down the hall, but the Stübli-restaurant attracts locals disenchanted with the uptown scene. Staying here means one more connection to get you to the slopes—a brief bus ride or a quick, 10-minute walk—but it's friendly and authentic, and you save a bundle. ⊠ *CH-1936,* ☎ *027/7712147,* FAX *027/7712147. 14 rooms. Restaurant, Stübli. AE, MC, V.*

Nightlife and the Arts

DANCING

The **Farm** (⊠ Rhodania Hotel, rue de Verbier, ☎ 027/7716121) is the place to be seen in Verbier, with lines often forming in the street for the privilege of jiving to pop's back catalog while quaffing a bottle of vodka costing well into three figures in both franc and dollar terms. Apparently it is not the done thing to turn up before 1 AM. The club is closed Sunday. In the meantime you could head to the less pretentious **Scotch** (⊠ rue de la Poste, ☎ 027/7711656), whose slogan reads: "We may be small but we're cheap." **Marshal's** (⊠ Hotel Farinet, pl. Centrale, ☎ 027/7713572) caters to the techno generation; the popular **Crok** bar (⊠ rte. des Creux, ☎ 027/7716934) has live music on weekends.

MUSIC

For more than two weeks overlapping July and August the **Verbier Festival and Academy** hosts an impressive classical music festival; the 2000 festival included baritone Dmitri Hvorostovsky, cellist Mischa Maisky, and conductors James Levine and Zubin Mehta. To order tickets, call ☎ 027/7718282 or fax FAX 027/7717057.

Outdoor Activities and Sports

BICYCLING

Jet Sports (☎ 027/7712067) rents mountain bikes.

GOLF

The **Golf Club** (☎ 027/7715314) has two 18-hole courses.

MOUNTAIN CLIMBING

École d'Alpinisme de Verbier (☎ 027/7712212) offers guides and lessons.

PARAGLIDING

The **Centre Parapente** (☎ 027/7716818) gives paragliding lessons and sells equipment. **L'Envol** (☎ 079/4333545) paragliding school offers training and rentals.

SPORTS CENTERS

Verbier's **Centre Polysportif** (☎ 027/7716601) has indoor skating as well as a swimming pool, saunas, whirlpools, a solarium, curling, nine tennis courts, and squash.

Champex

④   *31 km (19 mi) south of Martigny, 51 km (32 mi) southwest of Sion.*

Clinging high above the Orsières Valley (famous for its raclette cheese), this delightful little family resort lies wrapped around a tiny mirror of a lake and surrounded by forested peaks, concentrating some of the prettiest scenery in the region—including views dominated by the massive Combin (4,314 m/14,150 ft).

Dining and Lodging

$$ ✕▥ Belvédère. This is the prototypical *relais de campagne* (country
★ inn): full of warm wood, cozy rooms with balconies, creaky pine-panel halls hung with historic photos, and doilies everywhere, crocheted by the owner herself. Set on a wooded hill above the lake and town, it offers breathtaking views all the way down to the Val d'Entremont. The café attracts local workers, and the restaurant serves the owners' fresh, straightforward *cuisine bourgeoise* made with produce from their own organic garden, as well as a variety of fondues. Watch for garlic-sautéed porcini mushrooms on toast, lamb fillet in sage with *Rösti* (hash brown potatoes), and muscat mousse with grape compote. The list of local wines includes some rare bargains. ✉ *CH-1938,* ☎ *027/7831114,* ℻ *027/7832576. 9 rooms. Restaurant, café. MC, V.*

$–$$ ▥ Auberge de la Forêt. On a quiet street facing the lake, this place has a few lake-view rooms with a comfortable, modern look. The fireplace and grill turn out authentic raclette. ✉ *CH-1938,* ☎ *027/7831278,* ℻ *027/7832101. 13 rooms. Restaurant, café. MC, V.*

Col du Grand St-Bernard

★ ⑤   *40 km (25 mi) south of Martigny, 69 km (43 mi) southwest of Sion.*

The Great St. Bernard Pass, breasting the formidable barrier of the Alps at 2,469 m (8,101 ft), is the oldest and most famous of the great Alpine crossings, and the first to join Rome and Byzantium to the wilds of the north. Used for centuries before the birth of Christ, it has witnessed an endless stream of emperors, knights, and simple travelers—think of Umberto Eco's *The Name of the Rose,* with its two friars crossing on donkey back in howling winter winds. Napoléon took an army of 40,000 across it en route to Marengo, where he defeated the Austrians in 1800.

You'll have an easier time crossing today than Napoléon did: if you simply want to get to Italy quickly, you can take the swift tunnel that opens out on the other side, above the Valle d'Aosta. But by skipping the tiny winding road over the top, you'll miss the awe-inspiring, windswept moonscape at the summit and the hospice that honors its namesake. In 1038, the story goes, Bernard of Menthon, bishop of Aosta, came to clear the pass of brigands. When he reached the top, he found a pagan temple, which he covered with his chasuble. The shrine immediately crumbled to dust and, by the same power, the brigands were defeated. There Bernard established his hospice.

The **hospice of St. Bernard** served international travelers throughout the Middle Ages. Kings and princes rewarded the hospice by showering estates upon the order. By the 12th century, it owned 79 estates in England alone. Nowadays its residents—Augustinian canons—train as mountain guides and ski instructors and accommodate young groups. Behind the hospice, there's a kennel full of the landmark's enormous, furry namesakes: the famous St. Bernard dogs, who for centuries have helped the monks find travelers lost in the snow. They supposedly came to Switzerland with silk caravans from central Asia and were used by

Romans as war dogs; nowadays they're kept more for sentimental than functional reasons. The most famous was Barry, who saved more than 40 people in the 19th century and today stands stuffed in Bern's Naturhistorisches Museum (Museum of Natural History; ☞ Chapter 9). Souvenir stands sell plush versions of St. Bernards on either side of the pass. ☎ 027/7871236. ☜ *Kennel: 6 SF.* ☉ *July–Aug. 8 AM–10 PM.*

ISÉRABLES, SION, AND THE VAL D'HÉRENS

The Rhône Valley is most fertile just east of Martigny, its flatlands thick with orchards and vegetable gardens, its south-facing slopes quilted with vineyards. The region nurtures a virtual market basket of apples, pears, carrots, and delicate white asparagus, a specialty of early spring. The blue-blood crop of the region is grapes: this is one of the primary wine-producing regions in the country, and the fruity Fendant and hearty red Dôle (a blend of pinot noir and gamay grapes) appear on every region's lists, as well as the Dôle Blanche, actually a rosé. Once Valais wines were poured from hinged-lid tin or pewter pitchers called *channes*; reproductions are sold throughout the region. Also from the orchards come potent, intensely perfumed eaux-de-vie (or schnapps), especially *abricotine* (from apricots) and *williamine* (from pears).

This patch of Valais demonstrates the contrasts of this dramatic region: over the fertile farmlands looms the great medieval stronghold of Sion, its fortress towers protecting the gateway to the Alps. Jutting sharply up into the bluffs to the south are the isolated mountain villages of Isérables and Évolène.

Isérables

★ ➏ *24 km (15 mi) southwest of Sion.*

This is a rare opportunity to visit one of the scores of eagle's-nest towns you'll glimpse as you pass through the region's valleys. Set on a precarious slope that drops 1,000 m (3,280 ft) into the lowlands, it has narrow streets that weave between crooked old stone-shingle mazots, the typical little Valais barns balanced on stone disks and columns to keep mice out of winter food stores.

Since the arrival of the cable car in recent times, Isérables has prospered and modernized itself considerably. Yet the inhabitants of this village still carry the curious nickname Bedjuis. Some say it is derived from "Bedouins" and that the people are descended from the Saracen hordes who, after the battle of Poitiers in 732, overran some of the high Alpine valleys. Certainly some of the people here—stocky, swarthy, and dark-eyed—seem different from most others in the canton.

Sion

★ ➐ *158 km (98 mi) south of Bern.*

Rearing up spookily in the otherwise deltalike flatlands of the western Valais, two otherworldly twin hills flank the ancient city of Sion. Sion folk are seen as a little "different," not only by the Swiss in general but even by their fellow Valaisans. They are fiercely proud and independent, as reflected in the fanatical support for their soccer team (very rare in a country much keener on winter sports) and their dogged attempts to snatch the Winter Olympics. They failed for 2002 and, in a surprise upset, also lost the bid to host the 2006 Winter Olympics, to Turin, Italy. Because there's a dearth of quality hotels in Sion, the town is not as hospitable to travelers as the tourist-oriented ski resorts around it.

Crowning the higher hill, **Tourbillon,** is a ruined château built as a bishop's residence at the end of the 13th century and destroyed by fire in 1788. ✉ *Free.* ⊘ *Mid-Mar.–mid-Nov., Tues.–Sun. 10–6.*

On the other hill, **Valère,** is an 11th-century church. The two hills together are a powerful emblem of the city's 1,500-year history as a bishopric and a Christian stronghold. From the top of either hill you'll have a dramatic view of the surrounding flatlands and the mountains flanking the valley.

The town itself can be comfortably explored on foot in an afternoon, unless you lose yourself in one of its museums or labyrinthine antiques shops. The **Old Town,** down rue de Lausanne (take a left when leaving the tourist office, map in hand), is a blend of shuttered 16th-century houses and modern shops. The grand old **Maison Supersaxo** (House of Supersaxo) was built in 1505 by Georges Supersaxo, the local governor, to put his rivals to shame. This extravagantly decorated building includes a Gothic staircase and a grand hall whose painted wood ceiling is a dazzling work of decorative art. ⊠ *Tucked into a passageway off rue Supersaxo.* ✉ *Free.* ⊘ *Weekdays 8–noon and 2–6.*

The imposing **Hôtel de Ville** (Town Hall) has extraordinary historic roots: though it was built in the 1650s, there are transplanted stones in the entrance bearing Roman inscriptions, including a Christian symbol from the year AD 377. The 17th-century doors are richly carved wood, and the tower displays an astronomical clock. Upstairs, the **Salle du Conseil** (Council Hall) is also adorned with ornate woodwork. ⊠ *At intersection of rue de Conthey and rue du Grand-Pont.* ✉ *Free interior visits only with guided walking tour of the town (8 SF) from the Sion tourist office.*

The **Musée Cantonal d'Archéologie** (Museum of Archaeology) displays a collection of excavated pieces, including fine Roman works found in Valais. The narrow, cobbled rue des Châteaux leading up toward the twin fortifications passes graceful old patrician houses, among them the museum. ⊠ *12 rue des Châteaux,* ☎ *027/6064700.* ✉ *4 SF.* ⊘ *Tues.–Sun. 10–noon and 2–6.*

The cathedral, **Notre-Dame du Glarier** (Our Lady of Glarier), is dominated by its Romanesque tower, built in the Lombard, or Italian, style and dating from the 12th century; the rest of the church is late Gothic in style. ⊠ *rue de la Cathédrale.*

Just across from the cathedral, the **Tour des Sorciers** (Sorcerers' Tower) is the last remnant of the walls that once ringed the town. ✉ *3 SF.* ⊘ *Tues.–Sun. 2–6.*

★ In the **Église-Forteresse de Valère** (Church-Fortress of Valère), high above the town, you'll observe a striking example of sacred and secular power combined—reflective of the Church's heyday, when it often subjugated rather than served its parishioners. Built on Roman foundations, the massive stone walls enclose both the château and the 11th-century **Église Notre Dame de Valère** (Church of Our Lady of Valère).

This structure stands in a relatively raw form, rare in Switzerland, where monuments are often restored to Disneyland perfection. Over the engaging Romanesque carvings, 16th-century fresco fragments, and 17th-century stalls painted with scenes of the Passion, there hangs a rare **organ** in swallow's-nest form, its cabinet painted with two fine medieval

Christian scenes. Dating from the 14th century, it is the oldest playable organ in the world, and an annual organ festival celebrates its musical virtues (☞ Nightlife and the Arts, *below*). The church also houses the **Musée d'Histoire** (History Museum), which displays a wide array of medieval chests and sculptures. There are periodic guided tours, but they're not given in English. ☎ 027/6064710. ✆ *Church 3 SF; museum 5 SF; combination ticket 6 SF.* ☉ *Tues.–Sun. 10–noon and 2–6; guided tours of museum 1st Sat. of month, 2:30.*

OFF THE BEATEN PATH	**GRANDE DIXENCE DAM –** Veer right past Vex up the narrow mountain road that leads about 16 km (10 mi) up the Val d'Hérémence to the Grande Dixence Dam, a gargantuan monolith of concrete built in the mid-1960s at the improbable altitude of 2,364 m (7,754 ft). Only the Swiss could have accomplished such a feat of Alpine engineering—an achievement that brings them millions on millions of kilowatt hours every year. The potential energy is impressively apparent because the now-vast Lac des Dix backs up some 4 km (2½ mi) into the barren, abandoned valley.

Dining and Lodging

$$$$ ✕ **Supersaxo.** One of the few restaurants in Sion enjoying a reputation beyond the city walls, Supersaxo serves excellent cuisine in sleek surroundings. Look for the rabbit terrine and the roasted breast of peahen served with vanilla-scented potato "leaves." If the elaborate evening menus are beyond your price range, you can always pop into the brasserie and treat yourself to lunch, when a *plat du jour* (daily special) costs just 20 SF. ✉ *Passage Supersaxo,* ☎ 027/3238550. *MC, V.*

$$$–$$$$ ✕ **Pont-du-Diable.** Perched above the Rhône slightly east of Sion in the
★ little village of Chandolin, the Pont-du-Diable basks in a panoramic view of the valley. The seasonal menu reflects the best, most characteristic flavors of the area, with dishes such as fillet of sole wrapped around paper-thin slices of garlic and tender asparagus braised in virgin olive oil. The dining room is charmingly rustic; the service is both gracious and friendly. From Sion, drive northeast toward the Col du Sanetsch; it's about a 15-minute trip. ✉ *Chandolin,* ☎ FAX 027/3953030. *AE, DC, MC, V. Closed Sun.–Mon., 1st week of Jan., and early Aug.*

$$$ ✕ **L'Enclos de Valère.** If you've worked up an appetite climbing the Tourbillon, you may want to stop here in the Old Town on your way back down. Unfussy service, fine regional cuisine, and a 15 SF lunch special make it a welcome break. In summer you can eat outside on a shady terrace. ✉ *18 rue des Châteaux,* ☎ 027/3233230. *AE, MC, V. Closed Christmas–Jan. and Sun.–Mon. Oct.–Apr.*

$$ ▥ **Du Rhône.** This spare cinder-block property could be an American motel if it weren't for the illuminated antiquities visible from the north windows. At the edge of the Old Town and handy to the castle walks, it makes a comfortable, no-frills base for your explorations. ✉ *10 rue de Scex, CH-1950,* ☎ 027/3222891, FAX 027/3231188. *45 rooms. Restaurant. AE, DC, MC, V.*

$ ▥ **Du Midi.** On the edge of the Old Town and now absorbed into the upper floors of a downtown shopping block, this was once a freestanding roadhouse, a loner in the shadow of the city's twin citadels. Its small guest rooms are nothing fancy but are a decent value for the price. ✉ *29 pl. du Midi, CH-1950,* ☎ 027/3231331, FAX 027/3236173. *12 rooms. Restaurant, brasserie. AE, DC, MC, V.*

Nightlife and the Arts

Sion attracts world-class musicians and scholars to its festivals celebrating the medieval organ in its church-fortress Valère (☞ Exploring, *above*). The **Festival International de l'Orgue Ancien Valère** (International Festival of the Ancient Valère Organ; ☎ 027/3235767) takes place from July through the beginning of September.

En Route   The Val d'Hérens, south of Sion, is a valley lined with improbably high mountain farms and pastures. Here you will find the **Pyramides d'Euseigne** (Pyramids of Euseigne), a group of bizarre geological formations: stone pillars formed by the debris of glacial moraines and protected by hard-rock caps from the erosion that carved away the material around them. The effect is that of enormous, freestanding stalagmites wearing hats. A car tunnel has been carved through the bases of three of them. Six-day hiking tours of the Val d'Hérens (available from mid-June to mid-October) can be booked through the Sion tourist office (☞ Visitor Information *in* Valais A to Z, *below*).

Évolène

❽   *23 km (14 mi) southeast of Sion, cross the main highway and head south toward Vex.*

In a broad, fertile valley, Évolène is a town of ramshackle mazots and wooden houses edged with flower-filled window boxes that provide a picturesque setting for vacationers—mostly French—and mountaineers, who tackle nearby Mont-Collon and the Dent-Blanche. If you're lucky, you'll see some of the older women villagers in the traditional dress of kerchiefs and flowered cottons that they still favor.

Les Haudères

❾   *5 km (3 mi) south of Évolène, 28 km (17 mi) southeast of Sion.*

This tiny but popular vacation retreat is little more than a scattering of chalets in a spectacular, isolated mountain valley. Farther on, the little skiing and mountaineering resort of **Arolla** (2,010 m/6,593 ft) is custom-made for those seeking a total retreat in Alpine isolation.

CRANS-MONTANA AND THE VAL D'ANNIVIERS

Spiking north and south of the crossroads of Sierre, you'll find polar extremes: a sunny, open plateau, home to the glamorous resorts of Crans and Montana, and the wild, craggy Val d'Anniviers, which leads to the isolated forest retreat of Grimentz.

Crans-Montana

❿   *12 km (7 mi) north of Sierre, 19 km (11¾ mi) northwest of Sion.*

This well-known twin sports center rises above the valley on a steep, sheltered shelf at 1,495 m (4,904 ft) and commands a broad view across the Rhône Valley to the peaks of Valais Alps; its grassy and wooded plateau shares the benefits of Sierre's sunshine. Behind it, the **Rohrbachstein** (2,953 m/9,686 ft), the **Gletscherhorn** (2,943 m/9,653 ft), and the **Wildstrubel** (3,243 m/10,637 ft) combine to create a complex of challenging ski slopes. Every September, the 18-hole golf course is the site of the annual Swiss Open, a period the locals describe as "party week." The most direct route to Crans-Montana is from Sierre, just southeast, either by car, postbus, or funicular.

The resort towns themselves are highly developed and charmless, lacking the regional color and grace of Zermatt. The streets are lined with modern shops and hotels, and car traffic is almost always heavy. As in Verbier, all hotels are signposted. The crowds are young, wealthy, and international, although only a cynic would go so far as to describe the ambience as overbearingly vacuous.

Skiing

The pearl of the region is the **Plaine Morte,** a flat glacier 5 km–6 km (3 mi–3½ mi) long, perched like a pancake at an elevation of 3,000 m (9,840 ft), which has snow year-round. A cross-country ski trail (watch out for your lungs at this altitude) of 10 km–12 km (6–7½ mi) is open and maintained here seven months of the year. You can also downhill-ski on the gentle slopes in summer; in winter, the descent from the Plaine Morte follows wide and relatively easy pistes as far as one or two chutes. The ascent on the gondola from **Violettes Plaines-Morte,** virtually under assault during the high season and in good weather, will in itself justify your stay in Crans-Montana. Expert skiers may prefer the **Nationale Piste,** site of the 1987 world championships. The incredibly steep-pitched **La Toula** is also a challenge for pros. A one-day lift ticket costs 56 SF; a six-day pass costs 265 SF.

Dining and Lodging

$$$$ ✕⊡ **Aïda-Castel.** In a resort that mushroomed during the 1960s and
★ seems to be frozen in that decade, this warm and welcoming complex is refreshingly au courant. The public areas have carved or aged wood, terra-cotta, and stucco; the rooms have hand-painted furniture and some stenciled ceilings. The amenities are all top quality. The very popular public restaurant, La Hotte, serves Italian fare, some prepared on the open grill, as well as raclette made at fireside—so good that reservations are essential. The hillside location is moderately isolated, with great southern views from nearly every balcony. ⊠ *CH-3962 Montana,* ☎ *027/4854111,* 🆆 *027/4817062. 61 rooms. 3 restaurants, outdoor pool, hot tub, sauna, exercise room, meeting room. AE, DC, MC, V.*

$$$$ ⊡ **Crans-Ambassador.** A stylized château with a three-peak roofline and direct access to the slopes, this dramatic modern structure stands apart from the twin towns and offers some of the resorts' finest views south. Each room has a balcony or terrace, and the back rooms look onto shaggy pine forests. The interiors are anonymously sleek, warmed up by occasional touches of wood; all the baths sparkle. After a hard day's skiing, you might want to treat yourself at the phytothermal center. ⊠ *CH-3962 Montana,* ☎ *027/4854848,* 🆆 *027/4854849. 70 rooms, 10 suites. 2 restaurants, piano bar, indoor pool, sauna, exercise room. AE, DC, MC, V.*

$$$$ ⊡ **Grand Hôtel du Golf.** This is the blue blood of the lot, a grand, old,
★ genteel resort oasis with urbane good taste and every amenity. Built by English golfers in 1907 and owned by the same family since 1914, it's been modernized outside and carefully tended within. The perfectly turned-out rooms are done in pastels. In addition to a formal restaurant and a homey café, there's a fine bar completely paneled in oak. Manicured grounds adjoin the 9- and 18-hole golf courses. ⊠ *CH-3963 Crans,* ☎ *027/4854242,* 🆆 *027/4854243. 76 rooms, 8 suites, 2 apartments. Restaurant, bar, café, in-room VCRs, indoor pool, hair salon. AE, DC, MC, V.*

$$$–$$$$ ⊡ **Mirabeau.** Done in pastels straight out of suburbia, this attractive midtown property's views are not spectacular—you can see the street and other hotels. However, it's at the hub of the downtown dining and shopping scene. ⊠ *CH-3962 Montana,* ☎ *027/4802151,* 🆆 *027/ 4813912. 45 rooms. Restaurant, bar, health club. AE, DC, MC, V.*

$$–$$$$ ⊡ **Le Green.** What was once a rustic, welcome alternative to Crans glitz has succumbed: decorated in jazzy, bright *style golf,* this has become another pricey four-star option. Most rooms have a balcony and face south. Facilities include a brasserie, a pine-deck bar, and a sauna-solarium. ⊠ *CH-3963 Crans,* ☎ *027/4813256,* FAX *027/4811781. 32 rooms, 2 suites. Restaurant, bar, brasserie, sauna, exercise room. AE, DC, MC, V.*

$$–$$$ 🏨 **La Prairie.** Wally Cleaver might have stayed here on a school ski trip: there are rough-hewn fireplaces everywhere, and the young, rec-room atmosphere is downright wholesome. Built in the 1930s, the updated rooms glow with pine, and the baths are very modern. The hotel is away from the noisy center but conveniently placed. ⊠ *CH-3962 Montana,* ☎ *027/4854141,* FAX *027/4854142. 32 rooms. Restaurant, bar, outdoor pool. AE, DC, MC, V.*

$–$$ 🏨 **Regina.** On the main shopping street in Montana, this is a spare, tidy city inn with the rare option of inexpensive rooms (bathrooms are down the hall). Although their decor is dated (wood paneling, all-weather carpet), some rooms have balconies that overlook the valley. There's a cozy lounge downstairs as well as a wonderful bakery—so breakfasts are homemade and fresh. ⊠ *CH-3962 Montana,* ☎ *027/4813522,* FAX *027/4801868. 24 rooms. Breakfast room. AE, DC, MC, V.*

Nightlife

DANCING

If you've ever wondered what Salvador Dalí would have produced if he'd illustrated a vodka ad, then head for the **Absolut** (☎ 027/4816596), a nightclub in Crans. At 15 SF for a beer you might find the prices pretty surreal, too. **Pub Georges et Dragon** (☎ 027/4815496) is a lively international meeting place, with a DJ every night of the season. Up in Montana, the small but convivial **Amadeus** (☎ 027/4812495), beneath the Olympic Hotel, is a popular après-ski venue with the young crowd; the **Number Two** (☎ 027/4813615) hockey bar is comparatively cheap, popular with locals, and described by some as a bit wild.

Outdoor Activities and Sports

BICYCLING

The **Avalanche Pro Shop** (⊠ Montana, ☎ 027/4802424) rents mountain bikes for 40 SF per day and 130 SF for six days. A map of possible routes is available at the tourist office (☞ Visitor Information *in* Valais A to Z, *below*).

GOLF

Crans and Montana have one 18-hole **golf course** and two nine-hole courses (☎ 027/4859797).

TENNIS

The **Centre de Tennis Au Lac Moubra** (☎ 027/4815014) has seven indoor courts.

En Route   East of the city limits of Sierre and south of the Rhône, follow signs southward for Vissoie. Here you enter the **Val d'Anniviers,** a wild and craggy valley said to derive its name from its curious and famous (among anthropologists, at least) nomads, known in Latin as *anni viatores* (year-round travelers). Some claim they are descended from the Huns who straggled into the area during the 5th century. Since the development of modern roads, the Anniviards no longer follow their ancient pattern: migrating down into the valley around Niouc in spring, moving to Sierre in summer to cultivate collectively owned vineyards, and returning to their isolated villages to hole up for the winter. The ancient practice disappeared in the 1950s, but many residents are the nomads' descendants.

Grimentz

⑪ *20 km (12½ mi) south of Sierre.*

With a population of 370, this ancient 13th-century village has preserved its weathered-wood houses and mazots in its tiny center, although anonymous hotels have sprung up near the ski facilities above.

Skiing

Grimentz shares transit facilities with **Zinal** (☞ *below*) and **Chandolin** in the Val d'Anniviers. Though they're separated by wilderness, each can provide a day's skiing, with easy access for variety the next day. Grimentz's trails, while limited, should meet everyone's needs. There's a hair-raising expert run from **Pointe de Lona** (at 2,900 m/9,512 ft) all the way back down to the parking lot (at 1,570 m/5,150 ft). Beginners can enjoy equally spectacular sweeps from **Orvizal,** starting at 2,780 m (9,118 ft), back to town. The upper runs are reached by ski tows only; a cable car has been added to the first level. **Grimentz,** at 1,570 m (5,150 ft), has eight tows, one chairlift, one cable car, 50 km (31 mi) of downhill runs, and 22 km (14 mi) of cross-country trails. A ski pass, which costs 36 SF for one day, 172 SF for six days, offers access to all Val d'Anniviers facilities, including 46 lifts and 250 km (155 mi) of downhill runs.

Dining

$$ ✕ **Le Mélèze.** Warm your feet by the central fireplace, open on all sides, in the old, all-wood café and restaurant on the edge of Grimentz that serves raclette, crepes, and generous hot meals. ☎ *027/4751287. AE, DC, MC, V. Closed mid-May–June and Nov.*

Zinal

⑫ *25 km (16 mi) south of Sierre.*

Summer travelers can veer down a tiny forest road from Grimentz toward Zinal, with the Weisshorn dominating the views. Zinal (1,675 m/5,494 ft) is another isolated mountaineering center with well-preserved wood houses and mazots. It is worth building enough time into your itinerary to stop over in one of these windswept mountain aeries and walk, climb, ski, or relax by the fire.

ZERMATT AND SAAS-FEE

Immediately east of Sierre, you'll notice a sharp change: *vals* become *-tals,* and the sounds you overhear at your next pit stop are no longer the throaty, mellifluous tones of the Suisse Romande but the lilting, guttural Swiss-German dialect called Wallisertiitsch, a local form of Schwyzerdütsch. Welcome to Wallis (*vahl*-is), the Germanic end of Valais. This sharp demographic frontier can be traced back to the 6th century, when Alemannic tribes poured over the Grimsel Pass and penetrated as far as Sierre. Here the middle-class cuisine changes from *steak-frîtes* (steak with french fries) to veal and Rösti.

Zermatt

★ ⑬ *29 km (18 mi) south of Visp, plus a 10-km (6-mi) train ride from Täsch.*

Despite its fame—which stems from that mythic mountain, the Matterhorn, and from its excellent ski facilities—Zermatt is a resort with its feet on the ground, protecting its regional quirks along with its wildlife and its tumbledown mazots, which crowd between glass-and-concrete chalets like old tenements between skyscrapers. Streets twist past weathered-wood walls, flower boxes, and haphazard stone roofs until they break into open country that slopes, inevitably, uphill. Despite the crowds, you are never far from the wild roar of the silty river and the peace of a mountain path.

★ Hordes of package-tour sightseers push shoulder to shoulder to get yet another shot of the **Matterhorn** (4,477 m/14,685 ft). Called one of the wonders of the Western world, the mountain deserves the title: though it has become an almost self-parodying icon, like the Eiffel Tower or the Empire State Building, its peculiar snaggle-tooth form, free from competition from other peaks on all sides, rears up over the village, larger than life and genuinely awe-inspiring. Leaving the train station and weaving through the pedestrian crowds, aggressive electric taxi carts, and aromatic horse-drawn carriages along the main street, Bahnhofs-trasse, you are assaulted on all sides by Matterhorn images: on post-cards, on sweatshirts, on calendars, on beer steins, on candy wrappers, it looms in multiples of a thousand, the original obscured by resort build-ings (except from the windows of pricier hotel rooms). But breaking past the shops and hotels onto the main road into the hills, visitors seem to reach the same slightly elevated spot and stop dead in their tracks: There it is at last, up and to the right, its twist of snowy rock blinding in the sun, mink-brown weathered mazots scattered romantically at its base. Surely more pictures are taken from this spot than from any-where else in Switzerland.

It was Edward Whymper's spectacular—and catastrophic—conquest of the Matterhorn, on July 14, 1865, that made Zermatt a household word. Whymper stayed at the Hotel Monte Rosa (☞ Dining and Lodging, *below*) the nights before his departure and there named his party of seven for the historic climb: Michel Croz, a French guide; old Peter Taugwalder and his son, young Peter, local guides; Lord Francis Douglas, a 19-year-old Englishman; Douglas Hadow; the Reverend Charles Hudson; and Whymper himself. They climbed together, pair-ing "tourists," as Whymper called the Englishmen, with experienced locals. They camped at 11,000 ft and by 10 AM had reached the base of the mountain's famous hook. Wrote Whymper of the final moments:

The higher we rose the more intense became the excitement. The slope eased off, at length we could be detached, and Croz and I, dashing away, ran a neck-and-neck race, which ended in a dead heat. At 1:40 PM, the world was at our feet, and the Matterhorn was conquered!

Croz pulled off his shirt and tied it to a stick as a flag, one that was seen in Zermatt below. They stayed at the summit one hour, then pre-pared for the descent, tying themselves together in an order agreed on by all. Croz led, then Hadow, Hudson, Lord Douglas, the elder Taug-walder, then the younger, and Whymper, who lingered to sketch the summit and leave their names in a bottle.

I suggested to Hudson that we should attach a rope to the rocks on our arrival at the difficult bit, and hold it as we descended, as an ad-ditional protection. He approved the idea, but it was not definitely de-cided that it should be done.

They headed off, "one man moving at a time; when he was firmly planted the next advanced," Whymper recalled.

Croz . . . was in the act of turning around to go down a step or two himself; at this moment Mr. Hadow slipped, fell against him, and knocked him over. I heard one startled exclamation from Croz, then saw him and Mr. Hadow flying downward; in another moment Hud-

son was dragged from his steps, and Lord Douglas immediately after him. All this was the work of a moment. Immediately we heard Croz's exclamation, old Peter and I planted ourselves as firmly as the rocks would permit; the rope was taut between us, and the jerk came on us both as on one man. We held; but the rope broke midway between Taugwalder and Lord Francis Douglas. For a few seconds we saw our unfortunate companions sliding downward on their backs, and spreading out their hands, endeavoring to save themselves. They passed from our sight uninjured, disappeared one by one, and fell from precipice to precipice on to the Matterhorn glacier below, a distance of nearly 4,000 feet in height. From the moment the rope broke it was impossible to help them. So perished our comrades!

A "sharp-eyed lad" ran into the Hotel Monte Rosa to report an avalanche fallen from the Matterhorn summit; he had witnessed the deaths of the four mountaineers. The body of young Lord Douglas was never recovered, but the others lie in the grim little cemetery behind the Zermatt church, surrounded by scores of other failed mountaineers, including a recent American whose tomb bears the simple epitaph I CHOSE TO CLIMB.

In summer, the streets of Zermatt fill with sturdy, weathered climbers, state-of-the-art ropes and picks hanging at their hips. They continue to tackle the peaks, and climbers have mastered the Matterhorn literally thousands of times since Whymper's disastrous victory.

It's quite simple to gain the broader perspective of high altitudes without risking life or limb; the train trip up the **Gornergrat** on the Gornergratbahn functions as an excursion as well as ski transport. Part of its rail system was completed in 1898, and it's the highest open-air rail system in Europe (the tracks to the Jungfraujoch, though higher, bore through the face of the Eiger). It connects out of the main Zermatt train station and heads sharply left, at a right angle to the track that brings you into town. Its first stop is the **Riffelberg**, which, at 2,582 m (8,469 ft), offers wide-open views of the Matterhorn. Farther on, from **Rotenboden**, at 2,819 m (9,246 ft), a short downhill walk leads to the **Riffelsee**, which obligingly provides photographers with a postcard-perfect reflection of the famous peak. At the end of the 9-km (5½-mi) line, the train stops at the summit station of **Gornergrat** (3,130 m/10,266 ft), and passengers pour onto the observation terraces to take in the majestic views of the Matterhorn, Monte Rosa, Gorner Glacier, and an expanse of scores of peaks and 24 other glaciers. If you ski or hike down, the cost of the trip is just 37 SF. ⊠ *Leaves from Zermatt station.* 🕾 *63 SF round-trip.* ☉ *Departures every 24 mins 7–7. Bring warm clothes, sunglasses, and sturdy shoes.*

Zermatt lies in a hollow of meadows and trees ringed by mountains—among them the broad **Monte Rosa** (4,554 m/14,937 ft) and its tallest peak, the **Dufourspitze** (at 4,634 m/15,200 ft, the highest point in Switzerland)—of which visitors hear relatively little, so all-consuming is the cult of the Matterhorn. In the mid-19th century, Zermatt was virtually unheard-of; the few visitors who came to town stayed at the vicarage. It happened, however, that the vicar had a nose for business and a chaplain named Seiler. Joseph Seiler convinced his little brother, Alexander, to start an inn. Opened in 1854 and named the Hotel Monte Rosa, it is still one of five Seiler hotels in Zermatt. In 1891, the cog railway between Visp and Zermatt took its first summer run and began disgorging tourists with profitable regularity—though it didn't plow through in wintertime until 1927.

The town is a car-free resort (there's a reason for those carriages). If you're traveling primarily by car, you can park it in the long-term lot in Täsch, where you catch the train into Zermatt. *See also* Getting Around *in* Valais A to Z, *below.*

Skiing

Zermatt's skiable terrain lives up to its reputation: the 74 lift installations are capable of moving well above 50,000 skiers per hour to reach its approximately 245 km (152 mi) of marked pistes—if you count those of Breuil in Italy. Among the lifts are the cable car that carries skiers up to an elevation of 3,820 m (12,532 ft) on the Klein Matterhorn, the small Gornergratbahn that creeps up to the Gornergrat (3,100 m/10,170 ft), and a subway through an underground tunnel that gives more pleasure to ecologists than it does to sun-loving skiers.

This royal plateau has several less-than-perfect features, however, not least of which is the separation of the skiable territory into three sectors. **Sunegga-Blauherd-Rothorn** culminates at an elevation of 3,100 m (10,170 ft). **Gornergrat-Stockhorn** (3,400 m/11,155 ft) is the second. The third is the region dominated by the **Klein Matterhorn;** to go from this sector to the others, you must return to the bottom of the valley and lose considerable time crossing town to reach the lifts to the other elevations. The solution is to ski for a whole day in the same area, especially during high season (mid-December to the end of February, or even until Easter if the snow cover is good). On the other hand, thanks to snowmaking machines and the eternal snows of the Klein Matterhorn, Zermatt is said to guarantee skiers 2,200 m (7,216 ft) of vertical drop no matter what the snowfall—an impressive claim. A one-day lift ticket costs 60 SF; a six-day pass costs 296 SF. A **ski school** (⌧ Skischulbüro, Bahnhofstr., ☎ 027/9662466) operates during the high season, from mid-December until April.

Dining and Lodging

Many Zermatt hotels, especially larger ones, decide on a year-by-year basis to close during low season, which lasts from "melt-down" (anywhere from late April to mid-June) until "pre-season" (November through mid-December). If you plan to travel during the low season, be sure to call ahead.

$$$–$$$$ ✕ **Restaurant Gourmetstübli.** Dining here is like having a table in an eagle's nest with a view of the Matterhorn. The menu flies far afield; choices could include sushi, creamy curried pumpkin soup, duck breast with blood-orange sauce, and New Zealand venison. ⌧ *Grandhotel Schönegg,* ☎ *027/9674488. AE, DC, MC, V. Closed mid-Apr.–May and Oct.–Nov.*

$$–$$$ ✕ **Grill-Room Stockhorn.** The tantalizing aromas of melting pungent cheese and roasting meat on the open grill should sharpen your appetite the moment you step across the threshold into this low-slung, two-story restaurant. This is a great place to fortify yourself with regional dishes; the service and the clientele are equally lively. ⌧ *Hotel Stockhorn,* ☎ *027/9671747. AE, MC, V. Closed mid-May–mid-June and Oct.*

$$ ✕ **Findlerhof.** Whether for long lunches between sessions on the slopes,
★ for the traditional wind-down après-ski, or for a panoramic meal break on an all-day hike, this mountain restaurant is ideal. It's perched in tiny Findeln, between the Sunnegga and Blauherd ski areas. The Matterhorn views from the wraparound dining porch are astonishing, the winter dining room cozy with pine and stone, and the food surprisingly fresh and creative. Franz and Heidi Schwery tend their own Alpine garden to provide spinach for the bacon-crisped salad and rhubarb and berries for their hot desserts. It's about a 30-minute walk down from the Sunnegga Express stop and another 30 minutes back down to Zermatt. ⌧ *Findeln,* ☎ *027/9672588. MC. Closed May–mid-June and mid-Oct.–Nov.*

$$ ✕ **Zum See.** This alternative to Findlerhof, beyond Findeln in a tiny
★ village (little more than a cluster of mazots) of the same name, serves
light meals of a quality and inventiveness that would merit acclaim even
if it weren't in the middle of nowhere at 1,766 m (5,792 ft). In sum-
mer its shaded picnic tables draw hikers rewarding themselves at the
finish of a day's climb; in winter its low-ceiling log dining room sets
skiers aglow with an impressive assortment of brandies. Regional spe-
cialties are prepared with masterly care, from wild mushrooms in pas-
try shells to rabbit, Rösti, and *foie de veau* (calves' liver). ⊠ *Zum See,*
☎ *027/9672045. Reservations essential après-ski. MC, V. Closed mid-
Apr.–June and Oct.–mid-Dec.*

$ ✕ **Elsie's Bar.** This tiny log cabin of a ski haunt, directly across from
the Zermatt church, draws an international crowd for cocktails. Light
meals include cheese dishes and escargots. ⊠ *Kirchepl.,* ☎ *027/
9672431. AE, DC, MC, V.*

$$$$ ✕▦ **Julen.** The decor here happily shuns regional kitsch. Instead,
★ rooms have a Bavarian style: century-old spruce-wood decor paired
with primary-color carpets and silk curtains; each suite has a green-
tile stove. A three-floor sports center includes an elaborate Roman bath
where you can indulge in various therapies. The main restaurant of-
fers international cuisine, while the welcoming Stübli serves unusual
dishes prepared with lamb (such as lamb's tongue in capers) from local
family-owned flocks. ⊠ *CH-3920,* ☎ *027/9667600,* 𝔽𝔸𝕏 *027/9667676.
27 rooms, 5 suites. 2 restaurants, café, minibars, indoor pool, sauna,
exercise room. AE, DC, MC, V.* ✍

$$$$ ✕▦ **Mont Cervin.** One of the flagships of the Seiler dynasty, this luxuri-
★ ous, urbane mountain hotel is never grandiose, in either scale or attitude.
Built in 1852, it's unusually low-slung for a grand hotel. Its restaurant
has a light, modern ambience; you might try a salad of peahen and goose
liver with powdered cashew nuts and ginger-honey vinegar. Dessert
lovers shouldn't miss choices like caramelized frozen bananas with
chocolate sauce. Jacket and tie are required only for the Friday gala buf-
fet. The Residence, across the street through a handy tunnel, offers chic,
luxurious apartments. ⊠ *CH-3920,* ☎ *027/9668888,* 𝔽𝔸𝕏 *027/9672878.
101 rooms, 40 suites. 2 restaurants, bar, minibars, no-smoking rooms,
indoor pool, sauna, hair salon, meeting rooms. AE, DC, MC, V.* ✍

$$$$ ✕▦ **Zermatterhof.** This luxurious, faultless hotel was built in 1879, so
★ they have had more than a century to get things exactly right. Rooms
in multifarious shades and styles of wood have either granite or mar-
ble bathrooms, where you can lie back and enjoy the ultimate in Alpine
decadence—nibbling a chocolate Matterhorn while your back is mas-
saged by Jacuzzi bubbles. The formal restaurant serves ambitious French
cuisine, while the glass-dome Rôtisserie La Broche is your chance to try
regional specialties such as "Findler Hay Soup," with smoked lamb. ⊠
CH-3920, ☎ *027/9666600,* 𝔽𝔸𝕏 *027/9666699. 60 rooms, 26 suites. 2
restaurants, 2 bars, no-smoking rooms, indoor pool, hot tub, sauna, 9-
hole golf course, exercise room, meeting rooms. AE, DC, MC, V.* ✍

$$$–$$$$ ✕▦ **Pollux.** This modern hotel is simple and chic, with its straight-
forward rooms trimmed in pine and leatherette. It's small-scale, and
none of its windows looks onto the Matterhorn, but its position di-
rectly on the main pedestrian shopping street puts you in the heart of
resort activities. The restaurant is based on a village square, with gar-
den furniture and a central fountain; an appealing, old-fashioned Stübli
draws locals for its low-price lunches, snacks, and Valais cheese dishes.
If you're traveling with kids, ask for one of the joining rooms; in these,
children get a 60% reduction. ⊠ *CH-3920,* ☎ *027/9664000,* 𝔽𝔸𝕏 *027/
9664001. 35 rooms. Restaurant, Stübli, sauna, dance club, meeting
rooms. AE, DC, MC, V.*

$$$$
★ 🏨 **Hotel Monte Rosa.** Alexander Seiler founded his first hotel in the core of this historic building, expanding it over the years to its current scale. (This was the home base of Edward Whymper when he conquered the Matterhorn in 1865.) Behind its graceful, shuttered facade you'll find an ideal balance between modern convenience and history in the burnished pine, flagstone floors, original ceiling moldings, fireplaces, and the Victorian dining hall. The beige-oriented room decor is impeccable; southern views go quickly and cost more. The bar is an après-ski must. ⊠ *CH-3920,* ☎ *027/9673333,* 𝔽𝔸𝕏 *027/9671160. 44 rooms, 5 suites. Restaurant, bar, minibars, sauna (at Mont Cervin), meeting room. AE, DC, MC, V. Closed mid-May–mid-June.* ⌘

$$$$
★ 🏨 **Into the Hotel.** You can't get any closer to the mountains than this— Zermatt's extraordinary new hotel is built into a rock wall in the middle of town. This glass-and-steel structure is rife with high-tech innovations. For instance, the ultramodern guest rooms have combination bed-and-sofas on turntables, controlled by touchscreen panels. In the Presidential suite, the whirlpool bath can be raised through the glass roof, which opens hydraulically. And the Mediterranean restaurant has a retractable fountain and mobile fireplace. Try out the nightclub or meditation room, both built into the rock, or slip into the Turkish bath in the wellness center. Who has time for skiing? ⊠ *CH-3920,* ☎ *027/9667171,* 𝔽𝔸𝕏 *027/9667100. 43 rooms, 2 suites. Restaurant, bar, no-smoking rooms, indoor pool, sauna, exercise room, dance club, meeting room. AE, DC, MC, V.* ⌘

$$$
🏨 **Europe.** This tasteful lodging has rooms—many with a Matterhorn view—outfitted in cherry wood and, in some cases, dark-blue carpets and curtains. Over breakfast you can read the hotel's own daily news briefing and squeeze your own orange juice. You can also use the excellent sports center at its sister property Julen (☞ *above*), just a minute's walk away. The restaurant serves guests only. ⊠ *CH-3920,* ☎ *027/9662700,* 𝔽𝔸𝕏 *027/9662705. 22 rooms. Restaurant, bar, minibars, no-smoking rooms. AE, DC, MC, V.*

$$–$$$
🏨 **Parnass.** Across the street from the roaring river, with views east and south to the Matterhorn, this simple '60s structure offers a cozy, clublike lounge, knotty-pine rooms, and private pension dining with unusually adventurous and successful cooking. In winter, annual regulars rub shoulders by the fireplace in this exceptionally welcoming hotel. ⊠ *CH-3920,* ☎ *027/9671179,* 𝔽𝔸𝕏 *027/9674557. 32 rooms. Restaurant, no-smoking rooms. MC, V.* ⌘

$$–$$$
🏨 **Touring.** Its reassuringly traditional architecture and snug, sunny rooms full of pine, combined with an elevated position apart from town and excellent Matterhorn views, make this an appealing choice for travelers who want an informal alternative to the chic downtown scene. Hearty daily menus are served to pension guests in the cozy dining room (the same menu is available in the Stübli), and a sunny enclosed playground has lounge chairs for parents. ⊠ *CH-3920,* ☎ *027/9671177,* 𝔽𝔸𝕏 *027/9674601. 20 rooms. Restaurant, Stübli, playground, meeting room. MC, V.*

$–$$$
🏨 **Romantica.** Among the scores of anonymously modern hotels cloned all over the Zermatt plain, this modest structure—unremarkable at first glance—offers an exceptional location directly above the town center, no more than a block up a narrow, mazot-lined lane. Its tidy, bright gardens and flower boxes, its game trophies, and its old-style granite stove give it personality, and the plain rooms—many in pastel colors— benefit from big windows and balconies. You can also stay in one of the two *Walliserstudel,* tiny (but charming), 200-year-old huts in the hotel's garden. Views take in the mountains, though not the Matter-

horn, over a graceful clutter of stone roofs. ⊠ *CH-3920*, ☎ *027/ 9662650*, 𝔽𝔸𝕏 *027/9662655*. *13 rooms. AE, DC, MC, V.*

$$ ⊡ **Alphubel.** Although it's surrounded by other hotels and close to the main street, this modest, comfortable pension built in 1954 feels off the beaten track—and rooms on the south side offer large, sunny balconies. The interiors are a little institutional, but there's a sauna in the basement, available to guests for a small charge. ⊠ *CH-3920*, ☎ *027/ 9673003*, 𝔽𝔸𝕏 *027/9676684*. *31 rooms. Restaurant, sauna. AE, MC, V.*

$$ ⊡ **Mischabel.** One of the least, if not *the* least, expensive hotels in this pricey resort town, the Mischabel provides comfort, atmosphere, and a central situation few places can match at twice the price: southern balconies frame a perfect Matterhorn view—the higher the better. Creaky, homey, and covered with *Arvenholz* (Alpine pine) aged to the color of toffee, its rooms have sinks only and share the linoleum-lined showers on every floor. A generous daily menu, for guests only, caters to families and young skiers on the cheap. ⊠ *CH-3920*, ☎ *027/ 9671131*, 𝔽𝔸𝕏 *027/9676507*. *28 rooms. Restaurant. MC, V.*

Nightlife

GramPi's Bar (☎ 027/9677788), on the main drag, is a lively young-people's bar, where you can get into the mood for dancing downstairs with a Lady Matterhorn cocktail. The newly renovated **T-Bar** (☎ 027/ 9674000), below the Hotel Pollux, plays more varied music then the generic disco-pap of the ski resorts, and its walls and ceilings are interestingly adorned with ancient skiing equipment, which somehow looks more comfortable than the garish space-age wear of today.

Outdoor Activities and Sports

MOUNTAIN BIKING

Mountain biking is severely limited by Zermatt authorities to prevent interference with hiking on trails. About 25 km (15 mi) have been set aside, however. A map is available at the tourist office (☞ Visitor Information *in* Valais A to Z, *below*). Bikes can be rented at **Slalomsport** (☎ 027/9662366).

MOUNTAIN CLIMBING

The Matterhorn is one of the world's most awe-inspiring peaks, and many visitors get the urge to climb it. However, this climb must be taken seriously; you have to be in top physical condition and have climbing experience to attempt the summit. You also need to spend 7–10 days acclimatizing once in the area. Less experienced climbers have plenty of alternatives, though, such as a one-day climb of the Riffelhorn (2,980 m/9,774 ft) or a half-traverse of the Breithorn (4,165 m/13,661 ft). For detailed information, advice, instruction, and climbing guides, contact the **Alpin Center Zermatt** (☎ 027/9662460).

TENNIS

The **Alpenresort Hotel** (☎ 027/9663000) has three courts; rental equipment is available. The **Gemeinde** (☎ 027/9673673) maintains nine public courts, but you must reserve a day in advance.

Shopping

Zermatt may be Switzerland's souvenir capital, offering a broad variety of watches, knives, and logo clothing. Popular folk crafts and traditional products include large, grotesque masks of carved wood and lidded *channes* in pewter or tin, molded in graduated sizes; they are sold everywhere, even in the grocery stores of tourist-conscious resorts.

SPORTS EQUIPMENT AND APPAREL

Zermatt's streets are lined with stores offering state-of-the-art sports equipment and apparel, from collapsible grappling hooks for climbers to lightweight hiking boots in psychedelic colors. You'll see plenty of the new must-have walking sticks—pairs of lightweight, spiked ski poles for hikers to add a bit of upper-body workout to their climb. Although prices are consistently high, the selection is dazzling.

Bayard (⊠ Bahnhofpl., ☎ 027/9664950; ⊠ Bahnhofstr., ☎ 027/9664960) heads the long list of sporting-goods stores. **Glacier Sport** (☎ 027/9672719) specializes in ski equipment and accessories. **La Cabane** (☎ 027/9672249) is the best source for trendy sports clothing.

Grächen

⑭ *28 km (17 mi) south of Visp.*

From the valley resort village of St. Niklaus, a narrow, winding road crawls up to this small, tame family resort nestled comfortably on a sunny shelf at 1,617 m (5,304 ft). Little more than a picturesque scattering of small hotels, chalets, and mazots, it concentrates its business near a central parking lot and closes the rest of its streets to car traffic. Small and isolated as it is, there are enough shops and cafés to keep visitors occupied on a foggy day. This is a place to escape tourist crowds, hike high trails undisturbed by the traffic you find near the larger resorts, or ski a variety of fine trails on the Hannigalp. Grächen makes a heroic effort to keep families happy, offering a staffed and supervised winter-sports area, with ski and toboggan lifts, playgrounds, and even igloos, free of charge, for children under six years old.

Dining and Lodging

$$$–$$$$ ✕🏨 **Walliserhof.** Directly in the center of town, this eye-catching dark-wood, Valais-style chalet is ringed with balconies; in summer geraniums spill from every window. The interior is bright and elegant, and rooms glow with warm knotty pine. An "oasis of vitality" provides spa-type treatments such as herbal massages and facial peels. The restaurant serves basic French fare in a formal setting of candles and crisp linens. ⊠ *CH-3925,* ☎ *027/9561122,* ℻ *027/9562922. 25 rooms. Restaurant, café, sauna, exercise room, hot tub, dance club. AE, MC, V.*

$$ ✕🏨 **Désirée.** Though the rooms are institution-modern, they have a number of family rooms, the balconies take in mountain views, and the restaurant-Stübli downstairs is rich in smoky, meaty local atmosphere, serving Valais and Italian specialties. It's in the center but above traffic; access is by electric cart. ⊠ *CH-3925,* ☎ *027/9562255,* ℻ *027/9562070. 22 rooms. Restaurant, Stübli, sauna, exercise room. AE, DC, MC, V. Closed late Apr.–mid-June and late Oct.–mid-Dec.*

$$ ✕🏨 **Hannigalp.** The oldest hotel in town, this welcoming landmark
★ built in 1909 and run by the same family for 90 years has been completely modernized without losing its regional character. The rooms have been updated to spare, blond-wood simplicity; most have balconies. The amenities are remarkable for the price. Headed by the owner himself, the kitchen creates straightforward French and international cuisine for the restaurant and regional specialties to serve in the cozier bar. It is in a quiet, car-free zone. ⊠ *CH-3925,* ☎ *027/9562555,* ℻ *027/9562855. 22 rooms. Restaurant, bar, indoor pool, hot tub, sauna, tennis court. MC, V. Closed late Apr.–mid-June and late Oct.–mid-Dec.*

Saas-Fee

⑮ *36 km (22 mi) south of Visp.*

At the end of the switchback road to Saas-Grund (1,559 m/5,114 ft) lies a parking area where visitors must abandon their cars for the length of their stay in Saas-Fee. But even in the parking lot you'll be amazed, for the view on arriving at this lofty (1,790 m/5,871 ft) plateau is humbling. Saas-Fee lies in a deep valley that leaves no doubt about its source: it seems to pour from the vast, intimidating **Fee Glacier,** which oozes like icy lava from the broad spread of peaks above. *Fee* can be translated as "fairy," and although Saas-Fee itself is a tourist-saturated resort, the landscape could illustrate a fairytale. The town is at the heart of a cirque of mountains, 13 of which tower to more than 4,000 m (13,120 ft), among them the **Dom** (4,545 m/14,908 ft), the highest mountain entirely on Swiss soil.

Skiing

The first glacier to be used for skiing here was the **Längfluh** (2,870 m/9,414 ft), accessed by gondola, then cable car. The run is magnificent, sometimes physically demanding, and always varied. From the Längfluh you can take a lift to reach *the* ski area of Saas-Fee, the **Felskinn-Mittelallalin** sector (3,000 m–3,500 m/9,840 ft–11,480 ft). Felskinn harbors its own surprise: in order to preserve the land and landscape, the Valaisans have constructed a subterranean funicular, the Métro Alpin, which climbs through the heart of the mountain to Mittelallalin, that is, halfway up the Allalinhorn (4,027 m/13,210 ft); tourists debark in a rotating restaurant noted more for the austere grandeur of its natural surroundings than for the quality of its food. Felskinn-Mittelallalin's exceptional site, its high elevation, its runs (15 km/9 mi), and its ample facilities (cable car, funicular, and five ski lifts) have made Saas-Fee the number one summer-skiing resort in Switzerland. It is also one of two official European snowboard centers sanctioned by the International Snowboard Federation. A one-day lift ticket costs 58 SF; a six-day pass costs 270 SF.

Dining and Lodging

$$$$ ✕🏠 **Waldhotel Fletschhorn.** High on a forested hillside above the re-
★ sort, this quiet *Landgasthof* (country inn) is a sophisticated retreat. The baths are sizable, and although the rooms have ultramodern fittings, they're mellowed with pine paneling, antiques, and serene views. Half board includes innovative French cuisine based on local products: reindeer with wild mushrooms, stuffed quail with polenta in pinot noir. (The chef also runs culinary courses at the hotel.) Reservations are essential at the restaurant. Manager Hansjörg Dütsch provides transportation from town. ✉ CH-3906, ☎ 027/9572131, 🆑 027/9572187. *15 rooms. Restaurant, hot tub, sauna. AE, DC, MC, V. Closed late Apr.–early June and mid-Oct.–early Dec.* 🐾

$$$$ 🏠 **Ferienart Walliserhof.** Switzerland's first low-energy hotel has repositioned itself after a major renovation and expansion in winter 2000/2001. It has pumped up its amenities, with whirlpools in 33 rooms, a mock-glacier pool with a waterfall, a "wellness zone" with every sort of thermal and medicinal bath, a Balinesian restaurant, an art gallery, and more. The generously sized rooms have modern birch furnishings and granite bath vanities. For a splurge, try one of the suites; the Adlerhorst, for instance, has a Turkish steam bath and built-in fireplace. The international staff gives the hotel a lively atmosphere, and although it's in the center of town, it still has panoramic views on all sides. ✉ CH-3906, ☎ 027/9581900, 🆑 027/9581905. *43 rooms, 5 suites, 4 apartments. 4 restaurants, café, piano bar, indoor pool, hair salon, massage, sauna, exercise room, pro shop, nightclub. AE, DC, MC, V.* 🐾

$$$$ 🏠 **Saaserhof.** What this hotel has going for it is location: it's near the best lift facilities. Rooms are either in generic dark wood or modern pastels; the restaurant, open to nonguests, focuses on French-influenced cuisine. ✉ CH-3906, ☎ 027/9573551, 🆑 027/9572883. *40 rooms, 5 suites. Restaurant, bar, hot tub, sauna. AE, DC, MC, V.*

$$$–$$$$ ⊡ **Allalin.** Families will especially appreciate the flexibility and up-to-
★   date design of the suites and rooms here, all with kitchen equipment
and balconies. In high season guests usually pay half pension and eat
one meal per day in the restaurant—no great punishment, as the kitchen
is surprisingly sophisticated—although a breakfast-only arrangement
can be made. Built in 1928, the hotel feels warm, bright, and natural.
It's on the hill just east of the center and a block from the main park-
ing, and all doubles but one have a spectacular southern or southeast-
ern view. ⊠ CH-3906, ☎ 027/9571815, ⨳ 027/9573115. 16 rooms,
11 suites. Restaurant, bar, café, kitchenettes, sauna. AE, DC, MC, V.

$–$$ ⊡ **Britannia.** Compensating for its brand-new architecture with light
carved pine in every corner, this tidy, fresh, simple lodging is in the heart
of town, near resort shopping on the main pedestrian street. The best
balconies face south and east; the dining room also has a tantalizing
view. ⊠ CH-3906, ☎ 027/9571616, ⨳ 027/9571942. 19 rooms.
Restaurant, bar. AE, MC, V.

Outdoor Activities and Sports

MOUNTAIN CLIMBING

The **Swiss Mountaineering School** (☎ 027/9574464) conducts daily
guided forays all year round; you can rent season-appropriate equipment.

SPORTS CENTER

The **Bielen Recreation Center** (☎ 027/9572475) has a four-lane swimming pool, children's pool, whirlpools, steam baths, sauna, solarium,
and a pair of tennis courts.

TENNIS

Kalbermatten Sports Ground (☎ 027/9572454) is an ice rink in winter and a seven-court tennis club in summer.

BRIG AND THE ALPINE PASSES

This region is the Grand Central Station of the Alpine region; all
mountain passes lead to Brig, and traffic pours in (and through) from
Italy, the Ticino, central Switzerland, the Berner Oberland—and, via
the latter, from Paris, Brussels, and London and Rome.

Brig

16 *209 km (129 mi) southeast of Bern.*

A rail and road junction joining four cantons, this small but vital town
has for centuries been a center of trade with Italy. It guards not only
the Simplon route but also the high end of the Rhône Valley, which
leads past the Aletsch Glacier to Gletsch and the Grimsel Pass (toward
Meiringen and the Berner Oberland) or the Furka Pass (toward Andermatt and central Switzerland). The fantastical **Stockalperschloss,** a
massive baroque castle, was built between 1658 and 1678 by Kaspar
Jodok von Stockalper, a Swiss tycoon who made his fortune in Italian
trade over the Simplon Pass. Topped with three gilt onion domes and
containing a courtyard lined by elegant Italianate arcades, it was once
Switzerland's largest private home and is now restored. Group tours
in English are available upon request. To get here from the station walk
up Bahnhofstrasse to Sebastienplatz, then turn left onto Alte Sim-
plonstrasse. ⊠ Alte Simplonstr., ☎ 027/9216030. ⛦ 5 SF. ☉ June–
Sept., Tues.–Sun., guided tours at 10, 11, 2, 3, 4, and 5; May and Oct.,
Tues.–Sun., guided tours at 10, 11, 2, 3, and 4. Closed Nov.–Apr.

En Route Above the eastern outskirts of Brig is the entrance to the **Simplon Tunnel,** which carries trains nearly 20 km (12 mi) before emerging into

Italian daylight. The first of the twin tunnels—the world's longest railway tunnels—was started in 1898 and took six years to complete.

Simplon Pass

⑰ *23 km (14 mi) southeast of Brig.*

Beginning just outside Brig, this historic road meanders through deep gorges and wide, barren, rock-strewn pastures to offer increasingly beautiful views back toward Brig. At the summit (2,010 m/6,593 ft), the **Simplon-Kulm Hotel** shares the high meadow with the **Simplon Hospice**, built 150 years ago at Napoléon's request and now owned by the monks of St. Bernard. Just beyond stands the bell-towered **Alt Spital**, a lodging built in the 17th century.

From the summit you can still see parts of the old road used by traders and Napoléon, and it is easy to imagine the hardships travelers faced at these heights. Look north toward the Bernese Alps and a portion of the massive Aletsch Glacier. Beyond the pass, the road continues through Italy, and it's possible to cut across the Italian upthrust and reenter Switzerland in the Ticino, near Ascona.

Riederalp

⑱ *13 km (8 mi) north of the Brig.*

The bleak and stony ascent of the Val de Conches, or Goms as it is called by the locals, follows the increasingly wild, silty Rhône to its source, with mountain resorts threading into the flanking heights. Within the valley, Riederalp is best known as the home of Art Furrer, who became famous in the United States as one of the pioneers of freestyle skiing. On his return to Switzerland, he came to this resort and established a freestyle ski school available to nearly every good skier.

On a rugged, treeless plateau, the resort is accessible only by cable car from **Mörel**, and its views over the Italian Alps are rivaled only by the staggering views over the Aletsch Glacier on the secondary ascent by cable car up to **Moosfluh**. A swift gondola up to Moosfluh, reputedly the fastest in Europe, holds 12 people. Riederalp borders the preserved pine stands of the **Aletsch Forest,** one of the highest in Europe. From Fiesch, just up the valley from Mörel, you can ascend by cable car all the way to the top of the **Eggishorn** (2,927 m/9,600 ft). This extraordinary vantage point looks over the entire sweep of the Aletsch and its surrounding peaks.

Skiing

At 1,900 m (6,232 ft), with a peak of 2,700 m (8,856 ft), **Riederalp** has seven lifts and 30 km (19 mi) of downhill runs, a third of which are expert. A one-day lift ticket (including access to the whole Aletsch ski area) costs 43 SF; a six-day pass costs 208 SF. As you leave Ried behind and head up toward Gletsch, the Goms valley narrows and becomes **Obergoms,** stretching from Münster to Oberwald. Here you'll find not only superior snow conditions, but rustic, picture-book villages and the most beautiful cross-country skiing trails in the Alps with the exception of those in the Upper Engadine (☞ St. Moritz *in* Chapter 4). The 85 km (53 mi) of trails run along the valley at an altitude of 1,300 m (4,265 ft) rising to 1,450 m (4,757 ft) below Gletsch. Freestyle skier Art Furrer's **ski school** (Skischule Forum Alpin; ☎ 027/9284488) is still up and running.

Gletsch

⑲ *48 km (30 mi) northeast of Brig.*

Summer travelers may want to travel the distance to the tiny resort of Gletsch, named for its prime attraction: the glacier that gives birth to the Rhône. The views over the Bernese and Valais Alps are magnificent. From Gletsch, you can drive over the Furka Pass directly or over the scenic Grimsel Pass (2,130 m/7,101 ft) to the Bernese Oberland. Or you could see the area the turn-of-the-20th-century way by taking the **Realp/Gletsch steam train.** After 20 years in storage, the Realp/Gletsch steam engine now pulls itself up to the Gletsch glacier cog by cog, passing through fantastic Alpine scenery, over bridges and through tunnels as it crosses the Furka Pass. A one-way trip takes an hour and a half. Board at Realp or Obenwald; you can return via shuttle bus for a change of pace (included in the round trip ticket). ☎ 027/9701079. ✉ *80 SF round trip.* ☉ *June–Sept. (depending on weather).*

Furka Pass

★ ⑳ *11 km (7 mi) east of Gletsch, 59 km (37 mi) northeast of Brig.*

Making the final ascent of Valais, drivers arrive at Oberwald, starting point of the train tunnel through the Furka Pass, which cuts over the heights and leads down to central Switzerland. Spectacular views and stark moonscapes are punctuated by the occasional Spielberg-esque military operations—white-clad soldiers melting out of camouflaged hangars carved deep into solid-rock walls. The sleek, broad highway that snakes down toward Andermatt shows Swiss Alpine engineering at its best.

VALAIS A TO Z

Arriving and Departing

By Car

Valais is something of a dead end by nature: a fine expressway (**A9**) carries you in from Lac Léman (Lake Geneva), but to exit—or enter—from the east end, you must park your car on a train and ride through the **Furka Pass** tunnel to go north or take the train through the tunnel under the **Simplon Pass** to go southeast. (The serpentine roads over these passes are open in summer; weather permitting, the Simplon road stays open all year.) You also may cut through from or to Kandersteg in the Berner Oberland by taking a car train to Goppenstein or Brig. A summer-only road twists over the **Grimsel Pass** as well, heading toward Meiringen and the Berner Oberland or, over the **Brünig Pass**, to Luzern.

By Plane

Geneva's Cointrin (☎ 022/7177111) serves international flights and is nearest the west (French) end of Valais; it's about two hours away by train or car. **Zürich's Kloten** Airport (☎ 1571060) brings you closer to the east (German) side, but the Alps are in the way; you must connect by rail tunnel or drive over one of the passes.

By Train

There are straightforward rail connections to the region by way of Lausanne to the west and Brig/Brigue to the east. The two are connected by one clean rail sweep that runs the length of the valley. For **information** call ☎ 0900/300300.

Getting Around

By Car

If you want to see the tiny back roads—and there's much to be seen off the beaten path—a car is the only solution. The **A9** expressway from Lausanne shrinks, at Sierre, to a well-maintained highway that continues on to Brig. Distances in the north and south valleys can be deceptive: apparently short jogs are full of painfully slow switchbacks and distractingly beautiful views. Both Zermatt and Saas-Fee are car-free resorts, though you can drive all the way to a parking lot at the edge of Saas-Fee's main street. Zermatt must be approached by rail from Täsch, the end of the line for cars (there is a central, secure, long-term parking lot). Car trains through tunnels under mountain passes, either to Kandersteg or under Furka Pass, can be claustrophobic and time consuming: think of them as the world's longest car washes.

By Train

The main rail service covers the length of the valley from Lausanne to Brig. Routes into the tributary valleys are limited, although most resorts are served by cheap and reliable postbuses running directly from train stations. There is a train station in the main tourist magnet, **Zermatt** (☎ 027/9664711). The **Brig-Visp-Zermatt Railway**, a private narrow-gauge system, runs from Brig to Visp with connections to Zermatt. You can call any of the three stations for information.

On Foot

This is one of the hiking capitals of Switzerland, and it's impossible to overstate the value of setting off on a mountain path through the sweet-scented pine woods and into the wide-open country above timberline. The trails are wild but well maintained here, and the regional tourist office (☞ Visitor Information, *below*) publishes a thorough map with planned and timed walking tours. Ask for *Sentiers valaisans;* it's written in English, French, and German.

Contacts and Resources

Emergencies

Police: Crans-Montana (☎ 027/4866560); **Sion** (☎ 027/6065656); **Verbier** (☎ 027/7656320); **Zermatt** (☎ 027/9666920). **Medical assistance: Crans-Montana** (ambulance, ☎ 144); **Sion** (ambulance, ☎ 144); **Verbier** (☎ 144); **Zermatt** (ambulance, ☎ 027/9672000). **Late-night pharmacies** (☎ 111).

Guided Tours

BUS

Guided coach tours of Valais, including lodging and dining packages, are offered by **Valais Incoming** (⊠ 6 rue du Pré-Fleuri, Sion, ☎ 027/3273599, FAX 027/3273591).

HELICOPTER

Sion's **Air-Glaciers** (☎ 027/3291415) proposes several itineraries out of Sion for groups of four or six who want a bird's-eye view of Valais—from a helicopter. Prices range from 341 SF for 10 minutes on up into the thousands for personalized itineraries.

VINEYARDS

Wine lovers can trace the best Valais *vignobles* (vineyards) firsthand by following a list provided by the **OPAV** (Office de Promotion des Produits de l'Agriculture Valaisanne; ⊠ 5 av. de la Gare, Sion, ☎ 027/3222247 FAX 027/3228789), which promotes agriculture in the region; you must arrange the visits yourself.

Visitor Information

The main tourist office for Valais is in **Sion** (✉ 6 rue Pré-Fleuri, CH-1951, ☎ 027/3273570, FAX 027/3273571, ✍).

Local offices: **Brig** (✉ Train station, CH-3900, ☎ 028/222222). **Crans-sur-Sierres** (✉ CH-3963, ☎ 027/4850800). **Grächen** (✉ CH-3925, ☎ 027/9572727. **Martigny** (✉ 9 pl. Centrale, CH-1920, ☎ 027/7212220). **Montana** (✉ av. de la Gare, CH-3962, ☎ 027/4850404). **Riederalp** (✉ CH-3987, ☎ 027/9286050). **Saas-Fee** (✉ CH-3906, ☎ 027/9581858). **St-Maurice** (✉ CH-1890, ☎ 024/4854040). **Sion** (✉ pl. de la Planta, CH-1950, ☎ 027/3228586). **Verbier** (✉ CH-1936, ☎ 027/7753888). **Zermatt** (✉ CH-3920, ☎ 027/9670181).

12 VAUD

LAUSANNE, MONTREUX, LES ALPES VAUDOISES

The verdant vineyards of La Côte and Lavaux, the rugged Alpes Vaudoises, and two graceful waterfront cities—Lausanne and Montreux—comprise one of Switzerland's most diverse regions. Centered around Lac Léman, also known as Lake Geneva, this French-speaking canton harbors some of the country's most famous cathedrals and castles, as well as Alpine retreats, balmy lake resorts, and picturesque wine villages.

Updated by
Kay
Winzenried

IF PRESSED TO SELECT JUST ONE REGION, you can experience a complete cultural, gastronomic, and scenic sweep of Switzerland by choosing Vaud (pronounced Voh). It has a stunning Gothic cathedral (Lausanne) and one of Europe's most evocative châteaux (Chillon), palatial hotels and weathered-wood chalets, sophisticated culture and ancient folk traditions, snowy Alpine slopes and balmy lake resorts, simple fondue and the legerdemain of some of the world's great chefs. Everywhere there are the roadside vineyards that strobe black-green, black-green, as the luxurious rows of vines alternate with rich, black loam.

This is the region of Lac Léman, or Lake Geneva, a grand and romantic body of water. Its romance—Savoy Alps looming across the horizon, steamers fanning across its surface, palm trees rustling along its shores—made it a focal point of the budding 19th-century tourist industry, an object of literary fancy, an inspiration to the arts. In a Henry James novella, the imprudent Daisy Miller made waves when she crossed its waters unchaperoned to visit Chillon; Byron's Bonivard languished in chains in the fortress's dungeons. From their homes outside Montreux, Stravinsky wrote *The Rite of Spring* and Strauss his transcendent *Four Last Songs*. Yet at the lake's east end, romance and culture give way to wilderness and farmland, to mountains with some peaks so high they grow grazing grass sweet enough to flavor the cheese. There are resorts, of course—Leysin, Villars-Gryon, Château-d'Oex—but none so famous as to upstage the region itself.

Throughout the canton, French is spoken, and the temperament the Vaudoise inherited from the Romans and Burgundians sets them apart from their Swiss-German countrymen. It's evident in their humor, their style, and—above all—their love of their own good wine.

Pleasures and Pastimes

Châteaux

Home to magnificently restored Chillon, the most visited if not the best château in Switzerland, Vaud offers a variety of smaller draws as well, including Coppet, Nyon, Prangins, Rolle, Allaman, Aubonne, and Rougemont. Most house museums and offer beautiful views.

Dining

Because of its fortuitous position, draped along a sloping, sunny shore and facing a sparkling lake backdropped by looming peaks of the French Alps, the Lake Geneva shore draws weekenders and car tourists who speed along the waterfront highway, careening through cobbled wine towns, gastronomy guides on the dashboard, in search of the perfect lunch. As in all great wine regions, *dégustation* and *haute gastronomie* go hand in hand, and in inns and auberges throughout La Côte and Lavaux (the two stretches of vineyard-lined shore) you'll dine beside ascoted oenophiles who lower their half-lenses to study a label and order a multicourse feast to complement their extensive tastings.

With a host of Europe's renowned chefs to please, from the retired Fredy Girardet to the latest Michelin star aspirant, the Vaud table teases and gratifies. The culinary delights of the region range from the *cuisine du marché* (cuisine based on fresh market produce) of top-drawer chefs to the simplest fare: *papet Vaudois,* a straightforward stew of leeks, potatoes, and cream served with superb local sausages; delicate *filets de perche* (local perch fillets, sautéed in butter and served by the dozen); and even *malakoffs,* egg-and-Gruyère fritters, which hark back to soldiers of La Côte fighting in the Crimean Wars.

Though nowadays fondue is de rigueur in any Alpine setting, Vaud is the undisputed capital of the Swiss national dish and one of its most loyal custodians. In the Pays-d'Enhaut (Highlands) and on the slopes of the Jura Mountains, the cattle head uphill every summer, and production of the local cheese soars—the nutty hard cheese known as Gruyère, whether or not it comes from that Fribourgeois village. It is sold at various stages of its production: young and mild, ripe and savory, or aged to a heady tang.

The concept of fondue is elementary: grated cheese (generally a Gruyère and Vacherin blend, perhaps with a handful of Appenzeller) is melted in a pot with white wine, garlic, and a dash of kirsch. Diners sit in a circle around the pot, dipping chunks of bread into the bubbling mixture with long, slender forks. Many restaurants prefer to serve it in an adjoining *carnotzet*, or Stübli (the French and German version of a cozy drinking parlor)—not only to re-create a rustic Alpine experience but also to spare fellow diners the fierce aroma of cheese and garlic as well the smell of the fuel used to keep the pot's mixture warm and liquid.

It is a dish at its best when the windows are thick with frost. To accompany it, you drink fruity white wine or plain black tea—never red wine, beer, or (shudder) cola. And halfway through, you down a stiff shot of kirsch—the reviving blast called the *coup du milieu* (shot in the middle). A mixed salad of winter crudités—grated carrots, celery root, beets, or cabbage—is indispensable to digestion.

To experience Vaud's best cuisine, look for *déjeuners d'affaires* (business lunches), plats du jour, and prix-fixe menus, which can offer considerable savings over à la carte dining.

CATEGORY	COST*
$$$$	over 75 SF
$$$	45 SF–75 SF
$$	25 SF–45 SF
$	under 25 SF

Prices are per person for a three-course meal (two-course meal in $ category), including sales tax and 15% service charge.

Lodging

It's a pleasure unique to Vaud to wake up, part floor-length sheers, and look out over Lake Geneva to Mont Blanc; a series of 19th-century grand hotels with banks of balconied lake-view rooms were created to offer this luxury to such grand-tourists as Strauss, Twain, Stravinsky, and Henry James. Yet there's no shortage of charming inns offering similar views on an intimate scale. Up another 1,200 m (3,936 ft) you'll find the antithesis to an airy lakefront inn: the cozy, honey-gold Alpine chalet, with down quilts in starched white envelopes, balustrade balconies with potted geraniums, and also panoramic views.

The hotels of Lausanne and Montreux are long on luxury and grace, and low prices are not easy to find. Especially at peak periods—Christmas–New Year's and June–August—it's important to book ahead. Many hotels have been increasing in-room facilities; minibars, direct phone and fax lines, safes, and business centers are now the rule rather than the exception. Small auberges in the villages along the lake and the vineyards offer traditional dishes and simple comforts. Up in the Pays-d'Enhaut and the Alps southeast of the lake, there are comfortable mountain hotels in all price ranges—though rates are naturally higher in the resorts themselves. Charges are generally not as steep as those in the Alpine resorts of Graubünden or Valais.

CATEGORY	COST*
$$$$	over 325 SF
$$$	215 SF–325 SF
$$	130 SF–215 SF
$	under 130 SF

Prices are for a standard double room, including breakfast, tax, and service charge.

✍ *following the text of a review is your signal that the property has a Web site, where you will find details and, usually, images; for a link, visit www.fodors.com/urls.*

Mountain Sports

The Alpes Vaudoises are home to lovely, not overly developed high-altitude resorts—Leysin, Villars-Gryon, Les Diablerets, Château-d'Oex—where you can experience all levels of skiing difficulty and all the Swiss Alps atmosphere you could wish for. Summer opens trails and high-altitude passes for hikers and mountain bikers. You could also take on a more unusual activity, such as strenuous river-gorge expeditions, breathtaking paragliding and hot-air ballooning, even mountain surfing (zipping downhill on a skateboardlike scooter with handlebars).

Museums

Lausanne is a city of museums and galleries, not only covering history, science, and the fine arts, but eclectic subjects as well—the Olympics and *l'art brut* (raw art), for example. And all along the shore you'll find tiny, meticulous museums covering local history, from the strong influence of the Romans to wine making, the military, and, at Nestlé's Alimentarium, the history of food.

Wine

As one of the main wine-producing regions in Switzerland, Vaud can't be savored without sampling the local vintages. If you're only tangentially interested, check the blackboard listings in any café for local names of *vins ouvert* (open wines), sold by the deciliter: the fruity whites of Épesses and St-Saphorin of Lavaux (between Lausanne and Montreux); the flinty Luins, Vinzel, and La Côte variations between Lausanne and Geneva. If time allows, plan a drive worthy of Albert Finney and Audrey Hepburn in *Two for the Road*, steering that rental car down narrow, fountain-studded stone streets in tiny wine villages, stopping at inns and *vignobles'* (vineyards') dégustations to compare. (Do designate a driver.) Local vintners welcome visitors year-round, except during harvest, which is usually in October. Some vineyards have sophisticated tasting rooms; at others, a family member gathers guests around a tasting barrel within the working cellar. If there is a particular winemaker you want to visit, phone ahead for an appointment. If you are doing a full flight tasting, it is appropriate to buy a bottle unless you find the label not to your liking. In July and August you can head for a Saturday market in Vevey, where vendors sell wine wholesale and tasters carry a glass from booth to booth. For a boost in your knowledge of wine cultivation, processing, and labeling, track farther east to the Musée de la Vigne et du Vin (Museum of Viticulture and Wine) in Aigle.

Exploring Vaud

Lac Léman, or Lake Geneva, is a graceful swelling in the Rhône River, which passes through the northern hook of the Valais, channels between the French and Vaudoise Alps, then breaks into the open at Bouveret, west of Villeneuve. It is shared by three of Switzerland's great French cities, grandes dames of the Suisse Romande: Lausanne, Montreux, and Geneva (☞ Chapter 13). The southern shore lies in France's Haute-Savoie. The north portion of the lake with its green hillsides and the cluster of nearby Alps that loom over its east end make up the canton of Vaud.

Numbers in the text correspond to numbers in the margin and on the Vaud and Lausanne maps.

Great Itineraries

You could easily spend a full Swiss vacation in Vaud, flying directly in and out of Geneva Cointrin. You can move quickly into the heart of the region by car or rail. Visit the shore towns of Coppet, Nyon, and Morges; then dig into Lausanne's urban graces and crawl through delightful wine villages en route to Montreux. After exploring the castles and museums along the lakefront, head straight up into those mountains that have been looking over your shoulder.

IF YOU HAVE 3 DAYS

Drive the shore highway through **Coppet** ① to **Nyon** ② to visit the Roman museum and medieval castle that juts over the lake. Spend a day exploring the lively waterfront city of ☷ **Lausanne** ⑥–⑰, then set out for the winding road, La Corniche de la Vaud, visiting a vignoble or two at Épesses or St-Saphorin. You'll end up at the lakefront town of ☷ **Montreux** ⑳, with its fabled **Château de Chillon** ㉑.

IF YOU HAVE 5 DAYS

Begin in ☷ **Lausanne** ⑥–⑰ and spend two days savoring the Old Town and the hyperactive waterfront. Follow the Corniche route east as it winds its way through the vineyards of Lavaux, stopping as thirst and hunger dictate. The market-centered harbor-front town of ☷ **Vevey** ⑲ deserves a leisurely visit. Take in the highlights of the glitzy, Riviera-like city of ☷ **Montreux** ⑳ before threading your way through the grand halls and cells of **Château de Chillon** ㉑. Hop a late train from Montreux or take the half-hour winding drive for an overnight in the brisk mountain air of ☷ **Villars-Gryon** ㉓. Break in the new day with an Alpine hike or stroll, before heading back down the steep canyon to main route connections that speed you west for an afternoon among Roman and medieval structures in **Nyon** ②.

IF YOU HAVE 10 DAYS

Expand on the five-day program by spending more time outside the cities in the wine villages and mountain resorts. After launching your tour with a few days in ☷ **Lausanne** ⑥–⑰, go west along the Route du Vignoble to Rolle, Aubonne, **Allaman** ③, **Morges** ④, and **St-Sulpice** ⑤, overnighting in ☷ **Nyon** ② (lake steamers are an alternative transport for hopping from town to town). After taking in this section of Vaud, backtrack east past Lausanne. Pick up the Corniche Road for stops in Cully, Épesses, and St-Saphorin to taste the local wines. If you arrive in ☷ **Vevey** ⑲ on a Saturday, you may need a few extra hours to peruse the market and sample fresh produce, cheese, and local vintages. Next stop: the resort town of ☷ **Montreux** ⑳ paired with a visit to the **Château de Chillon** ㉑. Leaving the lake behind, zigzag your way into the Alpes Vaudoises. Spend a couple of nights in ☷ **Villars-Gryon** ㉓ to hike, ski, or bask on a sunny balcony. Cross the Col des Mosses and the Gorges du Pissot into ☷ **Château-d'Oex** ㉗ for another day or two of hiking and studying the folkloric chalets that link the region culturally to Gstaad and the Berner Oberland (☞ Chapter 10). In winter the passes are often closed. If snow is blocking your way, return to Montreux to board the Montreux–Oberland–Bernois Railroad (MOB), a spectacularly panoramic train ride.

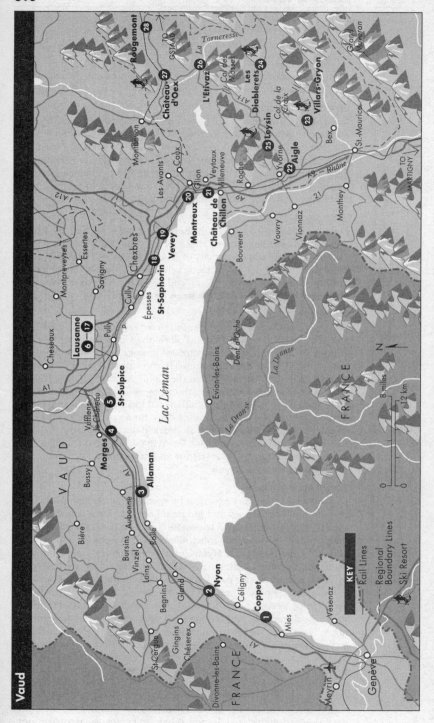

When to Tour Vaud

The lake sparkles and clouds lift from Mont Blanc from spring to fall; November tends to be drizzly gray, then winter brightens things up above the plain (as they call the flatter terrain surrounding the lake). Crowds monopolize Montreux and Chillon year-round but overwhelm it in July (jazz festival time) and August (Europe-wide vacations). It's worth aiming for concert and dance season in Lausanne: from September through May. Prime ski time in the Alpes Vaudoises is from late December through Easter, and prices go up accordingly. Early spring brings daffodil season in Les Avants and the tulip festival in Morges. Remember that at these latitudes summer daylight extends until 9 PM, allowing you to pack a lot into one day; the reverse is true in winter.

LA CÔTE AND LAUSANNE

Just northeast of Geneva, La Côte (the shore) of Lac Léman (Lake Geneva) has been settled since Roman times, with its south-facing slopes cultivated for wine. It is thus peppered with ancient waterfront and hillside towns, castles, and Roman remains. A car is a must if you want to wind through tiny wine villages, but do get out and walk—if only to hear the trickling of any number of Romanesque trough fountains. Be willing to traverse a few times from the slopes to the waterfront and back if you're determined to cover all the region's charms; sticking exclusively to either the diminutive Route du Vignoble or the shore road deprives you of some wonderful sights. You'll end your rural tour in the sophisticated city of Lausanne.

Coppet

① *9 km (6 mi) south of Nyon, 46 km (28 mi) southwest of Lausanne.*

Its pretty, arcaded main street, with occasional peeks through to the jettied waterfront, makes Coppet a pleasant stop for a stroll. But it is ★ the **Château de Coppet** that puts this lake village on the map. Enclosed within vast iron gates, the château has been kept in its original 18th-century form, with luxurious Louis XVI furnishings arranged in a convincingly lived-in manner; its grounds, with grand old trees, hidden courtyards, and stone stairs, are equally evocative.

The château, built in the 1300s, was restored when purchased in 1784 by Jacques Necker, a Genevan banker who served as financial minister to France's Louis XVI. The turmoil of the French Revolution and Necker's opposition to Napoléon led him into exile in this splendid structure, where his remarkable daughter, Madame de Staël, created the most intriguing salon in Europe. Her intellectual sparkle and concern for the fiery issues of the day attracted the giants of the early Romantic period: Lord Byron, the Swiss historian Jean-Charles Sismondi, the German writer August Wilhelm von Schlegel, and British historian Edward Gibbon. Part of the château is still occupied by family descendants, but you can see the interior on a guided tour. (The language of the commentary is generally chosen according to the language of the tour participants.) ⊠ *3 chemin des Murs, just uphill from the waterfront highway,* ☎ *022/7761028.* ⚹ *9 SF.* ☉ *Apr.–Oct., daily 2–6. Closed Nov.–Mar.* ✎

For the house-tour hound, the small **Musée Régional du Vieux-Coppet** (Regional Museum of Old Coppet), in a 15th-century residence on the arcaded Grand-rue, displays the restored furnishings of a local 19th-century bourgeois family. There's a noteworthy instrument in the music room: part piano, part violin. ⊠ *30 Grand-rue,* ☎ *022/7763688.* ⚹ *3 SF.* ☉ *Apr.–Oct., Tues.–Sat. 2–5. Guided tours by request. Closed Nov.–Mar.*

OFF THE
BEATEN PATH

CÉLIGNY – Six kilometers (4 mi) north of Coppet on the shore road, bear left inland at the first sign for Céligny, where you'll discover the endearing village that was home to Richard Burton during the last years of his life. With its lakefront, small port, lawns for sunbathing, and a pier, it provides the best swimming opportunities for miles around. The enclave is wholly charming: rows of vineyards, a historic (but private) château and church, a village square adorned with flowers, a fountain, and its best-kept secret, the wonderfully *sympa* (friendly) Hôtel du Soleil. From there you can walk to the village cemetery, the smaller one hugging the edge of the forest, to visit Burton's simple grave. Rumor has it that Elizabeth Taylor has already purchased the adjacent plot.

Dining and Lodging

$$$ ✕▥ **Hôtel du Lac.** First ranked as a *grand logis* in 1628 to distinguish it from a common roadhouse, this historic inn still feels like an exclusive men's club, catering to power-lunchers and well-heeled travelers. It fronts on the main road and is accessible by boat, with a sycamore-shaded terrace; an awning-covered restaurant; and rooms with exposed beams, niches, and antiques. Its inventive restaurant draws a regular clientele for its exquisite open-grill specialties such as sea bass with fennel or veal kidney with mustard sauce. Reservations for the restaurant are essential. ⊠ *51 Grand-rue, CH-1296 Coppet,* ☎ *022/7761521,* 🖷 *022/7765346. 12 rooms, 7 suites. Restaurant, bar, free parking. AE, DC, MC, V.*

$–$$ ✕▥ **Hôtel du Soleil.** Lured by the charm of Céligny and the chance to
★ own a 300-year-old building, Californian chef John Olcott and his German wife, Catrin, have established a wonderful auberge. For years the building lay dormant, until the couple took it over in 1996 and renovated every nook and cranny, including the seven sweet guest rooms up the winding stone staircase. Whether in the café up front or the quieter restaurant in back, the decor is a minimalist showcase for the chef's fetching presentations, such as *mâche* (lamb's lettuce) salad with seared fresh scallops in a blood-orange vinaigrette. Although part of the menu changes frequently, the local standards, which include *Rösti* (shredded fried potatoes), perch, and pasta, never vary. Be sure to save room for the *tarte crème brûlée.* You'll need a reservation in order to snatch a table from the locals; a reservation is essential in summer for a table on the terrace. ⊠ *10 rte. des Coudrées, CH-1298 Céligny,* ☎ *022/ 9609633,* 🖷 *022/7760800. AE, DC, MC, V. Restaurant closed Tues. No dinner Mon.*

Nyon

❷ *9 km (4 mi) north of Coppet, 27 km (17 mi) southwest of Lausanne.*

Lovely Nyon, with its waterfront drive, shops, museums, and a castle dominating its cliff-top Old Town, was founded by Julius Caesar around 45 BC as a camp for war veterans. The Romans called it Noviodunum and developed the entire region for miles around. Flanked by
★ a statue of Caesar, the **Musée Romain** (Roman Museum) contains an attractively mounted collection of sumptuously detailed architectural stonework, fresco fragments, statuary, mosaics, and earthenware. The museum was built atop foundations of a 1st century AD basilica; a pristine miniature model inside and an excellent trompe l'oeil artist's impression of the palace on the outside wall of the museum evoke the remarkable original structure. A complete listing of the exhibits in English is available upon request. ⊠ *rue Maupertuis,* ☎ *022/3617591.* 🎟 *6 SF; pass for all Nyon museums 12 SF.* ☉ *Apr.–Oct., Tues.–Sat. 10–noon and 2–5, Sun. 10–5; Nov.–Mar., Tues.–Sat. 2–5, Sun. 10–5. Guided tours by request.* ✎

Dominating Nyon's hilltop over the waterfront, the **Château de Nyon** is a magnificent, multispire 12th-century fortress with a terrace that takes in sweeping views of the lake and Mont Blanc. Within its spacious rooms you can visit the **Musée Historique** (Historical Museum), which covers the history of Nyon and focuses on a fascinating part of its heritage: after the French Revolution, Nyon became a great porcelain center, creating flower-sprigged tea sets, vases, and bowls, of which fine examples are on display. At press time the museum was under extensive renovation and will not reopen until 2005. ✉ *pl. du Château,* ☎ *022/3615888.*

Along with the views from the château-museum's terrace, don't miss the town's waterfront promenade below, where boats and swans bob in the waves. Nestled in a charming floral park that parallels the water, the **Musée du Léman** exhibits models of Lake Geneva steamers, sculling kayaks, and private yachts as well as sizable lake-water aquariums, housed in a shuttered 18th-century hospital. ✉ *8 quai Louis-Bonnard,* ☎ *022/3610949.* 🎫 *6 SF; pass for all Nyon museums 12 SF.* 🕐 *Apr.– Oct., Tues.– Sun. 10–noon and 2–6; Nov.–Mar., Tues.– Sun. 2–6.*

★ The 18th-century **Château de Prangins** was opened in 1998 as the Suisse Romand branch of the **Musée National Suisse** (Swiss National Museum). The château's reincarnation was nearly two decades in preparation, with its four floors detailing (in four languages, including English) Swiss life and history in the 18th and 19th centuries. For instance an exhibit might describe the country's history of international exports. Surrounded by parks and gardens (the estate once stretched all the way to Rolle), the museum is also a major venue for cultural events and regional celebrations. If you're traveling with kids, you'll get a price break; there's free admission for children up to age 16. ✉ *3 km (2 mi) northeast of Nyon,* ☎ *022/9948890.* 🎫 *5 SF.* 🕐 *Tues.– Sun. 10–5.* 🐾

OFF THE BEATEN PATH

ST-CERGUE – From Nyon you can take a beautiful ride into verdant Jura Range resort country on the private mountain railway Nyon–St-Cergue–La Cure (☎ 022/9942840) up to St-Cergue, 20 km (12 mi) to the north, and beyond. Note the contrast between the old rolling stock, museum pieces in themselves, and the modern, bright-red coaches. St-Cergue is a quaint time-capsule resort that flourishes in both summer and winter—the first hint in Vaud of bigger Alpine sprawls to come—with good ski facilities for children, modest skiing for adults, mushing (dogsled races), and fine cross-country trails. It's also the birthplace of snowshoeing, the hot winter sport that involves lightweight plastic *raquettes de neige.* If you find yourself here in late September or the first week of October, be sure to take in the annual *Fête Desalpe,* the ritual parade of cows coming down from the mountains. It lasts all of a Saturday morning, allowing hundreds of cows to file through the streets in amazing floral headgear.

GINGINS – Between Nyon and St-Cergue, detour west to the village of Gingins. Tucked away in the crossroads of this hamlet is the **Neumann Foundation,** where you can absorb the exceptional color and design of its glass collection. The glowing glassworks include art nouveau pieces designed by L'Ecole de Nancy founders Auguste and Antonin Daum and Emile Gallé and American artist Louis Comfort Tiffany. ✉ *6 km (3.7 mi) northwest of Nyon,* ☎ *022/3693653.* 🎫 *8 SF.* 🕐 *Thurs.–Fri. 2–5, weekends 10:30–5.*

Dining and Lodging

$$ ✕ **Auberge du Château.** This reliable restaurant, just steps from Nyon's château, serves straightforward Swiss fare and plats du jour, includ-

ing veal five different ways (such as scalloped veal with lime and fresh ginger) and game in autumn. In summer, a big terrace lets diners study the château; in winter, broad windows take in the view. ⊠ *8 pl. du Château,* ☎ *022/3616312. AE, DC, MC, V. Closed Wed. Oct.–Apr.*

$$–$$$ 🗉 **Château de Bonmont.** This manor house is surrounded by one of the region's finest golf courses and outfitted with all the trappings of a baronial country estate: wool tapestries, harlequin-patterned parquets, marble fireplaces, and glistening crystal chandeliers. Rooms are named after nobility—Louis XV and Louis Philippe, for instance—and are decorated in period styles. Many look out onto the lawns and gardens. ⊠ *8 km (5 mi) north of Nyon, CH-1275 Chéserex,* ☎ *022/3699900,* 🅵🅰🆇 *022/3699909. 8 rooms. Restaurant, bar, indoor pool, massage, sauna, aerobics, 18-hole golf course, tennis, horseback riding, free parking. AE, MC, V. Closed Jan.–Feb.* 🦞

$$–$$$ 🗉 **Hôtel Ambassador.** Terra-cotta stucco and peaked dormers set off this petite hotel on Nyon's main thoroughfare. Request one of the "under the roof" rooms; these have hand-hewn dark wooden beams, floral bedding, and compact modern baths. Stone walls and polished wooden beams lend a sophisticated air to L'Amphithéâtre, the hotel's intimate restaurant, which serves fresh lake fish and tasteful, uncomplicated fare. The quiet garden terrace with its view of the castle (which is illuminated at night) is an exquisite spot for a glass of wine or a light meal. Breakfast is included. ⊠ *26 rue St-Jean, CH-1260,* ☎ *022/9944848,* 🅵🅰🆇 *022/994486. 20 rooms. Restaurant. AE, DC, MC, V.*

En Route Twelve kilometers (7 miles) northeast of Nyon, the lakefront village of **Rolle** merits a detour for a look at its dramatic 13th-century **château,** built at the water's edge by a Savoyard prince. Seek out the Moinat Antiques and Decoration shop in town for a sample of what it takes to furnish a grand country home.

Route du Vignoble

36 km between Nyon and Lausanne.

Parallel to the waterfront highway, threading through the steep-sloping vineyards between Nyon and Lausanne, the Route du Vignoble (Vineyard Road) unfolds a rolling green landscape high above the lake, punctuated by noble manors and vineyards. Luins, home of the flinty, fruity white wine of the same name, is a typical pretty village. Just up the road, the village of Vinzel develops its own white wines on sunny slopes and sells them from the wine cellars (*vin-celliers*) that inspired its name. It is also the best source for a very local specialty, the *malakoff*. These rich, steamy cheese-and-egg beignets have always been a favorite of the Vaudois, but after the Crimean Wars they were renamed after a beloved officer who led his army of Vaud-born mercenaries to victory in the siege of Sebastopol. The Route du Vignoble continues through Bursins, home of an 11th-century Romanesque church—and of the venerable actor Peter Ustinov. Drivers can choose to follow it all the way to Morges or cross under the autoroute to view lakefront castles and the Swiss National Museum, in the Château de Prangins (☞ Nyon, *above*). The road is clearly signposted throughout.

Dining

$ ✕ **Au Coeur de la Côte.** Following ROUTE DU VINOBLE signs on the Jura side of the A1 autoroute after exiting at Gland, head up the vine-lined slopes to Vinzel, where this modest village inn and its flowered terrace overlook the vineyards and the lake beyond. Here you can taste the commune's Vinzel, or fill up on two or three hot, rich, Gruyère-based malakoffs, served with pickles and mustard, any time of day from 11:30

AM to 9:30 PM. ⊠ *Vinzel, along Rte. du Vignoble,* ☎ *021/8241141. Reservations not accepted. MC, V. Closed Mon.*

Allaman

❸ *17 km (10 mi) northeast of Nyon, 20 km (12 mi) west of Lausanne.*

This village is little more than a cluster of stone and stucco houses and red-tile-roof barns; the streets are so narrow that two cars can barely pass. The main draw is the stately 16th-century **Château d'Allaman,** built in the 12th century by the barons of Vaud, then reconstructed by the Bernois after a 1530 fire. It has been converted to a stunning antiques mall, its narrow halls and stairwells lined with beeswaxed armoires and ancestral portraits, all for sale at lofty prices through private entrepreneurs who rent space within. The château's vaulted crypt offers wine dégustations for potential buyers as well. For antiques, collectibles, and art at more reasonable prices, head to the annex next door, known as **La Grange,** the château's erstwhile stables and barn. ⊠ *Between Aubonne and Allaman, signposted,* ☎ *021/8073805 or 021/ 8088239.* 🖼 *Free.* ☉ *Wed.–Sun. 2–6.*

Morges

❹ *9 km (5 mi) northeast of Allaman, 8 km (5 mi) west of Lausanne.*

On the waterfront just west of the urban sprawl of Lausanne, Morges is a pleasant lake town favored by sailors and devotees of its Fête de la Tulipe (Tulip Festival), held annually from mid-April to mid-May. Its château, built by the duke of Savoy around 1286 as a defense against the bishop-princes of Lausanne, now houses the **Musée Militaire Vaudois** (Vaud Military Museum), which displays weapons, uniforms, and a collection of 10,000 miniature lead soldiers. In the Général Henri Guisan Hall, you'll find memorabilia of this World War II general, much honored for keeping both sides happy enough to leave Switzerland safely alone. ⊠ *Le Château,* ☎ *021/8012616.* 🖼 *5 SF.* ☉ *Feb.–mid-Dec., weekdays 10–noon and 1:30–5, weekends 1:30–5.*

In the heart of town a 15th-century courtyard-centered mansion, once home to renowned engraver Alexis Forel and his wife, displays the holdings of the **Musée Alexis Forel.** Although most of Forel's exceptional engravings are in the Musée Jenisch, in Vevey (☞ *below*), here you can experience his surroundings. Thick-beamed salons filled with high-back chairs, stern portraits, and delicate china remain as they were in the 1920s, when musicians and writers like Stravinsky, Paderewski, and Rolland gathered for lively discussions and private concerts. An attic room has a selection of 18th-century puppets and porcelain dolls. ⊠ *54 Grand-rue,* ☎ *021/8012647.* 🖼 *5 SF.* ☉ *Tues.–Sun. 2–5:30.*

The oar-powered warships of the Greeks, Romans, and Phoenicians once crossed the waters of Lake Geneva. Now you can follow in their wake on **La Liberté,** a reconstruction of a 17th-century galley. This brainchild of historian Jean-Pierre Hirt is part public works project, part historical re-creation. Unemployed workers helped handcraft the 55 m (183 ft) vessel; at press time, you could visit the shipyard to watch pieces of the ship being carved and fitted. The ship was due to launch on the day of the summer solstice in 2001. ⊠ *45 rue de Lausanne,* ☎ *021/8035031.* 🖼 *5 SF.*

One kilometer (½ mile) west of Morges, the tiny village of **Tolochenaz** honors a beloved long-term resident in the **Pavillon de Audrey Hepburn.** Founded in 1996, the contemporary, white, shoeboxlike building is a few minutes' walk from the village cemetery where the star is buried, a bit farther from La Paisable, the gracious, shuttered manor house where she lived for 26 years. Exhibits of photographs, posters, and Academy Awards chronicle her artistic and humanitarian achievements, but equally touching is the sentiment with which the villagers volunteer their time to keep her memory alive. ⊠ *Chemin des Plantées, Tolochenaz,* ☎ *021/8036464.* ⊡ *10 SF.* ⊙ *Mid-Mar.–mid-Nov., Tues.–Sun. 10–6; mid-Nov.–mid-Mar., Tues.–Sun. 1:30–5.*

Dining and Lodging

$$$–$$$$ ✕🏨 **Hotel Fleur du Lac.** The sun-splashed Mont Blanc falls into direct view as the draperies are pulled back from south-facing windows. Just out of town, but on the main route to Lausanne, this lakefront oasis is surrounded by abundant seasonal plantings and stately old trees. Innkeepers Elsbeth and Rodolphe Schelbert attend to your every need without hovering. Trained in top-starred restaurants, chefs deliver exceptional results to bistro and dining-room patrons. Fresh perch, a regional favorite, tastes even better when served lakeside. Book well in advance, as their guest return rate is unusually high. Reservations are essential for the restaurant. ⊠ *70 rue de Lausanne, CH-1110,* ☎ *021/8815811,* 𝖥𝖠𝖷 *021/8115888. 31 rooms, 7 suites. Restaurant, bar, free parking. AE, DC, MC, V.* 🕸

OFF THE   **VUFFLENS-LE-CHÂTEAU –** Two kilometers (1 mile) northwest of Morges,
BEATEN PATH   this village is known for its namesake château, a 15th-century Savoyard palace with a massive donjon and four lesser towers, all trimmed in fine Piedmont-style brickwork. It is privately owned, but the grounds are open to the public.

St-Sulpice

❺ *5 km (3 mi) east of Morges, 3 km (1¼ mi) west of Lausanne.*

Just west of Lausanne, turn right toward the waterfront to visit St-Sulpice, an ancient village and site of one of the best-preserved 12th-century
★ Romanesque churches in Switzerland. The severe but lovely **Église de St-Sulpice** (Church of St. Sulpice) was built by monks from Cluny Abbey in Burgundy; its painted decoration softens the spare purity of its lines. Three original apses remain, although the nave has disappeared; the short bell tower is built of small stone blocks likely brought from the ruined Roman township at nearby Vidy. At one time the home of 40 monks, the adjoining priory was converted into a private residence in the 16th century. Today the church earns new renown as a venue for classical music concerts. ⊠ *chemin du Crêt, at the dock.* ⊡ *Free.*

Lausanne

66 km (41 mi) northeast of Geneva.

"Lausanne is a block of picturesque houses, spilling over two or three gorges, which spread from the same central knot, and are crowned by a cathedral like a tiara. . . . On the esplanade of the church . . . I saw the lake over the roofs, the mountains over the lake, clouds over the mountains, and stars over the clouds. It was like a staircase where my thoughts climbed step by step and broadened at each new height." Such was Victor Hugo's impression of this grand and graceful tiered city. Voltaire, Rousseau, Byron, and Cocteau all waxed equally passionate about Lausanne—and not only for its visual beauty. It has been a cultural center for centuries, the world drawn first to its magnificent Gothic cathedral and the powers it represented, then to its university, and during the 18th and 19th centuries to its vibrant intellectual and social life. Today the Swiss consider Lausanne the most desirable city in which to live.

Lausanne's importance today stems from its several disparate roles in national and world affairs. Politically, it is the site of the Tribunal Fédéral, the highest court of appeals in Switzerland. Commercially, although it is by no means in the same league as Zürich or Bern, it figures as the headquarters for many multinational organizations, corporations, and sports federations. On a major international rail route and a vital national junction, Lausanne serves as a trade center for most of the surrounding agricultural regions and the expanding industrial towns of Vaud. This prosperity spills over into the arts; there's a surprising concentration of dance companies—including that of Maurice Béjart—as well as several theaters, jazz cellars, and a pair of excellent orchestras. Lausanne is also the world's Olympic capital; the International Olympic Committee has been based here since 1915 (its founder, Baron Pierre de Coubertin, is buried nearby at Montoie Cemetery).

The balance of old and new has not always been kept. The first 20 years after World War II saw an immense building boom, with old buildings and whole neighborhoods pulled down to make way for shining new office blocks and apartment buildings—an architectural exuberance that has given Lausanne a rather lopsided air. Rising in tiers from the lakeside at Ouchy (360 m/1,181 ft) to more than 600 m (2,000 ft), the city covers three hills, which are separated by gorges that once channeled rivers; the rivers have been built over, and huge bridges span the gaps across the hilltops. On one hill in particular, modern skyscrapers contrast brutally with the beautiful proportions of the cathedral rising majestically from its crest. For the sake of hygiene, atmospheric alleys and narrow streets have mostly been demolished, yet the Old Town clustered around the cathedral has been painstakingly restored.

For walking in Lausanne you should bring comfortable shoes, as the city's steep inclines and multiple layers add considerable strain to getting around. There are plenty of buses and a Métro (subway system), but to see the concentrated sights of the Old Town, it's best to tackle the hills on foot.

A Good Walk

Begin in the commercial hub of the city, the **place St-François** ⑥ (nicknamed Sainfe by the Lausannois), where you'll see the former Franciscan **Église St-François**. Behind the church, take a near hairpin turn right onto the fashionable main shopping street, the ancient **rue de Bourg** ⑦. At the top of rue de Bourg, rue Caroline leads you left and left again over the **Pont Bessières,** where you can see the city's peculiar design spanning gorges and covered rivers.

Crossing the bridge and bearing right brings you up into the Old Town. On your left, the imposing palace of the Old Bishopric now houses the **Musée Historique de Lausanne** ⑧. Straight ahead, at the top of rue St-Étienne in the place de la Cathedral, towers the tremendous **Cathédrale de Notre-Dame** ⑨, which is on par with some of France's and England's finest churches.

With the cathedral on your left, walk up the narrow passage of rue Cité-Derrière to the place du Château and its namesake monument, the **Château St-Maire** ⑫, a stern, castellated structure. As you face the château, turn left and walk down the rue Cité-Devant. On your right you will see the **Ancienne-Académie** ⑬ halfway between the château and the cathedral. As you pass the cathedral, again on your left, veer right toward a flight of wooden steps that leads down to the second, more dramatic **Escaliers du Marché,** a wood-roof medieval staircase. At the bottom of the 150 covered steps, you'll run into the place de la Palud and the **Hôtel de Ville** ⑩, the seat of the municipal and commu-

Lausanne

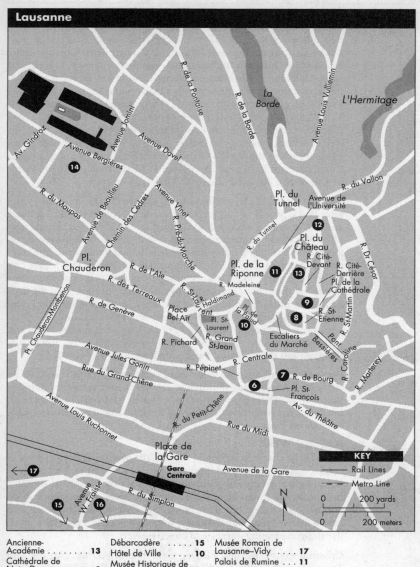

La Borde

L'Hermitage

Avenue Louis Vuillemin

Av. Gindroz

Avenue Bergières

Avenue Jomini

Avenue Davel

R. de la Pontaise

R. de la Borde

R. du Vallon

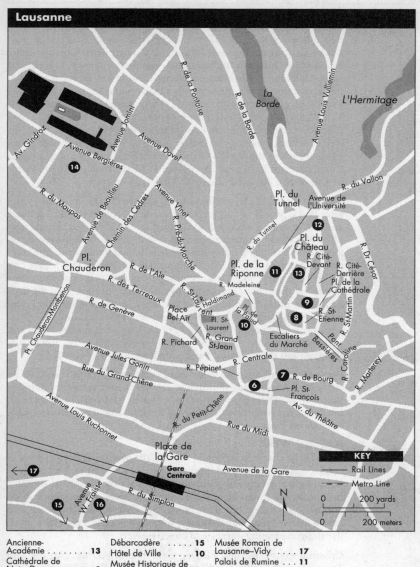**14**

R. du Maupas

Avenue de Beaulieu

Chemin des Cèdres

Avenue Vinet

R. Pré-du-Marché

R. du Tunnel

Pl. du Tunnel

Avenue de l'Université

12

Pl. du Château

R. Dr. César

Pl. Chauderon

R. de l'Ale

R. des Terreaux

R. de Genève

R. St-Laurent

Pl. de la Riponne

R. Madeleine

11

13

R. Cité-Devant

R. Cité-Derrière

Pl. de la Cathédrale

R. St-Martin

R. Dr. César

Pt. Chauderon-Mauborget

Place Bel-Air

R. Haldimand

Pl. de la Palud

9

8

R. St-Étienne

Pl. St-Laurent

10

R. Grand St-Jean

Escaliers du Marché

Pont Bessières

R. Caroline

Avenue Jules Gonin

R. Pichard

R. Pépinet

R. Centrale

7

R. de Bourg

R. Marterey

Rue du Grand-Chêne

6

Pl. St-François

Avenue Louis Ruchonnet

R. du Petit-Chêne

Rue du Midi

Av. du Théâtre

Place de la Gare

17

Gare Centrale

Avenue de la Gare

N

15

Avenue W. Fraisse

16

R. du Simplon

KEY	
	Rail Lines
	Metro Line

0   200 yards

0   200 meters

nal councils. Turning right, just up rue Madeleine from the place de la Palud, you will come upon the place de la Riponne and the imposing **Palais de Rumine** ⑪, which houses a pack of museums covering subjects from archaeology to zoology.

Some of Lausanne's other worthwhile museums take a bit of extra effort to reach. A long hike up avenue Vinet, northwest of the Old Town, will take you to the **Collection de l'Art Brut** ⑭, an unusual museum of fringe art across from the Beaulieu convention center. South of the Old Town, the waterfront community of **Ouchy** can be easily reached by the steep funicular Métro; there are stations across from the Gare Centrale (train station) and under the rue du Grand-Chene in the Flon (city center, a bit west of the Old Town). Ouchy's **Débarcadère** ⑮ has all the typical quayside attractions—vendors, people strolling on a promenade, and a relaxed atmosphere. Just east of Ouchy, on a hillside overlooking the lake, the dramatic **Musée Olympique** ⑯ conveys the history and disciplines of the Olympic Games. It's less than half a mile from the Débarcadère along the quai de Belgique, which turns into the quai d'Ouchy. West of Ouchy at Vidy (just off the Lausanne-Maladière exit from E25/A1) is the **Musée Romain de Lausanne–Vidy** ⑰, where you can see a reconstructed private Roman home. Like the Musée Olympique, this is easy to get to on foot; it's just under a mile from the Débarcadère.

TIMING

You can tour the Old Town in a couple of hours following the above route (do not reverse the order unless you're keen to walk up instead of down the Escaliers du Marché). But that's without stopping: if you have time, plan a full day to include visits to at least a few of the museums and the cathedral, not to mention some unique shops off the place du Palud. Or you could spend your afternoon in Ouchy and the nearby museums; getting to Ouchy by car or funicular takes under 10 minutes, while walking down the Avenue d'Ouchy from the Gare Centrale to the Débarcadère takes about 15 minutes. Remember that, except for the Musée Olympique (in summer), museums are closed on Monday.

Sights to See

⑬ **Ancienne-Académie** (Old Academy). Originally the first school of Protestant theology in Europe (1536), the edifice later became home to the city's university and is now a secondary school. ⊠ *7 rue Cité-Devant.*

★ ⑨ **Cathédrale de Notre-Dame** (Cathedral of Our Lady). A Burgundian Gothic architectural treasure, this cathedral, also called the Cathédrale de Lausanne, is Switzerland's largest church—and probably its finest. Begun in the 12th century by Italian, Flemish, and French architects, it was completed in 1275. Pope Gregory X came expressly to perform the historic consecration ceremony—of double importance, as it also served as a coronation service for Rudolf of Hapsburg as the new emperor of the Holy Roman Empire. Rudolf brought his wife, eight children, seven cardinals, five archbishops, 17 bishops, four dukes, 15 counts, and a multitude of lesser lords, who must have crowded the church's exquisitely proportioned nave.

Viollet-le-Duc, a renowned restorer who worked on the cathedrals of Chartres and Notre-Dame-de-Paris, brought portions of the building to Victorian Gothic perfection in the 19th century. His repairs are visible as paler stone contrasting with the weathered local sandstone; his self-portrait appears in the face of King David, harp and scroll in hand, to the right of the main portal. Streamlined to the extreme, without radiating chapels or the excesses of later Gothic trim, the cathedral wasn't always so spare; in fact, there was brilliant painting. Zealous Reformers plastered over the florid colors, but in so doing they unwittingly preserved them, and now you can see portions of these splendid shades restored in the right transept. The dark and delicate choir contains the 14th-century tomb of the crusader Otto I of Grandson and exceptionally fine 13th-century choir stalls, unusual for their age alone, not to mention their beauty. The church's masterpiece, the 13th-century painted portal, is considered one of Europe's most magnificent. At press time, constant repairs and renovation shrouded the structure in scaffolding.

Protestant services (the cathedral was reformed in the 16th century) exclude nonworshiping visitors on Sunday from 10 to 11:30. You may want to come instead for the evening concerts given on an almost-weekly basis in spring and autumn; call ahead for a precise schedule. ⊠ *pl. de la Cathédrale,* ☎ *021/3167161.* ⊙ *Apr.–Oct., weekdays 7–7, weekends 8–7; Nov.–Mar., weekdays 7–5:30, weekends 8–5:30.*

★ ⑫ **Château St-Maire.** The fortresslike elements of this 15th-century stone cylinder certainly came into play. The castle was built for the bishops of Lausanne; during the 16th century, the citizens wearied of ecclesiastical power and allied themselves with Bern and Fribourg against the bishops protected within. Before long, however, Bern itself marched on Lausanne, put a bailiff in this bishops' castle, and stripped the city fathers of their power. The Bernese imposed Protestantism on the Lausannois, and their Catholic churches and cathedral were ransacked to fill the coffers of Bern. Today the Château St-Maire is the seat of the cantonal government. ⊠ *pl. du Château.*

★ ⑭ **Collection de l'Art Brut.** This singular museum focuses on the genre of fringe or "psychopathological" art, dubbed *l'art brut* in the 1940s by French artist Jean Dubuffet. His own collection forms the base of this ensemble of raw material from untrained minds—prisoners, schizophrenics, or the merely obsessed. Strangely enough, the collection is housed in the Château de Beaulieu, a former mansion of Madame de Staël, she of the sophisticated salons. The exhibits range from intricate yarn and textile pieces to a wall full of whimsical seashell masks. One of the most affecting works is a panel of rough carvings made by an asylum patient in solitary confinement; it was shaped with a broken spoon and a chamber-pot handle. You can get here by walking up avenue Vinet or by taking Bus 2 from place St-Laurent in the direction of Le Désert. ⊠ *11 av. des Bergières,* ☎ *021/6475435.* ▦ *6 SF.* ⊙ *Tues.–Sun. 11–1 and 2–6.* ✐

⑮ **Débarcadère** (Wharf). The main boat traffic comes from the white steamers that land here. In fine weather, the waterfront buzzes with nightlife—strollers, diners, people lingering in outdoor cafés, roller skaters, artisans selling their wares. It's as if sedate Lausanne lifts her skirts a bit at the shoreline. ⊠ *pl. du Port, Ouchy.*

⑩ **Hôtel de Ville** (Town Hall). This building, constructed between the 15th and the 17th centuries, is the seat of municipal and communal councils. A painted, medieval **Fontaine de la Justice** (Justice Fountain) draws strollers to lounge on its heavy rim. Across from the Town Hall, you can watch the **animated clock,** a modern work with moving figures that was donated to the city by local merchants; the figures appear every hour on the hour. A street market is held in the square every Wednesday and Saturday morning. ⊠ *2 pl. de la Palud,* ☎ *021/3152223.* ▦ *Free.*

⑧ **Musée Historique de Lausanne** (Lausanne Historical Museum). The Ancien-Évêché (Old Bishopric) holds a wealth of both temporary and permanent historical exhibits about the city. Don't miss the 250-square-ft scale model of 17th-century Lausanne, with its commentary illuminating the neighborhoods' histories. Also look for the re-created 19th-century shop windows. ⊠ *4 pl. de la Cathédrale,* ☎ *021/3310353.* 🖾 *4 SF.* ⊘ *Tues., Wed., and Fri.–Sun. 11–6, Thurs. 11–8.*

★ ⑯ **Musée Olympique** (Olympic Museum). With high-tech presentation and touching mementos, this complex pays tribute to the athletic tradition in ancient Greece, to the development of the modern Games, to the evolution of the individual sports, and to the athletes themselves. There are art objects—an Etruscan torch from the 6th century BC, Rodin's *American Athlete*—7,000 hours of archival films and videos, interactive displays, photographs, coins and stamps, and medals from various eras throughout Olympic history. A museum shop, a lovely café overlooking the lake and sculpture park, and occasional Sunday-afternoon classical concerts complete this ambitious, world-class endeavor. Brochures and guided tours are available in English. ⊠ *1 quai d'Ouchy,* ☎ *021/6216511.* 🖾 *14 SF.* ⊘ *May–Sept., Mon.–Wed. and Fri.–Sun. 9–7, Thurs. 9–8; Oct.–Apr., Tues., Wed., and Fri.–Sun. 10–6, Thurs. 10–8.* 🕮

⑰ **Musée Romain de Lausanne-Vidy** (Lausanne-Vidy Roman Museum). This is the current incarnation of the restored remains of the late Roman communities Lousonna and Vidy, both of which flourished here from 15 BC into the 4th century. A private home, complete with a well and decorative murals, has been reconstructed and used as the centerpiece for a permanent exhibition on the ancient settlements. The displays include a small treasure trove of coins, votive figures, and objects from daily life—carved combs, toga pins, jewelry. You can get guided tours in English of the museum and neighboring archaeological sites on request. The site is west of Ouchy, just off the Lausanne-Maladière exit from E25/A1. ⊠ *24 chemin du Bois-de-Vaux, Vidy,* ☎ *021/6251084.* 🖾 *4 SF.* ⊘ *Tues., Wed., and Fri.–Sun. 11–6, Thurs. 11–8.*

Ouchy. Officially a separate township, Ouchy can easily be reached by the steep funicular Métro across from the Gare Centrale (train station) and from the Flon (city center). It serves as Lausanne's port, and it's a fashionable place to live. The resort area is dominated by the **Château d'Ouchy** (Ouchy Castle), now a hotel; its tower dates from the Middle Ages.

⑪ **Palais de Rumine.** Built at the turn of the century, this enormous neo-Renaissance structure houses several museums, all with a local spin. The **Musée Cantonal de Géologie** (Cantonal Geology Museum) has an excellent fossil collection, including a mammoth skeleton. Besides its collection of regional fauna, the **Musée Cantonal de Zoologie** (Cantonal Zoology Museum) has a rare collection of comparative anatomy. The top exhibit at the **Musée Cantonal d'Archéologie et d'Histoire** (Cantonal Archeology and History Museum) is the gold bust of Marcus Aurelius discovered at nearby Avenches in 1939. The **Musée Cantonal des Beaux-Arts** (Cantonal Museum of Fine Arts) has an enlightening collection of Swiss art, not only by the Germanic Hodler and Anker but also by Vaud artists—especially Bocion, whose local landscapes are well worth study during a visit to this region. Each museum has some descriptions or an abbreviated guide in English. There are no combination entrance tickets, but all museum admissions are free the first Sunday of each month. ⊠ *6 pl. de la Riponne. Cantonal Geology Museum:* ☎ *021/6924470.* 🖾 *4 SF.* ⊘ *Tues.–Thurs. 11–6, Fri.–Sun. 11–5. Zoology museum:* ☎ *021/3206790.* 🖾 *4 SF.* ⊘ *Tues.–Wed. 11–6, Thurs. 11–8, Fri.–Sun. 11–5. Archaeology and history museum:* ☎ *021/3163430.* 🖾 *4 SF.* ⊘ *Tues.–Thurs. 11–6, Fri.–Sun. 11–5. Fine arts mu-*

seum: ☎ *021/3163445.* 🎫 *6 SF.* ⊙ *Tues.–Wed. 11–6, Thurs. 11–8, Fri.–Sun. 11–5*

❻ Place St-François (St. Francis Square). The brick-paved square is dominated by the massive post office and the former Franciscan **Église St-François** (Church of St. Francis), built during the 13th and 14th centuries. From 1783 to 1793, Gibbon lived in a house on the site of the post office and there finished his work on *The Decline and Fall of the Roman Empire.* In those days, the square, now reserved for pedestrians, was a popular riding circuit.

NEED A   An espresso or bite to eat at this see-and-be-seen gathering spot oppo-
BREAK?   site the church is a welcome respite from climbing cobblestone streets.
                Restaurant Place Saint François (✉ 5 pl. St-François, ☎ 021/3202751)
                serves decadent pastries and inventive light meals in a sleek blond-wood
                setting. Just behind the restaurant is an epicurean boutique chock-full of
                gourmet items including private-label products from regional gastro-
                nomic star Philippe Rochat (☞ Dining and Lodging, *below*).

---

❼ Rue de Bourg. Once a separate village isolated on this natural ridge, this is now the fashionable main shopping street (☞ Shopping, *below*). Narrow and cobblestoned, it's lined with platinum-card stores like Hermès and Louis Vuitton; boutiques have been built into the centuries-old buildings, though some have added fittingly modern facades. Tony stores notwithstanding, the street has its down-to-earth moments; on weekends a fresh-produce market makes things even more crowded.

Dining and Lodging

$$$$ ✗ **La Grappe d'Or.** In this relaxed but classic firelighted French restau-
★   rant, imaginative modern cooking is prepared by Bavarian chef Peter Baermann and impeccably served under the discreet supervision of his wife, Angelika. Try the fillet of venison with a sauce of figs and red wine, scallops with potato gnocchi, or the hearty *cardons* (cardoons; an artichokelike vegetable cultivated in Geneva and Lyon) in foie gras. Pastries are extraordinary. ✉ *3 Cheneau de Bourg,* ☎ *021/3230760. Reservations essential. AE, MC, V. Closed Sun. No lunch Sat.*

$$$$ ✗ **Restaurant de l'Hôtel de Ville–Philippe Rochat.** Secure in his posi-
★   tion as heir to the legendary chef Fredy Girardet, Philippe Rochat reigns as culinary don of the region. It's a quick drive east from Lausanne to his understated manse. Service and presentation are spectacular, if a notch less ceremonious than in Girardet's era, and the food remains absolutely stellar. For these finely orchestrated prix-fixe menus and à la carte selections, the ingredients are key—lamb raised in the Pyrénées, cardoons grown in the village. Pace yourself, reserving time and room for selections from the immense cheese cart or celestial desserts. Make reservations as far ahead as possible. ✉ *1 rue d'Yverdon, Crissier, 7 km (4 mi) east of Lausanne,* ☎ *021/6340505. Reservations essential. AE, MC, V. Closed Sun.–Mon., and late July–mid-Aug.*

$$–$$$ ✗ **Café Beau-Rivage.** As if turning its back on the aristocratic Beau-
★   Rivage Palace that shelters it, this young, lively brasserie-café faces the lake and the Ouchy waterfront scene. Its flashy brass-and-Biedermeier dining area and bar fill with smart Lausannois and Grand Tour internationals enjoying trendy cuisine du marché, *bollito misto* (pot-au-feu with beef, veal, and poultry), and citron risotto. Despite the brasserie atmosphere, there are no paper place mats: linen, silver, and monogrammed damask set the BCBG (*bon chic, bon genre*) tone. In summer the pillared terrazzo terrace (protected from embarcadero traffic by rose gardens) is the place to be seen. ✉ *pl. du Général-Guisan, Ouchy,* ☎ *021/6133330. Reservations essential. AE, DC, MC, V.*

$$ ✕ **À la Pomme de Pin.** In the Old Town behind the cathedral, this win-
some *pinte* (wine pub)—one of Lausanne's oldest—produces an eclec-
tic menu ranging from French to Italian to Swiss (rabbit and Rösti,
anyone?) along with reasonable plats du jour, served both in the ca-
sual café and the adjoining linen-decked restaurant. ✉ *11–13 rue Cité-
Derrière,* ☎ *021/3234656. AE, MC, V. Closed Sun. No lunch Sat.*

$$ ✕ **Café du Grütli.** Tucked in between the place de la Palud and the covered stairs to the cathedral, this is a typical old-style Suisse Romand
restaurant, with a bentwood-and-net-curtain café on the ground floor
and a simple, more formal dining room upstairs. There are several fondues as well as brasserie classics—boiled beef vinaigrette, rabbit in mustard sauce, profiteroles, and tart Tatin (upside-down apple tart). Have
one of several open Vaud wines or a *café pomme* (coffee with a side
shot of apple eau-de-vie) with the locals, who unwind here with the
daily papers. ✉ *4 rue de la Mercerie,* ☎ *021/3129493. DC, MC, V.
Closed Sun. No dinner Sat.*

$$ ✕ **La Petite Grappe/Il Grappolino d'Oro.** The next generation of Baer-
manns (☞ La Grappe d'Or, *above*) opened a casual bistro where a
younger crowd gathers to dine and swap sound bites. The dining
rooms, which fill two levels in a narrow row house, are hung with bril-
liantly colored art. Like the parent restaurant, this offshoot has an in-
novative chef; the daily menu for under 40 francs is a steal since many
elements are pulled from La Grappe d'Or's pantry. Although reserva-
tions aren't essential, they're strongly recommended. ✉ *15 Cheneau
de Bourg,* ☎ *021/3118414. AE, MC, V. Closed Sun.*

$ ✕ **Bleu Lézard.** A cross section of Lausanne urbanites—hip artists, yup-
★ pies, shoppers, university students—fights for tables at this stylish
restaurant. Sample dishes such as aubergine carpaccio, duck breast in
violet vinegar sauce, and marrow crisps and grapes, all for remarkably
low prices. A tongue-in-cheek decor of found-object art and easygoing
waiters dressed in whatever khakis and flannels they found near the bed
that morning add to the laid-back ambience. Mixed drinks along with
live jazz, Latino, and disco music draw a nocturnal clientele downstairs
in the cellar. ✉ *10 rue Enning,* ☎ *021/3123830. AE, MC, V.*

$ ✕ **Café Romand.** All the customers seem to know each other at this
★ vast, smoky dining institution, where shared wooden tables and clat-
tering china create the perfect ambience for fondue feasts, mussels, *chou-
croûte* (sauerkraut), or a sausage plate. Prominent members of Lausanne's
arts community swarm here after rehearsals and concerts and are
known to toast each other loudly across the crowded room. ✉ *2 pl.
St-François,* ☎ *021/3126375. MC, V. Closed Sun.*

$ ✕ **Manora Crocodile.** If you're fed up with heavy Vaud cheese dishes
and local sausage, this cheery self-service chain offers startlingly in-
expensive options. Stir-fries sizzle in huge woks under silent no-smoke
hoods; there are also iced pitchers of fresh-squeezed fruit juices, four
sizes of salad, a fruit bar, a pasta station, and a daily risotto. No one
dish costs more than 20 SF, and the no-smoking dining room is a life-
saver in this city of chain-smokers. ✉ *17 pl. St-François,* ☎ *021/
3209293. Reservations not accepted. No credit cards.*

$$$$ ⊡ **Beau-Rivage Palace.** Of the scores of deluxe hotels in Switzerland,
★ this gleaming grande dame stands apart, its neoclassical structure
seamlessly restored to period opulence, its vast waterfront grounds man-
icured like a country manor estate. It opened in 1861 as the Beau-Ri-
vage (the Palace wing and Renaissance cupola were added in 1908),
but every inch of marble, crystal, and polished mahogany sparkles like
new. Rooms have plenty of modern touches—remote light controls,
maid lights, towel heaters, and phones sprouting from every surface—
as well as classic comforts such as wing chairs, Asian rugs, and bal-
conies with lake views. Among the facilities is a pair of first-class

restaurants: the romantic La Rotonde and the Café Beau-Rivage, with up-to-the-minute brasserie fare. Jacket and tie are required at La Rotonde. ✉ *17–19 pl. du Port, CH-1000,* ☎ *021/6133333,* 𝔽𝔸𝕏 *021/ 6133334. 155 rooms, 20 suites. 3 restaurants, 2 bars, in-room data ports, minibars, in-room safes, indoor-outdoor pool, beauty salon, sauna, 2 tennis courts, exercise room, playground, concierge, meeting rooms, parking (fee). AE, DC, MC, V.* ✌

$$$$ 🏨 **Lausanne Palace & Spa.** This Edwardian landmark—smaller than
★ the Beau-Rivage and distinctly urban in setting and style—stands on a hill high over the lake, with layers of city scenery draped behind. It faces a city street, so to take advantage of its views you need a back room—though three-quarters of the rooms have balconies. The room decor varies from Empire reproduction to cool modern, with period details such as inlaid wood and dramatic art deco baths. A Centre de Bien-Être (Wellness Center) centers on a sleek, calming Aveda spa. Its stunning indoor pool is flanked by mosaiclike murals; trim white columns reach to an undulating ceiling. Programs include meditation, massage, aromatherapy, yoga, and tai chi. The adjacent restaurant, Côte du Jardin, has a light menu that can be a welcome respite in the land of cheese and Rösti. Another of the hotel's restaurants, the street-side, Parisian-style Brasserie du Grand-Chêne, is decidedly hip and engaging. ✉ *7–9 rue du Grand-Chêne, CH-1002,* ☎ *021/3313131,* 𝔽𝔸𝕏 *021/ 3232571. 119 rooms, 31 suites. 3 restaurants, 2 bars, in-room data ports, minibars, in-room safes, indoor pool, beauty salon, spa, massage, sauna, health club, nightclub, concierge, meeting rooms, parking (fee). AE, DC, MC, V.* ✌

$$$–$$$$ 🏨 **De la Paix.** This turn-of-the-century business-class hotel in the center of town has all the amenities of a Best Western property and wonderful lake views. The rooms facing the lake are done in warm shades of pumpkin and terra-cotta; those on the backstreet side are considerably humbler. Its bar, Jacky's, is a Lausanne institution. ✉ *5 av. Benjamin-Constant, CH-1002,* ☎ *021/3107171,* 𝔽𝔸𝕏 *021/3107172. 111 rooms, 6 suites. Restaurant, bar, café. AE, DC, MC, V.* ✌

$$$–$$$$ 🏨 **Hotel Victoria.** If you need to stay near the train station, try this polished, business-oriented hotel. Though it's on the busy avenue de la Gare, it's well buffered from noise. Plaid sofas and modern artwork rub elbows with a marble staircase and a 17th-century tapestry. Rooms have plenty of work space and well-lighted desks; only 10 are air-conditioned. Since the hotel is geared toward businesspeople, you can often land a reduced weekend or holiday room rate. Although there's no restaurant on the premises, there are plenty of choices in the neighborhood. ✉ *46 av. de la Gare, CH-1001,* ☎ *021/3420202,* 𝔽𝔸𝕏 *021/3420222. 51 rooms, 4 suites. Breakfast room, bar, no-smoking floor, exercise room, free parking. AE, DC, MC, V.* ✌

$$$–$$$$ 🏨 **Mövenpick.** This is a business-style chain hotel across the street from a busy marina. One of the nicer of the newest hotels that stretch along the lake in Ouchy, it's a five-minute drive from the city center. Rooms, à la Laura Ashley, are spacious for a European hotel, but those facing the lake can be noisy. ✉ *4 av. de Rhodanie, CH-1001,* ☎ *021/6127612,* 𝔽𝔸𝕏 *021/6127611. 258 rooms, 7 suites. 3 restaurants, piano bar, no-smoking rooms, sauna, exercise room, free parking. AE, MC, V.* ✌

$$$–$$$$ 🏨 **La Résidence.** Within four graceful 18th- and 19th-century villas near
★ the waterfront at Ouchy, this polished small hotel complex has been modernized without ruffling its gentility or disturbing its graceful stone arches, marble floors, or discreet gardens. The complex includes the Hotel L'Angleterre, where Lord Byron penned *The Prisoner of Chillon;* at press time, renovations were planned through 2001, although the hotel will remain open continuously. Other buildings are slated for overhauls to maintain their grand style and sumptuous decor. Personal

service from the attentive staff makes this the delightful antithesis of a grand-hotel experience. It's the best of both worlds: guests may use the facilities of the Beau-Rivage Palace next door. ⊠ *15 pl. du Port, CH-1000,* ☎ *021/6133434,* FAX *021/6133435. 60 rooms. 2 restaurants, bar, pool, concierge, parking (fee). AE, DC, MC, V.*

$$$–$$$$ 🏨 **Royal Savoy.** Here you can not only stay in an enormous Victorian castle but also enjoy a broad, private landscaped garden and park, with outdoor swimming pool, terrace restaurant, and strolling musicians. The rooms themselves are lovely—something more expensive hotels sometimes seem unable to achieve—with florals and jewel tones, delicate period reproduction desks and chairs, and French doors that open onto balconies over the lawns and lake. ⊠ *40 av. d'Ouchy, CH-1000,* ☎ *021/6148888,* FAX *021/6148878. 99 rooms, 9 suites. 2 restaurants, bar, pool, sauna, exercise room. AE, DC, MC, V.* ✎

$$–$$$ 🏨 **Des Voyageurs.** In a narrow town house in the city center, this is a comfortable, friendly hotel, with pleasant decor and impeccable maintenance. The rooms' modern stamp (modular dormitorylike furniture and computer/fax access) is tempered with Victorian details; the oak stairways, stained glass, and period breakfast room individualize what could have been an anonymous urban space. ⊠ *19 rue Grand-St-Jean, CH-1003,* ☎ *021/3199111,* FAX *021/3199112. 33 rooms. Breakfast room, no-smoking rooms. AE, DC, MC, V.* ✎

$$–$$$ 🏨 **Élite.** Directly uphill from the train station on a surprisingly quiet street, this hotel is a tranquil little enclave. Most rooms have a view of fruit trees and a garden; ask for a fourth-floor room for a spectacular lake view. Although the modular furnishings are standard, they're warmed by the beige, peach, and rose color scheme. The hotel has been in one family for 50 years, and it shows—from the solid renovation and modern touches (electric doors, piped-in music) to the squeaky-clean maintenance. There are kitchenettes available. ⊠ *1 av. Ste-Luce, CH-1003,* ☎ *021/3202361,* FAX *021/3203963. 33 rooms, 1 suite. Breakfast room, air-conditioning, minibars, no-smoking rooms, free parking. AE, DC, MC, V.* ✎

$$ 🏨 **Château d'Ouchy.** Here you pay for the privilege of staying in a 12th-century castle that was converted into a pseudo-medieval hotel in the 19th century. The interiors are dated modern and a little faded. If you really want medieval atmosphere, spring for the deluxe top tower room ($$$$), which has wraparound views through Romanesque windows. There are a Parisian-style brasserie and a popular waterfront veranda with pasta and pizzas. ⊠ *2 pl. du Port, CH-1006,* ☎ *021/6167451,* FAX *021/6175137. 36 rooms, 3 suites. 2 restaurants, bar, dance club, free parking. AE, DC, MC, V.* ✎

$$ 🏨 **City.** This once-faded urban hotel, at the hub of the downtown crossroads, underwent a profound and daring renovation, transforming itself from a steam-heated dinosaur into a spectacular architectural showcase with curving chrome planes, a two-way escalator flanked by a sleek waterfall, and breathtaking views of the city, especially from the glassed-in breakfast room. Slick and soundproof, with fresh duvets, pink-tile baths, videos, hair dryers, and room service, the City is a value-priced model for its peers. ⊠ *5 rue Caroline, CH-1007,* ☎ *021/3202141,* FAX *021/3202149. 51 rooms. Breakfast room, in-room VCRs. AE, DC, MC, V.*

$$ 🏨 **Regina.** One of the best things about this tiny lodging is the owners' friendly service; the couple spent over a decade in the United States, so the language barrier is nonexistent. The guest rooms are squared away with color-coordinated carpets and upholstery. Those in the back are quiet, with roofline views; a few rooms are scheduled to be added to the top floor in fall 2000. Although the rooms don't have bathtubs, they all have private bathrooms with showers. The hotel is in the pedestrian zone of the Flon area. ⊠ *18 rue Grand-St-Jean, CH-*

1003, ☎ 021/3202441, ⅀ 021/3202529. 36 rooms. Breakfast room, in-room safes, minibars, free parking. MC, V. 🐾

$ 🏨 **Hôtel de L'Ours.** Wedged into a busy V-shape intersection and hidden behind the facade of a student-filled Italian restaurant, this basic lodging accommodates a budget *porte-monnaie* (wallet). Checking in at the reception window feels like an exchange at the local bus station. The staircases and paint job may be worn, but rooms are tidy. All have their own bathrooms with shower. ⊠ *2 rue du Bugnon, CH-1005, ☎ 021/3204971, ⅀ 021/3204973. 20 rooms. Restaurant, café, minibars. AE, DC, MC, V.*

Nightlife and the Arts

Lausanne is one of the arts capitals of Switzerland, sharing with Geneva the **Orchestre de la Suisse Romande.** It has also hosted the great ballet company of **Maurice Béjart** since his exodus from Brussels. The **Opéra de Lausanne** performs in its eponymous hall. The event seasons generally run from September to May; summer brings outdoor concerts and more casual events. For ticket outlets contact the Lausanne Convention and Tourist Office (☞ Visitor Information *in* Vaud A to Z, *below*). The tourist office's calendar of monthly events and the *Reg'art* (published bimonthly in French) give information on upcoming activities. Check out the daily newspaper *24 Heures* for listings as well.

BARS

One of the chicest and liveliest gathering spots in Lausanne is the **Café Beau-Rivage** (☎ 021/6133330), in the luxury hotel of the same name (☞ Dining and Lodging, *above*); there's a sophisticated armchair-filled lounge, a a Parisian-style brasserie with wicker-and-marble decor, and live music nightly. In the tiny wine bar just inside the hotel's lower lobby entrance you can sip local or imported vintages. The Lausanne Palace (☞ Dining and Lodging, *above*) serves the after-hours crowd in the stately **Le Bar du Palace.** For a lighter atmosphere meet at the stylish, pared-down **LP Bar** (☎ 021/3313131), also in the Palace.

Galerie St-François and environs have a number of bars. At **Le Café des Artistes** (, ☎ 021/3434401) you can follow the bouncing ball for karaoke. For late-night imbibing head to **Le Fellini** (⊠ Galerie St-François, ☎ 021/3434400), which serves until 2 AM.

CLASSICAL MUSIC

The **Opéra de Lausanne** (⊠ 12 av. du Théâtre, ☎ 021/3101600) performs in its eponymous hall. **Théâtre-Municipal Lausanne** (⊠ 12 av. du Théâtre, ☎ 021/3126433), like a tattered bomb shelter deep underground in the heart of Lausanne, is one of the city's central performance venues for concerts, opera, and ballet, including the riveting experiments of Maurice Béjart. The **Théâtre de Beaulieu** (⊠ 10 av. des Bergières, ☎ 021/6432111), right across from the Collection de l'Art Brut (☞ Exploring, *above*), hosts full-scale performances of orchestral music, opera, and dance in its larger hall; this is where the Orchestre de la Suisse Romande performs. The Orchestre de Chambre de Lausanne plays at the **Salle Métropole** (⊠ 1 pl. Bel-Air, ☎ 021/3111122).

DANCING

Since most nighttime activity is centered in the Flon or place St-François neighborhoods, it's easy to sample several hot spots. If you pass a crowded club where the music is to your taste, duck in—it's probably one of the happening locations too new or ephemeral to list. The popular **D Club** (⊠ 4 rue de Grand Pont, ☎ 021/3515142) is decked out with works of contemporary European sculptors. Inside the discotheque **La Griffe** (⊠ 2 pl. de la Gare, ☎ 021/3110262) you'll find a DJ, video screen, and light show. **Le Gibo** (⊠ Galerie St-François, ☎ 021/

3120935) offers tropical atmosphere and dance music. The club crowd comes from as far away as Zürich and Basel for techno concerts and live performances at **Le Mad** (⊠ 23 rue de Genève, ☎ 021/3121122).

JAZZ CLUB

Le Chorus (⊠ 3 av. Mon Repos, ☎ 021/3232233) has a renowned jazz cellar and also serves food and drinks. For acoustical jazz, drop in at **Pianissimo** (⊠ Foyer du Théâtr'Onze, 11 rue des Deux-Marchés, ☎ 021/3120043).

NIGHTCLUBS

The Lausanne Palace's upscale **Brummell** (⊠ 7 rue du Grand-Chêne, ☎ 021/3120920) has Las Vegas–type dancing shows and a cabaret.

THEATER

Théâtre Kléber-Méleau (⊠ 9 chemin de l'Usine-à-Gaz, Lausanne-Malley, ☎ 021/6258400), at Vidy, offers a variety of French-language theater, old and new. **Théâtre Vidy-Lausanne** (⊠ 5 av. Émile-Jacques-Dalcroze, ☎ 021/61945445), also west of Lausanne's center, presents classical and contemporary theater in French.

Outdoor Activities and Sports

BIKING

Gare CFF de Lausanne (train station; ⊠ 1 pl. de la Gare, Baggage Service, ☎ 051/2242162) rents bikes. You must make a reservation at least one day in advance; in summer three days is recommended. For a lakefront ride check out a set of wheels at **Kiosque d'Ouchy** (⊠ 2 pl. de la Navigation, ☎ 021/6162383).

SAILING

La Nautique (⊠ 1 pl. du Vieux-Port, ☎ 021/6160023) has a clubhouse, changing rooms, and a crane. The **École de Voile de Vidy** (⊠ Port de Vidy, ☎ 021/6179000) is a sailing school with rentals.

SKATING

Open-air ice skating rinks in the Lausanne area stay open from October to March. **Patinoire de Montchoisi** (⊠ 30 av. du Servan, ☎ 021/6161062) has 35,000 square ft of surface. **Patinoire de la Pontaise** (⊠ 11 rte. Plaines-du-Loup, ☎ 021/6484142) attracts urban crowds. Rental skates are available at both rinks.

SWIMMING

In Lausanne the pool **Piscine de Montchoisi** (⊠ 20 av. du Servan, ☎ 021/6161062) makes artificial waves; it's open from May through August. **Bellerive Beach** (⊠ 23 av. de Rhodanie, ☎ 021/6178131) has access to the lake and three pools, one Olympic-size, plus generous lawns and a self-service restaurant. The covered pool at **Mon-Repos** (⊠ 4 av. du Tribunal-Fédéral, ☎ 021/3234566) stays open all winter, closing only July–August.

Shopping

The main shopping circle centers on **place St-François, rue St-François, rue de Bourg,** and **rue du Grand-Pont.** Less-expensive shopping is along **rue St-Laurent** and **rue de l'Ale.**

BOOKS

Librairie Payot (⊠ 4 pl. Pépinet, ☎ 021/3413331) carries mass-market French books and a good assortment in English.

DEPARTMENT STORES

Bon Génie (⊠ 10 pl. St-François, ☎ 021/3204811) has clusters of designer areas on several levels. The large department store **Globus** (⊠ rue Centrale at rue du Pont, ☎ 021/3429090) has splendid food halls on the basement level.

LINENS

Coupy (✉ 4 rue Madeleine, ☎ 021/3127866) has a large selection of duvets, pillows, and linens. **Drafil** (✉ pl. St-Laurent, ☎ 021/3235044) carries a lovely line of trousseau goods, all made in Suisse Romande. **Langenthal** (✉ 8 rue de Bourg, ☎ 021/3234402) is the central source for towels, sheets, and embroidered handkerchiefs, mainly Swiss made.

MARKETS

There are fruit and vegetable markets in Lausanne along **rue de l'Ale, rue de Bourg,** and **place de la Riponne** every Wednesday and Saturday morning. **Place de la Palud** adds a flea market to its Wednesday and Saturday produce markets and is the site of a handicrafts market the first Friday of the month from March through December.

TOYS

Davidson Formation (✉ 20 rue Grand St-Jean, ☎ 021/3232522) has a unique collection of educational toys and English-language books. **Franz Carl Weber** is the main Swiss source for international toys (✉ 23 rue de Bourg, ☎ 021/3201471).

WATCHES

The place St-François has most of the watch shops. **Bucherer** (✉ No. 5, ☎ 021/3206354) sells Rolex and Piaget. **Junod** (✉ No. 8, ☎ 021/ 3122745) carries Blancpain. **Grumser** (✉ 10 rue de Bourg, ☎ 021/ 3124826) specializes in Baume & Mercier. **Roman Mayer** (✉ No. 12 bis, ☎ 021/3122316) carries Audemars Piguet, Ebel, and Omega.

LAVAUX VIGNOBLES AND MONTREUX

To the east of Lausanne stretches the Lavaux, a remarkably beautiful region of vineyards that rise up the hillsides all the way from Pully, on the outskirts of Lausanne, to Montreux—a distance of 24 km (15 mi). Brown-roof stone villages in the Savoy style, old defense towers, and small baronial castles stud the green-and-black landscape. The vineyards, enclosed within low stone walls, slope so steeply that all the work there has to be done by hand. Insecticides, fungicides, and manure are carried in baskets, and containers are strapped to men's backs. In early October pickers harvest the heavy, round fruit, carrying the loads to the nearest road, emptying them into vats, and driving them by tractor to the nearest press. Some Lavaux vintages are excellent and in great demand, but unfortunately, as with so much of Switzerland's wine, the yield is small, and the product is rarely exported. From May to October, especially on weekends, you'll find a winegrower's cellar in every village and some of the private châteaux-vignobles open for tastings (and, of course, sales).

Cully

The cluster of businesses, homes, barns, and cellars in Cully epitomizes the Lavaux lifestyle. Although it's not as picturesque as some lakeside or hill towns, in this narrow crossroads you can get a sense of what a vintner's life is really like, full of hard work and good eating. There are few reasons to stop, except the paramount one: to pause long enough to absorb the rich seasonality. The town is just off the Corniche Road.

En Route The scenic **Corniche Road** stretches some 17 km (10 mi) through
★ Lavaux, threading above the waterfront from Lausanne to Vevey, between the autoroute and the lakeside Route 9. This is Switzerland at its most Franco-European, reminiscent in its small-scale way of the Riviera or the hill towns of Alsace. You'll career around hairpin turns on

narrow cobbled streets, with the Savoy Alps glowing across the sparkling lake and the Dents du Midi looming ahead, hand-painted signs beckoning you to stop and taste the wines from the vineyards on either side of the road. Stop to gaze at roadside overlooks or wander down a side lane into the fields of **Riex, Epesses, Rivaz,** or the **Dézaley,** the sources of some of Switzerland's loveliest white wines and typically magical little Vaudois villages.

Dining and Lodging

$$$$ ✕⊞ **Auberge du Raisin.** Fashionably dressed families, romantic couples, and international business teams gather here to celebrate birthdays, weddings, and deal closings. In the center of the animated room, rotisserie hooks and spits twirl in a raised-hearth grill, as the chef seasons, times, and dispatches meats to the waiters (side dishes are synchronized in the kitchen). The wine list is fittingly thorough with both local and French vintages. After dinner there's no need to budge; you can overnight in the auberge's guest rooms. Checked spreads cover the draped four-posters and the brightly painted armoires and chests are a change from the usual fruitwoods; some of the large baths have skylights. Reservations are essential for the restaurant. ✉ *1 pl. de l'Hôtel de Ville, CH-1096,* ☎ *021/7992131,* 🆇 *021/7992501. 7 rooms, 3 suites. AE, DC, MC, V.* ✎

St-Saphorin

⑱ *15 km (9 mi) southeast of Lausanne.*

At the end of the Corniche Road, just west of Vevey, St-Saphorin is perched just above the water. With its impossibly narrow, steep cobbled streets and ancient wine makers' houses crowded around fountains and crooked alleys, this is a village that merits a stop. It lies along the ancient Roman highway, and its small church sits atop Roman foundations. There's a tiny museum of Roman artifacts (including a sizable millstone) in the church. Go through the low door near the altar; you can see the museum whenever the church is unlocked and services are not being held. The guides are all in French, but even without a guide it's easy to chart the church's expansion through its ruins.

Dining

$$ ✕ **Auberge de l'Onde.** Once the main *relais* (stagecoach stop) between
★ the Simplon Pass and Geneva, this is a vineyard inn out of central casting, groaning with history and heady with atmosphere: Igor Stravinsky and Charlie Chaplin were among the artists loyal to its charms. The ambience is equally seductive in its tiny wood-panel café, where locals read the papers over a chipped pitcher of St-Saph, as they call it, and a plate of butter-fried lake perch, or in its dainty beamed dining room lined with ancient crockery and lighted with grape-wood sconces. Some regulars complain that the kitchen is not quite as good since management passed to the younger generation, but you can still get excellent silver-platter service (two helpings) of very local *omble chevalier* (salmon trout) in sorrel sauce and bubbling-hot fruit gratins. White-bloused waitresses hover with a good bottle of the local *récolte* (vintage), while day-tripping connoisseurs sniff and roll the almond-perfume wine over their tongues. ✉ *St-Saphorin,* ☎ *021/9213083. AE, V. Closed mid-July–mid-Aug.*

Vevey

★ ⑲ *2 km (1 mi) east of St-Saphorin, 19 km (12 mi) east of Lausanne.*

This soigné waterfront town was the setting for Anita Brookner's evocative 1985 novel *Hotel du Lac,* about a woman retreating to a lake resort to write; her heroine was attracted to the site, in part, because of its slightly stuffy 19th-century ways. In the 1870s Henry James captured this mood of prim grace while writing (and setting) *Daisy Miller* in the Hotel des Trois Couronnes. Indeed, despite its virtual twinning with glamorous Montreux, Vevey retains its air of isolation and old-world gentility. Loyal visitors have been returning for generations to gaze at the **Dent d'Oche** (2,222 m/7,288 ft) across the water in France and make sedate steamer excursions into Montreux and Lausanne: today there are some who come just to see the bronze statue of Charlie Chaplin in the waterfront Rose Park and to take the funicular or mountain train up to Mont Pèlerin. Yet Vevey is a great walking town, with more character in its shuttered **Old Town,** better museums, landmarks, and shops, and more native activity in its wine market than cosmopolitan Montreux can muster.

Vevey is a marketing center for wines of the region, and the local white is sold in summer at its Saturday market on the waterfront, alongside fruits and vegetables; you buy your own glass and taste *à volonté* (at will). Vevey is also the hometown of Nestlé, the chocolate and milk products giant; its laboratories and world headquarters are based here.

Among the notables who have been drawn to Vevey as a place to live or merely to sojourn are Graham Greene, Victor Hugo, Jean-Jacques Rousseau (who set much of his *Julie, ou la Nouvelle Héloïse* here), Dostoyevsky, Gustave Courbet, Oskar Kokoschka, Charlie and Oona Chaplin (buried in the cemetery at Corsier), and Swiss native Édouard Jeanneret, known as Le Corbusier. By following an excellent brochure/map published by the tourist office, you can travel "On the Trail of Hemingway"—and to the homes and haunts of some 40 other luminaries.

★ Le Corbusier's **Villa le Lac,** a low-slung, single-story white house built directly on the Vevey waterfront, was constructed for his parents in 1923; it remains unaltered, with his original furnishings and details preserved within. Shingled in corrugated sheet metal, with a white-metal railed balcony looking over the water and a "birdhouse" chimney in molded concrete, it is typically sculptural and, in a modest way, visionary. ⊠ *On western outskirts of Vevey, just west of marina, Corseaux,* ☎ *021/9235371.* ▣ *Free.* ☉ *Guided tours Apr.–mid-Nov., Wed. 2–5.*

A controlling financial power in the region, Nestlé sponsors an unconventional museum in Vevey, the **Alimentarium.** Exhibits on food and food production are displayed in a grand 19th-century mansion. At press time the museum was closed for renovation; it's scheduled to reopen in stages beginning in summer 2001. ⊠ *Between quai Perdonnet and rue du Léman,* ☎ *021/9244111.*

The **Musée Jenisch** owes its considerable inventory of the works of the Expressionist Oskar Kokoschka to his retirement on Vevey's shores. If it is strictly the Kokoschkas you want to see, you may need to plan ahead. His works are not always on display, but advance arrangements can be made to view the holdings in the archives. The museum's partner wing, the **Cabinet Cantonal des Estampes** (Cantonal Print Collection) contains a rich assortment of engravings, including some by Dürer and Rembrandt. ⊠ *2 av. de la Gare,* ☎ *021/9212950,* ▣ *8 SF– 12 SF.* ☉ *Mar.–Oct., Tues.–Sun. 10:30–noon and 2–5:30; Nov.–Feb., Tues.–Sun. 2–5:30.*

The **Musée Historique du Vieux Vevey** (Historical Museum of Old Vevey) occupies a grand 16th-century manor house, briefly home to Charlotte de Lengefeld, wife of Friedrich von Schiller. It retains some original furnishings as well as collections of arms, art, keys, and wine-making paraphernalia. The first floor serves as headquarters for the Brotherhood of Winegrowers, the organization that stages the mammoth Fêtes des Vignerons (Winegrowers' Festival). The festival is held roughly every 25 years; you can get a taste of the most recent celebration (1999) from the costumes, photographs, and memorabilia on display. ⊠ *2 rue du Château,* ☎ *021/9210722.* ⌁ *4 SF.* ⊙ *Mar.–Oct., Tues.–Sun. 10:30– noon and 2–5:30; Nov.–Feb., Tues.–Sun. 2–5:30.*

The **Musée Suisse de l'Appareil Photographique** (Swiss Camera Museum) displays an impressive collection of cameras, photographic equipment, and mounted work. It also hosts *Images,* a biennial multimedia show held in the fall of even-numbered years. ⊠ *6 Anciens-Fossés,* ☎ *021/9252140.* ⌁ *5 SF.* ⊙ *Apr.–Oct., Tues.–Sun. 11–5:30; Nov.–Mar., Tues.–Sun. 2–5:30.*

In the neighboring village of La Tour-de-Peilz, the **Musée Suisse du Jeu** (Game and Toy Museum) fills a 13th-century castle. Games of strategy and chance are represented in displays spanning centuries, ranging from dice to video games. Its excellent gift shop is stocked with Legos, puzzles, and board games. Tours and notes are available in English. ⊠ *Château, 1.5 km (1 mi) east of Vevey on route 9,* ☎ *021/ 9444050.* ⌁ *6 SF.* ⊙ *Tues.–Sun. 2–6.*

Dining and Lodging

$$$$ ✕ **Restaurant Denis Martin Le Château.** Owner Denis Martin creates a chic, magnetic atmosphere here, attracting well-heeled locals and Nestlé executives. His seven-course Discovery menu might lead off with duck liver with pineapple chutney and honey vinaigrette, followed by herb-steamed lobster and tomato confit. Only the chef knows what the dessert of the moment might be—no doubt, a splendidly sweet surprise. ⊠ *2 rue du Château, in cellar of Musée Historique du Vieux Vevey,* ☎ *021/ 9211210. Reservations essential. AE, DC, MC, V. Closed Sun.–Mon.*

$$–$$$ ✕ **Les Temps Modernes.** This alternative restaurant/club is named after the film starring Vevey's most famous resident, Charlie Chaplin. An artsy crowd mingles with buttoned-down financiers, and Chanel-suited ladies sit next to baggy-clothed skaters. The decor is equally mixed: an industrial space with flea-market-modern furniture. (Since the building is a converted factory, it's difficult to heat; wear an extra layer in cold weather.) Menu selections are sophisticated and well presented: rabbit fillet atop mixed greens with raspberry vinaigrette or breast of guinea hen with fresh lemon thyme definitely merit a try. The performance space is connected to the dining room by a wide hallway; one evening the beams pulse with hot Latin music, another the familiar rhythms of concert jazz. Open jam sessions and concerts pack the house. Admission to the club ranges from gratis to 20 SF, depending on the performer. ⊠ *6B rue des Deux Gares,* ☎ *021/9223439. No credit cards. Closed July–Aug.*

$–$$ ✕ **Café de La Clef "chez Manu."** Jean-Jacques Rousseau stayed here in 1730, making this café as much a landmark as the pillared marketplace in front of it. No one seems to mind the uninspired decor of tile floors, salmon-pink walls, and the odd potted palm; the locals line up for lunchtime tables to savor such well-prepared traditional specialties as fondue and *filets de perches* (perch fillets—for something different, try them curried), along with *julienne de légumes au bouillon safrané* (fresh fish and vegetable soup with saffron). ⊠ *1 rue du Théâtre,* ☎ *021/9212245. MC, V. Closed Sun.*

$$$$ ✕⊡ **Le Mirador.** Anchored on a ledge above Vevey, this combination ★ spa resort and elite conference center is set among the meadows and modest villages of Mont Pèlerin. Breathtaking panoramic views encompass the lake, the Alps, and the vineyards—it's easy to spend hours on the terrace absorbing it all. Once in your room, draw back the tasseled drapes for more peaks-and-water views. The luxurious spa has a wide-ranging treatment menu, from jet-lag relief to skin care. The exercise facilities are equally extensive, including jogging trails, an indoor-outdoor pool, and a golf simulator. Amusing lifelike sculptures of everyday people by American artist J. Seward Johnson are scattered around the property, though they seem a bit out of place among the traditional oil paintings and stained-glass windows. Guest privacy is closely guarded; you'll have to guess which celebrity or corporate chief arrived by helicopter or commandeered the hotel's private yacht. Formal and casual meals with health-conscious options are served in separate, elegantly furnished restaurants or on the terrace. ⊠ *5 chemin du Mirador, CH-1801,* ☎ *021/9251111,* FAX *021/9251112. 87 rooms, 15 suites. 2 restaurants, bar, in-room safes, minibars, in-room VCRs, indoor-outdoor pool, beauty salon, spa, 2 tennis courts, health club, volleyball, library, concierge, business services, helipad, free parking. AE, DC, MC, V.* ⊗

$$$$ ⌨ **Des Trois Couronnes.** Honeycombed by dramatic atrium stairwells and thick with alabaster and faux marble, this regal landmark was Henry James's home base when he wrote (and set here) the novella *Daisy Miller* (the antiheroine strayed unchaperoned to Chillon and, having thus flown in the face of Victorian propriety, met her end). A vast lakefront terrace overlooks the pollards, the promenade, and the steamers that still carry their cargo of headstrong women toward Chillon. A change of ownership may continue the improvements needed to keep the grand old place up-to-date and justify its top-of-the-line rates. ⊠ *49 rue d'Italie, CH-1800,* ☎ *021/9213005,* FAX *021/9227280. 55 rooms, 10 suites. Restaurant, bar, café, beauty salon, free parking. AE, DC, MC, V.* ⊗

$$$-$$$$ ⌨ **Du Lac.** Anita Brookner set her novel *Hotel du Lac* in this lesser sister of the Trois Couronnes (☞ *above*): its readers may be disappointed to find the hotel lacking the discretion, refinement, and even the stuffiness she so precisely described. Instead, there are plenty of reminders that this is a link in the Best Western chain. Though some rooms are done in prim florals or chic burled wood, others retain the kelly-green carpet and mustard chenille of another era in decorating. Its location is the hotel's main attraction, as there are a sheltered terrace restaurant, garden, and pool all just across the street from the waterfront. ⊠ *1 rue d'Italie, CH-1800,* ☎ *021/9211041,* FAX *021/9217508. 56 rooms. Restaurant, café, pool, parking (fee). AE, DC, MC, V.* ⊗

$$$-$$$$ ⌨ **Hotel Pavillon.** The best of old and new can be found here. Frescoes from the 1920s of a winegrowers' festival cover the ceiling of La Brasserie, the old-fashioned restaurant, while a new annex of guest rooms is wired with up-to-the-minute technology (ISDN lines, fax connections, and acoustical insulation). The colors are strong—plaid spreads and geometric print draperies in bold orange and red, cherry-wood furniture, carpets dominated by dark green or blue. The 15 older rooms are comfortably furnished in subdued aqua-and-pink stripes with multicolor rattan; they do not have air-conditioning. The hotel is adjacent to the train station, making it convenient for early departures. ⊠ *pl. de la Gare, CH-1800,* ☎ *021/9236161,* FAX *021/9211477. 80 rooms, 5 suites. 2 restaurants, bar, snack bar, exercise room, parking (fee). AE, DC, MC, V.* ⊗

$$ ⌨ **Des Négociants.** Handy to the market and by the lake, this is a comfortable, no-nonsense lodging. Its arcaded, shuttered facade is in sharp contrast to the laminated, foursquare interiors, but the top floor has a dormer room of knotty pine that is suitable for families, and all baths are tiled. ⊠ *27 rue du Conseil, CH-1800,* ☎ *021/9227011,* FAX *021/9213424. 23 rooms. Restaurant. AE, DC, MC, V.* ⊗

Outdoor Activities and Sports

Interconnected **hiking trails** (signposted in several languages, including English, and including informative tidbits) span the length of the shore from Ouchy to Chillon, traversing vineyards and traffic arteries from the lakefront to hillside villages. Walking the entire 32-km (19-mi) *parcours viticole* takes about eight and a half hours, but you can also break it into smaller segments—and allow time for wine tastings. (If you're doing a portion of the trail, you can easily catch a train back to your starting point, as there are hourly stops in nearly every village.) Speaking of trains, if the distance and grade of the trails seem too much, you can take the bright yellow coaches of the **Train des Vignes** (vineyard train) through the rows of pinot noir, gamay, and chasselas vines. The train starts from Vevey's station near the waterfront and ends more than 2,000 ft above sea level in the village of Puidoux-Chexbres; its timetable is part of the regular CFF schedule.

Shopping

Saint-Antoine, a modern, multilevel complex diagonally across from the train station, clusters large and small retailers within its glass panels. An extra bonus: its underground parking is a smart alternative to the cramped, restricted parking in the Old Town. Boutiques and galleries in the Old Town east of place du Marché also deserve attentive shopping.

OFF THE
BEATEN PATH

BLONAY–CHAMBY RAILROAD – From Vevey and Montreux, a number of railways climb into the heights, which in late spring are carpeted with an extravagance of wild narcissi. If you like model railroads, you will especially enjoy a trip on the Blonay–Chamby Railroad line, whose real steam-driven trains alternate with electric trains on weekends only. The trains make a stop at a small museum of railroad history in between. You can depart from either end; parking is more plentiful in Blonay. The trip takes about 20 minutes each way, not including a browse in the museum. ⊠ *Case Postale 366, CH-1001 Lausanne,* ☏ *021/9432121.* ☒ *Round-trip ticket 12 SF.* ☉ *Trains run May–Oct., Sun. 9:40–6 and Sat. 2–6.*

Montreux

⓴ *4 km (2 mi) southeast of Vevey, 21 km (13 mi) southeast of Lausanne.*

Petite Montreux could be called the Cannes of Lake Geneva—though it might raise an eyebrow at the slur. Spilling down steep hillsides into a sunny south-facing bay, its waterfront thick with magnolias, cypresses, and palm trees, the historic resort earns its reputation as the capital—if not the pearl—of the Swiss Riviera. Unlike the French Riviera, it has managed, despite overwhelming crowds of conventioneers, to keep up appearances. Its Edwardian-French deportment has survived considerable development, and though there are plenty of harsh new high-rises with parking-garage aesthetics, its mansarded landmarks still unfurl orange awnings to shield millionaires from the sun.

The site where Stravinsky composed *Petrouchka* and *Le Sacre du Printemps* and where Vladimir Nabokov resided in splendor, Montreux and its suburbs have attracted artists and literati for 200 years: Byron, Shelley, Tolstoy, Hans Christian Andersen, and Flaubert were drawn to its lush shoreline. When its casino opened in 1883, tourism began in earnest. Today, Montreux is best known for its history-making Montreux Jazz Festival, which takes place each July; with Vevey, it also sponsors a Festival International de Musique (International Festival of Music) in September.

★ Certainly the greatest attraction at Montreux and one of Switzerland's must-sees is the **Château de Chillon,** the awe-inspiring 12th-century castle that rears out of the water at Veytaux, just down the road from and within sight of Montreux. Chillon was built on Roman foundations under the direction of Duke Peter of Savoy with the help of military architects from Plantagenet England. For a long period it served as a state prison, and one of its shackled guests was François Bonivard, who supported the Reformation and enraged the Savoyards. He spent six years in this prison, chained most of the time to a pillar in the dungeon, before being released by the Bernese in 1536.

While living near Montreux, Lord Byron visited Chillon and was so transported by its atmosphere and by Bonivard's grim sojourn that he was inspired to write his famous poem "The Prisoner of Chillon." He charts the prisoner's despair and brief moments of hope, culminating in the realization on release that "these heavy walls to me had grown/A hermitage—and all my own!/ . . .So much a long communion tends/To make us what we are:—even I/Regain'd my freedom with a sigh." Like a true tourist, Byron carved his name on a pillar in Bonivard's still-damp and chilly dungeon; his graffito is now protected under a plaque.

In high season visitors to Chillon must now file placidly from restored chamber to restored turret, often waiting at doorways for entire busloads of fellow tourists to pass. Yet the restoration is so evocative and so convincing, with its tapestries, carved fireplaces, period ceramics and pewter, and elaborate wooden ceilings, that even the jaded castle hound may become as carried away as Byron was. While you're waiting your turn, you can gaze out the narrow windows over the sparkling, lapping water and remember Mark Twain, who thought Bonivard didn't have it half bad. ⊠ *CH-1820 Veytaux, less than 3 km (2 mi) south of Montreux,* ☎ *021/9633912.* 🎫 *7 SF.* ☉ *Nov.–Feb., daily 10–noon and 1:30–4; Mar. and Oct., daily 10–noon and 1:30–4:45; Apr.–June and Sept., daily 9–5:45; July–Aug., daily 9–6:15.* 🐾

NEED A
BREAK? The lunch and tearoom set (ladies with poodles, Brits in tweeds, fashion plates in Gucci) regularly descends on **Zurcher** (⊠ 45 av. du Casino, ☎ 021/9635963), the irresistible *confiserie* on Montreux's main drag. A green salad, the *potage du jour* (soup of the day), and a chocolate-striated torte make a great quick meal. The café is closed on Monday.

Dining and Lodging

$$$$ ✕ **Le Pont de Brent.** Tucked on a hillside next to its namesake bridge
★ in the unassuming Montreux suburb of Brent, this small but elegant establishment ties with Philippe Rochat's restaurant for the honor of the best table in Switzerland. Who would guess that the green-shuttered windows and pale stone exterior of this unassuming building screen showstopping cuisine? Norman chef Gérard Rabaey performs alchemy with local ingredients to turn out dishes almost too pretty to eat: pastry filled with frogs' legs, truffles, and celery root, lobster and scallop lasagna with parsley jus, caramelized pears with honey ice cream. All is warm here, from the ocher walls to the welcome and service. ⊠ *Rte. de Brent, 7 km (4½ mi) northwest of Montreux, Brent,* ☎ *021/9645230. Reservations essential. MC, V. Closed Sun. and Mon., last 2 wks of July, late Dec.–early Jan.*

$$ ✕ **Du Pont.** In the Old Town high on the hill over Montreux's waterfront, this bustling, old restaurant-café takes its food and its customers seriously. You can relax in the smoky café (where jeans aren't out of place) or enjoy full service and pink linens in the lovely dining room upstairs. Suit your whim: the menu and the prices are exactly the same, including a cheap daily special—and whether you order them

upstairs or down, the German-born chef (who spent years in Italy) will personally grate your white Alba truffle. ✉ *12 rue du Pont,* ☎ *021/ 9632249. AE, DC, MC, V.*

$$ ✕ **Auberge La Cergniaulaz.** Follow the winding road from Les Avants past Sonloup to this postcard–perfect carved-gable chalet. It may look like a simple mountain restaurant, but the kitchen turns out sophisticated meals. Look for seasonal specialties like mushrooms in puff pastry with cream sauce or the peppery rabbit stew with polenta gratin and paper-thin fried onion rings. Daily preparations are chalked on slate; little English is spoken. You won't be able to tell the bankers from the farmers; many walk up for the exercise and culinary reward. ✉ *Les Avants,* ☎ *021/9644276. No credit cards. Closed Mon.–Tues.*

$$$$ ✕▦ **L'Ermitage.** Freestanding on its own waterfront-garden grounds, ★ this genteel, intimate retreat offers top-drawer *haute gastronomie* and a few luxurious rooms upstairs. The guest rooms are lightened with fresh flowers, lacquered cane furniture, and lake views; many rooms have balconies. Chef Étienne Krebs's exceptional menu may include cannelloni of rabbit stuffed with foie gras, fillet of veal with turnip tagliatelle and truffles, or pineapple fritters with ginger ice cream. The ultimate splurge: his seven-course "let yourself go" menu, a parade of delicately orchestrated surprises. The main restaurant is closed Sunday and Monday; there's a terrace for alfresco dining open daily in summer. ✉ *75 rue du Lac, CH-1815,* ☎ *021/9644411,* FAX *021/9647002. 7 rooms. Free parking. AE, DC, MC, V. Closed late Dec.–late Jan.* ✍

$$$$ ✕▦ **Le Montreux Palace.** Dominating the hillside over the Grand-rue ★ and the waterfront, the silver mansards and yellow awnings of this vast institution flag the Palace as a landmark, though its aristocratic interiors are now filled with cell-phone-chatting travelers. It was first opened in 1906, a colossal Belle Epoque folly of stained glass, frescoes, and flamboyant molded stucco. Author Vladimir Nabokov lived among the furbelows for for the last 20 years of his life. Much of that excess has been tempered with age and updated facilities, including a cyber-café and Switzerland's first Harry's New York bar. Across the street is the hotel's pavilion (Le Petit Palais) with a large conference center and tearoom. Lakeside rooms are appropriately posh; mountainside rooms, in the back, miss out on the hotel's raison d'être: a commanding Lake Geneva view. Reservations are recommended in all restaurants; a jacket and tie are required in La Veranda. A chic street-side café bearing the chef's name, Guignard, is getting great reviews for light lunches and theater dinners. Follow a dish such as smoky duck salad with delicate mushrooms or scallop brochettes with a custard or handmade chocolates. ✉ *100 Grand-rue, CH-1820,* ☎ *021/9621212,* FAX *021/9621717. 185 rooms, 50 suites. 4 restaurants, 2 bars, in-room data ports, in-room safes, no-smoking rooms, pool, beauty salon, tennis court, exercise room, nightclub, concierge, convention center. AE, DC, MC, V.* ✍

$$$–$$$$ ✕▦ **Hôtel Victoria.** Noël Coward stayed in Room 49 some 40 years ★ ago while his chalet was being renovated in nearby Les Avants (the playwright had a penchant for high places). Since 1869 this superb Relais & Châteaux hotel set in its own park above Montreux has drawn its share of celebrities and royalty, who come not to be seen but to see the glories of the lake from this unique vantage point—and to be pampered without pomposity. The current owner oversees every detail, from the foot-high down seat cushions in the grand salon to the hand-painted stenciling in the corridors and the freshly cut flowers everywhere. The dining room could be a Coward stage set, its opulence tempered by the occasional eccentric guest. Room decor mixes fine art with soothing pastels, swish amenities, and often a balcony. A lap pool, a lighted tennis court, and a French restaurant serving excellent light cuisine complete this elegant country-house fantasy. ✉ *CH-1823 Glion,* ☎ *021/*

9633131, ⊠ 021/9631351. *50 rooms, 9 suites. Restaurant, bar, breakfast room, minibars, pool, tennis court, sauna, exercise room, piano, library, free parking. AE, DC, MC, V.* 🕮

$$$–$$$$ 🏨 **Hotel Righi Vaudois.** Ascend in a funicular from Veytaux for a stay 700 m (2,300 ft) above Montreux. From the wraparound porch of this 1860s country house you'll have a different experience of the often touristy resort town—this is a quiet neighborhood. Ruby Oriental runners on buffed parquet lead through genteel salons with cushiony sofas and marble fireplaces. There are also acres of private gardens to explore. Antiques, botanical prints, and English country–style accents appoint the guest rooms; the spacious, modern baths shine with polished tile. ⊠ *Glion-sur-Montreux, CH-1823,* ☎ *021/9611881,* ⊠ *021/9611512. 48 rooms, 10 suites. Restaurant, bar, tennis court, free parking. AE, DC, MC, V.* 🕮

$$–$$$ 🏨 **Hôtel Villa Toscane.** Only steps from the sleek, glass-paneled Auditorium Stravinski, this *garni* hotel (without restaurant) stays on the side of homey, not fussy. The building is a turn-of-the-century villa; stained-glass windows filter light into the mahogany stairwell. Sitting areas, fireplaces, and kitchenettes in the larger rooms make longer stays more comfortable. Salmon-and-gray decor is spruced up with Tiffany lamps and black-accented burl-wood desks and cabinetry. The portable air-conditioning units look like small jukeboxes. ⊠ *2–8 rue du Lac, CH-1820,* ☎ *021/9638421,* ⊠ *021/9638426. 39 rooms, 4 suites, 1 apartment. Breakfast room, bar, sauna, free parking. AE, DC, MC, V.* 🕮

$$ 🏨 **Masson.** If you're traveling by car or enjoy being away from the down-
★   town resort scene, look up this demure little inn on a hillside in Veytaux, between Chillon and Montreux. Since it was built in 1829, it's had only four owners, and the current family takes pride in its genteel period decor and up-to-date technology, including color television with remote headphones so one guest won't disturb another. There are floral prints, brass beds, pristine linens, buffed parquet, and expansive lake views from the numerous balconies. The breakfast buffet is generous, with homemade breads and jams. ⊠ *5 rue Bonivard, CH-1820 Veytaux,* ☎ *021/9660044,* ⊠ *021/9660036. 35 rooms. Restaurant. AE, MC, V. Closed Oct.–Apr.* 🕮

Nightlife and the Arts

Montreux's famous festivals and arts events are listed in a seasonal booklet published by the tourist office; tickets are sold from its booth at the waterfront. The renowned **Montreux Jazz Festival** takes place every July in the ultramodern Auditorium Stravinski (⊠ 95 Grand-rue). The more sedate, classical **Festival International de Musique** (International Festival of Music) shares venues with Vevey from August through September; it's also held in the Auditorium Stravinski. For tickets to these popular events, contact their **ticket office** (☎ 021/9622119) as far in advance as possible (although the schedule is not released until May). In summer Montreux offers a variety of free outdoor concerts from its bandstand on the waterfront near the landing stage.

BARS

The **Montreux Palace** (☞ Dining and Lodging, *above*) has a swank Harry's New York Bar with a pianist after 5. An urbane, designer-clad crowd flocks to the **Mayfair Café** (⊠ 52 Grand-rue, ☎ 021/9636468) to take in the afternoon sun and make plans for the evening.

CASINO

The **Casino** (⊠ 9 rue du Théâtre, ☎ 021/9628383) has dancing, slot machines, a billiards room, and an ethnic restaurant. A 5 SF gambling limit applies.

DANCING

A DJ spins at the **Backstage Club** (⌧ 100 Grand-rue, ☎ 021/9633444), Montreux's hottest scene for dancing. You can glide along the lake as you dance on the **Bateau Dansant** (☎ 084/8811848), which departs from the landing stage on Wednesday at 7:25 PM and 9 PM throughout July and August.

Outdoor Activities and Sports

SAILING AND WATER SPORTS

Pedal boats are popular along Montreux-Vevey's waterfront. Rentals are available at **Albert Morisod** (⌧ By convention center, ☎ 021/9633936). **Jean Morisod** (⌧ At quai du Casino, ☎ 021/9633160) also rents them.

Cercle de la Voile de Montreux (⌧ Clarens, ☎ 021/9604171) is the local sailing club. Montreux offers its hotel guests free and supervised use of its waterfront facilities for windsurfing and waterskiing; in the afternoon a fee is charged at the **Ski-Nautique Club** (⌧ Clubhouse du Casino, ☎ 021/9634456).

La Maladaire (☎ 021/9645703) in adjoining Clarens has an Olympic-size indoor pool. The **Casino** (⌧ 9 rue du Théâtre, ☎ 021/9628383) has a pool on an outdoor terrace with a bar.

OFF THE
BEATEN PATH

LES AVANTS – The Montreux–Oberland–Bernois Railroad (MOB) line leads to the resort village of Les Avants (970 m/3,181 ft) and then on to Château-d'Oex, Gstaad, and the Simmental. Noël Coward bought his dream home in Les Avants, at No. 8, Route de Sonloup. Ernest Hemingway wrote to his family and friends of its fields of daffodils—and, more in character, of its bobsled track.

LES ALPES VAUDOISES

At the eastern tip of Lake Geneva, the Alps on the French and Swiss sides close in on the Rhône, and the lakefront highways begin a gradual, ear-popping ascent as the scenery looms larger and the mountains rise around you. The high-altitude Alpine resorts of Villars-Gryon, Leysin, and Les Diablerets each have their charms for winter-sports fans and summer hikers; a visit to any one of the three would suffice for a mountain retreat. On the other hand, the Pays-d'Enhaut, over the Col des Mosses, is a rustic, lower-altitude region surrounded by rocky ridges and velvet hillsides sprinkled with ancient carved-wood chalets; either Château-d'Oex or Rougemont would serve well as home base for a sojourn in this gentle resort area. You can make a beeline from one to another, but rail connections are limited and driving often torturous; you'd do well to choose one dreamy spot and stay put—by the fireplace, on the balcony—for as many days as your itinerary allows.

The resorts of the Vaud Alps, although anything but household words to most ski buffs, offer the bonus of a transportation linkup and lift-ticket package with the sprawling Gstaad Super-Ski region (☞ Chapter 10). This skiing mecca takes in the entire Saanen Valley from Zweisimmen to Château-d'Oex and even dovetails with the parallel valley resorts of Adelboden and Lenk, justifying a visit for skiers who want to cover a lot of territory during their stay.

Aigle

㉒ *17 km (10 mi) south of Montreux, 38 km (24 mi) southeast of Lausanne.*

On a smooth plain flanked by the sloping vineyards of the region of Le Chablais, Aigle is a scenic wine center. Its spired and turreted **Château de Savoie,** originally built in the 13th century, was almost completely destroyed—and then rebuilt—by the 15th-century Bernese.

The **Musée de la Vigne et du Vin** (Museum of Viticulture and Wine), in the Château d'Aigle, displays casks, bottles, presses, and wine-makers' tools within its wood-beam chambers. Some living quarters are reproduced, and there's even a collection of costumes worn over the centuries at the local Fête des Vignerons. ⊠ *Château d'Aigle,* ☎ *024/ 4662130.* ☞ *8 SF, 9 SF combination ticket with International Museum of Wine Labels.* ☉ *Apr.–June and Sept.–Oct., Tues.–Sun. 10–12:30 and 2–6; July–Aug., daily 10–6; Nov.–Mar., tours by appointment.*

A timbered attic in an adjacent warehouse shelters a separate museum, the **International Museum of Wine Labels,** which chronicles a history of prestigious vintages in its collection of labels from more than 50 countries dating back 200 years. You need go no farther for a tasting; the Pinte du Paradis wine bar is just downstairs, overlooking the vineyards. ⊠ *Maison de la Dîme,* ☎ *024/4662130.* ☞ *4 SF, 9 SF combination ticket with Museum of Viticulture and Wine.* ☉ *Apr.–June and Sept.–Oct., Tues.–Fri. 10–12:30 and 2–6, Sat. 9–noon; July–Aug., Tues.–Fri. 10–6, Sat. 9–noon.*

Chasselas grapes are cultivated on the steep shale and sandstone terraces by Aigle and Yvorne; these local wines flare with exuberance. Generations of the Badoux family have tended the land around Aigle held by *murailles* (stone walls), producing a signature wine identified by the lizard on the label. Their **La Boutique des Grands Vins,** a lovely wine shop, is just the place to scout a local find. Browse the shelves for select vintages, etched decanters, and corkscrews. ⊠ *18 av. du Chamossaire,* ☎ *024/4686885.* ☉ *Weekdays 8–noon and 1:30–6; Sat. 8–noon.*

OFF THE BEATEN PATH

SWISS VAPEUR PARC – Where the Rhône empties into Lake Geneva, between Vaud and France, families may want to visit the Swiss Vapeur Parc (Swiss Steam Park), a miniature railway circuit laid out in a green park. There you can straddle the tiny models and cruise around a reduced-scale landscape. It also includes a full-blown water park. ⊠ *CH-1897 Le Bouveret,* ☎ *024/4814410.* ☞ *10 SF.* ☉ *Mid-May–late Sept., weekdays 1:30–6, weekends 10–6; late Apr.–mid-May and late Sept.–Oct., Wed. and weekends 1:30–6. Closed Nov.–mid-Apr.*

AQUA PARC – This newly opened (late 1999) indoor water park stays open year-round; it's geared toward both children and adults. Captain Kid's Land and Jungle Land are filled with pirate-themed flumes, chutes, and slides. Paradise Land mimics a Caribbean getaway for adults, complete with a swim-up bar. Families get a discount rate. ⊠ *CH-1897 Le Bouveret,* ☎ *024/4815081.* ☞ *31 SF.* ☉ *Sun.–Thurs. 10 AM–midnight, Fri.–Sat. 10 AM–1 AM.*

En Route   At **Roche,** on the highway between Villeneuve and Aigle, there's a massive 15th-century stone barn that was built by the monks of Grand St-Bernard on a scale as big as an airplane hangar and divided into three great pillared naves. The building itself would be worth the detour, but today—after extensive restorations—it houses the **Musée Suisse de l'Orgue** (Swiss Organ Museum), a vast collection of instruments that had been without the cathedral-scale space required for display until it arrived in this gargantuan barn. There's an ornate Louis XVI organ case, an 18th-century pedal board, a neo-Gothic harmonium, and even an Emmental home organ. The curator leads three one-hour tours a day (in French) and demonstrates the instruments. ☎ *021/9602200.* ☞ *5 SF.* ☉ *May–Oct., Tues.–Sun. 10–noon and 2–5. Closed Nov.–Apr.*

Villars-Gryon

★ ❷ *15 km (9 mi) southeast of Aigle, 53 km (33 mi) southeast of Lausanne.*

At 1,300 m (4,264 ft), this welcoming ski center spreads comfortably along a sunny terrace, the craggy peaks of Les Diablerets (3,210 m/10,528 ft) behind it and before it a sweeping view over the Rhône Valley all the way to Mont Blanc. Balanced along its ridge and open to the vast space below, its busy little downtown—sports shops, cafés, resort hotels—tapers off quickly into open country. Though it's thriving with new construction, Villars retains a sense of coziness and tradition, and some of its family-owned hotels have preserved the feel of mountain lodges that's rare these days in Switzerland. What Villars lacks in glitz, it amply compensates for with unpretentious good cheer. A network of lifts connecting with Les Diablerets make this a good choice for skiers or hikers who want to experience Suisse Romande relatively unspoiled. The boarding schools headquartered in the area keep the town animated with teen adrenaline, backing sports like snowboarding, mountain biking, in-line skating, and rock climbing.

Skiing

For serious skiers, Villars itself nicely balances sophistication and Alpine isolation, offering some of the best-developed options and including a new and very accessible link to **Les Diablerets Glacier.** The main ski area over the village can be reached easily either by cable car to **Roc d'Orsay** (2,000 m/6,560 ft) or by cog railway from the center to **Bretaye;** either site allows access to the lifts that fan out over a sunny bowl riddled with intermediate runs and off-trail challenges. From Bretaye, you can also take lifts up to **Grand Chamossaire** (2,120 m/6,954 ft) for gentle, open runs. Trails from **Chaux Ronde** and **Chaux de Conches** are easy enough for beginners, but the more advanced can find jumps and trees enough to keep them more than alert. Just beyond Villars, the linking resort of **Gryon** presents a few more options and a change of scenery, again with trails for all levels of skill. **Villars** itself has 45 lifts, 120 mi (75 mi) of downhill runs (including the Diablerets Glacier), and 44 km (27 mi) of cross-country trails One-day lift tickets cost 49 SF; five-day passes are 201 SF.

Dining and Lodging

$–$$ ✕ **Le Refuge de Frience.** A few scenic kilometers from Villars en route
★ to Gryon, this 18th-century Heidi-esque chalet combines the grist of Alpine legend with good, honest food. Three cheery rooms glowing with log fires under low, beamed ceilings give way to unfettered views of the mountains and, in summer, of cows roaming the slopes. You won't see tourists here; it's a word-of-mouth place that packs in locals and weekend expats in the know. They go for the fondue and raclette, river trout, and plates of fresh regional mushrooms—and wine spouting from an old *fontaine,* a wrought-iron contraption rarely seen in restaurants. ⊠ *Alpe des Chaux, 4½ km (3 mi) from Villars,* ☎ *024/4981426. MC, V. Closed Tues. and Apr.–May.*

$$–$$$ 🏨 **Le Bristol.** This resort hotel, the poshest in town, rose from the ashes of an older landmark and—despite the Colorado-condo exterior and the jutting balcony for every room—is now furnished with a light, bright, and convincingly regional touch. The interiors are mostly white with mauve touches and carved blond pine, and picture windows are angled to take in the views. There are good health facilities and a choice of attractive restaurants, including a terrace above the valley. ⊠ *av. Centrale, CH-1884,* ☎ *024/4963636,* 🖷 *024/4963637. 87 rooms, 23 suites. 2 restaurants, bar, minibars, indoor pool, hot tub, sauna, exercise room, squash, free parking. AE, DC, MC, V.* ❧

$$ ⊞ **La Renardière.** This group of three classic chalets, set back from the resort center and surrounded by tall firs, hasn't budged from its '50s mountain lodge identity; it's still got its golden pine, plaid curtains, and log bar. The lounges and sitting areas have fireplaces; the rooms are simple, done in pine and chenille, with the customary color scheme of orange and brown. In the traditional restaurant, linens, crystal, and fresh flowers soften the rustic edges, and there's an agreeable terrace café that serves good lunches under the firs. ⊠ *rte. des Liyeux, CH-1884,* ☎ *024/4952592,* FAX *024/4953915. 20 rooms, 5 suites. Restaurant, bar, café. AE, DC, MC, V.*

$ ⊞ **Alpe Fleurie.** From the minute you check in, you'll know this is a family-run, family-oriented hotel: there are faded snapshots of children and dogs over the reception desk. Launched in 1946, this chalet-hotel has been updated steadily, and the rooms show a thoughtful mix of modern textures and classic pine. It stands on the valley side of the main street, and south-facing rooms have terrific views. Local residents hit the restaurant for their favorite Vaudoise specialties. ⊠ *av. Centrale, CH-1884,* ☎ *024/4953464,* FAX *024/4963077. 17 rooms, 2 suites. Restaurant, bar, café, minibars, free parking. AE, DC, MC, V.*

$ ⊞ **Écureuil.** Although there's a restaurant downstairs and a carnotzet for fondue, nearly every room in this warm family-run inn has a kitchenette, so you can make yourself at home mountain cabin–style. Opened in 1947 and now run by the son of the founder, the hotel has lots of homey touches: books and magazines, swing sets, and a piano parlor. An older stone-base chalet on the grounds offers bigger rooms; both buildings stand across the street from the Bristol and therefore don't have direct access to those Villars views. ⊠ *av. Centrale, CH-1884,* ☎ *024/4952795,* FAX *024/4954205. 27 rooms. Restaurant, café, Ping-Pong, free parking. MC, V.*

Outdoor Activities and Sports

GOLF
Precipitously sited, the **Golf Club Villars** (⊠ av. Centrale, ☎ 024/4954214), open from June to October, has 18 holes.

SKATING
Nonskiers can amuse themselves at a centrally located indoor **skating rink** (⊠ Chemin de la Gare, ☎ 024/4951221). Ice skates are available for rent.

SPORTS CENTER
The **New Sporting Club** (⊠ Rte. du Col de la Croix, ☎ 024/4953030) hosts all kinds of activities, from badminton to wall climbing. It also has an outdoor pool.

SWIMMING
In the same building as the skating rink in Villars, there's an **indoor pool** (☎ 024/4951221).

OFF THE
BEATEN PATH   **MINE DU SEL –** Children inured to the thrill of cable cars, narrow-gauge
↻   railroads, and steam trains might brighten at a journey to the center of the earth in the Mine du Sel (Salt Mine) at Bex, just off the southbound Route 9. First dug in 1684, this ancient underground complex bores into the mountain as far as Villars and covers some 50 subterranean km (30 mi). After an introductory audiovisual show, you ride a narrow-gauge train into the depths and take a guided walk through the works. Wear sturdy shoes and warm clothing as the temperature stays at 63°F (17°C) year-round. ⊠ CH-1880 Bex, ☎ 024/4630330. ☞ 15 SF. Prior booking essential, even for individuals. ◷ Apr.–mid-Nov., with 2¼-hr-long tours leaving daily at 10, 2, and 3.

Les Diablerets

㉔   *19 km (12 mi) northeast of Aigle, 59 km (37 mi) southwest of Lausanne.*

In summer, car travelers can cut along spectacular heights on a tiny 13%-grade road over the Col de la Croix (1,778 m/5,832 ft) to get from Villars to the small neighboring resort of Les Diablerets (1,160 m/3,806 ft). Train travelers will have to descend to Bex and backtrack to Aigle. Les Diablerets lies at the base of the 3,209-m (10,525-ft) peak of the same name—which sheds the dramatic namesake 3,000-m (9,840-ft) glacier. The village was named after the folklore tale of devils that played skittle among the desolate glacier peaks. The compact handful of hotels, shops, and steep-roof chalets is strung along a winding road. The valley brightens only when sun finds its way over crags and crests, which may be why skiing is guaranteed year-round and the Swiss team trains here in summer.

Skiing

The connection of Les Diableret's ski facilities with those of Villars adds considerably to ski options—including summer skiing on the glacier itself and some dramatic intermediate peak-top runs at **Quille du Diable** and **Scex-Rouge.** There's one gravity-defying expert slope, directly under the gondola, from **Pierre-Pointes** back to the valley. From Scex-Rouge, a popular run carries you around the top of the **Oldenhorn** and down to **Oldenegg,** a wide-open intermediate run through a sheltered valley. At 1,250 m (4,100 ft), **Les Diablerets** has six cable cars, 18 lifts, 120 km (75 mi) of downhill runs, 30 km (19 mi) of cross-country trails, and 6 km (4 mi) of prepared tobogganing trails. Lift tickets cost 49 SF for a one-day pass and 233 SF for a six-day pass. These prices include Glacier 3000, the aerial cableway, which links Pillon, Cabane, and Scex-Rouge (reduced family prices are available).

Dining and Lodging

$$–$$$ ✕⊡ **Grand-Hôtel.** Carved wooden eaves and ornate balconies frame this chalet-style hotel. It practically breathes Alpine ambience, from the heavy, carved blond-wood furniture to the starched white mile-high duvets. The café and brasserie are true to type, serving traditional cheese dishes. The hotel is just minutes from the lifts—and it has outstanding, inspiring views. ⊠ *chemin du Vernex, CH-1865,* ☎ *024/4923551,* ⅢX *024/4922391. 60 rooms, 4 suites. Restaurant, café, bar, minibars, indoor pool, parking (fee). AE, DC, MC, V. Closed late Apr.–Jun. and Oct.–Nov.*

Leysin

㉕   *16 km (10 mi) northeast of Aigle, 54 km (33 mi) southeast of Lausanne.*

From the switchback highway A11, a small mountain road leads up to this family resort, which has easy skiing and a spectacular, sunny plateau setting, looking directly onto the Dents du Midi.

Skiing

Small-scale and cozy, Leysin offers a widespread network of lifts that allows you to cover a lot of varied ground on easy-to-medium slopes. From Berneuse, a peak 2,049 m (6,720 ft) above Leysin, you can muster up your courage in Kuklos, a revolving restaurant, and head for the **Chaux de Mont** (2,200 m/7,216 ft), where an expert run winds along a razorback ridge and through the forests to town. At 1,250 m (4,100 ft), Leysin has two cable cars, 18 lifts, a shuttle train, and 60 km (37 mi) of ski runs, as well as skating, curling, ski bob, and 36 km (22 mi) of cross-country trails. Snowboarding hotshots swarm the slopes; Leysin is home to the European championships. Lift tickets cost 40 SF; a six-day pass runs 233 SF.

PAYS-D'ENHAUT

Separated from the high-altitude Alpine resorts by the modest Col des Mosses (1,445 m/4,740 ft) and isolated, high-altitude family ski centers (Les Mosses, La Lécherette), the Pays-d'Enhaut (Highlands) offers an entirely different culture from that of its Vaud cousins. Here the architecture begins to resemble that of the Berner Oberland, which it borders: deep-eaved wooden chalets replace the Edwardian structures of the lakelands, and the atmosphere takes on a mountain-farm air. The Pays-d'Enhaut once belonged to Gruyères, then was seized by Bern; when Vaud was declared a canton, the Pays-d'Enhaut went with it. A stone's throw up the valley, you cross the Sarine/Saanen and the so-called Rösti Border, where the culture and language switch to Bernese German. This is still Gruyère cheese country and also the source of one of Switzerland's most familiar decorative arts: *papier découpé*, delicate, symmetrical paper cutouts. They are cut in black, often with simple imagery of cattle and farmers, and fixed on white paper for contrast. The real thing is a refined craft and is priced accordingly, but attractive prints reproducing the look are on sale at reduced prices throughout the region.

L'Etivaz

㉖ *21 km (13 mi) northeast of Aigle, 59 km (37 mi) southeast of Lausanne.*

Visitors to the Pays-d'Enhaut who cross the Col des Mosses first pass through the village of L'Etivaz, where a Gruyère-style cheese is made from milk drawn exclusively from cows grazed on pastures of elevations between 1,000 m and 2,200 m (3,280 ft and 7,216 ft). The sweet, late-blooming flowers they eat impart a flavor that lowland cheeses can't approach. The very best L'Etivaz cheese—Rebibes—is aged for three years in the cooperative here until it dries and hardens to a Parmesan-like texture; then it's shaved into curls and eaten by hand. Feel free to stop in at the **cooperative;** one of the workers in rubber boots will be happy to sell you brick-size chunks of both young and old cheeses at prices well below those at resort groceries.

Dining and Lodging

$ X▦ **Du Chamois.** For four generations a single family has coddled guests
★   in this weathered-wood chalet. Its bookcases are full of rainy-day reading, and its meals simple, impeccable presentations of trout, cheese, omelets, and steaks. Warm gold pine planking covers nearly every surface, and historic photos, lace curtains, and local paper cutouts add the grace notes. The baths are up to date, while the rooms are simple and genuinely homey. ⊠ *CH-1831,* ☎ *026/9246266,* FAX *026/9246016. 15 rooms. Restaurant, café, tennis court, playground. V.* 🐾

En Route   Clinging to a precarious cliff-side road between L'Etivaz and Château-d'Oex, drivers penetrate the canyon wilderness of the **Gorges du Pissot,** where sports lovers in wet suits "canyon"—literally, hike the river bottom—under the white waters of the Torneresse River (☞ Outdoor Activities and Sports *in* Château d'Oex, *below*).

Château-d'Oex

㉗ *33 km (20 mi) northeast of Aigle, 64 km (40 mi) east of Lausanne.*

At the crossroads between the Col des Mosses highway to Aigle and the Valais and the route to the Berner Oberland lies Château-d'Oex (pronounced *day*), a popular sports resort that connects, in these days of sophisticated ski transit, with the greater Gstaad ski region. Its perhaps even greater claim to fame these days is ballooning, with periodic hot-air-balloon competitions that draw mobs of international enthusiasts and fill hotels throughout the region. In spring 1999 the Breitling *Orbiter 3* balloon launched from the valley floor for its record-breaking nonstop trip around the world. The town itself is a mix of Edwardian architecture with weathered-wood chalets, spreading over a green forest-top hillside above the highway. It heads the French end of the valley of the Sarine River—also known, in the Berner Oberland, as Saanenland.

★ In Château-d'Oex's small center, the **Musée Artisanal du Vieux Pays-d'Enhaut** (Artisan and Folklore Museum of the Old Highlands) gives you insight into life in these isolated parts. Complete interiors are evocatively reproduced: two kitchens, a farmer's home, a cheese maker's house, and a carpenter's studio. Marvelous wood carving and ironwork, a variety of ceramics, plus displays of old papier découpé, furniture, and popular art round out the collection. ⊠ *Grand-rue, CH-1837,* ☎ *026/9246520.* ▢ *5 SF.* ☉ *Tues., Thurs., and Fri. 10–noon and 2–4:30, weekends 2–4:30.*

Le Chalet is a reproduction of a mountain cheese maker's home, with afternoon demonstrations over an open fire. Visitors sit at café tables (and are sold drinks or cheese dishes) while they watch the hot labor of stirring milk in a vast copper vat. Regional crafts and dairy products are on sale downstairs. ⊠ *CH-1837,* ☎ *026/9246677.* ▢ *Free (a purchase or consumption is expected).* ☉ *Sat.–Thurs. 9–6, Fri. 9 AM–11 PM. Demonstrations Sept.–June, Tues.–Sun. 9:30–11:30 and 2–4;, July–Aug., Tues.–Sun. 2–4.*

Skiing

Château-d'Oex has cable-car links to **La Braye** and the expert and intermediate trails that wind back down. At 1,000 m (3,280 ft), it has one cable car, two chairlifts, 10 lifts, 50 km (31 mi) of downhill runs, and 30 km (19 mi) of cross-country trails. A one-day lift ticket costs 33 SF; a six-day pass costs 166 SF. La Braye also has an equipment test center where you can try out the latest snowboards and skis.

Dining and Lodging

$ ✕ **Buffet de la Gare.** Though you'd be better off driving five minutes up to L'Etivaz for equivalent (but better prepared and served) middle-class cuisine, this easygoing and convenient train-station café draws a regular local crowd for light meals and a dependable plat du jour. Stick with *croûtes* (rich toasted-cheese sandwiches) and salads, and opt for the casual—and smoky—café rather than the more formal restaurant, though it's fun to watch the trains roll by the latter. ☎ *026/9247717.* MC, V.

$$–$$$ ✕▤ **Bon Accueil.** Occupying a beautifully proportioned 18th-century
★ weathered-wood chalet, this is the quintessential French-Swiss country inn. The rooms mix aged pine planking, spindle furniture, and antiques, and under the old low-beam ceilings the floors creak agreeably. If you prefer quieter though smaller accommodations, take a room—perhaps with a sun terrace—in the new building (connected by lawn

and tunnel to the old). Up-to-date amenities, immaculate appointments, pastel accents, and fresh flowers—inside and out—keep standards at a well-above-rustic level. The restaurant (reservations are essential) is even more civilized, and the menu offers a range of specialties, from simple lake fish to such intricate creations as freshwater fish roasted in pinot noir accompanied by *choucroûte* (sauerkraut) and fried leeks. Meals are served in a warm dining room with a brick fireplace, much waxed wood, and pewter accents. For winter nights there's a firelighted stone cellar bar with low-key jazz. ⊠ *CH-1837,* ☎ *026/ 9246320,* FAX *026/9245126. 20 rooms. Restaurant, bar, sauna. AE, DC, MC, V. Closed mid-Oct.–mid-Dec.*

$$ ⤫⊞ **Ermitage.** Hoteliers Fabio and Françoise Piazza spent nearly a decade converting this once-ordinary mountain hotel into a unique, cozy inn. Timbered ceilings and stenciled detailing warm up the amply sized rooms, which are furnished with traditional, blond-wood armoires and fluffy cotton-encased duvets. The terrace is the perfect perch for watching balloon takeoffs—it overlooks the launch field. The carnotzet's meals—cassoulet, coq au vin, and other heartwarming dishes—are drawn from Piazza's grandmother's recipes. An excellent five-course prix-fixe meal (and at 85 SF, a great value) has the faithful driving up from glitzy Gstaad. ⊠ *CH-1837,* ☎ *026/9246003,* FAX *026/9245076. 16 rooms, 4 suites. Restaurant, café, minibars, playground, free parking. AE, DC, MC, V.*

$$ ⊞ **La Rocaille.** The pitched roof and balconies of this chalet look lovely whether banked with snow or framed by geraniums. Spic-and-span interiors, starched linens, and friendly service make it an annual favorite among balloonists and skiers. Although it's technically on the edge of town, nothing is more than a few minutes' walk away. Sometimes balloons creep so close to the eaves and terrace that you can hear the rush of burners and the pilot's commands. ⊠ *CH-1837,* ☎ *026/9246215,* FAX *026/9245249. 12 rooms. Restaurant, bar, café, minibars, in-room safes, free parking. AE, DC, V.*

Outdoor Activities and Sports

In summer the slopes turn into mountain-surfing runs. Mountain-bike shops rent big-wheeled scooters on which you can race downhill.

BALLOONING

The hot-air-ballooning center in Château-d'Oex offers accompanied flights year round. To arrange one, contact the tourist office (☞ Visitor Information *in* Vaud A to Z, *below*). An annual festival gets off the ground in late January. On Friday night a *night glow* is held. Scramble to the top of the hill that has the church (look for the steeple) for a stunning view of brilliantly colored, backlighted balloons choreographed to music.

BICYCLING

In this graceful region of rolling hills and steep climbs, mountain bikes can be rented at **Planète Sports** (☎ 026/9244464). Also try **Palaz Bike** (☎ 026/9244251).

RAFTING, HYDROSPEED, AND CANYONING

Several gorges near Château-d'Oex offer excellent rafting, as well as two unusual white-water sports. Hydrospeed involves floating the waters in flippers and wet suit; canyoning has you hiking the river bottom clad in wet suit, life jacket, and helmet. **Rivières et Aventures** (⊠ Case Postale 68, CH-1837, ☎ 026/9243424) organizes hiking, rafting, and kayaking excursions to the Gorges du Pissot (☞ *above*). You can also arrange supervised initiations into these sports through the tourist office (☞ Visitor Information *in* Vaud A to Z, *below*).

SKATING
There's an outdoor rink at the **Parc des Sports** (☎ 026/9246700). Rental ice skates are available at Planète Sports (☞ Bicycling, *above*).

SWIMMING
In summer Château-d'Oex opens a heated 50-m **open-air pool** with restaurant (☎ 026/9246234).

Rougemont

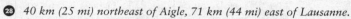 **40 km (25 mi) northeast of Aigle, 71 km (44 mi) east of Lausanne.**

Though this historic village is now being encroached on by sporty Gstaad—its beautiful wooden barns and ornately decorated chalets crowded out by modern resort lodgings—it retains its ancient monuments. The striking Romanesque **church,** with its deeply raked roof and needle-sharp spire, was built between 1073 and 1085. The exterior wall of the 16th-century **château** behind the church is emblazoned with the *grue* (crane) of Gruyères, harking back to the Pays-d'Enhaut's earliest loyalties. (The château is privately owned and closed to the public.)

Skiing
Rougemont has **La Videmanette,** a cable run that drops you off for leisurely, moderate skiing back to the village, or on up to trails that wind over toward Gstaad. From the second stop up the Videmanette, there's also a 4½-km (3-mi) sledding run. A regional ski pass permits access to lifts, rail lines, and buses in all ski villages at a reduced rate. A daily pass costs 44 SF; a weekly pass is 233 SF.

VAUD A TO Z

Arriving and Departing

By Car
There are two major arteries leading to Lac Léman (Lake Geneva), one entering from the north via Bern and Fribourg (**A12**), the other arcing over the north shore of Lake Geneva from Geneva to Lausanne (**A1**), then to Montreux and on south through the Alpes Vaudoises toward the Grand St. Bernard Pass (**A9**) in canton Valais. They are swift and often scenic expressways, and the north-shore artery (A1 and A9) traces a route that has been followed since before Roman times. Secondary highways parallel the expressways, but this is one case where, as the larger road sits higher on the lakeside slopes, the views from the expressway are often better than those from the highway. Be sure, however, to detour for the Corniche Road views between Lausanne and Montreux.

By Plane
Geneva's **Cointrin** (✉ 55 km/34 mi southwest of Lausanne, ☎ 022/7177111) is the second-busiest international airport in Switzerland, servicing frequent flights from the United States and the United Kingdom on **Swissair** as well as other international carriers. From Cointrin, Crossair (☎ 061/3253636 for central reservations; 1553636 toll free within the country), Switzerland's domestic line, connects to secondary airports throughout the country.

By Train
Lausanne lies on a major train route between Bern and Geneva, with express trains connecting from Basel and Zürich. From Geneva, trains take about 30 minutes and arrive in Lausanne up to four times an hour; from Bern, they take a little more than an hour and arrive twice an hour. TGVs (high-speed trains) run from Paris four times a day and

take 3 hours and 40 minutes. The Pendolino train has two departures a day between October and May: one to Milan and one to Venice. From June to September two more departures are added. A daily ICE, the German high-speed train, goes directly to Cologne; other hourly departures head to Germany with a change in Basel or Bern.

Getting Around

By Boat

Like all fair-size Swiss lakes, Lake Geneva is crisscrossed with comfortable and reasonably swift **steamers.** They sometimes run more often than the trains that parallel their routes. With a Swiss Pass (☞ Train Travel *in* Smart Travel Tips A to Z) you travel free. For boat schedule and docking information contact **Compagnie Générale de Navigation** (☎ 084/8811848) or pick up a timetable in any tourist office.

By Bus

A useful network of **postbus** routes covers the region for the resourceful traveler with plenty of time; some routes are covered only once or twice a day. Schedules are available from tourist offices (☞ Visitor Information, *below*) and rail stations. In smaller towns you can also check with the post office. Lausanne has a good city bus network. The Vevey–Montreux city service is extremely convenient, as it's hard to find a parking place in these towns. If you have a Swiss Pass, you can travel free on city buses and funiculars in Montreux, Vevey, and Lausanne.

By Car

A web of **secondary highways** cuts north into the hills then winds east of the southbound expressway into the Alpine resorts, giving the driver maximum flexibility.

By Train

Trains along the waterfront, connecting major Lake Geneva towns, are swift and frequent. There are also several **private rail systems** leading into small villages and rural regions, including the **Montreux–Oberland–Bernois Railroad** line (MOB; ☎ 021/9898181), which climbs sharply behind Montreux and cuts straight over the pre-Alps toward Château-d'Oex and the Berner Oberland. There is also the **Blonay–Chamby Railroad** line (✉ Case Postale 366, CH-1001 Lausanne, ☎ 021/9432121). The Swiss Pass is accepted on these private lines, but there may be an additional fee for panoramic excursions. Inquire at local tourist offices or train stations about a regional pass that combines rail, boat, bus, and cable-car excursions on these private lines at a reduced fee. It can be used for unlimited travel for three out of seven days and discounts on the other four days.

Lausanne itself has a tiny but essential **Métro** that every seven minutes connects the waterfront at Ouchy to the train station and the place St-François above. It runs until midnight; tickets are less than 3 SF, and a day pass costs 6.50 SF.

Contacts and Resources

Emergencies

Vaud (☎ 117). **Police:** Château-d'Oex (☎ 026/9244421); Montreux (☎ 021/9632121); Villars (☎ 024/4955321). **Ambulance:** Château-d'Oex (☎ 026/9247593); Montreux (☎ 144); Villars (☎ 024/4951537). **Hospitals:** Aigle (☎ 024/4688688); Lausanne Centre Hospitalier Universitaire Vaudois (emergency services; ☎ 021/3141111); Montreux (☎ 021/9666666). **Medical and dental referrals:** Lausanne (☎ 021/6529932). **Late-night pharmacies:** (☎ 111). **Auto breakdown:** Touring Club of Switzerland (☎ 140).

Guided Tours

ORIENTATION

Both branches of the **Lausanne tourist office** (✉ Gare Centrale, 9 pl. de la Gare 9; ✉ 4 pl. de la Navigation) run a daily two-hour coach trip into the Old Town, including a visit to the cathedral and an extended city coach tour that takes in the Lavaux vineyards.

Walking tours led by local historians in Lausanne, Vevey, and Montreux are increasingly popular. They are organized by the town's tourist office and are given daily between May and September. English-speaking guides are often available, but you should call in advance to check. Most local tourist offices offer three daily general tours during the summer: one to Gruyères; one to Chamonix and Mont Blanc; and one to the Alps by coach and the other by Montreux–Oberland–Bernois Railroad line's *Panoramic Train* to Les Diablerets and Château-d'Oex (☞ Getting Around, *above*). To ensure a tour with English commentary, reserve in advance.

VINEYARD TOURS

The **Office des Vins Vaudois** (✉ 6 ch. de la Vuachère, CH-1005 Lausanne, ☎ 021/7296161) offers carefully marked walks—not personally guided—through the vineyards, passing production centers, winegrowers' homes, and *pintes* (pubs) for tasting along the way. Write for the *Guide du Vignoble Vaudois* for itineraries, hours, and addresses of suggested stops. Vevey's **Le Train des Vignes** (vineyard train) runs through the area's vineyards; some outings include tastings and cellar tours. Inquire at Vevey's tourist office (☞ Visitor Information, *below*).

Visitor Information

The **Office du Tourisme du Canton de Vaud** (✉ 60 av. d'Ouchy, CH-1000 Lausanne, ☎ 021/6177202, FAX 021/6177240, ✆) has general information on the region.

Regional offices: **Château-d'Oex** (✉ CH-1837, ☎ 026/9242525). **Les Diablerets** (✉ CH-1865, ☎ 024/4923358). **Lausanne** (✉ 2 av. de Rhodanie, CH-1000, ☎ 021/6137321). **Leysin** (✉ CH-1854, ☎ 024/4942244). **Nyon** (✉ 7 av. Viollier, CH-1260, ☎ 022/3616261). **Montreux** (✉ 5 rue du Thêâtre, CH-1820, ☎ 021/9628484). **Morges** (✉ rue du Château, CH-1110, ☎ 021/8013233). **Vevey** (✉ Case Postale 27, CH-1800, ☎ 021/9222020). **Villars-Gryon** (✉ CH-1884, ☎ 0953232).

13 GENEVA

The birthplace of Calvinism and the International Red Cross, home to the European headquarters of the United Nations, and a stronghold of private banks and exclusive boutiques, Geneva is, in many ways, a paradox. It is Switzerland's most cosmopolitan city, a high-profile crossroads of wealth, influence, and cultures from around the world.

Updated by
Jennifer
McDermott

T HIS GRACEFUL, sophisticated Swiss city at the southwestern tip of Lac Léman (Lake Geneva) shares more than 96% of its borders, as well as its language, with France. To the north and west lie the Pays de Gex, to the south and east the Haute-Savoie. The River Rhône flows south from Geneva's *centre ville* to the Mediterranean; the canton as a whole commands panoramic views of the French Alps and the Jura. The combination of Swiss efficiency and French savoir faire gives Geneva a chic polish, while the infusion of international blood from the UN adds a heterogeneity rare for a population of only 180,000. Rolls-Royces purr past haute couture shops and manicured lakeside promenades even as international civil servants convene yet another conference or assembly.

Geneva was known for enlightened tolerance long before Henri Dunant founded the International Red Cross here in 1864 or the League of Nations moved in (1919). It gave refuge to religious reformers John Calvin and John Knox as well as to the writers Voltaire, Victor Hugo, Alexandre Dumas, Honoré de Balzac, and Stendhal. Lord Byron, Percy Bysshe and Mary Shelley, Richard Wagner, and Franz Liszt all escaped to Geneva when scandal erupted at home.

There were limits to this tolerance, however. With the rise of Calvinism in the mid-16th century, the city government forced the liberal philosopher (and Geneva native) Jean-Jacques Rousseau into exile. Nonbelievers left the city, even as it absorbed waves of Protestant refugees. The English fled Bloody Mary, Protestant Italians the wrath of the pope, Spaniards the Inquisition, Huguenots the oppressive French monarchy— and Geneva flourished as a stronghold of Protestant reform.

The conservative Genevois still seem to hear Calvin tsk-tsking in their ears as they hurry by some of the world's most expensive stores and palatial hotels. Well-heeled and well-traveled foreigners often indulge themselves the most, as executives jet in and out, and Middle Eastern oil money flows in.

But Geneva does let down her discreet chignon twice a year. Every August the city organizes a 10-day-long party, Les Fêtes de Genève, that draws huge crowds to the waterfront for a spectacular grand finale of fireworks set to music. The Fête de l'Escalade (Festival of the Escalade), in December, celebrates Geneva's independent spirit as demonstrated on the night of December 11–12, 1602. The duke of Savoy, coveting Geneva and hoping to restore it to Catholicism, sent his men to scale the city walls with ladders, but an alert sentry sounded the alarm, and the entire population turned out to fight. One resourceful housewife emptied a *marmite* (pot) of hot soup over the Savoyards scaling her walls—hence the festival's commemorative chocolate cauldrons. The city's 18 dead are remembered with a parade, and the usually decorous Genevois take to the streets of the Old Town in costume.

Pleasures and Pastimes

Churches
The Romanesque-Gothic Cathédrale St-Pierre, the ruins of its predecessors, and the Auditoire de Calvin provide an overview of Geneva's Catholic and Reformed personae.

Dining
Geneva has more restaurants per capita than New York City, and its chefs excel at everything from *haute gastronomie* to traditional bistro fare to creative ethnic food.

Like that of Lyons, only 150 km (94 mi) to the southwest, Geneva's rich, earthy local cuisine emphasizes *abats* (organ meats), *andouillettes* (chitterling sausages), potatoes, and onions. Menus are seasonal; some dishes may be had only at specific times of year. *Cardon* (cardoon, a locally grown, thistlelike vegetable available in winter) is baked with cream and Gruyère. Lac Léman yields abundant fish—perch, trout, *féra* (related to salmon), and *omble* (char)—in summer. *La chasse* (wild game) turns up between late September and mid-December. Year-round standards include *pieds de cochon* (pigs' feet), *fricassée de porc* (pork simmered in wine), *longeole* (unsmoked pork sausage stuffed with cabbage and fennel), *petit salé* (salt pork), tripe, and *boudin noir* (rich, rosy-brown blood pudding).

Prices at the top spots can be dry-mouth high, but—as in most Swiss cities—you'll save considerably by choosing a prix-fixe menu or a lunchtime *plat du jour*. It is possible to eat well at even the plainest corner bistro, but if you want to splurge, starting with truffles and foie gras, ending with *poire William* (a pear-based eau-de-vie), and plumbing the depths of great French-Swiss wine lists, there's no limit to what you can spend here.

Museums
Privately sponsored collections of contemporary works, French painting, primitive art, and Asian ceramics complement Geneva's six impressive (and free) public art and history museums. The Palais des Nations, still 100% functional as the European seat of the United Nations, is a living museum of 20th-century history. The Musée International de la Croix-Rouge (International Red Cross Museum) puts modern conflict and its aftermath into uncomfortable perspective.

Neighborhoods
The well-preserved cobbled streets of the *Vieille Ville* (Old Town) are captivating, but many of the city's less prominent areas are also worth a visit. Sailboats line the Left Bank *quais*; Little Spain, Portugal, and Lebanon coexist with red-light zones between the *gare* and the rue des Pâquis; and 19th-century mansions surround rue François-Le Fort. Carouge, to the south, is full of artists and craftspeople, and the university there activity revolves around the Plaine de Plainpalais.

Shopping
Many of Geneva's stores and galleries are devoted to those with deep pockets. The rue du Rhône alternates Gucci and Valentino with diamond-studded watches and jewels; the Old Town bulges with leather-bound books, antiques, designer furniture, and exclusive galleries.

EXPLORING GENEVA

The canton of Geneva pads the southwestern tip of Lac Léman, then bulges farther west into France. The city itself follows the lake as it narrows into the River Rhône. The two halves of this bisected center—Rive Droite (Right Bank, on the north side) and Rive Gauche (Left Bank, to the south)—have distinct personalities. The Old Town, the main shopping streets, and two-thirds of Geneva's museums fill the historic Rive Gauche. The Rive Droite includes the International Area and many handsome hotels. Most of the main neighborhoods are easily explored on foot; the International Area, on the northern edge of the city, is a short bus or cab ride from downtown.

Numbers in the text correspond to numbers in the margin and on the Geneva map.

When it Comes to Getting Local Currency at an ATM, Same Thing.

Whether you're in Yosemite or Yemen, using your Visa® card or ATM card with the PLUS symbol is the easiest and most convenient way to get local currency. For example, let's say you're in France. When you make a withdrawal, using your secured PIN, it's dispensed in francs, but is debited from your account in U.S. dollars. This makes it easy to take advantage of favorable exchange rates. And if you need help finding one of Visa's 627,000 ATMs in 127 countries worldwide, visit **visa.com/pd/atm**. We'll make finding an ATM as easy as finding the Eiffel Tower, the Pyramids or even the Grand Canyon.

It's Everywhere You Want To Be®

SEE THE WORLD
IN FULL COLOR

Fodor's Exploring Guides bring all the great sights vividly to life with hundreds of photographs, fascinating historical background, and colorful anecdotes. Detailed maps and practical information keep you headed in the right direction.

Pair a **Fodor's** Exploring Guide with your trusted Gold Guide for a complete planning package.

Great Itineraries

IF YOU HAVE 2 DAYS

Allow yourself an hour to stroll the city's horseshoe-shape waterfront, with its 15-ft-wide working flower clock and spectacular Jet d'Eau, then climb up into the Old Town and head for the starkly beautiful Cathédrale St-Pierre. Have lunch on place du Bourg-de-Four, then window-shop your way to the Musée d'Art et d'Histoire. The next day head for the International Area. Spend the morning at the Palais des Nations, the afternoon at the Musée International de la Croix-Rouge. Nights are for outdoor concerts (in summer) and hearty dinners with a glass or two of Genevois wine.

IF YOU HAVE 3 DAYS

Start your first day with a brief stroll along the waterfront, then head for place Neuve and the Musée Rath. Stop by the Monument de la Réformation before you climb into the Old Town. The cathedral and its archaeological site, the Auditoire de Calvin, the 14th-century Maison Tavel, the Musée Barbier-Mueller, and any number of art galleries and antiques shops will fill the afternoon. Start the next day with coffee on the place du Bourg-de-Four, then wander through the Musée d'Art et d'Histoire, the Collections Baur, and the Musée de l'Horlogerie. On your third day head north to the International Area. Spend the morning at the Palais des Nations, the afternoon at the Musée International de la Croix-Rouge, and end with a quick tour of the Musée Ariana.

IF YOU HAVE 4 DAYS

After the three days described above, devote your fourth day to museums that are off the beaten track. Spend a morning at the jewel-like Musée d'Histoire des Sciences and have lunch in the Jardin Botanique, then cross town to the cutting-edge Musée d'Art Moderne et Contemporain.

Right Bank and Left Bank

Geneva is centered on water. Grand hotels line the Right Bank, the Left Bank bristles with luxury shops, and monuments, parks, and fountains relieve the big-city bustle on both sides. Climb into the ancient, peaceful heights of the Left Bank's Vieille Ville (Old Town), and you'll find high-caliber museums, boutiques, and sidewalk cafés.

A Good Walk

Begin your walk from Cornavin, the main train station. Follow the pedestrian underpass through the shopping center below the **place de Cornavin** ① to the top of rue du Mont-Blanc, and stroll down this partially pedestrian shopping street to the lake. The view from the busy Pont du Mont-Blanc, which spans the last gasp of Lac Léman as it narrows into the Rhône, includes the entire city center and the **Jet d'Eau** ②, which spouts from March to October. Mont Blanc hovers in the distance like a sugar-dusted meringue.

Turn back to the Right Bank, make a right on rue du Mont-Blanc, and follow the plane trees down quai du Mont-Blanc, past the Belle Epoque paddle steamers operated by the Compagnie Générale de Navigation. On your left you'll see the elaborate **Monument Brunswick** ③, the tomb of Charles II, duke of Brunswick. Opposite the Hôtel Beau-Rivage, on your right, is a statue of Sissi, Empress Elisabeth of Austria, who was stabbed to death here in 1898. Follow the quay until it veers due north; on the jetty to your right are a white lighthouse and **Les Bains des Pâquis**, public beaches with a year-round sauna, changing rooms, restaurants, and protected space to swim and sunbathe. The views of the city from here are outstanding.

Head back to the Pont du Mont-Blanc and continue straight onto quai des Bergues. In the center of the river, off the pedestrians-only Pont des Bergues, the romantic **Ile Rousseau** ④ harbors a statue of its namesake and an 18th-century-style pavilion.

Cross to the middle of the pedestrian Pont de la Machine, follow either walkway around the tourist information booth, and keep to the left of the Ile de la Cité. The **Tour de l'Ile** ⑤ is the only remnant of the island's early 13th-century château.

On the Left Bank cross place Bel-Air to the historic center of the banking district, rue de la Monnaie (literally, Small Change Street). Follow the tram lines to the right, turn left onto rue de la Corraterie, and continue past the city walls that bore the brunt of the 1602 Savoyard attack. To your immediate right when you reach **place Neuve** ⑥ is the **Musée Rath** ⑦. The **Grand Théâtre**, to its right, resembles the Palais Garnier in Paris. At the far end of the square is the graceful Conservatoire de Musique.

Walk straight through the gates of the historic Parc des Bastions. To the right is the **Université de Genève**, founded by Calvin in 1559. The enormous **Monument de la Réformation** ⑧ dominates the left side of the park. Sit down on the terrace steps—made of Mont Blanc granite—to take it all in. Then keep walking toward the back of the park, exit, and turn left onto rue de St-Léger.

As you pass under a white-stone bridge and begin to climb, the present falls away and 16th-century houses ease you into the picturesque Vieille Ville (Old Town). When you reach the bottom of the tiered plateau and medieval marketplace known as **place du Bourg-de-Four** ⑨, climb the steps and angle uphill to the left on rue de l'Hôtel-de-Ville. Cut right into place de la Taconnerie. Across the street from Christie's auction house, if symbolically miles away, is the small Gothic **Auditoire de Calvin** ⑩, Geneva's 16th-century training ground for Protestant missionaries.

Circle around the back of the Romanesque-Gothic hybrid **Cathédrale St-Pierre** ⑪ and enter between the columns of its facade. The Calvinist interior is austere, but the **Chapel of the Maccabees** has been restored to neo-Gothic splendor. Climb the **north tower** for a great view of the city, then exit the cathedral and take the stairs on the left of the main doors down to the **site archéologique** ⑫. Once you've resurfaced after an underground tour of the ruins, head straight to rue du Puits-St-Pierre and Geneva's oldest house, the **Maison Tavel** ⑬, now a historical museum.

Next, turn left onto rue Calvin. Across the street from John Calvin's residence (No. 11), the **Musée Barbier-Mueller** ⑭ keeps its private collection of "primitive" art in permanent rotation. Continue down rue Calvin and turn left up rue de la Pélisserie by the plaque commemorating author George Eliot's visit to Geneva in 1849–50. Turn left again onto the Grand-Rue. The birthplace of Jean-Jacques Rousseau (No. 40) and Ferdinand Hodler's painting studio (No. 33) are tucked between designer boutiques, antiques stores, and art galleries. Follow this shopping artery to the cannons by the city's 17th-century **Arsenal**. The sober facade of the **Hôtel de Ville** ⑮, across the street, shields the seat of today's cantonal government.

Take rue de l'Hôtel-de-Ville back to place du Bourg-de-Four, cross the square, and dip down rue Etienne-Dumont. Curve left along the promenade du Pin to the **Petit Palais** ⑯, an elegant town house filled with the **Musée d'Art Moderne**'s private collection of French art.

Cross back to the intersection of rue Etienne-Dumont and promenade de St-Antoine and take the first steps down for a quick tour of the Old Town parking garage—it's built carefully around the massive remains of Geneva's medieval ramparts. Ride the elevator back up and cross the bridge to visit the **Musée d'Art et d'Histoire** ⑰. When you've exhausted its many rooms of archaeological treasures and fine paintings, exit and hang a right on rue Charles-Galland. Six gilt cupolas crown the 19th-century **Église Russe,** whose interior is decorated in neo-Byzantine style. Turn right on rue François-Lefort, left on rue Munier-Romilly. At the end of the block on the right is the **Collections Baur** ⑱, a superb private museum of Asian ceramics, jade, and lacquerware.

Return to rue Charles-Galland and follow it right to boulevard des Tranchées; turn left and head for place Émile Guyénot. The modern black-and-white building off to the right is the **Musée d'Histoire Naturelle** ⑲. Behind it, set back from route de Malagnou, is the **Musée de l'Horlogerie et de l'Émaillerie** ⑳. From here it's a quick walk back to the waterfront via rue Ferdinand-Hodler and boulevard Jaques-Dalcroze, or you can catch Bus 8 for the Right Bank.

TIMING

This orientation walk (sans museum visits) takes about three hours if followed at a steady clip. If you have time, stretch it out over a few afternoons and peruse the museums and shops. Note that many museums close on Monday.

Sights to See

✎ *following the text of a review is your signal that the property has a Web site, where you will find details and, usually, images; for a link, visit www.fodors.com/urls.*

⑩ **Auditoire de Calvin** (Protestant Lecture Hall). John Calvin founded his academy here in 1559 and taught missionaries his doctrines of radical puritanical reform. Protestant refugees from around Europe also gathered to worship in this sober Gothic chapel. Calvin encouraged his followers to hold services in their native English, Italian, Spanish, German, and Dutch. From 1556 to 1559, the Scots reformer John Knox preached here as well. Today the Auditoire is shared by the Church of Scotland, the Dutch Reformed Community, and the Waldensian Church of Italy. The Church of Scotland welcomes visitors to its Sunday-morning service at 11. ✉ *1 pl. de la Taconnerie,* ☎ *022/3118533.* 🎫 *Free.* ⊙ *Mon.–Sat. 10–noon and 2–5.*

★ ⑪ **Cathédrale St-Pierre** (St. Peter's Cathedral). Construction of this towering cathedral began in 1160 and lasted 150 years, by which time the Romanesque structure had acquired Gothic accents. The massive neoclassical facade was added in 1750. The interior is generally quite austere, as it was stripped of its colorful frescoes in 1536. However, the lavish 15th-century **Chapel of the Maccabees,** to the right of the main entrance, was restored to pre-Calvinist glory in 1875, and the contrast between its decoration and the nave's stern beauty speaks volumes about Calvin's influence. The panoramic view from the **north tower** (to the left at the far end of the nave) is worth the climb. ✉ *cour St-Pierre,* ☎ *022/3117575.* 🎫 *North tower 3 SF.* ⊙ *Oct.–May, Mon.–Sat. 10–noon and 2–5, Sun. 11–12:30 and 1:30–5; June–Sept., daily 9–7.*

★ ⑱ **Collections Baur.** Swiss collector Alfred Baur bought this quiet, graceful mansion to house his collection of Far Eastern art—Switzerland's largest—shortly before his death in 1951. Today well-conceived temporary exhibits span more than 10 centuries of Asian art, displaying delicate jades and rose and celadon porcelains from China, medieval Japanese stoneware, elaborate sword fittings, and exquisite Japanese

Geneva (Genève)

Rue Louis Favre

Rue de la Servette

Rue des Grottes

Rue du Jura

Rue de Lyon

Rue Voltaire

Rue Jean-Dassier

Rue de Malatrex

Rue de Mandement

James-Fazy

Rue Necker

Pl. de
Cornavin

Rue Pradier

**Gare de
Cornavin** ➊

**Basilique
Notre Dame**

Rue du Mont-Bla

Place
des
22
Cantons

R. de Chantepoulet

Rue des-Terreaux-de-Temple

Rue de Cornavin

Rue J.-J.-Rousseau

Rue du C

R. des
Corps-Saints

Rue du
R. Grenus

Place
Grenus

Rue des Étuves

Quai des

R. A. Vallin

R. du Temple

Place
St. Gervais

➎

Pont de l'Ile

Rhône

i
Machine

Quai des Forces Motrices

Pl. des
Voluntaires

Quai de la Poste

Rue du Stand

Pl.
Bel-Air

Rue du

Rue
Confé

Rue du Stand

Rue des Rois

Rue de l'Arquebuse

Blvd. Georges-Favon

Synagogue

Rue François-Diday

R. de la Cité

R. de
la Tertasse

Graf

*Cimetière
de
Plainpalais*

R. Hesse

Blvd. du Théâtre

Rue de la Corraterie

Rue de

Blvd. de St.-Georges

Pl. du
Cirque

R. Bovy-Lysburg

Calame

Rue du Général-Dufour

Grand Théâtre

Pl.
Neuve

Rampe

Rue du Vieux-Billard

Rue des Bains

Av. du Mail

Rue
Gourgas

➏

**Conservatoire
de Genève**

Promenade des Ba

Rue

N

Blvd. Georges-Favon

Blvd. Conseil-Général

**Musée d'Art Moderne
et Contemporain
& Centre d'art
Contemporain**

*Plaine
de
Plainpalais*

Rue
De-Candolle

**Universi
de Gene**

Rue des
Vieux-Grenadiers

KEY

i Tourist Information

Tram Line

0   220 yards

0   200 meters

Université

Rond-Point
de Plainpalais

Blvd. de
Philos-
ophies

Rue St Ours

B

➐

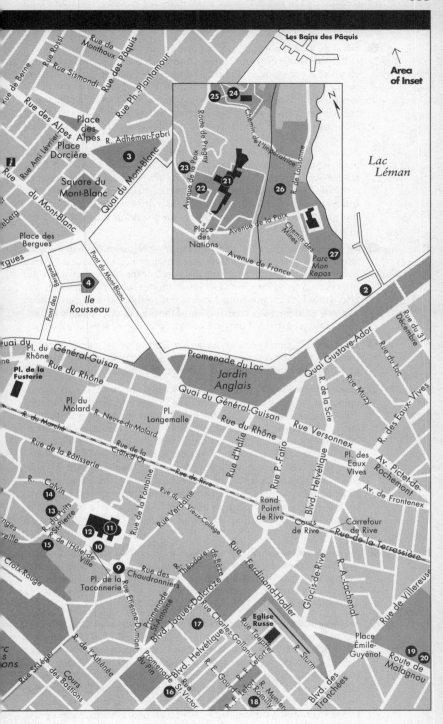

Les Bains des Pâquis

↑
Area of Inset

Rue de Monthoux
Rue de Rossi
Rue de Berne
Rue Sismondi
Rue des Pâquis
Rue Ph.-Plantamour
Rue Ami Lévrier
Place des Alpes
Place Dorcière
R. Adhémar-Fabri
3
Square du Mont-Blanc
Quai du Mont-Blanc
du Mont-Blanc
i
Rue
erg
Route de Pregny
Route de la Paix
Chemin de l'Impératrice
Chemin de Lausanne
Lac Léman
Avenue de la Paix
Avenue de la Paix
Avenue des Mines
25 **24**
23
22 **21**
26
Place des Nations
Chemin des Mines
Avenue de France
Parc Mon Repos
27
2

Place des Bergues
rgues
Pont des Bergues
Pont du Mont-Blanc
4
Ile Rousseau
uai du Rhône
Pl. du Rhône
Général-Guisan
Pl. de la Fusterie
Rue du Rhône
Pl. du Molard
R. du Marché
R. Neuve-du-Molard
Pl. Longemalle
Promenade du Lac
Jardin Anglais
Quai du Général-Guisan
Rue du Rhône
Quai Gustave-Ador
R. de la Scie
Rue Muzy
Rue du lac
Rue des Eaux-Vives
Rue Versonnex
Rue de la Rôtisserie
Rue de la Croix-d'Or
Rue de Rive
Rue de la Fontaine
Rue du Vieux-Collège
Rue Verdaine
Rue d'Italie
Rue P.-Fatio
Blvd. Helvétique
Pl. des Eaux Vives
Av. Pictet-de-Rochemont
Av. de Frontenex
R. Calvin
14
13
R. du Puits
R. St-Pierre
R. de l'Hôtel-de-Ville
12 **11**
15
10
9
Pl. de la Taconnerie
Rue des Chaudronniers
R. Théodore-de-Bèze
Rond-Point de Rive
Cours de Rive
Carrefour de Rive
Rue de la Terrassière
Rue Ferdinand-Hodler
Glacis-de-Rive
R.-A.-Lachenal
Rue de Villereuse
Promenade St-Antoine
Blvd. Jaques-Dalcroze
Rue Charles-Galland
17
Rue Etienne-Dumont
Croix-Rouge
R. de l'Athénée
Promenade du Pin
Blvd. Helvétique
R. E. Gourd
R. F. Lefort
R. F. Lefort
Rue St-Victor
16
Eglise Russe
Rue Toepffer
R. Sturm
Lefort
R. Munier
R. Romilly
18
Place Émile-Guyénot
Route de Malagnou
Blvd. des Tranchées
19 **20**
Rue St-Léger
Cours des Bastions
c
s
ons

lacquer boxes. General texts in English introduce each room. ⊠ *8 rue Munier-Romilly,* ☎ *022/3461729.* ☎ *5 SF.* ☉ *Tues.–Sun. 2–6.*

⓯ Hôtel de Ville (Town Hall). The government of the Canton of Geneva still inhabits this elegant vaulted compound, but the horses and sedan chairs that once clogged the cobbled ramp to the State Council Chamber on the third floor have disappeared. The oldest part of the building, the **Tour Baudet** (Baudet Tower), dates from 1455. But the star is the **Alabama Hall,** which became the birthplace of the human rights movement and the International Red Cross when 16 countries signed the first Geneva Convention here on August 22, 1864. The League of Nations convened its first Assembly in the hall on November 15, 1920, and it is still used for official functions. (In case you're wondering about the un-Swiss name, the hall was named after the ship at the center of a British-American dispute that was settled here in 1872.) The tourist office (☞ Geneva A to Z, *below*) works a brief visit into its weekday-morning walking tour of the Old Town whenever possible. ⊠ *2 rue de l'Hôtel-de-Ville.*

❹ Ile Rousseau. The liberal 18th-century philosopher Jean-Jacques Rousseau was the son of a Genevois watchmaker. He praised Geneva in his writings on education and politics, but the conservative city did not take kindly to his views. His statue on this former city bastion was effectively hidden, positioned facing out to the lake and surrounded by trees, until the 1861 construction of the pont du Mont-Blanc (Mont-Blanc Bridge) provided the perfect sight line. ⊠ *Off pont des Bergues.*

❷ Jet d'Eau. Originally a safety valve for Geneva's water supply system, Europe's tallest fountain gushes 140 m (460 ft) into the air over the Left Bank between March and October. ⊠ *Off quai Gustave-Ador.*

★ **⓭ Maison Tavel** (Tavel House). Geneva's oldest house traces the development of the city's urban life from 1334 to the 19th century. The vaulted cellars and the ground-floor kitchens display medieval graffiti, local coins, 15th-century tiles, and a guillotine. Seventeenth-century ironwork, doors, and other fragments of long-demolished Genevois houses fill the first floor; the second floor recreates a bourgeois home complete with 18th-century wallpaper. In the attic you'll find the Magnin Model, an enormous replica of Geneva as it looked before the city walls came down in 1850. Temporary exhibits rotate through the basement, such as a show of photographs of the city dating back to the mid-19th century. ⊠ *6 rue du Puits-St-Pierre,* ☎ *022/3102900.* ☎ *Free.* ☉ *Tues.–Sun. 10–5.* ✎

❸ Monument Brunswick. Charles II, the famously eccentric duke of Brunswick, died in Geneva in 1873 and left his fortune to the city with instructions that his tomb be given prominence and modeled on the Scaligeri mausoleum in Verona. ⊠ *Bounded by rue des Alpes, quai du Mont-Blanc, and rue Adhémar-Fabri.*

★ **❽ Monument de la Réformation** (Wall of the Reformers). Conceived on a grand scale—it measures 100 m (325 ft) long and 10 m (30 ft) high—this monument, a phalanx of enormous granite statues, pays homage to the 16th-century religious movement spearheaded by Guillaume Farel, John Calvin, Théodore de Bèze, and John Knox. Their solemn 15-ft-tall likenesses are flanked by smaller statues of major Protestant figures, bas-reliefs, and inscriptions connected with the Reformation. Oliver Cromwell is surrounded by bas-reliefs of the Pilgrim fathers praying on the deck of the *Mayflower* and the 1689 presentation of the Bill of Rights to King William III by the English Houses of Parliament. The Reformation's—and Geneva's—motto, Post Tenebras Lux (After Darkness, Light), spreads over the whole. ⊠ *Parc des Bastions.*

★ ⑰ **Musée d'Art et d'Histoire** (Museum of Art and History). The city's huge archaeology, fine-arts, and applied-arts collections moved from the over-crowded Musée Rath to this custom-built museum in 1910. Among the noteworthy holdings are the Egyptian art collection, the largest in Switzerland, and the finely crafted Escalade-era weapons. The fine-art collection includes the 15th-century *Miracle of the Fishes,* by Swiss painter Konrad Witz, in which Christ paces the waters of a recogniz-able Lake Geneva, an impressive array of Alpine landscapes, and a rich range of contemporary art. Plans are afoot to add several new galleries of classic musical instruments in 2001. ✉ *2 rue Charles-Galland,* ☎ *022/4182600.* ☞ *Free.* ☉ *Tues.–Sun. 10–5.* ☜

OFF THE
BEATEN PATH

MUSÉE D'ART MODERNE ET CONTEMPORAIN (Museum of Modern and Contemporary Art; MAMCO). Concrete factory floors and fluorescent lighting frame this gritty collection of mind-stretching, post-1965 art. The building's spare, bleak lines highlight permanent displays of work by Jenny Holzer, Sol Le Witt, Nam June Paik, Dennis Oppenheim, and Jean-Michel Basquiat. Take Bus 1 (direction Rive) from the train station to the École de Médécine. Walk back one block and turn left down rue des Vieux-Grenadiers. The entrance is the last doorway on the right. Back-ground information in English is available upon request for the many temporary exhibits. ✉ *10 rue des Vieux-Grenadiers,* ☎ *022/3206122.* ☞ *9 SF.* ☉ *Wed.–Sun. noon–6, Tues. noon–9.*

CENTRE D'ART CONTEMPORAIN (Center for Contemporary Art). Geneva's Kunsthalle (art institute) has been encouraging new work and organiz-ing exhibits by cutting-edge international contemporary artists since it opened in 1974. Its shows have included work by Cindy Sherman, Kiki Smith, Robert Mapplethorpe, Nan Goldin, Pippilotti Rist, and Tony Oursler; there is a parallel program of performances and lectures. The center is in the same former factory as MAMCO (☞ *above*). ✉ *10 rue des Vieux-Grenadiers,* ☎ *022/3291842.* ☞ *4 SF.* ☉ *Tues.–Sun. 11–6.*

★ ⑭ **Musée Barbier-Mueller.** Josef Mueller began to acquire fine "primitive" art from Africa, Oceania, Southeast Asia, and the Americas in 1907; today his family's vast, inspired collection of sculpture, masks, shields, textiles, and ornaments spans six continents and seven millennia. A small selection is on view at any given time, displayed like jewels in this warm, spotlighted vault of scrubbed stone. Three downstairs galleries are de-voted to pre-Columbian America, Africa, and Southeast Asia. ✉ *10 rue Calvin,* ☎ *022/3120270.* ☞ *5 SF.* ☉ *Daily 11–5.*

☁ ⑲ **Musée d'Histoire Naturelle** (Museum of Natural History). Local school groups enthusiastically support this museum; it is overrun with kids, even on weekends. Large, evocative wildlife dioramas complete with sound effects are the biggest draw for young children; older kids can study the evolution of man, precious stones, Swiss geology, exotic birds, or the his-tory of the solar system. Gigantic crystals, a case full of polyhedrons, beehives, *Tyrannosaurus rex* footprints, and a multimedia display on plate tectonics round out the collection. All labels are in French. ✉ *1 rte. de Malagnou,* ☎ *022/4186300.* ☞ *Free.* ☉ *Tues.–Sun. 9:30–5.*

⑳ **Musée de l'Horlogerie et de l'Émaillerie** (Museum of Watchmaking and Enameling). The permanent collections here include exquisite timepieces from as far back as 1550, many crafted in Geneva. There's also a re-production of a watchmaker's workshop, an assortment of ornate music boxes, and intricate enameled watchcases. One display traces the history of timekeeping from the sundial to the wristwatch. Fittingly, the Palladian-style villa echoes with clock chimes every hour. ✉ *15 rte. de Malagnou,* ☎ *022/4186470.* ☞ *Free.* ☉ *Wed.–Mon. 10–5.*

★ **❼ Musée Rath.** Switzerland's original fine-arts museum, inaugurated in 1826 and named for its late benefactor, Simon Rath, housed Geneva's growing collections of art and archaeology until they overflowed to the Musée d'Art et d'Histoire (☞ *above*) in 1910. Now the Rath hosts three temporary exhibitions of archaeology and contemporary art each year. Upcoming shows include a major archaeological survey of Ostia, the port of Rome (spring 2001). ✉ *pl. Neuve,* ☎ *022/4183340.* 🎟 *Up to 10 SF, depending on the exhibit.* ⊙ *Tues. and Thurs.–Sun. 10–5, Wed. noon–9.* 🐾

⓰ Petit Palais–Musée d'Art Moderne (Museum of Modern Art). In this Second Empire–style mansion, a collection of French art tracks the evolution of modernism from 1870 to 1930. The École de Paris, pointillism, and cubism are well represented; Caillebotte's *Pont de l'Europe* is one of the stars. Works by Chagall, Foujita, Kisling, de Lempicka, Picasso, Renoir, Tarkhoff, and Van Dongen round out the permanent collection. Up to three temporary exhibits are held each year. ✉ *2 terrasse St-Victor,* ☎ *022/3461433.* 🎟 *10 SF.* ⊙ *Weekdays 10–6, weekends 10–5.*

❶ Place de Cornavin. The train station anchors this Right Bank transportation hub. Here you can catch a tram to Carouge, pick up a cab, or get on a bus to the airport, the Left Bank, or the International Area (☞ *below*). ✉ *Top of rue du Mont-Blanc.*

★ **❾ Place du Bourg-de-Four.** Vestiges of the ancient roads that led south to Annecy and Lyon and east to Italy and the Chablais are still visible in this layered Old Town square. Once a Roman cattle market, later flooded with Protestant refugees, it is still the quintessential Genevois crossroads. Shoppers, lawyers, workers, and students strike a delicate balance between scruffy bohemia, genteel tradition, and slick gentrification as they meet for drinks around an 18th-century fountain. ✉ *Intersection of rue Verdaine, rue des Chaudronniers, rue Étienne-Dumont, and rue de l'Hôtel-de-Ville.*

NEED A
BREAK?

La Clémence (✉ 20 pl. du Bourg-de-Four, ☎ 022/3122498), an old and much-loved sidewalk café named for the largest of the cathedral bells, serves its breakfast *tartines* (baguettes with butter and jelly) and coffee in the middle of the busy square.

❻ Place Neuve. Aristocratic town houses overlook Geneva's opera house, the Musée Rath (☞ *above*), the Conservatoire de Musique, and the wrought-iron entrance to the Parc des Bastions. The proud statue at the center of the square honors General Guillaume-Henri Dufour, four-time leader of Switzerland's federal army and a key figure in the 1847 Sonderbund separatist conflict. ✉ *Intersection of blvd. du Théâtre, rue de la Corraterie, rue de la Croix-Rouge, and rue Bartholoni.*

★ ⛱ **⓬ Site archéologique.** Archaeologists found layer upon layer of ancient remains underneath St. Peter's Cathedral (☞ *above*) when its foundations began to falter in 1976. Excavations have so far yielded remnants of two 4th-century Christian sanctuaries, mosaic floors from the late Roman Empire, portions of three early churches, and an 11th-century crypt. The first Romanesque cathedral on this site was erected in 1000; today audioguides in English and careful lighting explain the (reinforced) underground maze that remains. ✉ *Cour St-Pierre,* ☎ *022/3117575.* 🎟 *5 SF.* ⊙ *June–Sept., Tues.–Sat. 11–5, Sun. 10–5; Oct.–May, Tues.–Sat. 2–5, Sun. 10–noon and 2–5.*

❺ Tour de l'Ile. The lone surviving fragment of Bishop Aymon de Grandson's 13th-century fortified château served as a prison during the Reformation. It is not open to the public. ✉ *Pont de l'Ile.*

International Area

Along the northern edge of the city, 10 minutes by car or bus from the pont du Mont-Blanc, is Geneva's humanitarian and diplomatic zone, with the Palais des Nations as its core. Modern office buildings for branches of the UN are threaded between 19th-century villas, which house nongovernmental organizations, embassies, and a handful of museums.

A Good Walk

Take Bus 8 (direction OMS) from the train station to place des Nations. Get off here for a good look at the front of the **Palais des Nations** ㉑, European headquarters of the United Nations, then walk up avenue de la Paix to the visitors' entrance (stay on the bus until the next stop, Appia, if you'd rather skip the walk uphill). The Italianate palace set back from the road on your right is the **Musée Ariana** ㉒, home to the Musée Suisse de la Céramique et du Verre. The **Musée International de la Croix-Rouge** ㉓, a fiercely moving museum that traces the history of humanitarian assistance, lies directly opposite the visitors' entrance to the Palais.

Avenue de la Paix becomes route de Pregny as it continues up the hill past one of the three campuses of the International School of Geneva, on the right, and the American Mission to the UN, on the left. Turn right on chemin de l'Impératrice to the Château de Penthes. The peaceful grounds of this 19th-century mansion are open to the public; the building itself houses the **Musée des Suisses à l'Étranger** ㉔, a permanent exhibit focused on the Swiss people outside Switzerland. The **Musée Militaire Genevois** ㉕, set in one of the Château's former stables, traces local military history.

Continue along chemin de l'Impératrice as it winds toward the leafy **Jardin Botanique** ㉖; you'll find the gardens spread out on both sides of the road just after a small underpass. Enter by the main gate, on the right, and wander past pink flamingos, greenhouses, and huge trees to the exit gate at place Alfred-Thomas. Cross the busy intersection and follow rue de Lausanne to the right. Enter the **Parc Mon Repos** through the gate to the left of the Perle du Lac restaurant, and head straight for the **Musée d'Histoire des Sciences** ㉗. This museum, in the stunning Villa Bartholoni, has a backdrop of breathtaking views. Bus 4–44 will take you back to the train station from here, or you can stroll through the gardens toward the quai Wilson and the center of town.

TIMING

You can easily devote a full day to this part of town—there's a lot of territory, both literal and figurative, to cover. Be sure to wear your walking shoes, check opening times in advance, and balance the museum shuffle with brisk walks in the fresh air.

Sights to See

🦢 ㉖ **Jardin Botanique** (Botanical Garden). These 69 restful acres are a legacy of Geneva's 19th century fascination with botany. The arboretum harbors trees that predate 1700; there are also an aviary, a deer park, a rose garden, and a seed bank. Exotic hothouses, Alpine rock plants, and an area devoted to scent and touch are highlights. ⊠ *1 chemin de l'Impératrice,* ☎ *022/4185100.* 🎫 *Free.* ⊙ *Apr.–Sept., daily 8–7:30; Oct.–Mar., daily 9:30–5.*

★ ㉒ **Musée Ariana.** This superb Italianate palace, built in 1884, is now home to the Musée Suisse de la Céramique et du Verre (Swiss Museum of Ceramics and Glass). Its enormous collections of stoneware, earthenware, porcelain, and glass span seven centuries, emphasizing the exchange of styles and techniques between East and West. Head to the basement to see temporary exhibits on contemporary ceramics. ⊠ *10 av. de la Paix,* ☎ *022/4185450.* ☞ *Free.* ☉ *Wed.–Mon. 10–5.* ☙

★ ㉗ **Musée d'Histoire des Sciences** (Museum of the History of Science). Age-old sun dials, astrolabes, microscopes, globes, and barometers are displayed like jewels in walk-around glass cases here. This is Switzerland's only museum to document the evolution of modern science; the exquisite neoclassical building, the Villa Bartholoni, dates from 1828. ⊠ *128 rue de Lausanne,* ☎ *022/4185060.* ☞ *Free.* ☉ *Wed.–Mon. 1–5.* ☙

★ ☾ ㉓ **Musée International de la Croix-Rouge** (International Red Cross Museum). State-of-the-art technology illuminates human kindness in the face of disaster in this painstakingly nonjudgmental museum set in a custom-built bunker. Powerful statues of bound, hooded figures guard the glass-and-concrete entryway; the exhibits within are balanced but often grim.

Audiovisuals show the postbattle horrors at Solferino that moved Henri Dunant to form the Red Cross. There are endless aisles of file boxes filled with seven million records of World War I prisoners. In a replica of a 3 m–by–2 m (10 ft–by–6½ ft) concrete cell, 34 footprints make the conditions for its 17 political prisoners poignantly clear. But good deeds are also dramatized, from that of the proverbial Samaritan to those of Clara Barton. Samples from modern aid efforts include disaster relief kits and snapshots used to reunite Rwandan families after the 1994 genocide.

The **Mur du Temps** (Wall of Time), a simple time line punctuated by wars and natural disasters that have each killed more than 100,000 people, puts the overall story into sobering perspective. The earthquakes, volcanic eruptions, and plagues of distant history give way to ever-deadlier wars in the modern era. Guided tours and museum literature are available in English. ⊠ *17 av. de la Paix,* ☎ *022/7489525; 022/ 7489506 for tour reservations.* ☞ *10 SF.* ☉ *Wed.–Mon. 10–5.* ☙

㉕ **Musée Militaire Genevois** (Geneva Military Museum). Switzerland may not have waged war outside its borders since 1292, but the military has not been idle. The weapons, uniforms, flags, and documents on display in this former stable tell the colorful story of Genevois soldiers from 1813 to the present. ⊠ *18 chemin de l'Impératrice,* ☎ *022/ 7349021.* ☞ *Free.* ☉ *Apr.–Dec., Wed.–Sat. 2–5, Sun. 10–noon and 2–5; Jan.–Mar., weekends 2–5.*

㉔ **Musée des Suisses à l'Étranger** (Museum of Swiss Citizens Abroad). The ivy-covered **Château de Penthes** bulges with documents, models, paintings, and objects set in ornate 19th-century rooms, illustrating Switzerland's relations with the outside world from the 13th century to the present. Displays on the Swiss Guards dominate the first and second floors. The third covers Swiss artists, inventors, archaeologists, chocolatiers, and even the Genevois pathologist who performed President Kennedy's autopsy. ⊠ *18 chemin de l'Impératrice,* ☎ *022/ 7349021.* ☞ *5 SF.* ☉ *Apr.–Dec., Tues.–Sun. 10–noon and 2–6; Jan.–Mar., weekends 10–noon and 2–5, Tues.–Fri. by request.*

NEED A
BREAK?

Have a generous plat du jour or a slice of homemade fruit tart on the summer terrace at **Cent Suisses** (⊠ 18 chemin de l'Impératrice, ☎ 022/ 7344865), a lunch-only spot on the grounds of the Château de Penthes.

★ ㉑ **Palais des Nations** (Palace of Nations). This monumental compound was built between 1929 and 1936 for the League of Nations; it became the European branch of the United Nations in 1946. Today the

Palais is the largest center for multilateral diplomacy in the world—it hosts some 7,000 conferences and 25,000 delegates each year—and the largest nexus for United Nations operational activities after New York. The group of five architects who won permission to design the original building in 1926 followed a style that has, ironically, come to be known as fascist; they created a superb example of the severe blend of art deco and stylized classicism that Mussolini and Hitler favored.

You'll need to show your passport and join a tour to see the interior of the Palais. Its interwar architectural details are preserved intact. High points include the **Assembly Hall,** the largest of the 34 conference rooms, where the UN General Assembly and scores of world leaders have met, and the ornate **Council Chamber,** home to the Conference on Disarmament, which glows with allegorical murals by Catalan artist José Maria Sert. Some conferences allow members of the public to attend their sessions. Tours last about an hour and are given in English. There are no set starting times.

The Museum of the League of Nations and the United Nations Philatelic Museum are quartered in the Palais as well. Admission to both collections is included in the general entrance fee, and their hours are the same as the Palais's. The Palais also hosts temporary exhibitions and film screenings; the literature in the UN bookstore covers everything from world hunger to peacekeeping. ⊠ *14 av. de la Paix,* ☎ *022/ 9074896.* ⌑ *8.50 SF.* ☉ *Apr.–June and Sept.–Oct., daily 10–noon and 2–4; July–Aug., daily 10–5; Nov.–Mar., weekdays 10–noon and 2–4.* ✍

DINING

Geneva's restaurants, regardless of their cultural leanings, take advantage of seasonal produce; menus change three or four times a year. Most kitchens offer lunchtime plats du jour that allow you to dine for a reasonable price, even at expensive establishments. Be sure to plan ahead: many of the top spots close on weekends, and it's a good idea to make reservations wherever you go.

CATEGORY	COST*
$$$$	over 90 SF
$$$	60 SF–90 SF
$$	30 SF–60 SF
$	under 30 SF

Prices are per person for a three-course meal (two-course meal in $ category), excluding drinks, sales tax, and 15% service charge.

$$$$ ✕ **Le Béarn.** French chef Jean-Paul Goddard has been building his restaurant's reputation for modern, light, and creative seasonal cuisine since 1979. Duck-breast carpaccio with apricot chutney, rabbit with sage, subtle but sweet tarragon sorbet, and a spectacular truffle soufflé are highlights. Be sure to consider the dessert cart and the French-Swiss wine list. The warm, sunken Empire-style dining room fills with bankers at midday. ⊠ *4 quai de la Poste,* ☎ *022/3210028. AE, DC, MC, V. Oct.–Apr., closed Sun., no lunch Sat. May–Sept., closed weekends.*

$$$$ ✕ **Le Chat Botté.** Richard Cressac's kitchen does not stray far from the French classics, but it does them well. Foie gras with truffles, Bresse chicken, veal in cream sauce, and warm chocolate pear tart are served in a discreet, understated dining room or, for the ultimate summer dining experience, on the lakefront balcony-terrace. The wine cellar is exceptional. ⊠ *13 quai du Mont-Blanc,* ☎ *022/7166920. Reservations essential. AE, DC, MC, V.*

Geneva Dining and Lodging

KEY

ℹ️ Tourist Information

— Tram Line

0   220 yards

0   200 meters

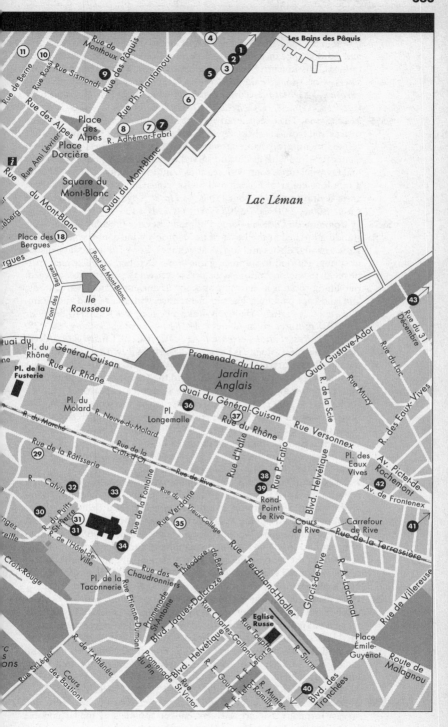

Les Bains des Pâquis

Rue de Monthoux

Rue de Berne

Rue Rossi

Rue Sismondi

Rue des Pâquis

Rue Ph. Plantamour

Place des Alpes

Rue Ami Lévrier

Place Dorcière

R. Adhémar-Fabri

Square du Mont-Blanc

Quai du Mont-Blanc

Rue du Mont-Blanc

Lac Léman

Place des Bergues

Pont des Bergues

Pont du Mont-Blanc

Ile Rousseau

Quai du Rhône

Pl. du Rhône

Général-Guisan

Rue du Rhône

Pl. de la Fusterie

Promenade du Lac

Jardin Anglais

Quai du Général-Guisan

Quai Gustave-Ador

Rue du 31 Décembre

Rue du lac

Pl. du Molard

R. Neuve-du-Molard

Pl. Longemalle

Rue du Rhône

R. de la Scie

Rue Muzy

Rue des Eaux-Vives

R. des Eaux-Vives

Rue Versonnex

R. du Marché

Rue de la Rôtisserie

Rue de la Croix-d'Or

Rue de Rive

Rue d'Italie

Rue P.-Fatio

Blvd. Helvétique

Pl. des Eaux Vives

Av. Pictet-de-Rochemont

Av. de Frontenex

R. Calvin

R. du Puits St-Pierre

R. de l'Hôtel-de-Ville

Rue de la Fontaine

Rue du Vieux-Collège

Rue Verdaine

Rond-Point de Rive

Cours de Rive

Carrefour de Rive

Rue de la Terrassière

Croix-Rouge

Pl. de la Taconnerie

Rue des Chaudronniers

R. Théodore-de-Bèze

Rue Etienne-Dumont

Promenade St-Antoine

Rue Ferdinand-Hodler

Glacis-de-Rive

R. A.-Lachenal

Rue de Villereuse

Rue St-Léger

Cours des Bastions

R. de l'Athénée

Promenade du Pin

Blvd. Jacques-Dalcroze

Rue Charles-Galland

Promenade St-Victor

Eglise Russe

Rue Toepffer

R. Sturm

R. E. Gourd

R. F. Lefort

R. F. Lefort Romilly

R. Munier

Place Émile-Guyénot

Route de Malagnou

Blvd. des Tranchées

i

11 10 9 4 1 2 3 5 6 8 7 7 18 43 29 36 37 32 33 38 39 35 34 30 31 31 42 41 40

$$$$ ✕ **Les Continents.** The dining room remains traditional—Victorian wood panels, creamy linen, chandeliers—but there is exciting new blood in the kitchen. Chef Didier Quesnel's particular yen for foie gras and seafood appears in dishes such as duck liver roasted with caramelized quinces. His inventive dessert selections could include chocolate and sweet-wine sponge cake, or cappuccino of baby bananas with mascarpone. ✉ *Hotel Intercontinental, 7–9 chemin du Petit-Saconnex,* ☎ *022/9193350. AE, DC, MC, V. Closed weekends.*

$$$$ ✕ **Le Cygne.** The exceptional view of Mont Blanc provides a welcome distraction from the slick, somewhat dated decor, but Olivier Villette's refined menu grabs your attention as soon as it arrives. Roast lamb shank flavored with garlic and served with zucchini in basil is a perennial favorite; turtle soup with scallops is more adventurous fare. There's a fabulous cellar of French and Swiss wines and a caravan of dessert carts waiting to circle your table. ✉ *Hotel Noga-Hilton, 19 quai du Mont-Blanc,* ☎ *022/9089085. AE, DC, MC, V.*

$$$$ ✕ **Domaine de Châteauvieux.** Philippe Chevrier presides over an out-
★ standing kitchen at the heart of the canton's wine country; he emphasizes seasonal dishes and top local vintages. Look for asparagus dishes in spring, seafood in summer, game come October, and a special truffle menu in winter. Antique wine presses crown the old stone courtyard; the dining room is a charming space with ancient beams, warm stone, and landscape paintings. The summer terrace, with its vineyard and mountain views, is particularly lovely. Take a boat up the Rhône to Peney or drive 10 minutes from Geneva. ✉ *Peney-Dessus, Satigny,* ☎ *022/ 7531511. Reservations essential. AE, DC, MC, V. Closed Sun.–Mon.*

$$$$ ✕ **Le Lion d'Or.** Cologny is Geneva's Beverly Hills with a view, and this
★ culinary landmark takes full advantage of its real estate—the summer terrace overlooks the city, the lake, and the Jura. Local celebrity chefs Gilles Dupont and Tommy Byrne give seafood and seasonal menus a sophisticated edge; line-caught sea bass is roasted to perfection, cardons are served au gratin with truffles. Herbs are extra fresh, as they come from a kitchen garden just below the terrace. The wood-paneled bistro next door shares the restaurant's kitchen but not its prices—grab a cab and come for lunch. ✉ *5 pl. Pierre-Gautier, Cologny,* ☎ *022/ 7364432. AE, DC, MC, V. Closed weekends.*

$$$ ✕ **La Favola.** Run by a Ticinese chef from Locarno, this quirky little
★ restaurant may be the most picturesque in town. The tiny dining room, at the top of a vertiginous spiral staircase, strikes a delicate balance between rustic and fussy, with lace curtains, embroidered tablecloths, polished parquet, and a rough-beam ceiling sponge-painted in shades of ocher and rust. The food mixes simplicity and chic: homemade pastas melt on the tongue, the carpaccio is paper-thin, and the tiramisu is divine. ✉ *15 rue Calvin,* ☎ *022/3117437. No credit cards. Closed Sun. No lunch Sat.*

$$$ ✕ **La Perle du Lac.** The dining room stays open from February to December, but this chalet-style former guesthouse in Geneva's Right Bank waterfront park comes into its own in summer. The large flowered terrace looks straight out over the lake at Mont Blanc; the Mouettes Genevoises boats dock right in front. The French-accented seasonal menu highlights fish such as *rouget barbet* (red mullet), turbot, and *cabillaud* (cod). The list of French wines is exhaustive. ✉ *126 rue de Lausanne,* ☎ *022/9091020. AE, DC, MC, V. Closed Mon. and Jan.*

$$$ ✕ **Roberto.** Roberto Carugati and his daughter, Marietta, have perfected an easy formality that lures lawyers, bankers, politicians, and fashionable Italians to their red-gold dining room. Parmesan cheese arrives in lieu of bread; the menu features eggplant carpaccio with coriander, pasta in saffron sauce, buttery sole with tarragon, and risotto served from shining copper and silver pots. Unusual and rare Italian wines loosen the elegance as the night wears on. ✉ *10 rue Pierre-Fatio,* ☎ *022/ 3118033. AE, MC, V. Closed Sun. No dinner Sat.*

$$$ ✕ **Le Vallon.** A rosy facade, lace curtains, and hanging grapevines set
★ the scene for a memorable meal at this century-old restaurant on the edge of town. Each dish, served on individually selected china, is a work of art. Everything on the menu—whether sausage, terrine, or a succulent *tarte Tatin* (caramelized apple tart) in calvados cream—is made in-house. ✉ *182 rte. de Florissant, Conches,* ☎ *022/3471104. MC, V. Closed weekends.*

$$ ✕ **Les Armures.** Everyone from street sweepers to President Clinton has come to this Old Town institution. The dining rooms have dark beams, heavy wrought iron, and authentic medieval arms; the robust Swiss menu includes fondue, raclette, *filets de perches* (perch fillets), *Schübling* (sausage), and *Rösti* (hash browns). They serve until midnight, unusually late by Geneva standards. ✉ *1 rue du Puits-St-Pierre,* ☎ *022/3103442. AE, DC, MC, V.*

$$ ✕ **Au Pied-de-Cochon.** Crowded, noisy, smoky, and gruff, this clattering white-tile bistro is anchored by its ancient beams and worn zinc bar. The simple dishes include andouillettes, boudin noir, longeole with lentils, and the namesake pigs' feet, served grilled, poached, or boned. ✉ *4 pl. du Bourg-de-Four,* ☎ *022/3104797. AE, DC, MC, V.*

$$ ✕ **Bistrot du Boeuf Rouge.** A belle epoque cash register weighs down
★ the bar, and the menu groans with rich, unadulterated Lyonnaise cuisine at this brisk, brass-accented bistro. Boudin noir with apples, homemade rillettes, andouillettes, and féra fillets are served with a light gratin *dauphinois*; the tender filet mignon barely requires a knife. Try the chestnut and citrus mousse or a silken flan *au caramel* for dessert. Each dish arrives for inspection on a decorated silver tray. ✉ *17 rue Alfred-Vincent,* ☎ *022/7327537. AE, DC, MC, V. Closed weekends.*

$$ ✕ **Bistrot du Boucher.** There's no question as to what dominates the menu here—the waiters wear butcher's aprons. The sign over the kitchen door reads BEWARE OF COW, but there's nothing to fear. Aperitifs are on the house, each dish is presented at your table prior to carving, and the steak tartare is mixed to your taste. Cow posters, figurines, and paintings add a sense of humor to the dignified art nouveau woodwork, bright tiles, and stained-glass ceiling. ✉ *15 av. Pictet-de-Rochemont,* ☎ *022/7365636. AE, MC, V. Closed Sun. No lunch Sat.*

$$ ✕ **Brasserie Lipp.** Green and white tiles, mustard-yellow ceilings,
★ warm wood, and bustling waiters in ankle-length white aprons bring this Parisian clone to life. Genevois intellectuals of all stripes linger over classic brasserie fare such as *choucroûte* (sauerkraut), veal blanquette, and heaping platters of seafood. The odd location, on the third floor of a slick shopping center, is balanced by a spectacular summer terrace at the foot of the Old Town. The kitchen stays open from noon until 12:45 AM (later than most). ✉ *Confédération-Centre, 8 rue de la Confédération,* ☎ *022/3111011. AE, DC, MC, V.*

$$ ✕ **Les Fous de la Place.** This confident spot on the edge of place Neuve pulls in trendy young professionals for ever-changing creative cuisine at reasonable prices. Asian and Middle Eastern flavors seep into the classic brasserie-style cooking; the slim red settees, saffron tasseled drapes, and scarlet cone lamps give the dining room a hint of decadence. Ask for a table on the sun-filled rooftop terrace in summer. ✉ *21 rue de la Corraterie,* ☎ *022/3105340. AE, DC, MC, V. Closed Sun.–Mon. No lunch Sat.*

$$ ✕ **Hôtel-de-Ville.** Behind its somewhat bedraggled lace curtains, this smoky, steamy brasserie packs in civil servants and art dealers, who settle onto wooden banquettes for typical Genevois *filets de perches* (perch), longeole, mussels, and beautifully garnished game platters in season. It serves until midnight. ✉ *39 Grand-Rue,* ☎ *022/3117030. AE, DC, MC, V.*

$$ ✕ **Jeck's Place.** Even by Geneva's standards, this halogen-lighted, peach-
★ accented restaurant presents a staggering mix of cultures. Owner Jeck
Tan, a native of Singapore and a graduate of the Swiss Hotel School,
greets you warmly in English at the door and presents a menu written
in Malay, Chinese, Thai, and French. The food, whether it's smooth
deep-fried bean curd with peanut sauce, chicken in a delicate green curry,
fried *mee hoon* vermicelli, or spicy roast duck *au diable*, is excellent.
The service is irreproachable. ✉ *14 rue de Neuchâtel,* ☎ *022/7313303.
AE, DC, MC, V. No lunch Sat.*

$$ ✕ **Le Lyrique.** Black-and-white floor tiles offset warm-yellow walls and
★ high wedding-cake ceilings in this relaxed café-brasserie in the heart
of Geneva's musical quarter. Portraits of Beethoven, Verdi, Strauss, and
Liszt watch as pretheater diners choose homemade pasta with scampi,
summer gazpacho, steak tartare, or one of the many alluring desserts.
Though it's normally closed on weekends, the restaurant stays open
whenever there's a performance at the Grand Théâtre, next door. ✉
12 blvd. du Théâtre, ☎ *022/3280095. AE, DC, MC, V.*

$$ ✕ **L'Opera Bouffe.** This trendy spot serves traditional bistro food with
★ a contemporary twist, courtesy of the Syrian chef. The setting is ca-
sual-chic, with wine stacked floor to ceiling and opera trilling in the
background. Don't pass up the warm *tarte Tatin* (caramelized apple
tart) with Gruyère cream. ✉ *5 av. de Frontenex,* ☎ *022/7366300. AE,
DC, MC, V. Closed Sun.–Mon. No lunch Sat.*

$$ ✕ **Le Relais de l'Entrecôte.** *Steak frites* with a pat of herb butter is served
★ in most Genevois restaurants, but the perfectly spiced *sauce maison*
and tender morsels you can expect here are truly exceptional. A crisp
green salad sprinkled with walnuts and thin, golden fries will accompany the only option on the menu; don't worry, there's a second portion on the way. A meal like this virtually requires a bottle of robust
house wine. The elegant, popular dining room is wedged between
haute couture emporia and decorated with gigantic belle epoque
posters. ✉ *49 rue du Rhône,* ☎ *022/3106004. MC, V.*

$ ✕ **Café du Grütli.** Black-clad filmmakers, actors, photographers,
dancers, and students from the nearby Université de Genève congre-
gate in this sun-soaked, smoky restaurant on the ground floor of the
Grütli arts center. Crème brûlée spiked with pistachio follows salmon
and perch carpaccio or penne with Gorgonzola and vodka, and there
are lots of daily specials. You can even soak up a bit of culture—undubbed classic films are screened in the basement, and the artwork on
the walls is for sale. ✉ *16 rue du Général-Dufour,* ☎ *022/3294495.
AE, DC, MC, V.*

$ ✕ **Chez Léo.** Intense, trendy locals descend on this tiny bentwood-and-
★ posters corner bistro for lunch, then linger over coffee. Look for a variety of homemade ravioli and tortellini, veal *piccata* in a
raspberry-vinegar or mustard sauce, and a noteworthy *tarte au citron*
(lemon tart). ✉ *9 rond-point de Rive,* ☎ *022/3115307. MC, V. Closed
Sun. No dinner Sat.*

$ ✕ **L'Echalotte.** Polished wood banquettes, good food, and low prices
★ draw local artists and journalists here; the seasonal menu stretches from
vegetarian options to abats. Buttery *crème de courge* (pumpkin soup),
the signature *onglet a l'echalotte* (steak in shallot butter), and a sinful
chocolate terrine are served promptly with casual flair. ✉ *17 rue des
Rois,* ☎ *022/3205999. MC, V. Closed weekends.*

$ ✕ **Taverne de la Madeleine.** Plain and simple, in terms of both decor
and cooking, this big, friendly Swiss canteen is a sure bet. It's got history on its side; the building dates from the 1600s. Choucroûte appears
in November and December; *filets de perches* (perch) may be had
year-round. The city's temperance league owns and operates the Tav-
erne, so it serves no alcoholic beverages, and the kitchen closes at 4

PM. ✉ *20 rue Toutes-Âmes,* ☎ *022/3106070. AE, DC, MC, V. Closed Sun. No dinner.*

$ ✕ **Le Thé.** A three-course meal at this tiny hole-in-the-wall Chinese
★ tearoom costs less than appetizers of similar quality elsewhere. The
choices, all *à la vapeur* (steamed), include succulent rice-flour crepes
stuffed with shrimp, dim sum, and steamed bread. There are more than
20 kinds of green tea alone; appropriately enough, delicate red-clay
teapots (for sale) line the walls. The six tables fill up fast—call ahead
or drop by after 1:30 for lunch. ✉ *65 rue des Bains,* ☎ *079/4367718.
No credit cards. Closed Sun.*

LODGING

Spending the night in Geneva can be financially taxing—rates are
comparable to those in most European capitals—but you'll limit the
damage if you can take advantage of special weekend or group deals.
One side effect of Geneva's popularity as a convention center is the
willingness of the hotels to drop rates at nonpeak times. Book well in
advance, since large blocks of rooms fill up during major events, and
remember that rates plummet most dramatically at luxury hotels.

CATEGORY	COST*
$$$$	over 350 SF
$$$	220 SF–350 SF
$$	140 SF–220 SF
$	under 140 SF

**Prices are for a standard double room, including breakfast, tax, and service
charge.*

✎ *following the text of a review is your signal that the property has
a Web site, where you will find details and, usually, images; for a link,
visit www.fodors.com/urls.*

$$$$ ☷ **D'Angleterre.** The balancing act between Victorian style and modern
★ amenities here is perfectly carried off. Broad satin pinstripes cover walls
and settees throughout the hotel; each hallway stocks leather-bound books
in several languages. Rooms have fine British antiques, dark green and
pale yellow accents, and wood-edged baths. Some also have balconies
with wrought-iron café tables and views of Mont Blanc. The Library bar
has a working fireplace and live jazz Thursday through Saturday; Tea
Roux, the spectacular winter-garden restaurant, serves light meals and
afternoon tea. ✉ *17 quai du Mont-Blanc, CH-1201,* ☎ *022/9065555,*
FAX *022/9065556. 39 rooms, 6 suites. Restaurant, bar, in-room safes, minibars, sauna, exercise room, meeting rooms. AE, DC, MC, V.*

$$$$ ☷ **Les Armures.** Original 17th-century stonework, frescoes, painted
beams, and tapestries adorn the lobby and some rooms in this low-key
hotel at the heart of the Vieille Ville. You can count on marble baths,
thick bathrobes, somber antiques, cable TV, and individual modem connections in each room. Two very quiet rooms give onto a tiny inner courtyard; those overlooking rue du Perron have picturesque cobblestone views.
✉ *1 rue du Puits-St-Pierre, CH-1204,* ☎ *022/3109172,* FAX *022/3109846.
24 rooms, 4 suites. Restaurant, bar. AE, DC, MC, V.* ✎

$$$$ ☷ **Beau-Rivage.** Hushed and genteel, this grand old Victorian palace
maintains much of its original splendor. The building centers on a four-
story atrium with a murmuring fountain. Rooms have period furniture, dramatic swagged fabrics, enormous baths, and a pervading sense
of romance. Front rooms overlook the Jet d'Eau and Mont Blanc; all
have 19th-century architectural details. The Mayer family's warm hospitality has made the hotel a Geneva landmark—their guest list since
1865 has included Richard Wagner, Jean Cocteau, and Sissi, Empress

Elisabeth of Austria. ✉ *13 quai du Mont-Blanc, CH-1201,* ☎ *022/ 7166666,* FAX *022/7166060. 91 rooms, 6 suites. 2 restaurants, piano bar, in-room safes, minibars, no-smoking rooms, meeting rooms. AE, DC, MC, V.*

$$$$ 🏨 **Des Bergues.** Creamy fabrics, graceful statues, and unpretentious, ★ friendly service give the oldest and least self-conscious of Geneva's grand hotels an inner glow. Guests are seated in the low-key marble lobby to register as if they were shopping for jewels. The Louis-Philippe elegance, crystal chandeliers, 1834 architectural details, and luxurious marble bathrooms mesh seamlessly with modern conveniences such as private fax machines and modem connections in all rooms. You can even request an aquarium for your suite. The sunny Le Pavillon restaurant serves a extraordinary afternoon tea. ✉ *33 quai des Bergues, CH-1201,* ☎ *022/9087000,* FAX *022/9087090. 107 rooms, 15 suites. 2 restaurants, bar, meeting rooms, beauty salon, baby-sitting, laundry service, parking (fee). AE, DC, MC, V.*

$$$$ 🏨 **President Wilson.** There's no trace of hotel hush in this expansive ★ hotel (yes, named for Woodrow). Huge, fragrant flower arrangements punctuate the public areas; 17th-century tapestries, colorful paintings, and Greco-Roman stonework balance green marble floors, sleek wood, and comfortable chairs throughout. Many of the stylish, modern rooms take in sweeping views of the lake, Cologny, or the French Alps. The heated outdoor swimming pool is a rare treat in the middle of the city. ✉ *47 quai Wilson, CH-1211,* ☎ *022/9066666,* FAX *022/9066667. 206 rooms, 30 suites. 3 restaurants, lobby lounge, piano bar, no-smoking rooms, pool, beauty salon, spa, health club, meeting rooms, business services, parking (fee). AE, DC, MC, V.*

$$$$ 🏨 **Le Richemond.** Crimson satin and velvet, fringed braid, moiré, lush floral carpets, pastel silks, and 18th-century antiques make this opulent, slightly stuffy 1875 landmark feel like a movie set. The place is for real, though, and it's not stuck in the past: all of the luxurious rooms have Internet access and voice mail. Individual balconies overlook the Brunswick Monument; Rolls-Royces angle for space outside. Famous guests have included Colette, Charlie Chaplin, and Marc Chagall. ✉ *Jardin Brunswick, CH-1201,* ☎ *022/7157000,* FAX *022/7157001. 67 rooms, 31 suites. Restaurant, piano bar, beauty salon, exercise room, meeting rooms. AE, DC, MC, V.*

$$$$ 🏨 **Swissôtel Genève Métropole.** The city owns this imposing 1854 Left Bank palace, now separated by six lanes of traffic from its former estate, but Swissôtel is in charge of the current steady renovation. Half the hotel will be finished by 2001. Each new bathroom has a television perched in a watertight alcove and a shower as well as a bathtub. All windows are triple-glazed to ensure silence. Massive scrubbed-stone arches give the place a grand air, but the ambience is relaxed and unfussy. High-voltage rue du Rhône shopping is literally just outside, and the wraparound view from the roof is the envy of the city during Fêtes de Genève fireworks. ✉ *34 quai Général-Guisan, CH-1204,* ☎ *022/ 3183200,* FAX *022/3183300. 115 rooms, 13 suites. Restaurant, piano bar, meeting rooms. AE, DC, MC, V.*

$$$ 🏨 **Ambassador.** Don't let the airport lounge–style lobby fool you— ★ each room in this central Right Bank hotel is fresh, colorful, and full of natural light. Many of the huge doubles would be called suites elsewhere, and bathrooms gleam with white tile. You'll pay more for a room with a view, but it's worth it to see the sun rise over the Old Town across the river. ✉ *21 quai des Bergues, CH-1211,* ☎ *022/9080530,* FAX *022/ 7389080. 83 rooms. Restaurant, meeting room. AE, DC, MC, V.*

$$$ 🏨 **Cornavin.** The comic book character Tintin made this hotel famous ★ with *L'Affaire Tournesol* (*The Sunflower Affair*). But even if Tintin hadn't rushed through in 1956, the interior design's deft manipulation of natural light and the world's longest nine-story clock pendulum in the lobby would bring it attention. The current management added three floors, a spectacular glassed-in breakfast hall, sleek cherry-wood furniture, and ingenious frosted-glass bathroom walls. The train tracks run just behind the hotel, but all windows are soundproofed. The dozen large triples and six interconnecting doubles are great for families. ⊠ *Gare de Cornavin, CH-1201,* ☎ *022/7161212,* FAX *022/7161200. 162 rooms, 4 suites. In-room safes, meeting rooms. AE, DC, MC, V.* ⊱

$$$ 🏨 **De Berne.** Most edges in this solid, spacious, well-maintained business-class hotel have been softened with polished wood, touches of brass, and warm colors. Mont Blanc is visible from the deluxe fifth floor, the buffet breakfast is generous, and double-glazed windows keep the noise of 24-hour street activity at bay. The kebab stands and cheap shoe stores on rue de Berne surround the center of Geneva's modest red-light district, but this not a dangerous part of town. ⊠ *26 rue de Berne, CH-1201,* ☎ *022/7154600,* FAX *022/7311173. 81 rooms, 8 suites. Restaurant, bar, meeting rooms. AE, DC, MC, V.* ⊱

$$$ 🏨 **Tiffany.** Glass elevators, a handful of rooms, and a dignified salon
★ were added in 1999, but the belle epoque spirit of this boutique hotel is unchanged, from the obligatory stained glass to the art nouveau–ish bed frames. Bathrooms in the new section are especially plush—fluffy bathrobes, ornate tiles, towel warmers, halogen lights—and each of the pair of new suites has a Jacuzzi. The painted ceiling in the graceful brasserie is a work of art; the English bar has a fine selection of whiskies, brandies, and cigars. ⊠ *1 rue des Marbriers, CH-1204,* ☎ *022/7081616,* FAX *022/7081617. 43 rooms, 3 suites. Restaurant, bar, lounge. AE, DC, MC, V.* ⊱

$$ 🏨 **Domaine de Châteauvieux.** A 10-minute drive west from downtown
★ Geneva will take you to the largest wine commune in Switzerland; vineyards undulate over the landscape on all sides of this former château. All the rooms were completely overhauled in 2000. Their delicate stenciling, marble sinks, and bright calico reflect a happy marriage of good taste and warm country spirit. The Domaine is a retreat to space and quiet; its hilltop views are fabulous. The restaurant of the same name (☞ Dining, *above*) may prove hard to resist. ⊠ *Peney-Dessus, CH-1242 Satigny,* ☎ *022/7531511,* FAX *022/7531924. 17 rooms, 1 suite. Restaurant, meeting room. AE, DC, MC, V.* ⊱

$$ 🏨 **International et Terminus.** This modest hotel is a sure sellout when there's a big conference in town. The current three-year renovation project should be finished in 2001, at which point all rooms will have spanking-new tile bathrooms, light wood furniture, pastel color schemes, and amenities such as minibars, safes, and cable TV. The hotel is just down the hill from the train station. All windows are double-glazed. ⊠ *20 rue des Alpes, CH-1201,* ☎ *022/7328095,* FAX *022/7321843. 60 rooms. Restaurant. AE, DC, MC, V.* ⊱

$$ 🏨 **Le Montbrillant.** Nineteenth-century beams and stone walls accent clean lines, rose fabrics, and crisp blue-gray trim at this family-run hotel less than 50 m (150 ft) from the back of the Gare Cornavin. Double-glazed windows keep it quiet; front rooms have a terrific view of the TGV as it arrives from Paris. The third floor is off-limits to smokers. Studio apartments on the fifth floor have kitchenettes, dormer windows, cathedral ceilings, and monthly rates. ⊠ *2 rue de Montbrillant, CH-1201,* ☎ *022/7337784,* FAX *022/7332511. 58 rooms, 24 studios. 2 restaurants, bar, meeting room, free parking. AE, DC, MC, V.* ⊱

$$ 🏨 **Suisse.** Colorful trompe-l'oeil scenes decorate the elevator doors, and a model tall ship or clipper guards the landing on each floor of this stylish corner hotel facing the train station. The narrow lobby is sponge-painted in warm shades of peach. The large, bright rooms have enormous, impeccable bathrooms; they're also soundproof. ⊠ *10 pl. de Cornavin, CH-1201,* ☎ *022/7326630,* ℻ *022/7326239. 57 rooms. Restaurant, bar. AE, DC, MC, V.*

$ ★ 🍴 **Bel'Espérance.** The Salvation Army owns this former *foyer pour dames* (ladies' boarding house) tucked away near place du Bourg-de-Four. Its spectacular terrace, conference facilities, bright yellow and blue rooms, tiled baths, and graceful Louis-Philippe–style breakfast salon put it on a par with much pricier hotels. Monthly rates, no-smoking rooms, self-service laundry facilities, and communal kitchen space are available; each studio has a kitchenette. Alcohol is not available here. ⊠ *1 rue de la Vallée, CH-1204,* ☎ *022/8183737,* ℻ *022/8183773. 38 rooms, 2 studios. Restaurant, meeting room. AE, DC, MC, V.* 🐾

$ ★ 🍴 **Central.** Christine and Erik Gangsted have engineered a complete overhaul (1999–2000) of this bargain hotel at the top of a Left Bank shopping street, and the transformation is impressive. The decor reflects the family ties to Bali, with warm Indonesian wood, intense pastel greens and blues, and sponge-painted terra-cotta. Each room is decorated with tasteful prints and paintings; baths have showers instead of tubs. All but the bunk-bed budget option have tiled showers and sinks with the toilet down the hall; you are guaranteed a balcony and breakfast in bed. Ask for a large room if you'll be traveling with kids. ⊠ *2 rue de la Rôtisserie, CH-1204,* ☎ *022/8188100,* ℻ *022/8188101. 27 rooms, 1 suite. AE, DC, MC, V.*

$ 🍴 **De la Cloche.** Christian Chabbey and his mother, Esther, keep friendly watch over their guests in this first-floor apartment. The flocked wallpaper and creaky parquet floors suit the kindly spirit of the place. All bathroom facilities were installed or renovated in 2000; five of the eight rooms share a toilet down the hall, and three have showers. Two rooms overlook a quiet inner courtyard. ⊠ *6 rue de la Cloche, CH-1201,* ☎ *022/7329481,* ℻ *022/7381612. 8 rooms. AE, DC, MC, V.*

$ ★ 🍴 **St-Gervais.** Red tartan carpeting and creamy linen warm the garretlike rooms in this old Right Bank inn. The tiny, wood-paneled café on the ground floor doubles as a breakfast room. Most major bus lines stop right around the corner, and the lake is a five-minute walk away. ⊠ *20 rue des Corps-Saints, CH-1201,* ☎ ℻ *022/7324572. 21 rooms, 1 with bath, 1 with shower. Breakfast room/café. AE, DC, MC, V.*

$ 🍴 **Des Tourelles.** Once worthy of a czar, now host to summer backpackers, this stripped-down Victorian town house has enormous bay-window corner rooms, creaky wooden floors, colorful quilts, new furniture, and spectacular river views. The hallways are gloomy and a bit scuffed, but each bright room has a complete modular bathroom and a mini-refrigerator. Bring earplugs if you like your windows open: there is plenty of noise from both river and traffic. ⊠ *2 blvd. James-Fazy, CH-1201,* ☎ *022/7324423,* ℻ *022/7327620. 23 rooms. Breakfast room. AE, DC, MC, V.* 🐾

NIGHTLIFE AND THE ARTS

The weekly *Genève Agenda* lists concerts, performances, museums, restaurants, and clubs in French and English. It is available free at tourist information booths, box offices, and most hotels. The monthly *Genève Le Guide* includes bilingual (French/English) film synopses as well as theater, music, dance, museum, and restaurant reviews. Pick up a free copy at tourist information booths, or buy one (3 SF) at any kiosk.

Nightlife

Genevois nightlife can be chic and exclusive, centered on trendy cafés and bistros, or linked to a pub circuit lifted whole from the British Isles.

Wherever you go, you'll find someone who speaks English—the international crowd likes to party.

Bars and Pubs

The opulent decor at **Le Baroque** (⊠ 12 pl. de la Fusterie, ☎ 022/3110515) pulls in hip young bankers armed with cell phones. Luxury hotel bars provide piano music, cocktails, and discreet service; the **Beau-Rivage** (☞ Lodging, *above*) is particularly genteel. **La Clémence** (⊠ 20 pl. du Bourg-de-Four, ☎ 022/3122498) fills with students and explodes into the street. English is the lingua franca at **Flanagan's** (⊠ 4 rue du Cheval-Blanc, ☎ 022/3101314) until closing time, at 5 AM. **Mr. Pickwick's Pub** (⊠ 80 rue de Lausanne, ☎ 022/7316797) serves fish-and-chips, shows English football, and staves off the homesickness of British expats. You'll find Guinness on tap, Kilkenny beer, and Irish accents at **Mulligan's** (⊠ 14 rue Grenus, ☎ 022/7328576). The **Roi Ubu** (⊠ 30 Grand-Rue, ☎ 022/3107398) draws young people to the Old Town like a magnet.

Dancing

Arthur's (⊠ 20 rte. de Pré-Bois, ☎ 022/7917700) spins house music and packs some 1,500 people onto multilevel dance floors. Live rhythm and blues on weeknights at the **Griffin's Club** (⊠ 36 blvd. Helvétique, ☎ 022/7351218) draws a black-tie crowd studded with famous names. **L'Interdit** (⊠ 18 quai du Seujet, ☎ 022/7389091) alternates high-voltage techno with flamboyant disco classics. Multiple dance floors at **Macumba** (⊠ 403 rte. d'Annecy, St. Julien-en-Genevois, ☎ 0033/450492350), just across the French border to the south, throb with '80s music, salsa, current hits, and classic rock. **Le Petit Palace** (⊠ 6 rue de la Tour-de-Boël, ☎ 022/3110 033) fills up on weekends with techno music and energetic young people. The DJ will play anything but techno at **Shakers** (⊠ 3 rue de la Boulangerie, ☎ 022/3105598), an Old Town cubbyhole with stone walls and cheap drinks. **L'Usine** (⊠ 4 pl. des Volontaires, ☎ 022/7813490), a much-loved former factory by the river, favors funk, hard rock, punk, grunge, and live bands.

Jazz Clubs

The hip young crowd at **AMR–Sud des Alpes** (⊠ 10 rue des Alpes, ☎ 022/7165630) prefers musical improvisation and contemporary jazz. The midriver restaurant **Aux Halles de l'Ile** (⊠ 1 pl. de l'Ile, ☎ 022/3115221) presents classic New Orleans jazz every Friday and Saturday night. Musical styles at the **Chat Noir** (⊠ 13 rue Vautier, Carouge, ☎ 022/3434998) range from Brazilian ethnojazz to blues to Celtic techno.

The Arts

Geneva supports an unusually rich arts scene for its size. The city's mix of cultures all but guarantees a steady influx of foreign artists and influences, with the result that most season programs are a mix of performers from Switzerland and abroad. Tickets usually remain on sale up to the day of performance, and you can buy directly from the theater. **Globus Grand Passage** (⊠ 48 rue du Rhône, ☎ 022/3195640) and the **tourist information booth** on pont de la Machine (☎ 022/3119827) are alternate sources.

Film

Most movies are dubbed, but undubbed English-language films are always screened somewhere in town. Check local newspaper listings for the initials *v.o.,* short for *version originale*. The **CAC Voltaire** (⊠ 16 rue du Général-Dufour, ☎ 022/3207878) organizes classic film minifestivals (undubbed) in the basement of the Grütli Arts Center. From late

June to mid-August the outdoor **Cinélac** (Port-Noir, Cologny) screens
a different movie each night against the sweeping backdrop of the lake
and the Jura. Many of their picks are undubbed English-language hits.

Music and Dance

The **Bâtiment des Forces Motrices** (⊠ 2 pl. des Volontaires, ☎ 022/
3221220) was built in 1886 to pump drinking water to the city; two
of the original turbines still adorn the lobby. Now its **Salle Théodore-
Turrettini** hosts traveling companies and local artists for a varied program of classical music, opera, and modern dance. Recitals, chamber
music concerts, and a major annual solo competition take place at the
Conservatoire de Musique (⊠ pl. Neuve, ☎ 022/3196060). The **Grand
Théâtre** (⊠ pl. Neuve, ☎ 022/4183000) ranks among the best opera
houses in the world and stages eight full-scale operas, two ballets, and
five recitals each season (September to June). The luscious red velvet
and cutting-edge technical facilities date from a 1998 overhaul. Jean-
Marie Blanchard will replace Renée Auphan as artistic director in
summer 2001. The list of artists who have performed with **L'Orchestre
de la Suisse Romande** (☎ 022/8070017), in the gilt bijou **Victoria Hall**
(⊠ 14 rue du Général-Dufour, ☎ 022/3283573), reads like a who's
who of classical music.

Theater

The children's theater **Am Stram Gram** (⊠ 56 rte. de Frontenex, ☎
022/7357924) makes magic with every production, whether drawing
inspiration from obscure myth, lyric poetry, Shakespeare, or contemporary writing. The creative performances are all in French. Artistic
Director Anne Bisang has brought international classics (translated into
French), contemporary drama, and innovative staging to the venerable **Comédie de Genève** (⊠ 6 blvd. des Philosophes, ☎ 022/3205001).
The more intimate **Théâtre du Grütli** (⊠ 16 rue du Général-Dufour, ☎
022/3289868) fills its spare, flexible space with experimental theater,
modern dance, and foreign plays (translated into French).

OUTDOOR ACTIVITIES AND SPORTS

Golf

The private 18-hole **Golf Club de Genève** (⊠ 70 rte. de la Capite,
Cologny, ☎ 022/7074800) rents equipment and welcomes nonmembers from Tuesday to Friday before noon between March and November. Lush fairways, spectacular views, and public access distinguish the
18-hole course at the **Domaine de Divonne** (⊠ Divonne-les-Bains, ☎
0033/450403434) just over the border in France.

Ice-Skating

You can skate outdoors for free in the heart of town from mid-December
to late February at the **Patinoire de Noël** (⊠ pl. du Rhône, ☎ 022/
9097000), which stays open daily until 11 PM. Indoor skating and lessons
are available Tuesday through Sunday from October to March at the
Patinoire des Vernets (⊠ 4–6 rue Hans-Wilsdorf, Acacias, ☎ 022/
4184022). Both rinks rent skates.

Sailing

Les Corsaires (⊠ 33 quai Gustave-Ador, ☎ 022/7354300) provides group
sailing lessons in English upon request and rents paddle-, motor-, and
sailboats.

Skiing

Geneva is surrounded by great downhill skiing, most of it in the French
Alps. From early December until mid-April ski buses depart daily from
the **Gare Routière de Genève** (⊠ pl. Dorcière, ☎ 022/7320230) for

Chamonix, Les Contamines, Flaine, and Morzine-Avoriaz. Trips take 1½–2 hours, and the 50–55 SF fare includes a ski-lift pass. The special **red mountain train** (☎ 022/3601314) ferries cross-country skiers from Nyon (15 minutes by train from Geneva) to St-Cergue's huge network of trails (☞ Chapter 12).

Swimming

Skeptics claim it's unsafe to swim in the cleaned-up waters of Lake Geneva, but the city's beaches are crowded from the moment they open in April until closing time in October. Take Bus 2 to the end of the line for the outdoor pool, lake access, and water slide at **Genève-Plage** (⊠ Port-Noir, Cologny, ☎ 022/7362482). The sauna and snack bar at **Les Bains des Pâquis** (⊠ 30 quai du Mont-Blanc, ☎ 022/7322974) stay open through the winter when the beach is closed. The **Piscine de Carouge** (⊠ 53 rte. de Veyrier, Carouge, ☎ 022/3432520) includes an Olympic-size outdoor pool, volleyball courts, and a water slide next to the River Arve. The indoor **Piscine de Varembé** (⊠ 46 av. Giuseppe-Motta, ☎ 022/7331214) stays open year-round.

Tennis

Nonmembers are welcome at the **Open Club de Bellevue** (⊠ 47 rte. de Collex, Bellevue, ☎ 022/7741514) during off-peak hours. The **Tennis Club du Bois Carré** (⊠ 14 chemin des Bûcherons, Vessy, ☎ 022/7843006) also offers badminton and squash. The **Tennis Club de Champel** (⊠ 41 rte. de Vessy, Vessy, ☎ 022/7842566) has indoor and outdoor courts. Same-day reservations are required. All of these are easy to reach via cab or public transport. You can rent equipment from local sports stores.

SHOPPING

General opening hours are weekdays from 9 to 6:30 and Saturday from 9 to 5. Shops in the downtown area close at 8 on Thursday.

Auctions

As a jewelry capital rivaled only by New York and an international center for Swiss watchmakers, Geneva regularly hosts high-profile auctions by the major houses. **Antiquorum** (⊠ 2 rue du Mont-Blanc, ☎ 022/9092850) deals exclusively in contemporary and antique time-pieces. **Christie's** (⊠ 8 pl. de la Taconnerie, ☎ 022/3191766) adds wine to its glamorous biannual jewelry sales. **Sotheby's** (⊠ 13 quai du Mont-Blanc, ☎ 022/7328585) holds previews twice a year at the Hôtel Beau-Rivage.

Department Stores

Globus Grand Passage (⊠ 48 rue du Rhône, ☎ 022/3195050) links the main Left Bank shopping streets. Service is good, and the kitchen goods, men's clothing, and fresh food sections are exceptional. **Bon Génie** (⊠ 34 rue du Marché, ☎ 022/8181111) sells expensive designer clothing and cosmetics on floor after hushed floor.

Markets

Les Halles de Rive (⊠ 17 rue Pierre-Fatio/29 blvd. Helvétique) sells fresh cheeses, meats, and pasta Monday through Saturday. A fruit-and-vegetable market fills the **boulevard Helvétique**, just outside, on Wednesday and Saturday mornings. **Place de la Fusterie** welcomes arts-and-crafts vendors every Thursday. The **Plaine de Plainpalais** hosts a polyglot flea market all day Wednesday and Saturday.

Shopping Streets

Geneva's two principal shopping streets run parallel along the Left Bank. **Rue du Rhône,** closest to the river, is the epicenter of luxury shopping. One block in, at the foot of the Old Town, is the less expensive, trendier street known variously as: **rue de la Confédération, rue du Marché, rue de la Croix-d'Or,** and **rue de Rive.** Galleries, antiques shops, bookstores, and boutiques line the **Grand-Rue** and the streets radiating from **place du Bourg-de-Four. Rue du Mont-Blanc,** on the Right Bank, is choked with souvenir stores.

Specialty Stores

Antiques
Antiquités Scientifiques (⌂ 19 rue du Perron, ☎ 022/3100706) buys, sells, and restores telescopes, barometers, and other scientific instruments. Browse gorgeous art deco furniture and 1930s jewelry at **Ars Nova** (⌂ 6 rue Calvin, ☎ 022/3118660). **Au Vieux Canon** (⌂ 40 Grand-Rue, ☎ 022/3105758) deals in extravagant English silver. **Buchs (Berndt)** (⌂ 34–36 Grand-Rue, ☎ 022/3117485) sells gilt mirrors and old-master frames. **Galerie 5** (⌂ 5 pl. du Bourg-de-Four, ☎ 022/3107824) is full of graceful, well-polished English furniture. **Rue des Belles Filles** (⌂ 6 bis rue Étienne-Dumont, ☎ 022/3103131) is a treasure trove of vintage clothing, jewelry, and knickknacks.

Books
À Montparnasse (⌂ 37 Grand-Rue, ☎ 022/3116719) deals in unusual old books, prints, and maps. **Elm Books** (⌂ 3 rue Versonnex, ☎ 022/7360945) stocks English-language titles for all ages. **Galerie Bernard Letu** (⌂ 2 rue Calvin, ☎ 022/3104757) carries an inspired multilingual range of art and photography books. Head to **Librairie Ancienne** (⌂ 20 Grand-Rue, ☎ 022/3102050) for leather-bound and gilt first editions. **Librairie Archigraphy** (⌂ 1 pl. de l'Ile, ☎ 022/3116008) displays art, design, and architecture books in a setting worthy of its subjects. **Librairie Jullien** (⌂ 32 pl. du Bourg-de-Four, ☎ 022/3103670) has sold books old and new since 1839. **L'Oreille Cassée** (⌂ 9 quai des Bergues, ☎ 022/7324080) captures the market for hardcover *bandes dessinées* (comic books). The commercial chain **Payot** (⌂ 5 rue de Chantepoulet, ☎ 022/7318950; ⌂ 16 rue du Marché, ☎ 022/3197940) serves French, English, and German readers.

Chocolate
Silky, handmade white-chocolate truffles top the selection at **Arn** (⌂ 12 pl. du Bourg-de-Four, ☎ 022/3104094). **Auer** (⌂ 4 rue de Rive, ☎ 022/3114286) was the first to make bite-size *pavés glacés,* creamy cobblestone-shape chocolates. **Du Rhône** (⌂ 3 rue de la Confédération, ☎ 022/3115614) has sold bittersweet hot chocolate since 1875. **Merkur** (⌂ 13 rue du Mont-Blanc, ☎ 022/7322719; ⌂ 32 rue du Marché, ☎ 022/3102221) has Swiss-theme gift boxes, individual bars, and huge champagne truffles. **Rohr** (⌂ 3 pl. du Molard, ☎ 022/3116303; ⌂ 42 rue du Rhône, ☎ 022/3116876) models its smooth, rich signature truffles after Geneva garbage cans. Sugary chocolate *moules du lac* (shaped like mussels) are the house specialty at **Zeller** (⌂ 1 pl. Longemalle, ☎ 022/3115026).

Jewelry
There's no ceiling on the price of precious baubles in Geneva. **Bucherer** (⌂ 26 quai du Général-Guisan, ☎ 022/3196266) sells luminous pearls and diamonds of all sizes. **Bulgari** (⌂ 30 rue du Rhône, ☎ 022/3177070) favors heavy gold necklaces and rings crusted with jewels. **Chopard** (⌂ 8 rue de la Confédération, ☎ 022/3113728; ⌂ 27 rue du Rhône, ☎

022/3107050) will wrap your wrist with a diamond-studded watch. **Cartier** (✉ 35 rue du Rhône, ☎ 022/8185454; ✉ 90 rue du Rhône, ☎ 022/3102040) sets its rubies, emeralds, and diamonds in a variation on its trademark panther. **L'Arcade** (✉ 20 rue de la Corraterie, ☎ 022/3111554) showcases Edith Moldaschl's unique line of costume jewelry from 1930 to 1960. **Ludwig Muller** (✉ 2 rue de la Cité, ☎ 022/3102930) draws inspiration from commedia dell'arte and uses rare blue gold.

Watches

Geneva watchmakers are known for unparalleled excellence. **Bucherer** (✉ 45 rue du Rhône, ☎ 022/3196266) carries more prestigious, indestructible Rolex models than anyone else in town. **Franck Muller** (✉ 1 rue de la Tour de l'Ile, ☎ 022/8180030) creates refined, complicated modern timepieces in the best Swiss tradition. **Patek Philippe** (✉ 41 rue du Rhône, ☎ 022/7812448) still occupies the original 1839 building where the winding mechanism behind all watches was invented. **Piaget** (✉ 40 rue du Rhône, ☎ 022/8170200) wraps its ultraflat watch movements in platinum and gold. The oldest manufacturer of watches in the world, **Vacheron-Constantin** (✉ 1 rue des Moulins, ☎ 022/3103227), sold its first sober design in 1755.

GENEVA A TO Z

Arriving and Departing

By Bus

Long-haul bus lines arrive from and depart for points across Europe at the **Gare Routière de Genève** (bus station; ✉ pl. Dorcière, ☎ 022/7320230), off rue du Mont-Blanc in the city center.

By Car

The **A1** expressway along the northern shore of Lac Léman connects Geneva to the rest of Switzerland by way of Lausanne. Autoroute links to Bern (**A12**) and Martigny (**A9**) part company above the city. The scenic southern shore of the lake gives access to the Valais via Évian-les-Bains, in France. Grenoble (to the south), Lyons (to the southwest), and Chamonix (to the southeast) are all between a 1- and 2-hour drive on the French **A40** expressway (l'Autoroute Blanche). No matter how brief your foray onto any expressway in Switzerland, you will need a *vignette,* or road-tax sticker (☞ Car Travel *in* the Gold Guide).

By Plane

Cointrin (✉ 5 km/3 mi northwest of city center, ☎ 022/7177111) is Geneva's airport and the second-largest international airport in Switzerland. Several airlines fly directly to Cointrin from London; **Swissair** (☎ 800/221–4750 in the U.S.; 0171/434–7300 in London; 0848/800700 in Geneva) has daily service to New York as well as hourly connector flights to its hub in Zürich. **Crossair** (☎ 0171/434–7300 in London; 0848/852000 in Geneva) links Geneva with Basel, Zürich, Lugano, and most major European cities.

BETWEEN THE AIRPORT AND THE CITY CENTER

By Bus. The No. 10 bus runs regularly between the airport departure level and downtown Geneva. The ride takes about 20 minutes; the fare is 2.20 SF.

By Limousine. All drivers employed by **Globe** (☎ 022/7310750) speak English. **Privilege** (☎ 022/7383366) rents chauffeur-driven Mercedes and a stretch Rolls-Royce.

By Taxi. Taxis are plentiful but expensive. You'll pay at least 25 SF to reach the city center, plus 1.50 SF per bag.

By Train. Cointrin has a direct rail link with the **Gare Cornavin** (✉ pl. Cornavin, ☎ 0900/300300), Geneva's main train station. Trains run about every 15 minutes from 5:30 AM to midnight; the six-minute trip costs 5 SF each way.

By Train

Both domestic and international services use the **Gare Cornavin** (✉ pl. Cornavin, ☎ 0900/300300). Direct express trains arrive from most Swiss cities every hour, and the French TGV provides a fast link to Paris.

Getting Around

By Bicycle

Bike lanes are ubiquitous downtown; these are marked with a yellow line and a yellow bicycle symbol on the pavement. Yellow signs indicate routes throughout the canton. **Genèv'Roule** (✉ 17 pl. Montbrillant; ✉ Les Bains des Pâquis, ☎ 022/7401343) rents bicycles starting at 5 SF per day; it's open from May to October.

By Boat

The **Compagnie Générale de Navigation** (CGN; ✉ Jardin Anglais, ☎ 022/3125223) provides transportation on belle epoque steamers between Geneva and Swiss lakeside towns such as Nyon, Lausanne, Vevey, and Montreux, as well as the French towns of Yvoire, Thonon, and Évian-les-Bains. The fare is included for holders of the Swiss Pass (☞ Train Travel *in* the Gold Guide); those with a Swiss Boat Pass (☞ Boat Travel *in* the Gold Guide) pay half price.

Smaller-scale lake connections, including a shuttle service across Geneva's harbor, are operated by the **Mouettes Genevoises** (✉ 8 quai du Mont-Blanc, ☎ 022/7322944) between April and October.

By Taxi

Taxis (☎ 022/3314133) are immaculate, and the drivers are polite, but do expect a 6.30 SF minimum charge plus 2.90 SF per kilometer (about ½ mi). In the evening and on Sunday the rate climbs to 3.50 SF per kilometer. Cabs will not stop if you hail them; go to a designated taxi stand (marked on the pavement in yellow) or call.

By Tram and Bus

Geneva's public transportation network is cheap, comprehensive, clearly marked, and efficient. Almost every bus stop has a machine selling tickets; instructions are given in English. For 2.20 SF you can use the system for one hour, changing as often as you like between buses, trams, and the Mouettes Genevoises (☞ Getting Around by Boat, *above*). A *carte journalière*—available for 5 SF from ticket machines, most newsstands, and the Transports Publics Genevois (TPG) booths at the train station and Cours de Rive—buys all-day unlimited travel in the city center. Holders of the Swiss Pass travel free on Geneva public transport.

Contacts and Resources

Consulates

Australia (✉ 2 chemin des Fins, ☎ 022/7999100). **Canada** (✉ 5 av. de l'Ariana, ☎ 022/9199200). **New Zealand** (✉ 2 chemin des Fins, ☎ 022/9290350). **United Kingdom** (✉ 37–39 rue de Vermont, ☎ 022/9182400). **United States** (Consular Agent; ✉ 29 rte. de Pré-Bois, ☎ 022/7981615).

Emergencies

Police (☎ 117). **Ambulance** (☎ 144). **Hospital** (✉ Hôpital Cantonal, 24 rue Micheli-du-Crest, ☎ 022/3723311). **Doctor referral** (☎ 022/3222020). **Pharmacies *de garde*** (☎ 111) are open 24 hours.

English-Language Bookstores

Titles sold at **Elm Books** (⌧ 3 rue Versonnex, ☎ 022/7360945) come directly from Britain and the United States. **Payot** (⌧ 5 rue de Chantepoulet, ☎ 022/7384709; ⌧ 16 rue du Marché, ☎ 022/3197940) tucks English-language best-sellers in with French books.

Guided Tours

BOAT

Swissboat (⌧ 4 quai du Mont-Blanc, ☎ 022/7324747) operates guided cruises on Lake Geneva daily from April to October. Recorded commentary is available in English; boats leave from quai du Mont-Blanc opposite the Monument Brunswick. The **Mouettes Genevoises** (⌧ 8 quai du Mont-Blanc, ☎ 022/7322944) provide tours of the Rhône and Lake Geneva's southwestern tip. You're given a printed text (ask for the English version) and a map when you board at quai du Mont-Blanc. River cruises have recorded commentary in English and depart from place de l'Ile.

ORIENTATION

Key Tours (☎ 022/7314140) runs two-hour bus-and-minitrain tours of the International Area and the Old Town. They leave from the place Dorcière bus station daily at 10 and 2 between May and October, and at 2 daily from November to April. Each tour costs 35 SF, and commentary is in English. Between May and October, if the weather is good, you may also catch the minitrain (independent of the bus tour) at place Neuve for a trip around the Old Town, on quai du Mont-Blanc for a tour of the Right Bank parks, or in the Jardin Anglais for a ride along the Left Bank quays. Each loop lasts about 30 minutes; the cost is 6.90 SF.

Key Tours also offers daylong bus excursions into the Geneva countryside, up the lake to Montreux/Chillon, and farther afield to Bern, Gruyères, Zermatt, Interlaken, and, in France, Chamonix.

SPECIAL INTEREST

The **United Nations** leads English-language lecture tours of the Palais des Nations (☞ Exploring Geneva, *above*). Tours last about an hour and cost 8.50 SF.

WALKING

Geneva's **tourist office** (☞ Visitor Information, *below*) organizes a walk through the Old Town every Saturday at 10 and twice each weekday from June to September; expect to pay 12 SF. Private tours are available upon request from the **Guide Service** (☎ 022/9097021) on pont de la Machine. English-language audio tours of the Old Town provided by the tourist information booth at 18 rue du Mont-Blanc cover 26 points of interest. The rental fee for the map, cassette, and player is 10 SF plus a 50 SF deposit.

Travel Agencies

American Express (⌧ 7 rue du Mont-Blanc, ☎ 022/7317600). **Carlson Wagonlit Travel** (⌧ 5 rue du Nant, ☎ 022/7372230). **Touring Club Suisse** (⌧ 8 Cours de Rive, ☎ 022/4172040).

Visitor Information

You can write to the administrative office of the **Office du Tourisme de Genève** (⌧ Case Postale 1602, CH-1211 Genève 1, ☎ 022/9097000, FAX 022/9097011, ✍). You'll find **tourist information booths** at the airport (⌧ Cointrin arrivals, ☎ 022/7178083), on the Right Bank (⌧ 18 rue du Mont-Blanc, ☎ 022/9097000), and even in the middle of the river (⌧ pont de la Machine, ☎ 022/3119827).

14 PORTRAITS OF SWITZERLAND

Skiing Switzerland

Books and Videos

Winter Activities Chart

Vocabulary

SKIING SWITZERLAND

TWO CABLE-CAR RIDES and thousands of feet above the resort village of Verbier, we sit in a mountain restaurant. On the table in front of us are one *café renversé*, two cups of hot chocolate, one tiny glass of bubbly white *Fendant* wine from Sion. Our legs tired from a long day of skiing, we catch our breath before the evening run, while the slopes and pistes below empty themselves of skiers and fill up with evening light. Outside, the sun hovers only inches above the horizon. Mont Blanc is an island of ice rising out of a sea of summits along the Franco-Swiss border. Peaks and passes stretch as far as the eye can see, an art director's Alpine fantasy in late light.

Verbier skiing is one reason I've returned to Switzerland in winter, faithfully, for the past 25 years. This is a giant of a ski area in a region of giant ski areas, perched high in the French-speaking, southwest corner of Switzerland, draped over four mountain valleys, embracing six villages, a labyrinth of interconnected lifts (more than 100), interlaced slopes (too many to count)—a ski area you can't explore in a week or even exhaust in a season.

For passionate skiers every trip to Switzerland is a homecoming. All our skiing archetypes originate here. White sawtooth horizons point to the sky, picture-postcard chalet roofs poke up under great white hats of snow, necklaces of lifts and cable cars drape themselves over the white shoulders of fairy-tale mountains, and runs go on forever.

These are big mountains, with vertical drops twice the length of those of the Rockies. In the Alps you can often drop four, five, or six thousand vertical feet in one run. Here runs are so long that halfway down you need a break—which you'll find at a little chalet restaurant in the middle of nowhere, where the views are as exhilarating as the schnapps that's so often the drink of choice.

These are pure white mountains, too, whiter than we're used to. In the Alps, the tree line is low, often only 1,000 m (3,000 ft) above sea level, and ski areas stretch upward from there. The skier's playing field is white on white; marked pistes are white rivers of groomed snow snaking down equally white but ungroomed flanks of Alpine peaks. There are more treeless bowls than you can count, than you can hope to ski in several skiers' lifetimes.

When European skiers tell you that the western Alps are higher and more glaciated, more likely to have good snow in a dry year, and that the eastern Alps are lower in elevation but full of charm, with more intimate, more richly decorated villages, they are usually referring to the difference between the French Alps and Austria. In fact, they could just as well be talking about the mountains and ski resorts of southwest Switzerland versus those of eastern Switzerland, Graubünden, and the Engadine; for Switzerland, with its many cantons, is a microcosm that mirrors the diversity of skiing all across the greater Alps. You can test your credit-card limits at the Palace Hotel in worldly St. Moritz, hear the Latin echoes of Romansh as you ride the cog railways of modest Kleine Scheidegg, or ponder the hearty existence of hearty mountain farmers among the peaks of French-speaking Valais—but always, the local mountain culture will be part of your ski experience.

As varied as the regions are the people who ski them. Depending on which canton you ski, you may hear the lilting singsong French of Vaud and the western Valais, the incomprehensible Swiss German of the Berner Oberland and eastern Wallis, or the haunting Latin echoes of Romansh in the high valleys of Graubünden. The ski pistes of Switzerland are the polyglot crossroads of Europe, where stylish Parisians in neon outfits rub elbows with Brits in navy blue, Munich businessmen in Bogner suits, and Swedish students with punk haircuts. And yet, when you're surrounded by mountains that will outlast fashions, lifetimes, and languages, such differences fade, and the mountains are all you can see.

We walk uphill through knee-deep powder toward the summit of the Allalinhorn—the friendliest of Canton Wallis's many 4,000-m (13,120-ft) peaks. Early morning sunshine rakes the corniced ridges around us; the village of Saas-Fee still hides in shadow below. With climbing skins glued to the bottom of our skis, we've shuffled up the Feegletscher to earn a morning's bliss in deep untracked snow. This glacier highway is taking us above the domain of passes and ski lifts and groomed slopes, into a world of icy north walls, pure knife-edge ridges, undulating mile-long coverlets of fresh powder, summits of whipped meringue, and snow crystals sparkling at our feet. Munching cheese and chocolate as we climb, thinking that we must look like silhouettes in one of Herbert Matter's prewar Swiss travel posters, breathing deeply, climbing slowly, we daydream our way to the top. Our tracks, like zippers in the snow, stretch up to a vanishing point in the midnight-blue sky above.

T'S A SOFT APRIL morning at Les Diablerets, a ski area on the frontier between francophone Vaud and the German canton of Bern. It's already 11 AM and the frozen corn snow is only now softening up on the wide glacier beneath the dark, thumblike peak of the Oldenhorn. From the topmost lift we can see west toward Lake Geneva, south toward the giant peaks of the Valais, and east toward the dark brooding peaks of the Berner Oberland. An observation deck on the roof of the Alps reveals mountains filling space to its farthest corners, to the hazy horizon, waves on a wind-tossed sea, frozen white, as far as one can see. On the deep valley flanks below Les Diablerets, winding west toward the Rhône Valley, another winter's worth of cow manure has performed its annual alchemy: the slopes are greening up with no respect for common-sense color—pastures of eye-dazzling kelly green under dark forests and crags. Only a few miles away, down the eastern German-speaking side of the mountains, the chic resort of Gstaad seems deserted; its jet-set winter guests have already hung up their skis and headed for the Mediterranean. The mountains are ours for a day.

At the top of the lift we break through the clouds. A sea of fog fills the Rhône Valley below us, a fluffy false plain, punctured only by snowy peaks, stretching to the horizon. Somewhere under these clouds is Lake Geneva, and far across, Les Dents du Midi ("The Teeth of Noon") rise out of the clouds like ice-sheathed knuckles. Villars-Gryon is a ski resort so small most American skiers have never heard of it, even though it's bigger than half the ski areas in Colorado. Alone, we ski along the edge of the piste, where the slope steepens and drops away in a succession of rocky ledges. Just over the border that separates the skier's world from the mountaineer's, we see a lone ibex, posing on a rock outcrop against the clouds, scimitar-shape horns swept back in wide twin arcs. We christie to a stop, stand in awe wishing we had cameras, and realize eventually that the ibex is not going to bolt. These are its Alps, its domain; we are the newcomers, birds of passage, intruders. It feels like a privilege to share the roof of Europe with this ibex, a privilege that our Swiss hosts have slowly earned over 700 years by farming basically unfarmable mountainsides, by making this land their domain. We push off, the cold winter snow squeaking under our skis. Behind our backs the ibex still stares off into the distance.

These images stay with me, indelible as the Alps themselves. Say the word *Switzerland* and I see the gentle slopes of the Plateau Rosa above Zermatt, perforated by the dotted lines of T-bars, peppered with tiny, bright-color skiers, slopes lapping in white waves against the base of the Matterhorn. Near Saint-Moritz, I see the blue-green crevasses of the Morteratsch Glacier, a frozen white-water rapid spilling down from the Diavolezza ski area: ice walls, blue ice caves, a labyrinth of ice. I see the three giants of the Berner Oberland, the Eiger, the Mönch, and the Jungfrau—the Ogre, the Monk, and the Virgin—shadowy 13,000-ft-high northern faces that loom above the toy skiers and runs of Grindelwald and Wengen.

That Switzerland has some of the best skiing in the world goes without saying. In the end, though, it's not the skiing I remember, or the runs, or the trails, or my turns. It's the mountains I remember. And so will you.

— Lito Tejada-Flores

BOOKS AND VIDEOS

Books

Wilhelm Tell, by Friedrich von Schiller, is the definitive stage version of the dramatic legend. *The Prisoner of Chillon,* by Lord Byron, is an epic poem inspired by the sojourn of François Bonivard in the dungeon of Chillon. *A Tramp Abroad,* by Mark Twain, includes the author's personal impressions—and tall tales—derived from travels in Switzerland. *Arms and the Man,* by G. B. Shaw, was the source of Oscar Straus's Viennese operetta *The Chocolate Soldier;* both are about a Swiss mercenary with a sweet tooth.

Novels set at least partially in Switzerland include *Daisy Miller,* by Henry James (Lac Léman, Chillon); *Tender Is the Night,* by F. Scott Fitzgerald; *A Farewell to Arms,* by Ernest Hemingway; Thomas Mann's *The Magic Mountain,* (Davos); Albert Cohen's *Belle du Seigneur* (Geneva); and *Hotel du Lac,* by Anita Brookner (Vevey).

The best-known children's book set in Switzerland is, of course, *Heidi,* by Johanna Spyri (Maienfeld). *Banner in the Sky,* by James Ramsey Ullman, is a powerful children's book about a boy's attempt to climb Switzerland's most challenging mountain.

La Place de la Concorde Suisse, by John McPhee, was developed from a series of *New Yorker* pieces the author wrote after traveling with members of the Swiss army. *Heidi's Alp,* by Christine Hardyment, a first-person account of a family traveling in a camper-van in search of the Europe of fairy tales, includes an adventure with a latter-day alm-uncle in a cabin above Maienfeld. *A Guide to Zermatt and the Matterhorn,* Edward Whymper's memoirs of his disastrous climb up the Matterhorn, is now out of print, but it may be available in a library (excerpts appear in Chapter 11, Valais). In *The Climb Up to Hell,* Jack Olsen details the dramatic 1957 Eiger expedition. *Terminal,* by Colin

Forbes, is a murder-mystery tale containing fantastic descriptions of Swiss cities.

There have been several books published on the recent findings of the Swiss banks' handling of Jewish and Nazi funds during and after World War II. Among these are *Nazi Gold: The Full Story of the Fifty-Year Swiss-Nazi Conspiracy to Steal Billions from Europe's Jews and Holocaust Survivors,* by Tom Bower, and *Hitler's Silent Partners: Swiss Banks, Nazi Gold, and the Pursuit of Justice,* by Isabel Vincent.

Videos

Heidi is undoubtedly the best-known film to be shot in Switzerland. Make sure you see the 1937 version directed by Allan Dulan, starring Shirley Temple. Swiss air must agree with James Bond; several films have Swiss scenes in them, including 1995's *GoldenEye* and *Goldfinger* (1964); *On Her Majesty's Secret Service* (1969) shows dazzling ski scenes of the Schilthorn in central Switzerland. You can also get glimpses of Swiss scenery in the 1994 version of *Frankenstein. Trois Couleurs Rouge (Three Colors Red),* the last in director Krzysztof Kieslowski's trilogy, and a big hit in Europe, is set in Geneva's Old Town, while Peter Greenaway's 1993 *Stairs* shows Geneva through the director's unique artistic vision. *The Unbearable Lightness of Being* follows a couple fleeing from the 1968 Russian invasion of Czechoslovakia. The moving *Reise der Hoffnung (Journey of Hope),* directed by Xavier Koller in 1990, centers on a Kurdish family fleeing Turkish persecution to seek sanctuary in Switzerland. In French director Claude Chabrol's *Rien Ne Va Plus (The Swindle;* 1997), Isabelle Huppert and Michel Serrault play a pair of con artists who attempt an out-of-their-league scam; a section was shot in Sils-Maria, and a Swiss Army knife comes into play.

Winter Activities of the Resorts

Resort	Lift-Ticket Cost (SF) * (one day/six day)	Elevation (m/ft)	Number of Lifts	Lift Capacity (number of riders per hour in thousands)	Maintained Trails (km/mi)	Snowmaking
Arosa	49/219	1,800–2,650 m 5,900–8,700 ft	16	21.7	70/43	❄
Crans-Montana	56/265	1,500–3,000 m 4,920–9,843 ft	39	38.6	160/100	❄
Davos-Klosters	54/268	1,560–2,844 m 5,118–9,330 ft	54	46.0	320/199	❄
Flims-Laax	59/324	1,160–3,292 m 3,808–10,798 ft	29	42.0	220/140	❄
Gstaad-Saanenland	50/233	1,100–3,000 m 3,600–9,843 ft	66	53.0	250/160	❄
La Vallée de Conches (cross-country)	n/a	1,300–1,450 m 4,265–4,757 ft	n/a	n/a	n/a	❄
Le Val D'Anniviers	40/210	1,350–3,000 m 4,430–9,843 ft	45	25.0	250/155	❄
Les Portes du Soleil (Champery and 14 linked Swiss and French areas)	48/219	1,000–2,500 m 3,280–8,200 ft	219	228.8	650/400	❄
Verbier (including 6 linked areas of Quatre-Vallées)	56/282	820–3,330 m 2,690–10,925 ft	100	74.0	400/248	❄
Saas-Fee	58/270	1,800–3,600 m 5,900–11,800 ft	26	26.4	100/50	❄
St. Moritz (Upper Engadine)	53/274	1,950–3,300 m 6,396–10,824 ft	55	65.0	350/34	❄
Grindelwald-Wengen (Jungfrau Region)	52/244	1,300–3,450 m 4,265–11,300 ft	45	40.0	213/132	❄
Zermatt	62/306	1,260–3,820 m 4,132–12,530 ft	73	70.7	245/152	❄

*varies according to extent of areas selected to ski in
ⁱdepending on type and quality of snow, as well as grooming of slopes

Average Annual Snowfall (cm/in)	Difficulty of Terrain: % Beg/Int/Exp	Cross-Country (km/mi of trails)	Glacier Skiing	Heli-Skiing	Para/Hang Gliding	Ice-Skating	Luge Runs	Skibob Runs	Ballooning	Accommodations (bed in hotels, chalets, and apartments)
692/272	31/57/12	26/16			❄	❄	❄			❄	8,000
518/204	38/50/12	40/25	❄	❄	❄	❄	❄	❄	❄		40,000
491/193	29/50/21	75/46			❄	❄	❄	❄			24,250
440/173	50/30/20	60/37	❄	❄	❄	❄	❄		❄		10,800
627/247	40/40/20	127/75	❄	❄	❄	❄	❄	❄	❄		12,300
522/206	n/a	180/53				❄					20,000
348/137	30/40/30	82/51		❄	❄	❄	❄	❄			20,000
619/244	25/40/35	250/155		❄	❄	❄					93,000
491/193	32/42/26	42/33	❄	❄	❄	❄	❄	❄			25,000
357/141	25/25/50	54/34	❄			❄	❄				7,600
368/145	35/25/40	180/112	❄	❄	❄	❄	❄	❄	❄		36,500
389/153	30/50/20	17/10		❄	❄	❄	❄	❄			10,000
434/131	30/40/30	10/6	❄	❄	❄	❄					13,500

WORDS AND PHRASES

	English	French	French Pronunciation
Basics			
	Yes/no	Oui/non	wee/no
	Please	S'il vous plaît	seel voo **play**
	Thank you	Merci	mare-**see**
	You're welcome	De rien	deh ree-**enh**
	Excuse me	Pardon	pahr-**doan**
	Hello	Bonjour	bohn-**zhoor**
	Goodbye	Au revoir	o ruh-**vwahr**
Numbers			
	One	Un	un
	Two	Deux	deuh
	Three	Trois	twa
	Four	Quatre	**cat**-ruh
	Five	Cinq	sank
	Six	Six	seess
	Seven	Sept	set
	Eight	Huit	weat
	Nine	Neuf	nuf
	Ten	Dix	deess
Days			
	Today	Aujourd'hui	o-zhoor-**dwee**
	Tomorrow	Demain	deh-**menh**
	Yesterday	Hier	yair
	Morning	Matin	ma-**tenh**
	Afternoon	Après-midi	ah-pray-mee-**dee**
	Night	Nuit	nwee
	Monday	Lundi	**lahn**-dee
	Tuesday	Mardi	**mahr**-dee
	Wednesday	Mercredi	**mare**-kruh-dee
	Thursday	Jeudi	**juh**-dee
	Friday	Vendredi	**vawn**-dra-dee
	Saturday	Samedi	**sam**-dee
	Sunday	Dimanche	**dee**-mawnsh

*Prevalent Swiss-German dialect

German	German Pronunciation	Italian	Italian Pronunciation
Ja/nein	yah/nine	Sí/No	see/no
Bitte	**bit**-uh	Per favore	pear fa-**voh**-reh
Danke	**dahn**-kuh	Grazie	**grah**-tsee-ay
Bitte schön	**bit**-uh **shern**	Prego	**pray**-go
Entschuldigen Sie *Äxgüsi	ent-**shool**-de-gen-zee **ax**-scu-see	Scusi	**skoo**-zee
Guten Tag *Grüezi *Grüss Gott	**goot**-en **tahk** **grit**-zee groos got	Buon giorno	bwohn **jyohr**-noh
Auf Widersehen *Ufwiederluege *Tschüss (*familiar*)	Auf **vee-der**-zane oof-**vee-der**-lawgah choohs	Arrivederci	a-ree-vah-**dare**-chee
Eins	eints	Uno	**oo**-no
Zwei	tsvai	Due	**doo**-ay
Drei	dry	Tre	tray
Vier	fear	Quattro	**kwah**-troh
Fünf	fumph	Cinque	**cheen**-kway
Sechs	zex	Sei	say
Sieben	**zee**-ben	Sette	**set**-ay
Acht	ahkt	Otto	**oh**-to
Neun	noyn	Nove	**no**-vay
Zehn	tsane	Dieci	dee-**eh**-chee
Huete	**hoi**-tah	Oggi	**oh**-jee
Morgen	**more**-gehn	Domani	do-**mah**-nee
Gestern	geh-**shtairn**	Ieri	ee-veh-ree
Morgen	**more**-gehn	Mattina	ma-**tee**-na
Nachmittag	nahkt-**mit**-ahk	Pomeriggio	po-mer-**ee**-jo
Nacht	nahkt	Notte	Noh-teh
Montag	**mohn**-tahk	Lunedì	**loo**-neh-dee
Dienstag	**deens**-tahk	Martedì	**mahr**-teh-dee
Mittwoch	**mit**-vohk	Mercoledì	**mare**-co-leh-dee
Donnerstag	**doe**-ners-tahk	Giovedì	**jo**-veh-dee
Freitag	**fry**-tahk	Venerdì	**ven**-air-dee
Samstag	**zahm**-stahk	Sabato	**sah**-ba-toe
Sonntag	**zon**-tahk	La Domenica	lah doe-**men**-ee-ca

	English	French	French Pronunciation

Useful Phrases

	English	French	French Pronunciation
	Do you speak English?	Parlez-vous anglais?	par-lay-vooz awng-**gleh**
	I don't speak French/German/Italian.	Je ne parle pas français.	juh nuh parl pah fraun-**seh**
	I don't understand.	Je ne comprends pas.	juh nuh kohm-prawhn **pah**
	I don't know.	Je ne sais pas.	juh nuh say **pah**
	I am American/British.	Je suis américain/anglais	jhu sweez a-may-ree-**can**/awn-**glay**
	I am sick.	Je suis malade.	juh swee ma-**lahd**
	Please call a doctor.	Appelez un docteur s'il vous plâit.	a-pe-lay uhn dohk-**tore** seel voo **play**
	Have you any rooms?	Est-ce que vous avez une chambre?	Ehskuh vooz ah-vay-oon **shahm**-br
	How much does it cost?	C'est combien?	say comb-bee-**enh**
	Do you accept . . . (credit card)	Est-ce que vous acceptez . . .	Ehskuh voo zahksehptay . . .
	Too expensive	Trop cher	troh **shehr**
	It's beautiful.	C'est très beau.	say tray boh
	Help!	Au secours!	o say-**koor**
	Stop!	Arrêtez!	a-ruh-**tay**

Getting Around

	English	French	French Pronunciation
	Where is . . .	C'est où . . .	say oo
	The train station?	la gare?	la gahr
	The post office?	la poste?	la pohst
	The hospital?	l'hôpital?	lo-pee-**tahl**
	Where are the rest rooms?	Où sont les toilettes?	oo sohn lay **twah**-let
	Left	A gauche	a **gohsh**
	Right	À droite	a **drwat**
	Straight ahead	Tout droit	**too drwat**

Dining Out

	English	French	French Pronunciation
	Waiter/Waitress	Monsieur/Mademoiselle	muh-**syuh**/mad-mwa-**zel**
	Please give me . . .	S'il vous plait, donnez-moi . . .	see voo **play** doh nay **mwah**

*Prevalent Swiss-German dialect

German	German Pronunciation	Italian	Italian Pronunciation
Sprechen Sie Englisch?	Shprek-hun zee **eng**-glish	Parla inglese?	**par**-la een **glay**-zay
Ich sprech kein Deutsch.	ihkh **shprek**-uh kine doych	Non parlo italiano.	non **par**-lo ee-tal-**yah**-no
Ich verstehe nicht.	ihkh fehr-**stay**-eh nikht	Non capisco.	non ka-**peess**-ko
Ich habe keine Ahnung.	ihkh hah-beh kine-eh **ah**-nung	Non lo so.	non lo **so**
Ich bin Amerikaner(in). Engländer(in).	ihkh bin a-mer-i **kah**-ner(in)/**eng**-glan-der(in)	Sono americano(a)/ Sono inglese.	**so**-no a-may-ree-**kah**-no(a)/**so**-no een-**glay**-zay
Ich bin krank.	ihkh bin **krahnk**	Sto male.	sto **ma**-lay
Bitte rufen einen Arzt.	**bit**-uh **roof**-en ine-en **ahrtst**	Chiami un dottore per favore.	kee-**ah**-mee oon doe-**toe**-ray pear fah-**voh**-reh
Haben sie ein Zimmer?	**Ha**-ben zee ine **tsimmer**	C'e una camera libera?	chay **oo**-nah **cam**-er-ah **lee**-ber-eh
Wieviel kostet das?	**vee**-feel **cost**-et dahs	Quanto costa?	**kwahn**-toe-**coast**-a
Nehmen Sie . . .	**nay**-men zee . . .	Posso pagare . . .	**pohs**-soh pah-**gah**-reh . . .
Es kostet zu viel.	es **cost**-et tsu feel	Troppo caro	**troh**-poh **cah**-roh
Das ist schön.	dahs is **shern**	É bello(a).	eh **bell**-oh
Hilfe!	**hilf**-uh	Aiuto!	a-**yoo**-toe
Halt!	hahlt	Alt!	ahlt
Wo ist . . .	**vo** ist	Dov'è . . .	doe-**veh**
Der Bahnhof?	dare **bahn**-hof	la stazione?	la sta-tsee-**oh**-nay
Die Post?	dee **post**	l'ufficio postale?	loo-**fee**-cho po-**sta**-lay
Das Krankenhaus?	dahs **krahnk**-en-house	l'ospedale?	lo-spay-**dah**-lay
*Das Spital?	dahs shpee-**tahl**		
Wo ist die Toilette?	vo ist dee twah-**let**-uh	Dov'è il bagno?	doe-**vay** eel **bahn**-yo
Links	links	a sinistra	a see-**neess**-tra
Rechts	rechts	a destra	a-**des**-tra
geradeaus	geh-**rod**-uh ouse	Avanti dritto	a-**vahn**-tee **dree**-to
Herr Ober/ Fraülein	hehr **oh**-ber **froy**-line	Cameriere(a)	kah-meh-**ryeh**-reh(rah)
Bitte geben sie mir . . .	**bit**-uh gay behn zee-**meer**	Mi dia pear-fah-**voh**-reh . . .	mee **dee**-a

English	French	French Pronunciation
The menu	La carte	la cart
The bill/check	L'addition	la-dee-see-**ohn**
A fork	Une fourchette	ewn four-**shet**
A knife	Un couteau	uhn koo-**toe**
A spoon	Une cuillère	ewn kwee-**air**
A napkin	Une serviette	ewn sair-vee-**et**
Bread	Du pain	due penh
Butter	Du beurre	due bur
Milk	Du lait	due lay
Pepper	Du poivre	due **pwah**-vruh
Salt	Du sel	due sell
Sugar	Du sucre	due **sook**-ruh
Coffee	Un café	uhn kahfay
Tea	Un thé	uhn tay
Mineral water *carbonated/still*	De l'eau minéral *gazeuse/non gazeuse*	duh loh meenehrahl gahzuhz/noh(n) gahzuhz
Wine	Vin	venh
Cheers!	A votre santé!	ah vo-truh sahn-**tay**

*Prevalent Swiss-German dialect

German	German Pronunciation	Italian	Italian Pronunciation
Die speisekarte	dee **shpie**-zeh-car-tuh	Il menù	eel may-**noo**
Die Rechnung	dee **rekh**-nung	Il conto	eel **cone**-toe
Eine Gabel	**ine**-eh-**gah**-buhl	Una forchetta	oona for-**ket**-a
Ein messer	I-nuh-**mess**-ehr	Un coltello	oon kol-**tel**-o
Einen Löffel	I-nen **ler**-fuhl	Un cucchiaio	oon koo-kee-**ah-yo**
Die Serviette	dee zair-vee-**eh**-tuh	Il tovagliolo	eel toe-va-lee-**oh-lo**
Brot	broht	Il pane	eel **pa**-nay
Butter	**boo**-tehr	Il burro	eel **boo**-roh
Milch	meelch	Il latte	eel **lot**-ay
Pfeffer	**fef**-fehr	Il pepe	eel **pay**-pay
Salz	zahlts	Il sale	eel **sah**-lay
Zucker	**tsoo**-kher	Lo zucchero	loh **tsoo**-ker-o
eine Kaffee	**ine**-eh **kah**-feh	un caffè	oon kahf-**feh**
einen Tee	**ine**-en tay	un tè	oon teh
Mineral wasser	mi-neh-**raal**-**vahs**-sehr	L'acqua minerale	l'ah kwa mee-neh-**rah**-leh
mit gas/ohne gas	mit gahz/**oh**-nuh gahz	*gassata/naturale*	gahs-**sah**-tah/nah-too-**rah**-leh
Wein	vine	Il vino	eel **vee**-noh
Zum Wohl! *Proscht	zoom vole prosht	Salute!	sah-**loo**-teh

INDEX

NOTES

NOTES

NOTES

NOTES

NOTES

NOTES

NOTES

NOTES

NOTES

NOTES

NOTES

NOTES

NOTES

NOTES

NOTES

NOTES